MW01130862

COUNTRY MUSIC
A CULTURAL AND STYLISTIC HISTORY
SECOND EDITION

JOCELYN R. NEAL

New York   Oxford

Oxford University Press

Oxford University Press is a department of the University of Oxford.
It furthers the University's objective of excellence in research, scholarship,
and education by publishing worldwide. Oxford is a registered trade mark of
Oxford University Press in the UK and certain other countries.

Published in the United States of America by Oxford University Press
198 Madison Avenue, New York, NY 10016, United States of America.

For titles covered by Section 112 of the US Higher Education
Opportunity Act, please visit www.oup.com/us/he for the latest
information about pricing and alternate formats.

Library of Congress Cataloging-in-Publication Data

Names: Neal, Jocelyn R., 1973-author.
Title: Country music : a cultural and stylistic history / Jocelyn R. Neal.
Description: Second edition. | New York : Oxford University Press, [2018]
Identifiers: LCCN 2018018243 (print) | LCCN 2018018428 (ebook) | ISBN
  9780190908751 (ebook) | ISBN 9780190499747
Subjects: LCSH: Country music–History and criticism. | Country musicians. |
  Country music–Political aspects. | Country music–Social aspects.
Classification: LCC ML3524 (ebook) | LCC ML3524 .N42 2018 (print) | DDC
  781.64209–dc23
LC record available at https://lccn.loc.gov/2018018243

9 8 7 6 5 4 3

Printed by LSC Communications, Inc., United States of America

Contents

Chapter 3: **New Traditions, Cowboys, and Jazz** 65

Part II: **World War II and After: Nationalism and Country Music (1940s and 1950s)**

Chapter 4: **Honky-Tonk and Rockabilly Revolution** 101

Part III: Coast to Coast: Outsiders, Outlaws, and Tradition (1960s and 1970s)

Chapter 7: California Country and Country Rock 211

Chapter 8: Classic Country 239

Chapter 14: **Redefining Country in a New Millennium** 433

Chapter 15: **Breaking Borders** 469

Preface

This book has grown from two seeds: one is a deep passion for country music of all stripes, styles, eras, and varieties; the other is an insatiable curiosity to understand the music, from the notes, rhythms, and words of the songs to the very human performances, the music's endlessly varied meanings, and what it can teach about history, about culture, and about the essence of human relationships. The book offers a journey through a century of country music, presenting information about the music, musicians, fans, and historical contexts, along with explorations of several important themes and issues that arise from that study. It is designed either for a one-semester, college-level course on country music or for use with country-music units and topics within the framework of a course on American music or popular music. Individual chapters within the book can also be used in many other contexts to investigate specific time periods, artists, and topics.

Coverage

The book presents a chronological history of the development of country music. It begins with the source materials from which country music emerged, then traces the music from its earliest recordings in the 1920s through the present. The book covers the developments of different musical styles, the evolution of the music industry, and the changing ways that the music relates to popular culture and different historical contexts. It includes information on an extensive number of country stars, songwriters, and industry personnel. It does not, however, attempt to be comprehensive on that front. It will instead give the curious reader the tools, information, and big-picture understanding to figure out how other bands and artists fit into the history of country music, while country music encyclopedias and websites can readily provide basic biographical information about bands and artists not covered in this book.

The main focus of this book is American commercial country music. There are thriving country music scenes in other areas of the world, and some coverage of them is provided here. The main narrative, however, explores the music in its native home. The attention to American commercial country music is an inclusive one: the book covers bluegrass, alternative country, western swing, and many other styles at length, and examines geographic centers far beyond the main production sites.

In the intervening years since the first edition appeared, the field of country music scholarship has expanded, with significant new research by Diane Pecknold, Dene Hubbs, Jeremy Hill, Travis Stimeling, Charles Hughes, Murphy Henry, Lee Bidgood, and many others. I have attempted to weave that new scholarship into the text throughout the book so that students will have access to the most contemporary ideas possible. This expansion of scholarship on country music is exciting, and students at all levels should be encouraged to reach beyond this textbook.

Approach

As explained in the Introduction, the book focuses on three interpretive themes that run throughout the history of country music: cultural identity; authenticity; and otherness, specifically the ways in which country music remains distinct from mainstream popular culture.

The book carefully and consistently avoids making any arguments about what music is or is not "real" country, and instead takes the stance that the student of country music should ask questions about "how" and "why" rather than merely assign categories. The fastest way to stall one's learning is to declare a song "country" or "not," or a performance "authentic" or "not." Asking students to think beyond such binary judgements will lead to far more insight and understanding. Individual instructors and students will have varying personal tastes for country music, and their interpretations of these issues will encompass many different perspectives. These are to be encouraged and can lead to very insightful class discussions and supplemental research projects.

This course of study can be undertaken from a variety of disciplines, including but not limited to music, history, cultural studies, American studies, English, sociology, and communications. The book assumes no formal musical training on the part of either the student or the instructor. Supplemental materials are included for students in a music discipline or those seeking more technical study of the music itself. These include an appendix on song form and a few musical examples that are not essential to the main body of the book.

Layout

The structure of the book will readily align with a typical one-semester or one-quarter course syllabus. The book is laid out in five parts, each of which covers approximately two decades and features three chapters. Each part begins with a brief overview that presents the major developments covered in the unit and situates them in a broader historical context. Each chapter contains the following:

1. A main narrative that covers the musical and cultural history of one era.
2. Two artist profiles that explore the biographies of key figures.
3. Three detailed listening guides that connect specific recordings to the ideas presented in the chapter. These listening guides form a core component of the book and should be a major part of the student's experience, because they link the ideas and main narratives to the sound of the music.
4. Comparative listening, identified as a "Listen Side by Side" exercise. These exercises guide close readings of two or more songs in relation to each other, where comparisons yield better understanding of the main themes of this book. These also serve as useful stimuli for in-class discussions.
5. Several essays that offer in-depth exploration of a single topic. These essays fall in one of seven categories: history, musical style, the music business, culture, technology, songwriting, and issues of identity (such as race, class, and

gender). For instance, the musical style essays provide definitions and dis-cussions of different musical styles such as western swing or countrypolitan, and the technology essays provide concise discussions of key developments in music technology that have had a major impact on country music. These essays will help students and instructors explore threads in these categories across the whole span of country music and tailor their courses to their specific disciplinary interests.

6. A playlist that suggests additional listening beyond the three songs covered in the listening guides. Together, the listening guides plus these additional playlists offer approximately eight songs associated with the main topics, issues, and ideas covered in that chapter.

7. Suggested sources for additional reading.

8. Review materials, including questions that are suitable for class discussion or writing assignments.

Four appendices are also provided. Appendix A is an introduction to song form that covers technical vocabulary and ways to analyze a song's form. These skills are essential to any close reading or analysis of individual songs. Appendix B offers a basic introduction to the instruments commonly heard in country music. Each entry describes the instrument's role in the history of country music and suggests songs where the instrument can be readily heard. Appendix C provides a glossary of key terms. And Appendix D presents a timeline of events in country music history along with touchstone events in American history.

The listening guides that appear throughout this book require some technical explanation. The timings shown for the start of each section align with the first structural downbeat of that section. This approach is consistent throughout the book and matches the accepted methodology for formal analysis of popular music. Students without a formal musical background may think more casually of sections starting with the singer's lyrics, which in many instances may be either pickup notes or after-beat patterns and may therefore occur a few seconds before or after the timing listed in the book. Therefore, students who are not focusing as much on the music-analytic aspects of this subject matter may treat those timings as general guidelines, while students taking a more rigorous approach to the musical analysis and music theory will be able to use them to identify specific structural features of the songs.

Source Materials

Along with this textbook, students will need access to recordings. Students and instructors have a variety of resources at their disposal to help in this task. Listening to the recordings is essential, and students should rely on those recordings as a primary source throughout their study. Students should also consult song lyrics; these are readily available on many internet sites, in liner notes to recordings, and of course through firsthand transcription of the recordings.

Outcomes

The student outcomes for any course in the history of country music are determined by the specific disciplinary approach and course design that the instructor chooses. This book will support a wide variety of learning outcomes, including but by no means limited to the student's ability (a) to recognize by ear many different styles, eras, trends, individual artists, and major themes in country music; (b) to interpret the varied meanings of country music within different historical and cultural contexts; (c) to use country music as the creative lens through which to study different people, cultures, places, and times; and (d) to explain country music's role and identity as a genre within popular culture.

Most of all, I invite instructors and students alike to incorporate this book into their personal explorations of country music. I hope that, in the course of their studies, students will encounter country music they love, country music they hate, country music that confuses them, and country music that inspires them. I encourage them to engage all of that music with a heightened sense of curiosity and critical inquiry. The music has much teach us all about human relationships, history, and culture. Enjoy the journey!

Acknowledgments

I am deeply grateful to the many people who have helped me write this book. Richard Carlin guided its creation with his extensive expertise and his own passion for the subject matter. Hannah Whitcher and the publication team of editors were invaluable throughout the publication process.

Thank you to the many reviewers for Oxford University Press who have provided productive suggestions and insights throughout the book's existence.

Colleagues who share my deep interest in country music have offered their own expertise, including Nate Gibson, Joti Rockwell, and Travis Stimeling. Fellow speakers at conferences, including Jewly Hight, Barry Mazor, Jon Weisberger, Fred Bartenstein, James Akenson, Don Cusic, Erika Brady, Diane Pecknold, Russell Johnson, and so many more have stimulated my thinking. The many students who have enrolled in my country music classes over the past decade, served as teaching assistants, and undertaken country music research projects with me have all helped me shape this book, including Christa Bentley, Gina Bombola, Meg Orita, and more. And I am grateful to the professors who inspired me to pursue this path of scholarship in the first place and made such study possible, including Betsy Marvin, Dave Headlam, and John Covach,

I owe the greatest debt to my family for their support of this project. My parents instilled in me a love both of music and of teaching. My children, Caelen, Rhiannon, and Liadan, are the center of my world. They have grown up surrounded by both this music and the research that led to this book. May they follow a pathway in life enriched both by music and by an endless desire to understand both the people and the culture of all the music they encounter. It is to them I dedicate this work.

Introduction: Heading into the Country

What is country music? It is an indelible part of American popular culture, interwoven with our sense of identity and our retelling of history. It is nostalgic, yet focused on the present. Some of it has been called hillbilly music, but at times the music has purged itself of all hillbilly associations. It is rural in origin, yet has always been reliant on an urbanized commercial industry. It is primarily white in terms of its racial and ethnic associations, but inextricably dependent on a range of musical styles with strong racial and ethnic pasts, including black, Cajun, and Latin, and home to diverse artists and audiences. It is extremely popular, yet one of its main concerns is to differentiate itself from what we call pop music. It offers both a window on working- and middle-class life and a punch line for tasteless jokes as old as some of the tunes themselves. Ask five different fans to define it, and you will likely get five contradictory yet equally passionate answers. None of these characteristics produces a clear definition, yet the music's complexity is what makes studying it so rewarding.

Country as Genre

Country music is a **genre** of popular music whose boundaries are determined by the interactions of fans, the commercial music industry, and musicians. "Genre" means category, and this book—along with most studies of popular music— includes the opinions of the music's fans as an important way in which a genre is defined. **Popular music** is the term by which we identify mostly commercially produced and disseminated music that is a common part of its audience's daily lives. Popular music is generally popular (meaning lots of people like it), although some genres within popular music have much smaller fan bases. In the past, music that has not been considered part of popular music has included art music, which is sometimes called classical music, and folk music. Some scholars in previous decades considered art music to be music that was neither a product of nor intended for mass culture, and folk music to be that which was entirely outside commercial enterprise. Art music was described as intellectually cultivated and an expression of high culture, such as a Beethoven symphony. This music was taught in formal music appreciation courses and supported by grants and institutions of higher learning, with the assumption that it was good for people to study it and hear it. Folk music, by contrast, was considered the anonymous music-making that was simply part of oral traditions in local communities and families. It was valued by collectors in the early twentieth century precisely because it appeared to represent a grassroots, raw expression of regular people's culture.

These distinctions, however, do not hold up to critical examination. In recent years, scholars have explored how some art music is both extremely popular and highly commercial, and how folk music was never really isolated from the forces of commerce, meaning that the songs that people sang in their homes, churches, and gathering places often came from identifiable songwriters, published songbooks, and traceable commercial sources. Thus, any apparent distinctions between popular, art, and folk music, which were never clear-cut in the first place, are even more suspect in the twenty-first century's musical landscape. To further complicate these terms, so-called folk singers such as Peter, Paul, and Mary or the Weavers were very much a part of popular music in the mid-twentieth century, when "folk" became a genre within popular music. For our purposes, we mainly need to understand popular music as that which is created for mass consumption within the commercial marketplace. Popular music includes some art music and is continually interdependent with folk traditions. Finally, the definition of popular music is always closely tied to the cultural identity of its fans: the people who listen to it, the circumstances in which they listen to it, the reasons why they listen to it, and the meanings they find in it.

Different genres of popular music include rock, pop, jazz, blues, hip-hop, rhythm and blues (R&B), gospel, Latin, folk, and country; think of these as the different bins one might have seen in a conventional record store. Thus, we will consider country as one genre within the broad category of popular music. Most music fans listen to and like many different genres. Similarly, individual artists might perform music that belongs to more than one genre. Songs, and even performers, often cross over from one genre to another. These categories we call "genres" are constantly shifting and changing, but there are some characteristics that remain consistent in how we understand them.

One point of potential confusion is that one genre of popular music is commonly called **pop** music. Historically, pop music emerged as the genre most widely accepted by mass culture as represented by a generally (although not exclusively) white middle class. Bing Crosby, Kay Starr, Frank Sinatra, and Rosemary Clooney were all routinely described as pop singers in their day. In later decades, pop music describes a musical genre and performers that have achieved mass acceptance by a young mainstream audience without being subsumed into racially and stylistically differentiated genres such as hip-hop. Lady Gaga, Katy Perry, and Justin Bieber are examples of pop stars.

The relationship between pop and country is particularly complex. For instance, country fans and performers often complain that country music is crossing over into pop, or that a pop star is trying to make country records; at other times, they celebrate the fact that country music is being accepted by a pop audience. The ever-evolving tension between pop and country will form an important part of our study.

Some writers have proposed that musical genres are merely labels that the music industry applies to recordings in order to market them. That perspective, however, relegates fans to a passive role and discounts their power in defining musical genres.

Our approach will instead acknowledge the fans' role in this process. In recent years, record labels have on several occasions packaged a CD as "country" and offered it to the fans, who have resoundingly rejected it on the basis of genre. Conversely, some recordings that sound radically different from most country music have been embraced by fans and accepted as country music, a process that can radically change the genre. And finally, some music that sounds like country is made by musicians and listened to by fans who reject that label entirely. Fans are active participants in how genres are formed and defined, primarily through the ways that they identify and express themselves in relation to their musical preferences.

Definition of Country

Country music, as we will define it in this book, is a commercial genre that claims a lineage from early twentieth-century, rural, white, mostly Southern, working-class popular music. It is symbolically related to the cowboy, and it draws on a largely Protestant, evangelical theology for its underlying philosophy. Its songwriting relies on storytelling; sympathetic, working-class characters; clear narratives; and relatable experiences from everyday life. Stock references such as trucks, cowboy hats, family, small towns, church, "y'all," and countless others often signal a song's affinity with country music. Although its musical sound has changed radically over the past century, it retains associations with certain iconic instruments such as fiddles, steel guitars, banjos, mandolins, and acoustic six-string guitars, although not all of these instruments are present in all styles of country music, nor does their incorporation automatically mean that a recording is country. Country singers and musicians often use Southern vocal accents, verbal interjections, and particular techniques of playing their instruments to differentiate country from other genres. Artists' biographies come into play at various times in the music's history, when a singer's hometown, family, or occupation may be invoked to help define the genre. Country music often situates itself in particular geographic locations: small-town or rural America, the South, Texas, the West Coast. One additional determining factor is whether the people who think of themselves as country fans accept a particular performer or performance music as country.

Our text will address many different musical styles within country music. Musical **style** is difficult to define but refers to those characteristics that can be identified by listening to the music. It describes the particular approach to a performance, the use of instruments, and the musical arrangement, based on what one can actually hear in the performance or recording. It tells us what tradition that performance came from and provides clues as to when, where, and why the recording was made. Think of the country genre as a large umbrella that covers many different styles of music. Over the decades, the styles gathered under that umbrella have changed and evolved so that what we hear today (instruments, type of singing, musical arrangements, etc.) may not sound at all like what we might have heard on a country radio broadcast in the 1920s. Nevertheless, all of those styles come together in the idea of country as a genre, which is a larger category defined by fan identity, traditions, and lineage.

MAIN COUNTRY STYLES WE WILL STUDY

The main styles of country music that we will study include the following. Dates indicate when the style was most prominent; keep in mind, however, that many styles were present for several years before they became widely known, and many styles remained part of country music long after they faded from prominence. The chapters indicate where the main discussion of the style is found.

Hillbilly music	1920s–1930s	chapters 1 & 2
Western swing	1930s–1950s	chapter 3
Singing cowboy	1930s–1940s	chapter 3
Brother acts	1930s–1940s	chapter 3
Honky-tonk	1940s–1950s	chapter 4
Rockabilly	1950s	chapter 4
Bluegrass	1940s–1950s	chapter 5
Country teen crooners	1950s	chapter 6
Nashville sound	late 1950s–1960s	chapter 6
Bakersfield sound	1960s	chapter 7
Country rock	1960s–1970s	chapter 7
Progressive Bluegrass	1960s–1970s	chapter 7
Classic country	1960s–1970s	chapter 8
Outlaw	1970s	chapter 9
Southern rock	1970s	chapter 9
Countrypolitan	1970s–1980s	chapter 10
Neotraditional	1980s	chapter 11
New country	1990s–2000s	chapter 12
Country pop	1990s–2000s	chapter 12
Alt-country (postpunk)	1990s–2000s	chapter 13
Alt-country (retro)	1990s–2000s	chapter 13
Commercial country (roots revival)	2000s	chapter 14
Commercial country (honky-tonk themes)	2000s	chapter 14
Commercial country (Latin influence)	2000s	chapter 14
Commercial country (Southern rock influence)	2000s	chapter 14
Bro country	2010s	chapter 15
Country/hip-hop	2010s	chapter 15

Imagine for a moment that you are flipping through various radio stations. What clues do you hear that help you quickly identify the country station? Your responses might include the lyrics (the words of the songs), the instruments, or the overall timbre (the general description of the sound), which is often described as having a "**twang**." Imagine that you are shopping in a record store. What visual clues tell you which CDs are country? Your responses might include the types of clothing and accessories worn by the stars, the way that the stars are presented in the photography, or the props seen in the photographs and cover art. Imagine that you are attending a concert or a club with live music. What clues identify the genre of the performance? Your responses might include the wardrobe or modes of transportation favored by the audience members, the types of graphics used in advertising posters, or even the name of the venue. In other words, country music has many signifiers in its sounds, visual presentations, and fan identities. As part of our studies, we will examine where these signifiers come from, how they became part of country music, and what they mean, both to country fans and to others.

Is it Real? Issues of Authenticity in Country Music

The biggest issue in scholarship on country music is the idea of **authenticity**. Scholars have written extensively about the topic; many agree that authenticity is a quality or value that fans ascribe to music based on two general considerations. The first is listeners' perception that the music is traditional, "like it used to be," or from a source that is an accepted part of country's roots. In this sense, listeners might describe a performance as authentic if it sounds like country music from some earlier era, or if the fans believe the artists belong to the country music tradition (perhaps through their family's history or biography). The second consideration is listeners' perception of the music as original (as opposed to a copy or facsimile), genuine (as opposed to artificial), and honest. In this sense, listeners might describe a performance as authentic if they feel like the singer is telling a story based on his or her own experience and attempting to connect directly and honestly with the listener without any calculated or constructed mediation. These very complicated and nuanced ideas of authenticity sometimes conflict with each other. Yet together, they help explain how fans continuously make judgments about what is or is not "real" country music.

What passes that test of authenticity will vary from one fan to the next, and from one era to the next, as we will see. Many fans of alternative styles of country claim that the Top 40 country music on contemporary radio is not what they consider "real." Conversely, lots of fans of Top 40 country music are not fond of and do not value alternative styles of country music. In every period in country music's history, contrasting musical styles have existed, and fans have debated their perceived authenticity. Think again about the signifiers we just listed that help define country music. For each of those, there are contradictions, exceptions, and controversies: fans sometimes reject as inauthentic a performance or recording that has many of those signifiers; in other instances, fans embrace a performance, singer, or recording as country even if it lacks any of those common signifiers. For our purposes, we are not going to concern ourselves with what is or is not "real" country music, even though that is a debate into which music fans often enter. Frankly, asking whether or not a particular artist or song is "real country" is a question that leaves us dead in the water and teaches us nothing. Our task, as students and historians, is instead to study how and why these differences of opinion occur, what they mean in the larger history of the music, and how they help us interpret culture and meaning.

Goals and Themes

Our study of country music focuses on two main goals:

1. to understand the music's history.
2. to identify country's major musical styles and trace their development by ear.

The history of country music includes its important singers, songwriters, business practices, cultural institutions, and songs, all within social and cultural contexts. Most of our study will focus on those contexts as they occur in American history, although we will also examine the export, import, and influence of country music in foreign locations. Country music is a useful window through which to revisit the cultural history of the past century. The Great Depression, World War II, the Korean and Vietnam wars, the Cold War, conflicts in Afghanistan and Iraq, periods of economic upheaval, the changing face of American life, technological advances, new media, new forms of entertainment and communications, the civil rights movement, the women's liberation movement, and countless other global events and cultural milestones are reflected through the lens of country music. Similarly, country music has acted as a voice for different marginalized populations throughout the past century, offering those groups a chance to be heard. To that end, this study of country music is really a study of history viewed through country music.

Our second goal, which is to be able to identify country's major musical styles by ear and trace their development, requires that you immerse yourself in the sounds of country music rather than merely reading about it. Each concept and idea in this book should be reinforced by constant and careful listening to relevant recordings. At the end of this study, you should be able to listen to just about any country music recording and identify the general musical style, the time period, and the historical or social context in which it was made.

This book is constructed around three primary themes:

1. Cultural identity
2. Authenticity
3. The "otherness" of country

These themes provide a framework through which to interpret the information we have about country music. Think of them as a lens that you can use to examine the music and its cultural context. The question is never whether these themes can be applied to country music of a particular style, era, or artist (they are always applicable), but rather how you can use these lenses to make sense of the details and musical specifics of that style, era, or artist.

Cultural Identity

Both performers and fans have used country music to express who they are and to give a voice to their frustrations, goals, passions, concerns, and fears. Country music's content and meaning are often linked to its performers' and listeners' economic and social status, class, race, ethnicity, gender, political beliefs, religious beliefs, fields of employment, and family status. The fans and performers represent the full range and diversity of identities within any of these categories. That explains, for instance, how one performance can take on very different and even contradictory meanings for different listeners. Identity, namely who is making and listening to the music, the circumstances and major concerns in their lives, and the social, economic, political, religious, and historical contexts through which they are connecting to country music, will be a major focus of our investigation.

Authenticity

Scholars, fans, and performers alike have focused on authenticity as the most important value that listeners ascribe to country music. What it means, however, varies from one listener to the next, and from one moment or song to the next. We will see how the genre depends on fans and performers at any given time agreeing on what seems "authentic," whether it is a revival of an old style or—totally different—an emphasis on new songs written by the singer, or something else altogether. Competing definitions of authenticity also explain different scenes, movements, or styles within country music, why one group of fans heads to a bluegrass festival and claim that is authentic, while another group of fans heads to a stadium to hear a concert headliner sing songs that they feel they "relate to." Sometimes authenticity means abandoning or at least hiding any desire to achieve commercial success. Consider that in the minds of some fans, being an authentic artist and wanting to sell records are incompatible ideas. At the heart of this paradox, country music came into existence as a commercial music, but has always cultivated the notion that it eschews commercial success.

The best way to study how authenticity functions within country music is to discard entirely any urge you have to label some music as authentic and some other music as inauthentic. Rather than declaring what you think is or is not authentic, ask yourself how and why a group of fans relate in a particular way to an artist or song.

The "Otherness" of Country

Through a variety of ways, country music continuously differentiates itself from other genres, most significantly pop music. In order to maintain its distinction from pop, country music has to be noticeably different from the mainstream. At the same time, many forces within the country music industry push the genre toward mainstream acceptability and larger audiences, which simultaneously increase country's popularity and decrease its distinctive identity. Therein lies the problem: if country music gets too popular and acceptable to the mainstream audience, it literally becomes pop music. But if country becomes pop music, it no longer enjoys a unique identity as something different than mass, mainstream culture, and its very existence as a genre is threatened. Its "otherness," therefore, is the ways in which it remains culturally marginalized and noticeably different from mainstream pop. Being different can be both an asset and a liability. Throughout this book, we will trace the way the music has sometimes blended into the cultural mainstream, thereby diluting its distinctive identity, and at other times amplified its differences. We will also consider why fans and musicians consider this issue vitally important to country music.

Situating a Performer

This book does not offer a comprehensive catalog of all significant country musicians. Such a collection might well be impossible, although there are some encyclopedias, websites, and books about the history of country music that come close. Instead, this book provides a framework for understanding the major trends, developments, and issues within the genre. Bands and artists generally appear in this text when they are either innovators in an area or style that had lasting impact or representatives of a larger development. The literal constraints on the size of this book mean that many interesting, influential, and important musicians are not covered directly. It is possible—or even likely—that your favorite artist might not appear. Rather than be disappointed if your favorite band or artist is not featured in the book, consider instead that by the end of your studies, you will have the tools and knowledge to do further research on those bands or artists and to make sense of how, where, and why they fit into the larger history of the genre.

How to Listen

Listening to music is easy to do. Most of us listen casually almost all the time for pleasure, to accompany to other tasks, or as a means of socializing. But listening to music as part of a serious study requires a different approach. Recordings will be our main source materials, and we have to treat the listening experience as a focused task that deserves our full attention and significant time. Each chapter includes listening guides and a playlist, which should be studied as carefully as the text itself. And each chapter includes a "Listen Side by Side," which guides you through a detailed comparison of two or more recordings. Let these recordings be your primary texts; study and "read" them as closely as possible, as they are the focal point of this history.

Every country recording invites three layers of listening:

1. The first addresses the song as a text consisting of both music and, in most instances, lyrics. Hank Williams's "Your Cheatin' Heart," for instance, has some words, a tune, and some chords that together comprise that particular song.
2. The second layer addresses the recording as a particular performance from a specific time, place, and set of circumstances. The singer's voice (if there is a singer) is unique; the choice of instruments (including additional voices)

is part of that performance. Those instrumentalists are using different techniques, improvising (creating on the spot) particular harmonies or short musical enhancements for that one performance, and blending in ways that create an identifiable musical style. Each performance uses a specific arrangement of the song, meaning which verses or sections are included, omitted, or repeated, and with what chords and musical parts, harmonies, and enhancements. No two performances, even with the same musicians and the same song, are identical. All of these aspects of the performance are important in our listening comprehension.

3. The third layer addresses the mediation of the recording itself—in other words, the technology involved in capturing, manipulating, reproducing, and delivering the sound to our ears. When we listen to early-1920s recordings made on wax-coated discs without the benefit of electric microphones, for instance, we hear vestiges of that recording process. The same song recorded in a modern, digital studio with sound-processing software such as Auto-Tune will sound very different. Again, these aspects of the recording itself are essential to our understanding of the music and its context and meaning.

In order to get the full benefit from listening, make sure you are hearing the specific performance or version of the song described in this book. In other words, we are not listening just to the words and melody of a song, but rather to the whole performance, with all three layers, to find out what it can tell us about the people, place, time, and traditions in which that performance took place.

The Listening Methodology Chart suggests a strategy for approaching a recording in all three layers. When you listen to music, make sure you have the best possible speakers or headphones, a quiet space, time to play the music several times, and a way to take notes on what you hear. You may not be able to write down some features of the recording such as the melody and chord progression (the actual notes being played and sung), because these skills require advanced, specialized training. However, you will still be able to describe some features of those musical elements. As you listen, think about comparisons between the recording and the other music you know. If you hear two versions of the same song, what has changed, and what is the same? If you hear two different songs in the same general musical style, what do they have in common? By the end of the semester, you will have a large catalog of country music recordings in your head that you can use to understand large trends, developments, and significant changes over the entire history of the genre.

The recordings that we have represent only a tiny fraction of the country music that has been performed over the past century. For every record that we can hear, a performer may have played dozens of concerts live, sung privately with friends, and rehearsed hundreds of other songs for which there is no extant record. While it is essential to acknowledge this, we should also be grateful that we get to hear as much music from the past century as is now possible, particularly with the increasing access to reissues of older recordings and the easy accessibility through the internet to current artists' music. Thus, our study pays tribute to the technology of sound recording and how it contributes to our access to the past.

Listening Methodology		
The Song	**The Words**	**What do they mean?**
		How do they sound?
		How are they organized?
	The Melody	**What does it sound like?**
		How is it organized?
	The Chords	**What is the chord progression?**
The Performance	**Musical Style**	**What is the sound of the ensemble?**
		What is the arrangement of the song?
	The Singer	**What does the voice sound like?**
		What performance techniques are used?
The Recording	**How was the sound captured?**	**What were the conditions where the recording was made?**
		What technologies were used in the recording process?
	How is the sound delivered?	**What technologies were used in creating the final product?**

What is the story about?

What allusions or references are in the words?

What interesting vocabulary is used?

What poetic devices are used?

What is the form?

What is the rhyme scheme?

What words, phrases, or sections repeat?

What is its range (how high and low does it go)?

What are its rhythms and contours?

Does it quote or borrow from other sources?

What is the form?

Do phrases or sections repeat?

What chords are used, and does the progression borrow from other sources?

What instruments are used?

Are there identifiable instrumental techniques from a particular place or time?

What rhythmic patterns or groove are used?

What are the musical roles of the different instruments?

What mood is conveyed?

What is the overall organization and form of the song as performed?

Is the voice smooth or raspy, high or low? Does the singer use vibrato or a straight tone? Is the sound pinched or resonant?

Does the singer talk, yodel, use a regional accent, or sing flat?

Is there audience noise from a live performance? Are there other audible hints of the setting or location?

Is there evidence of electronic microphones? Multi-track recordings? Overdubbing?

Is the recording stereophonic or monophonic? Are there audible effects added to the sound such as reverb or Auto-Tune?

Are there uncorrected mistakes, tape hiss, cracks and pops, or other audible indicators of old recordings?

Getting Started

There is a certain irony in undertaking an academic study of country music, given that country music touts its own simplicity, transparency, and accessibility. For many years, the study of country music was seldom approached in any academic setting; only in the past decade has it become widely accepted in colleges and universities, and even today some institutions have yet to embrace it. One might even wonder whether the scholarly tools of critical analysis or of historical and social interpretation can be fairly applied to country music. The answer is "yes," and the results of investigating country music from an academic perspective are rewarding. We have a responsibility, however, to consider carefully the cultural context where the music resides.

Part of our responsibility is to be aware of the prejudices, personal tastes, and preconceived notions that we all bring to the subject. Reflect on your own assumptions about the genre: for some students, country music is deeply personal and closely connected to their sense of identity; for others, it is something that is never taken seriously on its own but that stands as a foil for other genres. What we want to do is move beyond our preliminary assumptions while simultaneously trying to understand different points of view about the music. We can never transcend our personal perspectives entirely, but the more aware we are of them, the better equipped we are to explore contrasting interpretations and attempt to understand the music's many facets of meaning.

In this course of study, you will probably hear some music you like and some music you dislike. However strong your responses in either case, remember that it should not matter if we love or hate the music; our goals are neither to like it nor to defend its aesthetic value. Try to concentrate on learning everything you can from each recording, each historical era, and each event or performance that we will examine. There is a vast world of country music that promises rich rewards for anyone willing to undertake its study.

PART I

The Early Years
(1920s and 1930s)

Fans love "firsts": the first country recording, the first disc to sell a million copies, the first star to achieve national fame. Historians, however, know that the any such claims are bound to tell only part of the story. Whenever we discover a "first," we should immediately think, "Yes, but what came before?"

The year 1923 marks the beginning of country music as a genre, but the country music backstory begins well before then, when the source materials, traditions, and audiences were already connecting through music that would come to be known as country. Not until 1923, however, did the formula for an identifiable genre come together, and even then, it was not recognizable as country through the same criteria we might use today. Country music came into existence when the commercial music industry captured the soundscape of a particular audience: working-class people, mostly but not exclusively white, in the Southern United States, in rural communities of the North and Midwest, and in the immigrant and migrant communities of the Southwest and West Coast. All of those populations had rich and diverse musical traditions that, up to that point, had been largely overlooked by the urban, industrial forces of culture that were shaping twentieth-century America. Over the subsequent two decades, this music came to represent a significant slice of American identity. By the time World War II broke out, country music was an established genre that included a broad array of musical styles, a well-supported business infrastructure, and two full generations of stars.

The first two decades of country are characterized by a lack of musical coherence. Its sounds included string bands, fiddlers, singers accompanied by guitar, harmonica wizards, and family groups singing and playing everything from traditional ballads to folk tunes, pop standards, cowboy songs, gospel hymns, and blues. Record executives were often dumbfounded when these recordings sold in impressive numbers, particularly because in many cases they neither cared for nor understood the music. Radio stations were primarily local and regional businesses that programmed a wide variety of musical styles and featured live, local performers. Within this early scene, there were no clear boundaries as to what was or was not country music. In fact, the main unifying characteristic of this music was the biographies of the performers. Country music, which at the time many people called "hillbilly music," functioned as a catchall category for performances by mostly white, mostly rural and Southern, working-class musicians intended for a similar audience. Thus, from its earliest years, aspects of identity through race, region, and class helped define the music.

During its formative years, country music was also heavily shaped by the social context and economic conditions of its audiences. In the 1920s, record numbers of farmers left their former occupation, moved to urban locations, and joined the industrialized labor force. This shift gave them both increased purchasing power and a desire to hear music that reminded them of homespun rural traditions. Conversely, new technologies such as radio stations gave rural Americans unprecedented access to professional entertainment. Furthermore, World War I had primed audiences for new forms of commercial music. During that war, many working-class Southerners ventured far from home for the first time through military deployment. Soldiers served in Hawaii and Europe in large numbers, and after the war returned home with an expanded cultural outlook. They were interested in hearing new musical styles and, at the same time, increasingly nostalgic for the sounds that represented home. This desire for both new and old paved the way for the success of early country stars.

The stock market crash in October 1929 launched a decade of economic woes for most country music fans. During the subsequent Great Depression, many forms of commercial entertainment experienced substantial growth as people sought affordable reprieves from the bleak outlooks in their daily lives. Country musicians were especially successful in this regard because they voiced a deep empathy for working-class life. Country musicians provided accompaniment for dancing, soundtracks for wildly popular Hollywood westerns, comfortingly familiar Saturday night radio shows, musical assurance of gospel salvation, and a whole lot of hell-raising fun along the way, all of which was welcomed by Depression-era audiences.

Country music was commercial music from its outset, a point that cannot be overstated. In the early 1920s, record executives sought new and different music to boost flagging record sales. Radio executives needed entertainment that would draw a loyal audience and thereby enable them to sell lots of advertisements. Publishers and record producers were motivated by their ability to make money from the royalties guaranteed by copyright law (see Chapter 2). Performers and songwriters were interested in getting paid, and for many of them, working as a professional musician was far more palatable than their other employment options. Together, these forces led to the creation of a genre out of a large collection of musical traditions. These commercial considerations did not undercut the artistic motivations of performers or songwriters, nor did they detract from the fact that fans loved the sound of the music and heard it as deeply authentic, a word that always demands careful and critical investigation.

Although many fans associate country music with the South, its geographic origins are far more widespread. The South, including its urban centers of Atlanta, Charlotte, Nashville, was a critical site in the development of the music, but it was not alone. The songwriting and recording industry centered in New York provided key opportunities in the early days, and Chicago, home to a large population of

Appalachian migrants, was a vibrant site for radio and records alike. In California, Hollywood's stars of the silver screen such as Gene Autry and Roy Rogers became celebrated musical heroes who introduced a cowboy image and fresh songs to country music, and Texas was an important crucible.

While the links between country music and American folk traditions of ballads and fiddle tunes are strong, country drew on a host of other musical styles. In many instances, the sources of those songs were professional film-score composers or other musicians whose backgrounds involved advanced formal musical training. Jazz music and various European traditions of folk music both worked their way into the dance music that spread across the Southwest and became known as western swing. New microphone technology allowed country singers to imitate the sophisticated popular crooners of the day and abandon the nasal, harsh vocal styles that had characterized much of the first generation of country records. By the late 1930s, the sound of country recordings, along with the instrumentation and the images associated with the performers, was radically different than it had been at the genre's start.

Some fans and performers resisted every change within the genre. Drums and electrified steel guitars, for instance, seemed practical to the musicians who were playing for rowdy, inebriated crowds in Southwestern dance halls, but partisans of the string bands in the Southeast decried their usage. Even while musicians coast to coast were adopting cowboy attire and naming their bands with western slogans, other stars claimed that cowboys were invading and threatening country tradition. Some record producers wanted performers to keep their sound as old-fashioned as possible, even when the musicians wanted to sing more pop songs. By contrast, radio executives sometimes accused bands of being too twangy, traditional, folksy, and hard-edged for their shows. These differences of opinion have persisted in country music to the present day. Even in these first two decades of country music, we see that one consistent characteristic of country music is that its sound, image, and social meaning are, in fact, constantly changing.

By the beginning of World War II, what had started as the happenstance recording of some rural Southern musicians had grown into a well-defined, thriving commercial genre of music. Several radio barn dances achieved national syndication, record sales persisted even through the Great Depression, and country music adopted the cowboy as its lasting, heroic, iconic image. Country music drew together many different musical streams and wove them into a musical genre that was both a thoroughly modern commercial product and a celebration of a rural, idealized past. It was poised to become a national phenomenon, ready to be exported around the globe by American servicemen and women and celebrated at home as part of the quintessential American identity. ❧

The Birth of Country Music

1

The elements of country music first came together in the early 1920s to create the new genre. All of the contributing elements existed before then, but it was their intersection during a unique time in American history that led to the emergence of country music. The five main elements that contributed to this new genre's formation were:

1. Diverse sources of music in the lives of working-class Americans
2. New technologies to deliver the music
3. Audiences eager to hear the music
4. The business structure of a music industry
5. Talented performers

These elements also contributed to the formation of other genres, most significantly jazz, during the same years. The beginning of country music also coincided with dramatic changes in commercial entertainment in general, and therefore many of the ideas and elements we will examine apply to these larger developments, as well.

These innovations took place during the 1920s, a decade when Americans were enjoying newfound prosperity after World War I. New technologies transformed people's lives across all economic classes: the automobile revolutionized transportation, record players became accessible even to working-class families, radio broadcasts brought music and news from faraway places into homes, and increased industrialization changed employment patterns in formerly rural populations. All of these developments fostered connections between rural families and urban communities. The basic principles of a capitalist economy drove all of these changes: record labels wanted to sell records, radio stations wanted to sell advertising, companies wanted to sell their products, musicians wanted to earn a living playing and singing, and people everywhere wanted gainful employment and to enjoy a better quality of life.

Understanding these five key elements, how they developed, and how they joined together to form country music will be the main focus of this chapter. Let's examine them one by one.

Musical Sources

Country music drew from many different sources of music in its early days. These included:

- traditional ballads
- cowboy songs
- fiddle and dance tunes
- gospel hymns
- blues
- jazz
- popular songs written for the vaudeville stage
- minstrelsy

The oldest of these musical sources were the traditional ballads, or songs that told a story, that had been passed down orally from generation to generation. These ballads have long been romanticized as folk songs originally from the British Isles, preserved in pristine form in the isolated mountains of Appalachia.

During the first decades of the twentieth century, song collectors traveled to that area to collect and compare these ballads. The best known of these is British folklorist Cecil Sharp (1859–1924), who spent two years from 1916 to 1918 collecting and transcribing British ballads in collaboration with Maud Karpeles (1885–1976) in the Appalachian Mountains. During that same era, Olive Dame Campbell (1882–1954) was working with her husband in the region and also collected songs. Sharp and Campbell published their findings in several different books, the best known of which was the jointly authored *English Folk Songs from the Southern Appalachians* (1917). This book made available both the words and the melodies for several hundred folk songs, most of which the authors traced back to old British and Scottish ballads. "Barbara Allen," which several early country singers recorded in the 1920s and '30s, is the best known of these. Many of the first generation of country singers recorded songs from this tradition, although they became less common in subsequent decades. What was important, however, was that in the first two decades of the twentieth century, these folk song collectors raised public awareness of the rich musical culture of the Southern Appalachians.

Along with the Appalachian ballads, cowboy songs also gained wider recognition because of the work of collectors and folklorists who were working in the American West at the same time. N. Howard "Jack" Thorp (1867–1940) collected the first book of cowboy songs in his 1908 volume *Songs of the Cowboy,* although it contained only lyrics and no music. Two years later, John Lomax (1867–1948) published *Cowboy Songs and Other Frontier Ballads* with both lyrics and music. Many of these songs were collected from working cowboys, and a few could even be traced to earlier British Isles sources, but some were composed by songwriters who were not cowboys but were merely writing lyrics depicting the American frontier. All of these traditions would persist in country music, and in the 1930s, the American cowboy would become a dominant image for country music.

A third significant source of musical repertory for early country performers was the fiddle and dance tunes that had become standards for community entertainment. Many of these started out as songs or ballads with words, but those words were discarded over time as the tunes became popular for dancing, such as "Turkey in the Straw," "Sallie Gooden" (sometimes spelled differently), "Soldier's Joy," and "Sourwood Mountain" (see Listen Side by Side). Fiddlers sometimes accompanied themselves by tapping their feet to create a rhythmic pattern. In the mountains of the Southeast, banjo players often played with the fiddlers at dances and community gatherings. Many cities held fiddle contests, and the winners were widely acclaimed. Atlanta's famous annual fiddle convention began in 1913, but others, in places such as Virginia, are documented as early as the mid-eighteenth century. All of these traditions brought fiddle and dance tunes into common usage in small towns and rural communities.

Gospel hymns provided an extensive source of music for the early days of country. In the mid- to late nineteenth century, a religious fervor swept across the nation. Traveling preachers hosted revivals and camp meetings across the American South, which included congregational singing. A new style of hymn, which emphasized repeated phrases, catchy rhythms, and musical refrains (short melodies that are repeated many times) grew out of this movement. Many composers, such as Fanny Crosby (who wrote "Pass Me Not, O Gentle Savior") and P. P. Bliss (who wrote "Almost Persuaded"), specialized in this new style.

An entire industry sprang up around these gospel hymns in the early twentieth century. In cities such as Chicago, Dallas, Atlanta, Nashville, and Chattanooga, publishing firms such as R. E. Winsett and Charlie Tillman produced inexpensive paperback hymnals containing newly composed hymns as well as established favorites. A copy with just the lyrics might cost 10¢ or 15¢, while a hymnal with both lyrics and music would be 25¢ or 35¢. Some of the publishing firms, including James D. Vaughan's company, hired professional vocal quartets to tour through the region and perform the hymns as a way of advertising. Other music publishers soon followed suit.

The Vaughan quartets, who went on the road starting in 1910, continued a previous tradition of touring and performing local concerts to advertise music. Earlier related projects included historically black Fisk University's Fisk Jubilee Singers, who toured as a fundraising effort for the Nashville-based university as early as 1871. The Vaughan quartets (Vaughan had, at one point, sixteen different groups touring to promote his music and songbooks) were extremely successful, and have garnered historical significance in some circles as arguably the first musicians to make a country record. Herein definitions of what is and is not country are contested, but the main Vaughan quartet's first recording (1921), a spiritual that the Fisk vocal groups had already recorded multiple times called "Couldn't Hear Nobody Pray," fits the bill as white, southern musicians singing in a folk-influenced style.

Some editions of these gospel hymnals printed the music in standard musical notation, but the more common editions used **shape notes**, a notation system that used different shapes, such as triangles and squares, for the different pitches in the musical scale. Two different types of shape notes appeared in print: an older, four-shape system, which originated around 1800, and a seven-shape system, seen in Figure 1-1, which emerged several decades later and was quite common among the hymnals that the first generations of country singers used. Traveling singing teachers hosted one- or two-week singing schools throughout the Southern Appalachians where local residents learned to read the shape notes and then took that musical knowledge back to their families and churches. Thus, gospel music was both a thriving industry and an integrated part of daily life for the people who would become the first generation of country singers. Women especially integrated the gospel songs into their daily lives, singing them while tending to children and chores. Many of the performers who became recording stars in early country music knew by heart dozens of gospel songs, such as "I Am Resolved," "Sweeping Through the Gates," and "The Old Rugged Cross," but they also frequently used these published hymnals to learn and perform even more gospel songs.

Listening Guide

"O Bury Me Not on the Lone Prairie" (1926)

PERFORMERS: Carl
T. Sprague (vocal
and guitar), with C.R.
Dockum (fiddle) and
H.J. Kenzie (fiddle)

SONGWRITER:
unknown; credited to
H. Clemens

ORIGINAL RELEASE:
Victor 20122

FORM: Strophic

STYLE: Hillbilly
(cowboy ballad)

Carl T. Sprague (1895–1979) was one of the first singers to bring cowboy songs into the emerging genre of country music. He grew up near Alvin, Texas, and worked as a ranch hand, all the while learning traditional cowboy songs from his uncle. After serving in the WWI, Sprague returned to college at Texas A&M (then the Agricultural and Mining College) where he sang on air with the amateur radio club that had been founded on the campus prior to WWI. When fellow Texan Vernon Dalhart found success in 1924 recording old-time mountain songs, Sprague traveled to New York to audition for Victor Records, with his repertory of working ranch hands' traditional cowboy songs. Sprague recorded from 1925 until 1929, but never pursued music full-time. He spent most of his life working at Texas A&M, and also served in the US Army.

"O Bury Me Not on the Lone Prairie," also called "The Dying Cowboy," appears in the many published volumes in the early twentieth century of songs collected from cowboys. It bears many similarities to even older folk songs, most specifically "The Ocean Burial," which starts with the words "O bury me not in the deep, deep sea," for which sheet music dates from at least 1850. The cowboy version was widely known by the end of the nineteenth century. When John Lomax published *Cowboy Songs and Other Frontier Ballads* in 1910, "The Dying Cowboy" was the first song in the collection, with nineteen complete verses and sheet music, and it also appears in the second edition of N. Howard Thorp's *Cowboy Songs* (1921).

The melody that Sprague sang in 1925 is very close to the one printed in Lomax's book: it has the mournful sound of a lamentation, sung in a minor musical key. The other singers who recorded the song in the 1920s used the same melody. By the 1930s, however, the words were being sung to a different melody, in a major musical key and with a more popular style. In 1939, the classic western film *Stagecoach*, starring John Wayne, used this song with its more pop-style melody as its theme song.

This song also sits at a crossroads of the various forces bringing country music into existence. It was a cowboy song that was present before the cowboy image became prevalent in country music. On the one hand, Sprague has been lauded by some historians because of his personal biography as a working cowboy who learned his songs on a ranch. On the other hand, he cultivated his performance style on a college campus, and traveled to New York to record. For this particular recording, two professional studio musicians were hired to play violins. And the song's widespread legacy came from its use in a Hollywood film. This recording is thus a great starting point to discuss how fans and historians value biography and performance practice in how they understand a particular recording's place in country music.

Sprague sings only six verses from the many that had been collected and published. The presence of the two fiddles is both representative of how common fiddles were in cowboy musical culture (more so than guitars, prior to the influence of Hollywood westerns), and a musical crossover from classical and theater performances, where violins were used for expressive emotional laments.

To a modern listener, this song's strophic form lacks the sort of climax or changes in energy level that we expect from more modern country music. The plaintive performance lacks any of the driving rhythms or even a chorus, which invites us to hear it in the context of its time and place.

Listen Side by Side Suggestion: Johnny Cash, "Bury Me Not on the Lone Prairie," *Johnny Cash Sings the Ballads of the True West* (1965).

TIME	FORM	LISTENING CUES	DISCUSSION
0:00	Introduction	Fiddle, accompanied by guitar	One fiddle plays half of the melody. The guitar plays only a few chords as accompaniment, and there is no driving rhythm.
0:16	Verse 1	"O bury me not..."	The first verse introduces Sprague's voice, accompanied only by the guitar. The text begins with a first-person declaration of the refrain, then switches to a third-person narration.
0:44	Verse 2	"He wailed in pain..."	Both violins provide subtle accompaniment and harmony here. The text is a third-person narration. Sprague sings the melody the same in each verse throughout the song.
1:14	Verse 3	"O bury me not..."	This verse begins with the same declaration as the first verse, which is the title of the song. This opening suggests that it might be a chorus, but the verse then continues with new words. Note that the odd-numbered verses all begin with the refrain.
1:42	Verse 4	"It matters not..."	This verse continues in the first-person narration of the dying cowboy. Both violins enter again, and the verse ends with the refrain (title).
2:12	Verse 5	"O bury me not...."	This verse advances the plot, recounting the actual burial and death of the cowboy. Here, as in verses 1 and 3, it opens with the refrain, and the violins are silent.
2:41	Verse 6	"And the cowboys now..."	The violins re-enter, accompanying only on the even-numbered verses. Note the rather abrupt ending of the song, which was typical in this era. The limitations of the technology meant that long ballads with lots of verses would simply stop at the end of a verse. The lowest note played by the violin at the very end reinforces the mood of the lamentation.

The blues formed an important musical source for early country music. One prominent form of blues music involves African American performers singing short verses (usually a rhymed couplet) over a repetitive chord progression played on guitar (see Appendix A). Sometimes called down-home blues or country blues, this musical style most often had lyrics that bemoaned love gone wrong and that were laced with double entendres or sexual metaphors. While the image of a solitary, introspective bluesman is common in American popular culture, blues performers frequently played for lively, raucous crowds (house parties) and engaged in group performances where each singer would **improvise** new verses in turn. Many other blues traditions influenced country music, including female performers, jug bands (in which a performer blew across the top of a ceramic jug to create bass notes for the ensemble), and ragtime-influenced blues performers. Among working-class Southerners, the blues was not an exclusively African American tradition. Both white and black performers played and sang blues music, and these performances appear frequently among early country music recordings.

The earliest vernacular (folk) music that record companies recorded was blues music. The first black vocal recording of a blues tune, Mamie Smith's "Crazy Blues" (1920), sold so well that record producers set out to find more blues performers. Those producers launched expeditions to the South, during which they recorded not only black blues artists but also a number of white country artists, thereby contributing to the emergence of the new genre.

Jazz grew out of the popular dance styles in New Orleans, drawing on many of the same musical sources that provided country music's foundation. By World War I, bands had taken the rhythmic patterns from ragtime, added a new element called **swing**, which involved unequal divisions of the musical beat, and used them to devise a new musical genre that emphasized improvisation and came to be known as jazz. By the early 1920s, record labels were recording this new music and distributing it widely. Country musicians heard recordings, and sometimes radio broadcasts, by Louis Armstrong, Jelly Roll Morton, and King Oliver, along with the larger dance bands such as Fletcher Henderson's. The strongest influence of jazz on country music would appear in the early 1930s, but even in the 1920s, country musicians were well aware of the developments in jazz.

Tin Pan Alley was the origin of many popular songs, and it became a major source of music for early country entertainers. Referring specifically to a neighborhood in New York City located between Fifth and Sixth Avenues on West 28th Street, Tin Pan Alley was the nickname given to a group of music publishers who set up shop there in the late 1880s. The term referred to the cacophony of song pluggers (performers hired to advertise new songs) banging out new compositions on pianos as a way of enticing prospective buyers. Those publishing firms employed songwriters who cranked out popular tunes for professional performers, especially stars of Broadway and vaudeville.

Vaudeville was a style of stage show that featured variety acts and whose performing troupes traveled a circuit of theaters, taking their acts from town to town and spreading newly popular songs to their audiences. Many country singers thought of themselves simply as entertainers rather than as belonging to any particular subcategory of country or hillbilly entertainers. As such, they emulated the most popular singers of their day and learned many of their songs from live performances, including vaudeville.

Two additional traditions of traveling stage show, namely **medicine shows** and **minstrel shows,** spread more songs throughout the communities from which country musicians would emerge. Medicine shows flourished from the late nineteenth century until the 1930s. Such shows were run by salesmen with no formal medical training who traveled from town to town hawking elixirs that promised myriad miracle cures. These salesmen hired entertainers to travel with them; when they set up in a town, the musicians would perform to draw a crowd to whom the salesmen could then pitch their wares. Those entertainers mastered the art of holding an audience's attention, and many early country musicians honed their stagecraft while performing with medicine shows.

Minstrel shows first emerged in the early nineteenth century as traveling theater troupes that entertained local audiences with performances of comedy and song-and-dance numbers. By the late nineteenth century, minstrel shows had evolved into a relatively fixed pattern for performances, a particular series of skits, speeches, songs, dances, and humorous dialogue. The performers were in blackface: both white and black actors used burnt cork to darken their faces and hands and present extreme racist stereotypes and mocking caricatures of African-American identity. The stock black characters that appeared in minstrel shows included Zip Coon, a foppish, dandy character who attempted futilely to put on high-class airs, and Jim Crow, a Southern rural slave character, often singing nostalgically about happy days on a plantation. The dialogue and music mainly represented how northern, urban whites thought Southern blacks sounded, acted, and danced. Many aspects of minstrelsy and blackface performance were abhorrently racist. Scholars have expanded our understanding of the tradition beyond that mere condemnation, however. One common interpretation focuses on the idea of a mask; even black performers in a minstrel show had to "black up" their faces to portray minstrel characters, which suggests that minstrelsy allowed performers to enact transgressive and subversive ideas about class, race, and resentment in public. For instance, while some aspects of the performances involved white entertainers mocking and dehumanizing blacks, other aspects provided a way for both white and black entertainers to push off those negative judgments onto the "masked," artificially blackened characters and thus insulate themselves while offering disguised social commentary on injustice.

Blackface minstrelsy's stock characters and stage practices, which were well known to working-class audiences, provided many of the models on which early country entertainers built their own performances. Blackface skits that relied on supposed Southern black dialects for part of their humor appeared at country barn dances as late as the 1950s. Many early country stars worked as blackface entertainers in their early careers, when they developed many of their onstage skills. And the hillbilly rube character who appears frequently in early country music—an unsophisticated hick who is often surprisingly clever and gets the best of the wiser, more sophisticated urban characters—was extremely similar to one of the stock characters found in the minstrel show. Many of the songs that were very popular among early country singers came straight from the minstrel stage: the fiddle tune "Turkey in the Straw," for instance, was known on the minstrel stage as "Old Zip Coon," and "Old Dan Tucker" had been a favorite minstrel song that subsequently became a country and bluegrass favorite in the early decades of the genre. Some scholars have gone so far as to suggest that country barn dance programs were essentially minstrel shows in which the performers did not "black up." Country music's indebtedness to minstrelsy radically complicates the racial identity of the music (see Chapter 2) and adds a burden to its history that it still carries to the present.

Drawing their songs from all of these sources and performance traditions, early country singers often passed the songs around orally and learned them by ear, with the result that the songs took on local variations and adaptations along the way. Thus, whatever their origins, by the time country singers recorded them, the songs had become personalized expressions of their performers' own identity.

New Technologies: Records and Radio

New access to sound in the early twentieth century revolutionized the way that middle- and working-class people heard music. Prior to the invention of radio and records, all music was live and only audible in the presence of the musicians. If you wanted to hear a singer, you had to be in the same place as that singer during the performance. There was no way to revisit that particular performance later or experience it in any setting away from the actual performer. For most people, especially in rural locations, music came from either traveling entertainers or members of the immediate family and community performing for each other.

All of that changed in 1877 when Thomas Edison invented the phonograph. Initially conceived as a way to record speech as either a novelty or as a means to dictate business correspondence, the phonograph used a stylus to transfer sound waves to a rotating cylinder. Many other inventors and rival companies continued the development of sound-recording technology, including, significantly, Emile Berliner, who patented his gramophone in 1887. Instead of recorded cylinders, this device used flat discs, which would eventually become the industry standard. Inventors continued to refine the various machines, and, by the dawn of the twentieth century, the concept of mass reproduction of sound recordings for entertainment purposes was well established. In those years, three record labels, Victor, Columbia, and Edison, successfully tapped into the market for recordings of high-class opera stars, and families across the country began purchasing record players for their homes. By World War I, record players cost anywhere from $15 for a basic model to $175 or more for a high-end player. In 1917, many of the patents that had protected phonograph and gramophone technology expired, which meant that start-up record labels could now compete, and a year later, sales of record players and records topped $158 million. The number of record companies expanded dramatically and, as a result, the major labels, such as Victor and Edison, found their profits increasingly squeezed.

RECORD INDUSTRY TERMINOLOGY

Much of the terminology that surrounds the record industry comes from the technology used in early recording sessions. For many years, recording equipment literally carved the sound waves into wax coatings on discs, which gave rise to the common saying that musicians "cut" or "waxed" tunes. Records consisted of large, flat discs with one song per side, so musicians talked about the number of "sides" they recorded during a particular session, which meant the number of songs.

By 1920, the record industry was near saturation. Too many new labels were competing for audiences, and sales were dwindling. A second factor threatening the economic success of the record labels was the advent of commercial radio broadcasts, which offered people a free alternative for hearing music. These conditions combined to motivate record companies to look for new music and markets. Their first find was blues performers, starting with Mamie Smith who recorded "Crazy Blues" for the OKeh label in 1920. The record's success launched OKeh into the big leagues and sparked widespread interest on the part of other labels to diversify their musical offerings and seek out both black and white musical performers in styles they had previously overlooked. The result was the emergence of both blues and country music as commercial genres, as record producers left the confines of New York City to find untapped talent in remote areas. That climate expanded the record business for country music at an astonishing rate in the early to mid-1920s.

ARTIST PROFILE

Fiddlin' John Carson (1874–1949)

Credited with the first commercial recording of hillbilly music, Fiddlin' John Carson brought old-time mountain music into the bustling, industrial urban south. Popular sources cite his birth year as 1868, but historians have documented that Carson was most likely born March 23, 1874, in Cobb County, Georgia. Carson worked odd jobs in his youth, including a stint as a water boy for black railroad construction crews, and taught himself to play the fiddle. In 1900, he moved his wife and children to Atlanta and took a job with the Exposition Cotton Mills, joining throngs of other migrants leaving the rural mountains to work in the growing cities. Carson was caught in a generation of workers who suffered repressive employment practices within the larger trend toward industrialization. Ironically, Carson's participation in a yearlong strike at the mill fostered his budding career as an entertainer, because it gave him both time to practice and the need to earn money during the strike to provide for his family.

During his years in Atlanta, Carson built his reputation both by busking on the street and through celebrated triumphs at fiddle contests. In 1913, he wrote several ballads about a sensational murder of thirteen-year-old Mary Phagan and the trial of her accused murderer, Leo Frank, which had captured the attention of the entire Atlanta community. Frank, Jewish and from Brooklyn, aroused strident anti-Semitism within the working-class white community in Georgia, who further resented Frank's social position as superintendent of the firm where Phagan worked. Carson captured those sentiments in his compositions and, after a mob lynched the likely innocent Frank, Carson played and sang these songs to the crowds who gathered at the county courthouse.

Carson took home top honors at the Georgia Old-Time Fiddlers' Convention contests and was frequently celebrated in the local press. By 1922, Carson had put together

Radio had been essentially a research project during World War I, but in the years that followed, it emerged as a wildly popular source of entertainment, especially for families in rural areas. Experimental broadcasts of concerts and sporting events took place in 1919, and by 1920 the first commercially licensed radio station was on the air. Soon thereafter, radio stations appeared across the country. By 1922, there were eighty-nine licensed stations operating in the South. Most were owned by corporations that used the stations as advertising, but in order to get an audience, the stations had to broadcast something that appealed to their prospective listeners. Their typical broadcast schedule consisted of fifteen- or thirty-minute segments of live entertainment, cultural programming, farm reports, and news, with each segment sponsored by a particular corporation or product. By 1930, approximately one out of three homes in America had a radio in it, and families without one often joined neighbors to hear favorite programs.

Radio stations played a crucial role in country music's early years by disseminating country music to an audience eager to hear it and by providing employment to the first generation of professional country entertainers. On March 16, 1922, the a string band and was earning a significant part of his income through entertaining. His daughter Rosa Lee Carson (1909–1992) joined his act under the nickname "Moonshine Kate," which enhanced their stage image as rural mountain folks.

Already a local celebrity, Fiddlin' John Carson performed on Atlanta's WSB station on September 9, 1922, as part of a Saturday night variety program. Fan mail poured in, and Carson became a regular performer. Atlanta business-man and furniture salesman Polk C. Brockman saw a potential market for recordings of Carson's music and set up a field session with producer Ralph Peer for OKeh Records. Carson cut two tunes at the first such recording session ever held in the South. Brockman cleverly took the newly pressed recordings to the opening night of the Fiddlers' Convention that year and sold an astonishing number. OKeh and Peer had stumbled onto a new commercial genre of music.

Carson continued to record over the next decade, specializing in old-time songs and eschewing the newer, popular tunes that many of the younger hillbilly entertainers adopted. His musical career was shaped by his various political involvements; he regularly performed at functions of the Ku Klux Klan, of which he was also a member, and he performed extensively on the campaign trail for Eugene Talmadge, among other activities. His political support earned him the job of elevator operator in the Georgia State Capitol, where he remained for many years. Carson passed away in 1949, still fiddling until the day he died.

Carson represents an older generation of commercial hillbilly entertainers who refined their stagecraft before the advent of radio. These entertainers passed their old-time tradi-tions and songs on to new generations through their records. Carson purportedly disliked the newfangled, popular styles that hillbilly musicians adopted in the 1930s and beyond. His music was very much a product of its time and place—a segregated, racially charged South where the rural way of life collided with urban industrialization.

Atlanta Journal's station WSB (whose call sign stood for their slogan, "Welcome South, Brother!") went on the air with a 100-watt transmitter, which they upgraded a few months later to 500 watts. On a clear night in the early 1920s, that station could be heard all the way to Canada and Mexico, reaching an estimated two million listeners. On September 9, 1922, WSB aired local entertainer Fiddlin' John Carson, accompanied by a string band. That was the first broadcast of what would come to be called country music. Listener response was astonishing. In those days, people wrote letters or sent telegrams to their radio stations to express their opinions of various shows. Fan mail poured in, and WSB continued to broadcast Carson and similar acts, opening doors for other local musicians who would also become country stars.

In Fort Worth, Texas, the *Fort Worth Star-Telegram* company's WBAP ("We Bring a Program") station went on the air on May 2, 1922. On January 4, 1923, the station broadcast an old-time fiddler on a square dance program, thereby in-augurating the radio barn dance tradition. By then, radio stations were becoming increasingly common. In Charlotte, North Carolina, three amateur radio fans pooled their resources to start WBT, which also got its commercial license in 1922 and would play a significant role in country music's development. But the two stations that would have the biggest impact on the fledgling country music industry were Chicago's WLS and Nashville's WSM.

Owned by Sears, Roebuck and Company, WLS ("World's Largest Store," the Sears advertising motto) went on the air on April 12, 1924. One week later, on April 19, the station advertised a "National Barn Dance" program, which featured an old-time string band playing square dance tunes. WLS's rural, folksy programming proved very popular with its audiences, and the station's managers subsequently expanded their offerings of that music. Before long, a slot on WLS was highly coveted among country musicians, and many of the stars of the 1930s honed their skills in front of the WLS microphones.

In Nashville, the National Life and Accident Insurance Company's WSM ("We Shield Millions," referring to the company's core business) began broadcasting October 5, 1925, with a 1,000-watt transmitter, a very powerful radio signal for its time. On November 28, WSM aired an unscheduled performance by old-time champion fiddler Uncle Jimmy Thompson. As had been the case in Atlanta when Fiddlin' John Carson played, the listeners' response was overwhelming. WSM executives were already contemplating a barn dance program like those at other stations, and Thompson's popularity tipped the scales. On December 26, 1925, WSM launched its regularly scheduled barn dance, which would become the Grand Ole Opry, the now-legendary show on which today's best-known country singers still aspire to perform.

The birth of country music as a commercial genre required some way for audiences to get the music, and the developments in both the record industry and radio during the early 1920s made that possible. Working-class people now had unprecedented access to music. Musicians had new sources of income. Competition between record labels and from the new medium of radio drove producers to try new styles of music they had previously ignored. And radio stations, driven by the ability to advertise commercial products to a huge population, were eager to support entertainers who could win over those targeted audiences.

Audiences

When the first country music records were released, record label executives were surprised by the astonishing number of people ready and waiting to buy them. Before the 1920s, record companies had ignored large segments of their prospective audiences—mainly working-class populations—especially in the South and rural Midwest. But in the years following World War I, those audiences gained economic and cultural power, and therefore the attention of the music industry.

During the 1920s, many different social forces brought newfound attention to the culture and music of rural Southerners, especially in the Appalachian Mountains. Henry Ford, best known for his mass-produced automobiles, decided that old-time music and dancing were culturally superior to what he perceived as moral degradation brought on by jazz and urban entertainment. Ford used some of his considerable wealth and influence to sponsor fiddle contests, publications, and events that promoted the supposedly pristine, uncorrupted music of old-time entertainers and advance his very narrow views on what was of cultural value. Among many upper-class people in the Northeast, Southern mountain culture was a romanticized ideal that counterbalanced the rush of modernization and the apparent demise of old-fashioned values in the 1920s. Their condescending and negative attitudes toward working-class Southerners are readily apparent, however. Newspaper articles described the population as ignorant, illiterate, inbred, and backward. Many others had good intentions and better opinions of the region and its people, but still viewed Appalachian culture through a lens of superiority; ballad collectors such as Olive Dame Campbell, for instance, wanted to help the rural people from whom she gathered songs to develop their own culture, which she thought needed outside assistance in order to flourish. These more positive attitudes brought both money and attention to that population, but they also propagated the myth that Appalachia housed an essentially primitive, idealized folk culture.

The people who would become the country music audience were experiencing dramatic changes in technologies, transportation, and exposure to the world beyond their local communities. As large industries built up the South, families who had previously lived in remote areas with little or no disposable income and limited interaction with urban culture moved to take advantage of new jobs. Within the Piedmont (the region just east of the Appalachians through Virginia, the Carolinas, and Georgia), the textile industry became the primary source of employment for many families. The employees held physically taxing, dangerous, and underpaid jobs without any protection from labor unions. Mills were hot, poorly ventilated, and crowded working environments, and little attention was paid to worker safety. Employees and their families often lived in company-owned housing, and the company owners often set up community-enrichment programs. Purported to raise the employees' standard of living, these housing arrangements and community programs in fact increased the dependence of the entire community on the employer, and thus further limited the workers' ability to stand up to unfair employment practices. Nonetheless, these community programs usually included musical education, and the close living and working quarters facilitated musical collaborations. Thus, the mill towns were fertile communities for both audiences and performers of early country music.

Outside of the Piedmont, the general industrialization that had accompanied World War I had a similar effect on audience development. Although wages were low, they still offered monetary income to a population that had previously had little access to commercial goods. Automobiles let people travel farther and faster than before, while radio brought the voices and sounds of places formerly only imagined. One lasting effect of the war was that many young people had traveled around the world, bringing home both exposure to new sounds and sights and a heightened nostalgia for local culture.

The Business of Music

The driving force behind the emergence of country music was money. Performers wanted to be paid for making music. Record executives wanted to sell records. Radio executives wanted listeners to hear advertisements so they would buy sponsors' products and services. And audiences had the money to make all of that happen. The business of country music was vital to its emergence as a genre.

For record labels, one pressing question was what to call this new music. Most of the record labels had catalogs, which were official listings of their recordings, organized by musical genre. As they began to record rural music, by both white and black artists, they realized that they did not know what to call this music or how to sell it. To the record companies, the factors that differentiated this music from other genres were neither the songs nor the musical performances themselves. Many of the same songs had been recorded earlier, but by trained classical singers. Instead, the record companies considered the music different because of the identity of the performers (poor, mostly self-taught musicians with rural Southern connections) and the intended audiences, whom the record executives assumed were much the same as the musicians. They also differentiated the musicians by race; the music by black and white musicians was sold in separate catalogs. For black performers, the term that the record labels chose was "race records." For white performers, record executives initially tried out a variety of descriptions including "Old Familiar Tunes" and "Olde Time Tunes," but the term that emerged as a prominent identifier for this music was "hillbilly."

The term **hillbilly** first appeared in print in 1900 in the *New York Journal.* In 1926, *Variety* magazine defined a hillbilly as "a North Carolina or Tennessee and adjacent mountaineer type of illiterate white whose creed and allegiance are to the Bible, the Chautauqua, and the phonograph. . . . The mountaineer is of 'poor white trash' genera." Yet in spite of such derogatory associations, early country performers reportedly assigned the term to themselves. In January 1925, Al and Joe Hopkins, Tony Alderman, and John Rector recorded six songs for producer Ralph Peer. When Peer inquired as to the group's name for the necessary paperwork and logs of the session, Al Hopkins reportedly replied, "Call the band anything you want. We are nothing but a bunch of hillbillies from North Carolina and Virginia anyway." Within a short time, "hillbilly" had become an accepted identifier for much of the music that would later come to be known as the first generation of country. Like many other terms, it has been used both affectionately and insultingly over the years; many country singers identified themselves as hillbillies as a way of expressing pride in their rural, Southern, working-class heritage, yet those same singers sometimes bristled when outsiders used the term. In this book, we will use the word "hillbilly" to describe the musical styles of the first generation of country music that was generally marketed under that term and whose performers often embraced it as a description of themselves.

Along with a name, the new musical genre required an image that distinguished it from other genres. When the first hillbilly performers began recording, most of them presented themselves as well-dressed entertainers. Over the next few years, however, that image changed into a stereotypical hillbilly costume, which created a visual brand for the music. The best illustration of this is a set of photographs of Dr. Bate's band, one of the regular groups on WSM's Grand Ole Opry. Dr. Bate (1875–1936), a well-respected local physician who also fronted one of the most popular dance bands in Nashville, began performing as a regular act from the earliest days of the Opry. Publicity photos show Dr. Bate's band as sharp-dressed entertainers in conservative suits (Figure 1-2). During the show's first few years, announcer George D. Hay and others pushed the entertainers on the Opry to adopt costumes and personalities of hayseed hicks. Dr. Bate's band was named the Possum Hunters, and new publicity photos showed them in tattered overalls and sloppy hats with ties askew and pants rolled up (Figure 1-3). While many of the first

Figure 1-2 Opry performers Dr. Bate and the Possum Hunters, 1926, dressed as professional entertainers.

Source: Courtesy of Country Music Hall of Fame and Museum.

Figure 1-3 Dr. Bate and the Possum Hunters, 1928, dressed in rustic hillbilly costumes as part of an advertisement.

Source: Courtesy of Country Music Hall of Fame and Museum.

generation of hillbilly musicians did come from poor, rural backgrounds, the images that audiences grew to associate with the music were costumed constructions of a stereotype that helped make the music seem even more different.

Although song **publishers** were not as visible to the music's audience as the performers and record labels, they were an essential link in the music business chain that connected performers and their audiences. Every time a song was sold on a record or on sheet music, the person or company who held the copyright to that song earned royalties. Thus, the copyrights to popular songs were valuable possessions, and publishers—who often controlled those rights—wielded significant power within the country music genre.

If this business infrastructure had not been in place, the transformation of folk music and musicians into a viable, even thriving, genre known as country music would never have taken place. Rather than tainting country music, the industry's infrastructure is an integral component of the genre that allows it to evolve. No one understood this better than the first generation of country entertainers. The $50 they earned for each song they sang was motivation to come back and make more records, and a regular spot on a sponsored radio show reached audiences that would then come to their concerts. Finally, although they saw it as a business, the early country performers were also fans; they, like their audiences, loved listening to many types of music on their home record players and radios, and many of them aspired to stardom like the pop icons of their day.

HOW THE SOUNDS GOT ON THE RECORDS

The way sound recordings were made changed radically during the 1920s. At the beginning of the decade, recordings were still made acoustically, which meant that the musicians sang or played their instruments directly into a horn-shaped device. The horn directed the sound waves into the recording equipment, where a mechanical process transferred the sound waves to a stylus that carved grooves into a wax-coated master disc.

In 1925, the major record labels began using electric microphones in the recording process. The microphone converted the music's sound waves into an electrical signal; this signal was then amplified and transmitted to the recording machine, where it was transferred by electromagnetic means to the cutter, which carved the grooves in the recording disc. Electric recording technology was much more sensitive and captured a much wider range of frequencies—low notes and high notes, loud sounds and quiet sounds. Electrical recordings allowed performers greater variation in volume and tone quality in their performance, including the option of softer "crooning" styles of singing, which, in turn, had a drastic effect on the musical styles in country music.

The Performers

The fifth and final element that contributed to the birth of country music was a group of talented, motivated, and creative performers. Literally hundreds of different musicians made hillbilly records during the first decade of country music's history, although only a few achieved any lasting fame. As they were carving out new territory as entertainers, there was no consistency in their choices of instruments, repertory, or singing technique, and the hillbilly-era recordings ranged widely in style. This brief survey of performers introduces only a small selection of entertainers, instruments, and musical styles from the early years of hillbilly recordings. The primary instruments and styles featured in this music are fiddlers, banjo players, harmonica players, string bands, and, of course, singers. In each case we see musicians walking a fine line between amateur and professional performers in these early years. Who got a chance to make records, and who parlayed those opportunities into full-time musical careers, was not entirely predictable from circumstances.

By most accounts, the first country recording was made by fiddler Alexander Campbell "Eck" Robertson (1887–1975). Originally from Arkansas, Robertson lived in Texas, where he was widely known as a champion fiddler. In June 1922, he and fiddler Henry Gilliland (1845–1924) traveled to Virginia to perform at a reunion for Civil War veterans. After the reunion, the pair hopped on a train to New York City, determined to make records.

Figure 1-4 Eck Robertson.

Source: Southern Folklife Collection, Wilson library, The Unviersity of North Carolina at Chapel Hill.

When they arrived, they talked their way into the Victor Talking Machine Company, where the studio engineers recorded them playing four duets on June 30. The next day, Robertson returned to the studio and played six more tunes, including "Sallie Gooden," a traditional fiddle tune that Robertson performed with a series of impressive variations. Victor's executives had no idea yet of the potential market for hillbilly recordings and only released one record, "Sallie Gooden," backed by "Arkansas Traveler." The record sold only a modest number of copies, and Robertson did not return to the studio until 1929. And while Robertson gets credited by most historians for making the first country record, the first bona fide country hit was also by a fiddle player, in this case Fiddlin' John Carson from Atlanta.

DeFord Bailey (1899–1982)

DeFord Bailey was one of the most popular performers on the Grand Ole Opry in the late 1920s and the first African American star of country music. Although he also sang and played both the banjo and guitar, Bailey was known as "The Harmonica Wizard." Audiences who heard him on the radio may not have known that he was black, but audiences who saw him perform live on Opry tours certainly did. Although most record companies catalogued all black artists in their "blues" series rather than their "hillbilly" series, based solely on the performer's race, the Brunswick label released Bailey's first commercial recordings in 1928 in their "hillbilly" series, further acknowledgement that he was accepted as an early country musician.

Bailey was born December 14, 1899, in Smith County, Tennessee, and grew up in railroad station hamlets outside Nashville. He suffered childhood illnesses that left him weak and short in stature but which also afforded him ample opportunity to develop his harmonica skills. He learned to imitate the sounds around him, including passing trains. He also absorbed the musical traditions of old-time fiddling from several relatives and described his influences as "black hillbilly."

Bailey first performed on radio in 1925 for Nashville's fledgling WDAD station. By July of the next year, he had joined the regular lineup of hillbilly performers on WSM's Barn Dance, where he inspired emcee George D. Hay to rename the show. In December 1927, WSM aired a network broadcast of Walter Damrosch's NBC *Music Appreciation Hour*, which had featured only a piece of modern classical music depicting a train ride. Immediately after that, Bailey stepped up to the microphone and played his signature piece, "Pan American Blues," which is a blues-influenced imitation of a train rolling down the tracks and blowing its whistle, all done on solo harmonica. Afterward, Hay quipped, "For the past hour we have been

Banjo players also featured prominently in the early days of hillbilly recording. Like Fiddlin' John Carson, Uncle Dave Macon (1870–1952) was part of an older generation who moved into the entertainment business as the forces of modernization passed him by in his other profession. Uncle Dave, as he was known, remembered firsthand the vaudeville acts and traveling stage shows of the late nineteenth century that had passed through his hometown in Tennessee. His musical influences included both white and black entertainers, from whom he adapted blues and comedy routines. As a young man, he ran the Macon Midway Mule and Wagon Transportation Company in Murfreesboro, Tennessee, just south of Nashville. But when the automobile put him out of business in 1920, he turned to his banjo for a new career. Before long, Uncle Dave was touring on the vaudeville circuit and gaining notoriety for his bawdy humor and catchy songs. His recording career was launched courtesy of the Nashville-based Sterchi Brothers, who owned a furniture company. Furniture dealers such as Polk Brockman in Atlanta and the Sterchis sold record players in their stores, along with records to play on them, which gave them a vested interest in developing new, local talent. The Sterchis sent Uncle Dave and fiddler Sid Harkreader to New York in 1924 to record for Vocalion Records. Macon's solo rendition of "Keep My Skillet Good and Greasy," accompanied by banjo, captures the energy and appeal that he used to win over live audiences, while representing an old-time style of banjo playing.

listening to the music taken largely from the Grand Opera, but from now on we will present the Grand Ole Opry."

Bailey made two sets of commercial recordings during his life. In 1927, Hay sent him to New York City, where he cut eight sides for Brunswick. A year later, Bailey took part in the first commercial recording session in Nashville, produced by Ralph Peer. Bailey remained a major star on the Opry until 1941, when he was fired. By then, the audience's preferences and tastes had changed, and Bailey's harmonica solos were not part of the current trends in country music. A conflict between performance rights organizations (who handle copyright royalties) also prevented him from playing his signature tunes on air, which left him with nothing to perform. He retired from the musical spotlight, appearing only a few times as he got older. Bailey spent the rest of his life in Nashville, doing odd jobs to make ends meet. In 2005, he was inducted posthumously into the Country Music Hall of Fame.

Figure 1-5 Deford Bailey with his harmonica attached to a megaphone.

Source: Courtesy of Country Music Hall of Fame and Museum.

Banjo contests were nearly as common in the Appalachian South as fiddle contests, and one admired champion was Samantha Bumgarner (c. 1880–1960). In 1924, she and her friend Eva Davis went to New York to make records. Without an appointment, they walked in on the executives at Columbia Records and convinced them to record twelve songs. "Aunt Samantha" did not, however, manage to launch a commercial career as a hillbilly artist. She made no more recordings for almost thirty years, but instead became a staple of the folk festival circuit.

Hillbilly recordings in the 1920s featured several harmonica players, although the instrument would not be common in country music again until several decades later. Along with Eck Robertson and Fiddlin' John Carson, Henry Whitter (1892–1941), a guitarist, harmonica player, and singer, was one of the first earliest recording artists of hillbilly music. In March 1923, he reportedly traveled to New York City and made a few test recordings for OKeh records. None of those were ever released, but in December of that year, following the commercial success of Fiddlin' John Carson, Whitter returned and made several successful records, including his best known, "Wreck on the Southern Old 97." Another early country music harmonica player was Dr. Humphrey Bate (1875–1936), who not only starred on Nashville's Opry but also introduced "Harmonica Wizard" DeFord Bailey (see Artist Profile) to the show's management.

Listening Guide

"Hallelujah Side" (1926)

PERFORMERS: Ernest Stoneman and the Dixie Mountaineers (Ernest Stoneman, vocal and guitar; Kahle Brewer, vocal and fiddle; Walter Mooney, vocal; Tom Leonard, vocal; Hattie Stoneman, vocal; Irma Frost, organ) Songwriter: Johnson Oatman Jr. and J. Howard Entwisle

ORIGINAL RELEASE: Victor 20224

FORM: Verse-chorus

STYLE: Hillbilly gospel

Ernest Stoneman (1893–1964) was perhaps the most enterprising of the first generation of country recording artists. Born and raised in Virginia's Blue Ridge Mountains, Ernest was the eldest son of a lay Baptist preacher, Elisha Stoneman. Elisha frequently took his children along when he traveled to preach at nearby churches. As the eldest surviving child, Ernest was in charge of leading the singing, an assignment that taught him dozens of gospel hymns. He also taught himself guitar, banjo, and especially autoharp with help and encouragement from his cousins.

Ernest's wife, Hattie Stoneman (née Frost [1900–1976]), and her younger sister, Irma Lee Frost, were largely responsible for Ernest's musical success. The girls' father, John William "Bill" Frost, was one of the better fiddlers in Galax, Virginia, and he contributed to Ernest's musical development by making a home-made banjo for Ernest and a cousin to practice on. Irma was an accomplished church organist and could read musical notation, while Hattie took after her father as a fiddler.

Never one to keep a job for long, Ernest was working as a carpenter when he heard a record made by his acquaintance Henry Whitter. Deciding that he could sing better, Ernest contacted two record labels and paid his own way to New York for an audition. During the first few years of his career, Stoneman cut records for at least six different labels, often with ensembles he put together with family members and assorted friends and neighbors. He redid songs that other singers had recorded and acted as a regional contact for record executives seeking other talented musicians from the southern Virginia area.

"Hallelujah Side" was a collaboration between Johnson Oatman, Jr., who wrote the words to this as well as other popular hymns such as "Count Your Blessings," and J. Howard Entwisle, who also composed the music for "Keep on the Sunny Side." The lyrics celebrated the joy found in God's grace for Christians as far superior to any possible earthly wealth, a theme common in the revivalist hymns and one that found resonance with audiences who themselves had little in terms of material wealth. Oatman and Entwisle published "Hallelujah Side" in 1898.

Hattie and Irma had a large collection of paperback hymnals from which the group sang at several recording sessions. On September 21, 1926, Ernest Stoneman and the Dixie Mountaineers recorded "Hallelujah Side" along with six other hymns for Victor Records. For accompaniment, they used guitar, fiddle, and pump organ. The rhythms of the hymn were driven mostly by Stoneman's guitar technique—the pattern of a bass note followed by three strummed chords was his signature. Ernest and Hattie sang the melody, Hattie in the higher soprano register and Ernest an octave below. The other musicians sang the harmony mostly as printed in the published version of the hymn, although, as they did for the group's other recordings, they simplified the rhythms and chords to suit their own style. The tinny, nasal timbre of their voices was a common style of singing in the Southern Appalachians, whose characteristics are further emphasized by the recording technology of that time. The group performed the hymn much as they would have in a local church setting, singing straight through verses and choruses.

Figure 1-6 Courtesy of Patsy Stoneman and Country Music Hall of Fame and Museum.

TIME	FORM	LISTENING CUES	DISCUSSION
0:00	Instrumental introduction	Fiddle, organ, and guitar	The organ's low notes stick out in the musical texture, while the fiddle plays the melody with the upper notes of the organ. The instruments play through the verse of the hymn.
0:21	Verse 1	"Once a sinner far from Jesus, I was perishing with cold. . ."	The voices enter tentatively at first. Ernest Stoneman sings the melody an octave below Hattie. The other voices fill in the four-part harmony. The verse ends with the song's title.
0:42	Chorus	"Oh, Glory be to Jesus. . ."	The chorus uses part of the same melody as the verse and ends again with the song's title.

Continued

Listening Guide

"Hallelujah Side" (1926) **Continued**

TIME	FORM	LISTENING CUES	DISCUSSION
1:02	Verse 2	"Though the world may sweep around me..."	The musicians continue straight into the second verse with no break after the chorus. The fiddle can be heard playing a decorative descant during this verse.
1:23	Chorus	"Oh, Glory be to Jesus..."	The chorus repeats. The lower men's harmony is clearly audible in this section.
1:42	Verse 3	"Not for all the earth's gold millions would I leave this precious place..."	The third verse celebrates the value of Christian salvation over earthly wealth.
2:03	Chorus	"Oh, Glory be to Jesus..."	The final chorus is identical to the earlier iterations. At the end, Stoneman's guitar chords can be heard in their typical note-strum-strum-strum pattern. The recording ends at 2:24; there was not enough time allowed by the recording equipment for another verse and chorus.

The singers on early hillbilly records ranged from instrumentalists such as Fiddlin' John Carson, Uncle Dave Macon, and Charlie Poole, who simply sang as part of their act although they were not particularly famous for their vocal talent, to professionally trained vocalists. These professional singers held obvious appeal for the record companies because they lived near the major recording studios, making it unnecessary to transport bulky equipment hundreds of miles. They also typically read music and were already familiar with recording studios' procedures. Yet their role in the early years of country music is ironic, given that in the 1920s, the performer's biography was the primary delineator of the country genre. Furthermore, fans have valued early country music in many cases for its perceived authenticity as an expression of lived, working-class rural experience, thus complicating the very notion of authenticity as fans have constructed it in country music.

String bands, usually consisting of one or more fiddles, banjo, and guitar, were also extremely common in early hillbilly recordings. Almost every radio station had one or more resident string bands, and most hillbilly musicians recorded with some version of a string band during the course of their careers. Groups such as Gid Tanner and the Skillet Lickers, from Atlanta, Georgia, brought the same humor, vocal patter, and excitement into the recording studio that made them regional favorites for dances and gatherings. On some records, such as the traditional fiddle tune "Soldier's Joy," the band members introduce the song just as they would to a live crowd, encouraging everyone to roll up the carpets and dance along. The Skillet Lickers included two of the biggest stars in early hillbilly music, blind vocalist and guitarist Riley Puckett and fiddler Clayton McMichen.

In North Carolina, Charlie Poole and the North Carolina Ramblers became major stars, as well. Charlie Poole (1892–1931) was, by all accounts, a hell-raisin' entertainer who even predicted his own untimely demise at age thirty-nine. In 1917, Poole went to work in the textile mills in Spray, North Carolina, but for musicians such as Charlie Poole and his bandmates, the drudgery of a mill worker's life was a powerful incentive to become paid performers. Determined to seek their own opportunities, in the summer of 1925, Poole, Posey Rorer, and Norman Woodlieff hopped a train to New York City. There they convinced Columbia executives to record four songs on the label's "Old Familiar Tunes" series. "Don't Let Your Deal Go Down" was their first release, and it sold a reputed 102,000 copies—a stunning success for that era and an illustration of the popularity enjoyed by string bands.

One of the most industrious bandleaders was Ernest Stoneman, a musician from the Galax, Virginia, area. Stoneman's primary instrument was the autoharp, but he often accompanied himself with guitar. At other times he fronted a well-known string band (see Listening Guide). His ensemble's membership was constantly in flux. Even the band's name changed frequently: when Stoneman recorded gospel hymns, his group was known as the Dixie Mountaineers, but when they recorded racier comedy numbers, they were called the Blue Ridge Corn Shuckers. Sometimes, changes in personnel and band names were merely attempts to circumvent exclusive contracts with any one record label. Stoneman, for instance, held contracts with multiple record labels at the same time, a practical move for someone trying to make a living in the recording business but one that required some careful maneuvering.

Vernon Dalhart (1883–1948) is the most famous of these early hillbilly music stars who was not, biographically speaking, a hillbilly. Raised in Dallas, Texas, Dalhart (born Marion Try Slaughter) trained as a classical musician specializing in light opera. He moved to New York City in 1910, where he worked as a professional musician and made records of popular songs. In 1924, Edison (one of the big three record labels) hired Dalhart to sing "Wreck of the Old 97," a version of the song that Henry Whitter had recently recorded that was proving quite popular. Dalhart's unprecedented commercial success as a hillbilly singer has been a point of consternation for many historians and fans; his trained voice and professionally accompanied New York studio sessions produced recordings that fans nonetheless heard and endorsed as the essence of country music.

Other singers, such as Bradley Kincaid (1895–1989), combined a smooth, trained vocal style with a personal investment in disseminating old-time folk songs that he collected. Born in Kentucky, Kincaid began performing on WLS's National Barn Dance in 1926 and made his first records a year later. Although Kincaid's voice had the same resonant, sweet, even polished sound as did many popular singers outside of country music, he spent his time researching old-time songs and attempting to preserve what he believed were authentic folk melodies. He then made recordings of many of those songs and published songbooks with his favorites, which sold extremely well. His career offers another illustration of the fact that the commercial aspects of the music business often involved selling music that was valued for its noncommercial nature.

Listening Guide

"The Little Old Log Cabin in the Lane" (1923)

PERFORMER: Fiddlin' John Carson (vocal and fiddle)

SONGWRITERS: Will S. Hays

ORIGINAL RELEASE: OKeh 4890

FORM: Verse-chorus

STYLE: Early hillbilly

Fiddlin' John Carson recalled finding the lyrics for this old minstrel song in an old copy of *Greer's Almanac*. It was originally composed in 1871 by Will S. Hays, a songwriter from Louisville, Kentucky. Several versions of the song had already been recorded by popular singers, including one sung in an exaggerated African American dialect and accompanied by banjo, imitating a typical nineteenth-century minstrel stage performance of the song. In the song's lyrics, an ex-slave waxes nostalgic for the supposed antebellum comforts of a Southern plantation, lamenting that his "Old Massa and old Missus" are now dead and that "darkies" are no longer in the fields, leaving him with only his old dog in a crumbling cabin. That theme was common in minstrel songs written in the decades after the Civil War. Carson tended to favor these sorts of pathos-drenched, old-time, nostalgic songs. In this instance, his choice of songs also played into the legacy of minstrelsy: a white performer impersonating a black slave on stage. Carson's performance is further charged with meaning if one considers his membership in the Ku Klux Klan and undeniably racist personal politics.

In June 1923, producer Ralph Peer came to Atlanta to record Carson, who sang two songs for him. Carson accompanied his singing with his own fiddle playing. For modern listeners, this recording immediately sounds old because of the narrow range of frequencies that it reproduces, the extensive surface noise, and the harsh, throaty timbre of the singer's voice. Consider how much of your perception of this recording comes from those sonic factors as you listen to it.

Texan Carl T. Sprague (1895–1979) was one of several singers from Texas and the West who added cowboy songs to the early hillbilly record business, even though their cowboy-themed contributions were initially overshadowed by the string bands and Appalachian mountain songs. Sprague's voice was quite polished, and he most often sang while accompanying himself with sparse guitar playing. With his focus primarily on traditional cowboy songs, Sprague highlighted what would be a lasting tension in country music between performances of traditional repertory and an emphasis on writing new songs.

Among the first generation of country musicians were many performers who were recruited by family members to serve as duet partners and band members. For instance, Rosa Lee Carson, known as "Moonshine Kate," partnered with her father, Fiddlin' John Carson, regularly. In their performances, she played a smart-tongued,

TIME	FORM	LISTENING CUES	DISCUSSION
0:00	Intro	fiddle	The first few notes are the fiddle player tuning up. Note the loud surface noise on the recording due to the technology Peer had available for the recording.
0:02	Instrumental verse	fiddle tune	The fiddle plays half of the song's verse. Listen to the double-stops, which means two notes played at once on the fiddle. Carson adds a few embellishments to the melody, personalizing the tune.
0:22	Verse 1	"Now I'm getting old and feeble…"	Carson sings the first verse, playing the melody on his fiddle along with his voice and adding a few double-stops for harmony.
1:01	Chorus	"The chimney's falling down…"	The verse and the chorus both end with the title of the song. Listen to the rhythmic syncopation (a short, catchy pattern) at 1:07 ("let's in the sunshine"); this variation illustrates Carson's musical sensibilities.
1:20	Instrumental verse	fiddle	Carson plays another fiddle solo here that comprises half the verse.
1:38	Verse 2	"Now this footpath has growed up…"	Carson sings the second verse, which is full of nostalgia and resignation. As is common with most early hillbilly performers, Carson leaves out the rests between vocal phrases that would keep the musical meter steadier (listen at 1:48 where "the pond" comes in early, for instance).
2:15	Chorus	"The chimney's falling down…"	The chorus is the same as earlier in the song.
2:34	Instrumental verse	fiddle	Carson begins another fiddle solo here like the two previous ones, but cuts it off awkwardly with a sudden high chord. In live performance, this song would have been sung and played in a longer version, but Carson was approaching the three-minute maximum duration for the recording equipment Peer was using, and thus had to end his rendition abruptly.

sassy female comedy character, a stage persona that even more famous female entertainers in country music would also adopt. Her recording of her father's composition "Little Mary Phagan" in 1925 established her as a solo singer, as well. Fiddler Rob Stanley's daughter Roba similarly left her mark on country music history when she recorded "Single Life" in 1925, a rousing tribute to the joys of being unmarried.

The full effects of these performers' contributions to country music would play out over many decades, as future country singers looked back to the first generation of stars and held to their traditions. Because the country music industry was so novel at the time, very few of these performers were able to eke out a living from their music alone. Most were essentially amateurs who happened upon opportunities to make a little money with their talent. Only a few achieved any reasonable level of fame or commercial success. In its first five years, the fledgling country music industry had birthed a new genre and laid a solid foundation for its future, but it had not yet coalesced into a cohesive musical entity, and it had not yet found any breakthrough superstars.

Summary

The story of country music in its first few years was as much about the technologies—radio and records—as it was about the music, as those developments drove the discovery and dissemination of music that had never before been captured and marketed. In its initial stages, the emerging genre of country music was defined almost entirely by the personal identity of both musicians and audiences: working-class, white, and rural. The record labels formalized these distinctions by isolating the music in the ways they catalogued and marketed it, thereby setting it up as distinct or "othered" from other popular genres. The historical evidence from this era shows clearly how the music was treated as a commercial entity from the outset—musicians seeking to be paid for their music, for instance—which challenges the way some later fans would reflect on the roots of country music as untainted by any of the forces of commercialization.

Finally, the sources from which the performers drew their music ranged across many different traditions, including stage music and popular tunes. These aspects of early country music were largely protected from the fans' discourses of authenticity that would later characterize the genre.

☆ **ESSAY: CULTURE**

 # Radio Barn Dances

Every Saturday night, families gathered around their radios to hear weekly radio broadcasts known as **barn dances**. These barn dances were variety shows that attempted to imitate the live performance atmosphere of community gatherings. Radio stations hired a regular cast of performers for their shows, which also featured guest stars. They offered steady employment to the musicians and gave rural listeners a chance to hear new songs and old favorites every week.

The earliest known radio barn dance occurred in 1923, when WBAP in Fort Worth, Texas, broadcast an old-time fiddler and accompanying band playing square dance music. Listeners inundated the station with enthusiastic praise, and WBAP continued to air similar programs. Prior to WBAP's broadcast, other radio stations had hosted old-time fiddlers, including WSB (Atlanta), where Fiddlin' John Carson played in 1922; WFAA (Dallas); and KFNF (Shenandoah, Iowa).

The first barn dance to achieve lasting fame was the National Barn Dance, which first aired on April 19, 1924, on WLS (Chicago). The station, managed by the Sears–Roebuck Agricultural Foundation, geared its programming toward the rural farmers who lived in the Midwest, along with the large population of Southerners who had migrated north in search of better economic opportunities. WLS's barn dance featured old-time fiddlers, comedy duos, string bands, vocal trios, folk singers, and some pop musicians. Early stars of the show included Mac and Bob, Karl & Harty, Linda Parker (known as Sunbonnet Sue), Bradley Kincaid, and the Cumberland Ridge Runners. In the 1930s, Gene Autry, Patsy Montana, Lulu Belle and Scotty, and Red Foley were all members of the Hayloft Gang, as the cast was called. In 1933, NBC began broadcasting a segment of the show on its nationwide radio network. Although the Grand Ole Opry would surpass the National Barn Dance in terms of fame, WLS cultivated an astonishing number of talented country stars and helped launch their national careers as recording artists.

The best-known barn dance started a year after WLS's, after Nashville's WSM broadcast old-time fiddler Uncle Jimmy Thompson on November 28, 1925. Within a matter of weeks, WSM established a regular Saturday-night barn dance program and hired as its host George D. Hay, nicknamed the "Solemn Old Judge," who had been working as the announcer for WLS's barn dance. In 1927, Hay renamed WSM's show the Grand Ole Opry. Its cast consisted of a variety of performers, including string bands, harmonica players, vocal duos and trios, and banjo players. Uncle Dave Macon, DeFord Bailey, and Dr. Humphrey Bate were early stars, while within a decade or so they were joined by the Delmore Brothers, Roy Acuff, Bill Monroe, Minnie Pearl, and Ernest Tubb. NBC picked up the show for national syndication in 1939. Like WLS's National Barn Dance, the Grand Ole Opry hosted a live audience in different theaters over the years, settling into Nashville's Ryman Auditorium in 1943.

The barn dance format proved so popular that other radio stations quickly followed suit. In 1933, WWVA in Wheeling, West Virginia, launched its Jamboree, while WBT in Charlotte, North Carolina, aired the Crazy Water Crystals Saturday Night Jamboree. John Lair, a regular performer and later music director for WLS's National Barn Dance, recruited fellow musicians to start the Renfro Valley Barn Dance in Cincinnati in 1937.

The barn dances were important marketing opportunities for early country performers. While the shows paid relatively little, their radio signals covered entire regions. That exposure helped secure audiences for their concerts during the rest of the week. The barn dance format also kept alive entertainment traditions that were part of old-time music and community gatherings and especially of minstrel shows but that did not translate well to records. Square dances, trick fiddling, spoken comedy, and character sketches (little skits that sometimes included singing) were all common on these programs. Some of the barn dances, including the Opry, featured blackface skits, and most showcased exaggerated hillbilly personas. The barn dances also illustrate clearly the commercial aspects of early country music. Companies sponsored segments of a barn dance, thereby providing the money to pay the musicians, who in turn advertised the product on air as part of their act. Many of the barn dances disappeared with the advent of television, although the Grand Ole Opry still broadcasts today. But during the first decades of country music's existence, they were an essential connection between old-time community entertainment and the new, commercial genre.

❧ Women in Early Country Music

Many conventional histories of country music highlight the men who were involved in the genre's creation. Male fiddlers, male singers, male record executives, and male radio stars all received most of the attention, and that situation might leave us wondering, where were all the women? The answer is complicated. Women were involved in every aspect of country music from its beginning, but social and economic conditions dictated that few of them became commercial stars, and fewer still were acknowledged for their roles.

For working-class women in the Appalachian communities and other Southern regions from which country music emerged, daily life was a struggle that left little time for pursuing a musical career. Hattie Stoneman (1900–1976), wife of Ernest, who frequently played her fiddle on her husband's records, bore fifteen named children, along with another eight pregnancies that ended in miscarriage, stillbirth, or infant death. Large families were the norm, and mothers carried the burden of crushing poverty when struggling to feed so many mouths. Singer Sarah Ogan Gunning (1910–1983) watched one of her babies literally starve to death. Ella May Wiggins (1900–1929) lost four children to whooping cough because she could not afford medical care; the experience inspired her to become a labor activist in the mill towns of North Carolina, where she quickly earned a reputation as one of the best songwriters in the area. Although these impoverished circumstances left few women with the resources or energy to become professional performers, music was a treasured form of inspiration and diversion within these women's homes, and many of the first generation of male country singers learned their ballads, gospel hymns, and sentimental songs from their mothers.

The few women who sought commercial recording success faced another obstacle: social propriety dictated that "nice girls" did not entertain publicly or travel without proper chaperones. Performing with one's family, however, was acceptable. Many women who made records or gained fame on radio shows in early country music did so as part of family ensembles: Sara and Maybelle Carter toured with Sara's husband, A. P. (see Chapter 2); Rosa Lee Carson (1909–1992) became her father, Fiddlin' John's, sidekick under the stage name Moonshine Kate; Andrew Jenkins recorded with his stepdaughter, Irene Spain; the Stoneman family recordings included both Ernest's wife Hattie and her sister Irma Frost; similarly, the Pickard family recordings included Obed's wife, Leila May, and their daughters.

Figure 1-7 Moonshine Kate was both Fiddlin' John Carson's daughter and his stage partner.

Source: Pictoral Press Ltd/Alamy Stock Photo.

Outside of family ensembles, women rarely made records during the first decade of country music. Exceptions include Roba Stanley (1910–1986), daughter of fiddle champion Rob Stanley, who started her career accompanying her father but quickly won her own fans and made several solo recordings, starting in 1924. A handful of women, including banjo virtuoso Samantha Bumgarner (c. 1880–1960) and her fiddle-playing friend Eva Davis, blazed a trail for later generations of female performers.

By the 1930s, female country musicians were a staple of radio barn dances in many cities. Yet the same limited themes prevailed in the stage names and stage characters that the women created: acts consisting of "sisters" (even when the performers were not actually related) and couples (even when the performers were not married to each other) were common, and many women played stock characters such as the tart-tongued, sassy mountain lass or the sweet and innocent ingénue that were already known to the audiences and deemed acceptable. Evidence also suggests that women were more present than some historical records appear to acknowledge, which was not an uncommon phenomenon in record-keeping. The roster of all performers on the Opry from 1925 to 1940, for instance, lists 238 acts, of which a mere 14 are female. But that number is certainly lower than the actual number of women performing on the Opry. Annotations in the records list wives and daughters appearing as part of the men's acts and suggest that many more did so without receiving credit.

In all these ways, country music reflected larger concerns facing working- and middle-class American culture in the 1920s and '30s. The 19th Amendment to the U.S. Constitution, which prohibited gender discrimination in voting, was ratified in 1920, and in its wake, many people feared the destabilization of the American family unit. Increased concerns about proper social behavior for women certainly had an impact on the emerging genre of country music, as did the realities of working-class life for many people scratching out a living in the American South. Those women who did make records and perform on radio often left behind a legacy of radical, independent thinking both in their song lyrics and through the very nature of their careers. The women in early country music deserve recognition for their extensive contributions—both in front of audiences and behind the scenes.

☆ ESSAY: MUSICAL STYLE

Hillbilly Entertainers

Within the study of popular music, **style** refers to a performance's musical arrangement, vocal technique, use of instruments, how those instruments are played, and what musical interpretation they offer. In other words, it identifies the trends, time, place, and approach to performance heard in the recording. After the 1920s, several very specific and readily identifiable musical styles emerge in country music, but during the first few years, few consistent, identifiable features of musical style are audible, mostly because the music industry as a whole was experimenting with this new genre. Nonetheless, there are a few characteristics of hillbilly musical style that we can identify.

Most of the hillbilly singers in the early 1920s used a nasal, harsh vocal technique that was part of many Southern traditional singing styles. This technique coincidentally happened to work well for making recordings on acoustic equipment that was not able to pick up softer sounds. The performers' approach to arranging a song was often to preserve as many of the song's verses as would fit in a three-minute recording, and instrumental solos tended to stick fairly close to the original melody. With a few exceptions, women tended to sing in a much lower pitch register than they do today.

Instrumentalists varied widely in their abilities. Some were virtuosos with astonishing technique. Many others, however, were entirely self-taught and had only rudimentary skills on their instruments. Thus, on many hillbilly recordings, we hear accompaniments that sound merely functional.

For this study, we will use the term "hillbilly" to identify the musical style of vernacular recordings from the 1920s into the early 1930s that were later labeled as the origins of country music. While some scholars use the term "old-time" to describe this music, only a modest portion of the songs and musicians from this era looked back nostalgically to yesteryear. The term "hillbilly" is adopted here, without any pejorative intent, to identify the historical context of the music and performers and to differentiate it from emergent styles in the 1930s.

LISTEN SIDE-BY-SIDE

"Sourwood Mountain"

Gid Tanner and Riley Puckett, 1924
(Columbia 245-D)
The Hill Billies, 1926 (Vocalion 5022)

Ernest Stoneman and the Dixie Mountaineers,
1926 (Victor 20235)
Bradley Kincaid, 1928 (Gennett 6417)

"SOURWOOD MOUNTAIN" is a folk song of unknown origins that made its way into the fiddle tune repertory of early country music. Cecil Sharp and Olive Dame Campbell collected it and published in 1917 in their *English Folk Songs from the Southern Appalachians*, labeling it a nursery song. But the published version is different from the many ways that musicians performed the song, and it does not capture its real musical life. These four recordings let us (a) compare the ways that a single song exists simultaneously in many different forms and versions, and (b) let us hear several different types of ensembles and performance styles that were common during the hillbilly era.

Gid Tanner and Riley Puckett perform it as a simple fiddle tune with banjo accompaniment. Tanner alternates between playing the fiddle tune in a high register and a low register. As with many performances in this old-time hillbilly style, the music could have been used to accompany dancing and sounds quite repetitive.

The Hill Billies recorded it in a typical string band style, where the fiddle solos are prominent, and Al Hopkins sings just three short lines in the whole recording, ending each line with the nonsense refrain, "Hey hick-ee-al day." Their recording, with fiddles, banjo, and guitars, has lively bounce in its rhythms. Tony Alderman plays the "shave and a haircut" ending on fiddle.

Ernest Stoneman and his Dixie Mountaineers also recorded it basically as a string band, but here Stoneman plays the harmonica, an instrument that was quite prevalent in 1920s hillbilly recordings, and adds vocals for the whole song. Stoneman sings longer verses and a different chorus and refrain, "Run, run, run and you better get away," than any of the other sources mentioned here.

Bradley Kincaid's self-accompanied version on guitar showcases the vocals and transforms the fiddle tune back into a folk song. Note the resonant, smooth vocals that are significantly clearer and easier to understand than on the versions that show off the instruments (in part, simply because the recording was made later), and the story takes a more comprehensible form in this version. Together, these four recordings show how diverse versions of the same song can coexist in popular memory. They also show the sonic difference between the string band performances and that of a solo singer, where the listener's attention is directed to very different aspects of the performance in each case.

PLAYLIST

Bailey, DeFord, "Pan American Blues" (1927)

Macon, Uncle Dave, "Keep My Skillet Good and Greasy" (1924)

Poole, Charlie, and the North Carolina Ramblers, "Don't Let Your Deal Go Down Blues" (1925)

Robertson, Eck, "Sally Goodin" (1922)

Stanley, Roba, "Single Life" (1925)

Tanner, Gid, and the Skillet Lickers, "Dance All Night with a Bottle in Your Hand" (1926)

FOR MORE READING

Berry, Chad, ed. *The Hayloft Gang: The Story of the National Barn Dance.* Urbana: University of Illinois Press, 2008.

Huber, Patrick. *Linthead Stomp: The Creation of Country Music in the Piedmont South.* Chapel Hill: University of North Carolina Press, 2008.

McCusker, Kristine M. *Lonesome Cowgirls and Honky-Tonk Angels: The Women of Barn Dance Radio.* Urbana: University of Illinois Press, 2008.

Miller, Karl Hagstrom. *Segregating Sound: Inventing Folk and Pop Music in the Age of Jim Crow.* Durham: Duke University Press, 2010.

Tribe, Ivan M. *The Stonemans: An Appalachian Family and the Music That Shaped Their Lives.* Urbana: University of Illinois Press, 1993.

Wolfe, Charles. *A Good-Natured Riot: The Birth of the Grand Ole Opry.* Nashville: The Country Music Foundation Press, 1999.

NAMES AND TERMS

Bailey, DeFord	Moonshine Kate	Stoneman, Ernest
Bate, Dr. Humphrey	National Barn Dance	string band
Carson, Fiddlin' John	Poole, Charlie and the	Tanner, Gid, and the Skillet
Dalhart, Vernon	North Carolina	Lickers
Grand Ole Opry	Ramblers	Whitter, Henry
Hay, George D.	Puckett, Riley	WLS
Hill Billies, The	Robertson, Eck	WSB
Kincaid, Bradley	shape notes	WSM
Lomax, John	Sharp, Cecil	
minstrel show	Sprague, Carl T.	

REVIEW TOPICS

1. In what ways is country music a product of the American South, and how have various regional identities defined the music?

2. How was the notion of authenticity important in the formation of the country genre, and what are some apparent contradictions and complications that appear in the music's early history?

3. Who, in terms of gender, race, and class, generally recorded country music in its first few years? Who were the exceptions, and why? How did the performers' identity shape the genre?

National Stars
on the Horizon

In the summer of 1927, a set of recording sessions took place that historian Nolan Porterfield has called the "Big Bang" of country music. The sessions, which were held in an old warehouse in Bristol, Tennessee, were obviously not the first recordings of hillbilly music, nor did they produce any records that sold millions of copies. These sessions filled a more important role in the history of country music: they provided a creation story for the genre that eventually grew to mythic proportions. Creation stories typically provide reference points that bring together many complicated occurrences into a simplified version of events. Easily remembered and easily retold, creation stories help unify a community around its shared history.

The origins of country music include many different events, performers, and types of music. It is difficult to give preference to one particular record, musician, event, or performance in the early days as "starting it all." Prior to 1927, no group of songs had become the standard repertory for country music, and—more important— no performers had achieved true national stardom. Furthermore, no single event, time, or place had been so influential as to become the symbolic headwaters of country music. When historians refer to the sessions as the Big Bang of country music, they do not mean that the sessions were literally the first country recordings, but rather that they were a catalytic event with such far-reaching repercussions that they became the symbolic point of origin for the genre.

The two main reasons that the **Bristol Sessions** gained legendary status are:

1. Several artists, who happened to become the first superstars in country music, were "discovered" at these sessions.
2. The sessions took place in the Appalachian Mountains, far from New York City, with musicians whose lives appeared to be the essence of what hillbilly music was all about.

The sessions marked a turning point in early hillbilly music toward more emphasis on singers than on instrumentalists, and the sessions launched the careers of national stars. The sessions also reinforced the vital role of record producers in how country music evolved in the early years. The producer, Ralph Peer, who was an extremely influential and powerful man within the music industry, had a hand in shaping the entire genre.

This chapter explores the music and careers of national stars who took on roles of significant cultural importance during the Great Depression and interwar years: Jimmie Rodgers, the Carter Family, and Roy Acuff. As celebrity figures, they represented not only the music they sang and the rural Appalachian white fans of their music, but also the broader values of American working-class culture and a growing nationwide audience. Their biographies, and the stories fans have told about them and their music for decades, have shaped the historical narrative of country music, and for that reason, many of those stories are recounted here. In their roles as musicians, as legendary figures within country music, and as representatives of the entire emerging genre, their influence persists to the present day.

Role of the Producer

The mastermind behind the Bristol Sessions, and arguably the man who launched the first national stars in country music, was record executive, **producer**, and publisher Ralph S. Peer (1892–1960). As a teenager, Peer developed an interest in sound recordings and went to work for Columbia Records, one of the largest record companies of that era. After serving in the Navy in WWI, Peer was hired by OKeh Records to supervise recording sessions. In 1920, he and Fred Hager recorded Mamie Smith singing "Crazy Blues," which was the first African American vocal blues recording (see Chapter 1). Peer immediately saw the enormous market potential for previously unrecorded styles of music, including black blues singers and their white hillbilly counterparts. Peer was instrumental in figuring out how to take recording-studio equipment on the road and set up temporary studios in remote locations, which he knew was a crucial step in finding local blues and hillbilly talent. But his most important contributions to the development of country music were his interests in copyright law, publishing, and royalties (see essay on Copyright).

Copyright law required anyone singing a song on a record to pay royalties to whomever held the copyright for that song—usually a publishing firm. Ralph Peer saw tremendous potential to make money from these royalties by licensing the copyrights to songs that the hillbilly artists wrote. There was a catch, of course: songs were only eligible for copyright protection if they were newly composed by the person who brought them to Peer—they could not be old folk tunes, traditional songs, or songs already under copyright by someone else. This situation created an interesting conundrum: the hillbilly music business thrived on music that sounded old, traditional, and nostalgic. Those were the types of songs that record label executives wanted to release. But there was more money to be made from new compositions. Thus, Peer's business model required songs that sounded old and traditional but that were in fact newly written and eligible for copyright registration. In the days before modern databases and computer search engines, it was extremely difficult to check on the copyright status of a song or to figure out who actually wrote it, especially if the performer had learned it orally. Furthermore, performers held differing views on what constituted an original composition. These circumstances meant that there were strong incentives for singers to claim they had written songs even when they had not and strong incentives for publishers to claim the copyright for those songs regardless of their actual origins.

In order to launch his new publishing business, Peer left OKeh early in 1926 and negotiated a deal with the Victor Talking Machine Company in which Peer received very little money from Victor but got to secure the publishing rights to songs he recorded. Peer began traveling primarily to Southern cities where he hoped to discover new talent for Victor. One of these trips was the carefully planned excursion that resulted in the Bristol Sessions. Bristol was an excellent choice for Peer's purposes; located on the border of Tennessee and Virginia, it had been a major stop on the Virginia and Tennessee Railway since 1856. With over 30,000 residents, Bristol boasted one of the largest population centers in the Appalachian Mountains at the time. Furthermore, Peer already had recording contracts with at least two sets of performers from the area, including Ernest Stoneman, so he was aware of the region's rich musical heritage and had connections that could help locate new talent for him.

Figure 2-1 Jimmie Rodgers (left), with Anita Peer, Ralph Peer, Carrie Roders (right), and Rodgers's daughter Anita (front).

Source: Southern Folklife Collection, Wilson library, The Unviersity of North Carolina at Chapel Hill.

He and two sound engineers arrived in Bristol on July 22, 1927, and set up a temporary recording studio in an empty warehouse on the main street. Peer visited and auditioned musicians while he was on his way to Bristol, so that by the time he arrived, he had lined up more than half of the nineteen acts he would record at those famous sessions. During the sessions, a local newspaper article reported on Stoneman's income from Victor Records, which had amounted to $3,600 the previous year. That article enticed even more local musicians to audition for Peer, and he filled the rest of his schedule with new talent.

The Big Bang

Among those with whom Peer had corresponded prior to arriving in Bristol were the Carter Family. On July 31, 1927, A. P. Carter, his wife Sara, and her young cousin, Maybelle (see Artist Profile), from Clinch Mountain, Virginia, piled into an old car and made the trip to Bristol. Maybelle was seven months pregnant with her first baby, and Sara's baby Joe and eldest daughter, Gladys, came, too (daughter Janette stayed with her grandmother). Such a trip was no small undertaking, given the poor conditions of roads in that region and the tendency of automobiles to break down. When the Carters got to Bristol, they put on their best Sunday suit and dresses and presented themselves with as much polish as they could muster.

The Carters were steeped in the musical traditions of the Appalachian Mountains. Their emphasis on Sara's singing and family vocal harmony offered exactly the sort of music Peer was looking for. Over the next two days, they recorded six songs, including "The Storms Are on the Ocean" and "Single Girl, Married Girl." Those records sold well enough that Peer invited the trio to travel to Camden, New Jersey (where Victor had its national headquarters), in May 1928 for another session. Many of the songs they sang there, including "Keep on the Sunny Side" and "Wildwood Flower," became huge **hits** and signature songs for the family. That session established them as stars, and set them on the professional path that would carry them forward until the early 1940s.

As the Carters continued to record over the next few years, most of the songs that they brought into the studio were the product of A. P.'s song-collecting trips. He was

The Carter Family and Their Legacy

Alvin Pleasant "A. P." Carter (1891–1960) · Sara Dougherty Carter (1898–1979)
Maybelle Addington Carter (1909–1978)

The Carter Family has earned the moniker "First Family of Country Music," not only for the nearly 300 recordings they made, but also for their family's legacy, as their children and grandchildren have remained in the music business. The Original Carter Family, as they came to be known, recorded from 1927 until 1941, when they went their separate ways. The ensemble consisted of Sara Dougherty Carter, who sang lead and played autoharp; Sara's cousin, Maybelle Addington Carter, who played the guitar and added vocal harmony; and Sarah's husband, Alvin Pleasant (who went by A. P.) Carter, who specialized in collecting songs, occasionally sang bass harmony, and acted as the group's manager.

A. P. was born in Maces Spring (which the locals call Maces Springs), Virginia, and the

Figure 2-2 The Carter Family in the Clinch Mountains, Virginia.

Source: Southern Folklife Collection, Wilson library, The Unviersity of North Carolina at Chapel Hill.

a wanderer by nature, and song collecting came naturally to him. Family members recalled him coming home with his pockets full of scraps of paper on which he had jotted down his discoveries. His daughter Janette went with him on several jaunts and recalled occasionally writing down song lyrics for her father. A. P. was never very good at remembering the melodies, and for many collecting trips, A. P. brought along his neighbor, Lesley Riddle (sometimes identified as Leslie Riddles), a black guitarist and singer. Riddle learned the melodies, then taught them to Sara and Maybelle so family home remained in the Clinch Mountain area. A. P. traveled a bit and worked on the railroads as a young man, but soon returned home and tried selling fruit trees to earn a living. He met Sara, who lived just a few miles away, when she was barely sixteen, and the two married in 1915. Sara and A. P. started singing and performing together and even auditioned for a record label (although they did not receive an invitation to record). In 1926, Maybelle married A. P.'s brother Ezra and joined the ensemble.

The trio worked at various radio stations throughout the 1930s and became the quintessential musical hillbilly family; their audiences saw a group that represented wholesome values, motherhood, church, and old-fashioned mountain music. However, the relationships between the three performers were not always what they seemed. Sara and A. P. divorced in 1939—a scandalous decision for that time—but the group continued to perform together for a few more years. Finally, in the early 1940s, the trio parted company.

After the original group broke up, Maybelle and her three daughters, Helen, June, and Anita, continued to perform as "Mother Maybelle and the Carter Sisters," sometimes billing themselves as simply the Carter Family. In the early 1960s, the group began touring with Johnny Cash, a connection that led to a torrential love affair between June and Johnny. Johnny and June finally married in 1968, linking the Man in Black to the Carter Family legacy. June scored several hits, including winning two Grammy awards for duets with Cash, while her sister Helen also had some minor success as a country singer and Anita had a modest career as both a country and folk singer.

A third generation of family members also went into show business. Rosanne Cash, born to Johnny Cash and his first wife Vivian, scored several top ten country hits in the 1980s. Rosanne's then husband, Rodney Crowell, was also an extremely successful country singer in that decade. June's daughter from her first marriage, Carlene Carter, became a successful country singer in the 1990s. And June and Johnny's only child together, John Carter Cash, has also made his living as a singer. The family's fourth generation includes several professional musicians; for instance, Carlene's daughter, Tiffany Anastasia Lowe, is an indie rock singer based in Los Angeles.

Sara and A. P.'s children, Gladys, Janette, and Joe, worked to keep their family's music alive as well. Joe and Janette managed the Carter Fold, an old-time music performance venue on the site of the family's original home in southwest Virginia, which Janette's daughter Rita continues to run.

Since 1927, not a single decade has gone by without a major country hit from some member of the Carter family, which from the 1960s onward also included Johnny Cash. The group left their mark on country music not just from their stacks of records but also through the pedigree of four generations of singers and entertainers.

the family could add them to their repertory. This method of acquiring songs by oral transmission helps explain why so many of the Carter Family's recordings are clearly derived from preexisting gospel hymns and popular songs, but are seldom quite like the published versions. For instance, their classic "Wildwood Flower" was originally a vaudeville song published in about 1859, which made its way into oral tradition in the mountains. Over the years, the lyrics changed as people forgot bits of them or replaced unfamiliar words, either with more familiar references or with whatever

Listening Guide

"Can the Circle Be Unbroken (Bye and Bye)" (1935)

PERFORMERS:
The Carter Family
(A. P. Carter, vocal;
Sara Carter, vocal
and autoharp;
Maybelle Carter,
vocal and guitar)

SONGWRITERS: Ada
R. Habershon and
Charles Gabriel
(published gospel
hymn); A. P. Carter
(revised version)

ORIGINAL RELEASE:
Banner 33465

FORM: Verse-chorus

STYLE: Hillbilly
gospel

The features of "Can the Circle Be Unbroken" include standard elements that show up in many versions of the song and some elements that originate with the Carter Family. Ada R. Habershon and well-known songwriter Charles Gabriel published "Will the Circle Be Unbroken" in 1907, and it was recorded by several hillbilly artists prior to the Carter Family. A. P. changed the song's title from the more familiar "Will the Circle . . ." to "Can the Circle . . .", removed all the original verses, and wrote new ones about the death and burial of a mother, then claimed it was his own composition for copyright purposes.

By May of 1935, America had sunk into the depths of the Great Depression. Sales of the Carters' records had dipped and they were dissatisfied with their contract with Victor, so they switched to the American Record Company, a so-called dime-store or budget label, because its comparatively inexpensive records were sold in Woolworths and other discount stores and through mail-order catalogs. At their first session with the new label, the Carters recorded this song. While their instrumentation and general musical arrangements remained the same as in their first recordings, their overall sound had changed. Sara's voice was much lower, and the music sounds more ponderous than it did several years earlier. In all likelihood, the strains within the family were partly responsible: Sara had moved out two years earlier, leaving her children with A. P., and Maybelle's family had moved away to Washington, D.C. But the recording became one of their biggest hits and most covered songs ever. In both the folk and country genres, countless artists have sung the Carters' version—their verses and general musical treatment of the whole thing—although most frequently under the original title of "Will the Circle Be Unbroken."

approximated the sound. Sara's opening line, "Oh, I'll twine with my mingles," includes meaningless words, and the published version's "pale aronatus" became the equally nonsensical "pale and the leader" by the time Sara sang it. From these perspectives, the Carter Family were making records of the musical traditions in their home communities, where songs traveled fluidly, changing along the way in both their texts and melodies as people adapted them to personal performance abilities and contexts.

Although only a very small handful of their songs had actually been written by any of the trio, when the Carter Family brought these songs into the studio, Ralph Peer listed A. P. as the songwriter and filed copyright registrations for them as if they were newly composed originals. This approach allowed Peer as publisher to collect royalties (which he shared with the Carters) on these songs whenever they were recorded by the Carters—or anyone else, for that matter. From this perspective, the Carters were supplying Peer with exactly what he wanted: old-time, traditional songs that sold well yet could be copyrighted as new material.

TIME	FORM	LISTENING CUES	DISCUSSION
0:00	Instrumental introduction	guitar and autoharp	Maybelle strums a steady chord but does not play the song's melody here. Sara's autoharp is also on the recording, but hard to pick out.
0:07	Verse 1	"I was standing …"	Sara sings the first verse alone.
0:27	Chorus	"Can the circle …"	The trio sing in close, practiced harmony. The precision of their vocal harmony is much better than on their earlier records, reflecting several years of rehearsing and performing together.
0:45	Instrumental verse	guitar and autoharp	Maybelle plays the song's verse on the low strings of her guitar with her thumb-brush technique.
1:05	Verse 2	"Lord, I told the undertaker …"	Sara sings each verse alone. Her regional accent is clearly audible here.
1:24	Chorus	"Can the circle …"	Some of the phrases in the chorus have short pauses after them, and others flow directly into the next phrase. This pattern is unique to the Carter Family's version and alters the regular meter of the song.
1:43	Verse 3	"I followed close …"	Notice how familiar the melody has become after hearing two verses and two choruses already.
2:02	Chorus	"Can the circle …"	
2:20	Instrumental interlude	guitar and autoharp	Maybelle plays only the last phrase here of the verse on her guitar, which is different than the other guitar solos in the song.
2:30	Verse 4	"Went back home, Lord …"	Sara finishes the story about the mother who has passed away.
2:48	Chorus	"Can the circle …"	The recording wraps up with a final chorus, ending rather abruptly at almost exactly three minutes.

Peer recorded nineteen acts in Bristol between July 25 and August 5, including the Stonemans, Alfred G. Karnes, Henry Whitter, and Ernest Phipps and his Holiness Quartet, all of whom saw some commercial success. But the single biggest discovery of the entire session was Jimmie Rodgers (see Artist Profile).

Rodgers arrived in Bristol as part of a band; he had been performing with a group alternately called the Jimmie Rodgers Entertainers or the Tenneva Ramblers, and they auditioned together for Peer. After the audition, however, a heated dispute broke out among the band members over how the group should be billed (in other words, their band name). With no resolution forthcoming, Rodgers split from the group. The next day, August 4, 1927, Rodgers went to the studio alone and sang two songs, "The Soldier's Sweetheart" and "Sleep, Baby, Sleep." The traditional ballad and old lullaby both matched Peer's preference for old-time material. Although Rodgers had written neither, Peer put Rodgers's name on "The Soldier's Sweetheart" for copyright purposes; the other was too well known for Peer to attempt to copyright it, as it had been recorded only a few years earlier by another hillbilly star, Riley Puckett.

As had been the case with the Carters, Rodgers's songs from that first session sold only modestly, but they earned him another recording session. That November, Rodgers sang "Blue Yodel" (see Listen Side by Side), which became his first big hit and revolutionized the fledgling hillbilly music industry. "Blue Yodel" was first and foremost a blues tune: Rodgers had borrowed famous bits of poetry (two-line verses, specifically rhymed couplets) from black blues singers and strung them together in a

ARTIST PROFILE

Jimmie Rodgers (1897–1933)

Jimmie Rodgers, born September 8, 1897, near Meridian, Mississippi, is widely revered as the "Father of Country Music," its first major star, and the singer whose personal life and recordings came to represent the essence of country music. Rodgers's mother passed away when he was a young boy and his father traveled often, leaving him to be raised by an aunt. Already interested in entertaining at age thirteen, he ran off with a traveling medicine show that came through town on its way to Birmingham, Alabama. Rodgers was several hundred miles from home when he quit the show. The incident was evidence of his adventurous spirit and sometimes foolhardy business sense, which would shape his entire career.

As a teenager, Rodgers bounced between railroading jobs like those of his father and older brothers and intermittent employment as an entertainer whenever opportunities arose. He picked up both the ukulele and the guitar, although he never developed any real proficiency on either. Rodgers's personal life was marked by instability, trouble, and tragedy through those years. At age nineteen, Rodgers married Stella Kelly, but that union ended after only a short while, and in 1920 he wed Carrie Williamson, daughter of a minister. That familial connection proved invaluable in later years because

Carrie's sister, Elsie McWilliams, was a moderately proficient church organist who occasionally wrote songs. She became one of Rodgers's most valuable suppliers of new songs when, in later years, he ran short of suitable material for his recording sessions.

Rodgers's marriage added to the weight of his responsibilities as he searched for a way to provide for his young family. Carrie gave birth to two daughters, Carrie Anita (who went by Anita) and June Rebecca, who died of diphtheria when only a few months old. Compounding his personal trials, Rodgers was diagnosed with tuberculosis shortly after the passing of his infant daughter. By January of 1927, Rodgers had struck out at a number of jobs and moved his family to Arizona and back. He wound up again in Meridian and in need of financial support from his in-laws, very much down on his luck. That winter, Rodgers moved to Asheville, North Carolina. There he began working with a band consisting of brothers Claude and Jack Grant and Jack Pierce. In July, the quartet traveled to Bristol, mainly to see if Jack Pierce's father would help them acquire a more reliable car. While there, Rodgers made his first recordings and established himself as a solo entertainer.

The two songs that Rodgers recorded in August 1927 sold moderately well, but it was single story. His guitar playing was amateurish at best—he knew only a few chords and very simple patterns for adding in bass notes. And after each blues verse, he interjected a unique yodel that he had learned from a popular vaudeville theater tradition in which singers mimicked Austrian yodeling. To his fans, Rodgers's plaintive voice, with its nasal resonance, sounded honest and direct, both qualities that appealed to the listeners who bought his records in large numbers. And, to Peer's delight, Rodgers claimed to have written or co-written almost all the songs he brought into the studio, thereby assuring that both Rodgers and Peer could collect royalties on them.

Rodgers's next session that changed the course of musical history. In November 1927, although he had not heard from Peer in some time, Rodgers decided to go make more records. He traveled to New York, checked himself into an upscale hotel room (which he told the desk clerk to bill to the Victor company), and phoned Peer's office. Peer agreed to the session, and Rodgers recorded four songs, including "T for Texas," (see Listen Side by Side) which Peer issued under the title "Blue Yodel." "Blue Yodel" sold astonishingly well, and Rodgers was on his way to becoming a star.

Over the next five years, Rodgers adopted Texas as his new home—a geographic connection that would resurface decades later when new generations of country singers claimed Rodgers as part of the musical legacy of that state. He built a house in Kerrville, Texas, known as the Blue Yodeler's Paradise, and later relocated to San Antonio. He toured extensively while making a total of 114 different recordings. One of Rodgers's habits, amplified by Peer's willingness to try just about anything that would sell records, was to meet up with local bands and performers whenever he was preparing for a recording session and bring them with him to the session. As a result, his records feature accompanists ranging from small jazz ensembles to jug bands to Hawaiian ensembles. He did a duet with famed jazz trumpeter Louis Armstrong ("Blue Yodel

No. 9") (see Listening Guide) and recorded a set of musical skits with the Carter Family.

Rodgers was a bit of a rounder, fond of women, quick to imbibe alcohol, and slow to manage his money sensibly. In short, he lived the life that was recounted in many of his songs. In the spring of 1933, Rodgers's health declined significantly. He arranged one final recording session in New York, where he figured a dozen songs at $250 per side would yield a tidy sum for his family. His sessions began on May 17, where in spite of a weak and raspy voice, he recorded several songs that have become fan favorites. On May 24, 1933, Rodgers returned to the studio, this time accompanied by two professional session musicians because he was too weak to perform on his own. Toward the end of the day, Rodgers dismissed the session musicians and then sang one last song, ending his career alone with his guitar, exactly as he had begun it. The next day, Rodgers felt well enough to take a trip out to Coney Island, but on the way back to his hotel, he collapsed, and his ravaged lungs began to hemorrhage. On May 26, 1933, Jimmie Rodgers died. His casket was shipped home on a special train car attached to the Southern Railroad line that ran to Meridian, Mississippi. With that last fateful trip to his beloved Southland, Rodgers slipped into a new role as a country music legend.

CLEVER MARKETING STRATEGIES

When Jimmie Rodgers's "Blue Yodel" became a hit, Ralph Peer saw the potential for a sequel. He selected another of Rodgers's blues recordings and re-titled it "Blue Yodel No. II." The formula worked so well that Peer continued to use it, switching to Arabic numerals, with "Blue Yodel No. 3" and so on, until he had released twelve numbered "Blue Yodels" in the series. After Rodgers died, Peer chose one more of the blues-based recordings to issue as "Jimmie Rodgers' Last Blue Yodel." It proved to be a very successful branding and marketing strategy, especially when tied to Rodgers's moniker as "America's Blue Yodeler."

Figure 2-3 Jimmie Rodgers dressed as a dapper entertainer, just one of the costumes and personas he presented to his fans.

Source: Southern Folklife Collection, Wilson library, The Unviersity of North Carolina at Chapel Hill.

By the time he died of tuberculosis on May 26, 1933, Rodgers had completed a series of major concert tours and made 114 recordings in just shy of six years. Many of those songs went on to become standards in country music; "Blue Yodel No. 8," also called "Muleskinner Blues," became the signature piece for the first real bluegrass band, for instance. But the impact of his whole career was far greater than these details indicate.

The Carter Family, meanwhile, established a career built more on radio appearances than on sales, although they certainly did fine in terms of records. They continued recording throughout the 1930s with a mix of gospel tunes ("Can the Circle Be Unbroken," see Listening Guide), well-known popular songs ("Wabash Cannonball," which the Carters recorded before it became a signature song for Roy Acuff), and a few autobiographical tales ("My Clinch Mountain Home"). After passing through a series of radio station jobs, the family wound up at a border station, XERA, located near Del Rio, Texas, in the late 1930s. **Border stations** sat across the Mexican border and were not subject to U.S. radio regulations that limited a radio station's wattage (and thus how far it could be heard). Mexican-based stations could therefore operate at much higher wattages and blanket the United States with their signals, reportedly to the Canadian border. Most of the border stations provided advertising for medicines and elixirs of dubious usefulness and hired musicians to draw an audience for these products; XERA, for instance, advertised goat glands as a cure for impotence.

Long after Rodgers's death, the Carter Family enjoyed widespread exposure from their work at XERA, but it was both exhausting and hard on their families. Sara had moved out of A. P.'s home in 1933, although they continued to present their fans with a warm, family-centered image anchored by the presence of both Maybelle's and Sara's children. By the end of the 1930s, the strains had taken their toll, and the Carter Family's sound was already a bit dated. Of the three, Maybelle emerged as a new musical innovator with continued ambitions. Her name began to appear in songwriting credits toward the end

Figure 2-4 Jimmie Rodgers dressed as a railroad brakeman.
Source: Southern Folklife Collection, Wilson library, The Unviersity of North Carolina at Chapel Hill.

of their recording career, and she would enjoy several more decades of success as a performer. A. P. headed home to Virginia in 1941 and lived out his days secluded there, while Sara struck out for California with a new husband, leaving behind her life as a professional musician. But like Rodgers, the Carter Family's impact on country music far outpaced their actual recordings and musical performances.

The Long-Term Star

Jimmie Rodgers's career was tragically short, and although the Carter Family remained prominent figures in country music through the 1950s, the singer who became a national icon through his traditional approach to country music and reigned over the genre for over a half century was Roy Claxton Acuff (1903–1992). Although Acuff did not enter the music business until 1932, his

Figure 2-5 Jimmie Rodgers dressed as a cowboy.

Source: Southern Folklife Collection, Wilson library, The Unviersity of North Carolina at Chapel Hill.

approach to music and his stage presence were crafted in the same mountain traditions and medicine-show era as the first generation of country singers, and he kept those traditions as part of his trademark style. His allegiance to older musical traditions was balanced by a media-savvy awareness that the entertainment business was indeed a business. Unlike Rodgers and the Carters, who turned the publishing rights to their songs over to Ralph Peer, Roy Acuff set up his own publishing firm. And as a star on the Grand Ole Opry, Acuff became the name and face of the most famous roster of country musicians, sliding into the role of elder statesman and presiding over the show until his death in 1992. Historian Bill Malone has recounted how Japanese soldiers used a rallying cry of "To hell with Roosevelt; to hell with Babe Ruth; to hell with Roy Acuff," as the ultimate list of belittling insults when attacking US forces during WWII. The very fact that fans retell that story with pride illustrates the legacy that accompanies Acuff's name in country music history.

Born in Maynardville, Tennessee, Acuff was raised by a preacher father, who taught him to love music and baseball. Acuff set out to be a professional baseball player, but while recovering from a severe case of sunstroke, he practiced his fiddling instead. This change in interest led to an apprenticeship with Doc Hauer, a traveling medicine show performer. With Hauer, Acuff learned stagecraft that came from the older traditions of live entertainment that had deep roots in the nineteenth century. He figured out how to keep up a patter of jokes, balance a fiddle bow on his nose, and sing sentimental songs that held an audience's attention. The medicine show tradition had been a vibrant part of entertainment in the South for many decades, but Acuff's generation was the last of the country musicians to have experienced it firsthand—it would be a mere passing memory for later generations of country singers, and mark Acuff as of an older place and time.

Within a short while, Acuff was performing on a Knoxville radio station with a band called the Crazy Tennesseans. In spite of his success in Knoxville, like most other country singers in the 1930s, Acuff wanted to perform on the Grand Ole Opry. He finally got a guest spot in 1938, and shortly thereafter joined the cast, garnering attention for his performance of "The Great Speckle Bird," a song that would have been at home on the Opry a decade earlier in terms of its musical style. The Opry in the late 1930s was fraught with tensions between the hillbilly traditions on which it had been founded and newer trends toward popular (pop) music that were surfacing. Acuff found himself right in the middle. His fan mail, however, was heavily weighted toward the old-time traditions, and Acuff paid heed, setting his band's image and style squarely on the side of tradition. He changed the name of his band to the Smoky Mountain Boys (in spite of the fact that he had hired female musicians as band members), and fine-tuned them into one of the best-known backing bands in country music history. For all his allegiance to tradition, Acuff understood that the hillbilly personalities presented on the Opry were indeed performances of fictional characters and a way of branding the music. His band appeared in publicity shots in hayseed outfits, sometimes with teeth blackened out, all part of a purposeful "rustification" of the band to make them appear even more steeped in hillbilly tradition.

Acuff also knew that his audiences responded well to bands that included female performers. He brought guitarist Imogene "Tiny" Sarrett with his band when they first moved from Knoxville to the Opry. When Sarrett left the group, Acuff purposely sought another woman to join his band, this time banjoist Rachel Veach (1921–1980), cousin of Opry members Sam and Kirk McGee. Veach's presence in the band added to both their audience appeal and the quality of their musicianship, but it raised a problem for Acuff: codes of social behavior deemed it unseemly for a single woman to tour with a band, especially for a star such as Acuff who cultivated an image as a wholesome, upstanding traditional singer. But the idea that

Figure 2-6 Roy Acuff and his Smoky Mountain Boys, in a scene from the movie The Grand Ole Opry (1940); Acuff, center with fiddle; Rachel Veach, center; George D. Hay with his steamboat whistle, far right.

Listening Guide

"Blue Yodel No. 9" (1930)

PERFORMERS:
Jimmie Rodgers
(vocal), Louis
Armstrong (trumpet),
and Lillian Hardin
Armstrong (piano)

SONGWRITER: Jimmie
Rodgers

ORIGINAL RELEASE:
Victor 23580

FORM: Strophic blues

STYLE: Hillbilly blues

During the summer of 1930, Rodgers and his wife traveled to California for what was intended to be a restorative vacation and a chance for Rodgers to record at Victor's new West Coast studios. At the end of the recording sessions, Ralph Peer arranged a collaboration between jazz trumpeter Louis Armstrong (1901–1971), accompanied by Armstrong's wife, pianist Lil Hardin Armstrong, and Rodgers. Their duet, released as "Blue Yodel No. 9" but often called by its first line, "Standin' on the Corner," is an excellent illustration of the musical kinship between black blues and hillbilly music. The idea of Jimmie Rodgers and Louis Armstrong, a black musician originally from New Orleans who became a jazz legend, recording together is only odd if one forgets that jazz and country share many of the same historical roots.

The song's text, as sung by Rodgers, consists of six blues couplets. They form a more coherent storyline than most blues recordings, in which verses tend not to flow together in a logical plot. The storyline is similar to an old ballad known as "Frankie and Johnny" (which Rodgers also recorded), which recounts a scorned woman's revenge as she shoots her philandering man. There are moments of sheer awkwardness in the recording that result from Jimmie Rodgers's general inability to stick to regular phrases and musical timing. Both Armstrong and Hardin clearly had trouble following his timing. For instance, Rodgers crammed one of his verses into half the musical time of the others. But at other moments in this song, we hear Armstrong's jazz solo with piano accompaniment, a brief glimpse of the bigger musical landscape in which hillbilly music sat, as well as the wide range of styles and sounds that Rodgers's audience was hearing even just on his records.

This recording reminds us that the musical roots of country are much broader than just the old-time, traditional folk ballads of the Appalachian Mountains. Rodgers remains the undisputed first star of country music, and his best-loved recordings draw openly from music that is not white hillbilly in

the performers were actually portraying characters on stage, as with their hillbilly outfits and blackened teeth, came in handy again. Acuff pretended that Pete Kirby, his Dobro player, was Rachel's family chaperone and coined the nickname "Bashful Brother Oswald" for him.

Acuff wrote several songs that borrowed from old-time styles and traditions that became quite popular. To satisfy his fans' requests for copies of the lyrics, he printed songbooks and sold them for 25¢ at appearances and over his radio origin. This recording foreshadows many instances in later decades when country music again drew heavily on pop, jazz, blues, and other genres.

TIME	FORM	LISTENING CUES	DISCUSSION
0:00	Introduction	trumpet and piano	Armstrong plays part of the song's melody for the introduction.
0:14	Verse 1	"Standin' on the corner . . ."	Rodgers sings the opening verse, with Armstrong filling in between phrases.
0:32	Verse 2	"It was down in Memphis . . ."	The story continues in the second verse, which concludes with a yodel.
0:53	Verse 3	"I said you'll find my name . . ."	Rodgers compresses two lines of text into one musical phrase, effectively shortening the verse into half its original length. The page of lyrics that Rodgers sang from in the studio has this section marked as its own verse.
1:06	Verse 4	"Listen, all you rounders . . ."	Here Rodgers includes a verse with a shooting reference ("special") and rounders, similar to some of his other recordings. Armstrong gets more elaborate with his musical responses in this verse. This verse ends with a standard yodel.
1:28	Instrumental interlude	trumpet and piano	When Rodgers stops singing, Armstrong plays an improvised solo over the standard twelve-bar blues framework. Both Armstrong and Hardin sound relaxed in this section and show off their musical virtuosity.
1:53	Verse 5	"My good gal loves me . . ."	Rodgers stretches the rhythms of the song in his typical style on the word "cash."
2:10	Verse 6	"She come to the joint . . ."	The storyline in this blues verse, with an armed woman searching out her man, is common in other songs that Rodgers recorded. Rodgers ends the song with a yodel, and Armstrong closes the song with a traditional blues motive.

broadcasts. He recalled later that his wife, who handled most of the actual sales, was soon inundated with quarters. Just as Ralph Peer had done, Acuff recognized the lasting value in songwriting and controlling copyrights. In order to capitalize on that opportunity, he approached a songwriter, producer, and music industry insider named Fred Rose with a proposition: together they would start a new music publishing firm headquartered in Nashville. In 1942, Acuff–Rose set up shop and, building on the catalog of songs that Acuff already owned, went on to become one

Listening Guide

"The Great Speckled Bird" (1936)

PERFORMERS:
Roy Acuff & His
Crazy Tennesseans
(Roy Acuff, vocal;
Clell Summey,
steel guitar; Jess
Easterday, guitar;
Red Jones, bass)

SONGWRITER: Roy
Acuff

ORIGINAL RELEASE:
ARC 7-01-59

FORM: Strophic

STYLE: Hillbilly

This song takes us back in time and offers a glimpse of what a 1930s country music audience would connect with: a mournful metaphor about an isolated church and the singer's faith. Although the song is formally credited to Roy Acuff, he has never claimed to be its original author. Acuff learned the song from Charlie Swain, a member of the Black Shirts gospel quartet who also sang on the radio in Knoxville, Tennessee. Swain's source for the song was most likely members of the Church of God, a controversial congregation located about fifty miles from Knoxville. At least two other songwriters have claimed copyright credits for the song over the years, further complicating any attempts to establish its origins.

The melody of "The Great Speckled Bird" (originally released as "The Great Speckle Bird") is one of country music's best known; at least four different hits have used the same tune. Many historians have pointed out that the tune matches quite closely "I'm Thinking Tonight of My Blue Eyes," which had been recorded by the Carter family, among others. It was fairly common for songwriters to borrow an existing, well-known folk melody and simply add new lyrics to it, particularly in a time period when few country musicians could read traditional musical notation. In the 1950s, this same situation occurred when, first, Hank Thompson and, later, Kitty Wells recorded songs with new words that both used this melody. These songs that share only a tune are not the same as cover songs, but they do invoke the same sort of historical connections, tying these performances to the past in a way that resonates with country music's emphasis on tradition.

In 1936, Acuff used the song to earn a record deal from ARC. It matched his plaintive, personal style of singing and his taste for old-time music. Two years later, Acuff finally succeeded in obtaining an invitation to play on the Grand Ole Opry. The fan mail that poured in all praised his performance of "The Great

of the most influential publishing firms in country music. In so doing, Acuff framed his career as both singer and businessman, a move that had eluded both Rodgers and the Carters.

In 1939, NBC picked up the Grand Ole Opry for broadcast on its nationwide radio network. This change was significant because it transformed a regional show into a national one and rebranded country music as having more general appeal. Acuff had just recently joined the show, and the wider exposure turned him into a national star. From his position on the Opry, Acuff became a respected spokesperson for the older hillbilly styles of country music, and he used his influence to promote those styles on the Opry long after they had faded from prominence in

Speckled Bird," and on the strength of that response, Opry manager David Stone invited Acuff to join the cast.

Most of the musicians on this recording left Acuff's band shortly after he joined the Opry, and even the name of his band changed during those years. The group who became famous as Acuff's Smoky Mountain Boys came after this recording. But what did not change was Acuff's strong preference for old-time, sacred, and folk-infused music.

Throughout his long reign on the Opry, Acuff never abandoned his stalwart position that country music should be tied to rural, Southern musical tradition. This song's simple, strophic form (all verses) and its emotive Dobro fills (listen to Summey playing short, musical interjections between the vocal phrases) all illustrate Acuff's general approach to country music. This song also stands in stark contrast to the musical styles that were developing in more progressive parts of country music during these same years.

TIME	FORM	LISTENING CUES	DISCUSSION
0:00	Introduction	Dobro and fiddle	The sliding notes here are played on a Dobro. The rhythm guitar and bass set up a steady rhythmic foundation for the song.
0:16	Verse 1	"What a beautiful thought …"	Acuff sings, with the Dobro adding high slides between the phrases.
0:48	Verse 2	"With all the other …"	Some of Acuff's words are difficult to understand because of his strong accent.
1:18	Verse 3	"Desiring to lower …"	Listen to the lower notes on the Dobro at 1:45, which stand out from the rest of the song.
1:48	Verse 4	"I am glad …"	The lyrics defend a gospel-centered life.
2:19	Verse 5	"When He cometh …"	The lyrics offer a personal dedication to faith at the end. With no instrumental solos or other flourishes in the song, all attention remains on Acuff's delivery of the lyrics.

other strands of country. His resistance to musical changed marked Acuff as one of the last of his kind, a musician trained in the nineteenth-century entertainment traditions of the medicine shows who specialized in live performance, sentimental old songs, and the fiddling and string bands of Tennessee's past.

Country Music on the National Stage

The music and biographies of Jimmie Rodgers, the Carter Family, and Roy Acuff highlight a number of developments in country music as the genre matured on the national stage. What had been a few happenstance recordings and radio broadcasts of amateurs only a decade earlier had morphed into the domain of professional entertainers. By the early 1930s, five major developments had taken place in country music, each of which would leave an indelible mark on the genre:

1. Country music moved onto a national stage.
2. The traditional version of country music was defined.
3. Country stars' biographies were interwoven with their music.
4. The value of songs as intellectual property was recognized.
5. Stage personas made ideas of authenticity more complicated.

Country music moved onto a national stage

The emerging stars of country music were known as entertainers with individual personalities, rather than just the source of individual recordings. This shift in focus from song to singer accompanied a general rise in the popularity of these artists.

Jimmie Rodgers captured the hearts of the record-buying public beyond any one region or local area; by several accounts, even during the Great Depression, music fans everywhere would go into the local store and request a pound of butter, a sack of flour, and the latest Jimmie Rodgers record. In 1929, he made a short movie for Columbia Pictures called *The Singing Brakeman*, in which he sang three of his songs. That film lets us see just how captivating he was on stage. The Carter Family, with their extended stints on radio stations that blanketed the airwaves across huge swaths of the continental US, similarly reached a nationwide audience with both their music and their personalities. Roy Acuff completed this transformation, with his presence as an entertainer arguably outstripping the importance of any one song he sang. This focus on star singers on the blending of personal biography and musical output, and especially on songs with vocals rather than instrumentals, persists in country music today.

THE TRADITIONAL VERSION OF COUNTRY MUSIC WAS DEFINED.

With the songs of Rodgers, the Carters, and Acuff, the musical boundaries of traditional country music were squarely laid out: blues and bawdy comedy numbers, sentimental songs about family and home, gospel songs about heaven, and train songs and tales of local events, all accompanied by either guitar or a string band and often supplemented by vocal harmony. Although Rodgers died before new musical styles and pop influences began to encroach on the territory of traditional country music, Roy Acuff sat squarely in the middle of the debates that would ensue, courtesy of his role at the Opry. He held his course, remaining a staunch advocate for the styles of country music and the song topics that bespoke tradition from the Appalachian mountains and surrounding region.

Rodgers complicated these understood definitions of country music at the time by repeatedly defying any attempts to categorize him as an old-time, traditional, or folk musician. Many of his songs originated on vaudeville stages or were written by pop songwriters. He regularly borrowed heavily from African American performance techniques, including the types of interjections he added to the performances. Moreover, Rodgers had a penchant for collaborating with popular bands and ensembles, sometimes with musicians he had met only the night before a session. Far from being an anomaly, his duet with jazz trumpeter Louis Armstrong represents Rodgers's occasional efforts to make records that were contemporary, jazz influenced, and even pop in style. "Waiting for a Train," which he recorded with a small jazz combo he met in Atlanta, features a rousing clarinet and cornet (similar to a trumpet), just one of several jazz bands he collaborated with. Rodgers performed and recorded with a Hawaiian band (including ukulele), stride pianists (a style of playing jazz), African American jug bands, and a host of other musicians. One of Rodgers's lasting contributions was that he injected popular black musical styles into the core of country's traditions. Yet Rodgers is often considered the father of country music because he presented all of this music with his own plaintive signature vocal delivery, yodeling, and a white Southern working-class identity, which surpassed all the other elements in defining the sound.

COUNTRY STARS' BIOGRAPHIES WERE INTERWOVEN WITH THEIR MUSIC.

The powerful and lasting identities that these stars gave to country music were only possible because they also changed the fundamental relationship between the performer and the song. Before Jimmie Rodgers, listeners did not generally assume that singers were singing about their own experiences. Consider that at Rodgers's first recording session, he sang "The Soldier's Sweetheart." The song's lyrics are written in the first person ("Once I had a sweetheart . . ."), but from a female perspective. The speaker is a woman remembering her male lover who went to France to fight in World War I ("this awful German wahh," as Rodgers pronounces *war*). Audiences did not care that Rodgers, a man, was singing a "woman's song," because there was no assumption that the singer and the first-person character in the song were one and the same.

Over the span of their careers, these stars changed that. Rodgers sang about longing for his wife and daughter back home, about missing the South when he was away, about wild and reckless behavior, and about being worn down by "TB" (tuberculosis, which ultimately killed him). As his popularity grew, fans started to pay attention more to his songs' lyrics, believing that Rodgers was sharing his personal life, emotions, and foibles with the audience. With both the Carter Family and Acuff, their stoic gospel hymns and songs about mountain homes started to fuse with their public identities to the point that the songs sounded to their audiences like the musicians' own thoughts, ideas, and experiences.

By the end of his life, Jimmie Rodgers could not have gotten away with singing a serious first-person story from a woman's perspective, because country fans had fused the ideas of the singer and the protagonist (the lead or central character in the songs) into one person. Ballads written as third-person narratives (in other words, stories about some other characters, "he" and "she") were fine, but once a song adopted the pronouns "I" or "we," audiences wanted the singer to be believably telling a personal story. The groundwork was laid that connected singer to the song's characters, but the connection would not be cemented in place until Hank Williams (see Chapter 4).

THE VALUE OF SONGS AS INTELLECTUAL PROPERTY WAS RECOGNIZED.

The stories of these performers were, in part, stories about musicians' increasing savvy in the legal aspects of copyright and the business of music. Toward these ends, questions about who wrote a song, who arranged a song, who published a song, and who received royalties for a song occupied the fledgling country music industry. Ralph Peer's publishing strategies not only enabled the prominent careers of Rodgers and the Carters, but they were the engine driving them. Acuff continued in this thread: first selling songbooks of his fans' favorites like earlier radio stars had done, but then taking things a step further by setting up his own publishing firm. Although fans tend to focus on singers' biographies and musical output, the story of how country music built a business infrastructure and learned to capture the value of songs as intellectual property is fascinating.

STAGE PERSONAS MADE IDEAS ABOUT AUTHENTICITY MORE COMPLICATED.

One of the many ways that country fans treat the notion of authenticity is when singers are simply "their true selves," without pretense or performance. Up to the present, many country fans treasure the stars and the records from artists such as the ones addressed here as authentic, meaning, in this case, as a realistic depiction of the music and identity of the singers. Certainly Rodgers, the Carters, and Acuff were from rural, Southern working-class backgrounds (although Acuff's family was more highly educated and exposed to more middle-class life than the others). But as professional entertainers, they cultivated on-stage personalities that represented invented characters rather than just themselves.

Through their careers, Acuff, the Carters, and Rodgers defined the basic stage characters that would persist in country music. The first was the wholesome family who attended Sunday school and had deep roots in rural mountain communities. The other image that emerged was that of the hell-raising good old boy who would chase women with a stiff drink in hand, bemoan the hard knocks of working-class life, and ultimately wind up in need of either redemption or forgiveness, facing his own tragic mortality. Some historians have used the term "tragic troubadour" to describe this persona in country music. Jimmie Rodgers was the first major star to embody this identity, both in his songs and in his personal life.

It is important to note that neither Rodgers nor the Carters ever adopted the stereotyped comedic image of hillbilly hayseeds in hick overalls, although Acuff did to some small extent. The Carters donned suits and dresses for their publicity photos, and Rodgers alternately played up his personality as a classy entertainer, in his straw boater hat or bowler, or as a railroad brakeman, matching the rounder/blues lyrics of many of his songs. He occasionally even sported cowboy garb, a forerunner of the singing cowboys who would change the face of country music in the 1930s. The lasting images and iconic figures that Rodgers and the Carters presented were those of professional entertainers willing to present themselves in costume and in character, not "natural" hillbilly rubes. Roy Acuff on the other hand, took a similar stance to other musicians on the Opry and dressed in costumes to showcase hillbilly rube characters—the "rustification" of his presentation. These stories provide a great opportunity for us to reflect on how fans at different times have defined what they consider authentic, and how they understand the past and its music.

As the Great Depression rocked the foundations of working people's lives, country music poured into their homes in the voices and personalities of national stars. The infrastructure of the country music business was well-enough organized to be a profitable enterprise and to support even more expansion of the genre. And the sounds of traditional country music were ensconced in the records and radio broadcasts of these stars. New musical styles and images, however, namely those of western swing and the singing cowboy, were encroaching on country's traditions; they would challenge the status quo of hillbilly music, which itself was about to become both dated and too limiting for the scope of country music.

✴ ESSAY: MUSIC BUSINESS

 # Copyright

A songwriter's most valuable possession in the early days of country music was intellectual, rather than physical, property. Songwriters who held the copyright to their songs received royalty payments every time their song was sold on record, regardless of a copyright. Copyright is the bundle of rights that the original creator of a work—in our case, a song—controls. These generally include the right to print, publish, and sell the song, to make copies of it, and to perform it publicly. The rights pertain to the song itself, basically the words, melody, and chords, or, in other words, the intellectual property. It is interesting to note that a copyright can be bought and sold, just like a material possession. Stories abound in country music in which an unsuspecting songwriter sells all the rights to a song for only a few dollars, and only in retrospect realizes how valuable that copyright really was.

In 1909, the United States Congress passed a new copyright law that added a special provision. Under the new law, once a song had been recorded and sold, any other person was free to make a recording of that same song, with or without permission from the person who owned the song's copyright, as long as the copyright holder was paid 2¢ for every copy of the record with the song on it. These payments are generally known as mechanical royalties.

The payment structure in place in the early hillbilly recording industry had a major effect on the development of the genre. When a singer went into the studio to record a song, he or she was typically paid a fixed amount, often $25 or $50. The record label then sold the records for perhaps 75¢ apiece (during the Great Depression, the "budget" labels sold records for only 35¢). Sometimes the singer received royalties from the record label based on the actual sales, but in many instances, the singer did not receive any royalties or payments beyond that initial fee for the recording session. The holder of the song's copyright, on the other hand, was paid 2¢ for every record sold. If a song became a major hit and sold 100,000 copies, those royalties were worth $2,000. Furthermore, in many instances, more than one singer made recordings of the same song, especially if it became popular, and the song's copyright holder got paid for every one of those records, regardless of who the singer was or what label released the record. In other words, in the music business, there was often much more money to be made in songwriting than in performing.

In practical terms, only songs that were newly composed could be copyrighted. Traditional ballads were already in the public domain, meaning that anyone could use them without paying any royalties. Similarly, if a musician recorded a song that was under copyright to someone else, the musician only got the session fee. Thus, musicians faced a powerful incentive to write new songs, or at least to claim they had written them, so they could receive mechanical royalties.

In most instances, songwriters signed contracts with publishers, who then handled the copyrights of the songs, received the royalties, and split them with the songwriter according to an agreed percentage—often 75% to the publisher and 25% to the actual songwriter. Many producers and publishers turned a blind eye when musicians claimed to have written songs that they had actually learned from other sources, because of the financial incentive. This situation may help explain why A. P. Carter and Jimmie Rodgers have their names listed as "songwriter" for songs that they clearly did not write. The value of those copyrights, regardless of whether they were fairly claimed in the first place, is profound; the U.S. Congress has extended the duration of copyright protection, so many of the songs Jimmie Rodgers and A. P. Carter copyrighted in the late 1920s are still under protection today. This means that if a singer records one of these old Jimmie Rodgers songs or A. P. Carter songs, royalties are still paid to the publisher who controls the copyrights.

☆ **ESSAY: TECHNOLOGY**

 # Making Records in the 1920s

When Ralph Peer set up his portable recording studio in Bristol, Tennessee, in 1927, the equipment was very different than what musicians see today in the studio. Although Peer brought electric microphones and top-quality equipment for that era, the system still depended on several mechanical parts, and the actual recordings were still made on wax discs (called "masters"). A system of weights and pulleys kept the disc rotating at a steady speed during the recording session, although at the Bristol sessions, that equipment's speed was slightly off from what it should have been. The wax masters only held three minutes of music each, which determined the maximum length for a song. They were subject to all sorts of variances in the studio conditions; sound engineers sometimes positioned a lightbulb to warm and soften the wax so it would record better. And although the masters were reasonably sturdy, they sometimes sustained damage in transit back to the record company's production facilities.

The biggest differences, however, were that recordings could not be edited, spliced, or pieced together. Today, even a musician with just a microphone, a computer, and some free software can splice, edit, mix, mash up, and manipulate home-made sound recordings with great ease. The vast majority of the music we hear today is a combination of sounds that were never actually played or sung at the same moment in time, and many of which have been altered dramatically from what was actually played or sung. But in 1927, a recording captured exactly what was played and sung, all the way through the song in a single "take," or performance. If a musician missed a note, or if a singer forgot a word, the only options were either to use the recording in spite of the error or to perform the whole song again. Furthermore, all the instruments had to play at once—there was no way to add an extra instrument in at a later time. If an instrument was louder than the others, the sound engineer might move the performers around in the room to adjust the balance. And even with the advent of electric microphones, most families could not afford record players that had enhanced electric playback mechanisms, so listeners heard these records on acoustic record players that were subject to their own temperamental variances. When we listen to these recordings, we often hear moments that in today's studios would have been edited out long before the recording was released. But because there was no editing back then, we get to hear what the musicians sounded like actually playing through the song together.

★ **ESSAY: IDENTITY**

 # Race in Early Country Music

From its earliest recordings, country music was defined by the race of the performers. As we have already seen, record producers kept separate catalogs of recordings, listing black artists in the "race" catalog and white artists in the "hillbilly" catalog. But the racial identity of country music was far more complex than that. In the 1920s and '30s, the American South was still living under Jim Crow laws (a name referring to a character from blackface minstrelsy), which enforced segregation, often in violent and horrific ways. In most places, white and black audiences could neither eat together nor sit together at a concert. Racism was an ugly but very present part of life for many early country musicians. In 1928, for instance, Lee and Austin Allen, white brothers from Tennessee, recorded a blues tune in a traditionally black style, and their producer Frank Walker released it in the "race" catalog, even advertising it with a drawing of two black men. The Allen Brothers threatened to sue the record label because, they explained, they would be unable to get work as musicians if people thought they were black. Racism contributed directly to the development of the music in some cases, such as with Fiddlin' John Carson's association with the Klan. Whiteness, in the context of country music, was defined not only in opposition to blackness, either. Henry Ford, for instance, who founded the Ford Motor Company and mass-produced automobiles such as the Model T, used his resources to foster old-time music and culture not only because he saw it as culturally uplifting but also because he associated it with a racial purity and whiteness that aligned with his anti-Semitic views.

Early country music unquestionably owed a great debt to black cultural traditions and imitations of black cultural traditions (see Listen Side by Side). Blackface minstrelsy, with white performers impersonating black stereotyped characters, persisted in country music for years. The Opry featured blackface acts into the 1950s, and stars including Jimmie Rodgers and Bill Monroe (see Chapter 5) worked as blackface entertainers in their early careers. Blues tunes, such as those sung by Jimmie Rodgers, were learned from black musicians. In some of his blues performances, Rodgers inserted the call-outs and spoken interjections that were common among black performers and even adopted the dialect of those black entertainers at times. It is remarkable that Rodgers made records with black musicians, including the Louisville Jug Band and Louis Armstrong, given that such an undertaking was socially transgressive in segregated society.

Given the era in which they lived, white and black musicians interacted during those years to a degree that might seem surprising. Poverty fostered some of the interactions, as people of all races at the bottom of the socioeconomic ladder were often thrust together by circumstance, but at other times music was the binding force. Ernest Stoneman's daughter recalls a black banjo player staying at their home and playing music with them when passing through town; A. P. Carter took his black neighbor along on song-collecting trips; Jimmie Rodgers shared the stage with black entertainers in medicine shows; and Dr. Bates brought DeFord Bailey to the Opry, to cite a few examples.

In many instances, biographical accounts of country musicians' youth feature a black musician from whom the young performer absorbs musical knowledge: Hank Williams and Teetot Payne (Chapter 4) or Bill Monroe and Arnold Shultz (Chapter 5), for instance. The ubiquity of these stories throughout country music suggests an extremely complicated racial legacy in the genre, namely music that was socially coded as white but was conceived via the tutelage of black blues or street performers. Country fans both reinforce the whiteness of the music and celebrate its black roots. The relationship between music and racial identity is even more complicated in the post-2000 era, when artists have been both harshly criticized and lauded for audibly crossing into traditionally black musical styles.

Some historians have argued that, in some cases, musicians lived and worked in integrated racial spaces, and the segregation and distinctions between black and white music were imposed from outside by commercial forces. Others have argued that in some cases white performers mimicked black musical styles as a way of subjugating black culture and of exaggerating the way that music could represent racial difference, thereby propagating segregationist and racist attitudes. In all cases, country music's deep association with whiteness invites us to reexamine the times, places, and communities from which the music emerged.

☆ ESSAY: CULTURE

Cover Songs

A **cover song** is a performance of a song that has already been recorded or performed earlier by a different artist with whom the song is associated. For instance, when Dolly Parton recorded "Stairway to Heaven" in 2002, she was covering Led Zeppelin's "Stairway to Heaven." In some cases, fans may know the original and the cover; in other cases, they may only know one version of the song. Either way, the cover version gets some of its meaning from the fact that it is referring to an earlier performance and artist, even if that reference is quite abstract.

Cover songs have always been part of country music because they provide a way for new generations of singers to connect themselves to the music's history and pay tribute to musicians they view as their forerunners and inspirations. The first song that Bill Monroe (see Chapter 5) ever sang on the Grand Ole Opry was a cover of a Jimmie Rodgers song, for instance. Covers also introduce new audiences to old songs and artists. Southern rockers Lynyrd Skynyrd (see Chapter 9) talked about Jimmie Rodgers on stage before covering his "Blue Yodel" (which they called "T for Texas."). When fans know both versions, a cover song invites its audience to compare the two and draw connections. All of these aspects are extremely valuable in a genre where tradition is a defining principle.

Most historians consider a cover song to be different than a performance of a "standard." A standard is a song that is so widely known and performed by so many musicians that no one artist is associated with it. Many fiddle tunes, such as "Sourwood Mountain" (see Chapter 1), folk tunes, and gospel songs are considered standards. When a musician plays or sings a standard, the performance becomes part of an established tradition. A cover song, on the other hand, is one where the song was strongly associated with one particular artist.

Given the importance of Rodgers, Acuff, and the Carters in the early days of country music, many later artists covered their best-known songs as a way of drawing a connection to early country music. Acuff's signature song, for instance, was "Wabash Cannonball," and although he neither wrote it nor was the first to record it, it was strongly associated with him. Covers of that song were invoking its association with Roy Acuff. Over time, however, as more and more musicians perform a song, the song can begin to shift from a cover to a standard.

Whenever a cover appears in country music, we can investigate the origins of the song and compare versions. What has the cover artist kept the same and what has been changed? Why might some aspects of the song have changed? How and why is the cover artist connecting to a particular earlier performance? And what can we discover about the new artist's place and meaning in country music through the cover song? Cover songs will reappear throughout our study in many different time periods and contexts. Keep these questions in mind as we encounter them.

LISTEN SIDE BY SIDE

"Blue Yodel"	"Muddy Water Blues"
Jimmie Rodgers, vocals and guitar, 1927 (Victor 21142)	Freddie Spruell, vocals and guitar, 1926 (OKeh 8422)

Blues and country were two distinct categories of music in the 1920s, delineated by the racial identity of the performers. Record labels treated white and black performers differently, and because of both the social and the legal segregation of that time, those perceptions are ingrained in even today's listeners. We know from historical evidence and the recordings themselves, however, that musicians listened to each other across racial lines.

Our modern notions of what it means to write a song are also very different from the way songwriting was treated in the earliest days of country music. When musicians performed blues tunes, they often drew on a large collection of rhymed couplets (two lines of text that rhyme) and strung together a song from those pre-existing bits of poetry. Those shared lines of text were part of the common ground of the blues communities. When musicians recorded these songs, names of songwriters were attached to them, and royalties were distributed accordingly. Thus, what had been a communal tradition of borrowed texts were framed as individual songs.

"Blue Yodel" was Rodgers's first big hit, and Ralph Peer recorded his name as the songwriter. Many of the song's six verses, however, were in circulation by African-American blues artists prior to his recording of it. Historians and folklorists found another interesting phenomenon: in the years *after* Rodgers's hit records came out, those sections of the lyrics that were his own original work made their way into folk traditions and other songs, and song collectors discovered that they were being treated like part of a communal folk-music tradition rather than as one person's composition.

Freddie Spruell was one of the first musicians to make records we know as Delta blues in terms of their style. Although he was living at the time in Chicago, which was where he recorded "Muddy Water Blues," he was originally from Louisiana, and his performance style was generally that of the greater Mississippi Delta area, a style that blues legend Robert Johnson made even more famous in the 1930s.

Two important points emerge when comparing "Blue Yodel" and "Muddy Water Blues." The first is that we hear a black Delta blues number that has some of the same lyrics as "Blue Yodel." Spruell's second verse, "I'd rather drink muddy water, rather sleep in a real hollow log," is nearly identical to Rodgers's sixth verse. Other lyrics from "Blue Yodel" also appear in earlier blues songs.

Did Rodgers steal these lyrics? No; it was standard practice among musicians who sang blues tunes to swap and borrow lyrics from each other, and Rodgers's blues tunes contained a typical mix of his own original texts and stock blues phrases.

The second important point is that we can compare two similar recordings made within a year of each other, both solo male singers accompanied on guitar and with some lyrics in common, and compare the typical Delta blues musical style with the hillbilly style. Focus on the guitar styles:

Rodgers's steady pattern of low notes and simple strummed high notes is very different from Spruell's shuffle chords with a blues melody woven into them. Spruell does not yodel; his vocal performance includes more nuances and variations in pitch and rhythm, and his diction is harder to understand. Rodgers's voice is very distinctive, and the style of guitar, yodels, and singing on this recording are representative of the bulk of his career.

These two recordings offer a bigger window into the sounds and styles of popular music in the 1920s, and a sense of what a single fan might hear. As you listen to these two recordings, pay close attention to all the ways they each represent a shared musical tradition, and all the ways that they were marked as very different.

PLAYLIST

Acuff, Roy. "The Precious Jewel" (1940)

Acuff, Roy. "Wabash Cannonball" (1947)

Carter Family. "Keep On the Sunny Side" (1928)

Carter Family. "Wildwood Flower" (1928)

Rodgers, Jimmie. "Blue Yodel No. 8" ("Muleskinner Blues") (1930)

Rodgers, Jimmie. "Somewhere Down Below the Dixon Line" (1933)

FOR MORE READING AND VIEWING

Mazor, Barry. *Ralph Peer and the Making of American Roots Music.* Chicago: Chicago Review Press, 2014.

Neal, Jocelyn. *The Songs of Jimmie Rodgers: A Legacy in Country Music.* Bloomington: Indiana University Press, 2009.

Porterfield, Nolan. *Jimmie Rodgers: The Life and Times of America's Blue Yodeler.* Rev. ed. Urbana: University of Illinois Press, 1992; reprinted, Jackson: University Press of Mississippi, 2007.

Rodgers, Jimmie. *The Singing Brakeman* (short film). Columbia, 1929. In *Times Ain't Like They Used to Be: Early Rural and Popular Music, 1928–1935.* Newark: Yazoo Video, 2000.

Wolfe, Charles K. *Classic Country: Legends of Country Music.* New York: Routledge, 2001.

Zwonitzer, Mark, with Charles Hirshberg. *Will You Miss Me When I'm Gone?: The Carter Family and Their Legacy in American Music.* New York: Simon & Schuster, 2002.

NAMES AND TERMS

Acuff, Roy
border stations
Bristol Sessions
Carter, A. P.
Carter Fold
Carter, Maybelle

Carter, Sara
copyright
cover songs
creation story
Peer, Ralph
protagonist

Rodgers, Jimmie
standards
tragic troubadour
XERA

REVIEW TOPICS

1. How did the public personas of these national stars shape the development of country music?

2. Why have the Bristol Sessions achieved such mythological importance in country music's culture?

3. Examine today's country music and look for artifacts from Rodgers, Acuff, and the Carters such as cover songs, tributes, artists who mention their names in their song lyrics, or aspects of their biographies that have become country music lore. How have their legacies continued to shape country music?

New Traditions, Cowboys, and Jazz

The Great Depression coincided with the dawning of a new professional era in country music. Although in 1927 record sales of all genres had reached almost $70 million, by 1932 they had plummeted to a mere $11 million. Radio stations took up the slack by providing entertainment to people both in cities and in remote rural areas. Prohibition had gone into effect in January 1920, which unsurprisingly led to a rise in songs about ill-gotten booze and related illicit activities. The repeal of Prohibition came in April 1933, and in subsequent years, laws governing the sale and consumption of alcohol had a significant effect on country music's development. The biggest changes in country music, however, were the arrival of radically different musical styles, a new visual image associated with the music, and a shift in the geography of country music.

The growth and evolution of country music in the 1930s involved three main paths:

1. Radio shows, especially those based in the Southeast, cultivated traditional, old-time music and came to represent a nostalgic past during a decade of economic strife.
2. A fusion of jazz, dance music, and string band traditions occurred in Texas, leading to the development of western swing.
3. The Hollywood film industry brought a new hero to the silver screen and to the American imagination in the form of the singing cowboy.

In the wake of national stars such as Jimmie Rodgers, the Carter Family, and Roy Acuff, country music's distribution shifted from primarily regional marketing to much broader dissemination. The two most influential radio stations with regard to country music, WLS and WSM, both enjoyed "**clear channel**" status, which meant that no other station was allowed to broadcast on their assigned frequencies, and thus their signal reached far beyond their geographic home base. Nationwide radio networks such as CBS and NBC (which ran two networks at that time, known as Blue and Red) also affected the distribution model for country music. Their ability to broadcast a show from all their affiliate stations transformed the music into something intrinsically "American" in nature, where listeners coast-to-coast could hear the same programs. By the start of World War II, country music had outgrown its hillbilly associations and was starting to come together as a more cohesive and distinctive genre.

Barn Dance Radio Shows, Stars, and the Brother Acts

The mainstay of country music in the Southeast and Midwest was the old-time and hillbilly music on which the country recording industry had been founded. As a new decade dawned, radio programming became increasingly important to the developing of the genre. The National Barn Dance on Chicago's WLS station and the Grand Ole Opry on Nashville's WSM station gained stature as the premier programs, but across the Southeast and Midwest, almost every radio station hosted its own barn dance. In 1933, WWVA in Wheeling, West Virginia, began its Jamboree, which is second only to the Opry in number of years on the air. Atlanta boasted three different barn dance programs, and Charlotte, Knoxville, Louisville, Cincinnati, Des Moines, and Fort Worth featured at least one well-known show. The trend even spread to the West Coast. By the 1930s, the greater Los Angeles area was home to a huge population of migrants from the Midwest, the Southern Plains of Texas and Oklahoma, and the Southern region, especially Arkansas, as well as a growing minority population of Mexican-Americans. Country music appealed to all those residents. A half-dozen different stations in and around Los Angeles featured a barn dance program of some sort, although the musical styles on the West Coast were noticeably different than those of the Southeast.

Nowhere was the growing tension between old-time musical sensibilities and progressive musical styles more apparent than on the well-established barn dances. The Grand Ole Opry, for instance, had built its reputation on old-time string bands who played hoedowns, traditional hillbilly singers, and even comedy sketches with stereotyped hayseed characters. Many 1930's performers on the Opry followed in that tradition, such as the Dixieliners, a string band comprising fiddler Arthur Smith and Sam and Kirk McGee, who had worked with Uncle Dave Macon earlier in their careers. Comedy duos such as Lassus & Honey, who brought blackface minstrel show routines onto the Opry, and Sarie & Sally, whose characters were sassy mountain girls, continued to be very popular.

Change in the Opry's musical style came about primarily for business reasons. WSM's station managers were interested in hiring staff musicians who could not only play the Opry but also provide entertainment on other shows throughout the week that featured different genres of music. Musicians sought these sorts of employment opportunities, which allowed them to become full-time entertainers without other day jobs. The Vagabonds, a vocal group consisting of brothers Dean and Paul Upson and their friend Curtis "Curt" Poulton, got started while the Upsons were in college in Ohio, then earned some fame working radio stations around Chicago and St. Louis. They moved to the Opry in August 1931, at a time when station manager Harry Stone was working to improve the level of professionalism of the show. Stone and emcee George D. Hay disagreed in terms of musical taste: Hay advocated for old-time music, hillbilly images, and a folksy quality to the show, whereas Stone favored a more upscale image and music that kept abreast of popular trends. The Vagabonds were pop singers every bit as much as country; they worked up folk songs and traditional-sounding numbers for their Opry appearances, but the rest of their musical output was entirely in line with pop music (their biggest hits included "When It's Lamp Lighting Time in the Valley"). WLS's National Barn Dance faced similar tensions. Many of the biggest stars on the National Barn Dance sang and played old-time, traditional folk music in rural styles. A reasonable portion of the music on the show, however, was not tied to rural traditions at all, and pop vocal groups such as Ford and Glenn were also part of the cast.

In spite of the pop groups that occasionally found their home on these barn dances, 1930's country music in the Southeast and Midwest remained rooted in tradition. The one new musical development that had a lasting impact was the advent of the brother acts, a term that refers to duos (sometimes actual brothers, but often not) who sang in close harmony and accompanied themselves with string instruments (see essay on Brother Acts). These brother acts were a very practical response to the Depression, when larger bands cost radio stations more money because there were more people to pay. The duo format worked well for fifteen- and thirty-minute sponsored radio segments, and by the mid-1930s dozens of such acts were making names for themselves. The brother acts also filled an important role in the entertainment industry during the Depression. As the economy placed an increasing burden on families, the pervading mood in the nation turned toward sentimental reflections on home, faith, and family. Many of the brother acts specialized in gospel songs, sentimental ballads, and nostalgic reminiscences, which fit the format of duet singing with simple accompaniment particularly well. Corporate sponsors saw this music as wholesome and uplifting for their target audiences, and thus supported the acts financially.

The biggest stars of the Grand Ole Opry in the mid-1930s was a brother act. Alton (1908–1964) and Rabon (1916–1952) Delmore were born and raised in Alabama, where they learned to sing gospel hymns from old shape-note hymnals (see Chapter 1). Alton was also a gifted songwriter, a talent that would serve the brothers well throughout their professional career, because a steady supply of new material—and control of the copyrights for those newly composed songs—was an important part of a successful music career (see Chapter 2). Like the other brother acts, the Delmores were part of a second generation of country musicians who grew up hearing records and radio performances of the 1920s. They also were influenced by changing styles in pop music, including the way singers were able to use softer and more nuanced vocal styles because of advances in microphone technology. The Opry hired them in 1933, and the Delmores won over their audience with a sweeter, gentler vocal tone.

The Delmores devoted a lot of energy to building a loyal following among their fans by responding to fan mail, heeding song requests, and giving live performances in the surrounding area during the week. While the connection between fans and musicians is important in all genres of music, country in particular has always valued that bond. For instance, radio executives judged the success of early country radio broadcasts by the amount of fan mail that arrived at the station. Furthermore, the economic realities of country music meant that radio performers had to give live concerts regularly to earn a living. From the earliest days of the industry, country musicians understood that their fans demanded both access to the musicians and a perception that the stars really were "just one of them." These characteristics became part of the genre's core identity.

Figure 3-1 The Blue Sky Boys.

Source: Southern Folklife Collection, Wilson library, The Unviersity of North Carolina at Chapel Hill.

The Delmores' trademark sound was close-harmony vocals accompanied by guitar (Alton) and tenor guitar (Rabon). Unlike many of the other brother acts, who stuck to gospel songs and nostalgic, wholesome fare, the Delmores never shied away from blues-influenced numbers or songs with bawdy innuendos. One such hit was Alton's composition "Brown's Ferry Blues" (1933), which aptly demonstrates both their softer vocal styles and their penchant for playful lyrics with sexual overtones. The Delmore Brothers left the Opry in 1938 over a contract dispute, but continued to be a major force in country music. They adapted their musical style in the later 1940s to a lively hillbilly boogie style (see Chapter 4), but their brother act sound was a dominant part of 1930s country music.

The Blue Sky Boys, consisting of brothers Bill (1917–2008) and Earl (1919–1998) Bolick, from Hickory, North Carolina, followed the nostalgic sentiments of the 1930s in their music to an even greater degree than did the Delmore Brothers. They worked for the Crazy Water Crystals company (see essay on Sponsorship) and sang on several radio stations around the Southeast before landing a recording contract. First signed by producer Eli Oberstein (Ralph Peer's successor at Victor) in 1936, the brothers eschewed any music they thought immoral or unwholesome. On their radio shows and on their recordings, Earl accompanied them on guitar, while Bill's shimmering mandolin lines filled in around the vocals. Their harmony singing on hits such as "The Sunny Side of Life" (1936) and "The Dying Boy's Prayer" (1936) showed the influence of the older mountain styles of high lonesome tenor voices, which would later become the foundation of bluegrass music.

Literally dozens of other acts followed the same duet model, including the Callahan Brothers, the Shelton Brothers, Mac and Bob, Karl and Harty, the Dixon Brothers, and the Monroe Brothers. Although fewer in number, several women also adopted the duet formula, most memorably the DeZurik Sisters and the Girls of the Golden West. The most influential contribution of the brother and sister acts in the 1930s was to affirm the musical traditions of old-time folk songs and down-to-earth, gospel-infused performances. But more important than their contribution to 1930's country music was that brother acts became an established part of country music's identity. From the 1930s to the present, brother acts in many different guises have persisted: the Louvin Brothers in the 1950s, and the Everly Brothers, who crossed fluidly between country and rock 'n' roll, were both later incarnations of brother acts. Seminal bluegrass musicians, such as the Stanley Brothers, Jim and Jesse, and the Osborne Brothers, all grew out of that same tradition. Later generations included the Bellamy Brothers and the Judds (who were actually mother and daughter). In other words, the principle of close-harmony duet singing and a performance that drew on familial closeness far outlasted the traditional sounds of the 1930s.

On the barn dances, the big-name radio stars of the 1930s also kept alive the traditions of folk songs and old-time music. The biggest proponent of this was Opry star Roy Acuff (see Chapter 2). Many of the stars of WLS's National Barn Dance projected the same old-time sentiments and traditional musical preferences as the Opry's singers. Bradley Kincaid (see Chapter 1) continued to perform his vast collection of folk tunes on the show well into the 1930s. At the start of that decade, he was joined by John Lair (1894–1985), a fellow Kentuckian who wanted to promote what he perceived as authentic folk music. Lair formed the Cumberland Ridge Runners, a string band and vocal ensemble that specialized in old-time music. The National Barn Dance also boasted the best-known all-girl string band, the Coon Creek Girls, whose publicity photographs often showed them in antiquated long dresses posed in front of rural farm landscapes. Other nationally known stars were Red Foley (1910–1968) and Lulu Belle and Scotty Wiseman. Lulu Belle (born Myrtle Eleanor Cooper, 1913–1999) grew up in North Carolina and moved to Chicago to pursue a singing career. WLS initially hired her as a duet partner for Red Foley, but later teamed her with Scotty Wiseman (1908–1981). The duo sang in close harmony, relying heavily on the songwriting proficiency of Wiseman for new material. Lulu Belle adopted a sweet, homespun mountain-lass character on the radio, yet another instance where the performers' on-air personas were exaggerated stereotypes of country identities. The duo quickly became the darlings of their radio audience. Like the Delmore Brothers and countless other groups who performed on the radio in the 1930s, Red Foley, Lulu Belle, and Scotty took advantage of the crooning style of singing to soften and sweeten the sounds of country music. Yet their sound was firmly rooted in the traditions of homespun folk singing and mountain music, even though that was sometimes just a carefully fabricated presentation of tradition rather than actual old-time practice.

Although the radio shows in the Midwest and Southeast were home to lots of traditional, old-time influenced country music, some West Coast radio shows also included hillbilly singers. The most famous of these was a group known as the Beverly Hill Billies (decades before the television show of the same name). In 1930, radio station KMPC manager Glen Rice hired musicians to pretend that they were an uneducated, uncultured band who had stumbled straight from the hills and ridden their mules into the foreign territory of the Los Angeles radio station. Other folk-oriented performers on California's country radio shows included Woody Guthrie (1912–1967), who grew up on Jimmie Rodgers's music and spent a few years in

Figure 3-2 Lulu Belle and Scotty, stars of the National Barn Dance on WLS.
Source: Courtesy BenCar Archives.

the late 1930s as a hillbilly-folk singer and radio entertainer in California. Guthrie was part of a duo act with his brother Jack, who favored cowboy-themed songs, and later worked with duet partner Maxine Crisman (known on the air as Woody and Lefty Lou), singing more traditional country tunes. In 1940, Guthrie moved to New York and became a leading figure in the folk scene, bringing his knowledge and love of early country music into the movement that would become known as the folk revival.

Other stars kept alive the blues traditions that had been a big part of Jimmie Rodgers music. Louisiana native Jimmie Davis (1899–2000), for instance, began recording in Shreveport in 1928, singing in the style of Jimmie Rodgers. Throughout the 1930s, he was known for songs with blatant sexual innuendos (such as "Red Nightgown Blues"), most of them in a blues style, with some of his recordings accompanied by black musicians. Yet his best-known song was "You Are My Sunshine" (1940), which adopted the same sentimental, old-time feel that Roy Acuff had cultivated in many of his hits. Davis became governor of Louisiana in 1944, one of many country musicians from his generation who also entered politics.

The brother acts, string bands, and singing stars of the 1930s kept country music thoroughly grounded in notions of folk music and a nostalgic past. Gospel songs and religious themes were woven throughout the music, along with sentimental ballads and songs romanticizing rural America. The performers used costumes and adopted onstage characters to amplify the music's supposed old-time origins and traditional values. Yet as the decade continued, country music started to outgrow its hillbilly identity. The musicians had always had a love-hate relationship with the whole hillbilly image that was attached to the music. Many of them chafed at the perception that they were anything less than polished professionals, and quite obviously the image itself was nothing more than an act in most cases. If the musicians wanted to be taken more seriously, especially in an increasingly competitive entertainment industry and by a larger audience than they already had won, they needed a new set of images and characters that would transcend old stereotypes. They also needed to find a balance between the traditional folk and string band sounds of their past and new developments in pop music. During the 1930s, those two threads evolved in other regions of the United States, starting with the fusion of string band music and jazz in the Southwest.

Western Swing

Just where western swing fits in the history of popular music has been the subject of much debate. In its basic definition, western swing is dance music played in a jazz style by a hybrid of string bands and big bands, conceived in the 1930s and widely popular in the Southwest and on the West Coast through the 1950s. But is it jazz or country? Histories of jazz music tend to ignore or gloss over western swing. One reason for that is the way the music was marketed; record labels listed it in their hillbilly catalogues, and jazz fans and historians alike considered hillbilly music beneath their tastes. Another reason is that western swing has been incorporated by later generations of country music, so when historians look at its overall influence, they wind up with country stars such as George Strait rather than jazz performers. Finally, the music's cultural associations are generally with white, working-class rural fans and musicians associated with the Southwest, which simply is not the profile that jazz writers associate with the legacy of their music.

But histories of country music sometimes find it just as challenging to make sense of western swing. Western swing bands broke with string band traditions by incorporating all sorts of instruments such as drums and trumpets that were considered extremely radical (see essay on Western Swing). They performed current jazz and pop songs, wore stylish western suits, and presented themselves as hot dance bands None of these characteristics fit with the old-time folk perspectives that had been highly valued by record labels and musicians working in hillbilly music during the 1920s and early '30s. Bob Wills famously renounced any connection to the more traditional styles of country music when he declared in a 1946 interview, "Please, don't anybody confuse us with none of them hillbilly outfits." Even contemporary scholars sometimes insist that western swing should not be considered country music because, in their minds, country music carries connotations of being more "hick" or "low-class" than their ideas about western swing. Our definition of country music, however, is a broad and inclusive genre in which western swing played a critical role in breaking open the limited hillbilly traditions and allowing country music to expand.

In the early 1930s, musicians in Texas who grew up playing old fiddle tunes and string band music started hearing hot jazz styles on radio broadcasts and especially on records. They recognized the appeal of this music, especially for dancing. Unlike the Southeast, Texas and the Southwest had large immigrant populations from Germany and especially Eastern Europe (including today's Czech Republic) who brought with them partner dances, including waltzes, polkas, and schottisches. Dancing was an important pastime and form of entertainment in those communities. These regions were also a melting pot for other ethnic musical traditions. In East Texas, the influence of Louisiana's Cajun music spilled over; in South Texas, the Mexican styles of *norteño* and *conjunto* were commonly heard. Finally, fiddling was a well-established part of that musical culture. Fiddlers such as Bob Wills and his father won wide acclaim and, more importantly, were in high demand for dances and house parties. These combinations of influences were the recipe for western swing.

WHAT'S IN A NAME?

The term "western swing" was not applied to this music until long after it had been created. In the 1930s, the musicians simply described themselves as hot dance bands or hot string bands, where the term "hot" was an accepted code for "jazz-influenced with a strong rhythmic drive." The term "Texas swing" sometimes appeared, but it was not until 1946, when fiddler/bandleader Spade Cooley designated himself "King of Western Swing" as a means of marketing his band, that the style got its label.

The demographics of Texas encouraged the development of western swing. Families tended to live far apart, especially in West Texas, and social activities often revolved around community dances. The population included a significant number of ranch hands and oil field workers, many of whom were young, unattached people eager for entertainment. Although prohibition was repealed in 1933, many counties in Texas remained dry (meaning no liquor could be sold). As a result, large dance halls sprouted on county lines near those dry counties to draw the population from both areas. These raucous, lively dance halls required music and entertainment, and the environment fostered the development of the new musical style.

The bands who played these dance halls adapted to their audience's tastes. They played the hot jazz numbers that the audience wanted to hear and expanded their band's instrumentation so it could be heard in a loud dance hall. These western swing bands saw themselves as practical entertainers whose business model involved securing a sponsored radio show with which to build a fan base and then supplementing their meager radio income by playing dances. Unlike musicians such as Bradley Kincaid and John Lair, they were also unencumbered by any sense of responsibility toward preserving or promoting old-time folk singing or musical traditions.

Milton Brown (1903–1936) and his Musical Brownies were the first widely successful western swing band. Prior to forming the Musical Brownies, Brown had joined Bob Wills's Fiddle Band in 1930 as a vocalist. That ensemble, with Milton's younger brother Derwood as a guitarist, became the Light Crust Doughboys—thanks to their sponsorship by Burrus Mills, the makers of Light Crust flour—with a show on WBAP Fort Worth. Burrus Mills' advertising manager was the colorful Wilbert Lee "Pappy" O'Daniel (1890–1969), who hired the band. As he discovered their widespread popularity, O'Daniel became more involved in their activities, acting as manager and appearing on stage with them.

Both Brown and Wills found it increasingly difficult to work under O'Daniel's leadership. In 1932, Brown left to front his own band, the Musical Brownies. He hired classically trained fiddler Cecil Brower and jazz pianist Fred Calhoun, which expanded his band's abilities to play in a range of styles. Every Saturday night, the band appeared at the Crystal Springs Dance Pavilion just outside of Fort Worth, Texas, where they honed their musical skills and earned a large and loyal following. In 1934, the band began recording for Bluebird Records, which was the budget-priced subsidiary of Victor that sold records for only 35¢. Although they had added drums, piano, and electrified steel guitar to their ensemble, Brown's band remained, at its core, a string band: fiddle, guitar, banjo, and string bass. In 1936, Brown hired Cliff Bruner as a second fiddler, tapping into what would become a legendary tradition of twin Texas fiddling. The band's impact on popular music was tragically cut short when Brown died on April 18, 1936, from injuries sustained in a car accident a few days earlier. Sadly, Milton Brown did not live to see the full development of the musical style he helped pioneer but the musical style continued to thrive.

The band that slid into the western swing spotlight after Milton Brown's untimely death was Bob Wills (see Artist Profile) and his Texas Playboys. Wills was fiercely proud of his band's popularity with listeners. His onstage personality was always cheerful and brazenly outgoing, which matched a musical style that was entirely about entertaining a crowd in a dance hall. The sheer size of the Texas Playboys' lineup contributed to their bold sound—at their peak, Wills had twenty-two musicians in his band, often with three fiddle players sharing the stage. He cultivated a sound that moved continually away from the band's string band origins and closer to the big band jazz of his era. By the early 1940s, there was little musical difference between the types of songs, arrangements, and stage performance of the Texas Playboys and the jazz big bands that graced the ballrooms of New York City, except for the presence of the fiddles and banjos. Even the vocal styles matched popular music. The Texas Playboys' most popular recordings, such as "Right or Wrong" (1936), "New San Antonio Rose" (1940) (see Listening Guide), and "Roly Poly" (1945) featured the smooth singing of Tommy Duncan (1911–1967). Duncan had been working as a street entertainer when he auditioned for the Light Crust Doughboys in 1932 to replace Milton Brown. When Wills split from the band, Duncan insisted on going with him. More than any other feature of the western swing bands, the warm, smooth, resonant vocals of singers such as Duncan allowed the music to fit into the popular styles of that era and differentiated them from the hillbilly bands and mountain music traditions of the barn dances.

The western swing bands toured extensively, and as they did so, their musical style spread all across the Southwest and especially to California. In the 1940s, most towns had one or more dance halls that featured live music seven nights a week. Large dance bands such as the Texas Playboys were able to stay in business because it was common for people to go dancing several times a week. As western swing grew in popularity, several new bands gained prominence within the

Bob Wills (1905–1975)

Bob Wills had one of the most dominating personalities in country music. Born James Robert Wills on March 6, 1905, the son of a champion fiddle player and sometime farmer, Wills traveled with his family throughout his youth as they followed cotton-picking jobs. Along the way, Wills learned to fiddle, and by the time he was in his early teens, he was playing regular dance gigs with his family. Texas was home to a large number of traveling medicine shows, and in 1926, Wills spent a short time working for one.

Newly married and with a family to support, Wills made his way to Fort Worth, where in 1929 he put together the Wills Fiddle Band. In 1930, Milton Brown joined the band as vocalist, and they earned a sponsored radio show as the Aladdin Laddies. A year later, the band members switched their name to the Light Crust Doughboys, under the management of Wilbert Lee "Pappy" O'Daniel. The band provided steady employment, but Wills chafed under O'Daniel's heavy-handed leadership, and in 1933 Wills left to front his own band, the Texas Playboys. The new band settled in Tulsa, Oklahoma, where Wills drew on his musical interests in jazz, blues, and the burgeoning big band scene to expand the ensemble with horns, drums, piano, and electrified steel guitar. This change allowed the band to play old-time fiddle tunes and hot new jazz numbers with equal ease. As their fan base expanded, Wills

Figure 3-3 Bob Wills and his Texas Playboys. Wills is to the right of the microphone; Laura Lee Owens, who was one of Wills's vocalists, is standing on the right. *Source:* Courtesy of Country Music Hall of Fame and Museum.

drew the attention of the American Recording Corporation (ARC), and in 1935, the Texas Playboys made their first records at a temporary sound studio in Dallas, Texas.

That session resulted in one of the best-loved stories about Wills. As the band launched into their first piece, Wills let out a holler, started to call out names of band members who should take solos, and shouted encouragement to the musicians. For years, Wills had worked in raucous dance halls across the Southwest. Loud, inebriated crowds demanded a strong personality on stage, and Wills's method for both driving his band and keeping up the energy on stage was

style. The best known of those was fronted by fiddler Spade Cooley (1910–1969). Originally from Oklahoma, Cooley moved with his family to the Los Angeles area, where he was hired by western singer Jimmy Wakely. When Wakely began a film career in 1942, Cooley took over his band, hiring Sollie Paul "Tex" Williams (1917–1985), originally from Illinois, as his singer. Whereas Bob Wills had to holler out to them. He expected his musicians to be on their toes at all times and able to respond when he called on individuals to play solos, as well as to follow his verbal interjections. But in the studio, producer Art Satherley was taken aback by all the hollering and stopped the session. He asked Wills to please stop covering up the music with all his talking and hollering, but Wills turned to his band and announced, "Boys, pack up, we're going home." Satherley pleaded with Wills to stay, to which Wills replied, "By God! You want Bob Wills, you get Bob Wills, and I talk and sing and say what I want to when I feel like it." Such an assertive stance was rare in country music, where producers generally held all the cards and musicians did what they were told.

Wills expanded his band and refined his players' musicianship until the Texas Playboys could compete fairly head-to-head with such big bands as Tommy Dorsey's. World War II tore the band apart, with even Bob Wills joining the army for a short stint. But as the war wound down, Wills reassembled the band, and in December 1944 they headed to Nashville for a coveted appearance on the Grand Ole Opry. What transpired is a good reminder of just how different western swing was from the hillbilly traditions on which the Opry built its foundation. Wills's band was decked out in stylish western-cut suits and brought with them the musical sounds of the Southwestern dance bands, including a trumpet and—most controversial of all—drums. Drums were forbidden on the Opry stage. They smacked of modern innovation, jazz, urban styles, and morally questionable dance music. And they threatened the carefully cultivated, rural, rustic hayseed image that George D. Hay and others had devised to brand the show. The Opry's staff insisted that Wills's drummer Monte Mountjoy set up his drum kit behind the curtain. Bob Wills argued with the Opry management over the arrangement, and at the last second before they began playing, ordered his musicians to pull the drums out in front of the curtain. In retaliation, the Opry management refused to let Wills play an encore, even though the audience was clamoring for one. Wills had demanded that jazz and pop-influenced styles with nontraditional elements to be integrated into the Opry, and others would follow, although the Opry's regular house band was not allowed to include a drummer until 1974.

By the late 1940s, Wills's trailblazing was largely behind him. The big band styles of the previous decade had been supplanted by new developments in country music. Wills reduced the size of his band to a smaller ensemble of usually seven or eight musicians—a practical move that shrank his payroll, since changing public tastes in entertainment made well-paying dance gigs harder to find. He continued to tour and make recordings through the mid-1960s, when debilitating health problems finally took their toll. A new generation of country stars considered him an idol and, in 1973, Merle Haggard brought him back into the recording studio for a tribute album. Wills suffered a massive stroke during that session, and, sadly, passed away before the album was finished.

retained at least some loyalty to the string band and fiddle tradition during his early career, the California-based western swing bands of the 1940s, including Cooley's, were fully invested in matching the pop sounds of sophisticated dance orchestras. Cooley hired a full string section, horns, and accordion along with the typical dance-band instrumentation including drums and piano, and sometimes

Listening Guide

"New San Antonio Rose" (1940)

PERFORMER: Bob Wills and the Texas Playboys

SONGWRITER: Bob Wills

ORIGINAL RELEASE: OKeh 5694

FORM: AABA

STYLE: Western swing

In 1938, Bob Wills and his band recorded a fiddle tune known as "San Antonio Rose" that became reasonably popular with other musicians. Irving Berlin's music publishing firm in New York saw the song's potential and sent a representative to negotiate the song's publishing rights. To the representative's dismay, the song had no lyrics, which he figured would limit its appeal. He offered Wills a $300 advance if he would write lyrics for the song. Wills recruited several of his band members, including trumpeter Everett Stover, to help him work on the project, and together they knocked out what would become the best-known western swing tune ever. That was not the end of the story when it came to the words; the publishing executives decided the lyrics needed reworking as more of a cowboy-themed number with an altered melody. Wills was irate about the changes and had his attorney argue persuasively on his behalf. The Berlin firm finally relented, and by the end of the year, the published music matched what Bob Wills and his bandmates had written. Shortly thereafter, Bing Crosby recorded the song and turned it into an enormous pop hit, which presaged the era when country songwriters and publishers routinely supplied songs to pop singers (see Chapter 6).

At its heart, "New San Antonio Rose" had always been something of a pop song, with little traceable lineage to hillbilly music. On the April 1940 recording, Wills presented a full eighteen-piece big band that sounded in every respect like the dance-oriented jazz bands of that era. A trumpet section and saxophone section played in tight jazz harmonies; the rhythm section, with drums, bass, piano, banjo, and guitar, played a solid swing groove. Tommy Duncan's vocals were resonant, silky smooth, and tinged with vibrato. Most notable was the song's musical arrangement and form. Wills borrowed the sounds of Mexican mariachi bands that had infiltrated folk music traditions in Texas and translated that to a trumpet part that evokes San Antonio. Although the song matches the standard AABA form common to popular tunes of that era (see Appendix A), here the second section ("It was there . . .") has a slightly varied melody from the first section. The song also changes keys (called a musical modulation) right before the singer

even harp, to accompany Williams's vocals. Cooley also hired and featured female singers with his band, including Ginny Jackson and Carolina Cotton, whose yodeling connected the singing cowboys and western swing musical styles in a series of stunning performances. Tex Williams broke off from Cooley's band in 1946 and formed his own band, the Western Caravan, yet another instance where a musician honed his skills in someone else's band and then established a solo career.

enters, but it is done so seamlessly that it's almost impossible for a casual listener to tell. In every respect, this is a highly crafted musical performance that has no audible connection to any hillbilly hayseed tradition.

TIME	FORM	LISTENING CUES	DISCUSSION
0:00	Introduction	full band	This short instrumental introduction sets up the rhythmic pattern for the song.
0:04	Instrumental A-section	trumpets	Two trumpets play the tune in harmony. Bob Wills hollers over the band his signature, "Ah-ha," and "My San Antonio Rose!" just as he would in a live performance to get the audience involved in the song.
0:23	Instrumental A-section	trumpets	The trumpets continue the next section of the melody. At 0:40, the band modulates smoothly to a new key, just one illustration of the sophisticated musical arrangement of this song.
0:44	Vocal A-section	"Deep within my heart ..."	Tommy Duncan sings in a velvety baritone voice, backed by the saxophones. The piano provides fills between his phrases.
1:02	Vocal A-section	"It was there I found ..."	The piano is more audible between the vocal phrases here. Unlike most songs in this form, this second vocal A-section uses a slight variation on the melody from the previous A-section, which adds to the overall musical interest in the song.
1:21	Vocal B section	"Moon in all your splendor ..."	The trumpets enter in mariachi harmonies and rhythms behind this section. Wills hollers out several times.
1:39	Vocal A-section	"A broken song ..."	This AABA-pattern ends with the song's title.
1:57	Instrumental B section	trumpets	The two trumpets play the most memorable section of this song: the mariachi triplets.
2:15	Instrumental A-section	saxophones	As the saxophones enter for the last section of the song, Wills hollers, "All together now!" The close jazz harmonies of this saxophone section match what other big bands were using during this era. The song closes with a short trumpet flourish.

Although World War II broke up many of the big bands temporarily as their musicians served in the military, the western swing craze continued after the war. Dancing continued to be a popular pastime in both urban and rural areas, coast-to-coast. In 1943, *Life* magazine featured a couple on their cover doing a form of swing dancing called the lindy hop, accompanied by an article describing the national craze. Hollywood films featured swing music and dancing routinely, with the famous western swing bands often hired to perform in the movies. Bob Wills and his band appeared in well over a dozen major films along with two shorts (ten-minute features) that were exclusively about the band, all of which increased their fame and presence in popular culture, and Spade Cooley appeared in a number of westerns, as well.

By the end of the 1940s, the swing craze, which included western swing, was waning. In the early 1950s, the band leaders shrank the size of their bands to only a handful of musicians, partly as a cost-saving measure and partly to mirror newer trends in country music. Their multipart jazz harmonies were replaced by simpler, fiddle-based arrangements of songs. For instance, when Bob Wills and his Texas Playboys wrote and recorded "Faded Love" (1950), it sounded like an old fiddle tune. The trumpets and saxophones were long gone; instead, they used only eight instruments: three fiddles, electric guitar, piano, bass, drums, and a singer, plus three extra vocalists adding close harmony.

Radical changes in popular music during the 1950s relegated western swing to the sidelines. The swing bands and dance crazes of the previous decades had run their course. Jazz had long since turned to bebop, country to honky-tonk (see Chapter 4), and pop music toward newfangled rock 'n' roll. But western swing remained a part of the musical legacy of the Southwest, particularly tied to Texan lore. In later decades, musicians seeking to reconnect with a sense of history in Texas did so via western swing.

As for its impact on country music, western swing offered a lively, upbeat musical jolt of modernism that tied fiddle music to something other than a hayseed, rural past. Western swing was both contemporary and wildly popular. It also provided the musical foundation for the next major evolution in country music, namely honky-tonk. But it was its close musical cousin, the singing cowboy, who offered country music a new set of images and associations that would finally allow it to get past its hillbilly reputation.

Singing Cowboy

Symbolically, the hero who rescued hillbilly music from its cornball reputation was that star of the silver screen—the Hollywood cowboy with his noble horse, trusty sidekick, white hat, and rough-hewn, noble, masculine independence. Just as the movie version of the cowboy hero was not a literal depiction of working cowboys, the musical style of the singing cowboys was heavily influenced by people who were not cowboys at all. Nonetheless, the character, images, and sounds from these movie cowboys changed the course of country music and became permanent fixtures in the genre.

Traditional cowpuncher songs and western folk music about life on a ranch existed long before Gene Autry started strumming a guitar in movies. Many of those actual working-cowboy songs had been collected by John Lomax and others (see Chapter 1) and recorded by cowboy singers such as Jules Verne Allen and Carl T. Sprague. But the emergent musical style of the singing cowboy in the 1930s was primarily the creation of the Hollywood film industry.

B westerns, the film genre that featured the singing cowboy, were the result of a culmination of forces in the mid-1930s. In the late 1920s, new technology allowed movie studios to create "talkies," or pictures with sound. Al Jolson's *Jazz Singer* in 1927 was the first such film, and by 1929 the technology had advanced to the point that the sound picture *In Old Arizona* could be filmed outdoors. Audiences flocked to the theaters in the late 1920s and early '30s, both because they loved the new pictures with sound and because the economic woes of the country created a boom in the entertainment industries as people went to the movies to escape their worries for an hour or two. To satisfy audience demand, movie studios came up with the model of two movies coupled together: a longer A feature, made with more expensive stars, and a shorter, cheaper B feature that employed a formulaic plot and was quick and therefore inexpensive to produce. Meanwhile, the same growing sense of moral conservatism that propelled country singers in the Southeast toward gospel songs and sentimental ballads appeared in a new Production Code, to which all the major studios adhered, that censored any salacious content that could be deemed inappropriate. Another contributing factor was the growing Depression, which made it easy to cast businessmen, bankers, and urban-centered corporations as villains, while a cowboy represented a contrasting figure of stalwart honesty and independence, riding the open range in harmony with the land, which represented both literal and figurative freedom.

Figure 3-4 Gene Autry adverstising his radio show.
Source: Southern Folklife Collection, Wilson library, The Unviersity of North Carolina at Chapel Hill.

These factors came together in the B western. The hero in these storylines was a cowboy of unshakable moral code, fighting against corruption or corporate evil. The plots were formulaic, the production cost very little, and the values that the film portrayed were beyond reproach. Music added to the theatrical appeal of these films and helped fill out the skimpy plots. Memorable theme songs became important ways of branding and advertising the movies. In this new movie formula, the first singing cowboy star to emerge was who started his career as a stunt rider in live Wild West shows, then shifted to Hollywood in 1930, starring in films that featured both his riding skills and his singing and fiddling. Other actors also starred as singing cowboys during the early 1930s although, as was the case with John Wayne, sometimes their vocal performances were overdubbed. But until 1935, the singing cowboy character remained something of a novelty in Western films.

Listening Guide

"Back in the Saddle Again" (1939)

PERFORMER: Gene Autry

SONGWRITERS: Gene Autry and Ray Whitley

ORIGINAL RELEASE: Vocalion 05080

FORM: Verse-chorus

STYLE: Singing cowboy

Cowboy singer Ray Whitley (1901–1979) worked in New York in the early 1930s, then in 1936 headed to Hollywood where he began a successful movie career. In 1938, he penned "Back in the Saddle Again" for a movie called *Border G-Man*. Gene Autry heard the song and liked it. Whitley let Autry add his name as a cowriter to the song, a practice that was quite common. Whitley later explained that from his perspective, both he and the song benefited from that arrangement: on the one hand, Autry had greater incentive to record and promote the song because he now received a share of the songwriter's royalties, while on the other hand, Whitley's royalties would increase from the song's commercial success that Autry's fame brought. Autry's 1939 recording of the song became a major hit, and Autry adopted it as the theme song for his radio show, *Melody Ranch*. He also starred in a movie titled *Back in the Saddle* in 1941. This song's success illustrates the connections between film, radio, and records that fueled the development of country music in the 1930s.

"Whoopee-ti-yi-yo" was already a famous phrase, best known from "Git Along Little Dogies," a traditional song that had been published in John Lomax's *Cowboy Songs and Other Frontier Ballads* (see Chapter 1). "Back in the Saddle Again" combined that iconic phrase with frequent repetition of the song's title and a catchy tune, all of which created a memorable theme song for the radio show's audiences. The song's instrumentation includes two fiddles, which highlight the melody; accordion, which sets up a steady "trotting" rhythm that evokes the horse's hoofbeats; steel guitar, which fills in the sound between vocal phrases;

All that changed with the arrival of Gene Autry (1907–1998). Orvon Grover Autry was raised in Tioga, Texas, near Fort Worth. His father worked as a livestock trader, and Autry learned to ride a horse at a young age, a skill that would serve him well in his future career. Autry went to work as a railroad telegraph operator, but his passion was music, and in 1928 he moved to New York to audition for record companies. It was on this trip that he received the good advice to head back home and cultivate his yodeling and his cowboy songs. Like most country singers in the late 1920s, Autry was heavily influenced by Jimmie Rodgers, and like several other performers, he learned to imitate Rodgers quite successfully. For the next several years, Autry sang on radio shows in Oklahoma and cut a few records that were blatant imitations of Rodgers's style. By 1932, he was working on WLS's National Barn Dance in Chicago, where he landed a contract with producer Art Satherley of the American Record Corporation (ARC).

During the early 1930s, the National Barn Dance served as a musical gateway to the West Coast. Many of the entertainers who would become singing cowboys and

and string bass, which underpins the whole recording. Unlike many singing cowboy hits, this one had no vocal harmony. Autry's solo performance lets us hear his voice in its prime. The names of the accompanying musicians are not known except for Carl Cotner (fiddle), but they were mostly studio musicians who worked regularly with Autry in Los Angeles.

TIME	FORM	LISTENING CUES	DISCUSSION
0:00	Introduction	fiddle and accordion	The music's rhythms invoke a trotting horse.
0:18	Verse 1	"I'm back in the saddle . . ."	Notice how clear and smooth Autry's voice sounds, with clean diction. The song starts with the title.
0:35	Verse 1 continues	"Riding the range once more . . ."	Lyrics invoke images of both the open western landscape and the lone hero (armed and defending "law" that is "right"). Ends with the song's title.
0:53	Chorus	"Whoopee-ti-yi-yo . . ."	Traditional cowboy holler "Whoopie-ti-yi-yo" from the song "Git Along Little Dogies" plus the song's title creates the chorus.
1:09	Instrumental verse	fiddle and accordion	Fiddle plays the entire verse.
1:43	Verse 2	"I'm back in the saddle . . ."	Autry repeats the entire verse (both parts).
1:59	Verse 2 continues	"Riding the range once more . . ."	
2:16	Chorus	"Whoopee-ti-yi-yo . . ."	Chorus alternates the cowboy holler and the song's title. Ends with a steel guitar sliding up high.

western stars passed through Chicago. Two years after Autry moved to Chicago, Satherley engineered an opportunity for Autry to appear in a Hollywood western. Autry's first movie was a picture starring Ken Maynard called *In Old Santa Fe*. Maynard's producers found him become increasingly difficult to work with, so producer Nat Levine lined up Gene Autry to star in his next series, *Phantom Empire* (1935). Later that year, Autry starred in Republic Pictures' *Tumbling Tumbleweeds* and squarely established a new genre in film— the singing cowboy western. Autry's horsemanship was superb, as was his singing ability. His acting ability was inconsequential because the films usually cast Autry as himself, always supported by his comedic sidekick, Smiley Burnette. While churning out films, Autry continued to make records and tour, taking the singing cowboy identity that was his on-screen character onto the stage with him, and vice versa.

Other musicians with whom Autry collaborated, and who supplied songs for his films, significantly enhanced his commercial success. Topping that list were the Sons of the Pioneers, a quartet consisting of Bob Nolan, Tim Spencer, Leonard Slye,

Sons of the Pioneers (1933–)

To this day, there are fans who insist that country music and western music are two distinct genres. The Western Music Association, with its own awards, celebrates the differences and honors a long tradition of music that is tied to geographic places, values, and musical traditions. Cowboy poetry and close vocal harmony on prairie songs are the hallmarks of western music, as it is cultivated today as an explicitly non-commercial music. The roots of this music are, of course, intertwined with the roots of country music: in the 1930s, the commercial rise of the singing cowboy marked both the start of commercial western music and the reinvention of country music.

The Sons of the Pioneers sit in the crux of this relationship: they began as a talented vocal group writing sophisticated songs about cowboy themes for Hollywood movies, but ended up the lauded forefathers of today's western music and singing traditions. The core members of the original group had each moved to California to try to break into the entertainment business at the dawn of the Great Depression: Leonard Slye (1911–1998) was from Ohio; Bob Nolan (1908–1980) was from Manitoba, Canada; and Tim Spencer (1908–1974) had been living in Oklahoma most recently.

Leonard Slye specifically wanted to form a group that would focus on vocal harmony, and advertised for singers in the local paper. Nolan responded, and the two started singing together in 1931. Slye met Spencer in 1932 the same way. The three finally came together for the long term in 1933. The core group that would be known as the Original Sons of the Pioneers was completed in 1935 with the addition of fiddler Hugh Farr (1903–1980) and his brother, guitarist Karl Farr (1909–1961).

The Sons of the Pioneers were readily available to appear in Western films as supporting cast members and on-screen musicians as and fiddler Hugh Farr (joined later by his brother guitarist Karl Farr). They worked on radio stations around Los Angeles, where they perfected their three-part vocal harmony on cowboy-themed songs, many of which were composed by Bob Nolan. Those cowboy songs were perfect for the burgeoning western film industry, and by 1935, the Sons of the Pioneers were regularly appearing on screen, singing as part of the films' plots and providing theme songs such as "Tumbling Tumbleweeds" for the stars to sing.

To a 1930s audience, the singing cowboy was a hero worth emulating. Within a few short years, cowboy lore made its way into all corners of popular culture. Autry had combined his musical career as a country singer with the hero he played on screen. His vast popularity helped turn cowboy garb and western images into a major trend in country music. In his wake, singers chose western-themed nicknames ("Tex") and band names (the Drifting Cowboys) simply because of the widespread impact of the singing cowboy. Other musicians adopted the singing cowboy's clothing, song topics, and biographical tales as their own, even if their musical style was distinct from that of the Hollywood singing cowboy. For instance, the Girls of the Golden West, a sister act on WLS in the early 1930s, decked themselves the singing cowboy films grew in popularity. More significant, Spencer and Nolan were both talented songwriters, and they penned many of the cowboy-themed songs such as "Tumbling Tumbleweeds," "Cool Water," "Ride, Ranger, Ride," and "There's a Roundup in the Sky" that were both hit records for the group and featured numbers in major motion pictures.

Leonard Slye continued to pursue a film career while with the group, and in 1938, under the stage name Roy Rogers, starred in a film, joining the ranks of Gene Autry as a leading cowboy of the silver screen. Roy Rogers's career continued to diverge from the rest of the group, but Rogers's increasing stardom carried the group along, too, as the Sons of the Pioneers appeared in forty different films with Rogers during the early 1940s.

In the early 1950s, the Sons of the Pioneers, by they with a very different line-up, aired a regular radio program, *The Lucky U Ranch*, which they moved briefly to television in the early days of that media. During these years, their sound and stylings as all-American cowboys singing idyllic tales of the Old West played into the patriotic themes sought by Americans embroiled in the tensions of the Cold War. But as the decade rolled on, their relevance to mainstream popular culture faded.

The Sons of the Pioneers, like the other singing cowboys whose songs graced both film and airwaves in the 1930s, blended cowboy and prairie storylines with pop/crooner vocals. They sang in sophisticated three- and four-part vocal harmony, with their voices featured over relatively sparse accompaniment: usually just a fiddle, a guitar, and sometimes a bass. Their vocals were not marked by obvious regional accents. And like Gene Autry, Roy Rogers, and the pop stars of their day who regularly sang cowboy-themed songs, the Sons of the Pioneers were readily accepted as a pop music group, rather than being marked starkly as "country." Their music turned the cowboy and traditional western music into a polished Hollywood presentation of that very tradition, which carried widespread appeal.

out in leather fringe, boots, and cowgirl hats and concocted an elaborate (fictional) biography about their hometown, "Muleshoe, Texas," even though they were actually Millie and Dotty Good from Illinois.

Autry was not the only star to stamp such an impression on the American imagination. In 1938, Autry fell into a contract dispute with Republic Pictures, and in his place the film studio hired Leonard Slye, who had previously appeared in several westerns with the Sons of the Pioneers. Born in Cincinnati, Ohio, Slye (1911–1998) had already been auditioning for larger movie roles, and Republic slipped him into two of Autry's films, then gave him the starring role in *Under Western Stars*. He changed his name to Dick Weston, and then again to Roy Rogers. At the encouragement of the movie's producers, Art Satherley quickly launched a promotion for Rogers as a solo cowboy singer, knowing that hit records would improve his movie's success, and that successful movies would drive record sales.

Other singing cowboy stars emerged in the late 1930s, the most famous of whom is Tex Ritter (1905–1974). Ritter grew up in Texas and became interested in cowboy folklore and music while studying at the University of Texas, where he met several prominent folklorists, including John Lomax. After college, Ritter moved to

Listening Guide

"I Want to Be a Cowboy's Sweetheart" (1935)

PERFORMERS: Patsy Montana and the Prairie Ramblers (Tex Atchison, fiddle; Chick Hurt, mandola; Salty Holmes, guitar; Jack Taylor, string bass)

SONGWRITER: Patsy Montana

ORIGINAL RELEASE: ARC 5-11-56

FORM: strophic, with a refrain

STYLE: singing cowboy

Patsy Montana's biggest hit brings together many of the themes of this chapter. Originally from Arkansas, Montana grew up hearing the hillbilly music of 1920s, but her own sound drifted toward the western sounds and cowboy themes as they became more prominent in country music. The Prairie Ramblers had similarly started out as a string band from Kentucky, but by the time they recorded this song, they had adopted western-themed sounds, rhythms, and fiddling style. The B-side of this record, called "Ridin' Old Paint," features the band singing in the close harmony style of the Sons of the Pioneers.

Montana was known for her yodeling and energetic stage presence. This song is often cited as the first country song by a woman to sell a million copies, and it has become an anthem of independence for female country singers, covered by such artists as Patti Page, Suzy Bogguss, the Dixie Chicks, and LeAnn Rimes.

Montana and the Prairie Ramblers teamed up in Chicago on WLS as part of the Hayloft Gang and worked with producer Art Satherley, who was also responsible for Bob Wills's recordings. The band recorded this particular song while they were working for a year in New York, after which they returned to Chicago's WLS barn dance. Montana would later go to Hollywood and appear in *Colorado Sunset*, a western film in which she sang this song accompanied by a full singing cowboy-style band with close vocal harmony and an accordion. In other words, this song connects all the dots of country music's development in the 1930s—from hillbilly string bands and her youth in Arkansas, to working on a barn dance, adopting a western sound and theme, and winding up on the silver screen performing the polished singing cowboy music of the movies.

New York to pursue a theater career, and by 1933, he was hosting a radio program of old cowboy songs. Many of the songs that Ritter sang were the traditional music of working cowboys, and in 1932 he began to record for Art Satherley and ARC. With songs such as "Get Along Little Dogies" (1935), Ritter brought a dose of actual cowboy music into the midst of the Hollywood versions. About a year later, Ritter signed with a start-up movie studio as their star singing cowboy, and his music

TIME	FORM	LISTENING CUES	DISCUSSION
0:00	Introduction	Fiddle melody	The whole band plays the introduction, with Atchison's fiddle on the melody.
0:08	Refrain	Yodel	Montana's yodel functions like a chorus in this song, coming after each verse, and concluding the song, but it's not quite lengthy enough to be called a chorus, nor does it have any lyric content.
0:21	Verse 1	"I want to be . . ."	Note the specific references to activities (roping and riding), and place (the Great Divide) that position the song in the singing cowboy tradition, and the way the lyrics paint a picture: howling coyotes and a western sunset. The singing cowboys invoked lots of regional settings and depictions of activities to project their themes clearly.
0:53	Refrain	Yodel	Montana's yodel wraps up the verse conclusively. The sound of her voice and especially the bright yodel pierce through the texture of the band.
1:03	Instrumental	Fiddle	Here the fiddle plays a solo throughout a verse section. The mandola (a slightly larger version of a mandolin) can be heard filling in the sound and providing some counterpoint for the fiddle.
1:35	Verse 2	"I want to ride Ol' Paint . . ."	The lyrics here are linked to Montana's next recording, , "Ridin' Old Paint," which became the B-side of this record. Note the differentiation between the open range and the "city life."
2:07	Refrain	Yodel	This yodel is longer than the first two. Refrains and choruses often expand toward the end of a song.
2:20	Verse 1	"I want to be . . ."	The first verse repeats here, returning to the opening images and the title line of the song, which shows up twice.
2:52	Refrain	Yodel	Montana finishes the song with the yodel. Notice that the fiddle here plays in harmony with the yodel, creating the sound of a two-part yodel.

drifted toward the same sensationalized cowboy fare that Autry and Rogers were making famous.

The singing cowboy musical style spilled over to singers outside of the movies as well. Arkansas native Patsy Montana (1908–1996), born Ruby Blevins, went to college at UCLA, and while there, met Stuart Hamblen, a cowboy singer with a local radio show. A few years later, she traveled to Chicago to the World's Fair and, on a whim,

Figure 3-5 Patsy Montana.

Source: Southern Folklife Collection, Wilson library, The Unviersity of North Carolina at Chapel Hill.

auditioned at WLS. She was hired as a singer and fiddler with the Prairie Ramblers. In 1935, Montana wrote and recorded a song with the Prairie Ramblers called "I Want to Be a Cowboy's Sweetheart" (see Listening Guide). The song included bright, sassy yodeling, cowboy-themed lyrics, and a swing beat, all accompanied by a string band. It was essentially the female version of a singing cowboy tune, and it became an enormous hit. Although Montana recorded for almost another decade, it remained her signature tune. Montana knew Gene Autry from his days on WLS, and with his help she appeared in several Western movies, furthering the connection between the singing cowboy music and the characters that audiences saw on the silver screen.

The singing cowboy trend pulled in Jimmy Wakely, Eddie Dean, Ray Whitley, and countless other singers on the West Coast who built musical careers based on their performances of cowboy songs and supplemented their stardom with film appearances. What had started as Hollywood film producers finding a way to fill out their B westerns had grown into a musical phenomenon of its own. In 1940, Gene Autry began his own radio show, the *Melody Ranch*. Just over a decade later, Roy Rogers dove into the new field of television with his *Roy Rogers Show*. His recording, with wife Dale Evans, of "Happy Trails" encapsulated all the trends of the singing cowboys in one musical moment.

The crest of the singing cowboy's popularity was *High Noon*, a film starring Gary Cooper and Grace Kelly. The producers asked the film's classically trained composer, Dimitri Tiomkin, to write a theme song that would open the picture with a clear contrast between good and evil, between the hero and the villain, and that would capture the feel of the Wild West. Tiomkin's theme song, titled "High Noon" (1952) and sung by Tex Ritter, was a haunting depiction of the lonesome cowboy hero. It won two Oscars (one for best song) and marked the high point of the singing cowboy's reign in American popular culture.

By the 1950s, the western had been largely displaced in the film industry. In country music, new styles were on the horizon that made the singing cowboy sound dated and nostalgic. But during its reign, and in spite of its origins as the concoction of Hollywood producers, the singing cowboy permanently changed the look of country music. The singing cowboy's other contribution was one of imagination. The character that Gene Autry played on screen was not a real cowboy, but rather a movie hero presented as a cowboy. The music he sang was not the same folk music that working ranch hands had hummed, but rather songs written by professionally trained composers who were depicting this movie character and setting in sound. Yet audiences came to associate those movie sounds with the notion of a real cowboy. We can describe this process as a constructed authenticity: the singing cowboy from film came to represent authentic cowboys for the audience. This idea of a constructed authenticity became extremely important in country music during later decades, and it will remain an important part of our study.

Taking Stock on the Brink of World War II

Country music's developments during the 1930s illustrated the growing tension between the forces of tradition and the new musical styles that were emerging. The look and images associated with country music changed radically; the hillbilly label proved not only distasteful but also restrictive, and the cowboy was a welcome substitute.

Country music's complicated relationship with other genres became readily apparent with the conception of western swing. Western Swing and the singing cowboys both offered music that was heavily influenced by pop and jazz styles, and that appealed to audiences who were not invested in more traditional hillbilly music. These developments reduced the "otherness" of country music during this decade, bringing some of it closer to mainstream culture. Unlike today, in the 1940s, the figure of the cowboy was an ever-present part of the popular imagination: kids played dress-up as cowboys, movies featured cowboy heroes regularly, and pop singers, including Burl Ives and Frankie Laine, recorded quite a few pop songs that had cowboy and western themes ("Mule Train," "Rawhide"). As a result, even country music's newly adopted image of the cowboy did not distinguish it from mainstream culture; if anything, it brought them closer together.

Throughout all the changes, the commercial nature of country music played an increasing role in its evolution: corporate sponsors shaped the music's development; Hollywood film producers co-opted singers to make formulaic, budget-conscious films; and practical considerations of budgets and venues motivated musicians to conceive of new musical styles. The Hollywood singing cowboy and the jazz-infused western swing bands were both built on the idea that the musicians were performing characters on stage. Fans of this music were not concerned with notions of tradition or authenticity of a performer's biography. Instead, they connected with this music in the moment of performance, where authenticity came from the performers being completely invested in the music they were making.

For the most part, the musicians in these styles were still mostly white men from working-class backgrounds. Yet we see a significant number of women also performing, sometimes unbilled (their names were not publicized). Several women sang with the western swing bands, including Laura Lee Owens (Bob Wills), Ginny Jackson (Spade Cooley), and Carolina Cotton (both). And the singing cowboy movies often featured female performers (Dale Evans, Dorothy Page, and Patsy Montana, to name just a few). But the biggest presence of women in this era was in barn dances; WLS had a long roster of female stars, including Linda Parker in the early 1930s, Lula Belle, Girls of the Golden West, Louise Massey, and more. These women were known more for radio than for their recordings, and as a result, their names are not as well known as history favors musicians who left behind the biggest stack of records. Nonetheless, we get a portrait of the country singers in the 1930s: talented musicians who were well-versed in other genres of music, consummate professionals who had bold stage personalities and loyal fans.

The changes within country music in the 1930s left an indelible mark on the genre: the instrumentation from western swing, the dance-hall environment, and the images of the cowboy would remain in the genre from that point forward. Most significantly, country music was now poised to remain a contemporary force in popular culture as its audience underwent a major shift in demographics during and after WWII, and as television, pop music, and eventually rock 'n' roll would re-shape the entire musical landscape.

⋆ **ESSAY: MUSICAL STYLE**

 # Innovation in Western Swing

Western swing brought swing rhythms, jazz harmonies, a repertory drawn from popular music, improvisation, and innovations in instrumentation into country music. The style's name refers to the music's use of a rhythmic pattern known as swing, in which the music's rhythms subdivide the basic beat of the music into a longer and shorter pulse rather than into two evenly spaced pulses. If a tune is played in a swing style, the duration of each pair of short notes is altered so that the first note is almost twice as long as the second, as shown in example 3-1. The same melody can be played in "straight eighths," which is the term for music that is not swung, or in "swung eighths," the term for music where the notes are not played evenly but are instead swung, as shown in example 3-2. Scholars have documented that the exact ratio of the longer to the shorter division is never exactly 2:1, but that approximation is quite close. Try clapping a steady rhythm, and then clapping a swung rhythm (clapping so that the space between the claps alternates long-short-long-short-long-short-long-short).

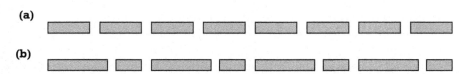

Example 3-1 A graphic illustration of swing rhythms, showing (a) the relative durations of notes in a nonswing style , and (b) the relative duration of those same notes played in a swing style, where the first of each pair of notes is almost twice as long as the second.

Example 3-2 The opening guitar melody from Bob Wills's recording of "Roly Poly" (1945), shown (a) in straight eighths, and (b) as it sounds when swung by Bob Wills's band.

The types of musical chords used in western swing were also different from other styles of country. Almost all the music that the Carter Family recorded used only a handful of simple, three-note chords that followed the same common patterns or progressions. The western swing bands, on the other hand, incorporated more complex chord progressions and jazz-derived harmonies, which often have more than three notes in each chord. Listen, for instance, to Spade Cooley's "Shame, Shame on You" (1945); the chord progression in this song is reminiscent of popular songs from Broadway show tunes or jazz standards, not the so-called three chords of early hillbilly music.

One reason for the different rhythms and chords in western swing is that the band leaders listened to the popular dance and jazz bands, live, on radio, and especially on records, and readily borrowed songs from them; Milton Brown's recording of "Who's Sorry Now" (1935) is one famous instance of that. While there were plenty of traditional fiddle tunes in their repertory as well, the western swing bands brought lots of blues and vaudeville songs into the mix. The attitude that old-time or traditional music was somehow better was not part of the western swing bands' thinking.

Improvisation, which occurs when musicians make up a new melody to play over the chords for a section of a song, is another characteristic of western swing. Other styles of country music have also included improvisation. For instance, when a mandolin player makes up a new harmony part or short bits of music to play in between the singer's phrases, that is a type of improvisation. What was different with western swing was the greater amount of improvisation and the emphasis placed on it. In jazz, ensembles often play the melody of a song together, and then for the next two or three minutes, take turns making up new melodies to go with the same chords. The musicians value the originality of the music that is created in that moment. Western swing musicians used this approach in performance. Listen to Milton Brown's recording of "Who's Sorry Now" (1935) while following this chart:

TIME	LISTEN FOR:
0:00	Fiddle: Cecil Brower plays the melody for the song through one time.
0:34	Piano: Fred Calhoun improvises (makes up on the spot) a new melody. This is called one "chorus" of the song, because the rest of the band is playing the same chords that they played under the original tune.
1:10	Steel guitar: Bob Dunn plays his electrified steel guitar here. He improvises a new melody over one chorus (which means one time through all the chords of the original tune). He takes a short "break" at 1:25, which means that the rest of the band stops playing for a moment at the end of the phrase so that Dunn can have a moment all to himself to play a fancy bit of music. This is a great example of the sound of Dunn's unique style of playing, which attempted to imitate the sound of a horn, rather than the slips and slides that would be common in other steel guitar players' styles.
1:45	Fiddle: Cecil Brower takes the next chorus, this time playing an improvised solo instead of the tune's melody. He takes a short musical break at 2:01, when the rest of the band momentarily stops playing for dramatic effect.
2:21	Vocal: Milton Brown comes in at the end of the song to sing the words to the original melody.

This recording consists of five "choruses," or times through the basic song. The first and last choruses use the song's melody. The three in the middle are all improvised. Notice that you can occasionally hear snippets of the original melody during these improvised solos, but for the most part they are original, different musical ideas that happen to fit with the same chords as the original melody.

Western swing's biggest effect on country music was its use of new instruments. Steel guitarist Bob Dunn (1908–1971) joined Milton Brown's band in 1934. Motivated by the loud venues where the band played, Dunn modified his Martin guitar to create the first electric steel guitar. With its electric pickup attached to an amplifier, the instrument had a bright, biting tone that cut through the noise in the clubs where the band played. A year later, steel player Leon McAuliffe brought the same innovation to Bob Wills's band. In order to better match the sound of the jazz bands that they heard on the radio, both Wills and Brown filled out their rhythm sections with piano; Fred Calhoun started playing for Brown in 1932. Wills hired drummer Smokey Dacus in 1935, a move that strongly differentiated western swing from the more traditional musical styles of that era. And he added a horn section (trumpets, saxophones, and sometimes trombones) to create the full sound of big band jazz. His guitarist Eldon Shamblin served as the professional music arranger for the band, allowing them to imitate the styles of the jazz ensembles. A few years later, the western swing bands based on the West Coast expanded further with full string sections (several violins playing carefully arranged music together) and even a harp (which is audible in Tex Williams, "I Got Texas in My Soul" [1946]), along with accordions, which had also become common in singing cowboy music. The vocalists in the western swing bands had none of the twangy, nasal timbres that were so popular among the 1920s hillbilly musicians. Instead, singers such as Milton Brown, Ginny Jackson, Tommy Duncan, and Tex Williams cultivated a smooth, resonant tone enhanced by vibrato and devoid of any extreme regional accents (although Wills himself was an exception on that front).

With all these characteristics, western swing is easy to identify by ear because it differs so dramatically from the other styles of country music popular in the 1930s. It shares some features with the singing cowboy style, especially the vocal timbres, use of accordions, and slick twin fiddles, but compared to the standard fare on Southeastern radio barn dance shows during the 1930s, it was radical music.

☆ ESSAY: MUSICAL STYLE

Singing Cowboys

The musical form and content of the singing cowboy recordings is more heavily indebted to pop music than to any folk tradition. The chord progressions, for instance, venture far beyond the three or four basic chords that were common in early hillbilly recordings or in the folk songs that working cowboys sang. In this heavily stylized music, the choice of instrumentation plays an important role. We hear lots of accordions, acoustic guitar, and smooth fiddles, but not the horn sections or drums that one finds in western swing, nor the banjos or Dobros that one finds in more traditional old-time country music. In the singing cowboy recordings, the fiddle players frequently use shimmering vibrato, where the pitch of the note wavers very slightly and rapidly, a technique more often associated with classical playing than with traditional hillbilly or working-cowboy styles of playing. The ensembles tend to be much smaller than the western swing bands. Gene Autry, for instance, often recorded with two fiddles, steel guitar, acoustic guitar, accordion, and bass. Later in his career, that basic sound was enhanced with a clarinet.

The male vocalists in the singing cowboy tradition in most cases had rich, baritone voices that matches the styles of pop crooners. Three- or four-part vocal harmony, frequently employing jazz chords, is a hallmark of the singing cowboy tradition, most notably in the Sons of the Pioneers' performances. Unlike the nasal sounds and high tenor harmony that sits above the melody in traditional hillbilly singing, the singing cowboys used smoother vocal styles with vibrato, and typically placed the harmony under the melody.

The most striking characteristic of the singing cowboy's style is the use of imagery in both the lyrics and the music. The lyrics for these songs were an extension of the singing cowboy's persona as it appeared in the movies: a lone, independent, yet loyally heroic character on a horse facing the wide open expanses of the western frontier. Prairies, cows, saddles, tumbleweeds, and long, dusty trails all made frequent appearances. The music for these songs used techniques of "text painting" to depict the settings in the sounds themselves. Trotting horse-like sounds appear as a clip-clop-clip-clop rhythmic pattern (and in Roy Rogers and Dale Evans's recording of "Happy Trails," the sound effect of horse's hooves is present). Echo effects suggest vast spaciousness (listen to the Sons of the Pioneers' recording of "Cool Water," where the repeated lyrics "Water, water, water . . ." are a sonic representation of the shimmering mirage of water in the desert).

The singing cowboy style and western swing music share many of the same features, and in some instances, a recording could be described as evincing both styles. The western swing bands adopted western or cowboy costumes, and performed plenty of songs about Texas, the open range, and cowboy themes; conversely, the singing cowboys were accompanied by western-swing style fiddles, swing rhythms, and the general sound of the western swing bands in many cases. In general, however, the singing cowboy style of country music was more of a musical depiction of the characters, settings, and plots of the western movies. The most significant feature of the singing cowboy, however, was the polished, smooth sounds, pop vocal timbres, jazz harmonies, and especially the accordions and style of fiddle playing, all of which were a musical world away from the traditional old-time sounds that were still in fashion on the barn dances of the Southeast and Midwest.

☆ ESSAY: MUSICAL STYLE

 # Brother Acts

The brother acts of the 1930s and their counterpart, the sister acts, established a clean, simple musical style and a cultural tradition that has remained in country music. Their sound is an easily recognized combination of vocal harmony and two string instruments. In most instances, the duo sings the melody with the harmony placed above it, on higher notes. Because the brother acts frequently used gospel tunes in their performances, many recordings also feature call-and-response or after-beat sections, where the person singing harmony sings a phrase after the person singing melody, which creates the effect of an echo (listen to, for instance, the Monroe Brothers, "What Would You Give in Exchange for Your Soul"). Their style of singing is influenced by the availability of better microphones and recording technology. While several of the brother acts retained their distinguishing regional accents and nasal twang, the vocal performances are not as strained or rough-hewn as hillbilly singers from even a half decade earlier.

The brother acts usually accompanied themselves with guitar plus one additional instrument, usually a mandolin, tenor guitar, or banjo. The guitar player was responsible for picking out the bass notes as well as filling in the chords. The other instrument provided occasional instrumental interludes and filled in behind the singers.

This two-voice style of country music remained popular throughout the 1950s, when it was largely supplanted by newer developments. However, certain vestiges of it remained. For instance, the vocal harmony technique of one person singing the melody and a second person adding just one line of harmony above it became a staple of the Bakersfield sound (see Chapter 7).

☆ **ESSAY: MUSIC BUSINESS**

Sponsorship

Bill Bolick of the Blue Sky Boys was once asked if he was bothered that a radio producer named one of his bands the Crazy Hickory Nuts. "At that time," he replied, "it didn't really bother me, because I was only thinking of the money I was getting out of it." Country music's increasing professionalism in the 1930s meant that musicians could actually earn a living with their art, but the realities of commercial sponsorship had a noticeable impact on the music's sound and development.

Commercial sponsorship had been a part of country music from its earliest days in countless ways. In the early days of traveling shows, musicians brought in a crowd so that the so-called doctor could pitch his cure-all elixir. As the record industry made headway into hillbilly music, Polk Brockman, the Sterchi Brothers, and others in the furniture business sponsored musicians and connected them with record labels because records brought customers into their stores. Large companies saw ownership of radio stations such as WLS and WSM as lucrative extensions of their advertising arms, while other companies happily purchased segments of time on radio stations. What happened in the 1930s built on an already-established pattern.

During the Great Depression, a boom in supposed cures for various forms of intestinal distress accounted for a major part of country music's development. In the late 1870s, a family discovered a mineral well with reputedly curative properties for all such ailments just west of Dallas. Entrepreneurs opened resort hotels at the site, and by the start of World War I, as many as twenty-one different mineral water

Figure 3-6 Crazy Water Crystals Box.

Source: Courtesy of Gene Fowler.

companies were selling the water and dehydrated crystals. The Crazy Water Crystals Company emerged as the leader, and in the 1930s began an aggressive advertising campaign. The Carolina-area salesman for the company convinced the company to sponsor a barn dance on Charlotte's WBT station, for which musicians would be hired solely to promote the product. At one time or another, many of the region's biggest stars, including Bill Monroe, worked for Crazy Water Crystals.

As the bands were essentially spokespeople, their sponsors decided what they sang, how they dressed, and even what the bands were called. Band names such as the Crazy Mountaineers and the Crazy Hickory Nuts were commonplace, and band names often changed when sponsors changed. In Texas, for instance, the same group of musicians was alternately known as the Aladdin Laddies and the Light Crust Doughboys, depending on whether their current sponsor was selling lamps or flour. Some musicians took these commercial relationships a step further; in 1953, the Martha White Flour Company hired Flatt & Scruggs to advertise for them, and the musicians turned the company's jingle into part of their regular repertory. The most sought-after recordings in country music for many years were those that Hank Williams made for the Mother's Best Flour Company, records that remained unavailable until fifty-five years after his death because of legal disputes. Obviously, the endless quest for fluffy biscuits was highly influential in country music's development.

While there was still plenty of bawdy humor and risqué joke telling to be found in country music, the influence of commercial sponsors pushed the performers toward music that was considered more religious, uplifting, and wholesome. These companies were attuned to their customers' attitudes and well aware that the music they sponsored would be associated not only with the performers but also with their corporate reputations. In all of these ways, sponsors such as the Crazy Water Crystals Company allowed a new generation of musicians to earn a living through their musical craft, but they also shaped the development of the music itself. Similar relationships are still an integral part of country music today.

LISTEN SIDE BY SIDE

"Wabash Blues"

Isham Jones and His Orchestra, 1921
(Brunswick 5065)
Milton Brown & His Musical Brownies, 1935
(Decca 5108)

Delmore Brothers, 1939 (Bluebird B-8204)
(Alton Delmore, guitar and vocals; Rabon Delmore, tenor guitar and vocals; Chuck Maudlin, fiddle; Smiley O'Brien, guitar; Joe Zinkan, string bass)

FOR THE MOST part, the brother acts and the western swing bands recorded different types of songs and had distinct musical styles: gospel hymns, sentimental ballads, train songs, and songs about home and family for the barn dance radio circuit; popular tunes about romance, songs about dancing and dances, western-themed tales, and lively jazz-styled blues tunes for the dance-hall stage. But both styles of country music were still part of the fabric of popular culture and sometimes found source material in the same pool of popular music. These cases remind us that the relationships between musical styles, and indeed between genres, are fluid.

One of the biggest hits of 1921 was a record made in New York by Isham Jones, a white bandleader in the jazz scene of the 1920s (dance bands who played jazz were often called "orchestras"). "Wabash Blues" (a completely different song than the folk tune "Wabash Cannonball," which the Carters and Acuff had recorded) had already become a standard, with accounts of it being played under the title "Trombone Jazz" several years earlier. Jones's recording topped the popular music charts for three months, and by the end of 1921, at least four more bands had recorded the same song.

The country musicians of the 1920s certainly were aware of popular tunes and recorded them along with all sorts of other types of music. Clayton McMichen, one of the fiddle players who had played on Jimmie Rodgers's records, recorded "Wabash Blues" in 1928, for instance.

Milton Brown's pioneering formula for western swing was to take jazz tunes and perform them with a hybrid band that was part jazz, part string band. Many of the early western swing recordings by Brown, Bob Wills, and others, were well-known, standard jazz tunes, as was the case here. In 1935, Brown recorded "Wabash Blues" in Chicago. Brown plays the opening melody on his fiddle, replacing the trombone from the original jazz version. Milton's brother Derwood sings lead, with Milton adding vocal harmony. Bob Dunn plays an improvised solo on his newly electrified steel guitar, and the piano is also audible throughout. In short, this is a great example of western swing treatment of a jazz standard.

Four years later, the Delmore Brothers, one of the most successful brother acts who had been stars of the Grand Ole Opry for years, recorded the song in South Carolina. Of all the brother acts of the 1930s, the Delmores were the ones who had always incorporated lots of blues and popular music in their performances. By 1939, the Delmores had expanded their duet formula to include more instruments, in this case fiddle, bass, and a second guitar. On this song Rabon plays the melody on his tenor guitar at the beginning, then the two sing in harmony. The fiddle solo in the middle reveals just how widespread the influence of jazz improvisation was in country music. Compare the fiddle solo here to Milton Brown's opening, however, and notice the nuances that Brown adds to his performance that are missing from the Delmores' version.

Pay attention to the sound of the Delmores' vocals, and listen to them in comparison to the Browns' vocals, also two brothers singing the same song in harmony. The pure, hollow tone of the Delmores without any vibrato, and especially the very end of the song with the high falsetto slide, is what marks them distinctively as a brother act from the 1930s southeast tradition. Throughout all of country music, the sound of the singers' voices—specifically the actual tone of their voice, treatment of vibrato, general singing techniques, and accents—remains one of the strongest indicators of what tradition or style of music they worked in, even more so than instrumentation, song choices, and melody and chords.

PLAYLIST

Blue Sky Boys, "Sunny Side of Life" (1936)

Brown, Milton and his Musical Brownies, "Who's Sorry Now" (1935)

Delmore Brothers, "Brown's Ferry Blues" (1933)

Lulu Belle and Scotty, "Remember Me (When the Candle Lights are Gleaming)" (1940)

Parker, Linda, "Take Me Back to Renfro Valley" (1933)

Sons of the Pioneers, "Tumbling Tumbleweeds" (1934)

Wills, Bob, "Take Me Back to Tulsa" (1941)

FOR MORE READING

Boyd, Jean A. *The Jazz of the Southwest: An Oral History of Western Swing.* Austin: University of Texas Press, 1998.

Cusic, Don. *The Cowboy in Country Music: An Historical Survey with Artist Profiles.* Jefferson, N.C.: McFarland & Company, Inc., 2011.

Green, Douglas B. *Singing in the Saddle: The History of the Singing Cowboy.* Nashville: Country Music Foundation Press and Vanderbilt University Press, 2002.

Kienzle, Rich. *Southwest Shuffle: Pioneers of Honky-Tonk, Western Swing, and Country Jazz.* New York: Routledge, 2003.

Russell, Tony. *Country Music Originals: The Legends and the Lost.* New York: Oxford University Press, 2007.

NAMES AND TERMS

Autry, Gene	Foley, Red	Satherley, Art
B western	Girls of the Golden West	singing cowboy
brother acts	Improvisation	Sons of the Pioneers
Brown, Milton	Lulu Belle and Scotty	Spencer, Tim
Cooley, Spade	Montana, Patsy	swing
Crazy Water Crystals	Nolan, Bob	western swing
Delmore Brothers	Ritter, Tex	Williams, Tex
Duncan, Tommy	Rogers, Roy	Wills, Bob

REVIEW TOPICS

1. How do the new musical styles of the 1930s relate to the cultural values that were established for country music in the 1920s?

2. Discuss ways in which the fans affected the development of country music during these years.

3. Why do you think the cowboy image has lasted so long in country music?

PART II

World War II and After: Nationalism and Country Music (1940s and 1950s)

From 1945 to the mid-1960s, American popular culture changed radically, and along with those developments came a major shift in the identity of the country music fan base. World War II had pulled America out of the Great Depression. It launched industrial growth and revealed the depth and strength of the American people. It took young American soldiers away from sheltered rural upbringings and shipped them around the globe, and brought women into the workforce in unprecedented numbers: in 1940, fewer than 14% of all married women worked outside the home, but by 1944 that number had risen to almost 23%. Congress passed the Servicemen's Readjustment Act (often called the G.I. Bill) in 1944, which, among many other benefits, paid for a college education for soldiers returning from World War II, a chance that many of them otherwise would not have had. With the revived American economic engine, increasingly industrialized landscape, and easier access to higher education, working-class families achieved a new level of prosperity and fundamentally altered the culture of their daily lives. An optimistic outlook swept the nation that was built on a deep, patriotic pride. Many soldiers returned home ready to settle down and raise a family. Within a few years, America experienced a population explosion, known as the "baby boom." When those babies became teenagers, unlike their parents' generation, they had both leisure time and access to disposable income. Those teen consumers became a powerful force within popular culture. They sought music that represented their youth in a new way; the result was rock 'n' roll, which radically redefined popular music from that point forward. In sum, the basic identity of the country music audience was rapidly changing.

Even before the arrival of rock 'n' roll, music of all genres underwent substantial shifts in the postwar years. In pop music, vocal harmony groups continued to thrive after the war; the Andrews Sisters and the Mills Brothers—some of the few black musicians who were regarded as mainstream pop stars—continued to score big hits. But pop music turned much of its attention to solo singers such as Frank Sinatra. By the 1950s, Tony Bennett, Rosemary Clooney, Kay Starr, Guy Lombardo, and Frankie Laine were major stars. During the 1940s, the main focus of jazz shifted from the big bands to bebop. Saxophonist Charlie Parker and trumpeter Dizzy Gillespie developed styles that emphasized virtuosic improvisation in small combos. In Chicago, Muddy Waters and Howlin' Wolf transformed downhome country blues into a new, electric urban blues played on electric guitars and with backing bands. Elsewhere, Louis Jordan, Big Joe Turner, and Roy Brown pioneered jump blues, a danceable style of music with swing rhythms and hot saxophone improvisation, with R&B vocalists. By the early 1950s, R&B singers such as Ruth Brown and black doo-wop vocal groups such as the Orioles and the Chords were making inroads with mainstream audiences. Latin dance music, especially the mambo, had also become popular in the United States, and those sounds infiltrated other genres of popular music.

Country music, meanwhile, worked hard to shed its remaining hillbilly imagery, which had been one of the major signifiers of the genre in previous decades. In the early 1940s, the music industry magazine *Billboard* still used the term "hillbilly" to identify white, working-class music that was not part of the mainstream pop scene. Many singers were becoming increasingly dissatisfied with this name, and in 1948, Ernest Tubb successfully petitioned Decca Records to change the way they listed country music in their catalogue. *Billboard* followed suit, briefly switching to "folk" and then settling on "country and western" as the new descriptive category. The addition of the term "western" reflected the impact of the singing cowboys in rebranding country music. It also freed country music from some of its own allegiance to tradition, which allowed the music increased relevance in the new, modern, postwar America.

With their hillbilly identity fading into the past, country musicians found that the borders between country and pop were increasingly fuzzy, and the "otherness" of country music was called into question. To the American public, there was little formal distinction between the genres of country and pop other than the way that record labels marketed their music. Established pop stars recorded songs with stereotypically country lyrics and sometimes even country sounds. Radio stations still played a variety of musical styles during each day, and would continue to do so until the late 1950s. Singers such as Gene Autry and Red Foley, whose main identity was linked to country music, had number one hits on *Billboard's* pop charts. In today's terms, we would describe these artists as crossover artists, meaning that their music crossed over from one chart (country & western) to another (pop), but what it really meant was that a few styles of country music had achieved nearly universal appeal.

Along with the changing identity of the country music audience, the musicians were shaped by different experiences and social contexts than earlier generations of country performers. Country stars in the 1940s and early '50s typically still grew up in rural, working-class families. Many considered Jimmie Rodgers and the Carter Family to be their primary musical inspiration, but their connection to those musicians came mainly from hearing their records played at home in the 1930s. Webb Pierce, Bill Monroe, Lefty Frizzell, and Johnny Cash, for instance, all covered Jimmie Rodgers songs early in their careers and talked about his importance in their musical development. But their lives took very different turns from the rural musicians of the 1920s and early '30s. One of those differences was the prevalence of military service; Rose Maddox's brothers, Howdy Forrester (Bill Monroe's fiddle player), and the Louvin Brothers served during World War II; Carl Smith, Ralph Stanley, and Ray Price in the mid- to late '40s; and Johnny Cash and George Jones during the Korean War, to name only a few. For some, military service was a time to develop songwriting and musicianship skills; for all of them, and for much of their audience, it meant displacement from home, physically and emotionally, which was reflected in their music.

The four primary musical styles covered in these chapters, honky-tonk, bluegrass, rockabilly, and the Nashville sound, were each forward-looking, progressive styles. Honky-tonk took root in the dance halls of the Southwest and West Coast, where wartime industries had brought huge populations of young workers. Bluegrass grew out of old-time string band music, but reinvented it as a hyperenergized, modern, showy and virtuosic style. Rockabilly fused honky-tonk with black popular styles such as jump blues to concoct a reckless, sexually charged music for teenagers. And finally, the Nashville sound marked country music's arrival at an apex of social acceptance: a sophisticated and mature new approach to country music that leveled the playing field between country and pop.

Yet through all these changes, strong threads of tradition continued to tie these musical styles to their predecessors. Not only were the musicians covering the songs of earlier country singers, but the very idea of celebrating (and remembering) a working-class identity grew in importance as the working-class population achieved economic and social upward mobility. The less evident the hillbilly roots of country were, the more symbolically important they became in the genre.

Honky-tonk and bluegrass were the last major styles of country music conceived before the age of television. Fans came to know country stars in the late 1940s through radio and records, where their voice was the only connection between singer and listener. That changed in the early 1950s. CBS, NBC, and ABC all launched network television broadcasts in 1947 and 1948. By 1950, Americans owned eight million televisions; by 1954, more than half of all households had a television in them; and by 1956, even the stalwart keeper of tradition, the Grand Ole Opry, had a televised segment. Fans who previously might never have seen their favorite singers in person could now see them, up close, in their living rooms. Television changed fans' perception of the music from a disembodied voice to a flesh-and-blood person in front of them. The sexual energy of the rockabilly stars came not only from the sounds of the music but also from the physical, visible presence of their bodies. And the sophistication and popular appeal of the Nashville sound stars was marked by their tuxedos and evening gowns. Country music would spend the next half century grappling with the repercussions of television.

Television was not the only technological advance during these years to re-shape country music. The time period covered in this unit saw the shift from mono-phonic recordings to stereophonic recordings; from the format of the single to the format of the long-play record; and from simple processes of recording music to complicated multi-track recordings with overdubs. Quite literally the sound of country records changed radically over this time span.

Our three main themes will continue to guide our exploration of these mid-century decades. Fans' investment in the concept of authenticity increased as the honky tonk singers increasingly personalized the stories they were telling in their songs, and as bluegrass became a foil for much of what else was happening in popu-lar music. The identity of both the fan base and the performers was reconceived after World War II, with the public image of country music morphing into that of pop stars by the early 1960s. And, finally, how country music preserved its distinc-tive or "othered" nature in the face of both its growing popularity and the onslaught of rock 'n' roll was a major issue in the early 1960s.

Throughout these chapters, keep in mind that country music spent these two decades responding to and being influenced by rock 'n' roll and, subsequently, rock music. The story of country music simply cannot be told without considering Elvis Presley, Buddy Holly, and Chuck Berry, all musicians who had roots in hillbilly and country music, who shook things up to the point that country music's very exis-tence was temporarily threatened; but when the dust settled, the same threads of tradition were still holding the genre together in an entirely new form. ⚜

Honky-Tonk
and Rockabilly
Revolution

orld War II marked the dawning of a different era for country music, when servicemen and women took the music with them around the world, when publishing firms began to set up shop in Nashville, and when musicians shed lingering hillbilly associations in favor of the images of cowboys and western entertainers. During those years, country music was shaped by two main developments: first, its radio stars polished up their hillbilly roots and took traditional country music to a nationwide audience and, second, a new style known as honky-tonk surged in popularity. Those trends held course until Elvis Presley burst onto the scene in 1954, ushering in a fusion of country and rhythm 'n' blues that shook up teen audiences everywhere. In the wake of those developments, the whole landscape of popular music changed.

New Radio Stars

Many of the musical developments from the 1930s continued into the next decade and beyond. As explored in Chapter 3, the singing cowboy was just hitting his (and, occasionally, her) stride in the 1940s, and western swing was in prime form. Simultaneously, the more traditional, old-time strands of country music were picked up by a new generation of superstars who had tremendous staying power. Comedienne Minnie Pearl, known for the price tag dangling off her hat and her shrill "Howdeeee!," joined the Grand Ole Opry in 1940 and remained there for five decades; Little Jimmy Dickens joined in 1948 and performed until his death in 2015. During the 1940s and '50s, well-established stars, including Roy Acuff and Red Foley, continued their reign over country music; both men hosted the nationally broadcast segments of the Opry and continued to make hit records such as Foley's "Peace in the Valley" (1951). Their music was heavily influenced by folk and hillbilly traditions, but in those years they sang with very little audible twang in their voices and focused on storytelling ballads, sentimental songs, and gospel hymns.

The most influential newcomer who joined them in the mid-1940s was Eddy Arnold (1918–2008). The son of a sharecropper from Henderson, Tennessee, Arnold started his music career touring with western swing and polka bandleader Pee Wee King. In 1943, he began singing on WSM; put together his own band, the Tennessee Plowboys; and signed a record contract with RCA Victor. A year later, he had his own segment on the Opry each week and was on his way to becoming

---

MUSICAL COMEDY

The potential for country comedy, long exploited by the Opry performers, was not lost on songwriters and musicians of the 1940s. Novelty songs held wide appeal in this era. Merle Travis (1917–1983) and Tennessee Ernie Ford (1919–1991) entertained with songs such as Travis's "So Round, So Firm, So Fully Packed" (1947). Pop singers also took advantage of the novelty song, such as Frankie Laine's "Mule Train" (1949), with whip-cracking whoops and a driving boogie rhythm laced with accordion. These pop songs that drew on country comedy were the start of a long-standing practice.

---

the undisputed biggest country star of his generation, with eighteen number one hits between 1946 and 1955. Arnold's band featured fiddle, steel guitar, guitar, and upright bass, along with occasional piano and mandolin. His voice was silky smooth, and he sang in a crooning style that won him a large female following. His songs included an unusual number of romantic numbers ("I'll Hold You in My Heart [Till I Can Hold You in My Arms]" [1947]), and even the heartbreak ones lacked any trace of bitterness ("Bouquet of Roses"). Fans adored his boyish good looks and sincere performances; he offered them the country-boy version of a pop star. Starting with "Anytime" in 1948, Eddy Arnold held the number one spot on *Billboard's* country chart for an astonishing sixty consecutive weeks, with a total of four songs.

Eddy Arnold, Red Foley, and others, including the singing cowboy stars such as Gene Autry, were making records and winning over radio audiences with country music, but some of their recordings were dangerously close to becoming indistinguishable from mainstream pop music. Only Arnold's affiliation with the Opry, his band's steel guitar, and his folksy connection to rural Tennessee kept him squarely in the country genre. He occasionally added in a signature western yodeling number such as "Cattle Call," which he recorded in 1944. Beyond that, however, he appeared to be a pop star in the making.

Country Music Culture in the Postwar Years

In the post-World War II years, two developments helped differentiate country music from other genres. One of those was a more definitive distinction between the genres of country and folk. In the early 1950s, popular culture confronted the new global order of a nuclear age and the Cold War. A growing fear of communism gave rise to the Red Scare, during which Senator Joseph McCarthy led aggressive inquisitions into "anti-American" activities. Many of the people who were investigated and blacklisted were musicians, filmmakers, and actors. Musicians involved in the folk movement, such as Pete Seeger, became targets of those investigations. Although country music and folk music shared the same historical roots—music of the "folk"—and both genres trace their origins to performers such as the Carter Family, this marked a historical division between the two genres. In the face of these political threats, country musicians sought to distance themselves from any "folky" associations, and on radio broadcasts and in stage patter, they reinforced patriotic positions while trumpeting the values of the American family and capitalist way of life.

The other development in the 1940s that set country music apart as a genre was a new style of music that reflected the fans' changing social environment: honky-tonk. A huge population of young people relocated during the war and shortly after. For instance, in just eight months in 1943, over 25,000 people from Texas, Oklahoma, and Arkansas moved to the greater Los Angeles area. They came for military duty, but also to work in shipyards, the aircraft industry, foundries, factories, and canneries. In other regions, similar relocations and realignments of employment took place among the population.

As they moved, these people became dislocated not only from their physical communities but also from their sense of the past. They took country music with them, but it evolved into forms that reflected their new communities. Just a decade earlier, country music had reveled in a rural way of life. Now its audiences were struggling to find their grounding in a modern setting, especially in cases where work had taken them into large communities of single people without the traditional stability of church, farm, and family. Many women had entered the workforce during the war, and at its end, they chose to keep their jobs in record numbers, thereby challenging older social mores. Changes in gendered norms within the audience affected country music. Men returned home from the war to find that their traditional roles had, in some cases, been filled. They sought to reestablish themselves within the fabric of their communities, to reconcile their sense of dislocation, and to keep pace with their rapidly changing cultural environment. Honky-tonk music became the sound of country music in this setting: the rhythmic pulse of Saturday nights spent drinking and dancing, nursing heartaches, and longing for an imagined idyll.

Honky-Tonk Roots

Within only a decade or so, honky-tonk music would come to symbolize the entire genre of country music. The term refers to a musical style, to the venues where that music was played, and to an attitude and philosophy represented by the major performers and songs within the style. The venues in which the music took root, which came to be known as honky-tonks, were taverns, roadhouses, and saloons, with plenty of alcohol and usually with a dance floor, associated with a working-class clientele, and often of suspect reputation. These venues dotted the landscape of the Southwest, especially Texas and California, although usage of the term expanded to include roadhouses in the Southeast. Roadhouses and drinking-and-dancing venues were sometimes also called juke joints, although

> ## ORIGINS OF THE TERM HONKY-TONK
> The first appearance of "honky-tonk" in print occurred in 1894, when the *Daily Ardmoreite*, a newspaper in Oklahoma, reported that "the honk-a-tonk last night was well attended by ball-heads, bachelors and leading citizens." In the first decades of the twentieth century, the term showed up in song titles and lyrics such as a Broadway number in 1918 called "Everything Is Hunky Dory Down in Honky Tonk Town," and other songs followed suit. The term showed up in country music when Al Dexter recorded "Honky Tonk Blues" for Vocalion in 1936, and by the early 1940s country musicians had recorded over a dozen songs with titles such as "Honky Tonk Mamas" and "Honky Tonk Rag." Hank Williams's "Honky Tonkin'" changed the term into a verb that meant heading out for an evening of lively drinking, dancing, and carousing in a tavern or roadhouse. When scholar Bill Malone wrote the first academic history book on country music in 1968, he used the term to label the musical style that took root in those very establishments, as it has been known ever since.

that term was more often applied to venues that catered to black patrons and featured R&B music.

The music played in these venues was the offspring of the fiddle-driven western swing that had graced those dance halls in prior years. It was loud, rhythmic dance music whose lyrics focused on the personal relationships and heartaches of the men and women who frequented these spaces. It embraced both up-tempo drinking and party songs and laments that wallowed in the depths of human misery, along with redemption-themed gospel numbers. Honky-tonk left behind most of the maudlin nostalgia for an imagined rural, folksy past. It was instead the product of the postwar industrialization and mobilization of the American working class.

It took a new singer, Ernest Tubb (1914–1984), to bring together all the elements that would form the honky-tonk style. In 1941, he recorded an abject lament of a man whose woman had left him that became prototypical honky tonk. "Walking the Floor over You," had a swing beat and electric lead guitar that reveal the lineage of the Texas roadhouses where Tubb learned his craft; the lyrics wallow in unending personal misery, and Tubb's vocals cut through directly to the listener. By mid-1940s, Tubb had expanded his band from the trio (rhythm guitar, bass, and electric guitar) heard on "Walking the Floor Over You" to a five-piece instrumentation (rhythm guitar, bass, electric guitar, fiddle, and steel guitar) that would become the standard in the style, and recordings such as "It's Been So Long Darling" (1945) and "Drivin' Nails in My Coffin" (1946) are prime examples of the fully formed honky-tonk musical style.

Honky-tonk ushered in songs about infidelity, sometimes called "cheatin' songs" in country music. In the 1940s, singing explicitly about this topic was still shocking and a violation of social taboos, especially if there was any implication of a woman's infidelity. One of the first of these was Floyd Tillman's "Slippin' Around" (1949). These songs would brand country music with a reputation that it still holds today as consisting of drinkin' and cheatin' songs. Honky-tonk also featured such raw, direct emotion in its lyrics that its songs became appealing source material for early rockabilly and rock 'n' roll singers. Elvis Presley, for instance, covered honky-tonk tunes, including Leon Payne's "I Love You Because" (1949). By the late 1940s, honky-tonk was an established musical style with strong connections to the cultural landscape of postwar America. It was drinking-and-dancing music, tied to the venues where it was featured, willing to address socially controversial topics of relationships and fidelity, and characterized by unfettered emotions and a confessional attitude that would be fertile inspiration for later generations of artists.

Figure 4-1 Ernest Tubb, holding the guitar he got from Jimmie Rodgers's widow.
Source: Courtesy of Country Music Hall of Fame and Museum.

The Louisiana Hayride

In April 1948, station KWKH launched a new barn dance program in Shreveport, Louisiana, called the Louisiana Hayride. This show proved particularly important in country music's history because it fostered the new musical style of honky-tonk, and in the next decade it would help launch rock 'n' roll as well. Unlike the Opry, the Hayride was not tied to a sense of nostalgia or tradition, nor did its leadership perceive themselves as any sort of protectors or gatekeepers of authenticity. The station had a powerful signal that gave it a long geographic reach, and a segment of the program was also distributed on both the CBS radio network and the Armed Forces Radio network, which guaranteed it a wide audience. The Hayride's management was willing to take chances with new, young, brash musicians, many of whom were honky-tonk singers still experimenting with their sound and honing their skills. Electric guitars and drums faced none of the opposition on the Hayride that they did on the Opry. Furthermore, the house band at the Hayride brought a strong R&B influence into their playing.

Shreveport was still under legalized segregation in the 1940s, and the ugly racism that was rampant in the South and beyond was certainly present. But at the same time, Shreveport also fostered a surprising degree of interaction between black and white musicians. Its red-light district had black and white bars and brothels next door to each other, where some of the best and most famous blues, boogie, barrelhouse, and folk musicians, including Lead Belly (Huddie Ledbetter), played regularly. Furthermore, KWKH broadcast an R&B show, which the staff musicians from the Hayride regularly listened to. Along with an R&B influence, the musicians who spent time on the Hayride also absorbed the rich Cajun culture of Louisiana (see essay on Cajun Country). All these factors combined to make the Hayride a hotbed of innovative country music activity in the late 1940s.

Honky-Tonk Heyday

Between 1947 and 1953, four country stars—Hank Williams, Webb Pierce, Lefty Frizzell, and Hank Snow—recorded some of the best honky-tonk in all of country music. Williams (see Artist Profile) has become the most famous, but in the early 1950s, the others were just as influential. Pierce (1921–1991) grew up in his native Louisiana as a devoted fan of Jimmie Rodgers. After serving in the army, he moved to Shreveport, landed a spot on the Louisiana Hayride during its first year, and signed with a small record label. In 1951, the major label

Figure 4-2 Webb Pierce and his Wandering Boys.
Source: Courtesy of BenCar Archives.

Decca picked up his contract, and with the release of the song "Wondering" (1952), he became a major honky-tonk star. Pierce's nasal, naturalized vocals that portray convincing pathos and misery fit perfectly into the honky-tonk aesthetic.

One of Pierce's lasting contributions to country music was actually the work of one of his band members. Pierce hired Bud Isaacs to play steel guitar for him, and in 1953 Isaacs added a foot-operated pedal to his steel guitar so he could change the pitch of a note while it was still sounding. This pedal steel sound, which stands out in the introduction to Pierce's hit "Slowly" (1954), was quickly imitated by other steel guitarists and became a musical signature of honky-tonk.

Lefty Frizzell (1928–1975) was also raised on the music of Jimmie Rodgers. Frizzell grew up in Texas and spent his early career performing in honky-tonks in Texas and New Mexico. In 1950, he caught the ear of a Columbia Records producer and began releasing honky-tonk records. His musical experiences in Texas lent a touch more western swing to Frizzell's sound than some of his contemporaries had, especially in his use of piano on many recordings. "If You've Got the Money I've Got the Time" (1950) shows off the humorous side of honky-tonk music in fine form. Frizzell toured with Hank Williams and joined the Opry. Like Williams's, Frizzell's professional life was scarred by problems with alcohol, and he also was hampered by business difficulties. In 1953, these problems knocked his career off track. Unlike Webb Pierce, however, Frizzell came back with a new musical style at the end of the decade and enjoyed a hugely successful second career, with hits in a much later musical style that sound nothing like his honky-tonk recordings.

Another fan of Jimmie Rodgers who turned into a major honky-tonk star was Canadian Hank Snow (1914–1999). In the 1930s, Snow toured and appeared on radio stations, yodeling and singing in the style of his musical hero. He moved to Nashville in 1945, by which time his recordings had shifted to a honky-tonk style. He joined the Opry in 1950. Snow's first big hit was "I'm Movin' On" (1950), which is built on a modified twelve-bar blues pattern (see Appendix A) and which foreshadowed Johnny Cash's rockabilly sound later in the decade. "Would You Mind" (1953), another of Snow's hits, is a solid illustration of the influence of Cajun-style fiddling in honky-tonk music.

Although Webb Pierce, Lefty Frizzell, and Hank Snow were distinctly different artists, the commonalities in their biographies, musical style, and song choices help illustrate the major themes in the honky-tonk era. These artists were inspired by the first generation of hillbilly musicians, drew specifically on Texan and Louisianan regional musical traditions, and fused their personal biographies into their songs. Their honky-tonk recordings used similar instrumentation and a marked, nasal, naturalized vocal style. Together, they represent a stylistic development that marked a major turning point in the history of country music.

ARTIST PROFILE

Hank Williams (1923–1953)

The legends surrounding Hank Williams's life far overshadow his biography. During his twenty-nine years, he was neither the biggest-selling country singer nor the one with the most hits, and yet his name has become synonymous with country music. Generations of country singers have written tribute songs, and fans treat both his life story and his music as sacred.

Hiram "Hank" Williams was born September 17, 1923, in Mount Olive, Alabama. His father, Lon, was disabled, and his mother, Lillie, was a strong-willed woman who was involved in Hank's career up to (and beyond) his

Figure 4-3 Hank Williams, stooped over the microphone, wearing one of his signature western suits; Don Helms's double-necked steel guitar, with finger picks on his right hand, is visible in the foreground.

Source: Courtesy of Country Music Hall of Fame and Museum.

death. During his childhood, Hank received a few music lessons, sold peanuts on street corners, and befriended an older African American named Rufus "Tee Tot" Payne, from whom he learned blues guitar and vocal styles.

In 1937, the family moved to Montgomery. There, Hank put together a band, which he dubbed the Drifting Cowboys in keeping with the trend toward western names, and began playing on the local radio station. In 1944, Hank married Audrey Mae Sheppard Guy. Two years later, at Audrey's encouragement, the two of them went to Nashville to meet with songwriter and music publisher Fred Rose. Rose first signed Hank Williams as a songwriter, but in December 1946, Rose offered him a contract to make records for the fledgling Sterling label. In 1947, Rose managed to get Hank a contract with the much larger label MGM, and he recorded his first big hit, "Move It on Over."

In August 1948, Hank joined the Louisiana Hayride on Shreveport's KWKH. In December, he recorded an old Tin Pan Alley tune called "Lovesick Blues." That song became a hit, and on the strength of it, Hank was finally invited to play the Opry in June 1949. His first performance was a stunning success: legends claim that he played as many as nine encores that evening, although biographer Colin Escott asserts that there were actually no encores on that segment of the show.

Hank's next few years were professionally good but personally unstable. Audrey had filed for divorce in 1948, although they reconciled later that year. Their son Randall Hank Williams (known later as Hank Williams Jr.) was born in 1949. Hank continued to write songs, record, and tour, with several number one records on the charts. His up-tempo tunes such as "Jambalaya" (whose Cajun influence is partly the result of his time working in Shreveport) and his heartbreak songs such as "Cold, Cold Heart" were both irrepressibly fun and pathetically sad. He recorded heartfelt gospel hymns under a pseudonym, Luke the Drifter, a common practice so that a singer's secular songs would not taint the piety of the sacred ones. Meanwhile, his health continued to deteriorate; he suffered from spina bifida and was in constant pain. To cope, he self-medicated with booze and narcotics, and frequent benders left his bandmates and manager Fred Rose extricating him from jail and all sorts of other unsavory situations.

By the fall of 1952, both Williams's career and his personal life were in shambles. Audrey had divorced him (again). The Opry fired him in August for failed appearances due to his drinking. He met Billie Jean Jones Eshliman, who at the time was dating fellow honky-tonk singer Faron Young. Hank and Billie Jean agreed to marry as soon as her divorce from her husband was finalized. Fred Rose was desperately trying to rescue Hank's career and managed to get him another slot on the Louisiana Hayride. Meanwhile, Hank had sent another girlfriend, Bobbie Jett, who was expecting his child, to live with his mother in Montgomery. In October, Hank and Billie Jean married, first in a secret, private ceremony, and then the next day at two public extravaganzas, to which fans purchased tickets.

Hank Williams's death is the most mythologized event in all of country music history. Hank spent Christmas in Montgomery. He was then supposed to play a New Year's Eve show in Charleston, West Virginia, and a New Year's Day show in Canton, Ohio. Foul weather prevented him from flying, so he hired a teenager named Charles Carr to drive him. They left Montgomery on December 30 and spent the night in Birmingham. The next morning, they drove to Knoxville, where Hank realized that in order to make the show on time, he would have to fly. He chartered a plane, but the weather forced them to turn around, and he canceled his appearance in Charleston. The pair checked into a Knoxville hotel briefly, where Hank received several shots of morphine and vitamin B_{12}. About 10:45 p.m., the hotel porters carried Hank to the car, and Carr and Williams left for Canton. In Blaine, a patrolman stopped Carr for speeding. The patrolman later recalled that Hank appeared already dead at that point. Carr continued north to Bristol, where he picked up a relief driver from a local taxi company for a short stretch of the trip. What happened next may never be known for sure, as witnesses disagree. They passed through Bluefield and Beckley, West Virginia, and likely stopped at a gas station on the edge of Oak Hill. At this point, Carr claimed to have discovered Hank's lifeless body. From there, they traveled to the Oak Hill hospital, where Williams was officially pronounced dead at 7 a.m., January 1, 1953.

Although that was the end of Hank Williams's life, it was the beginning of both the legend and a macabre circus. A vicious legal battle ensued for the rights to Hank's estate, with his mother, Audrey, and Billie Jean laying claim to various portions. Two days after his death, Bobbie Jett gave birth to his daughter, whom Lillie adopted. Both Billie Jean and Audrey went on tour as "Mrs. Hank Williams." Williams's reputation was at times whitewashed—some promotional copy reported that he had died in a car crash, which was more respectable than being the victim of alcohol, drugs, and hard living—and at other times exaggerated; he became the token representative for reckless behavior of all sorts.

After his death, Hank Williams filled a critical role in country music history. He only recorded for about six years, and died just before rock 'n' roll permanently altered the landscape of popular music. Unlike many of his honky-tonk contemporaries whose musical style and image adapted with the changing trends, Williams's style appeared frozen in time; he started out recording classic honky-tonk, and he died making the same kind of music. Furthermore, his biography had all the tragic pathos of a honky-tonk song. In the coming decades, when the country music community searched for a symbol of authenticity in country music, they settled on Hank Williams.

Listening Guide

"Your Cheatin' Heart" (1952)

PERFORMER: Hank Williams (Hank Williams, vocal, guitar; Tommy Jackson, fiddle; Don Helms, steel guitar; Chet Atkins, electric guitar; Eddie Hill, rhythm guitar; Floyd "Lightnin'" Chance, bass)

SONGWRITER: Hank Williams

ORIGINAL RELEASE: MGM K-11416

FORM: AABA

STYLE: Honky-tonk

Hank Williams went into the studio for the last time on September 23, 1952. By then, his personal life was in a shambles, but he cut four songs on that session, all of which were stellar. Williams had written "Your Cheatin' Heart," along with "Kaw-Liga," a month earlier while in Montgomery. Fred Rose had traveled down from Nashville to go over the new songs and likely edit them (Rose certainly had a major hand in "Kaw-Liga"). Then in September, Williams cut them in the Castle Studio in Nashville.

Historians speculate that "Your Cheatin' Heart" was aimed at Audrey. The lyrics are presented in the first person, addressing a second-person "you," the woman accused of being unfaithful. Because of this, the listener is drawn into a direct, intimate, and emotional rant, which makes the song feel even more personal and the singer more vulnerable—both important qualities in honky-tonk. The singer is miserably "walk[ing] the floor" himself, and predicts that the woman will end up alone, suffering the same emotional distress. Although the song's lyrics are more bitter than Ernest Tubb's "Walking the Floor over You" (1941), they clearly make reference to both that pioneering honky-tonk hit and the broader tradition of earlier honky-tonk songs.

The song's form (see Appendix A) reveals Fred Rose's effect on Williams's songwriting. Unlike the common verse-chorus form, this AABA pattern shows an influence from the Tin Pan Alley songwriting tradition and pop music in general, which was the tradition in which Rose had worked. The melodies in this song are so distinctive that it is easy to hear the pattern AABA, and it is an exceptionally clear example of the form. In this particular song, however, Williams used one segment of the lyrics twice: the section that begins "When tears . . ." comes back in the second half of the song, as well. The simplicity of the song's form and the repetition of lyrics create the effect of a chorus in the song, as seen in Example 4-1.

FORM

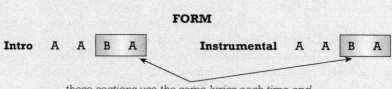

these sections use the same lyrics each time and
therefore behave like a chorus for the song

Example 4-1 Song form for Hank Williams's "Your Cheatin' Heart."

"Your Cheatin' Heart" was the first of Williams's records released after his death, which helped fuel its success. Williams's version reached number one on the *Billboard* "Top Country & Western Records" that spring. But long before then, Fred Rose had sent the song to pop producers, and both Joni James and Frankie Laine released pop versions of it in 1953. In the years that followed, the song became synonymous with both Hank Williams and honky-tonk.

TIME	FORM	LISTENING CUES	DISCUSSION
0:00	Introduction	steel guitar	The first three notes that Don Helms played on his steel guitar became a standard honky-tonk introduction for many years.
0:08	A-section	"Your cheatin' . . ."	Williams's voice quivers on several notes, creating a sense of vulnerability. The fiddle fills in between Williams's phrases.
0:22	A-section	"But sleep won't . . ."	Williams slides into several notes, as is common in honky-tonk. The steel guitar fills in between Williams's phrases.
0:38	B-section	"When tears . . ."	The raw, nasal sound of words such as "down" are hallmarks of honky-tonk.
0:53	A-section	"You'll walk . . ."	Williams's voice breaks slightly on "I do," which conveys the emotional intensity of the song.
1:07	Instrumental B-section	steel guitar	Don Helms's steel guitar slides into notes and adds a slight, wavering vibrato, creating what is often called the honky-tonk "cryin' steel guitar" sound.
1:23	Instrumental A-section	Fiddle	Tommy Jackson's fiddle playing uses double-stops, which means we hear him playing two notes as one throughout this solo.
1:38	A-section	"Your cheatin' . . ."	The nasal timbre on words such as "love" are a clear illustration of the naturalized vocals in honky-tonk.
1:53	A section	"The time will . . ."	Williams's voice cries on words such as "heart," illustrating why his fans perceived his music as so personal.
2:08	B section	"When tears . . ."	This section uses the same lyrics as the previous B section, which makes it (plus the subsequent A section) behave like a chorus for the song.
2:23	A section	"You'll walk . . ."	The steel guitar's short motive at the end of the song reinforces the honky-tonk sound. Williams's voice changes timbre drastically between the high notes and the low notes in this section.

The Honky-Tonk Image

As much as the honky-tonk musical style relied on the direct, raw, and personal communication between singer and listener, the honky-tonk image was gaudy in its excess. Many of the performers took their cues from the western swing musicians, whose stylish dress and boisterous stage presence won over their fans. But the honky-tonk singers went even further, embellishing their western-cut suits and cowboy garb with sequins, rhinestones, and lavish embroidery. The first major designer of these costumes was Nathan Turk, a tailor in California who had initially built his reputation working with film stars. In 1947, "Nudie" Cohn, a Russian-born immigrant, opened a shop in California and started to work with country singers. Cohn crafted "Nudie suits" to match the personality and name of country's biggest stars from the 1950s onward. Singer Porter Wagoner got wagon wheels on his, for instance, as a play on his name. Cohn's son-in-law, Manuel, launched his own business in the 1970s, which became the next go-to place for country singers looking for personalized high-fashion western wear. While the costumes that Cohn and others created did not affect the musical style, they certainly became part of the aesthetic, or artistic package, of honky-tonk. The glamorous, extravagant outfits captured the devil-may-care, playful side of honky-tonk and provided a foil both for the music's beer-drenched heartbreak songs and for the singers' personas as "regular folks."

Honky-Tonk Angels

Very few women recorded honky-tonk music during these years. Of those, Rose Maddox (see Listening Guide for "Pay Me Alimony"), Kitty Wells, Rose Lee Maphis, and Molly O'Day were particularly influential. O'Day was instrumental in the career of the most famous honky-tonk singer, Hank Williams. O'Day and her husband Lynne Davis met Williams and discovered the quality of his songwriting long before anyone else had taken notice. O'Day scored a hit with a song she learned from Williams, "Tramp on the Street" (1946), and subsequently with a song that Williams wrote, "I Don't Care if Tomorrow Never Comes" (1947).

Like O'Day, Rose Lee Maphis witnessed the development of honky-tonk music firsthand. Maphis (1922–) started out singing on barn dance radio shows on the East Coast, including as part of an all-girl band called the Saddle Sweethearts on Virginia's Old Dominion Barn Dance in the 1940s. She married Joe Maphis (1921–1986), and in 1951, right as the honky-tonk era was booming, the couple moved to California, where they changed their musical style to match the roadhouse honky-tonk that was popular there.

Shortly after arriving in California, Joe Maphis penned their biggest hit, "Dim Lights, Thick Smoke (And Loud, Loud Music)" (1952), in which a man accuses a honky-tonk angel of preferring dance halls and nightlife to staying home with her children (see Listen Side by Side in Chapter 5). The so-called honky-tonk angel was a stock female character that started to show up in country songs with increasing frequency. Up to that time, there had been relatively few female character types in country music: mamas, sweet young mountain lasses, tart-tongued comedic old maids, and cowgirls, for instance. In the imaginations of the songwriters, this new character, the honky-tonk angel, inhabited the dance halls and eschewed conventional domestic life. Her frequent appearance in song lyrics, along with the prevalence of "cheatin' songs," illustrated the country audience's ambivalence regarding the social changes, especially with regard to gender roles and the growing instability of traditional family relationships, that characterized the postwar cultural landscape.

Answer Songs

The honky-tonk angel character reappeared in a pair of honky-tonk recordings that brought the discussion of gender roles into the forefront of country music: Hank Thompson's "The Wild Side of Life" and Kitty Wells's answer to it, "It Wasn't God

Figure 4-4 Rose Maddox with the Maddox Brothers, decked out in their bright costumes designed by Nudie Cohn.
Source: Southern Folklife Collection, Wilson Library, The University of North Carolina at Chapel Hill.

Listening Guide

"(Pay Me) Alimony" (1951)

PERFORMER:
Maddox Brothers
and Rose (Rose
Maddox, vocals;
Fred Maddox,
bass; Cal Maddox,
rhythm guitar; Henry
Maddox, guitar;
Don Maddox, fiddle;
Gene Breeden,
guitar)

SONGWRITERS:
unknown

ORIGINAL RELEASE:
4 Star 45-1549

FORM: Verse-chorus

STYLE: Honky-tonk

This recording is a great example of the way honky-tonk fused with hillbilly boogie on the West Coast. California always fostered its own musical styles, which in the case of honky-tonk, retained the exuberance and excess of the western swing bands' stage shows.

Rose Maddox's personal biography was representative of the entire shift in working class culture that took place in the 1940s. Born into abject poverty about ninety miles outside of Birmingham, Alabama, Roselea Arbana Maddox (1925–1998) and her family set out for the promised riches of California in 1933. Her parents and five of their children hopped freight trains and hoboed their way to Modesto, where the family joined countless other migrants in farm labor. In 1937, disheartened by picking cotton all day, her older brother Fred decided to put together a family band. He talked his way onto a few radio shows, and then sought a sponsor. A local businessman agreed, but only if the band had a "girl singer." From that moment on, the band had a sponsor, and Rose was in the group.

Over time, the Maddox Brothers and Rose adapted their sound to the livelier dance beats of western swing. They purchased garish western costumes from tailor and costume designer Nathan Turk, who was most famous for rodeo outfits and had already outfitted bands such as Bob Wills's Texas Playboys. The band augmented their string band sound with electric guitars, which along with Rose's brash vocals and their choice of song lyrics moved them squarely into the honky-tonk musical style.

On this song, the Maddox Brothers filled out the pulsating rhythms of the band with several guitars, both acoustic and electric. The acoustic guitar's sock-rhythm accompaniment added percussive sounds, as did the upright bass. Shuffle-style fiddling provided contrast and counterpoint for Rose's vocals. Electric lead guitars sounded like they were brought back in time from the first years of rock 'n' roll, prescient of the rockabilly style that would soon emerge. Altogether, the band's signature sound was rough-hewn and homegrown. When they played gospel songs or ballads, they sounded like an old-time string band. But when they cut loose on livelier numbers such as this, they turned into a honky-tonk band infused with boogie and rockabilly.

The band's stage presence was unequaled; Rose explained, "People came to be entertained, and we entertained them!" Her brother Fred could never resist adding jokes into the song (yelling "Good morning, judge!" at the end of this recording) or playing pranks on the other musicians on stage. The family chemistry was important to their stage show as well—even though they were bedecked in outrageously elaborate costumes and clearly performing, they always came across as genuine to their audiences, partly because the natural camaraderie of the siblings could not be disguised.

This song is an early example of a feisty, outspoken, female perspective in country lyrics. Celebration of single life and complaints about the constraints of married life appear in country song lyrics from the first decade (the Carter

Family's "Single Girl, Married Girl") to the present. Rose Maddox contributed several songs on this topic, including "I Wish I Was a Single Girl Again." The singer's tale in "(Pay Me) Alimony" contrasts with the stereotyped image of the country sweetheart as a contented, domestic wife and mother.

TIME	FORM	LISTENING CUES	DISCUSSION
0:00	Introduction	electric guitar	Listen to the band members hollering during the introduction, bringing the sounds of live performance into the studio.
0:11	Verse 1	"Come all you pretty . . ."	Rose Maddox's voice has a strong southern accent. Fred frequently hollered out comments ("I'm a-listenin'!") while she was singing, which added humor to the performance. The band sets up a hard-driving boogie rhythm for this song. Listen to the instruments playing improvised melodies behind Rose's vocals.
0:30	Chorus	"To pay me alimony . . ."	Listen to the intricate electric guitar melody played behind Rose.
0:39	Instrumental verse	steel guitar, fiddle, electric guitar	The fiddle plays a duet with an electric guitar for the first half of this interlude. Then at 0:48, the electric lead guitar plays a blistering solo that foreshadows the rock 'n' roll guitar solos from the late '50s and even the surf rock guitar styles that would emerge from California later.
0:59	Verse 3	"He said that . . ."	The words get funnier (and more biting at the same time) as each verse unfolds (rhyming "stale bologna" with "alimony," for instance).
1:17	Chorus	"To pay me alimony . . ."	The repetition of the title stands out in this chorus.
1:26	Instrumental verse	electric guitar	This solo only covers half a verse. It features rhythmically sophisticated improvisation and would be entirely at home in a rockabilly recording a half-decade later.
1:37	Verse 3	"One day a message . . ."	The electric guitar's accompaniment behind Rose's vocals is some of the most exciting in this entire recording. The band's shout-out at the end of this verse keeps any of it from being too serious, and reflects the live, on-stage interactions that bands would cultivate in honky tonk performances.
1:55	Chorus	"Hooray for alimony . . ."	The comedy of this song is reinforced when Rose changes the words in this last chorus and ends with tongue-in-cheek advice for young women to "get yourself a handsome man and sue for alimony."

Who Made Honky Tonk Angels." The songs encapsulated the differences in gender identity and social propriety that surfaced in country music and culture during the period. Their lyrics addressed the swaggering men who frequented honky-tonks in search of loose women and drink and the women who questioned both the double standard regarding acceptable behavior and the feelings of abandonment on the home front.

"The Wild Side of Life," written by Texan songwriter William Warren and honky-tonk pianist Arlie Carter, was a huge hit for Hank Thompson in 1952. Warren and Carter had used the melody from Roy Acuff's song "The Great Speckled Bird," which itself was a traditional tune that had showed up in other songs. Over this borrowed melody, they wrote lyrics in which the singer bitterly castigates his wife for abandoning him, instead heading back to a supposedly glamorous nightlife as a honky-tonk angel where she waits to be "anybody's baby."

Songwriter J. D. Miller heard the song and thought the lyrics "I didn't know God made honky-tonk angels" were begging for a woman's response, so he penned an answer song, again using the same melody. In this version's lyrics, the female singer sits beside a jukebox and hears it playing "The Wild Side of Life," to which she responds with the answer song's title, "It *wasn't* God who made honky-tonk angels," and the stinging accusation "Too many times married men think they're still single," which, she explains, has been the downfall of many a "good girl."

This gender-focused discourse, realized in the form of songs, made "**answer songs**," a phenomenon became very popular in the early 1950s. Answer songs use the melody, topic, and story line of an existing song, along with lyrics that are re-written from the opposite gender's perspective. Honky-tonk music lent itself easily to this gender-based practice because of the style's first-person lyrics and confessional vocals. Answer songs became a way for the voices and opinions of women to join in the honky-tonk musical discourse.

J.D. Miller's song made its way to Kitty Wells (1919–2012), the best-known female honky-tonk artist and celebrated "Queen of Country Music," who built her solo career on the answer-song formula. Born Muriel Ellen Deason, Wells began singing on the radio as part of a sister act in 1936. A year later, she married country singer Johnny Wright, who toured with his duet partner Jack Anglin under the name Johnny and Jack. Wright suggested she take a new stage name, borrowing it from the traditional ballad "Poor Kitty Wells." By 1952, she was anxious to retire and stay home with her children. Instead, Paul Cohen, head of Decca's country music division, convinced her to record Miller's song.

Although written by a man, Wells's recording was an outspoken defense of women who had formerly been ostracized as "bad girls." Country fans raved about the song, but both the NBC radio network and the Opry censored it as too suggestive (presumably in its reference to a woman's promiscuity). That censorship is certainly a telling sign of the tensions about gender and social propriety that hung in the air in the early 1950s.

Wells's hit served as a model for a long line of similar answer songs, including "Paying for That Back Street Affair" (after Webb Pierce's "Back Street Affair"),

"Your Cold, Cold Heart Is Melted Now" (after Hank Williams's "Cold, Cold Heart," although this used the melody from "Your Cheatin' Heart"), and "Hey Joe" (after Carl Smith's "Hey Joe"). Wells became the most famous female honky-tonk singer of the 1950s; she never sought the spotlight, however, and was quick to deny any staunch feminist stance. Given the lyrics that made her famous, it is ironic that in interviews she always emphasized her private life as a wife and mother, and even published several cookbooks. She left it to the next generation of female country singers to take a more politicized personal stance through their song lyrics.

A Broader Soundscape

As much of an impact as honky tonk had on country music, it was not the only sound in the mix during the 1940s. Along with the continuation of hillbilly styles with some radio stars and the flourishing bluegrass sounds (see Chapter 5), country also had a

Figure 4-5 Kitty Wells.
Source: Southern Folklife Collection, Wilson Library, The University of North Carolina at Chapel Hill.

growing contingent of outside influences making bold appearances. Cajun music was one of those (see essay on Cajun Country). Hillbilly boogie was another. This particular style, whose main features were in the rhythms of the songs, evolved from boogie-woogie (sometimes also known as barrelhouse), a style created by black pianists in the 1920s. It first surfaced in Texas, Arkansas, and Louisiana, but soon thereafter spread to Chicago and other parts of the country. Although the earliest practitioners were pianists, boogie-woogie's features, especially the rolling and driving bass lines and syncopated rhythms, easily migrated both to guitar and to full bands. In the early 1940s, black R&B musicians transformed boogie into jump blues, while white country musicians started incorporating boogie music into their country performances, especially in honky-tonk venues. This rowdy, exciting dance music had many of the necessary characteristics to please a honky-tonk crowd and also allowed the performers to show off their virtuosic skills, especially on guitar.

Among the country stars who frequently performed boogie music were the Maddox Brothers and Rose, the Delmore Brothers (see Chapter 3), Merle Travis, and pianist Moon Mullican. One center for the production of country boogie was King

Example 4-2 Some typical boogie bass or guitar lines.

Records, an independent label founded in 1943 by Syd Nathan in Cincinnati, Ohio. Recordings such as the Delmores' "Freight Train Boogie" (1946), Travis's "Merle's Boogie Woogie," (1948), and Mullican's "Cherokee Boogie (Eh-Oh-Aleena)" (1951) were all major country hits on the King label. Country boogie became an important contributor to honky tonk, but even more significant was the way it paved the way for other fusions of R&B and country styles, a formula that would help spawn rockabilly and rock 'n' roll.

The Impact of Honky-Tonk

One last generation of country singers sang honky-tonk in the mid-1950s before the style gave way to newer trends away. Singers including Ray Price, Faron Young, Jim Reeves, and George Jones became major honky-tonk stars, but a musical revolution was looming. By the 1960s, all of these stars had changed their styles (as had Eddy Arnold) and left honky-tonk in the dust. That musical revolution was launched by rock 'n' roll. Although at its conception, honky-tonk was a modern, progressive music that displaced more traditional styles of country, it was also the last era before the genre underwent a far more radical transformation. In later years, many fans, musicians, and historians looked back to honky-tonk as representing so-called uncorrupted, "real" country music, invoking ideas about authenticity in the process.

A New Era

In the mid-1950s, country music underwent a radical change. Hank Williams was dead, and with him passed the era of honky-tonk music, when country captured the essence of the working-class white American's outlook with plaintive lyrics accompanied by fiddle and steel guitar. Americans found themselves in the midst of new prosperity and opportunity, but unsettled in their global politics: embattled in Korea against a known enemy, and embattled on the home front against an elusive political enemy, communism, that many predicted would threaten the very essence of the American dream. Yet a new generation was coming of age. These youth, known as the baby boom generation, were born at the end of World War II and in the years following. For the first time in American history, youth had plenty of leisure time, disposable income, and access to entertainment technology in the form of records and television. Especially in the South, these young people were also becoming aware of the growing civil rights movement. The music during these years changed in accordance with all of these factors, which contributed both directly and indirectly to the creation of rockabilly, a fusion of honky-tonk music with rhythm & blues (R&B), especially the style known as jump blues. This new music brought issues of race to the forefront of country music once again.

Setting the Stage: The Emergence of Rock 'n' Roll

Our story of rockabilly begins with the conception of rock 'n' roll, which emerged from the intersection of youth culture and the pulsating dance music that was part of R&B. In 1951, a Cleveland record store owner named Leo Mintz noticed that both black and white teenagers were growing more interested in R&B records. He convinced disc jockey (DJ) Alan Freed to broadcast R&B records on a late-night show, which caught the attention of white teenagers in the region. What Freed and others in the music industry discovered was an enormous, untapped potential audience for this music. Freed branched out into promoting concerts and dances a year later. While the major record labels in both country and pop music were still catering to adult tastes during those years, independent record labels and radio stations started cultivating bands whose music sounded reckless, young, and unrestrained and blended black and white musical traditions into a strain of R&B. Movies picked up on a similar theme of juvenile social rebellion, and the silver screen depicted this cultural movement in such films as *The Wild One* (1953), *Rebel Without a Cause* (1955), *Blackboard Jungle* (1955), and especially *Rock Around the Clock* (1956).

This intersection between white and black audiences and musical styles began even before the U.S. Supreme Court's decision in *Brown v. Board of Education*, a landmark ruling in 1954 that set in motion school integration. Although one segment of the population had already experienced some degree of integration through military service, racial tensions among working-class Southerners ran high. In the early 1950s, white teenagers' growing fascination with R&B was extremely disturbing to the older generation. Historians have described this generation of teenagers as searching for ways to rebel against the established cultural traditions of their parents, home, family, religion, and politics. In the

South these entities were all shaped by ideas of segregation, a Jim Crow society, and racial prejudice. In the eyes of these teens' parents, this music was not only tantalizing and seductive but destabilizing to the larger social order, largely for reasons of race. Mass efforts to stop white youth audiences from listening to R&B failed, and instead, the teens found the music even more enticing. Historian Michael Bertrand has suggested that musical interactions across these deeply entrenched racial boundaries, both with white audiences seeking out R&B and with white performers adopting traditionally black styles, laid the foundations for larger social reforms that accompanied the 1960's civil rights movement.

As testimony to his growing popularity, in 1954 Alan Freed was hired by a major radio station in New York City, where his radio show was called "The Rock and Roll Party." Freed continued to promote concerts and dance parties, centered on R&B music but pitched to white, middle-class teens. Partly through Freed's show and concerts, the phrase "rock and roll," which included connotations as a metaphor for sex, became the label for a new style of music. The first generation of rock 'n' roll stars included Chuck Berry, Little Richard, Fats Domino, Bill Haley, Jerry Lee Lewis, Buddy Holly, and, of course, Elvis Presley.

Most historians of popular music use the term "rock 'n' roll" to describe a particular musical movement that existed from approximately 1954 to 1959. They use the term "rock" to describe a larger musical genre, analogous to country or jazz. Within that perspective, rock 'n' roll is considered the first generation and style of rock music, with rock music going on to develop into a much broader genre. Keep in mind that prior to about 1954, there was no such thing as rock music: it simply had not yet been conceived. Thus, audiences in the mid-1950s had to make sense of new artists according to the existing stylistic and genre categories that were part of their vocabulary, namely R&B and country.

Memphis Rockabilly and Sun Records

Within rock 'n' roll, one of the most prominent styles was rockabilly—a term that emphasized the performers' connections to country music with the "-billy" from "hillbilly," and that initially was applied to white artists. Rockabilly developed in several different urban locations across the South, most notably Memphis, Tennessee, but also in Louisiana and Texas, as well as a few key sites outside of that region.

In the 1950s, Memphis was home to a large number of African American musicians steeped in R&B, as well as home to a rich gospel music tradition. It was also situated in southern Tennessee, where hillbilly music had long since taken root. Those musical practices came together in three important cultural settings. One was that working-class musicians knew and learned from each other, even across racial lines. Johnny Cash, for instance, recalled spending time in the black neighborhoods in Memphis, where he "met [black blues musician] Gus Cannon one day on the porch of his home. . . . I sat and listened to him, played with him, and it got to be quite a regular affair with me." Another was through concert venues; although they were living under legally enforced conditions of segregation, white and black teens attended mixed-audience concerts and dances long before they attended integrated schools in many areas. These interactions were not without tensions and occasional outbreaks of violence. For instance, black musicians experienced wretched accommodations, restrictions on such things as where they could wait backstage before their performances, refusals of service, and threats to their personal safety while performing in the South, yet they also found large and enthusiastic audiences there for their music. Another method by which music crossed the lines of segregation was radio stations; young people began listening to radio stations whose music had not previously been marketed to them. Community tensions surfaced in this arena as well: in some towns, civic pressure from white leadership compelled radio stations and jukebox operators to stop playing R&B under the pretext that it was inappropriate or immoral, thinly disguised objections to the music's racial associations. Yet in spite of the cultural barriers to musical integration, an audience of both black and white youth flocked to this music.

Sam Phillips's Sun Studios in Memphis was a key location for this fusion of hillbilly honky-tonk with R&B styles. An Alabama native, Phillips (1923–2003) entered the music business as a DJ, working initially in Muscle Shoals and later moving to Memphis in 1945. In 1950, he leased space at 706 Union Avenue in Memphis and opened the Memphis Recording Service. The studio was available for a fee to anyone who wanted to make a recording. Like many others in the music business during these years, Phillips was acutely aware of the growing appeal R&B stars had among a diverse audience. He also recognized that the youth market was interested in music that sounded different from the polished, mainstream pop that the major record labels were selling.

In 1951, pianist Ike Turner brought his band into Phillips's studio, including saxophonist Jackie Brenston, and they recorded an updated jump blues tune they called "Rocket 88," with Brenston singing lead. Phillips sold that recording to Chess Records in Chicago, and it is often cited as the first rock 'n' roll record. Phillips also produced records for blues stars, including Howlin' Wolf and B. B. King, during these years. Recognizing that he had access to some phenomenal talent in Memphis and that there was no reason to ship the recordings off to someone else's record label, Phillips decided to try his hand again at running a label. In 1952, he launched Sun Records.

Elvis Presley Makes a Record

In 1953, a young truck driver named Elvis Presley (1935–1977) walked into Phillips's studio to make a record. Born in Tupelo, Mississippi, Elvis had lived in Memphis since 1948, and had been auditioning as a singer for some time already. Phillips's secretary took notice of Elvis's vocal abilities, and in 1954, Phillips brought him back into the studio to try a few more recordings. Elvis had grown up on country music and was an avowed fan of Hank Snow, Roy Acuff, and Ernest Tubb, among others. Elvis's vocal style was steeped in Southern gospel, which he had sung all his life, and heavily influenced by both black gospel performances and the many black R&B musicians whom he had heard in Memphis. Phillips was sufficiently impressed that he recruited a local country duo, bass player Bill Black and guitarist Scotty Moore, to accompany Elvis at another session. While clowning around in the studio, the trio performed an impromptu rendition of a jump blues tune, "That's All Right (Mama)." A few days later, the trio of Elvis (playing rhythm guitar), Black (bass), and Moore (electric lead guitar) recorded a souped-up, rocking version of Bill Monroe's bluegrass tune, "Blue Moon of Kentucky" (see Listen Side by Side in Chapter 5). That recipe, country plus R&B, yielded rockabilly (see essay on Rockabilly).

Elvis's records quickly became popular with DJs, and he began to tour and perform. In October of 1954, he debuted on the Grand Ole Opry, although the Opry's establishment felt his style did not suit the staid demeanor of the show. Two weeks later, he appeared on the Louisiana Hayride. There, Elvis added a drummer to his band, which moved him even further away from country traditions. Drummer D. J. Fontana was a product of the Shreveport musical scene, where white and black musicians had forged musical connections for several years. In an interview with ethnomusicologist Tracy Laird, for instance, Fontana recalled going to black clubs after World War II to sit in with the bands, as well as mixed-race jam sessions: ". . . black, white, . . . they didn't care. If you played, come on, bring your horn, bring your drums, whatever." Such musical integration stood in stark contrast to the turbulent race relations that characterized their community in general, but it also provided the musicians the opportunity to develop this new hybrid sound. Fontana remained Elvis's drummer for more than a decade.

For the rest of 1954 and '55, Elvis toured with other country singers and won over teenage audiences with his rockabilly energy, gyrating hips, and sensuous vocal performances. While other white musicians, including Bill Haley and the Comets, had performed black R&B tunes before to great success, Elvis's vocals were different: he adopted not just the songs and general musical style but also specific vocal techniques from blues- and gospel-influenced styles, including his use of extreme

---

ELVIS AS COUNTRY

Students often think of Elvis as the "King of Rock 'n' Roll" and find it puzzling to view him as a country singer. Remember, however, that when he first started making records, it was as a country singer who happened to have a unique style and energy, and the category of "rock music" was not yet in existence. His musical style was different than the honky-tonk and more traditional country singers of the 1950s, but he began his career squarely within the country music genre. He performed on traditionally country shows and for country music fans. He routinely covered songs by honky-tonk and cowboy singers ("I Love You Because" and "I'll Never Let You Go," for instance). And, most important, country fans not only liked Elvis's records but also thought of them specifically as country hits. Throughout the 1950s, Elvis's records appeared at the top of the *Billboard* country charts. Many of the famous singles he made for the RCA record label, including "Heartbreak Hotel," were recorded in Nashville with top country session musicians, including Floyd Cramer, Chet Atkins, and, on other songs, a vocal quartet called the Jordanaires, all of whom recorded with the biggest stars in country music over the next decade (see Chapter 6).

registers (very high notes and low notes) and wildly expressive effects such as his growls and interjections. His rockabilly recordings were among the most popular within the growing rock 'n' roll fad.

In 1955, Sam Phillips sold his contract with Elvis Presley to RCA for $35,000 plus $5,000 in back royalties for Elvis. Fans have often wondered why Phillips was willing to part with the contract of an apparently rising star for what appeared to be, in hindsight, to be a modest payment. The answer helps explain how the economics of the music business affected independent labels like Sun. Phillips had a young star whose records were topping the charts and who was wildly popular with his audiences. By all appearances, he was in an excellent position. But Phillips also had a cash-flow problem. Sun Records had to pay up front costs for manufacturing, distributing, and promoting the records. Meanwhile, retailers were often able to delay paying Phillips for the records they sold, or pay only part of what they owed him at a time. Sun Records, as a small, independent label with little capital on hand, could not afford to promote Elvis across the national market. Meanwhile, RCA and the other major labels were increasingly aware of the growing market for rock 'n' roll, but they generally lacked the flexibility, local connections, and willingness to take risks that were needed to launch new artists. The Phillips-RCA deal, brokered by Elvis's manager, Colonel Tom Parker, addressed all these issues: RCA got a hot, rising star of rock 'n' roll; Elvis got a record label with the connections and raw capital to promote his career; and Phillips got an infusion of cash that allowed Sun Records not only to stay afloat but also to develop and promote his other talented artists, including Johnny Cash, Carl Perkins, Jerry Lee Lewis, and Roy Orbison.

Once Elvis left Sun Records, his style soon moved away from rockabilly. As rock 'n' roll gained a larger audience and the major record labels began to invest in it, the music continued to evolve. By the late 1950s, Elvis's recordings had few if any audible connections to traditional country music, his concerts were no longer connected to the country genre, and country fans no longer claimed him. But for the first few crucial years of his career, he was situated squarely in country music, and he brought to life a new style known as rockabilly that left a lasting mark on the genre.

Rockabilly as Part of Country Music

In 1955, another trio of musicians stepped into Sam Phillips's Memphis studio. Johnny Cash (see Artist Profile), with Luther Perkins (electric lead guitar) and Marshall Grant (bass), adopted a similar formula of blending boogie rhythms and jump blues with hillbilly honky-tonk music. Unlike Elvis, Cash was deeply invested in the sincerity of old country music, and his own songs sometimes delved into the darker recesses of country themes, including tales of heartbreak, suffering, and violence. To his fans, Cash was young, defiant, mysterious, and rebellious, and his version of rockabilly worked its way into the core of country music.

Johnny Cash (1932–2003)

Johnny Cash is both an enigma and an icon in country music. Many of his fans purport to like Cash but not country music; some think of him as connected more to rock than country; others know him only from the records he made in the 1990s and 2000s, when he was far removed from the mainstream country music industry. Yet Cash's music is deeply embedded in country, and he has been a critical part of the genre's evolution over the years. Cash's five main contributions to country music are:

1. a large number of rockabilly hits
2. substantial crossover success in rock and pop music
3. the dark, brooding "man in black" personality, which remains a counterbalance to lighter, pop-country trends
4. the songs he has written, many of which are covered regularly
5. the juxtaposition of his troubled, sinner songs and his gospel music, which represent that core duality in country music

Born J. R. Cash on September 12, 1932, in Kingsland, Arkansas, the second of seven children, he grew up working in cotton fields alongside his family. In 1950, he moved to Pontiac, Michigan, where he worked on an assembly line for a short time, then headed back to Arkansas, where he enlisted in the air force (and where he became John, since the air force would not accept a single initial as a first name). While stationed in Landsberg am Lech, Germany, Cash spent his leisure time playing the guitar and singing with friends, and wrote a number of his most famous songs. In 1954, Cash returned home and married his longtime girlfriend, Vivian Liberto. The couple moved to Memphis, where Cash found work as an appliance salesman. In his spare time, Cash began playing music with two auto mechanics, Marshall Grant and Luther Perkins. The

trio went to Sam Phillips's studio, where Cash sang gospel songs of the sort his mother had taught him as a child. Phillips flatly announced that gospel wouldn't sell, and convinced Cash to head toward secular music. Phillips also saw great potential in the unpolished sound of Perkins and Grant, who were known as the Tennessee Two, paired with the haunting, stoic, and deep voice of Cash's vocals, and kept the group's sound very minimalist.

Cash's first single, "Cry, Cry, Cry," made the national charts. In 1956, "I Walk the Line," which he wrote for his wife Vivian, reached number one. Cash was touring widely with various country variety shows, often with labelmate Elvis Presley. In 1956, Cash joined the Grand Ole Opry. By 1957, Sam Phillips had turned over most of his day-to-day recording work to producer Jack Clement, who pushed Cash toward more teen-friendly pop sounds ("Ballad of a Teenage Queen," for instance) and abandoned the stark minimalism of his early recordings. Cash signed with Columbia Records in 1958, partly because they promised to let him record gospel and have more say over his music. The next few years were less successful for Cash, who had fallen into drug addiction. His musical fortunes began to improve in about 1962, when he began touring with Maybelle Carter and her daughters Helen, June, and Anita. "Ring of Fire" (1963), which June cowrote with songwriter Merle Kilgore, marked a major return to the spotlight for Cash. For the next few years, he explored concept albums and folk revival topics, singing both western cowboy songs and songs of Native American heritage and social injustices, including "The Ballad of Ira Hayes." His first marriage dissolved, and in 1968 Cash married June Carter.

Cash's major career shift came in the late 1960s when he recorded a pair of live albums inside prisons. His concerts in 1968 at Folsom Prison, and a year later at San Quentin, hit at the peak of the country-rock phenomenon and established his public character as a brooding, outlaw figure. Although he had never served hard time and had only been incarcerated overnight on drug charges, Cash earned a reputation as residing on the outside of the law. Nonetheless, he enjoyed major commercial success during these years, and in 1969 hosted his own television show (his first guests were Bob Dylan and Joni Mitchell). During these years, he also solidified his image as the "man in black" with a song by that title. Throughout the 1970s, Cash experimented with movies, especially westerns, and continued to tour, although he had fewer and fewer hit singles. In 1985, he teamed up with Willie Nelson, Waylon Jennings, and Kris Kristofferson (see Chapter 10) to form the Highwaymen, a supergroup that recorded several classic country albums. His solo career, however, continued to decline, and by 1992, he was without a record contract altogether.

Cash's fortunes changed in 1994, when hip-hop producer Rick Rubin signed him to his new record label, American Recordings. Rubin saw the market potential of a legendary figure such as Cash in an era when hipster bands were increasingly fascinated by country rock, roots revival, and old hillbilly music. Cash and Rubin embarked on a series of award-winning albums that recaptured the stark, jagged minimalism and gothic song lyrics of Cash's early rockabilly days. They teamed him up with rock bands, and covered songs by a host of non-country artists. Both Cash's music and his legacy appealed to the alternative fan base during the late 1990s (see Chapter 14). Cash's rendition of "Hurt," by hard rock band Nine Inch Nails' Trent Reznor, sealed his reputation as a genre-defying patriarch of alternative country and roots rock. The accompanying video offered

viewers a tour through Cash's family memories, career highlights, and personal tribulations; when he died just seven months after filming the video, his fans treated it as his swan song.

Johnny Cash and June Carter Cash's romance was perhaps the most storied in all of pop culture, and her death in May 2003 devastated him. He passed away only a few months later. Their marriage had been one of the strongest forces in Cash's life. It tied him to country music royalty; the Carter Family, as the legendary first family of country music, automatically bestowed some weight on his career, simply by association. More practically, it gave him touring partners and access to an audience in the 1960s, when he badly needed that career boost. Cash always credited June with helping him battle his addictions and literally saving him from himself. Their story has lived on for fans in tribute songs (Heidi Newfield's recording of "Johnny and June," for instance), films (*Walk the Line* [2005], with Oscar-winning portrayals by Reese Witherspoon and Joaquin Phoenix), and, of course, their own duet recordings ("Jackson" [1968], which won a Grammy).

Figure 4-6 Johnny Cash and the Tennessee Two, Luther Perkins and Marshall Grant; note the basic rockabilly instrumentation.

Source: Southern Folklife Collection, Wilson Library, The University of North Carolina at Chapel Hill.

Listening Guide

"Folsom Prison Blues" (1955)

PERFORMER: Johnny Cash

SONGWRITER: Johnny Cash

ORIGINAL RELEASE: Sun 232

FORM: Strophic (twelve-bar blues)

STYLE: Rockabilly

Johnny Cash wrote "Folsom Prison Blues" while stationed in Germany. The origins of the song came to light, however, when Cash released it on his wildly popular *At Folsom Prison* album in 1968, when a pop singer and songwriter named Gordon Jenkins came forward to claim writer's credit for the song. Jenkins had written and recorded "Crescent City Blues" on a 1953 album that Cash owned, and from which he had lifted the melody, rhyme scheme, and some of the lyrics. At that time, Cash paid a settlement to Jenkins, and both names are credited on the song today. Considering that many fans today think of "Folsom Prison Blues" as the ultimate musical expression of Cash's dark, tortured, outsider persona, it is fascinating to hear the Jenkins version, on which vocalist Beverly Maher sings over a popular dance band with sweet horns and cocktail-style piano.

Cash's "Folsom Prison Blues" recording is early rockabilly in its most primal form: Cash played rhythm guitar; Luther Perkins picked out stark, minimalist guitar solos on his electric guitar; and Marshall Grant thumped out a bass line. This recording also illustrates Sam Phillips's talent for capturing his musicians in an unrestrained, raw performance. Perkins's guitar playing was rudimentary, and Grant was a self-taught bassist with almost no technical expertise. Phillips insisted on keeping the Tennessee Two as Cash's backing musicians because their sound had an exuberance that technical proficiency would obscure. Their sound was marked by a "boom-chuck-uh" rhythm that came from Grant's bass plus Cash's pulsing sock-rhythm guitar.

Where "Folsom Prison Blues" deviated from rockabilly's popular trends was in its story line and in Cash's vocals. The text is the musings of an unrepentant murderer doing time in Folsom Prison, listening to a train passing by and lamenting his lost freedom to roam and ramble. While that sort of tale had roots in country blues (similar themes were part of Jimmie Rodgers's songs, for instance, especially the various "Blue Yodels"), it did not match the dance-party and sexual-energy lyrics of most rockabilly tunes. Cash's voice was also different from most of the rockabilly stars. He avoided the extreme exaggerations of guttural grunts, yelps, and growls, although he did sing in extremely low registers. Those low notes (such as when he drops down at the end of each verse) became one of his signatures, and they offered some of the same seductive qualities that Elvis generated with his voice.

Although in the mid-1950s Cash had not yet adopted his "Man in Black" persona or cultivated his reputation for hard-living behavior, fans have looked back at this song as a way of finding the dark side in Cash's music from the very beginning. The line about shooting a man just to watch him die is often quoted by fans as the epitome of bad-boy country blues behavior, and fans measure other country singers in comparison to the pathos and gritty realism of those lyrics.

Those connections were further amplified when Cash opened his 1968 concerts in Folsom Prison with the song, and the version that was released on that live album, *At Folsom Prison,* appeared to fans to be a convict's own lament, sung from behind bars.

As is common in rockabilly, this song is based on a twelve-bar blues progression (see Appendix A), although Cash consistently drops the last bar of the pattern. The relationship of the text to the pattern of chords, however, is quite interesting. Each verse is four lines of text, organized as a pair of rhymed couplets. Country songwriting often relies on near rhymes or **slant rhymes**, which describes two words that share the same vowel sound but have different consonant sounds. Slant rhymes allow lyrics to sound more conversational and less stilted or formally constrained, while still invoking the structure of rhymed poetry. "Folsom Prison Blues" contains several instances of slant rhymes.

Lyrics	Rhyme
Line 1 . . . ends with bend	*a*
Line 2 . . . ends with when	*a*
Line 3 . . . ends with on	*b*
Line 4 . . . ends with –tone	*b*

Cash (and, before him, Jenkins) fit the four lines of each verse over the three sections of a twelve-bar blues progression in a pattern that can be traced back to African American boogie-blues recordings, especially in Memphis and further south in the Mississippi Delta area. Two famous blues artists who used this particular lyric form are Kokomo Arnold and Robert Johnson; the pattern is shown in Example 4-3.

"Folsom Prison Blues" Pattern

Relationship of text to music in each verse:

Lyrics:	*line 1,*		*line 2,*	
Chord progression:	**I**	**I**	**I**	**I**

	line 3,		*(pause in the vocal delivery)*	
	IV	**IV**	**I**	**I**

	line 4,		*(pause in the vocal delivery)*	
	V	**V**	**I**	*****

*In a standard twelve-bar blues progression, there would be an extra measure of music here. Cash, however, modifies the standard 12-bar blues progression by omitting the last measure. This lets him move more quickly to the next verse, but it also adds a sense of heightened tension and instability to the song's form. While most fans would not be consciously aware of the change in the pattern or its effects, anyone who is familiar with blues music would be subconsciously aware that the predicted pattern had been altered.

Example 4-3 Blues lyric structure as used in "Folsom Prison Blues" and earlier in some 1920s.

Continued

Listening Guide

"Folsom Prison Blues" (1955) Continued

TIME	FORM	LISTENING CUES	DISCUSSION
0:00	Introduction	guitar	Luther Perkins used a very simple guitar solo for the introduction. Notice the "freight train" boogie rhythms that start at the beginning of the song—these are the clicks and ticks that are created by the bass and the rhythm guitar.
0:06	Verse 1	"I hear the train …"	Cash strains a bit to sing the last note of the verse (on the word "San An-*tone*") because it is so low.
0:32	Verse 2	"When I was just …"	This verse includes arguably the most famous line in all of country music. Notice that the line stands out more because of the long pause in the vocal part after it.
0:58	Instrumental interlude	guitar	Here Perkins played a guitar solo on the upper strings of the guitar, much higher than he preferred. Toward the end of the solo (around 1:12), Perkins switches to playing simple chords, then fades out toward the end of the solo.
1:23	Verse 3	"I bet there's rich folks …"	Cash's voice includes hints of humor (where he laughs just a tiny bit while singing). Notice how his tone of voice changes on "…tortures me," which connects the song to a dark, desperate, and moody sound.
1:49	Instrumental interlude	guitar	Perkins again plays a solo over one verse of the song's chord progression, and again he resorts to playing simple chords at the end of the solo.
2:14	Verse 4	"Well, if they freed me …"	The train imagery here, especially the "lonesome whistle" and the description of the inside of the train, are reminiscent of earlier country songs, especially in the honky-tonk tradition.
2:39	Tag	guitar	Perkins ends with a low, rumbling guitar solo of only a few notes that is quite typical for his playing style.

Cash's labelmates at Sun Records included Carl Perkins (1932–1998), who walked into the studio in 1954 with a similar sound, that of a highly energized trio, backing his vocal antics. Unlike Cash and Elvis, Perkins had already been performing with a drummer, W. S. Holland, since 1953. The drums pushed his recordings even further afield from traditional country music, but Perkins, like Cash, toured and performed within the country genre. In 1956, Perkins released "Blue Suede

---

CROSSING OVER

In the mid-1950s, popular music experienced a large number of "crossover" hits, where a particular recording found success with an audience to whom it was not initially marketed, such as a country star showing up on the R&B charts. What this phenomenon really indicates is that the new musical styles did not line up with categories such as "country," "pop," and "R&B," which the trade magazines had ascribed to music based primarily on the audiences' class and race. The established genre categories simply did not account for white, middle-class teenagers who were interested in R&B, black teenagers who were interested in rockabilly, or teen audiences whose buying power displaced the stars of their parents' generation from the pop charts.

It is worth noting that neither country nor R&B lost their racial associations in the 1950s. White artists, including Elvis, occasionally appeared on the R&B charts, but black artists did not stake any claim to the country charts. Most crossover activity occurred on the pop charts; until that time, the pop charts had been out of reach for both country and R&B stars, with both of those genres relegated to "outsider" status within mainstream popular culture. With the advent of rock 'n' roll and rockabilly and the rise of the youth audience, hits that originated in the country or R&B markets routinely surged onto the pop charts. This happened so frequently that *Billboard* actually suspended publication of a separate R&B chart for a short time in the early 1960s because it became redundant once the R&B hits were all featured on the pop chart. The country charts, meanwhile, continued to reflect a core segment of the country audience, for whom whiteness remained a delineating characteristic of the music and their cultural identity.

Shoes," considered one of the all-time rockabilly classics. The song was a huge hit on the country charts, but it also **crossed over** onto both the pop charts and the R&B charts.

Sam Phillips continued his stint producing rockabilly stars with Jerry Lee Lewis (1935–) and Roy Orbison (1936–1988), although Orbison's biggest success would come after his rockabilly years. These musicians were working within the country genre and were widely embraced by large portions of the country audience. Nonetheless, the pulsating rhythms, frenzied vocals, hysterical teen fans, and sexual overtones that were rampant in rockabilly were shocking and offensive to more staid, conservative country fans, many of whom simply asserted that this music was not, after all, what they considered "real country."

Rockabilly Women

Women recorded rockabilly during the 1950s, but only in small numbers. The overtly sexual connotations of the music threatened the respectability of those few who ventured into the musical style, but those who did, notably Wanda Jackson and Charline Arthur, bravely paved the way for later generations of female rock and country artists. Wanda Jackson (1937–) was one of only a handful of women who sang rockabilly, and with that sound she left her mark on not only country but also rock 'n' roll, a genre even less welcoming to female singers in the 1950s. Jackson started performing at local concerts in Oklahoma when she was in high school. Her earliest music was in the core traditions of country, although she cultivated a pop image with costumes covered in fringe and sequins on short cocktail dresses. Most of her first recordings were straight-up honky-tonk. Jackson toured with (and briefly dated) a young Elvis Presley, who encouraged her to test out a rockabilly style. Jackson's voice easily adapted to the growling outcries and exaggerations of vocal effects that were valued in rockabilly. Unlike many of her contemporaries, who either stuck to more traditional country or moved entirely away from it, Jackson released different records and slipped back and forth between honky-tonk and hard-driving rockabilly, sometimes even in the same song, such as "I Gotta Know" (1956).

Charline Arthur (1929–1987) found her way into the music business through songwriting, as did many other country singers in the 1950s and '60s. From Henrietta, Texas, near the Oklahoma border, Arthur started singing on local radio stations as a teenager. Colonel Tom Parker, best known for managing Elvis's career, heard her music and helped her get a songwriting contract with the Hill & Range publishing firm, which specialized in country songs. From there, Arthur got a contract with RCA Records and began recording for producer Chet Atkins. Although her music was strongly laced with honky-tonk, she also delved into boogie and embraced enough of an R&B influence to connect her with early rockabilly. Although Arthur's fame was short-lived, other women followed her lead, including teenager Brenda Lee and Janis Martin, each of whom shaped a career that bridged country, pop, and rock 'n' roll.

Not only did these women make memorable recordings, they also changed the image of female country singers. Arthur in particular was known for wearing pants, for her outspoken opinions, and for her command of a stage. Singers such as Arthur challenged polite middle-class

Figure 4-7 Wanda Jackson, 1956.

Source: Courtesy of Country Music Hall of Fame and Museum.

norms of feminine, domestic decorum by behaving like "one of the boys." Their hardscrabble attitudes and strength of personalities reflected, instead, a growing independence in working-class women's identity in those years that had been sparked by the changes in gender roles during World War II; think, for instance, of the iconic image of Rosie the Riveter flexing her muscles on posters, and of the thousands of women who went to work and excelled in what had conventionally been men's jobs. Although the women's liberation movement was still a decade or so in the future, a strong, feminist, independent streak was emerging in country music.

Rock 'n' Roll and Country Connections beyond Sun

In the late 1950s, many other young singers steeped in country music's traditions entered the music business by merging country and rock 'n' roll. The Everly Brothers, Don (1937–) and Phil (1939–2014), grew up in Kentucky singing in their family's country band. Their father, Ike Everly, knew RCA producer Chet Atkins, and through his contacts, the brothers signed with Acuff-Rose as songwriters. They cultivated their country music heritage as a brother act (see Chapter 3), but with an updated sound that matched the rockabilly craze of the mid-1950s. In 1957, they signed with a small, independent label called Cadence Records, and released a number of hits, most famously "Bye Bye, Love." The Everly Brothers found their main audience within rock 'n' roll, but they kept alive the close harmony that tied them to traditional country music. They also maintained strong ties to the country music industry, and frequently worked with established, Nashville-based country songwriters. Many years later, when they experienced a lull in their career, the brothers returned to very traditional honky-tonk and hillbilly roots.

Unlike Elvis and the Everlys, who headed into rock rather than country as their careers blossomed, plenty of young rockabilly artists wound up back in more traditional country music. Among them are Waylon Jennings (1937–2002), Conway Twitty (1933–1993), and George Jones (1931–2013). Each of these artists would become a major star in the classic country era of the 1970s (see Chapters 8 and 9), yet each began singing in the hybrid rock/country/rockabilly scene of the mid-1950s. Waylon Jennings, for instance, started out as a bass player for early rock 'n' roll star Buddy Holly, whose music incorporated West Texas honky-tonk into its sound. Conway Twitty, originally from Mississippi, signed with Sun Records for a brief time in the mid-1950s, then switched to MGM, where he recorded several rock 'n' roll teen hits, styled in the same fashion as Elvis Presley's records during that time. In the late 1960s, he returned to country music, successfully marking a career path that other rock and pop stars would trace in later decades.

George Jones similarly launched a rockabilly career before he settled into the styles for which he is most famous. Jones grew up in East Texas, a fan of hillbilly and honky-tonk singers. After a short stint in the military, Jones signed with a regional, independent record label. In 1956 he moved to Mercury Records and cut several rockabilly tunes. "White Lightning" (1959), which featured dramatic, stop-time rhythms and rockabilly piano parts, reached the top of the country charts. Other records, including "Who Shot Sam," were quintessential rockabilly, complete with raw sound effects, rollicking piano, and a boogie-blues pattern. Jones kept pace with changes in country music, however, and by the mid-1960s, his style had mellowed and lost all traces of rockabilly.

Coming to an End

The rockabilly fad in country music was a brief one. For half a decade, the baby boomer audience, independent record labels, and a pervasive spirit of rebellion brought to life a new musical style that was equal parts country and R&B and that ushered in rock 'n' roll. But by 1959, the entire landscape of popular music had changed. Rock 'n' roll was still in its musical youth when, on February 3, 1959, a plane crash killed Buddy Holly, Ritchie Valens, and the Big Bopper (J. P. Richardson). Waylon Jennings missed being on the plane only because he gave up his seat at the last minute. Those three young stars were not the sum total of rock 'n' roll by any means, but the tragedy came to represent the end of an era (eulogized as "the day the music died" by songwriter Don McLean in "American Pie"), and the other stars of rock 'n' roll had lost their shine. Elvis Presley had been inducted into the army in 1958; Jerry Lee Lewis's reputation was tainted when, in 1958, a scandal broke about his marriage to a thirteen-year-old cousin; Chuck Berry was charged in 1959 with violating the Mann Act; and Little Richard had disavowed rock 'n' roll in 1957 and followed a calling into Christian ministry. The entire stable of artists who had put Sun Records on the map had jumped ship to other labels. Deejays and radio executives who had helped promote the music were under fire from accusations of payola, which was the practice of taking money and bribes in exchange for playing particular records, and which became illegal in 1960. In sum, by 1959, the first generation of rock 'n' roll, with its naive idealism and youthful energy, had passed.

Country music had also experienced the taste of the rewards—both economic and in terms of fame—afforded by crossover hits as country singers and recordings had briefly become that era's "popular" music. All those factors combined to end the rockabilly fad. By 1960, Johnny Cash was no longer recording anything that sounded like rockabilly, and he would not revisit the style until a few of his retrospective recordings in the mid-1990s.

Some country fans prefer to dismiss the entire rockabilly fad in country music as a momentary invasion by some outside force. Those fans view the intersection of rock 'n' roll and country music as a corruption of earlier, pristine hillbilly and traditional country music. What that perspective fails to consider is that rockabilly grew directly out of country music, motivated by the changes in audience and American culture in general during the 1950s. And, as always, when the identity of the fan base shifts, the music moves in a similar trajectory.

★ ESSAY: MUSICAL STYLE

Honky-Tonk

Honky-tonk music's characteristics include the following: five specific instruments, naturalized vocals, first-person confessional heartbreak lyrics, and stories in the texts that adopt a hell-raisin', good-times attitude balanced by a Sunday morning guilt trip.

The basic instrumentation for honky-tonk bands relied on five instruments: fiddle, steel guitar, acoustic rhythm guitar, electric lead guitar, and bass. In the 1940s, the steel players used console steel guitars (typically two guitar necks built into a wooden table-top platform); in the 1950s, players added new features to their steel guitars, most notably pedals. Famous honky-tonk steel players such as Don Helms and Bud Isaacs used particular musical gestures that became part of the style, such as starting on a low note and sliding to a high note. This sliding sound created the "cry" or "twang" for which honky-tonk is known. Fiddle players and steel guitar players typically took turns adding "musical fills," or short melodies, between the singer's phrases. Bass players still relied on upright, acoustic basses. The rhythm guitarists often used a "sock rhythm" style of playing, in which they would use their left hands to keep the strings from vibrating while striking the strings with their right hands, which created a percussive sound that was similar to a hi-hat in a drum set. The resulting "chuck" sound can be heard on beats 2 and 4 in honky-tonk recordings, and it adds a percussive effect to the music without actually using drums.

Beyond this core instrumentation, some honky-tonk artists included drums (especially in the 1950s) and piano. Other instruments appeared occasionally. Many honky-tonk recordings use swing rhythms and borrow from the western swing tradition in the rhythmic, danceable feel of their songs. Several leading stars of honky-tonk worked in East Texas and Louisiana, and particularly in the fiddling, one can often hear a Cajun influence.

The most important feature of honky-tonk music was the vocal style that most singers used. The vocal style does not feature any of the formal characteristics of a trained singer. Instead, the voice sounds "naturalized," or as if the singing is simply an extension of how a regular "guy" or "gal next door" might tell a story, with the expressive nature of speech appearing in the singing. Honky-tonk singers often allow cracks, pops, cries, quivers and breaks in their vocal performances when they increase the emotional impact of the song. They allow the timbre, or tone color, of their voices to vary between high notes and low notes, which a classically trained singer would try not to do. Many of them use a bright, nasal tone, which adds to the general characteristic some fans call twang in honky-tonk music. The effect of the honky-tonk vocals was that fans heard this music as honest, direct, and unmediated by the act of performance. In other words, the song came straight from the singer, without any fancy musical technique getting in the way.

Honky-tonk lyrics tended to adopt a first-person narrative approach ("I'm so lonesome I could cry"), which added to the audience's perception that the songs were the singer's own words. The lyrics also frequently address "you" in the text, which creates a sense of direct interpersonal communication (such as "Walking the floor over you").

Honky-tonk lyrics frequently describe an outlook on life that we can summarize as hard-living, devil-may-care Saturday night fun, with a corresponding guilt trip on Sunday morning. The philosophy of honky-tonk music was based on seeking empathy for the hard knocks of working-class life (especially when it came to heartbreak) and an evangelical Christian perspective on redemption. The songs describe human weakness, suffering, and indulgence in (sometimes sinful) pleasure along with accountability. That philosophy allowed both the singers and the fans to reconcile the "Live Fast, Love Hard, Die Young" songs with the gospel hymns that so many of the same artists recorded.

☆ ESSAY: CULTURE

 # Cajun Country

In the mid- to late 1950s, during the same years that rockabilly's infectious rhythms caught the attention of teenagers everywhere, Cajun music made significant inroads into country. Cajun music is the folk music of Acadians, people of French descent who, in the eighteenth century, were exiled from their Canadian settlements and relocated to Louisiana. Traditional Cajun music relies heavily on the fiddle and the accordion, and lyrics are often sung in French dialects. Throughout the nineteenth century, this music flourished at house parties and through local traditions. In 1928, Joe Falcon (accordion) and Cleoma Breaux (guitar) traveled to New Orleans and made the first commercial recordings of Cajun music for the Columbia Record Company. Mainstream American culture, however, stigmatized Cajun culture as poor and unsophisticated, and the recordings reached only a limited segment of the American listening public.

In the 1940s, many Acadians moved to Texas in search of war-era employment in port cities such as Port Arthur. Additional migration throughout the region meant that Cajun music thoroughly mixed with both western swing and honky-tonk. In 1946, Harry Choates (1922–1951), a band leader and fiddle player, recorded the Cajun waltz "Jole Blon" for an independent record label. Choates's version is a mid-tempo waltz with French lyrics sung in a distinctive, shrill tone. A number of radio disc jockeys took a liking to the recording, and with that publicity, "Jole Blon" became a huge hit. Within a few months of Choates's release, country artists including Roy Acuff did their own versions, which exposed an even larger audience to the song. This song's success pulled Cajun music toward broader acceptance and paved the way for more integration and ongoing musical exchanges between country music and Cajun music, most famously Hank Williams's "Jambalaya."

The most readily identifiable features of Cajun music, as it intersects with country, include:

1. The accordion and related instruments, with reedy, pulsing sounds
2. A rhythmic, two-beat pattern that emphasizes the weak beats (beats 2 and 4 when counting 1-2-3-4) and the subdivisions of the beats (the "ands" when counting 1-and-2-and-3-and-4-and) with pairs of straight eighth notes that produce a bouncing, lilting feel. The most common rhythmic pattern is shown in Example 4-4.
3. Fiddling that alternates long bow-strokes with two short ones (following the common rhythm showed in Example 4-4). Cajun fiddlers often play more than one note on the fiddle at once (called "double-stops"), using one of the notes as a drone pitch.

Example 4-4 Cajun fiddle rhythm commonly borrowed by country musicians.

In 1948, the Louisiana Hayride launched in Shreveport. The radio barn dance hosted country stars, including Webb Pierce and Hank Williams, but it also

Figure 4-8 Doug (with fiddle) and Rusty Kershaw.
Source: Gordon Gillingham photograph © Grand Ole Opry Archives.

employed Cajun musicians, most famously brothers Doug and Rusty Kershaw and Jimmy C. Newman. In the mid-1950s, these musicians became quite famous, and after a few years on the Hayride, those musicians were invited to join the Grand Ole Opry, thereby exporting Cajun music into the heart of country music. Those interactions have continued over the decades, with Cajun fiddling styles, rhythms, and references in song lyrics throughout country music. There have also been several times when Cajun music has surged in popularity within country. One such instance was the early 1990s, especially the New Country commercial country era, when songs such as Vince Gill's "Liza Jane" and "One More Last Chance," Mary Chapin Carpenter's "Down at the Twist and Shout," and even Garth Brooks's "Callin' Baton Rouge" put Cajun dance rhythms, the occasional accordion, and a distinctive Cajun fiddling style at the top of the country charts and all over country radio.

☆ ESSAY: MUSIC BUSINESS

 # Forces behind the Scene

Two incidents in the music business occurred in the early 1940s that increased the presence of country music nationwide and beyond. The first was a contract dispute between the National Association of Broadcasters (NAB) and the American Society of Composers, Authors, and Publishers (ASCAP). The NAB represented radio stations, while ASCAP was a performing rights organization that collected royalties and distributed them to composers who were members of the society when their songs were played on the radio or elsewhere. The contract between ASCAP and radio stations stipulated how much each station had to pay for the music they broadcast. The existing contract was scheduled to expire on December 31, 1940. In negotiating a new contract, ASCAP demanded a higher fee structure that the radio stations claimed would force them to pay $7.1 million, up from $4.3 million, in royalties. ASCAP further angered the radio stations by attempting to negotiate with small groups of them separately rather than deal with their appointed representatives. As a result, the radio stations were eager to find some way to license music that did not require them to deal exclusively with ASCAP.

ASCAP had been founded in 1914 as a practical way for its members to collect royalties. However, not all songwriters were members of ASCAP. The organization had strict rules governing who could join, and a complicated structure for distributing royalties that left newer members at a disadvantage. Most blues, folk, and hillbilly or country songwriters were not allowed to join ASCAP, whose leaders tended to look down their noses at songwriters who were not part of the social establishment, who did not read or write formal musical notation, and whose music they did not considered respectable, even if it was popular.

In response to the contract dispute with ASCAP, the broadcasters organized a new performing rights organization, Broadcast Music, Incorporated (BMI), in late 1939. Unlike ASCAP, BMI welcomed country songwriters and publishers, and set up a payment structure that was much fairer to the country songwriters. But the new organization needed songs, or else it would have nothing to license to the radio stations. BMI quickly built a catalog of songs that included lots of traditional, public domain numbers in new musical arrangements. But the real boon for BMI was that Ralph Peer's very successful publishing firm (see Chapter 2) became dissatisfied with its ASCAP contract. Peer's publishing houses switched to BMI, as did E.B. Marks, another highly respected publisher. With these two major additions to their catalog, BMI held licenses to enough music to meet the needs of radio stations, and country music was a disproportionately large part of that catalog. From January through October 1941, radio stations banned all ASCAP-licensed music and instead turned entirely to BMI music for their programs. Because so much of the BMI music was country, the genre and its songwriters got an enormous boost in exposure. Even after the contract disputes were settled, BMI continued to court country songwriters and publishers. In 1942, BMI even provided $2,500 in start-up funds to Roy Acuff and Fred Rose, whose Acuff-Rose publishing company would be the home of Hank Williams songs later in the decade. In other words, the ASCAP/NAB contract dispute both directly and indirectly granted country music tremendous national exposure in the early 1940s, and instigated the growth of Nashville's music-publishing empire.

The second music-business incident that benefited country music was a strike by the American Federation of Musicians (AFM) union after negotiations with record labels broke down. The strike, during which members of the musician's union refused to make any new recordings, began on August 1, 1942, leaving the record companies with only whatever stockpile of recordings they had amassed before the strike began. The first record companies to settle with the AFM in the fall of 1943 were Decca and Capitol, both of which featured large country divisions. Thus, when new recordings finally became available again, many of the first ones were country. The strike also exempted V-discs, which were made specifically to entertain American troops abroad. A disproportionate number of those consisted of country music, which helped spread country music internationally and introduced it to soldiers who would soon be returning home. Although neither the ASCAP/NAB dispute nor the AFM strike was targeted specifically at the country music genre, both incidents had a profoundly beneficial effect on the growth and dissemination of country music.

☆ **ESSAY: MUSICAL STYLE**

 # Rockabilly

Rockabilly in the mid-1950s was a unique style cultivated at Sun Records. Its musical characteristics are quite easy to spot and include:

- Three instruments: electric guitar, acoustic guitar, and acoustic bass
- Frequent use of the twelve-bar blues chord progression

- Swing rhythms and boogie patterns
- Percussive rhythms from slap bass and rhythm guitar
- Exaggerated vocal expressions
- Slap-back echo and reverberation added in the recording process
- Unbridled enthusiasm and careless energy
- Lyrics often about teen romance, sex, or partying

Rockabilly was a fusion of honky-tonk sounds with rhythm and blues, most specifically the jump blues tradition. The word "rockabilly" is most often used to describe white bands, even though the musical style blends both white and black musical traditions. The basic sound comes from the combination of three instruments as heard on both Johnny Cash's and Elvis Presley's early recordings: electric guitar, acoustic guitar, and acoustic bass. An acoustic bass provides both the foundation for the band and many of the percussive pops and slaps heard on the recordings. Bass players often adopted the "slap bass" style of playing that was common in R&B recordings, where the player snaps the strings so that they pop against the wood of the instrument's finger board as well as sounding the actual note. The acoustic rhythm guitar fills in the sound of the band with steady chords. In many instances, the rhythm guitarist would stop the strings from vibrating so that the resulting sound was a "chuck" noise, similar to the sock-rhythm playing heard in honky-tonk music. The guitarists also experimented with ways of adding even more percussion to the sound: Johnny Cash wove strips of paper between his guitar strings, for instance, to add a crackling noise to the music. The electric guitar contributed both brash solos and musical interjections between the vocal phrases. Although the style often came from those three instruments, some performers included drums in the basic rockabilly ensemble. Piano and saxophone were also common additions.

Rockabilly songs often relied on the twelve-bar blues chord progression or some slight variation of it. The songs used swing rhythms, which were common to the jump blues styles from which rockabilly evolved. And many of the rockabilly bands cultivated a "freight train" boogie sound, which emphasized the continual subdivisions of the beat and an intense wave of sound and energy. Johnny Cash's band was known for this particular sound. Rockabilly also employed lots of stop-time segments of songs, where the musicians stopped playing their steady chords and bass notes and instead played just one short chord per measure with a sharp chord (as heard on the introduction to "Blue Suede Shoes").

Rockabilly vocalists often used extreme exaggeration in their performances, sliding from very high, pinched notes to low, booming notes. They grunted, growled, snarled, and yelped in the performances. They interjected with call-out phrases such as "Ah, let's go, cat!" and "Right!" (both of which are heard from Carl Perkins in "Blue Suede Shoes"). Male performers often added guttural vocal interjections, which were interpreted as sexual utterances. To many of their fans, rockabilly vocals were an unfettered expression of both lustful desire and angst. Adding to the style's characteristics, record producers often added both reverberation and a slap-back echo effect on their recordings, where the sounds repeat themselves a fraction of a second later.

As was the case with Sam Phillips, rockabilly producers tended to cultivate performances that sounded under-rehearsed on purpose, and where audible enthusiasm was prized over technical precision. That unbridled energy and the reckless nature of the performances were important features of the music for millions of teenagers who were seeking a sonic form of rebellion. Most of the songs' lyrics addressed youth-centered topics: love, heartbreak, and rebellion.

Although rockabilly did not last long as a distinct musical style, many of its featured lingered in country music (and in rock music) for several decades and are still present today.

LISTEN SIDE-BY-SIDE

"In the Jailhouse Now"
Songwriter: Jimmie Rodgers
Jimmie Rodgers, 1928 (Victor 21245)
Webb Pierce, 1954 (Decca 29391)

TWO PERFORMANCES OF the same song, one from 1928 and one from 1954, readily reveal the differences between hillbilly and honky-tonk styles of country music. In February of 1928, Jimmie Rodgers (see Chapter 2) recorded "In the Jailhouse Now," a popular song from the burlesque and vaudeville stage traditions that had originally been sung by black entertainers. The song was a favorite among many different performers, including jazz dance bands, black jug bands, and blues artists, to name only a few. Even though Rodgers did not write the song (vaudeville performers Toots Davis and Eddie Stafford copyrighted it in 1915), he claimed his own arrangement, and over the years, wound up credited as the songwriter.

Rodgers's performance features his own guitar playing, plus his friend and sometime bandmate Ellsworth T. Cozzens on banjo. The guitar playing consists of Rodgers picking out bass notes, alternating with simple, strummed chords. Rodgers yodels in his typical style, and he is very free with the rhythms of his vocal phrases. For the banjo solos (at 1:02 and at 2:11 in the recording), Cozzens uses an old-time, frailing style of playing (striking the strings with the backs of his fingers rather than picking them). In terms of the song's form, Rodgers

sings a verse, then the chorus, followed by a yodel, and repeats that process for a total of three verses. Aspects of the 1920's recording process are also audible; one can easily hear moments when Rodgers misses a strum on the guitar, and the ending of the recording is surprisingly abrupt.

Webb Pierce grew up listening to his mother's collection of Jimmie Rodgers records, and when he starting recording and performing on the Louisiana Hayride, he frequently used Rodgers's songs. By December of 1954, Pierce was an established country star: he had already placed eight songs at the top of the *Billboard* country chart and was a member of the Grand Ole Opry. When he recorded "In the Jailhouse Now," he transformed the song into a honky-tonk hit, which wound up at as his ninth number-one on the *Billboard* country chart.

The instrumentation that Pierce used was electric lead guitar, rhythm guitar, steel guitar, bass, and fiddle, which was the classic honky-tonk lineup. Pierce supplemented this with a second fiddle player and additional rhythm guitars. The typical sock-rhythm "chuck" sound from the guitar adds a bit of percussion to the recording. A hint of boogie appears in the electric guitar (around 0:15). Pierce sings in a naturalized, nasal vocal style typical for honky-tonk. The Wilburn Brothers sing harmony on the recording. In terms of the song's form, Pierce alters the arrangement from Rodgers's version in two significant ways:

1. Pierce omits the yodel. Yodeling would have sounded quite out-of-date in 1954, and by leaving it out, Pierce makes the performance less about covering Rodgers and more a contemporary performance in his own style.
2. Pierce sings the chorus first, which catches the audience's attention right from the start with the catchiest part of the song, and he only sings two of the verses. Honky-tonk music often emphasized the danceable rhythms and memorable hooks in a song, rather than long recitations of verses.

Note also that in the last verse Jimmie Rodgers sings, "We took in every cabaret in town," using a word that refers to nightclubs that featured a variety of entertainment; such places were very popular in New York City in the 1910s. When Webb Pierce sings it, he changes the line to "We took in every honky-tonk in town," transforming the urban popular entertainment reference to one that was part of country culture in the 1950s.

Pierce's version was made in Castle Studios— one of the best in Nashville—under the direction of Owen Bradley, who would become one of the most influential and innovative producers in all of country music by the end of the decade (see Chapter 6). The honky-tonk recording reveals a directed professionalism that makes audible the transformation of the country music industry between 1928 and 1954.

PLAYLIST

Cash, Johnny, "I Walk the Line" (1956)

Frizzell, Lefty, "Always Late (With Your Kisses)" (1951)

Jones, George, "White Lightning" (1959)

Pierce, Webb, "Slowly" (1954)

Wells, Kitty, "It Wasn't God Who Made Honky Tonk Angels" (1952)

Williams, Hank, "Lovesick Blues" (1949)

FOR MORE READING

Bertrand, Michael. *Race, Rock, and Elvis*. Urbana: University of Illinois Press, 2000.

Brasseaux, Ryan André. *Cajun Breakdown: The Emergence of an American-Made Music*. New York: Oxford University Press, 2009.

Escott, Colin. *Good Rockin' Tonight: Sun Records and the Birth of Rock 'n' Roll*. New York: St. Martin's Press, 1992.

Laird, Tracey E.W. *Louisiana Hayride: Radio & Roots Music along the Red River*. New York: Oxford University Press, 2005.

Lang, Jeffrey J. *Smile When You Call Me a Hillbilly: Country Music's Struggle for Respectability, 1939–1954*. Athens: University of Georgia Press, 2004.

Peterson, Richard A. *Creating Country Music: Fabricating Authenticity*. Chicago: University of Chicago Press, 1997.

NAMES AND TERMS

Acuff-Rose	Frizzell, Lefty	Perkins, Luther
AFM strike	Grant, Marshall	Phillips, Sam
answer song	honky-tonk	Pierce, Webb
Arnold, Eddy	Jackson, Wanda	Presley, Elvis
Arthur, Charline	Jones, George	rock 'n' roll
ASCAP	Kershaw Brothers	rockabilly
BMI	Louisiana Hayride	Rose, Fred
boogie	LP record	Sun Studios
Cajun music	Maddox, Rose	teen crooner
Cash, Johnny	Maphis, Rose Lee	Tennessee Three
Choates, Harry	Memphis	Thompson, Hank
Cohn, Nudie	multitrack recording	Tubb, Ernest
Everly Brothers	novelty song	Wells, Kitty
Foley, Red	O'Day, Molly	Williams, Hank
Freed, Alan	Perkins, Carl	

REVIEW TOPICS

1. How does honky-tonk music both connect to country's past and open new avenues of development for its future?

2. What were the racial associations of country music in the 1940s and early '50s, and what factors contributed to and/or confounded those associations?

3. Discuss similarities and differences in the record labels' approaches and songwriting practices in country music of the 1940s and '50s compared with the earlier decades we have studied.

The Birth of Bluegrass

5

oday, some listeners think of bluegrass as an ancient mountain tradition that dates back to some primitive time in Appalachian history. In fact, the music known as bluegrass came into existence for the first time after World War II. In the mid-1940s, this new style was a youthful, energized, and thoroughly modern transformation of older string band music. In those early years, bluegrass was embedded in the country genre, just one more style among many. Yet over the next several decades, changes occurred in the music, in the audiences who liked it, and in the way that it was used in popular culture. Bluegrass became associated with notions of old-time, traditional, backwoods, and antimodernist ideas, and the music began to function more as a distinct genre that was separate from, rather than part of, country.

The Origins of Bluegrass

Bluegrass evolved from the string bands that were common across the southeast, but most especially in the region known as Appalachia, including the mountainous areas of eastern Kentucky and Tennessee, plus western North Carolina, Virginia, and West Virginia. String bands (see Chapter 1), which usually consisted of some combination of guitar, mandolin, banjo, and fiddle, served many purposes within local communities, including performing for the ubiquitous Saturday night dances and entertaining at various community functions, playing a mix of sacred and secular repertory. String bands made commercial recordings from the early 1920s onward, and the bands became a mainstay of radio stations in that decade. From the Fruit Jar Drinkers, who were on the Grand Ole Opry, to the all-girl Coon Creek Girls on the Renfro Valley Barn Dance, Gid Tanner and the Skillet Lickers in Georgia, or the Wills Fiddle Band (with Bob Wills) in Texas, string bands accounted for much of the country music that audiences heard on a daily or weekly basis throughout the 1920s and '30s.

The central figure in the history of bluegrass music, Bill Monroe (1911–1996; see Artist Profile), got his professional start in a string band with two of his brothers, Charlie (guitar) and Birch (fiddle). The trio, known as the Monroe Brothers, toured across the Midwest from about 1932 to 1934. By then, brother acts (see Chapter 3) were in high demand, and the string band's sound had been further refined from its previous incarnations, with increased attention to close vocal harmony and instrumental virtuosity. In that climate, Charlie got an invitation to join a radio show in Iowa in 1934. He took Bill with him (Birch stayed behind), and the Monroe Brothers earned a reputation as one of the best brother acts on the radio. In 1936, producer Eli Oberstein of Victor Records recorded the Monroe Brothers, who became even more popular as their records hit stores. But by 1938, the brothers were no longer getting along, and while performing in Raleigh, North Carolina, the

143

Bill Monroe (1911–1996)

Known as the "Father of Bluegrass," Bill Monroe is credited with the creation and dissemination of an entire musical style. Monroe was born September 13, 1911, near Rosine, Kentucky, the youngest of eight children. The family played music together, and Monroe picked up the mandolin, mainly because his brothers had already claimed other instruments. Monroe recalled learning musical skills from a black blues player named Arnold Shultz, along with Monroe's Uncle Pen Vandiver, a successful fiddler. Bill and his brother Charlie performed as the Monroe Brothers until a fight between them in 1938 dissolved the partnership. Charlie formed the Kentucky Pardners, and Bill hired his Blue Grass Boys. The band underwent personnel changes during World War II, but its lineup stabilized shortly thereafter with the addition of Lester Flatt and Earl Scruggs. For a few short years, Monroe's band was the crucible in which the new style of bluegrass was forged. Although Flatt and Scruggs left the Blue Grass Boys in 1948, Monroe retained his status as the revered figurehead of the musical style for another decade. By the late 1950s, however, other styles of country music had displaced bluegrass from the core of country music, and Monroe encountered difficulties keeping the band afloat economically.

Monroe's fortunes changed in the 1960s when folklorist/musician Ralph Rinzler brought Monroe's name to the attention of folk revival audiences, most significantly in a famous profile Rinzler wrote about him in *Sing Out!*, a major publication in the folk scene. Almost overnight, Monroe's reputation changed from an aging, crotchety band leader on the Opry to a celebrity and the founding father of the folk revival's much-loved bluegrass music. He rode that wave of success well into the 1970s. In the 1980s, he recorded a number of duets with younger bluegrass musicians, thereby passing down his legacy. He also remained a fixture on the Opry. In 1996, he suffered a debilitating stroke, and passed away just a few months later.

Monroe's most significant contributions to bluegrass include an innovative approach to playing the mandolin, his unique vocal sound, and a legacy of songs that he composed. Monroe developed a different style of mandolin playing in which he imitated the fluid and intricate melodies usually played on fiddle. This approach changed the mandolin's role in a band from a mainly supportive one to a leading one. He sang in an unusually high vocal range and with a tone that was piercing; his vocals spawned the "high lonesome" terminology for bluegrass. Finally, his role as a bandleader had a formative influence on all of bluegrass music: generations of musicians cut their professional teeth as members of his band, which was a rigorous training and proving ground. His influence spread even further through the musical careers of his former band members as they went on to successful careers. Countless songs pay tribute to him, his mandolin, his singing, and his songwriting, and he has remained the singular figurehead of bluegrass music.

two fought (questions about the provocation of this fight, whether ego, money, or women, remain unresolved) and went their separate ways.

Bill Monroe's experience in a string band and brother act proved crucial to the formation of bluegrass for several reasons. For one, Bill Monroe acquired years of experience on stage in front of an audience and developed incredible talent as a vocalist and mandolin player. During his extensive touring, and while working at several different radio stations, Monroe was exposed to diverse musical styles. And his bitter rivalry with his brother Charlie motivated him to put together a top-notch band and audition for the Grand Ole Opry, a critical step in disseminating his music more widely and transforming it into an established musical style.

Shortly after their split, Bill Monroe assembled a band he called the Blue Grass Boys and found work on radio stations, which he supplemented with concert appearances. In October 1939, Monroe and his band auditioned for the Opry and earned a spot on the show. To craft his band's sound, Monroe chose songs from many sources, including traditional string-band tunes that were essentially folk songs, but also more commercial songs, most notably hits by Jimmie Rodgers and other country stars. He then reshaped them with the rhythms and energy that he heard in contemporary styles such as jazz. He improvised (created new melodies for) solos that were adventurous and wandered further from the song's original melody than had been typical among either brother acts or earlier string bands. And his rhythms tended to use lots of **syncopation**. He played at breakneck speeds, and played and sang in higher keys than was common. All these characteristics came together in the song that he used for his Opry audition: "Muleskinner Blues."

Historians consider that performance the moment when bluegrass was conceived, even though Monroe's sound had not yet fully matured. "Muleskinner Blues"

Figure 5-1 Bill Monroe and his Blue Grass Boys in 1942 (from left): "Cousin Wilbur" Westbrook, "Stringbean," Howdy Forrester, Bill Monroe, and Clyde Moody; note the classic five-piece instrumentation.

Source: courtesy of Country Music Hall of Fame® and Museum.

Listening Guide

"Blue Moon of Kentucky" (1946)

PERFORMERS: Bill
Monroe and his Blue
Grass Boys

SONGWRITER: Bill
Monroe

ORIGINAL RELEASE:
Columbia 20370

FORM: AABA

STYLE: Bluegrass

"Blue Moon of Kentucky" is an anomaly among Monroe's late-1940s bluegrass recordings, but it is also a prime illustration of the range of songs within classic bluegrass. Monroe penned the song while driving from Florida back to his home state. The nostalgic song is set in slow triple meter (three-four time, sometimes called "waltz time"), and one can count 1 – 2 – 3 – 1 – 2 – 3 . . . along with the music. This gives the song a lilting rhythm and suggests the style of an old nineteenth-century sentimental song. The song's form positions it in the songwriting tradition of Tin Pan Alley; rather than the simple verse-chorus pattern of many folk songs, Monroe wrote the song in an AABA form, repeating the whole AABA pattern a second time in the recording. These AABA units are interspersed with fiddle and mandolin solos. The song's lyrics borrow from clichés similar to those of Bob Wills' "New San Antonio Rose": moonlit nights, lost love, and pining away under the stars.

The band for this session consisted of the most famous lineup in bluegrass history: Lester Flatt on guitar, Earl Scruggs on banjo, Bill Monroe on mandolin, Cedric Rainwater (Howard Watts) on bass, and Chubby Wise on fiddle. However, unlike most of that group's recordings, Flatt did not sing lead and Scruggs did not take a banjo solo. Instead, the song was a showcase for Bill Monroe, who sang without any additional vocal harmony and played an extended mandolin solo in the middle of the recording.

Although bluegrass is known for fast instrumental pieces with prominent banjo parts, there were a whole range of song types in bluegrass. Monroe's recordings of gospel songs, nostalgic waltzes such as this one, and blues numbers, among others, were all part of bluegrass. The vocal style heard here, with Monroe's high, piercing tenor voice singing the melody with occasional breaks and cries, and a hint of yodeling, illustrates the high lonesome sound that came to represent not only bluegrass music but also an idealized version of rural Appalachian culture.

This song gained further notoriety when Elvis Presley recorded it in a raucous rockabilly version in 1954. Comparison of the two highlights both the way that Monroe's music influenced the generation who would craft rock 'n' roll and how different their musical styles were.

was a cover of Jimmie Rodgers's "Blue Yodel No. 8," but Monroe's version changed its character. He sang it higher, faster, and with an elaborately drawn-out yodel that ended with a distinctive yelp in his voice. At the time, his band consisted of bass, mandolin, fiddle, and guitar. Although Monroe almost always played the mandolin, for this song, he switched to guitar. His pulsating guitar part provided the musical "drive" or energy (see essay on Bluegrass) that would become a critical characteristic of bluegrass.

The rest of the elements of bluegrass fell into place over the next five years. In 1942, Monroe hired a banjo player for his band named Dave "Stringbean" Akeman.

TIME	FORM	LISTENING CUES	DISCUSSION
0:00	Introduction	fiddle	The fiddle plays part of the melody, while the other instruments provide accompaniment.
0:14	A-section	"Blue moon of Kentucky..."	Bill Monroe's voice is particular piercing on this recording.
0:28	A-section	"Blue moon of Kentucky..."	Listen to the slight break or "cry" in Monroe's voice at the beginning of this section.
0:42	B-section	"It was on a moonlit..."	There are subtle hints of a yodel in this section, listen to the word "your" on "your love," for instance.
0:56	A-section	"Blue moon of Kentucky..."	The song form (AABA) means that the title line gets repeated a lot.
1:09	A-section (Instrumental)	mandolin solo	The tremolo technique is very clear here: Monroe plays the same note rapidly over and over on his mandolin so that the sound doesn't die away too fast.
1:23	A-section (Instrumental)	mandolin solo	Monroe plays two different notes at once in this solo, which lets the mandolin provide its own harmony.
1:36	A-section	"Blue moon of Kentucky..."	The whole AABA pattern repeats, beginning here.
1:50	A-section	"Blue moon of Kentucky..."	By this point in the recording, the lilting three-four waltz time lulls most listeners into a mellow mood.
2:04	A-section	fiddle solo	The understated fiddle solo here is a stark contrast to the typical banjo solos in bluegrass, which often have rapid-fire syncopated, showy passages.
2:18	A-section	fiddle solo	This fiddle solo continues the nostalgic, reflective mood of the song, while the mandolin provides a countermelody.
2:32	B-section	"It was on a moonlit..."	Monroe changes the melody here to incorporate more high notes (listen, for instance, to "night" at [2:34]).
2:46	A-section	"Blue moon of Kentucky..."	Notice at the very end of the song, Monroe's voice jumps up an octave to end on a falsetto high note (at [2:57]). This is a form of vocal yodeling, albeit a very understated one, just as Monroe yodeled in "Muleskinner Blues."

While banjos had been part of country music since its earliest recordings (recall Uncle Dave Macon or Charlie Poole, for instance, discussed in Chapter 1), the instrument would become a mainstay of bluegrass music. In 1945, the band's lineup crystallized as the most famous bluegrass ensemble in the music's history: Bill Monroe (mandolin), Chubby Wise (fiddle, 1915–1996), Howard Watts (bass, stage name Cedric Rainwater, 1913-1970), Lester Flatt (guitar, 1914–1979), and Earl Scruggs (banjo, 1924-2012). Flatt, from Overton County, Tennessee, sang lead on most of the band's recordings, and provided the strong, recognizable voice over which Bill

Monroe sang high tenor harmony. Flatt also was a remarkably talented guitarist who conceived the G-run (see essay on Bluegrass) and was particularly adept at playing the fast, syncopated songs that Monroe favored. Earl Scruggs (see Artist Profile) provided the single most identifiable element of the new musical style: a three-finger roll technique for playing the banjo, which is known as "Scruggs-style." By picking the strings with three fingers of his right hand (the thumb, index, and middle fingers), Scruggs was able to create syncopated banjo parts that added a heightened rhythmic energy to the songs. Prior to this innovation, many banjo players struck the strings of the banjo with their right hand closed into a partial fist, using techniques called frailing and clawhammer. Scruggs instead learned special three-finger techniques that were used in the North Carolina mountains by musicians such as Snuffy Jenkins and Charlie Poole, then modified that regional approach into his own style, with its emphasis on the rolling pattern of nonstop syncopation.

From 1945 to 1947, Monroe's Blue Grass Boys were a tightly rehearsed, virtuosic group of musicians who pioneered an original and distinctive style of string band music. Their records sold well, and they were widely regarded as part of country music's establishment. They toured extensively and played concerts with other country musicians, often with several different styles of country music appearing on the same program. Their music was not yet called bluegrass, however, nor had the style spread beyond Monroe's own band.

Monroe's band changed membership frequently, as did the lineups in bands of other styles. Monroe was a strict and demanding bandleader, and several of his musicians considered him difficult to get along with. Many of those musicians also realized that they could make more money as well as enjoy more artistic freedom if they fronted their own bands. In 1948, both Lester Flatt and Earl Scruggs left Monroe's band. The split was so acrimonious that Monroe attempted to stall Flatt & Scruggs's future career at several different times, and Flatt and Scruggs refused to appear at events where Monroe was playing. Within a few months of leaving, Flatt and Scruggs teamed up to form their own band, the Foggy Mountain Boys. Flatt and Scruggs continued to play music in the same basic style as when they were working for Monroe, which exported Monroe's sound from just one band to what would become a larger trend across many bands. Their departure also opened up slots in Monroe's band. Monroe filled those slots with young, talented bluegrass musicians, many of whom subsequently left to front their own groups or play with other ensembles. Monroe's band ended up serving as a sort of proving ground and professional training of the highest caliber for young bluegrass musicians who passed through its ranks over the years. That process helped spread bluegrass music to a large number of bands, and the style took on its own identity within country music.

First-Generation Bands

By the early 1950s, bluegrass had become a popular musical style in the Southeast, and several bands made names for themselves by playing music similar to Monroe's band. The two most significant were Flatt and Scruggs and the Foggy Mountain

ARTIST PROFILE

Earl Scruggs (1924–2012)

Over the span of Earl Scruggs' career, he changed from an architect and founding father of the new musical style into a progressive bluegrass artist experimenting with rock music and its intersections with roots music with a younger generation of collaborators. His personal relationships with fellow musicians ended in bitter fracture, first with Bill Monroe and later with his longtime collaborator Lester Flatt. Yet the importance of his initial contribution, the three-finger roll style of banjo playing that came to define bluegrass, cannot be overstated.

Scruggs was born in Shelby, North Carolina, and grew up playing banjo in the regionally distinct three-finger style with local string bands. He also worked in the textile mills, as had a full generation of North Carolina country musicians before him, which only served to motivate him toward a full-time career in music. In 1945, Bill Monroe invited Scruggs to join his band at their gig on the Grand Ole Opry. The combination of Scruggs's syncopated, aggressive banjo rhythms and Monroe's ability to drive the band toward a highly energized performance became the guiding force for the Blue Grass Boys in the late 1940s.

In 1948, Scruggs left Monroe's band, teamed up with Flatt, and married Louise, who became the new band's business manager. Scruggs credited her with turning them into a successful working band as opposed to just a bunch of people "out

picking and grinning." That business acumen differentiated them from the other bluegrass bands who struggled mightily in the changing landscape of the late-1950s music business.

Flatt and Scruggs named their new band after "Foggy Mountain Top," an old Carter Family song (see Chapter 2), which tied them to the early hillbilly tradition even while they were branching out into a more commercial, polished image. In 1969, Flatt and Scruggs parted ways over different visions of what direction to take their music in. Unlike Monroe, Flatt, and most notably Ralph Stanley, Scruggs left behind the core bluegrass approach that had become its own tradition and instead explored rock, folk rock, and other hybrid styles in the 1970s. The change cost him some attention from the hardcore bluegrass audience in those years, but it gained him a whole new following when he helped organize a groundbreaking recording session with the Nitty Gritty Dirt Band that brought together young California rockers with aging country legends such as Maybelle Carter, Jimmy Martin, and Roy Acuff (see Chapter 8). From that perspective, Scruggs embodied the idea of bluegrass as a musical style interacting with both country's past and its commercial present. Throughout his life, he remained one of the most celebrated figures in all of country music, with honors ranging from Grammy awards to a National Medal of Arts.

Boys, and Ralph and Carter Stanley and the Clinch Mountain Boys. While bluegrass was a relatively recent innovation in musical style, later generations of fans and musicians have looked back at this first generation of players and credited them with founding a tradition. Thus, the terms "classic" and "traditional" are sometimes used to describe the musical practices of this first generation of bluegrass artists.

Listening Guide

"Foggy Mountain Breakdown" (1949)

PERFORMERS: Flatt and Scruggs and the Foggy Mountain Boys

SONGWRITER: Earl Scruggs

ORIGINAL RELEASE: Mercury 6247

FORM: Strophic

STYLE: Bluegrass

Earl Scruggs modeled this banjo-focused showstopper on a tune called "Blue Grass Breakdown" that he had recorded in 1947 while in Bill Monroe's band. The chord progression and banjo melody are extremely similar, as is the structure of the song. "Foggy Mountain Breakdown" consists of just sixteen measures of music and three different chords. That unit, called a "chorus" in the Listening Guide, then repeats over and over, a total of twelve times in the recording, while first Scruggs and then Benny Sims (fiddle) improvise different solos over the chords. At the beginning, middle, and end of the recording, Scruggs plays the basic version of the tune with very little embellishment, which provides anchor points in the recording for the listener. At the end of each chorus, Flatt plays a distinctive G-run, which helps wrap up the chorus, gather the band together, and provide a rhythmic and melodic marker of the song's form.

Many of the distinctive traits of bluegrass banjo playing are audible in this recording. The syncopated rhythms show up throughout, as does the use of the drone note (a single pitch that repeats over and over within the pattern). Scruggs shows off the range of the banjo, moving from low to high and back again. Notes that slide from one pitch to another are also audible here. Mostly, however, it is the rapid-fire, staccato playing that sounds like a perpetual motion machine that most characterized bluegrass in the minds of many audiences.

Flatt and Scruggs's band had Sims on fiddle, Curly Seckler on mandolin, and Howard Watts (another alumnus of Bill Monroe's band like Flatt and Scruggs) on bass. In 1949, they sounded vibrant, relaxed, and loose, like they were thoroughly enjoying playing together. It is noteworthy that there are only banjo and fiddle solos in this recording; mandolin is curiously absent, a purposeful move on the part of Flatt and Scruggs to distance themselves from the sounds of Bill Monroe and his mandolin. "Blue Grass Breakdown," on which Scruggs modeled this piece, opened with a blistering mandolin solo. With "Foggy Mountain Breakdown," Flatt and Scruggs crafted an impressive banjo showcase, but really they were staking a claim to an independent identity as a band. The song eventually won Scruggs a Grammy after it was used in *Bonnie and Clyde*, and it provided them with a signature song (even sharing the name of their band) early in their career. But more than anything else, it redefined bluegrass in the minds of many listeners as fast-paced banjo-picking music.

Throughout the 1950s, Bill Monroe and his Blue Grass Boys remained one of the most successful groups, and they continued to be stars on the Opry. Flatt and Scruggs, meanwhile, signed a recording contract with Mercury Records in 1948 and found work on various radio stations in North Carolina, Tennessee, and Kentucky. Two years later, they moved to Columbia Records and started to focus more on

TIME	FORM	LISTENING CUES	DISCUSSION
0:00	Chorus 1	banjo	The first chorus presents the basic tune. Notice how at the end of every chorus, Flatt plays a distinctive G-run.
0:12	Chorus 2	banjo	On this second chorus, Scruggs plays the tune almost the same as in the first, which helps the listener get familiar with the pattern.
0:24	Chorus 3	banjo	Here Scruggs varies the tune a bit with more continuous patterns.
0:36	Chorus 4	fiddle	The first fiddle chorus uses long bow strokes and very few notes to outline the chord progression.
0:48	Chorus 5	fiddle	The second chorus with this fiddle solo continues the musical ideas from the first.
1:00	Chorus 6	banjo	Here Scruggs jumps to a higher register and plays a banjo solo. The "rhythmic drive" is particularly audible at 1:00.
1:12	Chorus 7	banjo	This chorus reaches the highest point on the banjo for the song, and then Scruggs systematically works back down to lower registers.
1:24	Chorus 8	banjo	This chorus is quite similar to Chorus 1 and reminds the listener about the basic tune in the middle of the recording.
1:36	Chorus 9	banjo	This chorus explores syncopation in the banjo patterns. Listen to the short pattern that repeats, starting at [1:45]. There, the banjo creates tension and excitement with a short, tumbling pattern of notes that repeats over and over again.
1:49	Chorus 10	fiddle	The fiddle imitates the sound of a train whistle at the beginning of this solo.
2:00	Chorus 11	fiddle	The fiddle starts in a high register, mimicking what the banjo had done in Chorus 6.
2:13	Chorus 12	banjo	The contrasts between the rapid-fire notes of the banjo and the long, drawn-out notes of the fiddle are made even more apparent here.
2:25	Chorus 13	banjo	Here Scruggs goes back to the original tune and repeats what we heard in Chorus 1. This signals that the song is wrapping up.
2:37	Tag	banjo	At the very end of the song, Scruggs plays a variation of "Shave and a haircut, two bits" as a short tag or punctuation on the end of the recording.

performing and recording original songs. Every few months, they moved to a different radio station, which allowed them continuous expansion into fresh territory and new audiences, thereby accumulating an even larger following.

Flatt and Scruggs contributed to bluegrass's development in four distinct areas: (1) as virtuosic performers, (2) as songwriters, (3) by changing their band's instrumentation, and (4) by their success with commercial sponsors and publicity. As performers, Scruggs's banjo playing and Flatt's vocals and guitar work were already admired by fans. As songwriters, many of their original compositions have since become bluegrass classics, the most famous being "Foggy Mountain Breakdown." Although Bill Monroe had included an accordion on several of his records shortly after World War II, and although he had used both harmonica and accordion on stage, the instrumentation of bluegrass had settled into a five-piece band: fiddle, banjo, mandolin, guitar, and bass. Flatt and Scruggs altered this, first by adding an additional acoustic guitar to their line-up, which gave a fuller and stronger rhythmic drive to their recordings. The sound of the second guitar moved the group closer to the sound of the most successful contemporary honky-tonk and traditional country singers, whose bands relied on a combination of rhythm guitar and a second guitar playing solos. Flatt and Scruggs's second change in instrumentation came in 1955, when they hired Burkett (Buck) "Uncle Josh" Graves. Graves had played bass for a number of Opry stars, but switched to Dobro in Flatt and Scruggs's band. Within a few years, many bluegrass bands adopted the Dobro as part of their standard instrumentation as well. In 1953, a representative from the Martha White Flour Company heard Flatt and Scruggs play and arranged for the company to sponsor the band on Nashville's WSM station. Flatt and Scruggs did not appear on the Opry program until 1955 (mostly because of Bill Monroe's antagonism toward them), but the sponsorship gave them a steady gig and widespread name recognition. It also continued the older, hillbilly tradition of bands taking on direct corporate sponsorship (see Chapter 3).

Figure 5-2 Flatt and Scruggs's band: Earl Scruggs (with banjo) and Lester Flatt (right); note the inclusion of the Dobro (center back) in their band.

Source: courtesy of Country Music Hall of Fame® and Museum.

> ## BLUEGRASS GETS A NAME
>
> Bill Monroe used the term "bluegrass" as a nostalgic reference to his home state of Kentucky when he named his band, and the term came to represent the whole musical style he and his band originated. According to several historians, Flatt and Scruggs were responsible for "bluegrass" coming to mean a particular musical style; at their concerts, fans often requested songs that they had performed or written while working for Bill Monroe in the 1940s. Given the extreme animosity between the two bands, fans referred to the songs obliquely as those "bluegrass songs," a reference to the name of Monroe's band, rather than request "Bill Monroe" songs. The term took on this new meaning, and by the mid-1950s was commonly used to describe the musical style.

Carter (1925–1966) and Ralph (1927–2016) Stanley also shaped the emergent style of bluegrass, mainly by anchoring it in more traditional sounds and styles. The Stanley brothers grew up in Dickenson County, Virginia, an area with a rich mountain music tradition. Ralph's mother taught him to play the banjo in the clawhammer style when he was a teenager. Both brothers served in the military during World War II. Upon their return, they decided to form a band in the tradition of the brother acts, with Carter on guitar and Ralph on banjo. They got a show on WCYB in Bristol, Tennessee, and they expanded their band to include mandolin, fiddle, and bass, calling it the Clinch Mountain Boys. The Stanleys were big fans of Bill Monroe, and for several years they copied his sound, his songs, and his musical style. They made recordings for an independent label which sold well in the Appalachian region, and which eventually caught the attention of other record labels. In 1949, they switched to Columbia Records. For a brief time in early 1951, the Stanleys disbanded, and Carter went to work for Bill Monroe, forging yet another direct tie between Monroe's band and the others in the emerging bluegrass scene. But in late 1951, the Stanleys regrouped and for the next fifteen years were heralded as one of the classic bluegrass bands.

The Stanley Brothers always maintained a more traditional sound than many of their bluegrass contemporaries. They often featured a high-baritone vocal arrangement, in which the melody was sung below two lines of harmony. Their vocal styles maintained the haunting, hollow sound of the Primitive Baptist religious tradition in which they were raised. They stuck to traditional repertory and instrumentation, and on occasion Ralph played banjo using older techniques. The Stanley Brothers kept the high lonesome sound (see essay on Bluegrass) alive later in the decade while many other bluegrass bands were moving in new directions. In 1966, Carter passed away from alcoholism, leaving Ralph to forge a solo career.

Bill Monroe, Flatt and Scruggs, and the Stanley Brothers formed the core of the first generation of bluegrass, but several other bands earned widespread fame during those years as well. Four additional groups are worth mentioning because their stardom lasted for decades and they proved extremely influential on later bands. Mac Wiseman (1925–) and Jimmy Martin (1927–2005) worked for Bill Monroe before each set out on his own. Banjoist Don Reno (1927–1984) worked for Monroe before teaming up with Red Smiley (1925–1972) to form Reno and Smiley. And brothers Jim (1927–2002) and

Figure 5-3 The Stanley Brothers.

Source: courtesy of Country Music Hall of Fame® and Museum.

Jesse (1929–) McReynolds combined as Jim & Jesse.

Certain commonalities emerged across the first generation of bluegrass bands. The musicians were mostly born in the 1920s, and almost all hailed from the rural Appalachian region. They grew up on country radio, listening to the brother acts and traditional bands such as Roy Acuff (see Chapter 2). They knew both commercial hits such as Jimmie Rodgers songs and folk ballads and fiddle tunes from the oral tradition. They knew each other, played in each other's bands, and blatantly copied each other's styles. They recorded widely in the early 1950s for major record labels, held jobs on local radio broadcasts with sponsors, and won audiences largely through their live performances. Their music was integrated into country; they played on country music concerts and tours and on the Grand Ole Opry, and their songs appeared on the various "Folk" and "Country & Western" *Billboard* charts that reported on recordings' popularity each week. For the first half of the 1950s, bluegrass was extremely popular in the Southeast, especially in Appalachia. By the second half of the 1950s, some bands were having a hard time competing for contracts because record companies turned their attention to other musical developments of those years, namely rockabilly (see Chapter 4) and rock 'n' roll, although a few, most notably Flatt and Scruggs, enjoyed unprecedented success. The 1960s, however, radically changed bluegrass music, directed it toward a different audience, and altered the way that fans interpreted its meaning.

Bluegrass Meets Folk

Around 1960, bluegrass music became the cultural site of a major clash regarding politics, musical meaning, and class identity. Up to that point, the music had been the domain of working-class Southerners, a combination of gospel songs and mountain ballads mixed with folk tunes, fiddle tunes, newly composed story songs, and lyrics about rural Appalachian life, pitched toward an audience that included older listeners as well as younger. Its performers and fans both viewed bluegrass as modern and forward-looking, albeit still respectful of older musical traditions. Yet around that time, the audiences caught up in the folk revival took an interest in bluegrass, which changed the music's audiences, interpretations, and regional and class identity. Many of the music's new fans were northeastern middle- and upper-class college-age people in cities and towns far outside Appalachia. For those audiences, bluegrass took on a very different meaning, one more strongly linked with an imagined rather than literal past; for the musicians, this attention was mostly welcome because it fostered more performance opportunities and more record sales.

The folk revival took root in the 1940s when musicians such as Woody Guthrie saw traditional folk songs as a way of connecting with working-class Americans and a means to promote labor unions, economic justice, and a left-wing political agenda. Musicians began to revive and perform old folk songs to resurrect and celebrate what they saw as a representation of working people's culture. At that time, it was relatively difficult to find 1920s and '30s hillbilly and blues recordings, even though there was growing interest in that music. In 1952, music collector Harry Smith compiled a six-volume set of LPs that contained old hillbilly and blues records, titled *Anthology of American Folk Music*. The album made available 1920s and '30s recordings that were previously unknown to urban listeners. For many young, aspiring musicians and political activists, the album was a gateway to music that represented natural folk culture, and its release contributed even further to the burgeoning interest in old-time music. Musicians such as Mike Seeger and Bob Dylan were among those who heard the album and were inspired to investigate folk music further.

Although the Harry Smith Anthology, as it was called, was a major event in the folk revival's history, many musicians, including Pete Seeger and the Weavers, were already performing acoustic versions of old folk songs. Their version of folk music was slowly moving into mainstream popular culture: the Weavers, for instance, placed songs such as "Goodnight Irene" on the pop charts and polished up the sound of folk music to widespread appeal. Yet folk music's assimilation into the popular mainstream was challenged in the early 1950s. The folk movement, with its leftist political associations and history of labor activism, faced staunch opposition from the political right in those years, as the Cold War fostered widespread fear of communism. In 1950, U.S. Senator Joseph McCarthy inflamed those fears in anticommunist speeches. That summer, an independent publication called *Red Channels* published a list of "suspected communists," which included prominent musicians and folklorists Pete Seeger and Alan Lomax. The ensuing period of heightened anticommunist activities and investigations was known as the Red Scare, and during that time the folk movement was heavily targeted.

One effect of these political developments was a deep rift between the genres of country and folk music. The two had been thoroughly interwoven from their start; both country music and the folk scene had shared musical roots in the Carter Family, Jimmie Rodgers, black blues musicians, string bands, and other vernacular recording artists from the 1920s and '30s. The protest songs of Kentucky coal miners or North Carolina textile workers were equally folk and country in their musical identities. Leading folk figures such as Woody Guthrie (see Chapter 3) were an integrated part of the country music scene in the 1930s. And both country and folk musicians touted the importance of tradition, chose songs that were anchored in working-class identity, and preserved older performance practices such as string bands and close vocal harmony. By the 1950s, however, the two were becoming distinct genres. Country music continued to be the working class's own music and carried a relatively conservative political identity, even while that audience's socioeconomic conditions were shifting in the postwar years (see Chapter 4). Folk music, meanwhile, had found an audience that included an upper-class cadre of young people attempting to position themselves against the political establishment, an audience that, for the most part, was distinct from the population of country fans. By the 1950s, country and folk were two distinct genres, marked by differences in geographic region, politics, and class identity.

After the flurry of anticommunist activities abated in the mid-1950s, the folk revival continued, though with less overtly political associations. In 1959, Alan Lomax, who was by then widely regarded as one of the twentieth century's leading folklorists and collector of folk songs, declared in a famous article that bluegrass was "folk music with overdrive," and that it was a new incarnation of the old folk traditions that he and other folk revivalists wanted to promote. This gave legitimacy to the music in the folk community, who had previously been largely unaware of bluegrass. Lomax organized a concert at Carnegie Hall in New York City of folk singers, bluesmen, gospel entertainers, and—a radical move—a bluegrass band, who earned the wildest acclaim from the New York City folk music audience. Bluegrass had become a source pool for the growing folk revival, and bluegrass musicians were its new stars.

The adoption of bluegrass into the folk revival affected the next generation of bluegrass musicians. Folk revivalists also altered the meaning and cultural practice of bluegrass:

- They touted the acoustic and interactive nature of the bluegrass musical performance as a pristine folk value.
- They equated the technical proficiency of the instrumentalists with a celebration of craft and traditional work.
- They separated bluegrass from other country music styles, which they did not embrace.
- They connected bluegrass to a live-festival and workshop tradition that continues to thrive today.

Many of the better-known bluegrass bands made records specifically for the folk revivalist audience during the late 1950s and early '60s, and published instructional booklets and song lyrics so the fans could learn the songs and the style themselves. The banjo in particular became the symbolic instrument of both bluegrass and the folk revival, and many enthusiastic urban, northern college students eagerly set out on pilgrimages to the Southern fiddle contests and conventions of the sort that Fiddlin' John Carson had played at in the 1910s and '20s (see Chapter 1). Some of the folk revivalist northerners who were fascinated by this music put together champion bluegrass bands. In 1960, for instance, one such group called the Greenbriar Boys won first place in the "old-time band" contest at North Carolina's famous Union Grove Fiddler's Convention. The Greenbriar Boys were considered outsiders from New York City—their mandolin player, Ralph Rinzler (1934–1994), was a college-educated son of a doctor. This marked a transformation in bluegrass's history, when a new group of participants without biographical connections to the first generation of bluegrass earned acceptance, and when the music shifted allegiances to a different genre.

The merging of bluegrass and the folk revival resulted in some bluegrass bands adopting the sweet vocal styles favored by commercial folk groups and losing some of the high lonesome sound of first-generation bluegrass. The most famous band to come out of this new bluegrass/folk context was the Country Gentlemen, which formed in 1957 in Washington, D.C. Even the Country Gentlemen's band name was an attempt to distance themselves from the rural, hayseed association of all the bands whose names ended with "boys." Although their membership has changed many times over the years, their classic lineup consisted of Charlie Waller, John Duffey, Eddy Adcock, and Tom Gray. Unlike most famous bluegrass bands, the Country Gentlemen did not include a fiddle player in their core group. They emphasized the smooth, resonant vocals that were popular with commercial folk singers such as the Kingston Trio, and their repertory included newly composed songs on "folk" topics as well as more traditional fare. Working in D.C. also gave them a different perspective on bluegrass music because they played for a largely urban and middle-class fan base.

The Country Gentlemen found major success in the mid-1960s with songs like "Bringing Mary Home," but they also started to affect the way that bluegrass was understood by its audiences. By the 1960s, some bluegrass fans adopted a traditionalist view of first-generation bluegrass and resisted any changes to the sound and style that stars such as Monroe had pioneered. In these fans' opinions, the Country Gentlemen were too much tied to the urban folk revival to be considered part of the lineage of bluegrass. For hard-core folk music enthusiasts, on the other hand, the Country Gentlemen were too commercial and musically polished, and not sufficiently invested in either traditional folk songs or the political content that more radical folk singers favored. Thus, the Country Gentlemen highlight the ongoing tensions about ideas of authenticity and tradition that were important to fans of both bluegrass and folk music.

Another musician who emerged from this collision of the folk revival and bluegrass music was Arthel Lane "Doc" Watson (1923–2012), from Deep Gap, North Carolina. Blind since a baby, Doc Watson grew up on traditional folk and mountain music and, like other musicians of his generation, heard countless radio programs and records in his youth—he has cited the Skillet Lickers (see Chapter 1), for instance, as one of his influences. He admired the guitar playing and singing of such country stars as Merle Travis and Joe Maphis (see Chapter 4, and Chapter 5's Listen Side by Side), as well as the guitar skills of the top Nashville studio session musicians such as Grady Martin. In the 1950s, Watson played electric guitar for a number of bands in and around Johnson City, Tennessee.

Watson's path to becoming a major star was through a local friend, Clarence "Tom" Ashley, an older banjo player who had recorded for Ralph Peer (among others) back in the 1920s. Ashley was famous among folk revivalists because one of his recordings showed up on the 1952 Harry Smith *Anthology of American Folk Music*. In 1960, Ashley attended the Union Grove Fiddler's Convention, where he met folklorist and urban bluegrass performer Ralph Rinzler. Rinzler was thrilled to have found a performer from the *Anthology*, and promptly arranged a series of recording sessions at Ashley's home for later that summer. Ashley brought Doc

---

IN SEARCH OF THE OLD

The story of how Doc Watson was discovered illustrates how bluegrass's meaning had shifted since the first generation of performers. When Bill Monroe invented bluegrass, he was playing music that was progressive and modern. Yet when Ralph Rinzler met Watson, Rinzler was explicitly looking for a living incarnation of a historical tradition. Rinzler, who was in a culturally powerful position to record and promote music, did not want the music Watson initially offered him. Instead, Watson had to adopt an explicitly retrospective musical identity in order to get recorded. This situation shares much in common with the early 1920s recordings of hillbilly music, where producers from outside the musical culture were searching for music that, to them, sounded old or authentic. In order to get a record made, the musicians often obliged. It is worth noting that although he built much of his reputation on his acoustic, folk identity, decades later, Watson made some rockabilly recordings, including the album titled *Docabilly*.

Watson along with him to the sessions. Much to Rinzler's dismay, Watson launched into some rockabilly with his electric guitar—the sort of music he had been playing at gigs around Johnston City. Rinzler had no interest in recording something so contemporary and so far removed from his vision of old-time music. Shortly before Rinzler left, however, he discovered that Watson could also play folk tunes in older styles astonishingly well. Rinzler found an acoustic guitar for Watson to borrow and included Watson on the *Old Time Music at Clarence Ashley's* albums from those recording sessions. From that point forward, Watson embraced a reputation as a folk, acoustic, and bluegrass musician, and began to tour and perform widely. He was featured at the Newport Folk Festival in 1964, which was the premier stage for folk musicians during those years (and the site where Bob Dylan would shock his folk music fans by going electric just a year later).

Watson's style of playing is known as flat-picking. He uses a single pick, held in his right hand, to play the guitar, as opposed to finger-picking, a style in which the guitarist wears picks on individual fingers of the right hand, and then uses the thumb and two (or more) fingers to individually pluck strings. Watson's flat-picking was particularly impressive and earned him a reputation as one of the premier guitarists in bluegrass. Watson was adept at picking fiddle tunes on the guitar at breathtaking speed, which influenced the next generation of bluegrass players, notably Clarence White (see Chapter 7). His musical style, however, focused overall more on the combination of his voice plus guitar playing.

From Bluegrass and Folk to Commercial Country

In the 1960s, many bluegrass bands adapted their music and performance style to the changing audience of folk revivalists. The Osborne Brothers, for instance, listened to and learned from the first generation of bluegrass stars but allowed their own music to evolve beyond that tradition. Much as Flatt and Scruggs had done, the Osbornes managed to forge strong commercial connections with the mainstream country music scene and found acceptance both with bluegrass fans and with the broader category of country fans.

Born in Kentucky, Bobby (1931–) and Sonny (1937–) Osborne grew up in Ohio and began performing locally in the late 1940s. Bobby was drafted into the Marine Corps in 1951, and while he was serving in the military, Sonny worked in Bill Monroe's band. At various times, the brothers also played with Jimmy Martin and with the Stanley Brothers, thereby making the rounds of several of the top bluegrass bands of the early 1950s. In 1955, the brothers returned to Dayton, Ohio, and formed their own band. A year later, they released "Ruby Are You Mad," a fast-paced, classic bluegrass tune written by Cousin Emmy that showcased Sonny's virtuosic banjo playing as well as their distinctive vocals. The song was a hit with country audiences, not just bluegrass audiences. From their earliest performances, the Osbornes were interested in finding the broadest possible audience for their music, and they felt no obligation to adhere strictly to bluegrass traditions.

A few years later, in 1960, a group of folk music enthusiasts at Antioch College, a small liberal arts school in Ohio, planned a bluegrass concert for the campus, believing that there were lots of students who would like the music. The organizers of the event had attended country music festivals and concerts for many years. They patterned the Antioch concert after those festivals, and hired the Osborne Brothers as the headliners. Historians have pointed out the significance of this concert as the first time bluegrass was played on a college campus. Much like Lomax's Carnegie Hall concert a year earlier, this event was part of a trend, fueled by the folk revival, in which college-educated, Northeastern urban audiences started to embrace bluegrass. In many cases, these new fans of bluegrass had no personal connections with the nostalgic rural existence that they believed bluegrass represented, and little or no experience with country music.

At the concert, the Osbornes performed in their usual style, mixing in sentimental folk songs, bluegrass breakdowns that featured lightning-fast banjo finger-work, casual joke telling and banter with the audience, and gospel songs. That combination was the expected norm for a country music concert or radio broadcast, much like what Roy Acuff had been doing for years, and much like what the Osborne Brothers typically did on stage at the WWVA Jamboree. This particular college audience, however, had no investment in this performance tradition. Bobby Osborne's jokes fell flat, and their invitation to the audience to head up to Wheeling, West Virginia, to hear the band play on the traditional country barn dance was received with laughter by college students apparently unable to take seriously the idea that they would go hear anything so "hillbilly." Similarly, the gospel song they sang was not well received. But the college students whistled and cheered wildly for the numbers that were primarily instrumental breakdowns with elaborate banjo playing. That audience equated bluegrass with fast banjo-picking tunes rather than with the whole range of topics and songs that were part of the typical bluegrass performance up to that time. The idea that "bluegrass" meant fast instrumental tunes was a very restrictive view of what was actually a much more diverse musical tradition.

Listening Guide

"Rocky Top" (1967)

PERFORMERS: The Osborne Brothers

SONGWRITERS: Felice and Boudleaux Bryant

ORIGINAL RELEASE: Decca 32242

FORM: Verse-chorus

STYLE: Bluegrass

This recording is one of the best known in all of bluegrass, thanks to its associations with the University of Tennessee sports teams, countless remixes and cover versions, and the enduring popularity of its humorous lyrics. Yet it was written and recorded by nonbluegrass musicians, and depicts some of the most extreme (and harsh) stereotypes of backwoods Appalachian culture, making its widespread acceptance as a bluegrass hit somewhat anomalous.

The Nashville-based songwriting team of Felice and Boudleaux Bryant, husband and wife, penned a straightforward verse-chorus song, with each verse a humorous rhymed couplet in which the singer reminisces about a place and time in Tennessee—a rural, bygone era in Appalachia—where mountain folk culture was preserved, where modern problems such as smog and bills didn't exist, where the ideal girl was both wild and sweet, where the locals brewed moonshine and outsiders were not welcome, and most importantly, where life was "simple." The song played on stereotypes of Appalachian life as simplistic and superior to the rat race of a modern, urban lifestyle, much as it was portrayed in several television shows during the 1960s. Like most country-music humor, the song is simultaneously a genuine expression of nostalgia and a parody done through exaggerations.

The Osborne's recording featured Bobby singing a high lead part (the melody) and playing mandolin, with Sonny playing banjo. The recording also included Hal Rugg on steel guitar, an instrument that was atypical for bluegrass and instead tied the recording to mainstream country music. Hargus Robbins played piano, Jerry Carrigan played drums, Lawrence Blackwell played bass, Ray Edenton played guitar, and Grady Martin played guitar. These were essentially the best studio players working in Nashville's mainstream country scene (see Chapter 6) rather than part of the bluegrass scene. In other words, while the Osbornes were bluegrass stars, and the use of banjo and Appalachian stereotypes marked the song as a bluegrass hit for its audiences, it was a product of the core Nashville country music industry (songwriters, song form, studio musicians, instrument choices) that happened to borrow the trappings of bluegrass.

"Rocky Top" was a major hit on country radio. From the vantage point of mainstream country music in 1967 and '68, this was a bold, banjo- and mandolin-flavored bluegrass recording. But from the vantage point of bluegrass music, this was a commercial country song with a few elements of bluegrass tucked into it. Those two perspectives highlight the complicated way that bluegrass and mainstream country music related to each other during those years.

TIME	FORM	LISTENING CUES	DISCUSSION
0:00	Introduction	banjo	The banjo is the most prominent instrument here, but the steel guitar (atypical for bluegrass) is also audible.
0:07	Verse 1	"Wish that I was..."	The lyrics describe an anti-modernist nostalgia (no "telephone bills" or "smog"). Notice the steel guitar provides the fills here between the vocal phrases.
0:20	Verse 2	"Once I had..."	Notice the banjo fills that are clearly audible between the singer's phrases.
0:32	Chorus	"Rocky Top, you'll..."	On the chorus, the vocal harmony is lower than the melody, a unique feature of the Osborne Brothers' style. The end of the chorus repeats the song's title twice in a row, reinforcing it in the listeners' memories.
0:48	Verse 3	"Once two strangers..."	The cultural stereotypes that will become part of bluegrass' reputation are present here: backwoods people who are closed to outsiders, who live beyond the reach of both law and civilization. These depictions intrigued many of bluegrass' new fans.
1:00	Verse 4	"Corn won't grow..."	This verse is a humorous reference to Southern moonshiners.
1:12	Chorus	"Rocky Top, you'll..."	This chorus matches the earlier one.
1:27	Instrumental interlude	banjo	The banjo plays a solo over the verse of the song.
1:39	Instrumental interlude	mandolin, then banjo	The mandolin takes over the solo here—notice the change in timbre. This section of the song is an instrumental solo on the chorus (based on its phrase structure and chord progression). There is a dramatic moment of stop-time at [1:42]. Following that, at [1:45], the banjo takes the solo again.
1:54	Verse 5	"I've had years..."	Here we get just one verse (a rhymed couplet) rather than two before the next chorus. That keeps the song under the three-minute length.
2:06	Chorus	"Rocky Top, you'll..."	This section is a good illustration of the rhythmic "drive" in bluegrass: it feels like the musicians are constantly accelerating through this part of the song.
2:21	Tag	"Rocky Top..."	After the final line of the chorus, we get another repetition of the song's title. Here, the vocalist goes up higher than he is comfortable. This makes the audience even more aware of the extremely high register of the bluegrass vocals throughout this song.

Figure 5-4 The Osborne Brothers.
Source: Courtesy of Country Music Hall of Fame® and Museum.

The Osborne Brothers continued to gain popularity and signed with Decca Records in 1963. A year later, they were inducted into the Grand Ole Opry. But their biggest success came in 1967, when they recorded "Rocky Top" (see Listening Guide). "Rocky Top" marked an important moment in the history of bluegrass for two reasons: first, it placed a bluegrass recording right in the middle of mainstream country, and, second, it illustrated one progressive direction in which bluegrass was moving. During the 1960s, mainstream country's sound veered in a very different direction (see Chapter 6) than bluegrass. The rise of festivals that featured exclusively bluegrass bands (see essay on Bluegrass Festivals) and the music's association with the folk revival had increased the split between bluegrass and country music. Furthermore, some of the most popular representations of bluegrass were seen on television shows such as the Andy Griffith Show, which portrayed bluegrass as a backwoods mountain music with no modernist identity at all. In 1967, the Osbornes fused mainstream, modern country, and bluegrass, albeit in a stereotypically mountain-music tale about moonshiners written by a couple of professional songwriters in the Nashville establishment. In the wake of "Rocky Top," three-finger bluegrass-style banjo enjoyed a noticeable resurgence on country radio hits, and bluegrass music was woven back into mainstream country once again.

The Osborne Brothers were particularly successful at merging bluegrass music with the commercial mainstream in part because they broke with musical conventions in their bluegrass performances. Their vocal harmony was unusual, for instance, in that Bobby sang the melody as the highest vocal part, with all the other vocal harmony lower, as opposed to the typical bluegrass approach that sandwiched the melody in between two lines of vocal harmony. In terms of instruments, Bobby played mandolin and Sonny played banjo, both of which were conventional, but beyond that, they experimented in the late 1960s with piano, drums, and electric guitars. In spite of these musical traits, they were revered as huge stars within the bluegrass scene and kept their fans in both the folk revival and mainstream country. Their musicianship, especially their songwriting, their clever musical arrangements, and Sonny's banjo skills, also earned them the respect of the music industry in Nashville. While their recordings represent a hybrid of bluegrass style and mainstream commercial country, they also hint at a major development within the bluegrass scene in the late 1960s and early '70s, in which some bluegrass bands sought a progressive reinterpretation of bluegrass (see Chapter 7).

Bluegrass as Symbol and Soundtrack

The folk revival had a strong effect on bluegrass music in the 1960s, but a second factor in its development was the music's use in television and film settings, which connected bluegrass to particular cultural stereotypes, actions, places, and plots in the minds of the American public. These appearances of bluegrass in television and movies also brought the music into contact with different recording practices, which changed the sound of bluegrass in some instances. It is likely that many listeners today associate bluegrass with certain cultural meanings and identities based on how the music was used in movies and television shows, starting in the early 1960s.

Historian and folklorist Neil Rosenberg traces the first usage of bluegrass in a soundtrack to 1961, when it accompanied some experimental, avant-garde short films that showed sports footage sped up with time-lapse photography. From that point forward, bluegrass was often used to reinforce scenes of people rushing or of intense yet repetitive actions. The sound of bluegrass's syncopated banjo technique, the fast tempo of the breakdowns, and the idea of perpetual repetition, particularly in the way musicians play the same notes over and over as part of the instrumental technique for both mandolin and banjo, all became associated with those visual images: chases, repetition, frantic behavior, and chaos.

The most influential use of bluegrass came a year later, however, in 1962, when CBS's producers for the television show "The Beverly Hillbillies" chose Flatt and Scruggs to record the theme song, "The Ballad of Jed Clampett." The television sitcom explored the cultural clash when a family of backwoods hillbillies strikes it rich and moves to Beverly Hills, California. Although the show's premise is based on the supposedly irreconcilable differences between the high-class urbanites and the hillbillies, the sitcom usually made the high-class city folk the butt of the jokes, which subtly reinforced the notion that there was great value in the simplistic and heavily stereotyped rural mountain culture. Less than two decades earlier, country musicians had struggled mightily to get rid of their music's "hillbilly" association, which many of them thought demeaned their performances, yet this show revived those connections. The song was written by the show's producer and sung by Jerry Scoggins, who had worked as a vocalist and musician for Gene Autry and in the Hollywood film industry before. But Flatt and Scruggs were the instrumentalists on the recording, and it became known as a "Flatt and Scruggs tune." The show was immensely popular, and based on that television exposure, Flatt and Scruggs recorded the song and released it as a single, with Flatt singing lead; that version reached number one on *Billboard's* country charts, the first time that a bluegrass tune had done so. This very popular recording was essentially a Hollywood version of bluegrass, quite different in many respects from what the contemporaneous bluegrass bands were doing: the vocals were pitched lower (matching the sound of the television show's theme) and recorded with lots of reverberation, there is more percussion on the recording, and Scruggs' banjo is featured continuously throughout, rather than trading off with other instruments or showcasing the ensemble as a whole. In that last respect, the recording amplified the banjo's symbolic representation of hillbilly identity. Even though the recording was a Hollywood interpretation of bluegrass, the tune furthered the associations between bluegrass, comedy, and backwoods mountain-folk culture within the popular American imagination.

In 1967, *Bonnie and Clyde* used yet another Flatt and Scruggs performance, "Foggy Mountain Breakdown," as its theme song. In that setting, bluegrass combined references to recklessness, high-speed driving, and the thrill of the chase with references to the counterculture, living outside the establishment, and a low-class earthiness and sexual tension. A more extreme case of these elements coming together was 1972's *Deliverance,* in which an traveling Atlanta businessman plays an impromptu duet with a local boy from a remote and backwoods "hillbilly" region of the South, portrayed in the film as aloof, mentally slow, physically abnormal, and unwilling to communicate with the outsiders except through his music. The guitar/banjo duet, titled "Dueling Banjos," became symbolic of the rest of the film, which suggested that middle-class America perceived backwoods Appalachian culture as having a dark and depraved side. Bluegrass, in that setting, represented something that was exotic, foreign yet American, tantalizing yet disturbing all at once. But it was also firmly linked to antimodern culture. In the years that followed, those associations became clichés within television and film. Blackened teeth and banjos were the formula for comedy on shows such as the television program *Hee Haw*, and truckin' movies and car chases were accompanied by the twang of bluegrass banjos in *Smokey and the Bandit* (1978), *Urban Cowboy* (1980), episodes of *The Dukes of Hazzard* (1978), and countless other movies and TV shows.

The Relationship between Bluegrass and Country

Bluegrass began as a specific style of country music, then moved further from the mainstream sounds of country music, periodically reconnecting with it. It remained part of the Grand Ole Opry's broadcasts throughout these years, an indication of its continued inclusion in the genre of country music. Yet it developed a more independent identity as well, almost becoming its own genre. Occasionally, songs such as "The Ballad of Jed Clampett" brought bluegrass back onto country radio, although it is ironic that this particular recording was as much the product of a Hollywood producer, songwriter, and commercial singer as it was a Flatt and

Scruggs piece. "Rocky Top" was a similar case in the late 1960s. Most significantly, fans and historians alike have sometimes viewed bluegrass during the 1950s and '60s as a counterbalance to the other developments in mainstream country that moved closer to pop and rock. To those listeners, bluegrass represented something less commercial (even though bluegrass artists were plenty interested in selling records to their audiences) and more traditional (even though bluegrass artists were constantly experimenting).

Bluegrass continued to evolve after the 1960s, both as a part of country music and as an independent musical genre, and we will explore those developments in several later chapters. The meaning fans have ascribed to bluegrass since its inception in 1945 has always been full of contradictions. It is simultaneously a modern, virtuosic form of string-band music pioneered by Monroe in the mid-1940s and a reflection of an idealized old-time, homespun tradition. It encompasses the sounds of the politically leftist folk revival and the sounds of Bill Monroe's sincere gospel recordings. It is the soundtrack of the backwards, uncouth hillbilly who either mocks or threatens the urban sophisticate, yet it appeals to countless northern, urban musicians who aspire to both play and experience its culture. It is viewed as anticommercial, yet also as a musical tradition that is fully entwined with commercial sponsorship, down to the jingles that bluegrass bands have made famous. It is both long-haired hippy music and conservative, traditionalist music. These intrinsic contradictions make it a fascinating field of study.

⭐ ESSAY: MUSICAL STYLE

Bluegrass

The musical style of the first generation of bluegrass stars came to be regarded as "classic" or "traditional" bluegrass, terms that recognize how later generations of fans and musicians looked back to the music of Monroe, Flatt and Scruggs, the Stanley Brothers, and others. Later developments in bluegrass are often described using the sound of those first bands as a reference point.

Classic bluegrass relies on five instruments and a distinctive style of singing for its musical identity. The instrumentation for a bluegrass band is:

1. banjo
2. mandolin
3. fiddle
4. acoustic guitar
5. acoustic bass

Along with those basic instruments, bands have included harmonica, accordion, and—most famously—Dobro. The way that the instruments are played and the way that they interact with each other in the music is what distinguishes bluegrass from other string-band styles. The most distinctive feature is the banjo, which is played in a three-finger, "Scruggs-style" rolling pattern. The highest-pitched string on a five-string banjo behaves as a drone, or in other words, a single note that the player repeats quite often. The three-finger style makes frequent use of that drone, and it also creates syncopated rhythms, where accents occur against the beat of the music.

The interaction between the instruments is a crucial part of bluegrass. The guitar, banjo, fiddle, and mandolin each participate in a form of musical conversation, in which the instruments play different interacting melodies at the same time to match the chords of a particular song, and then respond to each other in a form of musical dialogue. Often during a song, one instrument will play a solo, while the others will add short musical commentary between the phrases of the solo instrument.

Bluegrass performers have devised short musical patterns or melodies that are idiomatic to the different instruments (in other words, they match the way the instrument works particularly well) and that pop up regularly in these musical conversations. These patterns act as a type of musical interjection or punctuation within the "conversation" between the instruments. The most famous of these patterns is called a "Lester Flatt G-run," so named because Flatt played it regularly to mark the end of musical sections or phrases in his recordings (see example 5-1). Listen to "Blue Grass Breakdown" (1947), recorded by Bill Monroe and his Blue Grass Boys. Every sixteen measures of music (approximately every eleven seconds), Flatt plays the basic G-run pattern. Note that there are many variations of this pattern, and Flatt often leaves out one or two of the notes when playing it. The basic gesture, however, is easy to recognize, and is a stock pattern in bluegrass. It marks the end of each segment of the music and helps keep the instruments together within the song's form. Although the G-run is one of the easiest short patterns to spot by ear, there are others as well, that you may start to recognize. Together, the bluegrass instruments engage in an improvised yet familiar conversation, based on a particular song's melody and chord progression. And within that musical conversation, each instrument has particular gestures or patterns that it commonly contributes.

Bluegrass bands that adhere to the style's early traditions use acoustic instruments rather than electric ones. This fact has been widely touted by fans who

Example 5-1 A "Lester Flatt G-Run" shown in conventional musical notation (top line) and in tablature (bottom line). Note that there are many variations of this pattern as well.

associate acoustic instruments with a form of cultural authenticity, or who perceive acoustic instruments to be more representative of uncorrupted folk culture. Bill Monroe famously refused to let the Osborne Brothers use electric pickups on their instruments at one of his festivals in an attempt to preserve that tradition. However, in spite of this allegiance to acoustic instruments, bluegrass has always included electric amplification, or, in other words, microphones.

Microphones are necessary to balance out the different instruments and the style of singing so that the melody and various solos can be heard over the rest of the band, and so that larger audiences can hear the music. In fact, microphones are an integral part of performing on stage for bluegrass musicians. Many bluegrass bands adhere to the performance tradition of the first generation of performers and use only one or two omnidirectional microphones for the whole band instead of one mike for each performer. Those microphones pick up the sound from many different directions. In order to control which voice or instrument is the loudest, the musicians literally move around the stage, letting the person singing the melody, or the person taking the solo, step up to the mike. With the banjo and guitar necks sticking out, and with fiddle bows flying, all this motion becomes a complicated choreography. Dobro player Buck Graves described the movement on stage as different musicians in Flatt and Scruggs's band came up to the microphone: "They used to call us a football team at the Opry. Earl was the quarterback, and I was the running back. Earl would hand it off to me, and I'd cut through that hole. One time we had this boy come in [to play with the band] . . . and he'd forgotten the patterns that we'd run. That poor boy, I remember, I caught him on the back of the head with my Dobro neck. Liked to plumb knock him off the stage." While the performers' movements on stage served a practical purpose in using the microphone to control the balance in the band, it was also fascinating for the audience to watch the musicians weave in between each other, leaning in for the vocal parts, trading places physically as well as musically.

The vocal style of bluegrass is often called "high lonesome" singing. The term was the title of a Country Gentlemen song, which John Cohen borrowed and used as the name of a documentary he filmed in 1963 that included footage of Bill Monroe's band. From that point forward, "high lonesome" became a common description of Bill Monroe's singing as well as the vocal style common among the first generation of bluegrass bands. It refers to a thin, clear, and high-pitched vocal sound, usually a straight tone without any vibrato, and often nasal. As was common among the brother acts (see Chapter 3) that preceded bluegrass, male bluegrass vocalists often sang in the very highest regions of their vocal range. To accompany the melody, bluegrass singers add two or sometimes three additional vocal parts. The usual arrangement of those vocal harmony parts, often called the "stack," is a high tenor harmony line, then the song's melody in the middle, and a lower baritone harmony line sung beneath the melody. If a fourth voice is present, it might add a low bass part beneath the other three, especially in gospel repertory.

The rhythmic characteristics of bluegrass include the rapid, repeated notes heard in the mandolin and the syncopated patterns that come out of three-finger banjo style. But the term most often used to describe bluegrass rhythm is "drive."

In the faster songs, the performers create a sense that the music is constantly accelerating, even if the tempo never actually changes. To create this effect, they start with a strong pulse that is easily perceptible in the performance, and they clearly articulate the beat and the subdivisions of that beat. The melodies then use syncopated rhythms and are played so that they are almost imperceptibly ahead of the beat. Those features combine to create what is known as "rhythmic drive."

The musical style also comes from the songs that make up traditional bluegrass. While ballads, waltzes (such as "Blue Moon of Kentucky," see Listening Guide), and gospel hymns are common in bluegrass, the style is best known for its instrumental "breakdowns." The term refers to compositions, typically without any vocal parts, whose rhythms are so fast that they almost "break down" the music from the sheer speed and musical agility. In earlier times, breakdowns were specifically designed for lively, rowdy dancing. Within bluegrass, breakdowns consist of a short main melody and a chord progression. The chord pattern repeats while the instrumentalists take turns improvising solos over the chords.

☆ ESSAY: IDENTITY

 # Women in Bluegrass

With bands called "Blue Grass *Boys*," "Foggy Mountain *Boys*," "Clinch Mountain *Boys*," the "Virginia *Boys*," and even the "Country Gentle*men*," not to mention all the "Brothers" in early bluegrass, one might fairly wonder where the women were. The answer is that among the first and even second generation of bluegrass musicians, there were not very many female performers, and those who were part of the scene earned very little recognition. The reasons for that include the difficult life of touring and gigging that was simply hard on any musician, but especially on women. The social mores of the 1940s and '50s did not condone "nice" women on stage entertaining for money, and enough of the men in the music business—both organizers and musicians—had reputations as womanizers that the concerns were well founded. Bands moved from radio station to radio station and traveled extensively just to make ends meet, and few women were willing to put up with the lifestyle. Beyond those practical considerations, bluegrass earned a reputation as "men's music"; the raucous string band music that came before it and the amped-up "overdrive" that folklorist Alan Lomax described in the music were not conducive to a female presence.

A few remarkable women were able to succeed in spite of those cultural barriers. Sally Ann Forrester (1922–1999), for instance, played accordion on quite a few of Bill Monroe's recordings in the mid-1940s. She was, by all accounts, a phenomenal musician, and some historians assert that Bill Monroe kept her husband and fiddle player Howdy Forrester in his band so that she would play for him, too. A few years later, Bessie Lee Mauldin joined the Blue Grass Boys as bass player. Although not on stage, Earl's wife Louise Scruggs (1927–2006) helped shape bluegrass by handling the bookings for Flatt and Scruggs and managing the band's appearances

Figure 5-5 Bill Monroe and his Blue Grass Boys, c. 1945; after he hired Lester Flatt (second from left), and with Sally Ann Forrester (right) on accordion (one of the first women in bluegrass).

Source: Courtesy of Country Music Hall of Fame® and Museum.

for many years. She had a hand in their most important business decisions and music selections, as well. As was the case in other styles of country music, more women began to appear on the scene by the 1960s, often through family groups. Banjo player Roni Stoneman, the youngest daughter of Ernest Stoneman (see Chapter 1), became famous both with her family's band and later for her work on the television show *Hee Haw.* Folk singer Alice Gerrard, who had been at the Osborne Brothers' 1960 Antioch College concert, teamed up with Hazel Dickens, who grew up in Kentucky mining-town poverty and channeled her biography into writing and performing activist folk songs. The duo, as Hazel and Alice, recorded several unforgettable albums, and helped pave the way for other women who entered bluegrass through the folk revival.

By the 1970s, more women were appearing in bluegrass music. Fiddler Laurie Lewis (1950–) put together an all-female bluegrass band with Kathy Kallick (who later fronted her own band as well), and they earned the respect of their audiences based on their musicianship. The trend continued into the 1980s, when more female-led bands began to appear, both in bluegrass and beyond. Emmylou Harris (1947–, see Chapter 13) recorded a landmark bluegrass album, *Roses in the Snow*, with her Hot Band, which included future stars such as Ricky Skaggs. Harris's band paved the way for later luminaries such as Rhonda Vincent (1962–) and Dale Ann Bradley. Fiddle player and vocalist Alison Krauss (1971–, see Chapters 13 and 14) not only fronted one of the most successful bluegrass bands of recent decades, but also scored mainstream hits with her bluegrass-infused recordings. Other female instrumentalists have occasionally been lauded by the bluegrass industry, most notably bassist Missy Raines (1962–), who took home seven awards from the International Bluegrass Music Association between 1998 and 2007, and Kristin Scott Benson (1976–), who was awarded IBMA Banjo Player of the Year 2008–2011. Today there is an increasing number of female stars, from Sierra Hull to Molly Tuttle, and many of the best new bands such as Flatt Lonesome and Mile Twelve include women. Nonetheless, bluegrass remains dominated by male performers. That situation simply makes Sally Ann Forrester and her few female colleagues all the more impressive for staking a claim to the music so early on.

☆ ESSAY: CULTURE

 # Bluegrass Festivals

Between the tradition of country jamborees and folk revival concerts, it is little wonder that bluegrass has taken up residence in the world of music festivals. The music's anticommercial and antimodern associations have never melded well with commercial radio, but have nested well in the setting of outdoor events that promise some sort of physical as well as musical escape from contemporary urban life. Furthermore, the improvisatory nature of the music, combined with the emphasis on interactions between the instruments and between the voices, lends itself to live performance rather than recordings.

The origins of the bluegrass festival are traced to 1961, when an all-day bluegrass event with six of the top bluegrass bands, including the Country Gentlemen, Bill Monroe, and the Stanley Brothers, took place at Oak Leaf Park in Virginia. Prior to that time, country music shows typically only had one bluegrass band on the lineup, but the audience responded well to this different approach. In 1965, the first full-fledged bluegrass festival took place at Fincastle, Virginia, near Roanoke. Organizers Carlton Haney and Ralph Rinzler patterned the event after a combination of folk festivals like the famous Newport Folk Festival and country music jamborees. Concerts, workshops, and plenty of participation from audiences in the form of picking sessions set the model in place for future festivals. In 1967, Bill Monroe launched his own event, which he named Bean Blossom. Popular culture embraced music festivals in many different genres during these years. The "Summer of Love" of 1967, which was a music-infused gathering of several thousand hippies in California as a type of impromptu festival, gave way to the legendary Monterey Pop Festival. Just two years later, Woodstock, in upstate New York, hosted what is now the best-known music festival. Bluegrass was merely jumping on the bandwagon, so to speak, with its burgeoning festival culture. By the early 1970s, annual festivals had sprung up in Colorado, the Midwest, and both coasts, and new ones appeared each year. One of the most influential is Merlefest in North Carolina, founded by Doc Watson in 1988, who named it in honor of his son who had passed away.

Bluegrass continues to favor the festival format, which helps distinguish the music from other styles of country. Ticket prices belie the music's supposed folk accessibility, but festival grounds remain the most conducive home to the music's continued evolution.

LISTEN SIDE BY SIDE
"Blue Moon of Kentucky"
Songwriter: Bill Monroe
Bill Monroe, 1946 (Columbia 37888)
Elvis Presley, 1954 (Sun 209)
Bill Monroe, 1954 (Decca 9-29289)

IN 1954, ELVIS PRESLEY was in Sun Studios trying to come up with a second tune to record for the other side of his first single, "That's All Right." Presley knew Bill Monroe's music well, especially from the late 1940s when Monroe had Flatt and Scruggs in his band. According to guitarist Scotty Moore's account, bass player Bill Black started clowning around with "Blue Moon of Kentucky," imitating Monroe's high-pitched singing. Presley and Moore joined in, and they worked up the song as their flip side.

Presley's performance took the song that Monroe had written and recorded in a classic bluegrass style and performed it in the rockabilly style. Notice the following changes:

- Rhythm: Monroe's recording was in triple meter ("waltz time"), where the music is counted 1-2-3. Waltzes were not part of the basic rockabilly or rock 'n' roll aesthetic. Instead, Presley switched to a quadruple meter ("four-four time"), where the music is counted 1-2-3-4.
- Instrumentation: instead of the five-piece acoustic bluegrass instrumentation, here we hear rhythm guitar (Presley), electric lead guitar (Moore), and upright bass (Black).

- Vocal style: notice Presley's pulsating interjections throughout the performance ("Well, I said . . ." and "uh-shining"), as well as the rhythmic pulsing of his vocals in the introduction ("You're gon-**na** bring **a'** me back **a'** my **a'**baby tonight").
- Style of playing: during the electric guitar solos (0:52 and 1:26), the slap-bass technique is clearly audible, where Black is creating percussive pops and snapping sounds.
- Story: Monroe's song is one of pure nostalgia and heartbreak. Presley adds a new line of text in his introduction, asking the moon to bring back his "baby" (the term itself hinting at the 1950s date). This transforms the song's story from one of passive reflection on loss into plea for a change in fortune ("bring me back my baby").

Elvis Presley's version of the song both pays tribute to the original artist and puts his own stamp of identity on it, in this case through quite a dramatic musical transformation, the two key elements of a cover song.

Monroe heard Elvis's version almost immediately upon its release and decided to rerecord the song himself. In 1954, Monroe took his band back into the studio to do another version of "Blue Moon of Kentucky." The first minute of the recording is stylistically very similar to his 1946 version, but after he finishes the song's lyrics, the band changes meters and speeds up the tempo dramatically. The rest of the recording is essentially Monroe's bluegrass band covering Elvis's rockabilly version, which was a cover of Monroe's original.

LISTEN SIDE-BY-SIDE

"Dim Lights, Thick Smoke (And Loud, Loud Music)"

Songwriters: Joe Maphis, Rose Lee Maphis, and Max Fidler
Flatt and Scruggs (1952)
Joe and Rose Lee Maphis (1953)

"DIM LIGHTS, THICK Smoke (And Loud, Loud Music)" illustrates the way that a song moves fluidly between musical genres, while also showcasing the sonic differences between honky tonk and bluegrass. The song echoes the themes of "The Wild Side of Life" and honky tonk more generally (see Chapter 4), with lyrics that accuse a woman of wanting to have "a drink with the first guy you meet" instead of being a loving wife and mother. The song's writer, Joe Maphis, was from Virginia, and started his musical career on the barn dances and radio shows of the 1940s. In 1951, he moved to California, where he built a career as a honky tonk musician along with his wife Rose Lee Maphis. He wrote the song in 1952, and shared writing credit with his friend Max Fidler, who published the song, and with Rose. Rose later recalled in an interview that he shared the writing credit with her so that together they would get two-thirds of the writers' royalties.

The chronology of the various recordings of the song runs counter to the typical story of a musician writing a song, and then another musician covering it. Maphis's publisher Max Fidler knew one of the Columbia Records A&R (artist and repertory) men—whose job included helping to find songs for their artists. Flatt and Scruggs had just recently signed with Columbia and were gearing up for a session. Thus, the song made its way from the songwriter to the publisher, to an A&R man, and then to a band that was about to do a recording session. In 1952, Flatt and Scruggs released the first recording of the song. The musicians in their band at this time were exceptional: fiddler Benny Martin, mandolinist Curly Seckler, and bassist Jody Rainwater (Charles Johnson). Three-part vocal harmony on the chorus and the instrumentation mark the song as distinctly bluegrass, and the fiddle's introduction is unexpected, a tad strident, and memorable.

A year after Flatt and Scruggs released the song, Joe and Rose Lee Maphis made their own recording. Rose sang a single line of vocal harmony above Joe's lead. Sock-rhythm guitar, electric lead, steel guitar, and a touch of fiddle create the essence of honky-tonk, and Maphis's vocals project the expected "cry" of the style. In this recording, the style and the lyrics line up exactly as one might expect in a honky tonk recording.

As years passed, the bluegrass version made its way onto a number of compilations and "Essentials" albums of Flatt and Scruggs's music, thereby becoming gaining stature as a "Flatt and Scruggs number." Furthermore, fans who look only at the chronology of the recordings might be led to believe that Flatt and Scruggs' was the "original" version, so to speak, and Maphis's version a cover.

The story of the song's origin is exactly the opposite: Maphis reported that he was inspired to write the song after seeing Buck Owens play at a legendary honky tonk. Thus, the origins of the song are reflective of the first-person experience of the writer, Maphis. Close comparison of the two versions lets us hear the differences in style between bluegrass and honky tonk quite clearly, while the story of the song's origins highlights the two styles' shared kinship—both musically and within the songwriting, publishing, and recording industries.

PLAYLIST

Country Gentlemen, "Fox on the Run" (1971)

Flatt and Scruggs. "The Ballad of Jed Clampett" (1962)

Monroe, Bill. "Blue Grass Breakdown" (1947)

Monroe, Bill. "Muleskinner Blues" (1940)

Stanley Brothers. "The White Dove" (1949)

FOR MORE READING

Cantwell, Robert. *Bluegrass Breakdown: The Making of the Old Southern Sound*. Urbana: University of Illinois Press, 1984.

Cohen, Ronald D. *Rainbow Quest: The Folk Music Revival and American Society, 1940–1970*. Amherst: University of Massachusetts Press, 2002.

Goldsmith, Thomas, ed. *The Bluegrass Reader*. Urbana: University of Illinois Press, 2004.

Henry, Murphy Hicks. *Pretty Good for a Girl: Women in Bluegrass*. Urbana: University of Illinois Press, 2013.

Rosenberg, Neil V. *Bluegrass: A History*, rev. paperback ed. Urbana: University of Illinois Press, 2005.

Stanley, Ralph. *Man of Constant Sorrow: My Life and Times*. New York: Gotham Books, 2009.

NAMES AND TERMS

Anthology of American Folk Music	flat-picking	Osborne Brothers
Beverly Hillbillies, The	Flatt, Lester	rhythmic drive
bluegrass	folk revival	Rinzler, Ralph
breakdown	Forrester, Sally Ann	Scruggs, Earl
Country Gentlemen	high lonesome sound	Stanley Brothers
"Dueling Banjos"	Lester Flatt G-Run	three-finger roll
	Monroe, Bill	Watson, Doc

REVIEW TOPICS

1. What aspects of class identity that are entangled with bluegrass, and how and why did the music appeal to people of very different social classes and backgrounds?

2. How is the basic tension between tradition and innovation realized in bluegrass music?

3. Discuss the conceptual differences between live performance and recordings as they pertain to bluegrass music and culture.

The Nashville
Sound and Musical
Innovation

From about 1957 to the 1960s and beyond, mainstream country music's style changed to the "Nashville sound." The phrase first appeared in print in 1958 in *The Music Reporter*, a trade magazine that kept tabs on the country music industry. Two years later, *Time* used it to describe the latest country offerings, and by the early 1960s it was a common way of labeling the new developments in country music. The Nashville sound blossomed in the late 1950s and the first few years of the 1960s. It characterized the music of a new generation of stars who were working with a few key **producers** and a small group of songwriters and session musicians. It also described the changes that an older generation of stars brought to their music, which in several cases revitalized their careers. By the mid-1960s, however, the musical style began to change subtly, and it became a foil against which other developments defined themselves. Within a decade, the sound evolved into the classic country style of the 1970s (see Chapter 8) while still maintaining many of the features that first appeared in the late 1950s. Ever since the 1960s, country music historians have been struggling over how to explain the Nashville sound and how to make sense of it within the history of country music. It is one of the most polarizing and polemical topics in all of country music, because it challenges the distinctions between country and pop as well as country's allegiance to tradition.

The Business Behind the Nashville Sound

Two main catalysts prompted the development of the Nashville sound. The first was the drastic change in popular culture and the role of music within teen culture that occurred with the arrival of rock 'n' roll in the 1950s (see Chapter 4). Musicians, record label executives, and fans alike were aware that the market for popular music of all genres had expanded. The second was a restructuring of country music that changed how artists managed their careers and how records got made in Nashville. Several savvy executives, including Steve Sholes, head of the country Artists and Repertoire (**A&R**) division at RCA, recognized that country music could reach and satisfy a larger audience than anyone had previously thought. As the major record labels—Columbia, Decca, RCA, and Capitol—paid more attention to country music, their producers and executives gained greater influence over the sound of the music. One component of the Nashville sound was a shift in power from the artists themselves to the producers and to the corresponding infrastructure of songwriters, publishers, recording studio technicians, and session musicians.

Chet Atkins (1924–2001)

Chet Atkins enjoyed three separate careers in country music, all rolled together: a finger-picking guitar player of unparalleled talent; the producer behind the Nashville sound; and the executive responsible for transforming the country music industry from the top down.

From Luttrell, Tennessee, Atkins grew up playing both fiddle and guitar. He was inspired by Merle Travis's style of playing, and made the guitar his home instrument. After he finished high school in Georgia, Atkins accompanied various country singers who had radio gigs. He worked in Knoxville, Nashville, Cincinnati, and Springfield, backing artists such as Maybelle and the Carter Sisters, Red Foley, and Johnnie and Jack. Atkins developed a finger-picking style, similar to Merle Travis's, that allowed him to play intricate melodies and harmonies at the same time, for which he earned wide acclaim. In 1947, Steve Sholes, who would later sign Elvis Presley to RCA, offered Atkins a recording contract as both a singer and a guitarist. Meanwhile, Atkins became one of the A-list session guitarists in Nashville. By the mid-1950s, Atkins's guitar albums were selling moderately well, and he enjoyed two chart hits.

Sholes, who was based in New York, began relying on Atkins to fill in as producer for RCA's recordings in Nashville. In 1955, Atkins became manager of RCA's Nashville studio. Two years later, Sholes turned exclusively to the pop division of RCA, mostly to handle Elvis Presley's burgeoning career, and Atkins took over Nashville's division of RCA. In that role, he signed artists to the RCA roster, handled the studio sessions, and had a hand in selecting the songs. Jim Reeves, Eddy Arnold, Don Gibson, and later Charley Pride were a few of the acts Atkins produced. His formula was to find the best possible songs from Nashville's larger community of songwriters, then to coach the artist into the full Nashville sound style (see essay on The Nashville Sound). In the case of artists such as Jim Reeves, who had been recording for years, this involved helping the singers literally change their vocal style. In these various roles, Atkins was largely responsible for conceiving the entire Nashville sound.

By the 1970s, Atkins relinquished his role as producer and returned more to guitar playing while cultivating his longstanding interest in jazz. In the early 1980s, he left RCA. Yet the significance of what he accomplished as a record producer in the late 1950s and early '60s continues to shape country music today.

Figure 6-1 Porter Wagoner (left) and Chet Atkins.
Source: Southern Folklife Collection, Wilson Library, The University of North Carolina at Chapel Hill.

Four record producers were primarily responsible for conceiving of the new musical style: Owen Bradley (1915–1998) at Decca, Chet Atkins (1924–2001) at RCA, Don Law (1902–1982) at Columbia, and to a lesser extent Ken Nelson (1911–2008) at Capitol were every bit as important in creating the hit records as the stars whose names appeared on those records. Of the four, both Bradley and Nelson had worked as bandleaders and performers in pop music, Bradley in Nashville and Nelson in Chicago. Don Law, originally from England, entered the record business as a bookkeeper and soon began working with Art Satherley, the producer responsible for the early careers of Bob Wills and Gene Autry, among others (see Chapter 3). By the 1950s, each was heading up the country division at his respective label, and each was poised to make major changes in the sound of the records he was producing. Atkins was already a highly respected guitarist (see Artist Profile). Bradley, along with his brother, guitarist Harold Bradley, saw a need for a high-quality recording studio in Nashville. Together, the Bradleys built a studio, which was available not only to Decca artists but to other labels as well. In that way, Owen Bradley integrated himself into another aspect of the music-recording process.

The recording process that these producers pioneered relied on a small group of exceptionally talented studio musicians who were available for hire by any of the record labels. Recording sessions were booked in three-hour segments, during which the musicians created a musical arrangement, then recorded the final version of the song, completing usually three or four songs during one session. They worked efficiently and collegially, partly because they had played together so much. They did not use regular printed music, but instead relied on a system of shorthand notation to keep track of the chords and sections of each song—a system that was very different from that used in New York studios. The top session musicians were known as the Nashville A-Team, and their collective sound was featured on almost all the records made in Nashville during those years, regardless of who the lead singer or star was.

SOME OF NASHVILLE'S A-TEAM SESSION PLAYERS

Guitar: Grady Martin, Hank Garland, Harold Bradley, Ray Edenton

Bass: Bob Moore, Henry Strzelecki

Piano: Floyd Cramer, Hargus "Pig" Robbins, Bill Pursell

Steel Guitar: Pete Drake, Buddy Emmons, Jerry Byrd

Drums: Buddy Harman, Jerry Carrigan

Backup Vocal Quartets: The Jordanaires, the Anita Kerr Singers

Harmonica: Charlie McCoy

The Musical Scene for the Nashville Sound

Owen Bradley and Chet Atkins were very attuned to four trends in the 1950s. The first of those was the way that country songs were routinely becoming pop hits when they were recorded by pop stars: pop vocalist Patti Page had a major hit with "Tennessee

Waltz" in 1950; Tony Bennett with "Cold, Cold, Heart" in 1951. The second was that rock 'n' roll had captured some of the audience that would conventionally have listened to country music, which meant that the country record labels and radio stations were scrambling to find a market for themselves. The third was that country music, and especially Nashville, held a huge reserve of talent plus the flexibility to work quickly and efficiently at getting records made. The fourth was that country singers were selling records in the pop market by finding a sound that blended traditional country music with other genres. This last point was particularly interesting to Atkins and Bradley.

Country Teen Crooners

Starting in the mid-to-late 1950s, a number of singers made records that were just as much country as rock 'n' roll in their sound, in that they lacked many of the typical signifiers of either genre, instead functioning as sugary-sweet pop music. Clean-cut, handsome young artists sang about teen romance, accompanied by a highly polished rock 'n' roll band, while adhering to country decorum. This music was "pop" at its most accessible; the songs and performers did not connect themselves either to traditional country or hillbilly identities or to the rebellion and social marginalization that was typical of rock. Instead, they came across as a far less threatening (and less racially transgressive) version of Elvis's teen ballads. The performers' vocal styles avoided the guttural expressiveness of rockabilly, the naturalized twang of honky-tonk, or the resonant polish of western swing; instead, these singers cultivated a sweet, innocent "crooner" sound. The country audience liked the results, and this music took up residence in the country genre and on the country charts.

George Hamilton IV (1937–2014) embodied this teen-crooner performer. He came from a middle-class family and was enrolled as a college student at the University of North Carolina when a local, independent record label convinced him to record "A Rose and a Baby Ruth" in 1956, a hit song with charming lyrics about a teenager too poor to buy his sweetheart a box of candy and a whole bouquet of flowers. Hamilton was not interested in tying himself to traditional country music (even his name was as far from a hillbilly identity as one could get). For a white, male singer such as Hamilton whose recordings were appealing to teens, however, the country music industry provided the infrastructure from which to market his music and build a career. Hamilton began performing on Connie B. Gay's country music television program, and through that television exposure gained an even bigger audience. In 1960, he moved to Nashville, and as the country music genre as a whole shifted more toward pop, he fit right in. Shortly thereafter, he was inducted into the Grand Ole Opry. His career as a country singer was both long and successful; for over a decade, every single record that he released made it onto the *Billboard* country chart.

Another of the teen crooners, Sonny James (1929–), from Alabama, grew up performing with his family's country band, much as the Everly Brothers had. After serving in the Korean War, James followed a similar career path as other mid-'50s country singers. He performed on the Louisiana Hayride, then moved into television, where he sang on the *Ozark Jubilee,* the best known of the country music television shows in the 1950s. Like Hamilton, James had a clean-cut, upstanding image and a sincere voice that appealed to a general and broad audience. In 1956, he released "Young Love," which reached number one on both the country and pop charts in 1957. James joined the Grand Ole Opry in the early 1960s, and a decade later scored sixteen number one country hits in a row.

While Sonny James and George Hamilton IV kept an upscale, classy identity throughout their career, even artists whose fame came from rougher or harder-edged country styles indulged in this teen crooner fad. Johnny Cash, for instance, recorded "The Ballad of a Teenage Queen" (1958) at the request of producer Jack Clement (Sam Phillips's assistant). The song was a simpering 1950s teen romance story. In spite of the jarring juxtaposition of Cash's haunting baritone vocals with the cornball lyrics about a starlet coming home to marry the boy who worked at the local candy

Figure 6-2 George Hamilton IV.

Source: Southern Folklife Collection, Wilson Library, The University of North Carolina at Chapel Hill.

store, the song topped the country charts and contrasted starkly with Cash's other 1950s, work such as "Folsom Prison Blues." Marty Robbins was similarly known primarily for his gunfighter ballads and cowboy songs, but in 1957 he recorded a number one country song in the teen-crooner style, "A White Sport Coat (and a Pink Carnation)," with lyrics about attending a high school prom.

Conceiving the Nashville Sound

The teen crooner style revealed to country music record executives the potential audience for music that was a carefully orchestrated blend of country, pop, and the most crossover-friendly parts of rock 'n' roll. Chet Atkins pulled these ideas together and came up with a strategy for country artists to make records that would appeal to the broader pop audience, beginning with the records he produced for Jim Reeves (1923–1964). Reeves, originally from Texas, signed a recording contract with an independent label in 1952 and spent the next several years touring, recording honky-tonk music, and performing on the Louisiana Hayride. After a few hits, he joined the Grand Ole Opry and signed with RCA. There, producer Chet Atkins added backup vocalists and sleeker, more sophisticated musical arrangements behind Reeves's vocals. The formula worked, and in 1957 Reeves had his first crossover hit, "Four Walls," which topped the country charts and peaked at an impressive number eleven on the pop charts.

The general formula for this new style involved downplaying the twang, steel guitar, and raw honky-tonk elements, essentially the same recipe that the teen crooner artists were using. Even the musicians who played on these crossover hits were often the same as those backing the rock 'n' roll stars; Elvis Presley, Roy Orbison ("Pretty Woman"), and countless other rockabilly and rock 'n' roll stars recorded not only in Nashville but also with the same session musicians that the country singers were using. What was different from the teen crooners, however, was that the Nashville sound recordings were not pitched at the teen audience. And most importantly, the core country audience accepted this style as the next direction for country music rather than as a separate tangent, offshoot, or aberration.

ARTIST PROFILE

Patsy Cline (1932–1963)

Patsy Cline is among the most famous female singers in country music. She is revered for the sheer power and expressiveness of her voice and her strong-willed personality. Yet the way fans remember Patsy Cline is also colored by her crossover success in the pop market; her role in the changing face of country music during the 1960s; her conflicts regarding record labels, managers, contracts, and choices of songs; and her tragic death at the peak of her career. In those regards, Cline's story encapsulates the main issues in country music during the 1960s.

Born in Winchester, Virginia, as Virginia Patterson Hensley, Cline grew up in a working-class white family in a small town sharply divided along lines of race and class. Cline was from the poor side of town, and her taste for country music and colorful clothes and her brazen personality all led the "society" ladies in town to look down on her, a slight that Cline never forgot.

As a teenager, Cline sang both country and pop songs at local venues, eventually winding up as the vocalist for a local country band. She married Gerald Cline in 1953 and took a modified version of her middle name plus his last name as her stage name. Her big break came in 1954 when she appeared on country promoter Connie B. Gay's television show in Washington, D.C. From there, she signed a record contract with 4 Star Records, a label based in California. The label's owner, Bill McCall, only allowed Cline to record songs for which he held the publishing rights. This situation, driven by copyright (see Chapter 2), limited Cline's choice of songs, which historians have argued hampered her early career.

Cline had a single hit, "Walkin' after Midnight," in 1956, a performance that was essentially a honky-tonk rendition of a pop song, with lots of steel guitar in the recording and none of the typical Nashville sound elements such as piano or backup singers. No major hits followed, though, and within a few years, her career had floundered. Nonetheless, Cline had begun to work in the studio with producer Owen Bradley through a licensing agreement between McCall and Decca Records, for which Bradley worked. She also landed a spot on popular entertainer Arthur Godfrey's national television program. In 1960, her contract with 4 Star Records finally expired and Decca picked her up, allowing her to continue working with Owen Bradley but now with the freedom to record songs by the top songwriters in Nashville. She also was inducted into the Opry.

For the next three years, Cline's career soared. On her records, she and Bradley cultivated the nascent Nashville sound into a full-fledged crossover phenomenon. Bradley shifted her from a brash vocal style best suited to live performances into a more expressive, nuanced pop-vocal style. The resulting recordings of songs such as "I Fall to Pieces" and "She's Got You" crossed over onto pop radio, and Cline became the figurehead for a new style of country music that was fully embraced by a wider audience.

In keeping with the overall trends in country music in the 1960s, Cline started wearing elegant evening gowns and cultivated a sophisticated image, one that bespoke respectability. The change to both her music and her personal style, however,

The Stars

The two biggest stars of the Nashville sound era were Jim Reeves and Patsy Cline (see Artist Profile). Like almost all the stars of the Nashville sound era, they began their careers performing in earlier styles; Jim Reeves, with "Mexican Joe," and

involved downplaying the more traditional cow-girl image of a country singer to which Cline had always aspired. Stories about her career often include tensions over this shift: Cline wanted to wear fringed singing-cowgirl outfits and sing traditional country music such as covers of Hank Williams and Bill Monroe songs, whereas her producer and record label were guiding her toward an uptown, upscale image and sound. To the extent that these stories are true, they reflect the basic conflicts within the country music genre during these years over how country music's past related to its present.

In 1963, Cline sang at a benefit in Kansas City, then got on a plane to fly home to Nashville with fellow Opry singers Hawkshaw Hawkins and Cowboy Copas, along with manager and pilot Randy Hughes. That plane crashed just ninety miles out of Nashville, killing all aboard, on March 5, 1963. For the next few years, Cline's music remained very much in the public's eye, as her label released several posthumous records. She drifted out of the spotlight in the 1970s when country music itself shifted away from the Nashville sound. But a series of high-profile events a decade later brought Cline back in the memory of country fans. In 1977, Loretta Lynn released a tribute album of Patsy Cline covers. Three years later, writer and entertainment executive Ellis Nassour published a biography of her. Canadian singer k. d. lang covered several of Cline's songs on critically acclaimed albums, and in 1985 a Hollywood film starring Jessica Lange called *Sweet Dreams* was released, which chronicled Cline's career and tumultuous relationships, including her troubled marriage to second husband Charlie Dick.

Today, Patsy Cline's role in the history of country music is complicated. She did not write

Figure 6-3 Patsy Cline on the Opry stage; note her cocktail dress.
Source: Courtesy of Country Music Hall of Fame and Museum.

her own material, and she recorded some of the most pop-styled, crossover country music of all time. Country fans usually devalue both of those characteristics in a genre where authenticity is often associated with distinctively hard-edged country music penned by the artist herself. On the other hand, Cline's personal story of a rise from poverty to success, burdened by stormy personal relationships and always struggling against the confines of the music industry, endears her to country fans. One of Cline's lasting contributions to country music is this balance between opposing ideologies, a model that will prove useful in considering the careers of later country stars.

Listening Guide

"Faded Love" (1963)

PERFORMER:
Patsy Cline

SONGWRITERS:
John Wills, Bob Wills

ORIGINAL RELEASE:
Decca 31522

FORM: Verse-chorus
(with refrain)

STYLE: Nashville
sound

Patsy Cline recorded "Faded Love" just a month before her death in a tragic plane crash, during what was the peak of her career. By 1963, Cline had enjoyed several crossover hits. She and producer Owen Bradley had crafted a style for her that showcased the sheer power of her voice while also delving into a more sentimental style. Bradley carefully cultivated the pop elements in her performances, even though Cline resisted many of those features. Her recording sessions during these years always included the best session musicians in the business: backup vocals from the Jordanaires, pianist Floyd Cramer, drummer Buddy Harmon, guitarist Grady Martin, and several others. For this particular session, which took place on February 4, 1963, over twenty musicians participated, included a large group of violinists, or "strings," in the parlance of popular music. Bill McElhiney, who was a formally trained trumpet player and one of the most respected musical arrangers in Nashville, wrote out the musical arrangements for the songs, which created a lush, full sound with no audible twang whatsoever.

This session was the first of four days in the recording studio, during which time Cline and Bradley were getting ready for a new album. While her sound had morphed into something unrelated to country music's honky-tonk and hillbilly past, Cline had never given up her personal preference for singing country music standards. For these sessions, she and Bradley picked almost all songs that had already been hits in one form or another—proven crowd-pleasers, in other words. About half the songs were pop standards, but about half were country standards. During those four days, she sang "Blue Moon of Kentucky" (Bill Monroe) and "Crazy Arms" (made famous by Ray Price), among others. In that vein, she and Bradley chose a Bob Wills western swing tune, "Faded Love," from 1950 (see Chapter 3). What is most interesting about her cover versions of classic country recordings is that although the song is ostensibly the same (same melody, chords, and lyrics), the entire musical and emotional effect changes dramatically; Cline slows down the tempo of "Faded Love" and adds vocal scoops, ornaments, and blues elements that show off her virtuosity as a singer. Although there are backup singers on the recording, they remain part of the supporting texture, and Cline sings the song as a personal lament of heartbreak. On Wills's original, the vocal harmony is featured prominently with the melody, so the performance sounds less like one person's individual story and the listener's attention is drawn to the ensemble as a whole. Cline's version eliminated the musical elements that characterized western swing, which distanced her performance from Bob Wills and his legendary status in country music: gone were the fiddling, the steel guitar, and the swing beat. It is well worth it to listen to the Wills version first to situate the song in its western swing origins, then compare Cline's Nashville sound rendition.

The inherent tension between Cline's pop musical style and her affection for more traditional country music was part of what made her so successful. Pop singers had been recording covers of standard country songs for years: the songs Cline chose for that session had already been covered by Jackie DeShannon, The Mills Brothers, Sam Cooke, Ricky Nelson, and countless others, none of whom would be described as country singers (although Nelson would later drift in that direction). Yet Patsy Cline was working as an insider in country music, one who continued to pitch herself as a country singer to her fans even while her recordings showed no audible markers of a country identity. Fans then and now see that tension—between Cline's pop style on the one hand and her devotion to the history of hard-edged, traditional country music on the other—as the way in which Cline rose above the pop-crossover music of her era to become a legendary country icon.

TIME	FORM	LISTENING CUES	DISCUSSION
0:00	Introduction	strings	Shimmering strings are heard from the very beginning. They slide from note to note, imitating the sound of a steel guitar. Part way through the introduction, the backup singers enter, which creates a thick texture.
0:23	Verse 1	"As I look …"	Cline back-phrases heavily from the beginning, singing far behind the beat of the music. The interplay of drums, piano, and guitar here are typical of the Nashville sound.
1:05	Chorus	"I miss you, darling …"	Right before the chorus, the strings play a fast, ascending scale that builds the listener's sense of anticipation and makes the arrival of the chorus even more climactic. Listen to Cline's vocal expressiveness here. She slips into a bluesy growl as she sings low notes, and she adds a tear to her voice several times. At the end of the chorus, her voice quivers and switches to a very vulnerable tone, mirroring the lyrics.
1:44	Instrumental interlude	strings	Between the vocal sections, the strings play a brief interlude.
1:57	Verse 2	"As I think of the past …"	The lyrics of this second verse reflect the sentimental and sometimes corny poetry that the western swing bands played. Cline sings the "mating of the dove" line straight, but at this slow tempo, those cliché lyrics stick out from the introspective description in the rest of the song.
2:39	Chorus	"I miss you, darling …"	Cline continues to back-phrase heavily here. Notice the intricate guitar playing (session musician Grady Martin), which was common in the Nashville sound era recordings.
3:19	Tag	"And remember …"	As she repeats the last line of the song, Cline switches into her bolder vocal sound. She often did this at the end of songs, a remnant from her live stage performances where a "big finish" was expected by the crowd. Yet at the very end of the song, Cline takes a breath close to the microphone and then lets the last note turn into a sob. Her performance drifts toward overdone schmaltz at that moment.

Listening Guide

"He'll Have to Go" (1959)

PERFORMER: Jim Reeves

SONGWRITERS: Joe and Audrey Allison

ORIGINAL RELEASE: RCA 47-7643

FORM: AABA

STYLE: Nashville sound

This recording, which reached number one on the *Billboard* country chart and number two on the *Billboard* pop chart, is the essence of the Nashville sound that altered country music in the late 1950s. The songwriters included Joe Allison, who was both a founding member of the Country Music Association and one of the key players in promoting country music's upscale image in the early 1960s. Producer Chet Atkins was the main innovator in terms of new instrumentation, adding reverb on the vocals, and the overall shift into the new style. The session musicians included a who's who of Nashville A-list players: Floyd Cramer on piano, Buddy Harman on drums, Hank Garland on guitar, Bob Moore on bass, Marvin Hughes on vibraphone (vibes), and the Anita Kerr singers providing backup vocals. Noticeably absent is the steel guitar. In its place, the shimmering tones of the vibes—an instrument with no traditional roots in country music whatsoever—appears in the arrangement. The vibes in particular mark the song as having crossed over into mainstream respectability.

By 1959, Jim Reeves (1923–1964) had changed his vocal style. Having left behind his honky-tonk techniques, Reeves now used more vibrato and sang in a lower range, which allowed him to create a smoother, more resonant and intimate sound. That approach worked well with songs such as this one, whose lyrics address a single, intensely emotional encounter. Like many of the Nashville sound era's hits, the text in "He'll Have to Go" gives the listener a very focused entry point into a story centered on a relationship and universal emotions in a moment in time—a telephone conversation of whispered intimacy, lips close to the phone. Only as the song progresses does the picture in the listener's mind expand from that tightly circumscribed view: the protagonist is somewhere with a jukebox; the woman is somewhere with another man. The attention, however, remains on the two voices connected by the phone line.

Patsy Cline, with "Walkin' after Midnight," were known to audiences through recordings in the honky-tonk style. But their primary fame came in the crossover Nashville sound work that they did. They each cultivated a personal image that was similarly uptown, sleek, and sophisticated to match their musical style; Reeves appeared in tuxedos and was known as Gentleman Jim for his classy stage presence and professional polish, while Cline appeared in bespangled eveningwear and furs, much as an urban popular singer would have dressed. Their songs (see Listening Guides) adhered to the model of the Nashville sound in every respect,

This song represents the dual features of the Nashville sound; the musical style erased any audible signifiers of its hillbilly past and exported country music to widespread popularity. Students often look back at this recording and wonder how and why it is considered country in the first place. The answer is mainly through the way that the larger country music audience saw itself and identified with a particular genre. Whatever perspective one brings to these complex issues of authenticity, though, the expressive power of Reeves's voice is admirable, as is the level of craftsmanship of both the songwriters and session musicians.

TIME	FORM	LISTENING CUES	DISCUSSION
0:00	Introduction	piano and vibes	The vibes and piano replace what would conventionally have been a steel-guitar introduction in earlier country styles.
0:09	A-section	"Put your sweet lips …"	Reeves's sensuous, velvety vocals start out as if this were a tender, romantic phone call. The end of this section twists the plot so that we find out the singer's lover is with another man. Notice how Reeves sings a low note on the word "low," a form of text-painting that entwines the melody and lyrics in the song.
0:44	A-section	"Whisper to me …"	The vibes become more prominent during this section, which creates some variation in the musical setting. Reeves adopts a more conversational style in this section, personalizing the text.
1:19	B-section	"You can't say …"	At this bridge section, the backup singers change to a repetitive rhythm that adds an urgency to the song.
1:37	A-section	"Put your sweet lips …"	The final section returns to the opening of the song, but here the listener already knows about the "other man," which changes how this text is understood.

and their audiences loved the records. Both had a strong presence on the pop charts during the early 1960s and were known for that crossover success.

Unlike Reeves and Cline, who did not write their own songs, Don Gibson (1928–2003) was a star both as a songwriter (see essay on A Professional Writer's Town) and as a singer. His recording of "I Can't Stop Loving You" (1958) is a perfect example of the typical Nashville sound recording: the performance still includes steel guitar and hints of a southern vocal accent, but it is mixed with piano, backup singers, and resonant reverb.

Pop Stars Make Country Albums

Record executives working in pop music took note of Nashville's recording studio system, the success of the local producers, and the commercial viability of the country music that was coming out of Nashville. While country songs had been making their way into the repertory of pop stars for several years, in the early 1960s the fad intensified. Pop stars started recording whole country-themed albums that consisted of covers of country hits; the cover art on several of these albums included hay bales, cowboy hats, and stereotypical country outfits for these usually classy pop stars—an ironic twist, since the country singers in the Nashville sound era often released albums with none of those "country" symbols. The best known of these albums were two volumes by R&B legend Ray Charles (1930–2004) called *Modern Sounds in Country and Western Music* (1962).

Figure 6-4 Jim Reeves.

Source: Southern Folklife Collection, Wilson Library, The University of North Carolina at Chapel Hill.

Charles's version of "I Can't Stop Loving You" became a number one pop hit, which encouraged more singers to release their own "country albums."

POP STARS MAKING COUNTRY ALBUMS

A brief sample of pop singers' country albums:

Connie Francis, *Country and Western Golden Hits* (1959)

Patti Page, *Patti Page Sings Country and Western Golden Hits* (1961)

Jaye P. Morgan, *That Country Sound* (1961)

Rosemary Clooney, *Rosemary Clooney Sings Country Hits from the Heart* (1962)

Nat "King" Cole, *Ramblin' Rose* (1962)

Kay Starr, *Just Plain Country* (1962)

Dean Martin, *Country Style* (1963)

Dean Martin, *Dean "Tex" Martin Rides Again* (1963)

Bing Crosby, *Bing Crosby Sings the Great Country Hits* (1963)

Perry Como, *The Scene Changes* (1965)

Many of these themed country albums, including Ray Charles's *Modern Sounds*, were not actually recorded in Nashville but rather in New York or Los Angeles. But others, including those by Rosemary Clooney, Jaye P. Morgan, Connie Francis, Dean Martin, Perry Como, and Burl Ives, were recorded in Nashville. A *Billboard* article published in June 1960 described the trend: "The sound coming out of Nashville which continues to catapult more and more locally recorded songs into the pop charts, is beginning to attract a growing number of artists and record execs who have heretofore recorded elsewhere." Not all of these visiting stars came to record country music. For instance, British pop sensation Helen Shapiro came to Nashville to make her third pop album, *Helen in Nashville* (1963), on which the Jordanaires appear. The Nashville studio system had earned a reputation in and out of country music for its professionalism and ability to produce extremely popular recordings.

Figure 6-5 Eddie Arnold.
Source: Courtesy of Country Music Hall of Fame and Museum.

BUT ARE THEY COUNTRY?

Pop and R&B stars' country albums were sometimes quite commercially successful, as with Ray Charles's hit, which reached number one on the *Billboard* pop chart. These recordings forged new connections between listeners, music genres, and artists. In that instance, R&B fans heard a song that was ostensibly "country," and country fans got to know an R&B artist. In spite of those connections, however, much of the core country audience did not receive these albums as "country music" per se. Ray Charles's single, for instance, never appeared on the *Billboard* country chart. This is not at all surprising to fans who listen to Charles's albums in particular: his musical arrangements were so far afield from country that they simply did not match the sonic profile of the genre. But there was more to it: in the early 1960s, race unquestionably played a role in a performer's acceptance by some country fans. There were factors beyond that as well. These recordings illustrate how genre was defined by aspects of identity and lineage, not just what songs or musical styles appear on an album.

Many of the biggest country stars from the 1950s joined in the trend and smoothly slipped into the Nashville sound by the end of the decade. Eddy Arnold, whose career predated the rise of honky-tonk, started experimenting with backup singers and an even more pop sound by the mid-1950s. By 1960,

Arnold had adopted the strings, backup singers, and pop-crossover stylings enthusiastically (see Listen Side by Side). Faron Young (1932–1996), from Shreveport, Louisiana, sang on the Louisiana Hayride in the early 1950s and recorded honky-tonk hits such as "Live Fast, Love Hard, Die Young." But by 1961, he, too, had adopted the new style. His recording of "Hello Walls" in 1961, penned by a then-unknown songwriter named Willie Nelson, used the Jordanaires as backup singers, vibes, piano, and vocal back-phrasing (see essay on The Nashville Sound). Porter Wagoner, Lefty Frizzell, and even George Jones also made the transition from honky-tonk to Nashville sound in the recordings.

Figure 6-6 Marty Robbins.

Source: Southern Folklife Collection, Wilson Library, The University of North Carolina at Chapel Hill.

The Songs

Two main themes appeared in the song lyrics of the Nashville sound recordings. The first was songs focusing on the universal emotions of love and heartbreak, told without elaborate narratives. These songs, such as "Four Walls," "I Fall to Pieces," "Sweet Dreams," "(I Can't Help You) I'm Falling Too," and countless others, worked in a crossover market because they had little or nothing in their lyrics that marked them as stereotypically country—they were not exclusively about the South, rural life, working-class identity, trains, prison, etc. Instead, they stuck mainly to the territory of lost love, unrequited love, cheating, regrets, and (less frequently) happy love.

While those songs that centered on love and lost love made up the bulk of the Nashville sound recordings, a second collection of topics also appeared. These focused on nostalgic depictions of the Old West, cowboys, and ballads about legendary folk heroes. Some scholars have described these as "**saga songs**" or "historical ballads." At the same time that mainstream country music was becoming more popular and downplaying its twangy, hillbilly roots in terms of its sound and image, these cowboy-themed and Old West–themed "saga songs" appealed to fans specifically because they connected with an imagined, idealized cowboy origin for the music. It was a way of making country music "very country" without actually tapping into the negative hillbilly/hayseed stereotypes that had plagued the music for decades. The folk revival had also brought story songs back into the public's consciousness. The result was that songs with an aura of folk tradition (even if they were actually new compositions) were back in vogue. Marty Robbins's "El Paso" (see Listening Guide) was a prime example of this phenomenon, a song about two cowboys in a gunfight over a Mexican dance-hall girl, complete with a mounted posse. Eddy Arnold used old cowboy and folk ballads as a bridge between his honky-tonk success in the 1940s and early '50s and his long string of hits in the early 1960s. The same year that Robbins recorded "El Paso," Eddy Arnold released the album *Thereby Hangs a Tale*, which featured songs about the Battle of Little Bighorn (General Custer's Last Stand); "Redheaded Stranger," involving a Wild West shootout; and that fantastical cowboy ballad, "(Ghost) Riders in the Sky." Arnold's versions of "Streets of Laredo," "Jim, I Wore a Tie Today," and "Cool Water" (which the Sons of the Pioneers had penned in the heyday of Hollywood's singing cowboys) all brought stories of Old West cowboys into the lush Nashville sound era.

The best known of these historical ballads are Jimmy Dean's recording of "Big Bad John" (1961), by Dean and Roy Acuff, and Johnny Horton's "The Battle of New Orleans" (1959), by Jimmie Driftwood. Like the various novelty songs in the honky-tonk era such as "Sixteen Tons," these recordings relied on stark, minimal accompaniments and held the listener's attention with their heroic tales of bravery. Dean's "Big Bad John" told of a mining accident in which the title character held up a cracking timber so that twenty men could escape before the mine collapsed. "The Battle of New Orleans" was an account of an 1815 battle between American and British forces, complete with a banjo playing "Dixie" and snare drums evoking soldiers marching.

Even Jim Reeves dove into the "saga song" trend when he was not recording heartbreak ballads. "Distant Drums" (released in 1966 after his death) followed a soldier heading off to war; "The Blizzard" (1961) was a pathetic tale of a man and his horse struggling home through a storm and freezing to death just a stone's throw from his waiting lover. Two of the most memorable of these songs were Lefty Frizzell's "Long Black Veil," in which the hero dies to protect the reputation of the married woman with whom he is having an affair, and "Saginaw Michigan," where a young man uses his wits and a clever ploy to win his girl's hand and send his meddlesome father-in-law on a fool's expedition in a gold rush.

A number of songs in this Nashville sound era borrow from Latin American musical traditions, both the Mexican mariachi sounds found in "El Paso" and syncopated dance rhythms taken from the cha-cha and other Latin dances. These elements had been embraced by American popular culture in the 1950s and early '60s, particularly in the form of a Latin dance craze that brought those rhythms into American jazz and popular music. As country music shifted more into the popular mainstream and assimilated pop music's sounds, these Latin sounds appeared with growing frequency in country hits. Songs such as Jim Reeves's "Rosa Rio," Johnny Cash's "Ring of Fire," and Marty Robbins's "Devil Woman," to name a few, illustrate that trend.

Listening Guide

"El Paso" (1959)

PERFORMER:
Marty Robbins

SONGWRITER:
Marty Robbins

ORIGINAL RELEASE:
Columbia 4-41511

FORM: AABA
(modified)

STYLE: Nashville
sound

"El Paso" represents two important aspects of country music during this Nashville sound era: a musical style that was not drenched in orchestral arrangements of strings (unlike so many of Patsy Cline and Jim Reeves's recordings) and a fascination with cowboys, the Wild West, and their symbolism in American culture. Typical descriptions of the Nashville sound as a musical style emphasize its use of piano, strings (violins, in particular), drums played with brushes, and smooth backup vocalists singing "oohs and ahs," while lacking steel guitar, fiddle, and that elusive quality called "twang" in the music. While that description holds true in many instances, it glosses over a more subtle trend during these years. The schmaltzy strings and syrupy piano heard in "Faded Love" and "He'll Have to Go" (see Listening Guides) characterized only a fraction of country recordings in the late 1950s and into the 1960s. More commonly, Nashville sound recordings simply featured a polished sound of subtle drums, virtuosic guitar-picking, backup vocals, and bass, which was the instrumentation on this recording. "El Paso's" guitar parts evoke Latin dance music, another common trait in this style. "El Paso" was also a classic instance of the Old West themes that popped up during this time. The song appeared on Robbins's album titled *Gunfighter Ballads and Train Songs*, which consisted of "saga songs" that lived up to the album's title.

Marty Robbins recorded "El Paso" for Columbia Records, which was headed by Don Law. Columbia had carved out a niche within country music for "outsider" characters, more hard-edged country music, and a strong tendency toward older, traditional influences. Johnny Cash signed with Columbia during these years, as did Lefty Frizzell, who released a cover album of Jimmie Rodgers songs around this time. Robbins was very much at home on the label.

The song structure of "El Paso" broke with convention. In the 1950s, country music still adhered to the standard formula of three minutes per song, a practice left over from the days when records could only hold that much music on one side. Its story ran for nearly five minutes, which the record company thought would alienate radio stations. Two versions of the song were released, one that omitted an entire section of the song. But fans preferred the longer version. The song rose to number one on the *Billboard* country chart, but also crossed over and became a number one pop hit as well.

The song's form comes from the AABA Standard Song Form pattern (see Appendix A), but it is modified slightly here. As with all AABA song forms, "El Paso" does not have a chorus. Instead, there are two different musical sections, with distinct melodies and chord progressions. The song follows the pattern of AABAA-BAAB... as if it were a continuously overlapping set of AABA units. There are two additional features worth mentioning. In the middle of the song, one A-section (at 2:09) is only half as long as the rest, likely the result of editing to make the song a bit shorter. And after each B-section, there is a short vocal phrase that leads into the next A-section, connecting the two. These bridging-phrases are marked in parentheses and with an asterisk (*) in the chart below: they are part of the subsequent A-section in terms of their meaning and phrasing, but they occur before the chord progression and rhythms start that A-section. This approach to musical form has an important effect in "El Paso": it keeps propelling the song forward through a very long story. Each time we get to what could be the end, the song's form pushes us into the next section. The song only concludes when the singer (as the protagonist) dies in the arms of his lover.

TIME	FORM	LISTENING CUES	DISCUSSION
0:00	Introduction	guitar	Grady Martin created a Mexican Mariachi sound on his guitar for this recording.
0:12	A-section	"Out in the West Texas town …"	This song is a long, narrative ballad. Right from the start, Robbins lets us know it will trace a dramatic story.
0:31	A-section	"Blacker than night …"	Felina is described in this song as both enticing and dangerous; the cowboy loves her, but knows that no good will come from it. She represents a complicated female character, neither exclusively good nor bad.
0:47	B-section	"One night a wild young …"	On the word "wind," Robbins and the two backup singers Jim Glaser and Bobby Sykes) together slide through a musical pattern that sounds like what trumpets would play in a Mariachi band.
1:11	A-section	"(So in anger I)* Challenged his right for …"	This section could have been the end of the song—the gunshot a final act. But instead, the song rolls forward.
1:30	A-section	"Just for a moment I stood …"	This section was cut from some released versions of Robbins's performance in order to shorten it.
1:48	B-section	"Out through the back door …"	At the end of each B-section, the music appears to change keys, but in effect it is only slipping back into the home key. That mirage of changing keys keeps the song sounding fresh throughout its almost five minutes.
2:09	A-section (half)	"(Just as fast as I)* Could from the West Texas town …"	The types of geographic references here (West Texas, New Mexico) are important within the western cowboy songs that were popular in these years. This is the only A-section in the recording that consists of only one, instead of two, long vocal phrases.

Continued

Listening Guide

"El Paso" (1959) Continued

TIME	FORM	LISTENING CUES	DISCUSSION
2:19	A-section	"Back in El Paso my life …"	Memories of Felina haunt the singer, and the crux of the song is found in the line that states his love is stronger than his fear of death. The listener knows that this is the start of a new section at 2:19, rather than a continuation of the previous one, because of the change in texture and the back-up singers' shift at that moment.
2:37	B-section	"I saddled up and away …"	Notice that the B-sections consist of two long vocal phrases. The first is fourteen bars long (counting "1 2 3" as one bar), and the second is eleven bars long. These are highly unusual lengths of sections. Although most listeners are not paying attention to this sort of feature, they are subconsciously aware that the form of the song does not conform to typical patterns of country music (or pop music in general).
2:59	A-section	"(And as last, Here I)* Am on the hill …"	Each of the long vocal phrases in this section is 11 bars long (counting "1 2 3" as one bar). This ebb and flow of phrases does not follow the typical patterns. The result is that the music sounds more exotic and connected to the various folk traditions within Mexican music.
3:17	A-section	"Off to my right I see …"	The singer is depicted here as the lone, isolated heroic figure riding into a certain doom. This romanticized independence, of an underdog accepting his fate as the sacrifice for love, resonates with the traditions in country music lyrics.
3:36	B-section	"Something is dreadfully wrong …"	The drama of the narrative pulls the listener into the experience as we hear the singer's own gradual realization that he has been shot.
3:57	A-section	"(But my love for)* Felina is strong …"	This section effectively feels like the end of the story, as the singer feels the rifle bullet enter his body.
4:16	A-section	"From out of nowhere …"	This last A-section suggests—surprisingly—that the narrative is actually going to continue, but then unexpectedly, the singer dies and the song ends in the middle of its expected AABA pattern.

Instrumentals

Many of the hits in the Nashville sound era did not have a lead vocalist. Instrumentals— recordings of just instruments, without a singer—were not only common but quite popular during this time. Instrumental recordings date back to the earliest days of country music; Eck Robertson, for instance, recorded with just his fiddle in 1922, and DeFord Bailey's harmonica solos were a major draw for the Opry broadcasts (see Chapter 1). In the intervening decades, however, instrumentals had been mostly displaced in mainstream country music by recordings with words and a lead singer. The one exception to that was bluegrass, where instrumentals continued to make up a significant part of the repertory throughout those years. With the arrival of the Nashville sound era, instrumentals resurfaced as part of mainstream country.

The most famous of the instrumental stars was pianist Floyd Cramer (1933–1997). Cramer worked on the Louisiana Hayride in the early 1950s, then moved to Nashville in 1955. Within a short time, he was playing on sessions for just about every artist recording in Nashville. His signature style was called "slip-note," in which Cramer played the key on the piano below the melody's note, followed a split second later by the actual melody note. The results sound like the pianist is missing the melody's note then correcting it (on purpose), or what in classical music would be called "grace notes." The effect is similar to the way a steel guitar or fiddle player can start on a lower pitch and then scoop or slide into the melody's note. In 1960, Cramer recorded "Last Date" with all the features of a Nashville sound hit, including the Anita Kerr singers filling in vocal "oohs" and "ahs," but with a piano solo in place of a lead vocalist. The song was a huge crossover hit, reaching number two on the pop charts (ironically, the song that beat it was an Elvis Presley record on which Cramer played). "Last Date" was so popular that several country singers, including Conway Twitty and Skeeter Davis, wrote lyrics for it so they could record it.

Other instrumentalists also made records during these years, notably Chet Atkins. With the exception of Cramer's, the instrumental records generally had narrower distribution and were known only among a smaller group of dedicated fans. But the very fact that they were making and selling instrumental albums in the first place illustrates the increased attention and respect that musicians other than the well-known vocalists received during the Nashville sound era.

The Second Wave of Nashville Sound Artists

Two tragic deaths cut short the Nashville sound's first wave of development, even though the basic musical style persisted throughout the 1960s and beyond. Patsy Cline died in a plane crash in 1963, and a year later Jim Reeves was killed when his private plane crashed just south of Nashville. The two biggest stars of the Nashville sound, the artists whose recordings had transformed country music into a part of the cultural mainstream, were gone. Popular music was also changing; in 1964, the same year Reeves died, the Beatles took America by storm, while a year later folk artist Bob Dylan shocked fans by plugging in an electric guitar and moving into folk-rock. In California, emerging styles of country music appeared as alternatives and counterweights to the Nashville sound (see Chapter 7). But within mainstream country music, and within the studios in Nashville, the style persisted, albeit in a toned-down version.

So prevalent was the Nashville sound that even those few holdouts who had steadfastly refused to adopt the style finally gave in. Ray Price (1926–2013), for instance, had stuck to his traditional honky-tonk sound clear through the 1950s, refusing to abandon the steel guitar and fiddle-driven accompaniment to his twang-filled, naturalized vocals. But by the mid-1960s, even Price had traded in his twang for a slicker, more uptown sound with strings, backup vocalists, and a smoother singing style.

One change within the Nashville sound was a shift in common song topics. Country hits in the mid-1960s included a large number of novelty songs. These kept to the basic musical style of the Nashville sound, but drew on decades-old traditions of country comedy to lighten the mood. West Virginian Little Jimmy Dickens, a figure on the Opry since 1948, entertained fans with such novelties as "May the Bird of Paradise Fly up Your Nose" (1965) and "Country Music Lover" (1967), whose lyrics play on the names of legendary country musicians.

Roger Miller (1936–1992) wrote the most popular novelty songs in the mid-1960s, which often combined nonsense syllables and infectious rhythms. From Fort Worth, Texas, Miller served in the Army during the Korean War, then made his way to Nashville, where he first found success as a songwriter. After several years of struggling to break into the business, Ray Price hired him to play in his band, and Miller secured a recording contract with a small label. By 1964, he was ready to give up on his country music ambitions, but he needed money to move west. He went into the studio with the intention of merely fulfilling his contract with the record label and drawing his paycheck. The songs he had written for that session included "Dang Me" and "Chug-a-Lug," which introduced Miller's pop vocal style, novelty lyrics, and incredible talent for rhythms that hold a listener's attention. The two songs reached numbers one and three respectively on the country chart and turned Miller into a star. His next hit, "Do-Wacka-Do," employed even more nonsense syllables, while "You Can't Rollerskate in a Buffalo Herd" (1966) took the compositional style a step further with nonsense ideas (the lyrics include "you can't go fishin' in a watermelon patch"). The results were a new type of Nashville sound recording, one that featured rhythmic inventiveness and particularly memorable, pop-styled hooks—catchy tunes that were simply fun to listen to.

A year after first scoring a hit, Miller released "King of the Road" (1965), which became his signature song in his signature style. The song displayed Miller's expressive vocals, which included crystal-clear diction, the occasional growl for effect, and a resonant baritone range, along with his penchant for masterful rhythmic control. The swinging bass line, finger-snaps, and patterns in the lyrics all played with the audience's sense of expectation. Yet the lyrics were uncharacteristically serious, compared to his novelty comic numbers. They revealed a greater depth of emotion and storytelling in his songwriting that fostered a long and very successful career

Figure 6-7 Roger Miller.

Source: Southern Folklife Collection, Wilson Library, The University of North Carolina at Chapel Hill.

as a songwriter, both in country music and later on Broadway. "King of the Road" reached number one on the country chart and number four on the pop chart.

By the time Miller started recording hit songs in the mid-'60s, a few strands of more traditional, hard-edged country music were making their way back into mainstream country music. The Nashville sound had already toned down the excesses of strings, piano, backup vocalists, and even the bell-like sound of vibraphones that had been so prevalent earlier in the decade. The traditional styles merged with this more mature Nashville sound, and in that guise, country music moved into its classic period (see Chapter 8), a seamless evolution of style and tradition.

Making Sense of the Nashville Sound

When asked to describe the Nashville sound, Chet Atkins famously referred to the sound of coins jingling in his pocket—indicating that he considered it to be a way to sell records and make money. Ever since its inception, the Nashville sound has been the subject of both admiration and scorn from country music scholars. Its commercial success, its crossover trends, and its polish—both in music and in image—are at the heart of the controversy. Did it sell out country's authenticity? Did it rescue a woefully old-fashioned or embarrassingly low-class music? Was it simply a natural evolution of directions in which country was already headed? Was it just a repackaging that did not alter the heart of country music?

At stake are the same issues of authenticity and distinctiveness that have characterized country music from its conception. If the Nashville sound was so popular that it was indistinguishable from pop music, then how could it still be country, given that part of country's identity was its opposition to the popular, middle-class mainstream culture? Some scholars have answered these questions by suggesting that the onslaught of rock 'n' roll threatened to kill the country music genre entirely, and that the Nashville sound was an unfortunate but necessary moment of selling out to commercial interests that was required to save country music. In 1979, scholars Bill Ivey and Douglas Green wrote, "The Nashville Sound is . . . in critical disfavor today . . . When it was in control, its successes came close to ruining otherwise fine . . . performances." Their view lambasted the producers and artists alike for "ruining" good country music, but they end with a redemptive view: "The fact remains that [Chet Atkins] and Owen Bradley and Anita Kerr and the rest of the Nashville sound's architects saved country music . . . from obscurity and maybe even oblivion." That perspective vilifies rock 'n' roll as something foreign that disrupted country music, ignoring the way rock 'n' roll emerged as an outgrowth of both country and R&B. Yet it is important to realize that in the late 1970s, many country fans, musicians, and industry personnel held that view, as it will help us to understand the tensions within country music in the 1970s.

More recent scholarship has suggested a very different interpretation of the Nashville sound, namely that it was an evolution from within country music, brought about by both social and economic forces. One of the most significant of these forces was the changing identity of the country audience. The Nashville sound's emergence occurred at the same time that the traditional country fan base—which consisted largely of working-class Southerners—found themselves in very different circumstances. In a move known as the "great white migration," a sizeable percentage of white Southerners whose families had worked in coal mines, as sharecroppers, and on farms left the region to join the industrial workforce in urban areas. This migration began after World War I and continued through the Great Depression and after World War II, further increasing in the 1950s. Between 1950 and 1960, for instance, a half million people moved out of West Virginia, many settling in or near Detroit, Cleveland, and Chicago. U.S. Route 23, running through Georgia, North Carolina, Tennessee, Virginia, and Kentucky before terminating in Michigan, even earned the nickname "the Hillbilly Highway" because of the prevalence of out-migration from the Southern regions.

These migrants often remained nostalgic for their former homes, and in many instances returned there, sometimes even seasonally. Yet they moved to take advantage of better employment opportunities, and as historian Chad Berry has described, many of them realized those goals. They increased their income and spent it on material goods, including better cars and nicer houses. They moved into the suburbs and assimilated quite successfully into the middle class. Throughout this process, however, they retained their sense of belonging to the South and their working-class roots. Thus, a large portion of the country music audience, still loyal to that music, underwent a major shift in their own cultural identity during these years. The Nashville sound both mirrored that shift and aligned with an expanded country music audience; the music shed its hillbilly identity just as its audience was doing the same thing. As its audience melded into the larger middle-class, suburban family population, country music quite literally became a musical representation of that lifestyle, which in turn gave it access to an even bigger audience.

The studio system that Chet Atkins and Owen Bradley ushered into Nashville was another reason why the Nashville sound merged so well with mainstream popular culture. Their system relied on powerful producers, an expert team of session musicians available for hire, and a precision music-making machine into which just about any star could be placed. This was the basic model on which pop music had relied for years, especially in New York and, to a lesser extent, Los Angeles. Thus, when pop producers took an interest in Nashville, they found they were able to work in that setting quite comfortably because it felt like familiar territory. There were also notable differences; many of the pop producers and singers who came to Nashville, including Connie Francis and Perry Como, commented in interviews how surprised they were by the unique notation system used in the studios there, called the Nashville Number System, and the session musicians' methods of working out arrangements by ear. Others noted the collegiality of the musicians and the more laid-back atmosphere. In spite of these differences, however, Nashville's studio system still fit with pop music's production model, and Nashville's infrastructure was in large part responsible for the crossover phenomenon of country music in the 1960s.

In sum, to a huge population of fans, the Nashville sound was great country music, professionally made by talented musicians, with which they connected. But the Nashville sound took country music to one extreme of pop assimilation, straining some fans' perceptions of authenticity and tradition in the music. This development provided the catalyst for an opposing style to take root, as we will see.

☆ ESSAY: MUSIC BUSINESS

 # The Country Music Association

By the late 1950s, the country music business was sorely in need of a central organization. The primary problem faced by country music publishers, musicians, and record labels was the general public perception that country music belonged to low-class, poor people. Radio stations relied on advertising dollars as their source of revenue, and thus were reluctant to play music whose audience they generally thought was too poor to interest potential advertisers. Disc jockeys had wielded tremendous power over what records were heard and which artists were popular, but that profession as a whole had recently come under intense scrutiny for unfair practices, bribery, and other assorted problems. Nonetheless, the only large, professional organization in country music was the Country Music Disc Jockey Association (CMDJA). Country disc jockeys had started meeting annually in 1950; two years later, radio station WSM (home to the Grand Ole Opry) began hosting an annual DJ Festival, and in 1953, the CMDJA was formed. The

CMDJA's weakness was that it represented only one branch of the growing country music industry and was not in a position to address the larger questions of image and marketing that country music faced. Recognizing these limitations, several artists and prominent country music executives campaigned for a different type of organization, and at the 1958 CMDJA meeting, a small group of people established the Country Music Association, which met formally for the first time in November 1958.

The Country Music Association (CMA) brought together different branches of the industry; publishers, artists, managers, DJs, radio executives, record labels, trade publications, and songwriters each had representatives on the board of the new organization. The CMA launched a systematic campaign to improve country music's public image. Representatives lobbied to convince radio station owners that the new country format would appeal to middle-class, suburban listeners, and that people who didn't think they liked country music actually did. The CMA's most important work, however, was to bring together the disparate strands of country music into a more coherent canon. Arguments about taste, musical style, tradition, and authenticity were commonplace during the 1950s, with fans, DJs, and executives weighing in on what styles were too twangy or too pop. Those arguments threatened to keep the music fragmented and splintered at the exact time in history that a more unified front promised economic rewards.

To build unity within the country music industry, the CMA first had to convince fans, artists, and the industry that there was such a thing as a genre of country music. The CMA then addressed its goals in three ways. The first was to establish the Country Music Foundation, whose mission was archival and academic. The Foundation provided a sense of intellectual grounding and cultural importance to the genre. The second act of the CMA was to found a Hall of Fame; this allowed the country music industry to craft an official history and legacy for the music. In 1961, the Hall of Fame welcomed its first three inductees: Jimmie Rodgers, Hank Williams, and Fred Rose. These choices not only made the legends of Rodgers and Williams into a celebrated part of the music's official history, but also acknowledged the importance of songwriters and music executives in the genre through the choice of Rose. The third act of the CMA that brought together country music into a more cohesive genre was launching an annual awards show, which began in 1967.

The CMA Awards gave the music industry an opportunity to publicly celebrate and crown the artists it considered to be at the top of the genre. These awards drew national focus to a few significant artists and allowed the music industry to make public its central focus and trends. Any such centralization comes at a significant cost, however, and the trade-off here was that artists who did not fall into the trends that the CMA Awards honored lost some cultural status within the country music scene. But within a decade of its formation, the CMA had taken a fragmented, scattered set of musical traditions and pulled them together into a mass-marketed, respectable musical genre. It had a dedicated foundation whose mission was to preserve and study the music, a clear sense of its own history, and a way to honor and promote its current stars.

⭐ **ESSAY: MUSICAL STYLE**

The Nashville Sound

The Nashville sound's main features included:

1. Instrumentation borrowed from mainstream pop recordings and the elimination or deemphasis of traditional country instrumentation such as banjos and fiddles
2. Smooth, resonant, crooner vocals
3. The incorporation of new studio technology into the recordings
4. New structural features in the songs themselves

Specific instrumentation is the most commonly cited characteristic of the Nashville sound. Nashville sound recordings tended to use drums, though often played with brushes instead of hard sticks. Piano was common, usually played in a "slip-note" style that imitated the traditional sliding notes of a steel guitar. Some recordings also featured vibraphones, which were common in popular music of the 1960s; their chime-like sounds were unlike anything heard in older styles of country music. Occasionally, other instruments sneaked into the Nashville sound as well. Trumpets made appearances, most famously on Johnny Cash's "Ring of Fire," and sometimes even organ.

In place of one or two fiddles, Nashville sound recordings employed whole sections of "strings." Although "violin" and "fiddle" are, in fact, two words that describe the same instrument, the terms are often used to distinguish styles of playing. Writers refer to "strings" on a recording, for instance, when there are a group of three or four violinists playing classical technique, such as vibrato, long, controlled bow strokes, and very precise pitches. Thus, the replacement of "fiddles" with "strings" did not involve any different actual instruments, but instead a noticeably different way of playing them.

Both acoustic and electric guitar were also common in Nashville sound recordings, which often featured virtuosic passages of intricate guitar work. Regarding the steel guitar that was ubiquitous in honky-tonk recordings, some published descriptions of the Nashville sound claim that it was not present in the Nashville sound recordings. The instrument was, in fact, present on many of the records from that era. What changed was not the presence of the steel guitar but the way in which it was used. In Nashville sound recordings, the steel guitar was no longer featured for the "crying" sound that stood out so prominently in the musical texture of honky-tonk recordings. Instead, it was blended smoothly into the accompaniment.

Nashville sound recordings often featured a tic-tac bass, which was the combination of an upright (acoustic) bass and an electric bass guitar playing the same note at the same time. The result was a crisper bass sound in which one could hear a slight pop at the beginning of the note, after which the sound settled into the fat resonance of the upright bass. Different musicians and producers created the tic-tac sound in different ways, sometimes combining an electric baritone guitar with the upright bass and sometimes combining a six-string electric bass guitar with the upright bass.

Nashville sound vocals used more vibrato, more chest voice, and a less nasal sound than earlier styles of country music. The male singers in particular tended to sing in a lower register, and with a less pinched, strained sound. Both male and female soloists blended many of the expressive techniques such as vocal cries and breaks into their performances, but they also used crooner techniques, such as singing very softly and close to the microphone or adding a controlled vibrato to their performance, in many recordings. The Nashville sound recordings also used backup singers, most commonly a vocal quartet. They sang harmony with the soloist, but they also sang neutral syllables such as "ooh" and "ah" to fill in the overall sound of the recording with a lush musical texture.

The singers on these recordings often back-phrased, which means that they sang the phrases of the song with a more improvised rhythm, generally hanging back behind the beat. This technique was common among pop stars, especially those who sang ballads. It made inroads into country music in the late 1950s as part of the larger crossover phenomenon. Patsy Cline heavily back-phrased her ballads in particular, but other singers used it, too. The overall effect was to draw attention to the vocals as an expressive and artful performance, in contrast with the naturalized style of honky-tonk vocals.

Nashville sound recordings used the full extent of available recording technologies. These include echo and reverb; stereophonic recording, which plays back the instruments in different spatial relationships to a left and right speaker; and overdubbing, which means that the final version is not merely the result of one live performance but rather the assembled layers from many performances.

Although writers seldom consider the structural details of a song in relation to musical style, in the case of the Nashville sound it is particularly relevant. The structure of the songs themselves became part of the style. The songs featured in Nashville sound recordings show a slightly different approach to songwriting than earlier country music (see essay on A Professional Writer's Town). Taken together, the elements of the Nashville sound created a distinctly different musical style that was a radical change for country listeners.

(see essay on A Professional Writer's Town)

☆ **ESSAY: SONGWRITING**

 # A Professional Writer's Town

During the Nashville sound era, Nashville turned into a songwriter's town. When country singers moved there in hopes of attaining stardom, they often got signed to a publishing firm long before they got a record deal, which made songwriting a major gateway into the country music business. In the 1960s, established country stars increasingly turned toward songwriting as a means of prolonging their careers. Finally, the fundamental level of craftsmanship within country songwriting changed dramatically.

The foundations for Nashville's songwriting community were laid in the 1940s, when country songwriters discovered that their songs were valuable far beyond the boundaries of country music. Songwriting had always been important in the country music industry; Ralph Peer was not the only producer who figured out that songs could generate money, and every artist knew that a supply of good material was absolutely essential. But Nashville—and country musicians—lacked the publishing firms and connections within the larger music industry to fully capitalize on songwriting's potential.

All that changed when Fred Rose (1898–1954) moved to town. Raised in St. Louis, Rose moved to Chicago as a teenager and worked as a nightclub and jazz pianist. From there, he went to New York, where he found some success as a popular songwriter. He was a skilled musician who, unlike most country singers, could read music fluently, and composed popular songs in the styles of Tin Pan Alley. Eventually, Rose went to Nashville and became a successful songwriter with hits for singing cowboy stars such as Ray Whitley and Gene Autry. In 1942, he saw tremendous potential in the music published field, and he partnered with Roy Acuff to open the Acuff-Rose publishing firm.

Fred Rose and his son Wesley, who worked for Acuff-Rose as well, found themselves with a rich catalog of high-quality songs that they knew could find audiences outside of any one genre. The Roses pitched their songs to producers and executives in the New York pop music scene, including Mitch Miller, the head of Columbia Records, Shortly thereafter, pop stars began recording country songs. In 1951, for instance, Tony Bennett turned Hank Williams's "Cold, Cold Heart" into an enormous pop hit. Countless others followed suit, integrating Nashville into the larger popular music industry.

After Acuff-Rose reached out to country songwriters, other publishers followed suit. In 1945, Hill & Range Music (a name chosen to entice singing cowboy songwriters) opened its doors, albeit in New York, not Nashville. In 1951, Tree Publishing launched in Nashville, and two years later, Cedarwood Publishing also opened shop there. The Nashville music business was in full swing, and the groundwork laid for a flourishing of professional songwriting.

Songwriting became the most accessible entry-point into the country music business for many new artists.

Figure 6-8 Fred Rose at the Piano.
Source: Courtesy of Country Music Hall of Fame and Museum.

Publishers were quick to sign new artists to a songwriting contract, because there were comparatively few costs involved up front. If the writer happened to become a big star who recorded his or her own songs, the publishing firm would earn sizable royalties. Roger Miller and Willie Nelson were just two of many stars who entered the country music business as songwriters during these years and later became stars as performers.

Many established country artists also turned increasingly toward songwriting as a primary part of their careers as they aged. Chief among these were Ira (1924–1965) and Charlie (1927–2011) Loudermilk, known as the Louvin Brothers. Born in Alabama and raised on gospel and hillbilly music, Charlie and Ira began performing as a brother act in the 1940s. They joined the Opry in 1955, long after the heyday of brother acts, and became ambassadors of that earlier style, carrying it forward to younger generations of country fans. But more importantly, the brothers, especially Ira, had a gift for songwriting. Their songs, published by Acuff-Rose, became a major resource for other singers, especially in the late 1960s and '70s.

During the 1960s, country songwriting was largely the domain of a very small group of songwriters. Harlan Howard (1927–2002), Don Gibson (1928–2003), and Hank Cochran (1935–2010) are among the best known, and collectively, they account for a sizeable percentage of Nashville sound hits: "I Fall to Pieces" (by Howard and Cochran, recorded by Patsy Cline), "Sweet Dreams" (by Gibson, recorded by Patsy Cline), and "Make the World Go Away" (by Cochran, recorded by Ray Price and Eddy Arnold) are among their most famous. Contributing to their success was the fact that fewer and fewer stars during these years were writing their own songs, as the roles of singers and songwriters began to diverge. Singers such as Patsy Cline and Jim Reeves needed professional songwriters to supply them with their material, which fueled the substantial growth of the songwriting community. One of the most successful teams of songwriters was husband and wife Felice (1925–2003) and Boudleaux (1920–1987) Bryant. Although they wrote most successfully for rockabilly and pop-influenced performers such as the Everly Brothers, they were a key part of the Nashville songwriting engine that was driving the development of country music throughout the 1960s.

The songs' overall level of craftsmanship also increased during this era. This is not to say that the songs are somehow inherently "better" than earlier country songs, because value judgments such as "better" or "worse" are both highly dependent on the individual listener's tastes, preferences, and personal interpretations of authenticity. However, what we can say about the craftsmanship is that—generally speaking—the songs from these professional writers in the 1960s had more consistent uses of sophisticated musical forms, a wider harmonic vocabulary (more chords in their chord progressions), more complicated poetic structures in terms of rhyming, allusions, and double meanings, and different topics for their storylines than country music from earlier years.

One of these changes was an increasing use of song forms and patterns that showed pop music roots. In terms of song form, the traditional verse-chorus patterns that were common in the hillbilly recording era and found on many honky-tonk songs gave way to more AABA song forms, which had a long history in pop music.

This more sophisticated and pop-influenced songwriting craftsmanship had surfaced in the work of Fred Rose and a few others in the late 1940s, but it had subsequently become commonplace in country music. In many instances, the country hits of the Nashville sound era were not only composed but also recorded as if they were pop hits, which helps explain why the songs were able to cross over into the pop market so easily.

The second change in the songwriting was a shift away from traditional rural, working-class references in the lyrics. Corollaries included the country music industry shedding its hillbilly-hayseed image and the performers trading their cowboy and hillbilly garb for uptown evening wear. These developments ran parallel to the changing demographics of the country audience as many traditionally working-class country fans relocated geographically and experienced a boost of upward mobility that resulted in a suburban, middle-class country audience. In other words, songwriting was very much an integrated part of the genre that both affected and reflected the larger cultural changes within country music. By the end of the Nashville sound era, songwriters had become an even more powerful constituency within the genre.

LISTEN SIDE-BY-SIDE

"Take Me in Your Arms and Hold Me"
Songwriter: Cindy Walker
Eddy Arnold, 1949 (RCA Victor 21-0146)
Eddy Arnold, 1961 (RCA Victor LSP-2337)

IN 1949, EDDY ARNOLD (1918–2008) recorded this classic country song by Cindy Walker, one of the few female country songwriters to achieve lasting recognition. The song reached number one on the country charts during the honky-tonk years. Twelve years later, in 1961, at the peak of the Nashville sound era, Arnold recorded it again. A comparison of the two recordings—sung by the same artist—lets us easily hear the shift in musical style that occurred between the honky-tonk era and the Nashville sound.

The first version was recorded the same year that Hank Williams made his Opry debut. It captures Eddy Arnold, known as the Tennessee Plowboy, at the height of his honky-tonk career (see Chapter 4), although even then his style exhibited a slight tendency toward pop music. On this performance, he incorporates a form of yodeling on the word "arms," where he flips from a low note up to a high note while letting his voice change into a head-tone sound (this is the same yodeling technique that Hank Williams often used in his hits, most famously "Lovesick Blues"). This type of yodeling does not involve the nonsense syllables "yo-del-ay-ee-oo," but rather involves the voice switching from a heavy, low register into a thin, high register rapidly, and with an audible change in the sound's color in the middle of a word. The accompaniment comes mainly from fiddle and steel guitar (which are heard together in the introduction). The bass and rhythm guitar set up a steady, duple, bouncing rhythm.

By 1961, Arnold had become a leading figure in the new Nashville sound era. Like many of the other artists who outlasted honky-tonk, Arnold changed his image to reflect the upscale, popular mode of country music in the 1960s. Arnold kept many of his old songs in his repertory, especially the old cowboy songs and heartbreak laments such as this one, and he kept his vocal yodeling technique. But he wrapped the songs in lush orchestral arrangements and left behind the plowboy image completely. Clad in a tuxedo, he performed in concert halls and noncountry venues coast to coast. The introduction to the 1961 version of "Take Me in Your Arms . . ." uses several violins, or "strings," playing with a shimmering, tremolo technique. The pianist, Bill Pursell, is busy throughout the song with tinkling fills, while the drums and strings pull the listener into the lilting shuffle rhythm. In keeping with the overall change in style, Arnold sings the song in a much lower key than he did in 1949, so that his voice sounds more full and resonant, and slows down the tempo dramatically. At this slower tempo, he leaves out two full sections of the song in order to keep the recording to a reasonable length. The stereophonic mix of the song highlights the changes in recording technology that had occurred between the two versions. Most striking is the way that Arnold's vocals are drenched in echo and reverb, both effects that are added in the recording process and that are strikingly different from the stark, naturalized sound of honky-tonk vocals.

Similar stylistic differences are apparent when one compares just about any honky-tonk or western swing song from the 1940s or early 1950s with 1960s cover versions of it. This is true when the cover is done by a country artist, such as Bob Wills's version of "Faded Love" and Patsy Cline's cover of it. But it is also true when the cover is done by a noncountry artist, such as Hank Williams's "I'm So Lonesome I Could Cry" sung in 1963 by Rosemary Clooney. Yet as we have seen elsewhere in this chapter, the country singers making these records saw them as heartfelt, genuine country performances, and thought of the Nashville sound merely as a new style of country music, just as honky-tonk or bluegrass had also been new styles at one time. Eddy Arnold, for instance, declared that he simply preferred the 1960s versions of his songs to the earlier ones as a matter of personal taste. Fans have not always agreed.

PLAYLIST

Cline, Patsy. "Walkin' after Midnight" (1956)

Cramer, Floyd. "Last Date" (1960)

Dean, Jimmy. "Big Bad John" (1961)

Frizzell, Lefty. "Saginaw Michigan" (1964)

Miller, Roger. "King of the Road" (1965)

Young, Faron. "Hello Walls" (1961)

FOR MORE READING

Brown, Maxine. *Looking Back to See: A Country Music Memoir.* Fayetteville: University of Arkansas Press, 2005.

Jensen, Joli. *The Nashville Sound: Authenticity, Commercialization, and Country Music.* Nashville: Vanderbilt University Press, 1998.

Jones, Margaret. *Patsy: The Life and Times of Patsy Cline*. New York: Da Capo Press, 1999 (originally published New York: HarperCollins, 1994).

Kosser, Michael. *How Nashville Became Music City U.S.A.: 50 Years of Music Row*. New York: Hal Leonard, 2006.

Pecknold, Diane. *The Selling Sound: The Rise of the Country Music Industry*. Durham: Duke University Press, 2007.

Streissguth, Michael. *Eddy Arnold: Pioneer of the Nashville Sound*. Jackson: University Press of Mississippi, 2009.

NAMES AND TERMS

Arnold, Eddy	Dean, Jimmy	Reeves, Jim
A-Team	Dickens, Little Jimmy	Robbins, Marty
Atkins, Chet	Gibson, Don	Rose, Fred
Bradley, Owen	Hamilton, George IV	Sholes, Steve
Charles, Ray	James, Sonny	slip-note piano
Cline, Patsy	Miller, Roger	strings
CMA	Nashville sound	Teen crooner
Cramer, Floyd	Price, Ray	tic-tac bass

REVIEW TOPICS

1. How did the studio system in Nashville affect the sound of the recordings in the early 1960s?

2. In what ways was the Nashville sound a continuation of earlier efforts to shift country music away from its hillbilly image, and in what ways was its approach different from what had occurred in the past?

3. Discuss the actual sound of these recordings, i.e., your response to hearing them, in relation to the meaning and role of the Nashville sound hits within the country genre.

PART III

Coast to Coast: Outsiders, Outlaws, and Tradition (1960s and 1970s)

By the middle of the 1960s, country music had found a place within the new landscape of popular music. Through the Nashville Sound, it had garnered the attention of the music industry at large, slipped into the mainstream, and secured a more respectable reputation for itself. But radical changes were on the horizon: as the soundtrack for a white, middle-class Americans, country would be called on to confront the social revolutions of the late 1960s and 70s. The music would catalog, critique, and influence the American public's response to the Vietnam War, the Civil Rights Act and the corresponding social movement, and the women's liberation movement.

Cultural developments outside of country had a profound influence on the genre. The folk revival hit country music full force in the 1960s, bringing new audiences to the genre while simultaneously adding confrontational politics to the mix. Meanwhile, radical new styles of rock music took root, and in many instances those styles both affected country music and borrowed heavily from it. Mainstream country music consciously crossed the border into the realm of pop, while resurrecting an exaggerated stereotype of its former hillbilly identity for comedic effect. And finally, a burgeoning movement within country, ideologically centered in the lone star state of Texas, cultivated a rebellion from within, which became the outlaw movement. In sum, country music engaged much more heavily with other musical genres and with the social issues that emerged during these years, while demanding attention as a major representation of American popular culture.

By the mid-'70s, country music was already a significant player in the music business. National trade organizations had launched awards shows and founded a Hall of Fame to canonize its founding fathers (the first seventeen inductees were men—the women had to wait longer for recognition, which says a lot about how these organizations viewed their own history). That generation of stars has since become the classic names in country music—Loretta Lynn, George Jones, Tammy Wynette, Conway Twitty, and Dolly Parton—and their styles of their music have become benchmarks of tradition. These developments culminated symbolically in 1974, when the Grand Ole Opry moved its live broadcast from the historic Ryman auditorium in downtown Nashville—a location rich in history but lacking amenities such as air-conditioning and decent parking—to a new, state-of-the-art facility with an accompanying theme park, some fifteen miles outside of Nashville in the suburbs. A year later, film director Robert Altman's *Nashville* used country music, its stars, and its city to offer a biting and satirical critique of modern America's cultural wasteland; the film simultaneously offended many within the core country audience and—partially through its widespread critical acclaim—brought a new audience to the genre. By then, country music had transitioned from a regional music into a national music and had fully assimilated into mainstream, middle-class American life.

During these years, the dominant issue within country music was how to maintain ties to the past while taking on a modern, forward-looking identity that matched its audience's outlook—the basic tension between tradition and innovation. One of the strongest modernizing forces that threatened country music's past traditions was television, which had been part of the country music scene since the early 1950s. Country singers wanted (and often got) to host their own shows, which gave them weekly access to huge audiences. The shows also meant that their physical appearance, stage personality, and ability to host, interview, and interact with other musicians became increasingly important. The potentially large television and movie market also motivated country singers to present themselves as high-class entertainers rather than to limit themselves to a particularly "country" audience. Stars such as Porter Wagoner and the Wilburn Brothers commanded long-running, popular shows focusing on country music. Others, such as Johnny Cash and Glen Campbell, fronted shows that were pitched mainly toward a pop audience; although those shows lasted only a few years, they still helped spread the popularity of country music in the late 1960s.

Politics shaped country music during those years as well. From World War II on, the country music industry had found a receptive audience among military personnel, many of whom came from working-class, small-town or rural backgrounds, and a disproportionate number of whom were Southern. Those ties grew stronger as country music was co-opted by the social conservatism that grew out of the Cold War. By the 1960s, country music was firmly linked to a nationalist, patriotic, and conservative political agenda, even while other genres of popular music, notably rock, adopted more radical and antiestablishment perspectives. Country song lyrics, however, espoused a variety of political perspectives during those years, just as individual fans held a wide variety of political opinions. In many instances, the lyrics of a single song could be interpreted in several conflicting ways by listeners. While country music became the soundtrack for what President Richard Nixon called the "silent majority," country music also appealed to musicians in various liberal and countercultural movements because it represented ideas of tradition, roots, and antimodernism. How various styles of country music could simultaneously invoke a conservative political stance and appeal to audiences with liberal and even radical leanings is one of the more intriguing features of the genre.

These chapters also address the ways in which country music intersected with other musical genres and major social movements during the late 1960s and throughout the 1970s. Many country singers in this period purposely sought mainstream acceptability. They mastered the art of being show-business entertainers to such an extent that they moved seamlessly between the worlds of Las Vegas, Hollywood, and Nashville. No other change in country music's history has provoked as much controversy as that one; proponents celebrated the uptown developments, while detractors complained bitterly about the loss of tradition. Yet, in spite of all of these developments, the music from this time period has retrospectively been celebrated as "classic country." Today's fans look back half a century at this music nostalgically as a golden age in the genre.

These chapters cover three major developments that occurred between the late 1960s and the late 1970s in country music. First, we will examine the response and reaction to the Nashville sound that occurred on the West Coast, along with folk and rock musicians' growing interest in country music, bluegrass musicians' fascination with musical experimentation, and country musicians' appropriation of rock music. Second, we will look at the continued evolution of mainstream country music as traditionalist or classic country music emerged from a fusion of the Nashville sound with honky-tonk aesthetics. And third, we will explore a revolution that occurred from within the core of the genre, which became the Outlaw movement and forged ties between country and Southern rock. More than in any earlier time period, these musical developments diversified the sounds of the genre and solidified its ties to other musical genres.

The three main themes of this book are relevant to understanding these musical developments. The identity of country musicians and fans during these years reflected the splits in the larger population: the audiences for Bakersfield music and for the country rock of the Byrds were simply not the same. Within the Outlaw movement, Willie Nelson famously described groups on opposite ends of the political spectrum sitting side by side at his concerts. And perhaps most significantly, the country songwriters themselves drew on different life experiences, including college educations and a range of new political perspectives. Authenticity shifted to a value most typically (but not always) attributed to first-person narratives in the music. And the relationship of country music to other genres shifted from one of differentiation (otherness) to one of complex interweavings. ❧

California Country and Country Rock

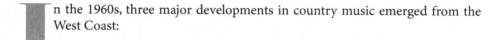

In the 1960s, three major developments in country music emerged from the West Coast:

1. The Bakersfield sound, which grew out of the working-class dance halls in the farming and oil-well communities north of Los Angeles.
2. Progressive bluegrass, which merged traditional bluegrass instrumentation with the experimental sounds of the 1960s, in particular folk rock.
3. Country rock, which evolved in the later '60s as more young rock musicians—many of whom had also played in bluegrass bands—turned to country music as a means of connecting with their musical roots.

These styles had been brewing for some time in California, where a unique combination of audiences and venues cultivated different sounds than in the Southeast. California also offered a unique opportunity for crossover influences, in these instances not from pop music but rather from rock and folk music. In each case, these West Coast developments stood in stark contrast to the traditions of mainstream country music as represented by Nashville, the Opry, and other such institutions. Each of these three developments in country music ran its course in a relatively short span of time. By the mid-1970s, the Bakersfield sound had merged into mainstream country music, while both progressive bluegrass and country rock had headed in different directions, continuing to thrive with a dedicated fan base outside of country. Yet all of these contributions would prove extremely influential for later generations of country musicians.

Out in Bakersfield

Bakersfield, California, sits approximately a hundred miles north of Los Angeles in the fertile, agricultural San Joaquin Valley, which also happens to have oil. In the 1930s and '40s, the region saw an influx of migrant workers from Oklahoma, Texas, and Arkansas who were escaping the Dust Bowl and looking for better opportunities for their families. Rose Maddox, for instance, had been part of this group (see Chapter 4). Like most of Southern California, Bakersfield and the neighboring working-class community of Oildale were made up of people who were displaced from home and family, working as wage-laborers in the boom period after World War II.

Their regular entertainment in the 1940s consisted of gathering for live music and dancing, which helped them both to keep aspects of their former culture alive and to forge a new community. During the heyday of western swing, more than eight dance halls in the area featured live music most nights of the week. Bob Wills was among the many bandleaders who brought his band to town for an extended engagement at one of these venues. By the 1950s, honky-tonks such as the Blackboard and Trout's (which finally closed in 2017) had opened their doors to the shift workers, particularly from the oil fields, who were looking for a place to unwind. Unlike today's nightclub scene, these venues employed live musicians nightly. And as had been the case in the Texas dance halls a few decades earlier (see Chapter 3), the practicalities of playing for a rowdy crowd who liked to dance and drink affected the music. The house bands in the 1950s were relatively small—usually five or six musicians—and drums and amplified electric guitars allowed them to be heard over the noise of the crowd. Country musicians working on the West Coast, such as Rose Maddox or Lefty Frizzell, were able to find performance opportunities quite easily. The sheer number of venues meant that several other bandleaders who did not attain fame outside the region also had successful careers, including Tommy Collins, Billy Mize, Bill Woods, and Wynn Stewart.

By the late 1950s, Bakersfield musicians had cultivated a unique musical style, which came to be called the Bakersfield sound. Historians have sometimes described this as a reactionary development that grew out of opposition to the Nashville sound. However, the two musical styles emerged at more or less the same time. Their

Listening Guide

"Mama Tried" (1968)

PERFORMER: Merle Haggard

SONGWRITER: Merle Haggard

ORIGINAL RELEASE: Capitol 2219

FORM: Verse-chorus

STYLE: Bakersfield sound

Merle Haggard wrote "Mama Tried" for a relatively unknown Dick Clark movie called *Killers Three* in 1968, but over time, fans have transformed the song into an autobiographical signature song for Haggard. When the song came out, Haggard was well into a successful run of hits. His first number one song had appeared almost exactly two years earlier, and since then he had become the dominant face of the Bakersfield sound.

In the late 1960s and early 1970s, country singers began to transform their biographies into signature songs. This trend reflected how fans were once again placing value on music that was tied directly to the personal experiences of the singers. Loretta Lynn's "Coal Miner's Daughter," Johnny Cash's "Daddy Sang Bass," and Dolly Parton's "Coat of Many Colors" were just a few of the many songs that functioned as minibiographies.

Like these other songs, "Mama Tried" had the essential elements of a country biographical song: references to family, religion, hard times, hard work, hard knocks, and personal strength. To that basic list, Haggard added the promise of both freedom and adventure of a rambling life in the form of train images. Of course, the details of the song contained poetic license rather than strict adherence to autobiography, as Haggard was not serving "life without parole." Together, "Mama Tried" and "I'm a Lonesome Fugitive," which had been his first number one hit back in 1966, defined Merle Haggard's personal story for legions of fans.

This song also showcases the mature Bakersfield sound: ringing guitars, the searing bite of a Telecaster, swing rhythms, drums, insistent bass lines, and sparse differences in sound were the direct results of the music-making environments in which each was conceived. The Nashville sound (see Chapter 6) was designed to take advantage of the full capabilities of the modern recording studio, and its producers were pitching the recordings to a growing radio audience that included pop-crossover listeners. By contrast, the Bakersfield sound artists created a musical style (see essay on Bakersfield Sound) that was firmly planted on the live honky-tonk stage, then imported it into the recording studio with few modifications. Where the Nashville sound represented shimmering strings and sophisticated, musical polish, the Bakersfield sound represented working-class music forged in a smoky honky-tonk.

The sound of Bakersfield music had its roots in the mid-1950s honky-tonk of artists such as Carl Smith, Lefty Frizzell, and Ray Price. Of particular importance was the "shuffle" rhythm, a variant of the swing rhythm that was commonly used by '50s-era R&B musicians. Shuffles were slightly different than "swing" tunes, mostly in that the shuffle pattern placed an accent on all four beats of the music, whereas the swing tunes often had a strong backbeat, or accent on counts 2 and 4. This difference is underscored by the use of a "walking bass" in shuffle tunes, in which

vocal harmony on the chorus of the songs. Here, Bonnie Owens contributes vocal harmony, Roy Nichols plays the electric guitar solos, and Haggard's voice sounds like he is trapped somewhere between accepting and defying his apparent fate.

TIME	FORM	LISTENING CUES	DISCUSSION
0:00	Introduction	electric guitar	Ringing guitar sounds, especially these patterns played on acoustic rhythm guitar, are a hallmark of these Bakersfield recordings. The electric guitar solo that enters at 0:05 is a memorable hook for this song.
0:12	Verse 1	"The first thing…"	This verse evokes the same rambling, train-riding hobo character that has been popular in country music since the days of Jimmie Rodgers.
0:32	Verse 2	"A one and only…"	This verse solidifies the ideas of family and religion that underpin the country music philosophy.
0:52	Chorus	"And I turned twenty-one…"	The drums play a swing rhythm here with a loud ride cymbal. Vocal harmony (two voices) fills in behind Haggard's solo.
1:11	Instrumental interlude	electric guitar	The solo uses the same melody that we heard in the introduction (and that will return at the end), then launches into a short but classic "Bakersfield Telecaster" sound.
1:21	Verse 3	"Dear old daddy…"	This verse continues the story line with a sincere tribute to his mother, and by extension, working-class women.
1:41	Chorus	"And I turned twenty-one…"	Notice the opening line of the chorus, which has become the symbolic identity of Merle Haggard much like one line from "Folsom Prison Blues" did for Johnny Cash.
1:59	Outro	electric guitar	This wraps up the song the same way it began.

the bass player plays notes on all four beats. Price helped popularize this rhythm, particularly in his 1956 recording, "Crazy Arms." Price used honky-tonk instrumentation, including fiddle and pedal steel guitar, with the addition of piano. The recording also featured a syncopated melody that used uneven note values (swing rhythms), the first of each pair of short notes being twice as long as the second. The walking bass is easily audible throughout. Unlike Nashville sound recordings with several backup vocalists, this recording featured just one backup singer, who sang a high harmony part over the melody. Shuffle patterns had occasionally shown up in country music prior to Price's 1956 recording, but "Crazy Arms" codified the style.

ARTIST PROFILE

Merle Haggard (1937–2016)

Merle Haggard is one of the few country singers who has been revered as a legend by almost all subsequent generations of country singers. His name, along with George Jones, Johnny Cash, and Hank Williams, appears in countless tribute songs and oblique references to the storied yesteryears of country music. Born in 1937 to parents who left Oklahoma during the Dust Bowl migration, Haggard grew up in Bakersfield, California, a town whose music scene he later helped turn into a national phenomenon. Haggard's family was working poor but not destitute. When he was nine, his father passed away, and Haggard's wild streak left him perennially in juvenile detention. Petty theft and fighting gave way to auto theft. In 1957, Haggard was arrested trying to rob a bar, and with his past record, he was sentenced to time in San Quentin prison. While there, Haggard decided to set a straighter course.

Upon release from prison, Haggard found work as a musician in the burgeoning scene around Bakersfield. By good fortune, Wynn Stewart hired Haggard to play in his western swing band for a stint in Las Vegas. From those connections, Haggard secured his first record contract with a small, independent label. Meanwhile, Buck Owens hired him to play bass for a short while with the Buckaroos. By 1965, Haggard had signed with Capitol Records, found modest success as a songwriter, and started to front his own band, the Strangers.

Haggard's sound picked up where Owens had left off: electric guitars searing through hard-driving honky-tonk dance hall music with steel guitar, memorable acoustic guitar patterns, loud bass, and drums. He began to perform with Owens's former wife, Bonnie, whom he married in 1965. And his songwriting turned more toward personal experience and the essence of the Bakersfield aesthetic, hard knocks of working-class life served with a heavy dose of irony. A good example of Haggard's classic sound is 1968's "Mama Tried" (see Listening Guide).

Throughout the 1960s, Haggard recorded exclusively in Capitol Records' Hollywood Studios. He released a number of live albums, something that fit well with the Bakersfield sound's concept of live, bold, raw country music. He also continued a trend that honky-tonk stars such as Webb Pierce and Lefty Frizzell had pioneered, namely paying tribute to and connecting with the first generation of

Ray Price's sound was soon adopted by the West Coast musicians, who found that it fit their musical tastes and performance venues well. Before long, the style was known as a "Bakersfield shuffle." Musicians such as Buck Owens further modified the style to a more generic "Bakersfield sound," which included the drums, electric guitar, and—a recent development—electric bass. The Bakersfield sound had additional distinctions that set it apart from the developments in Nashville. Among those were a tendency toward a simpler, verse-chorus type of songwriting and songs that were unapologetically grounded in working-class stories.

country singers, most notably Jimmie Rodgers. In 1969 Haggard released *Same Train, A Different Time*, an album of Rodgers cover songs. His debt to country music tradition was an important part of how the Bakersfield sound was perceived by fans, who saw it as tied to the hard-edged, twangy roots of the genre. During the 1960s, Haggard scored several number one hits, among them "I'm a Lonesome Fugitive," "Sing Me Back Home," "Hungry Eyes," "Mama Tried," and "Workin' Man Blues." Toward the end of the decade, he wrote and recorded two songs that entered the political fray: "Okie from Muskogee" and "Fightin' Side of Me" (see essay on "Okie from Muskogee" and Country Music Politics). Heated debates over the lyrics of those two songs have nearly overshadowed everything else from Haggard's output during those years.

In the early 1970s, Haggard's style drifted more toward mainstream country. He began recording in Nashville, and the defiant sound of the Bakersfield tradition receded from his records. In 1977, he switched to MCA Records, then to Epic a few years later. By the early 1980s, new trends in country music had passed him by. By the 1990s, Haggard had drifted into a new role as elder statesman within country music, recording occasionally for alt-country labels, and even touring with Bob Dylan.

Figure 7-1 Merle Haggard performing in 1969.
Source: Courtesy BenCar Archives.

Merle Haggard's personal troubles (several failed marriages and stints with alcohol and drugs) and financial troubles continued to plague him throughout his life. Honored as a legend, Haggard was the quintessential ramblin' man and lonesome fugitive whom mama tried but failed to save from his own troubled, honky-tonk soul.

Buck Owens (1929–2006)

Known as one of the leading figures in the Bakersfield sound, Owens's contributions to the development of country music in the 1960s were somewhat overshadowed in later years by his cohosting the comedic television program *Hee Haw*.

Alvis Edgar Owens Jr., who picked up the nickname Buck at a young age, was born in Sherman, Texas, but grew up in Arizona, where his family had moved during the Dust Bowl migration. He picked up the guitar at an early age and earned a job playing on a local radio station. In 1951, he moved with his young wife, Bonnie, and their baby to Bakersfield, California, looking for work in that region's thriving music scene. Within a short time, Bill Woods hired him to play in his successful western swing band, and Owens supplemented his income as a highly regarded session musician in Los Angeles, where he backed a number of big-name stars in the 1950s, including Faron Young and Wanda Jackson. During those years, his personal life was a wreck; Bonnie divorced him in 1953, unwilling to put up with his philandering ways.

By the mid-1950s, Owens had started to play guitar for Tommy Collins, who was enjoying some success as a country singer. Collins even got invited to Nashville to play the Opry, and took Owens along as part of his band. Owens's business sense was also apparent. He and Harlan Howard had teamed up as songwriting partners, and realizing that the economic potential for songwriters lay in the publishing rights, Owens and Howard launched Blue Book Music, a publishing firm that Owens would later take over on his own. Owen wanted to establish a solo career as a singer as well; he signed with two small labels, but failed to launch any hits. He moved briefly to Washington State, where he gained more experience playing in honky-tonks and dance halls. While there, he met a teenager named Don Rich, a talented fiddle player, guitarist, and vocalist, with whom he collaborated for nearly two decades.

Ken Nelson of Capitol Records signed Owens in 1957, and by the mid-1960s Owens had a string of number one singles on the country charts. Owens's formula for success was the honky-tonk barroom country music played nightly in local venues up and down the west coast: danceable, raucous heartbreak music. Very early in his career, when he found himself broke, he hocked his electric Gibson archtop guitar at a pawn shop. He failed to return for it on time, and lost it. That incident indirectly shaped the course of Bakersfield music; Owens needed a guitar, so he purchased a used Fender Telecaster from a friend. The distinctive twang and growl of the Telecaster guitar became the bedrock of the Bakersfield sound. His guitar, plus a sparse, minimalist honky-tonk texture, loud drums, and an affinity for rock 'n' roll, shaped Owens's music into

While the dance halls and honky-tonks of Bakersfield were the perfect environment for this new style to develop, its larger impact on country music came more from their proximity to Los Angeles, where session musicians, recording studios, and record labels—both small and large—provided the necessary infrastructure to market this music to a national audience. Most notably, Capitol Records opened its doors there in 1942 and had become a major label in country music by the 1950s. Without that gateway to the larger music industry, the local or regional style would the definitive style of an era. By the mid-1960s, his band, called the Buckaroos, relied on bass, drums, electric guitar, rhythm guitar, and steel guitar, plus the single line of high vocal harmony provided by Rich.

Situated in California, Owens was an important point of contact between country music and the growing genre of rock. His first number-one song, "Act Naturally" (1963) was a favorite of drummer Ringo Starr, who had the Beatles cover it (see Listen Side by Side). Conversely, Owens covered a number of rock songs, including Chuck Berry's "Johnny B. Goode," which wound up at the top of the country charts in Owens's version. While rock and country music were becoming increasingly distinct genres during the 1960s, Owens and the Bakersfield sound constituted one instance where the two not only met but actually merged.

Owens's hits continued well into the mid-1970s. However, in 1969 he signed on as cohost of a new television program, *Hee Haw*, that offered a half hour of cornball country comedy interlaced with country music performances. Fans came to associate Owens and cohost Roy Clark more with the stereotyped hayseed themes on the show and slapstick comedy than with his striking contributions to country music in the 1960s. In 1974, he suffered the biggest setback of his career when Don Rich was killed in a motorcycle accident. The loss of his friend and musical partner hit Owens hard, and friends claimed he never fully recovered.

Figure 7-2 Buck Owens and his Buckaroos (Don Rich, second from right).

Source: Southern Folklife Collection, Wilson Library, The University of North Carolina at Chapel Hill.

By the 1980s, Owens had left the spotlight as a singer, although he remained fully invested in the music business through his ownership in a number of radio stations. As the neotraditional movement (see Chapter 11) gained steam, however, newcomer Dwight Yoakam paid tribute to the Bakersfield sound and brought Owens out of retirement to record a new version of his anthem, "The Streets of Bakersfield," which Owens had originally done in 1973. The song's antagonistic, rambling loner with his own code of morals was an iconic representation of the Bakersfield musical tradition. Owens passed away in his sleep in 2006 after playing one last concert as his Crystal Palace venue in Bakersfield.

have never reached the national stage. But with Los Angeles's resources only a few hours away, the musicians had easy access to publishing firms, record labels, and studios that were in a position to market their music more broadly.

The two leading proponents of the Bakersfield sound were Buck Owens and Merle Haggard (see Artist Profiles). The two became major stars in country music while also cultivating the distinctive characteristics of the Bakersfield sound, both in their musical performances and in the images and attitudes associated with the sound.

Listening Guide

"Excuse Me (I Think I've Got a Heartache)" (1959)

PERFORMER: Buck
Owens

SONGWRITERS:
Harlan Howard and
Buck Owens

ORIGINAL RELEASE:
Capitol 4412

FORM: Verse-chorus

STYLE: Bakersfield
shuffle

In 1957, Buck Owens signed a contract with Capitol Records and began to fine-tune the sound of his own band. Over the winter holidays in 1959, he headed down to Hollywood to cut several songs, among them this one. Harlan Howard penned the words for it, inspired by a conversation he had with a local DJ named Bill Strength, whose wife was moving out at the time. Buck Owens wrote the music, as was common when Howard and Owens teamed up on a song. Even in its form, "Excuse Me" is as straightforward a song as possible—a simple verse-chorus pattern with only two verses, which is far more conventional a country song than the more pop-influenced AABA forms that were so popular among the Nashville sound performers at this time.

Owens's entire approach to making music was radically different than that of the Nashville sound artists such as Patsy Cline and Jim Reeves who were also topping the chart in the late 1950s. Owens played guitar and had earned his living for many years as a working musician in other people's bands. He wrote or cowrote many of his own songs. Within the recording studio, he had recently taken on more responsibility for how his records sounded. When Owens first signed with Capitol Records, producer Ken Nelson dressed his songs up with more backup vocals and musical arrangements that borrowed from pop music, much as the producers in Nashville such as Owen Bradley and Chet Atkins were doing at that time. However, the approach did not work with Owens—those songs floundered. Owens reportedly even offered to cancel the recording contract, but Ken Nelson decided instead to let Owens have more of a say in how the band sounded in the studio. As a result, Owens returned to the dance hall sound that he had cultivated in the honky-tonks in California and Washington State. Steel guitar, fiddle, honky-tonk piano, drums, and the shuffle rhythm became the foundation of his sound. On later recordings, Owens's Fender Telecaster guitar stole the show, but on "Excuse Me," the fiddle and steel guitar pulled the sound back to the heart of the honky-tonk era.

This session was the first collaboration in the recording studio between Owens and Don Rich, who traveled to Los Angeles during his winter break from school to participate in the session. Until his death in 1974, Rich was responsible for singing vocal harmony with Owens on almost every concert and recording, and that

In the 1960s, country music experienced a significant backlash from fans who felt that the Nashville sound had gone too far in its extremes of pop-crossover elements. They were craving a musical antidote that would—in their minds—return to the essence of country music, which they imagined as some ideal combination two-part sound was a key characteristic of the Bakersfield sound. He also took over the lead electric guitar later for the band, which freed Owens up to focus on singing. But at this relatively early stage in his career, Owens overdubbed his own vocal harmony, which means that he sang the melody and then, in another "take," sang the harmony part with himself on the tape, and Rich only played fiddle on this song.

"Excuse Me" is an excellent example of the Bakersfield shuffle rhythm, which arises from the interaction of several instruments' rhythmic patterns including especially the piano part. The recording was released in January of 1960, and it became Owens's highest-charting hit to date, topping out at number two on the *Billboard* charts. The Bakersfield sound, as heard in this early example, represents the places and traditions of the West Coast and how differently country music functioned there than in the Nashville establishments.

TIME	FORM	LISTENING CUES	DISCUSSION
0:00	Introduction	steel guitar	The opening of this recording shows a clear connection to the honky-tonk tradition. Steel guitar plays the melody, while the rest of the band including drums, bass, rhythm guitar, and piano, set up a shuffle rhythm.
0:08	Verse 1	"They just don't know…"	Notice how laid-back Owens's vocals sound against the driving, shuffle-pattern rhythm. The fiddle (played by Don Rich) provides a contrasting melody behind Owens's vocals. The reverb on the vocals makes the whole recording sound very different than the early 1950s honky-tonk.
0:35	Chorus	"Excuse me…"	One of the typical features of a Bakersfield recording is one backup vocalist singing harmony above the melody on the chorus, just as we hear here. The fiddle drops out, and instead, the steel guitar takes up the role of filling in contrasting melody behind the singers. Notice how the song's title shows up twice in the chorus.
1:01	Instrumental interlude	Steel guitar	The instrumental solo occupies exactly one verse of the song.
1:28	Verse 2	"I guess it's pride…"	The fiddle reappears here. Notice the sparse texture behind Owens's vocals.
1:55	Chorus	"Excuse me…"	The fiddle is replaced by steel guitar again for the final chorus. The whole song is over in less than two and a half minutes.

of hillbilly and honky-tonk. Although the Bakersfield sound offered plenty of contrast in its musical style alone, its ideology was what some fans found most appealing. The artists often wrote their own songs, then recorded them with essentially the same arrangements and instrumental lineups as they used in their live performances. The artists, especially those signed to Capitol Records, made their recordings in California, which meant that they were using different session musicians and were physically removed from Nashville, a fact that carried great symbolic importance to some fans. And rather than drawing significant influence from pop music, the Bakersfield artists were on the front lines of new developments in rock music and were borrowing readily from that scene. Patsy Cline did not cover Chuck Berry songs, for instance, but Buck Owens certainly did. As a result, the Bakersfield sound came to represent more than just an alternative to the Nashville sound. It gained meaning as a push-back against the Nashville sound. For its fans, the Bakersfield sound was the rightful heir of western swing and honky-tonk, music made by "cultural outsiders" who defiantly resisted assimilation into the pop mainstream (or, in other words, protected country's "otherness"), even when their music was, in fact, popular.

Even the professional and trade organizations in country music reflected the Nashville-Bakersfield tension. In 1964, the Academy of Country Music (ACM) was organized in California as an alternative to the Country Music Association (CMA). Its founders were displeased by the Nashville-centric nature of the CMA as well as its apparent preference for the crossover styles of country music. The ACM's mission, by contrast, included promoting and celebrating West Coast country music, including the developments in Bakersfield and the honky-tonk traditions that still thrived in the western states. The ACM launched an annual awards show in 1965 and named Buck Owens and Bonnie Owens as the top male and top female vocalists. Five years later, the ACM added an Entertainer of the Year award, which went to Merle Haggard, confirming the organization's West Coast leanings. The polarization represented by the two trade organizations mirrored the tensions within the country fan community.

Bluegrass Meets Folk-Rock

At the same time that Buck Owens and Merle Haggard were cranking out hot guitar licks and barroom lyrics, California was home to another development in country music. Bluegrass bands had taken up residence in California, where their music was integrated into the thriving folk scene, similar to what was happening on the East Coast (see Chapter 5). Many of the bands preserved the instrumentation and performance styles of Bill Monroe or Flatt and Scruggs; they stuck to acoustic instruments, sang folk songs or newly composed songs that used the same topics and general sound as older tunes, and emphasized those aspects of bluegrass that were most distinct from commercial country and from other genres. But some bands moved into what is called progressive bluegrass: they began to experiment with a wider selection of instruments including electric bass and guitars, flute, drums, and pianos, all used in ways that evoked the developments in folk-rock and, more generally, 1960s rock. These bands covered rock and jazz songs; they wrote new songs on unconventional topics that had no ties to the rural traditions or nostalgic story-telling of bluegrass; and, in many instances, they created strong connections with the musicians, audiences, and styles of jazz, folk, folk-rock, and psychedelia. Many of these progressive bluegrass musicians were young, and their own taste in music ranged from country and bluegrass far afield into those other genres. As a result, during the later 1960s sharp divisions appeared within bluegrass, with traditionalists on one side and progressive bluegrass musicians on the other.

One of the more acclaimed progressive bluegrass bands was, ironically, also known for their portrayal of stereotypical, traditional Appalachian mountain folk. The Dillards originated in Missouri with brothers Doug (1937–) and Rodney (1942–) Dillard, along with Dean Webb and Mitch Jayne. Doug played banjo, while Rodney covered both guitar and Dobro. In 1962, the band moved to Los Angeles to pursue their music. Their big commercial break came in 1963, when they were hired to play a family band named the Darlings on *The Andy Griffith Show*. Set in the fictional town of Mayberry, North Carolina, *The Andy Griffith Show* explored life in a slow-paced Appalachian town. On the show, the Darlings were an amusingly uncultured jug band who lived out of town in a backwoods mountain shack, with actor Denver Pyle filling in as the band's jug blower. Exposure from the television show helped the Dillards' musical career tremendously, as they appeared on a half-dozen episodes from 1963 to 1966. Yet while they were portraying a string-and-jug bluegrass band on screen, the Dillards were moving into increasingly progressive areas of bluegrass in their own concerts and recordings.

As on the East Coast, California boasted a musical melding pot in the 1960s that combined both the folk revival and the developments in rock, which ranged from the British Invasion and the Beatles (starting in 1964) to the growing psychedelic

Figure 7-3 The Dillards: (from left) Rodney Dillard, Doug Dillard, Dean Webb, and Mitch Jayne.

Source: Southern Folklife Collection, Wilson Library, The University of North Carolina at Chapel Hill.

scene that was centered in San Francisco a few years later. In the middle of all of that, a larger group of musicians that included Doug Dillard began to experiment with a fusion of folk music, bluegrass instruments, and the chord progressions, vocal harmonies, electric guitars, and drums from rock. The result was initially called folk-rock, best illustrated by the sounds of the Byrds and Bob Dylan in the mid-1960s. By 1968, when the Dillards released their fourth album, *Wheatstraw Suite*, their sound had migrated away from traditional bluegrass and into a new form called progressive bluegrass that layered folk vocals with bluegrass over a rock-band rhythm section. *Wheatstraw Suite* included a cover of the Beatles "I've Just Seen a Face," evidence of the band's direct absorption of rock music. The overall sound of this progressive bluegrass is clearly illustrated on "Listen to the Sound," where flutes and percussion weave around the mandolin and guitar, with chords, vocal harmony, and changes of key that are ripped straight from experimental rock music. The results are completely foreign to traditional bluegrass but have much in common with radical new developments in rock, specifically country rock, and many of the musicians from the progressive bluegrass scene collaborated with musicians from country rock.

The Dillards were not the only band to move into progressive bluegrass. Chris Hillman (1944–) was another California musician who moved fluidly between the bluegrass, folk, and country-rock communities during the 1950s and '60s. Hillman, who grew up near San Diego, was a big fan of California's best bluegrass bands in the 1950s, and took up mandolin and guitar. In 1962, he joined the Golden State Boys, who changed their band's name to the Hillmen. The group was only together for two years, but they represent the musical interactions that tied together bluegrass, folk-rock, country rock, and mainstream country music. Chris Hillman would later join the country rock band the Byrds, while their lead singer Vern Gosdin would become a major mainstream country star in the 1970s. In other words, the Southern California bluegrass scene was a critical crossroads in the overall development of 1960s music.

The growing psychedelia scene around San Francisco had a large bluegrass component. Jerry Garcia (1942–1995), for instance, was raised in the Bay Area, which housed a full musical array of rock, R&B, country, bluegrass, and folk in the 1950s. Garcia, who played both banjo and guitar, is best known for fronting the rock band the Grateful Dead, but in the early 1970s, he and other musicians whose backgrounds were a blend of rock and bluegrass formed Old and In the Way, a bluegrass group that leaned toward the progressive side with a cover of a Rolling Stones tune, for instance. Astute fans hear bluegrass elements in many of the Grateful Dead's recordings. Furthermore, many of today's progressive bluegrass bands adopt the jam format (extended improvisations and songs that last ten minutes or more in live performance) that the Grateful Dead made famous and draw equally on bluegrass and rock in their music.

During the late 1960s, bluegrass music headed down two different pathways. The traditionalists' music became more and more entwined with ideas about old-time music and culture, while progressive bluegrass branched out even further into rock and jazz; after only a few short years, it headed away from the country genre and found its niche audience among rock and bluegrass fans. Its lasting impact on country music, however, came largely from the country rock that it fostered.

FOLLOW-UP ON FIRST GENERATION BLUEGRASS

The development of progressive bluegrass affected the first-generation bands as well, including those outside of California. In March 1969, Lester Flatt and Earl Scruggs split up, an event that was highly symbolic of the larger changes that had occurred in bluegrass music by that time. After more than two decades of playing together, the two disagreed about the direction the band should take, about choices of music, and about the culture in which bluegrass music resided. Always more of a traditionalist, Flatt put together a new band that sounded much like the bluegrass of the early 1950s. Scruggs, on the other hand, teamed up with his sons—literally and symbolically a "new generation"—to form the Earl Scruggs Revue, a band that merged rock and bluegrass elements. Their sound was similar to the growing folk-rock and country-rock movements in California. The careers of Flatt and Scruggs metaphorically represent bluegrass: they joined musical forces to establish it as a style, and they parted ways as bluegrass itself splintered in several different musical directions.

Figure 7-4 The Earl Scruggs Revue: Earl Scruggs fronting a rock band.
Source: Courtesy of Country Music Hall of Fame and Museum.

Country Rock

Starting in the mid-1960s, many folk and rock musicians cultivated an interest in country music. At the time, country represented something grounded, rooted in American identity, and traditional. Folk legend Bob Dylan (1941–), for instance, came to Nashville in 1966 while recording *Blonde on Blonde*. Dylan's producer had suggested that they try working in Nashville, where they had easy access to a host of talented session musicians. This was part of the larger trend in the 1960s of non-country musicians heading to Nashville to record (see Chapter 6). Dylan was ready for a change of scenery, and the country-music tradition appealed to him, so he readily agreed. While the results were not really part of the country genre in any meaningful sense, the songs had a sparse texture and an earthiness that resonated with country music. A year later, Dylan returned to record *John Wesley Harding*, on which he added Pete Drake, one of country music's hottest steel guitar players. The culmination of Dylan's relationship with country music came, however, in 1969, when he returned again to record *Nashville Skyline*. During those sessions, Dylan and Johnny Cash sang a number of duets, including several old Jimmie Rodgers songs. The majority of the country music audience paid Dylan little attention, and the songs he released did not appear on the country charts at all. Dylan's own fans, however, labeled the album "country" in their perception.

The relationship between Johnny Cash and Bob Dylan formed an important connection between country music and the folk and folk-rock genres. In the mid-1960s, Cash had become interested in his ancestry, including the idea that he was of Native American descent. This turned his attention toward lineage, heritage, and the idea of folk identity in general. Motivated by his growing interest in folk music, Cash recorded a song that had originally been written by Peter LaFarge, a highly respected folk singer who was part of the Greenwich Village scene in New York, where Pete Seeger and Ramblin' Jack Elliott had hung out in the 1950s. LaFarge penned a ballad about the sad fate of World War II veteran Ira Hayes (1923–1955), who was one of the Marines who raised the flag on Iwo Jima. Upon his discharge from service, Hayes faced racial and cultural prejudice and was unable to make a stable life for himself in American society. He died from alcohol poisoning and exposure. LaFarge's ballad about Hayes was a scathing social critique of a society that abandoned its heroes to the fates of racial and cultural injustice. Cash recorded "The Ballad of Ira Hayes" in 1964, and, at Dylan's invitation, performed it at the Newport Folk Festival, the most famous and influential of the myriad folk festivals. When country radio stations did not embrace this activist ballad, Cash lashed out at the country music industry in a full-page *Billboard* magazine ad, in which he accused country radio's "D.J.'s, station managers, and owners" of not having enough "guts" to play a song that Cash described as "strong medicine." That moment helped define Cash as an outsider working against the mainstream country music establishment. It also forged a connection between the 1960s folk scene and a small segment of country music. Bob Dylan revived that connection when he came to Nashville in 1969.

Dylan's involvement with both Nashville and country music in the late 1960s was part of a larger trend of rock and folk-rock performers obsessed with country music. The majority of these artists already had some experience in the growing folk-rock scene in California and the progressive bluegrass scene. Many of them had played in bluegrass bands of one sort or another, and several of them had grown up listening to country music at home. Their basic philosophy was to take the rock music they played and fuse it with traditional country music into what

Gram Parsons called "cosmic American music." Similar developments were taking place during these years in Texas (see Chapter 9), where musicians such as Michael Murphey sang about "cosmic cowboys." Like Dylan, many of the California folk-rock bands decided to pursue their interests by recording albums that were what they perceived as authentic country.

At the front of this movement was the Byrds, a band from Los Angeles, California. Band member Roger McGuinn (1942–) spent his teenage years playing folk music in Chicago, then moved to New York to pursue a career as both a song-writer and performer. In 1964, he traveled to California to play at the Troubadour Club, which was one of the best-known venues for folk music at the time. While there, McGuinn met Gene Clark, and the two of them teamed up with David Crosby, Michael Clarke, and bluegrass musician Chris Hillman (who had played with the Golden State Boys) to form the Byrds. Although their musical backgrounds were mostly folk and bluegrass, the British Invasion and rise of the Beatles motivated the group to explore rock music from their folk perspective. They added the distinctive, jangling of an electric Rickenbacker twelve-string guitar to their band, and with their folk/rock hybrid sound began covering Bob Dylan songs. In 1965, the band recorded Dylan's "Mr. Tambourine Man," followed a year later by "Turn! Turn! Turn!" (written by folk legend Pete Seeger), in each case adding a rock feel to the songs' folk origins. By 1967, the Byrds were quite popular, and fans valued their specifically American identity, in contrast to the British Invasion bands. At this point, the Byrds' sound began to change: the band left folk influences behind and moved into more experimental, psychedelic rock sounds. Personnel had also changed, with Gene Clark leaving in 1966. As was often the case in young bands, egos and personalities clashed. In 1967, McGuinn and Hillman fired David Crosby, and drummer Michael Clarke also departed. In their place, McGuinn and Hillman

Figure 7-5 The Byrds who recorded Sweetheart of the Rodeo: (from left) Kevin Kelley, Gram Parsons, Roger McGuinn, Chris Hillman; they broke up shortly after.

Source: Southern Folklife Collection, Wilson Library, The University of North Carolina at Chapel Hill.

hired Kevin Kelley and a young keyboardist, guitarist, and vocalist named Gram Parsons (1946–1973). Parsons and Hillman were both interested in pursuing a more country sound; Parsons had grown up on country music and wanted to make an album that would be received as legitimate country.

At the urging of Parsons and Hillman, the band headed to Nashville. They selected a bunch of country songs, including ones by Merle Haggard, the Louvin Brothers (see Chapter 6), and songwriter Cindy Walker, which both Gene Autry and Hank Snow (see Chapter 4) had recorded. From the folk side, there were two Dylan tunes, one from Woody Guthrie, and one traditional folk song. Rounding out the album was a pair of songs Parsons had written and a cover of a southern soul tune by R&B star William Bell. Together, the band viewed the songs as a miniportrait of Americana: folk, country, and soul, all played sincerely by a rock band. The Byrds were determined to make the album as much a part of contemporary country music as possible. They hired well-known country session players, including Lloyd Green and JayDee Maness (both steel guitar), Clarence White (guitar), and John Hartford (fiddle, banjo, and guitar).

The resulting album, *Sweetheart of the Rodeo*, was not a commercial success. The core country audience was skeptical at best, and many country fans turned a cold shoulder to the band (see essay on The Byrds on the Opry). One reason for their lack of acceptance was that country music defined itself by far more than the sound of the music. Particularly in the volatile social context of 1968, fans were looking for an ideology and cultural identity in their music, not just the presence of a steel guitar. The long-haired hippie rock band from California who had a recent hit with "Eight Miles High," which many fans understood to be about drug use, did not earn a warm welcome from the country fan base. By the time the album was released, Gram Parsons and Chris Hillman—the two musicians from the group who were most interested in country music—were no longer in the band, and the Byrds abandoned their country-music ambitions. Even though it faced a hostile reception at the time, *Sweetheart* marked a seminal event in country music history: an established rock band turned to country to find both songs and a musical style that represented deep roots in an American identity.

After their departure from the Byrds, Hillman and Parsons formed the Flying Burrito Brothers, which earned a reputation as the foremost country rock band. The Flying Burrito Brothers' first album was *Gilded Palace of Sin* (1969), which solidified the country rock sound: part honky-tonk, part Bakersfield, lyrics tinged with emotional angst, and the musical wash of sound characteristic of late '60s psychedelia. In 1972, Parsons met a singer-songwriter named Emmylou Harris (see Chapter 13) who would go on to be a major country star in the 1980s, and the two spent the last two years of Parsons's life performing and recording together, leaving behind albums that have been celebrated by country rock fans for almost four decades.

Parsons's personal life was becoming increasingly unstable, and he suffered from drug and alcohol addictions. In 1973, Parsons died from an overdose of drugs and alcohol while vacationing in Joshua Tree National Monument in Southern California. His biographical drama continued, however. Two of Parsons's friends stole his body while it was being shipped home to his father and returned it instead

---

COUNTRY THROUGH A ROCK CRITIC'S EARS

The relationship between rock and country music has always been complicated. Because the rock audience is significantly larger than the country audience, the mainstream public's perception of country music is sometimes skewed by the preferences of rock fans and—more important—rock critics. And rock critics tend to disregard mainstream country and gravitate toward country's outsiders whose music sits on the fringes of the genre.

When *Rolling Stone* published its second edition of "500 Greatest Albums of All Time" (covering albums of any genre) in 2012, the only artists with any sort of country identity who showed up in the top 50 were Bob Dylan, Elvis Presley, the Eagles, and the Allman Brothers—basically country rock and southern rock artists, plus Presley, whose Sun Sessions would have been heard as country at the time. That list also included both Ray Charles's *Modern Sounds in Country and Western Music* (#105) and the Byrds' *Sweetheart of the Rodeo* (#120). Neither of these albums fared well with the country audience, but both ended up earning the acclaim of rock fans and critics, which in turn made them iconic parts of pop culture. Conversely, when country fans and critics compile country versions of a "greatest albums" list, they tend to name artists such as Willie Nelson and Johnny Cash, with the Byrds and Dylan appearing much further down their lists. In other words, county albums that become the most famous among rock audiences are not the same as the country albums that appeal the most to country audiences.

---

to Joshua Tree, where they attempted, with several gallons of gasoline, to fulfill their dead friend's wish to be cremated there. His death added to the artistic mystique surrounding him and fed his growing mythological status, much as Hank Williams's death had done twenty years earlier (see Chapter 4).

Country Rock Branches Out

After Gram Parsons and the Flying Burrito Brothers helped create country rock in the late 1960s, other bands continued that trend into the 1970s. Among those were the Eagles, also from California. In 1971, pop singer Linda Ronstadt hired Los Angeles session musicians Don Henley and Glenn Frey as a backup band for her upcoming project. They, in turn, brought in Randy Meisner and Bernie Leadon. Leadon had played with the Flying Burrito Brothers a few years earlier and was steeped in the sounds of country rock. He also had an affinity for bluegrass and played most notably banjo, along with mandolin and several other instruments. After the four finished working for Ronstadt, they decided to keep the group together as the Eagles.

In 1973, the band members recorded a **concept album**—an album with a central story or narrative that runs throughout all the songs—called *Desperado*, based on tales of an Old West gang of bank robbers. The Eagles dressed up in bandit costumes for the album's cover photograph and filled the album with songs they had written about the gang, suggesting metaphoric relationships between those Wild West outlaws and the band's own outlook on the world. The album's style is country rock, the same sounds

Listening Guide

"Will the Circle Be Unbroken" (1972)

PERFORMERS: The Nitty Gritty Dirt Band with guests

SONGWRITER: credited to A. P. Carter; an arrangement of a song by Ada R. Habershon and Charles H. Gabriel

ORIGINAL RELEASE: United Artists UAS-9801

FORM: Verse-chorus

STYLE: Country rock

Recorded in a week-long marathon session in Nashville, *Will the Circle Be Unbroken* was a landmark album in the history of country music. Several of the Nitty Gritty Dirt Band (NGDB) members grew up as fans of country music, and banjoist John McEuen had played in a bluegrass band in California before joining the NGDB. None of the NGDB members were over twenty-five years old when they made the *Circle* album, and in their minds, the older generation of country singers were musical heroes. They had shared the stage with Merle Travis in Los Angeles in the 1960s, but they had not yet met any of the other country legends who would eventually contribute to the album. Those connections came mostly through Earl Scruggs, whose sons were fans of the NGDB. They introduced the band to Scruggs, who became their point of contact for the rest of the country stars.

The concept for the album was one of pure happenstance. The young musicians invited the senior generation of country music legends to sing their signature country songs with the NGDB on a country album, and a remarkable roster was assembled: Roy Acuff, Maybelle Carter, Jimmy Martin, Doc Watson, Merle Travis, Earl Scruggs, Pete Kirby (who had been Acuff's Dobro player), Vassar Clements (who had played fiddle with Bill Monroe), and several others. The sessions took place in Nashville in August 1971. NGDB members recall sitting around with Doc Watson and Earl Scruggs at their homes, playing and singing and learning from the masters. Jimmy Martin schooled them in bluegrass vocal harmony; Roy Acuff worked up a number of his most famous tunes with them. The group took their musical ideas into the recording studio having rehearsed very little. Producer Bill McEuen, whose brother John was the NDGB's banjo player, kept the tapes rolling in the studio throughout the entire session, which was not standard practice. By coincidence, journalist Chet Flippo, who was at the time a well-known music writer for *Rolling Stone* magazine, happened to be in Nashville and caught wind of the sessions. He showed up and reported on this unusual gathering, and ended up writing liner notes for the album.

The album appeared in 1972 with extensive notes, photographs from the sessions, and three long-playing records that included not only the songs but also the studio banter. The album was a huge success, and much as Harry Smith's *Anthology of American Folk Music* had opened up the world of early hillbilly and blues recordings for an earlier generation of musicians in the 1950s, the *Circle* album reintroduced aging country stars to a whole new generation of listeners, including those who came to the album as rock fans of the NGDB. That casual dialogue allowed listeners a sneak peek into the exchanges between the stars of country music's early years and the newcomer rock musicians, who were bridging not only the rock/country division but also the generational division between 1960s and '70s youth and their parents' generation.

Since 1935, when the Carter Family had recorded this song, it had become a standard in the country, gospel, and folk genres; along the way, its title had changed from "Can..." to the more prophetic "Will..." The song also provided a metaphor for the different generations of musicians who came together to make this album, especially situated as it was in the early 1970s, when questions of tradition and roots loomed large in country music. Symbolic of the album's place in history, however, "Will the Circle..." was not the closing track on the album. Instead, when the album appeared it had Randy Scruggs (Earl's son) finger-picking a guitar version of Joni Mitchell's folkie ballad, "Both Sides Now" as its epilogue. The last word on this seminal country-rock gathering of the generations was given to the youth and the contemporary 1960s folk scene.

TIME	FORM	LISTENING CUES	DISCUSSION
0:00	Introduction	banjo	The banjo plays the song's melody in the introduction. Notice how full and busy the rest of the band sounds behind the banjo. That cluttered sound is characteristic of the country rock recordings of this era, and makes it easy to tell this is neither a classic bluegrass recording nor an early hillbilly recording.
0:21	Verse 1	"I was standing..."	Mother Maybelle (Maybelle Carter) starts the song with the verse that her brother-in-law, A. P., penned for the original Carter Family. Many different instruments play behind her, including fiddle and Dobro.
0:41	Chorus	"Will the circle..."	The whole group joins in for the chorus. Notice that Maybelle's voice still stands out. As the chorus continues, individual voices stick out at different places, which conveys the sense that this was an informal sing-along that just happened to be recorded.
1:02	Instrumental verse	fiddle and harmonica	Vassar Clements plays the fiddle solo here, while Nitty Gritty Dirt Band member Jimmy Fadden adds harmonica.
1:22	Verse 2	"Lord, I told..."	Jimmy Martin sings the second verse. His vocals are the essence of the high lonesome sound, tight and thin.
1:42	Chorus	"Will the circle..."	The chorus comes in again, similar to the first time. At the end of this section, we hear the singer call out to Doc Watson to take the next solo.
2:02	Instrumental verse	guitar	Doc Watson flat-picks the solo here.
2:22	Verse 3	"I will follow..."	Roy Acuff sings the third verse. The recording session took place shortly before Acuff's sixty-eighth birthday. His age is apparent in the timbre of his voice.
2:42	Chorus	"Will the circle..."	For the third chorus, the group takes a similar approach to the first two.

Continued

Listening Guide

"Will the Circle Be Unbroken" (1972) **Continued**

TIME	FORM	LISTENING CUES	DISCUSSION
3:03	Instrumental verse	Dobro	Acuff's longtime Dobro player, Pete Kirby (known as Bashful Brother Oswald), plays this solo.
3:22	Verse 4	"I went back home…"	Maybelle Carter finishes the recording. In her early sixties at the time of this session, Maybelle's verse about missing her long-gone family, sung in the presence of the next generation of country singers, became symbolic of a much larger story than is contained in the lyrics.
3:42	Chorus	"Will the circle…"	Maybelle's voice stands out from the rest of the group here.
4:02	Instrumental verse	banjo	Earl Scruggs plays the banjo solo here.
4:22	Chorus	"Will the circle…"	For the final chorus, the band drops out for the last few measures as the song slows to its end, punctuated by a final gesture from the Dobro.

that had been flowing out of Southern California for half a decade by then. As had been the case with the Byrds, the core country music audience was reticent to accept the Eagles as part of the genre. Although songs from the album such as "Tequila Sunrise" had an audible country style, they did not appear on the country charts for reasons that had more to do with the band's lineage and identity than its sound. A few years later, a whole wave of other artists with pop-rock backgrounds, including Linda Ronstadt, Olivia Newton-John, and John Denver, introduced a soft-rock sound to country music, while facing staunch resistance from some factions of the audience. In that mid-'70s climate, the Eagles placed a few songs on the country charts. That period of acceptance was brief, however, and by the late 1970s, most of what the Eagles were recording had little to do with country music. By the end of the decade, the band had split up.

The Eagles were not the only band to view themselves as outlaws or to employ country music's sounds to express that attitude. The term "outlaws" came to represent a movement among country singers who, in the mid-1970s, cast themselves as outsiders and took on the country music establishment (see Chapter 9). The photograph of the Eagles dressed as gun-toting outlaws helped pull together ideas of country music, the Wild West of yesteryear, and a rebellious rocker attitude. Although the Eagles sat more on the side of rock than country during their recording career, twenty years later the featured singers on a tribute album called *Common Thread: Songs of the Eagles* (1993) were all country stars. At that point, some twenty years after the Eagles had originally sung those songs, country music—rather than rock—was the genre that drew most directly from the 1970s country rock style and overall approach to performance. Like the Byrds and Flying Burrito Brothers, the Eagles have been lauded by later generations of country fans for their contributions to country rock much more enthusiastically than one might have guessed based on the band's original experiences in the '70s. This situation shows once again how the relationship between musical styles, genres, and audiences is constantly evolving.

Of all the California rock bands that sought to make inroads into country music during these years, the most successful was the Nitty Gritty Dirt Band (NGDB). In 1966, Jeff Hanna and Bruce Kunkel founded the Illegitimate Jug Band, so called because they did not really play the jug. Within a few years, the band had changed names and added banjo player John McEuen. Their style and sound were only tangentially related to country music, but they gradually gained a fan base among rock audiences on the West Coast. Their big break came when they recorded "Mr. Bojangles," by Jerry Jeff Walker, in 1970. Walker had been a major songwriter within the Greenwich Village folk revival scene of the 1960s (see Chapter 5), and would later become one of the most celebrated songwriters in his adopted state of Texas during the outlaw movement (see Chapter 9). Walker's song became a huge pop hit for the NGDB and won them a wider following.

By the early 1970s, the group's interest in country music had increased. John McEuen had played in bluegrass bands prior to joining. Hanna was fond of early rock 'n' rollers such as Chuck Berry, Buddy Holly, and Little Richard, but also the Everly Brothers, with their country leanings. Exchanges between rock and country, and more specifically bluegrass and hillbilly music, were already well established when the NGDB launched a project to record a country album with established stars.

Through happenstance meetings and the assistance of Earl Scruggs, the band headed to Nashville in 1971 to record (see Listening Guide). The road from California rock to Nashville was well traveled by then, but the NGDB's approach was different than their predecessors. They had less interest in making a contemporary country album, and were more invested in situating themselves in traditional country music. They assembled a group of older country stars, including Roy Acuff, Maybelle Carter, Doc Watson, and Earl Scruggs, with whom they would collaborate. The NGDB headlined the project, which, for audiences, defined it as country rock. Far more than just another record, the album became a folk documentary on a rock band's indoctrination into country traditions; the album contained three LPs and extensive liner notes, with studio banter and conversations between the participants included.

Released in 1972, *Will the Circle Be Unbroken* triangulated on country's relationship to its own past, to rock music, and to folk traditions. The NGDB's forays into country music were generally well received; the presence of country stars such as Acuff on the album certainly helped, as did the band members' obvious respect for and deference to their senior collaborators. Unlike the other country rock bands discussed here, who either headed away from country music and back into a rock identity or flamed out in self-destructive behavior, the NGDB took up residence in the genre. In subsequent decades, they continued to record country music, while occasionally focusing on rock.

California Country

Although Nashville has dominated the public's imagination of country music, in the 1960s and early 1970s California emerged as an equally important creative center. The intermingling of musical cultures there led to new developments in country music that were the direct result of folk, rock, and country musicians coming together in one place. All of these developments—Bakersfield sound, progressive bluegrass, and country rock—had complicated relationships with earlier generations of country music. All of them brought country music in some form or another to a broader audience. And all of them would become vitally important to later generations of country artists looking into the past for something that combined country tradition with an independent, even defiant rock attitude (see Chapter 13). Finally, these developments pushed the boundaries that determined what the country audience would or would not accept from its musicians, and provided essential checks and balances to the pop-crossover trends of the Nashville sound. All three developments pitted tradition against rock-influenced innovation, and all three thrived on being the "outsider" in comparison to mainstream Nashville.

⭐ **ESSAY: MUSICAL STYLE**

 # Bakersfield Sound

The Bakersfield sound had two main components:

1. A chugging, shuffle rhythm
2. The instrumentation used by the leading bands in Bakersfield, including the incorporation of electric guitar and bass.

The shuffle rhythm, often called a "Bakersfield shuffle," combines swing rhythms, where the notes are played in an uneven pattern of long-short-long-short, with a "walking bass line," where the bass player plays a note on all four beats of the measure, where one might count 1-2-3-4. In a shuffle pattern, any accompanying instruments, such as a rhythm guitar or piano, play the "chug-a-chug-a" rhythm that adds an accented chord played between each beat in the music.

The "Bakersfield sound" is also defined by the instrumentation and the way those instruments are played. At the heart of the Bakersfield sound is the Fender Telecaster guitar, a solid-body, dual-pickup electric guitar that was capable of playing twangy high notes that sounded like a steel guitar or gravelly, gritty low notes that cut through the rest of the band's sound. The second major contributor to the Bakersfield sound is the electric bass, rather than an acoustic upright bass, which pulled the sound closer to the rock music of the 1960s. The rest of the instrumentation included drums, rhythm guitar, steel guitar, and sometimes piano or fiddle. Vocal harmony in the Bakersfield sound is typically the stark, minimal harmony provided by one voice singing above the melody. While full backup quartets appear on some recordings, the style tends to avoid the syrupy "oohs" and "ahs" of the Nashville sound.

Bakersfield sound bands were known for creating a "freight train" sound, which described the charging, rumbling energy of the songs. Loud drums pounded out the beat, while the Telecaster guitars played just barely ahead of the beat, creating a sense of surging energy. Although the instrumentation and overall sound of Bakersfield recordings does not resemble bluegrass, both styles feature this characteristic, best described as "drive."

Bakersfield sound vocalists often included more of a naturalized tinge or nasal twang in their vocals. The lyrics often were tinged with abject, solitary yet stubborn bitterness and self-referential irony, although a few love songs sneaked in as well. The song lyrics depicted explicitly working-class characteristics and concerns. Most of the stars had worked their way into the industry by paying their dues on thousands of honky-tonk stages, playing for huge dance crowds. The sound they honed on stage persisted in the studio, and the distinction between the live and recorded versions of songs was minimal. Finally, the fans tended to value the idea that the stars were not only singing but also writing the songs in most instances, and that the songs reflected lived experience.

The Bakersfield sound was treated by fans and journalists as a counterbalance to many of the developments that the Nashville sound offered, as well as a continuation of the themes from honky-tonk and rockabilly that seemed to have been lost in the Nashville sound. Writer Martha Hume described the Bakersfield sound: "In contrast to its contemporary country cousin, the Nashville Sound, music made in Bakersfield was rawer." Historian Gerald Haslam summarized: "The music was indeed distinct... Bakersfield did come to symbolize western resistance to Tennessee's corporate control and cookie-cutter music." The important word there is "symbolize"; the meaning ascribed to the music by its fans far surpassed any intrinsic opposition found in the sounds themselves. By about 1970, many country singers had fused some aspects of the Nashville sound with many of the features of the Bakersfield sound, and the next wave of developments (see Chapter 8) in country music combined what had originated as opposing styles.

☆ **ESSAY: HISTORY**

"Okie from Muskogee" and Country Music Politics

In 1969, the United States was embroiled in a bitter political controversy over the Vietnam War. The hippie movement, widely associated with the political left and antiwar sentiments, was in full swing. Just a year later, the clash of political cultures would turn violent when National Guardsmen would shoot and kill student protestors at Kent State University in Ohio. Politics pervaded almost every aspect of American culture, including country music.

In the 1950s, country music and folk music had diverged largely over issues of political agendas (see Chapter 5). Although both genres claimed a lineage in the working-class music of people such as Jimmie Rodgers, the Carter Family, and Woody Guthrie, the folk scene had taken up an activist and even—at times—communist stance. By the 1960s, country music had staked out territory that leaned toward the political right. This was partly pure economics; working-class Southerners were drafted into the armed services in high numbers and thus tended to adopt a supportive view of the military. In any political controversy, each side finds a soundtrack, and the audiences who were dubbed the silent majority—the working- and middle-class Americans who were not actively involved in antiwar protests—settled on country music.

In 1969, Merle Haggard released "Okie from Muskogee," a song he had penned with bandmate Roy Edward Burris. The lyrics outlined the upstanding, clean-cut lifestyle of small-town America, represented by Muskogee, Oklahoma, as the place where hippie fashion, habits (smoking marijuana or experimenting with LSD), and acts of political protest (burning draft cards or rioting on college campuses) were condemned. As soon as the song came out, audiences responded to it with enthusiastic fervor, touting its representation of what they claimed were patriotic, wholesome American values and its denunciation of the counterculture that they thought was dragging down the country. But what Haggard had intended for the song was unclear.

Critics and historians have debated whether Haggard, whose parents were Okie migrants, wrote the song as a statement of solidarity with the silent majority or as a tongue-in-cheek dig at them. Interviews and explanations that he has offered over the subsequent four decades have done nothing to clarify the situation, as Haggard has made contradictory statements that equally support either interpretation. There are moments in the recording where one can hear a hint of laughter in his performance, yet at the time, fans rallied around it as an attack on the counterculture. Later in his life, Haggard has performed the song with humorous alterations to the lyrics, and several of his songs in the 2000s espoused a liberal political viewpoint.

Some historians have argued that "Okie" brought to light a large audience who rallied behind very conservative political sentiments, and Haggard pragmatically provided them with an anthem. Others have argued that Haggard was himself invested in that sentiment, at least at that time.

As commonly occurs in country music, songs can suggest multiple, even contradictory, interpretations, and that is part of the artistic value of music. Artists such as Johnny Cash and Merle Haggard have famously refused to provide any definitive explanations of their music's meaning, preferring instead to allow the ambiguities to enrich the songs. In order to understand the song's place in both the history of country music and the history of American culture, one must be willing to examine it from more than one perspective, and grant it the possibility of multiple interpretations.

 # The Byrds on the Opry

On March 15, 1968, the Byrds played the Grand Ole Opry in Nashville. The California-based country rock band was in town on a promotional tour for their album *Sweetheart of the Rodeo*, and their label, Columbia Records, had arranged for the performance. Opry management was understandably concerned about how the evening would go. The Opry presented a politically conservative face to its largely Southern conservative audience, and tensions over the Vietnam War ran high. The Byrds agreed to sing two Merle Haggard songs—a relatively safe bet because the audience revered Haggard as part of country music's establishment, and these songs would allow the newcomer-outsiders to pay tribute to a respected figure in country music. But all did not go according to plan, and when the dust settled, it appeared that the long-haired, rebellious, possibly drug-using, folk-friendly rock band was not welcome in the Opry—the Mother Church of Country Music.

The issues surrounding the Byrds' appearance on the Opry had little to do with actual musical style or sound. Indeed, when they recorded *Sweetheart of the Rodeo* the previous year, the Byrds had included many of Nashville's leading session musicians on the album, and they had put forth every effort to make it sound "country." Steel guitar player Lloyd Green—a highly respected session player in Nashville—even agreed to perform on the Opry with the band. Gram Parsons was a longtime fan of country music and was emotionally invested in the Byrds becoming a country band. They had missed their mark in terms of sound—their version of "Life in Prison," for instance, lacked the spare texture and mellow maturity of Haggard's recording, and some music critics even speculated that the album was intended as parody. But that alone was not enough to draw the ire of the Opry's audience. Instead, the backlash came from a clash of broader cultural traditions.

In 1968, the political leanings of the Grand Ole Opry performers tended toward open support of the president, and the country music audience remained closely tied to a demographic that was working-class, Southern, and serving in the Armed Forces. The Byrds, by contrast, had recorded a number of pacifist folkie songs, had ties to the folk scene with its overtly leftist political agenda, and were well known for "Turn! Turn! Turn!" (a song that originated with activist and folk music star Pete Seeger). In these contexts, music came to represent far more than just musical style or even specific lyrics. A country song was not just a particular melody with some chords and lyrics, but instead was a means of expressing cultural identity—in other words, the fans' way of saying who they are, what they think, and where their values are. In that heated political climate, the Byrds did not align with the country ideology, and they were viewed with suspicion, or at the least, skepticism.

Yet even those questions of identity were not what unseated the Byrds' attempt at finding a home in country music. When they got on the Opry stage, they had agreed to sing two Haggard songs. The audience greeted them with derision, tweeting at the "birds" and shouting derogatory comments about long-haired hippies, even though they had dressed conservatively for the show and had recently cut their hair shorter. After their first song, Haggard's "Sing Me Back Home," Gram Parsons went off-script and announced they would sing a Byrds original tune, "Hickory Wind," for their second number. The Opry management and the show's hosts that evening were furious, and the audience turned hostile. A few months later, a radio interview with famed country DJ Ralph Emery turned sour when Emery accused the band on air of being undesirable, dangerous hippies. The two incidents reinforced the worst of the negative stereotypes of the country music audience, and several of the band's members turned their backs on the genre to which they had tried so hard to connect. They even penned a scathing mockery of Emery in their song "Drug Store Truck Drivin' Man."

The Opry incident helps illustrate how country music represents more than just sound. In subsequent decades, country singers have looked back on the 1960s country rock era as influential. Gram Parsons inspired Emmylou Harris, who enjoyed mainstream success as a country star in the 1970s and '80s (see Chapter 13). Parsons also became a legendary icon in the alt-country movement of the 1990s. But at the time, the country audience rejected the Byrds as inauthentic, regardless of the sound of their music.

LISTEN-SIDE-BY-SIDE

"I've Just Seen a Face"

SONGWRITERS: Lennon/McCartney
(Paul McCartney)

The Dillards, 1968 (on *Wheatstraw Suite*)
The Beatles, 1965 (on *Rubber Soul*)

THROUGHOUT MUCH OF popular music's history, country differentiates itself strongly from other genres, preserving its "otherness" and thus core identity. At particular moments in history, however, those differences are subsumed in larger, shared aesthetics. Right around 1968, progressive bluegrass, country rock, folk rock, and even psychedelia found common influences and musical characteristics in what was really a "sound of an era" that both spanned multiple genres and challenged the notion of genre in the first place.

As is often the case, individual musicians listened to, liked, and borrowed from music outside of their home genres with great frequency, and never more so than during this time. British Invasion bands such as the Beatles (fronted by John Lennon and Paul McCartney, arguably the most significant band in rock history) had a robust knowledge of American popular music of all genres, and their drummer Ringo Starr was an avowed fan of country music. The Byrds, another band that figures prominently in the history of rock music, set out to make an album that they conceived of as country. And although country musicians were acutely aware of what was happening in rock music and sometimes covered rock songs, most of the time the direction of influence was that rock bands covered country songs. This song was one of the exceptions.

Of all the styles of music that were garnering significant attention in the late 1960s, progressive bluegrass was one of the most interesting for its combination of traditional roots and experimental new sounds. It both drew on early country music and hillbilly influences from its bluegrass lineage on the one hand, and incorporated the more progressive developments that were mainly happening in rock music on the other. *Wheatstraw Suite* was not the first time that an ostensibly bluegrass band had done an album with rock songs, or even specifically covered the Beatles. Two years earlier, the bluegrass band called The Charles River Valley Boys recorded *Beatle Country*, an album of all Beatles songs, but their performances were more in line with traditional bluegrass. By contrast, the Dillards took their sound much closer to the rock styles that they were covering, layering their bluegrass past with lots of new instruments (prominent steel guitar and electric bass, along with drums and strings) and different harmonies. Critics were quick to point out that the resulting album was not necessarily bluegrass at all, at least by old definitions.

Notably, *Wheatstraw Suite* was conceived as one whole artistic work. It opens with traditional Southern gospel; "Single Saddle" is a singing cowboy number that sounds like an affectionate parody in the context of the rest of the album. "Bending the Strings" is pure banjo-breakdown

bluegrass. And the last track opens with a mock radio market report. In between, the band presents recordings that are an equal blend of folk rock and country rock in terms of style.

Wheatstraw Suite is similar in many ways to the Byrds' *Sweetheart of the Rodeo*. It contains a mix of original tunes and covers: seven of its tracks were written by the Dillards or members of the band; the remaining six tracks were drawn from a combination of traditional tunes and contemporary country and rock songs, including ones from eclectic singer-songwriters. And similar to the Byrds, the Dillards brought in session players to add extra instruments to the recordings.

"I've Just Seen a Face" was an easy point of connection between the Beatles and the American progressive bluegrass scene because, out of all the Beatles' songs from this era, this one revealed their knowledge of and interest in American country music most obviously. Music critic Richie Unterberger and Paul McCartney himself have both described the Beatles' 1965 original as "country," so a band primarily known for bluegrass did not have to alter the song much at all to fit into their sound.

The Beatles' version starts with a slow introduction, followed by Paul McCartney's vocals over an uptempo two-beat groove. The phrases have an irregular length in terms of their number of beats. We hear vocal harmony only on the refrain, "Falling, yes, I am falling…". The Dillards' version keeps all those elements, losing the British accent that marked McCartney's vocals. The Dillards add banjo and steel guitar, along with vocal harmony throughout, including three-part harmony on the refrain. These changes seem to realize the original "country" intent of the Beatles' song more fully. We get a chance to hear the country side of rock and the rock side of country at this fascinating moment in history.

PLAYLIST

Byrds. "Hickory Wind" (1968)

Dillards. "Listen to the Sound" (1968)

Haggard, Merle. "Okie from Muskogee" (1968)

Hartford, John, "Back in the Goodle Days" (1971)

Owens, Buck. "Act Naturally" (1963)

FOR MORE READING

Cantwell, David. *Merle Haggard: The Running Kind.* Austin: University of Texas Press, 2013.

Einarson, John. *Desperados: The Roots of Country Rock.* New York: Cooper Square Press, 2000.

Haslam, Gerald W. *Workin' Man Blues: Country Music in California.* Berkeley: University of California Press, 1999.

Meyer, David. *Twenty Thousand Roads: The Ballad of Gram Parsons and His Cosmic American Music.* New York: Villard Books, 2007.

Price, Robert. *The Bakersfield Sound: How a Generation of Displaced Okies Revolutionized American Music.* Berkeley: Heyday, 2018.

Sisk, Eileen. *Buck Owens: The Biography.* Chicago: Chicago Review Press, 2010.

NAMES AND TERMS

ACM	Earl Scruggs Revue	Owens, Bonnie
Bakersfield sound	Flying Burrito Brothers	Owens, Buck
Beatles, The	folk-rock	Parsons, Gram
Byrds	Haggard, Merle	progressive bluegrass
Capitol Records	Hartford, John	Rich, Don
concept album	Hayes, Ira	shuffle rhythms
Dillards	Hillman, Chris	Telecaster guitar
Dylan, Bob	Nitty Gritty Dirt Band	Trout's Nightclub
Eagles	Old and In the Way	(honky-tonk)

REVIEW TOPICS

1. What characteristics of country music were so appealing to folk, rock, and bluegrass musicians in the 1960s?

2. Discuss the distinction between style and genre as it relates to the 1960s in country music. In this era, what does it mean to "sound like country?"

3. How do fans decide what a song such as "Okie from Muskogee" means, and can you think of other examples where multiple, contradictory meanings of the same song coexist in country music?

Classic Country

The landscape of popular music continued to change at a rapid pace in the 1960s. In Detroit, a new record label called Motown introduced a slick, polished R&B sound to audiences. From Great Britain, a wave of rock bands headed by the Beatles sparked a frenzy among fans that surpassed even Elvis Presley's meteoric rise in the 1950s. From the West Coast, American bands such as the Beach Boys turned surf rock into a national phenomenon. Within country music, we have already explored some of the developments that occurred where the folk revival met with country traditions (see Chapter 7). Together, these developments created a musical climate with little stability in any genre.

The 1960s were a turbulent time on many cultural fronts, all of which were reflected in popular music. Many Americans felt deep-seated anger over military actions and distrust of the Nixon-era government, while the specter of global conflict hung overhead in the form of the Cold War. Social revolution on the fronts of civil rights and women's liberation divided and destabilized many communities. As the baby boomers reached maturity, many of them openly rebelled against the measured order of 1950s Middle America in the form of drugs, free love, and disavowal of traditional community structures. One outcome was that young people launched the hippie movement. Rock music in particular reflected these changes. Music fans often think of the late 1960s as the era of the Monterey Pop Festival (1967) and Woodstock (1969). Although thousands of fans (mostly young) were at those events and found a means of expression in rock music, millions of other Americans found little if anything to connect with in the rock and pop music of that time.

White working- and middle-class people, especially those who were middle-aged and were in the midst of raising families, found that the social order, lifestyles, and community values on which they had been raised had eroded. The economy was deeply troubled; through the 1970s, the annual inflation rate, for instance, which typically was under 4%, skyrocketed to almost 14%. On the domestic front, legal and social changes more than doubled the divorce rate. The threads that had held together a working-class identity, namely pride in earning a living, confidence in the American Dream, and the stability of the traditional family unit, were unraveling. They turned to mainstream country music, which gave a voice to their concerns, interests, and fears.

The socio-economic changes after World War II that had lifted many country fans into a middle-class lifestyle had firmly taken root by this period. From the 1960s onward, a sizeable portion of the country music audience found themselves much more assimilated into middle-class, mainstream American life. These circumstances increased general concerns about defining and preserving country music's "otherness" or distinction from mainstream pop and popular culture. The circumstances also renewed fans' nostalgia for an imagined rural, working-class identity.

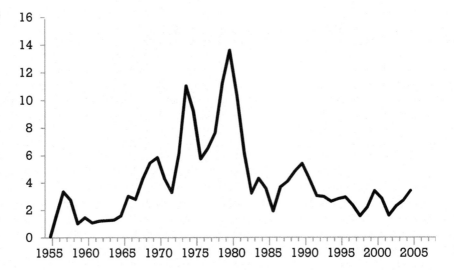

Figure 8-1 Average annual inflation (percent) in the United States (data source: Consumer Price Index).

At the time, many fans thought of the mainstream country music of the late 1960s and '70s simply as a continuation of the Nashville sound. However, the music's sound had evolved after the deaths of Patsy Cline and Jim Reeves (see essay on Classic Country) into its own distinctive style. When fans look back on it from today's perspective, they often use terms such as "classic" to describe that era's sound, similar to the way radio formats use the term "classic" to describe playing rock music of the '60s and '70s. Thus, we will adopt the term as a stylistic label for the mainstream country music from those years, even though at the time it was recorded, neither the artists nor the fans thought of it in that light. The other term that we will use is "traditionalist," which captures the way that the 1970s mainstream country stars were ideologically invested in country's past, even while making music that was thoroughly modern in its topics, musical style, and marketing. In subsequent

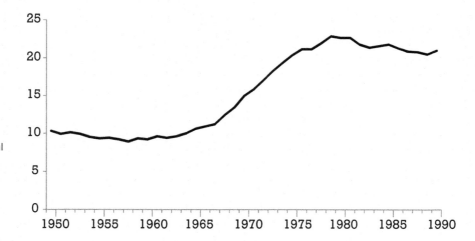

Figure 8-2 Annual divorce rate per 1,000 married women (data source: National Center for Health Statistics).

decades, fans have often credited the late 1960s and '70s with resurrecting a sense of tradition, partly because that era was sandwiched in between two periods of rampant pop-crossover excesses. Yet as time continues to pass, the way new fans think of that era is shifting once again, as we will explore at the end of this chapter.

The classic country era's lasting contributions to the genre included establishing:

- a larger group of female stars than had graced country music up to that time
- a generation of male singers who modernized honky-tonk
- a televised presence for country music that put it in just about every American's living room
- a means for middle-class white Americans to musically reflect on the changing social order

During these years, fans saw a proliferation of magazines and trade papers about country music, as well as the first academic book on the subject—scholar Bill C. Malone broke new ground when he wrote *Country Music U.S.A.*, which gave the genre a certain air of respectability. This era's stars were working in essentially a modern music industry, making both albums and singles in multitrack stereophonic studios, marketing their music on both radio and television, and actively touring and performing. This fact has helped the classic country stars to extend their careers several decades and take on a "classic" identity for later generations of fans; three decades later, many of them were still touring, and fans had easy access to television footage and relatively modern-sounding stereo recordings. At the end of the 1970s, mainstream country music had accompanied its fans through a decade of social change and was poised for its biggest crossover era yet.

Classic Country's Female Stars

Patsy Cline paved the way for a new generation of female country singers. Unlike so many of the women before her, Cline was not marketed as someone's wife or mother, but instead claimed the spotlight unapologetically for herself. Female fans loved her music, and she provided inspiration for young, aspiring singers to chase their own careers. The next wave of female country stars were not only singers, however, but also songwriters and businesswomen, who saw the potential to be fully integrated into the country music industry's operations. Three women in particular blazed trails in these areas: Loretta Lynn, Tammy Wynette, and Dolly Parton. They were by no means the only stars of that era; Lynn Anderson, Dottie West, Connie Smith, Jeannie C. Riley, Barbara Mandrell, and dozens of other women also caught the attention and affection of the country music fan base. But Lynn, Wynette, and Parton's contributions were particularly important, and all three left their marks as singers, songwriters, and entrepreneurs within the music industry. Collectively, they projected the varying points of view of working-class and middle-class mostly (but not exclusively) white American women during these years. Their biographies were also part of their legends: like the stars of the honky-tonk era, these women wove their real-life biographies into their stage personas, an aspect of country tradition that became increasingly important during the 1970s.

Listening Guide

"Coal Miner's Daughter" (1970)

PERFORMER:
Loretta Lynn

SONGWRITER:
Loretta Lynn

ORIGINAL ALBUM:
Coal Miner's Daughter (Decca DL-75253)

FORM: Strophic

STYLE: Classic country

This musical autobiography revealed a more nostalgic and introspective side of Loretta Lynn than most of her earlier well-known hits, which had earned her a feisty, feminist reputation. The musical setting borrows heavily from the Nashville sound tradition, with background vocalists; layers of accompanying instruments, including piano; and a sophisticated arrangement that complicates a simple, four-chord song with two modulations. That musical setting contrasts with the lyrics' nostalgia for a simple rural lifestyle, in spite of the impoverished conditions in which she was raised. Yet two of the most prominent instruments in that mix are a banjo and a steel guitar, which both evoke an older, more traditional approach to country music. In these regards, the song represents the dual nature of country music during the 1970s: it was a sophisticated entertainment industry that relied on notions of a simple, rural, working-class past for its identity.

Many artists during this era sang autobiographical songs through which their fans learned about their personal histories. These songs, such as Merle Haggard's "Mama Tried" (see Chapter 7) and Dolly Parton's "Coat of Many Colors," usually include common references to religion ("Sunday learning" or the Bible), family, poverty, and pride. Those aspects of a singer's biography were important in establishing his or her creditability as a country singer with the fans during the classic country period.

"Coal Miner's Daughter" is a strophic song, composed only of verses. To add interest within that structure, the musical arrangement changes what instruments are featured behind Lynn's singing in each verse, and the song modulates (changes key) twice.

Loretta Lynn née Webb (1935–) was born in Butcher Holler, Kentucky, the second of eight children in a poor coal miner's family. At age thirteen, she married Doolittle "Mooney" Lynn, and moved to the Pacific Northwest when he followed employment opportunities. By eighteen, Lynn had four children and was running the household on a sparse income—a life many country fans today can barely imagine. She was a fan of Patsy Cline's, and her husband purchased a guitar for her to cultivate that interest. Lynn began writing songs and performing locally, and in 1960 she signed with a small, independent label called Zero Records, based in Vancouver. She made a few records in Los Angeles for the label, then she and her husband set out to promote the records at radio stations themselves. They made their way to Nashville, where Lynn's single "I'm a Honky Tonk Girl" earned her sufficient acclaim to land her a guest appearance on the Opry and the attention of the Wilburn Brothers, an established brothers act who, by 1960, had their own television show and publishing firm. The Wilburns helped extract Lynn from her Zero

TIME	FORM	LISTENING CUES	REFERENCES
0:00	Introduction	steel guitar and banjo	Common in traditionalist country.
0:08	Verse 1	"Well, I was born …"	Banjo evokes ideas of place (Kentucky) and bluegrass.
0:37	Verse 2	"My daddy worked …"	Background singers enter. Note how the song connects the listeners to specific places.
1:03		Modulation: from the key of D to E-flat	Sophisticated musical arrangement of a very simple song form.
1:05	Verse 3	"Daddy loved …"	Regional accent connects Lynn to a specific place of origin ("worsh" for "wash" and "ev'r" for "every") Piano appears in the background to add interest to the arrangement.
1:32	Verse 4	"In the summertime …"	Background singers replace piano again.
1:58		Modulation: from the key of E-flat to E	Even novice listeners who have not had any formal training in music or music theory can hear these modulations. Notice how the whole recording sounds like it shifts and brightens at this exact moment.
2:01	Verse 5	"Yeah, I'm proud …"	Piano reappears, while Lynn sings the title of the song. Notice the grammar that evokes a working-class idiomatic style of speech ("The work we done …")
2:29	Verse 6	"Well, a lot of things …"	Steel guitar reappears. The song ends once again with the title line.

Records contract, secured a deal for her with Decca Records, promoted her on their television show and in concerts, and effectively launched her national career.

By 1966, Lynn had released several albums and a string of singles, some of which had landed in the top ten in *Billboard*'s country charts. Lynn established herself as an artist with a strong allegiance to country's past, covering songs by Hank Williams, Johnny Cash, and Ernest Tubb, among others. Her sound relied on the "boom-chuck" two-beat rhythms of honky tonk, with plenty of steel guitar layered into the mix. Her recordings made allowances for the contemporary Nashville trends with their inclusion of backup singers, tic-tac bass, and often elaborate piano parts as well. In those ways, Lynn's sound was the quintessential fusion of honky-tonk and the Nashville sound that came to define the classic country era.

Within a few short years, Lynn had carved out a reputation for outspoken, defiantly independent song lyrics that contradicted any assumptions that country women lacked their own opinions or voices. Her first number-one hit was her self-penned

"Don't Come Home A'Drinkin' (With Lovin' on Your Mind)" (1966), which offered a feisty ultimatum to a partying husband, along with a complaint that he never takes *her* out on the town but merely has his fun, then comes home expecting more. Other hits adopted a similar tone: "Fist City," "Your Squaw Is on the Warpath," "You Ain't Woman Enough (To Take My Man)," and "Women of the World (Leave My World Alone)." The lyrics to several of these songs featured a protagonist speaking directly to other women, which established a space within country music in which "housewives" defended their lives and families from "honky-tonk angels," two female characters that date back many decades in country music's history. Lynn's songs presented a very different brand of feminism than what made headlines in those years, however. Lynn's characters spoke from a vantage point as wives and mothers, fully intent on preserving those institutions even while demanding increased respect, while a far more liberal feminism was on display outside of country music.

Tammy Wynette (1942–1998) grew up picking cotton alongside her grandparents in rural Mississippi. She married before high school graduation, and at age twenty-three was a divorced mother of three, working in a hair salon. Opry star Porter Wagoner heard her sing locally and offered her a spot on one of his concert tours. Drawing on that experience, Wynette moved to Nashville in 1965, and was soon signed by Billy Sherrill, producer for Epic Records and the person most responsible for shaping the classic country era's sound. Sherrill (1936–2015) had initially trained under Sun Records' Sam Phillips, but by the mid-1960s he had crafted a vision for the new country sound. Sherrill's concept kept much of the sentimentality and lush musical arrangements of the Nashville sound era but blended it with honky-tonk elements. Also a songwriter, Sherrill shaped the careers of Wynette, George Jones, and Charlie Rich, along with others, all among the brightest stars of that era. As had been the case in earlier generations, Sherrill's role as producer had a significant and direct effect on the sound of country music.

On most of Wynette's recordings, Sherrill's production work exhibited many more elements of the Nashville sound style than did Lynn's recordings.

Figure 8-3 Tammy Wynette and George Jones performing on the Opry, 1969.

Source: Les Leverett photograph © Grand Ole Opry Archives.

Lush strings, lots of reverb added to Wynette's voice, silky backup vocals, and layers of instruments blended together graced many of her hits, although a heavy dose of steel guitar was also present. Sherrill had listened closely to the work of pop producer Phil Spector, whose "girl-group" R&B hits of the early 1960s revolutionized studio production with what was called a "wall of sound," consisting of many instrumentalists performing together to create an intensity and saturation of sound on the recording. Sherrill imported the approach into country music very successfully. Wynette had a huge voice that could belt out high notes, quiver with heartbroken misery, or take on the commanding volume that Patsy Cline had used a decade earlier, and it cut through even Sherrill's thick instrumentation. Sherrill and Wynette also relied on dramatic musical swells in many of their recordings, where a song would move rapidly from a quiet section into a full-throttle high point, with Wynette belting out high notes suddenly (listen, for instance, to "The Ways to Love a Man"). The effect was one of surging, raw emotion, but still wrapped in the rich, sophisticated orchestration of the Nashville sound. The formula worked; from 1967 to 1976, Wynette scored twenty-three top ten hits on the *Billboard* country charts, including a run of six number ones in a row. Fans adored the way she conveyed stories of broken hearts and familial anguish.

The biggest controversies surrounding Wynette's career grew out of her songs' lyrics and how they address marriage and gender relations. Most of the songs she sang were written by the stable of professional writers in Nashville, including Norro Wilson and Billy Sherrill, yet her fans thought of the lyrics as her own expressions and ideas. Wynette's first big hit, "Your Good Girl's Gonna Go Bad" (by Billy Sherrill and one of his songwriting partners, Glenn Sutton), was laced with tambourine, electric Telecaster guitar, and a sassy set of lyrics in which Wynette announces she will get "painted up, powdered up" and set out to experience the wild side of life, since that is apparently the sort of woman who caught her man's attention—yet

DOES THE SINGER MAKE A DIFFERENCE?

Some songs, such as "Stand by Your Man," are widely associated with one singer—in this case, Tammy Wynette. When a different person covers the song, the way fans hear and interpret it is sometimes jarringly different. Given the strongly gendered interpretations of "Stand by Your Man," one interesting experiment is to listen to a male country singer performing the song, as in Lyle Lovett's 1989 cover version. The musical accompaniment, lyrics, and just about every aspect of Wynette's performance are the same, only we hear Lovett's voice. Does the change in the singer's gender and vocal tone change how you understand the lyrics? Can you hear the song in his performance as an apology and request for tolerance, understanding, or forgiveness, spoken from a male perspective? What supporting evidence can you offer for either these or other interpretations of the song? How and why might some country fans tend to adopt one interpretation, while noncountry listeners might tend toward another? The multiplicity of meanings that songs such as this one offer are part of what make music such a rich form of cultural expression, and they are worthy of careful consideration.

another instance of the dialogue of wife versus honky-tonk angel. That perspective, however, was rare among Wynette's recordings. The majority of her hits counseled women to stick by their men even in the face of tribulation—a recommendation that was at odds with the more radical feminist perspectives that were frequently expressed during those years. "Stand by Your Man" (1968), which Sherrill and Wynette cowrote, was the lightning rod for much of that controversy: the singer apparently advises women to remain with their men even while suffering neglect and mistreatment. For decades, Wynette's hit has been touted by politicians, journalists, and critics of all stripes as evidence that country music is misogynistic, repressive toward women, and antifeminist. Hillary Clinton, wife of then presidential candidate Bill Clinton, invoked the song pejoratively in a 1992 television interview after allegations of her husband's long-time infidelity surfaced, saying on the CBS show *60 Minutes,* "You know, I'm not sitting here as some little woman standing by my man like Tammy Wynette! I'm sitting here because I love him, and I respect him…" That reference disparaged the song and—by extension—Tammy Wynette for apparently saying that a woman should put up with any and all mistreatment, suffer in silence, and remain passive and obedient. Other fans, however, hear the song differently and find humor and an expression of solidarity among women in the way that Wynette inflects some of the words in the song. This song offers a good example of the multiplicity of meanings that fans will ascribe to a single recording, based on their individual perspectives.

Figure 8-4 Dolly Parton in *9 to 5,* marking a new gender identity in country music.

Source: Photo by Michael Ochs Archives/Getty Images.

Dolly Parton entered the scene at approximately the same time as Wynette (see Artist Profile). Like Wynette's and Lynn's, Parton's contributions to country music include many songs that explore gender relationships. Parton's were less thematically consistent than Loretta Lynn's, but just as radical. Many young musicians today find it hard to imagine how difficult it was for a woman to break into the country music business in those years, especially since we now look back at Parton and others as superstars who are widely known even outside of country music. But in 1970,

ARTIST PROFILE

Dolly Parton (1946–)

With a career spanning more than four decades and covering almost all aspects of the music business, Dolly Parton is a major force within country music. Born January 19, 1946, in Sevierville, Tennessee, Parton is the fourth of twelve children raised in a poor sharecropping family. She made a few recordings as a young teenager, and immediately after graduating from high school moved to Nashville. Her uncle, Bill Owens, was an established songwriter there who helped her make contacts in the industry and cowrote several successful songs with her, including "Put It Off until Tomorrow" for singer Bill Phillips.

Her early attempts at a solo career floundered, but in 1967 Porter Wagoner hired her as his duet partner, known in the business as a "girl singer," for his successful television show. The term referred to the secondary or supporting role that these women held, where their primary task was to make the (male) star look and sound even better. The two began releasing extremely successful duets in 1967, and Wagoner served as manager for her solo career. For several years, Parton's solo releases floundered, but in 1970 her version of "Muleskinner Blues" reached number three on the *Billboard* country chart. Thereafter, she enjoyed a string of number one records, and her reputation as a star was firmly established.

Like many of her fellow country singers in the mid-1970s, Parton was interested in reaching a larger audience and expanding her career far beyond the conventional boundaries of country music. In what was a radical move for a country singer, Parton hired Sandy Gallin, who had experience in pop music but no ties to country music, as her new manager. She broke her contract with Wagoner in 1975, and a year later starred in her own short-lived television series. She incorporated elements of disco and R&B into her musical style and sought performance opportunities in conventionally pop venues, including Las Vegas. In 1980, Parton starred in the Hollywood film *9 to 5*, for which she also wrote and performed the theme song.

Parton's curvaceous figure, campy wigs, and glitzy costumes disguise a savvy businesswoman who has built an empire as a songwriter, producer, and brand marketer. She has shown remarkable abilities to transform her music and her identity to stay ahead of trends in country music. In the early 1980s, she scored crossover hits with pop-infused tracks such as "Islands in the Stream" (written by the Bee-Gees); in the late 1980s she recorded classic country songs with Emmylou Harris and Linda Ronstadt just as country was moving toward a neotraditional period; in the early 1990s, she released a line-dance country-pop hit; and in the late 1990s, she reoriented herself as a traditional bluegrass musician right before the roots movement and bluegrass revival crested. Her continued relevance after more than four decades in country music is indicative both of the way that country music holds to its traditions and past and of the way that it interacts with popular culture at large.

for instance, only four out of the twenty-three songs that reached the top of the *Billboard* country charts were sung by women. Producers, songwriters, studio musicians, and record executives were almost all male and, especially in the religiously and politically conservative South, the feminist movement had not yet changed perceptions of "appropriate" gender roles. In 1970, Parton's choice to sing "Muleskinner Blues," an outspoken, whip-cracking, traditionally "man's" song that both Jimmie Rodgers and Bill Monroe had made famous, took both musical and personal gumption, and it paid off—that was how she became a star in her own right.

Parton also faced the career limitations that came with being a country singer—which meant marginalization in the larger pop-music scene—as well as a woman, and actively sought strategies to overcome them. Her recording of the song "9 to 5" (1980) serves as a useful metaphor for and symbol of the complete transition of both gender roles and genre boundaries in country music from the mid-1960s to the start of a new era. Parton wrote the song, starred in the movie by the same title, and fully embraced the pop-influenced sound of a pulsating electric bass line, syncopated rhythms, and a full horn section. The symbolism continued with the character Parton played in the film, a woman working self-sufficiently outside the home, yet under-recognized and harassed by her unenlightened male boss. In just under fifteen years, the female perspective represented by country music was no longer limited to the domestic sphere. That shift in perspective, however, raised issues that have remained part of the country music discourse to the present day, as we shall see in the early 1990s (in songs like "Is There Life Out There," "He Thinks He'll Keep Her," etc.; see Chapter 12). Country music had paralleled the social transition of working- and middle-class America through the 1970s and emerged on the other side in a new social context.

Classic Country's Male Stars

The male country stars during the late 1960s and '70s were, for the most part, older than the previous generations of country singers had been in their respective heydays. Many had started out in rockabilly or rock 'n' roll, then moved into mainstream country music as their own interests and music had both matured. They represented a working- and middle-class, mostly white, middle-aged male voice wrestling with the demise of traditional masculine heroes as cultural values shifted away from celebrating working-class jobs that relied on physical prowess. High unemployment and inflation during the late 1960s and early 1970s threatened men's ability to provide for their families. Tensions surrounding social class and education ran particularly high among young men, because those who were in college or graduate school in many cases were not drafted and sent to Vietnam. Those without the means or ability to pursue a college education—a high percentage of whom were Southern and poor and had families who worked in the sectors of employment hardest hit by the economic downturn, in other words, many country fans—resented the situation. These concerns manifested themselves in country music, where the male singers gravitated toward songs about searching for meaning in life, about loss and a sense that things of value were slipping out of reach, and about abject loneliness (see essay on Gender in Classic Country).

The most famous of the male singers from this era is George Jones, who began his career in the mid-1950s as a rockabilly singer (see Chapter 4). His sound and style changed, however, after he began working with Tammy Wynette, whom he

George Jones (1931–2013)

George Jones's career illustrates both the larger trends in mainstream 1970s country music and the paradoxes within that tradition. Born September 12, 1931, in Texas, Jones started singing on the radio as a young teenager. Like many country singers of his generation, he served in the military from 1951 to 1953. A year later, he began recording rockabilly and honky-tonk tunes for Starday, a small record label based in Texas. From 1955 to 1960, several of his songs reached the *Billboard* top ten, and Jones moved to a larger label, Mercury Records.

Jones (known as the Possum, the nickname by which he is called in a number of country songs) is regarded by many country fans and historians as the quintessential honky-tonk singer who is able to convey raw heartbreak, vulnerability, and pathos in his performances. Yet his best-known recordings of the 1970s were extremely successful as a marriage of honky-tonk

themes and vocals with Nashville sound accompaniments produced by Billy Sherrill.

Jones's personal life added an autobiographical aura to his honky-tonk reputation. He struggled with alcoholism and drug use for much of his professional life, earning the nickname "No-Show Jones" because of many missed appearances. His marriage to Tammy Wynette lasted from 1969 until 1975. Their duets, recorded both during and after the marriage, captured their tumultuous relationship in song. Jones married Nancy Sepulveda in 1983 and credits her with helping him overcome his addictions.

Jones largely disappeared from country radio in the mid-1980s, although he has continued to release albums on small labels and tour. Following his induction into the Country Music Hall of Fame in 1982, he adopted a role as country music patriarch and keeper of tradition. His death in 2013 marked the closing of an era.

---

married in 1969. Through Wynette's connections, Jones teamed up with producer Billy Sherrill, who shaped the sound of his records for nearly two decades. Sherrill applied the same musical treatment he had used so successfully with Wynette. He allowed Jones the full range of vocal expression, from tears and cries to the quivers, wails, and scoops that conveyed raw, direct emotions as in honky-tonk, but he backed Jones with a full range of instruments, layered and mixed into a lush blend of the Nashville sound traditions. The combination let fans continue to associate Jones with honky-tonk traditionalism while keeping him in the mainstream sound of the 1970s. A consummate stylist, Jones relied on the professional songwriting teams in Nashville for most of his hits rather than writing them himself, even though his fans unmistakably heard the songs as "his own." His self-destructive, alcohol-drenched lifestyle only added to his appeal. Fans wanted and expected their country stars to be the literal embodiment of the songs they sang, and Jones offered them that type of authenticity. His career thrived through the 1970s and well into the next decade.

Listening Guide

"He Stopped Loving Her Today" (1980)

PERFORMER: George Jones

SONGWRITER: Bobby Braddock and Curly Putman

ORIGINAL ALBUM: *I Am What I Am* (Epic JE-36586)

FORM: Verse-chorus

STYLE: Classic country

This song appears on many fan and critic polls as the greatest country song of all time. It marked the beginning of a third era of George Jones's career, following on his early rockabilly recordings and his string of early 1970s classic country hits such as "The Grand Tour" and "A Good Year for the Roses." As one of the biggest stars during this classic country era, Jones specialized in beer-drenched heartbreak songs. During the late 1970s, Jones slipped out of the spotlight, until this song, penned by two longtime Nashville songwriters, reached the top of the country charts and restored his stardom. The momentum from this song carried Jones into a third period of success in his career and maintained his relevance to the country music audience through the early 1980s, even while most of country music has moved onto a more countrypolitan, pop-infused sound (see Chapter 10).

Both Bobby Braddock and Curly Putman had been working as songwriters in Nashville since the 1960s. They collaborated on "D-I-V-O-R-C-E," which Tammy Wynette released in 1968, and were two of the most prolific writers in the classic country era. They had worked for years with producer Billy Sherrill, who was at the helm for this recording. Combined with Jones's mature vocal work, "He Stopped Loving Her Today" was the created product of seasoned masters in the country industry.

The song catches the listener off guard with its lack of an introduction. The first line of text foreshadows the entire plot. Listeners often miss the early hints in the text that the protagonist (the "he" in the lyrics) is dead, and that the song takes place at his funeral. The singer is a bystander, serving as narrator; this approach, which uses a mostly third-person voice, was common in the classic country story-song era. In this song, however, the singer participates in the story and draws the audience into the text with the inclusive "we" ("we all wondered," for instance, if the former lover would show up at the funeral). Finally, Braddock and Putman craft one of the most dramatic scenes in all of country music with just a few words and a mere suggestion: the former lover dares to show up at the funeral, amid rampant speculation over whether or not she would come. Jones's spoken delivery compels listeners to enter the song's domain and see in their imaginations her arrival, adding details and realism to the scene that are not made explicit in the lyrics: the quiet buzz that ripples through the crowd, her demeanor, her facial expressions, and the (dead) protagonist's lack of response. Jones's ironic summation, "This time he's over her for good," employs dark humor and a wry outlook regarding a pathetic situation.

Certain aspects of the recording evoke honky-tonk musical characteristics, especially the emotionally raw account of abject misery and obsession over lost love. Jones's voice, the use of the recitation in the fifth verse, and the story line itself all connect to that tradition. The prominent guitar, steel guitar, and especially the crying harmonica are reminiscent of the harder-edged side of 1970s country. But at the same time, the full, lush string section, the dramatic musical swells, the backup singers, and the electric bass are indicative of the Nashville sound approach to production that Jones was known for. In this way, the musical style of this song illustrates the dual nature of this era's country music; it draws equally from the commercial pop stylings of the Nashville sound era and from the more traditional, honky-tonk–infused styles.

A note about the timings listed in this chart: for each section within the song, the timings mark where the formal unit begins (marked by the chords and the band's accompaniment), although Jones often starts singing a bit earlier with pick-up notes.

TIME	FORM	LISTENING CUES	REFERENCES
0:00	Verse 1	"He said I'll love you …"	Jones's voice opens the recording, which is unusual because it offers no introduction for convenient radio airplay (when the DJs introduce the song). There is intense foreshadowing in the opening line, where the protagonist predicts his own death.
0:29	Verse 2	"He kept her picture …"	The harmonica enters here as a response to each of Jones's lines. The abject misery of this man's broken heart is part of the pathos of country music.
0:53	Verse 3	"He kept some letters …"	There is a modulation (key change) right before this verse. Notice that the song gathers momentum as more instruments enter, most significantly the drums. The harmonica is replaced with a combination of steel guitar and string section. The lyrics provide a sense of time frame (the date 1962).
1:24	Verse 4	"I went to see him …"	The singer enters the narrative here when he says "I went …" Notice the harsh irony of the line "first time I'd seen him smile in years"; the protagonist finds relief from his misery only in death.
1:51	Chorus	"He stopped loving her …"	The chorus uses the music to create the sense of swelling emotion. Listen to the strings [1:51] that start low and race up to a high note. Jones's voice sounds like it's on the verge of crying.
2:17	Verse 5	"You know, she came to see …"	The back-up singers set the mood of this verse as reflective and contemplative. This is one of the most famous recitations in country music, where Jones speaks instead of sings the verse. It moves the song into the domain of a staged drama. Jones introduces another character into the story line here: the woman who had broken the protagonist's heart.
2:43	Chorus	"He stopped loving her …"	The same swelling line from the strings comes at [2:44]. At the very end of this chorus, the band drops out and we get just the vocalists with piano for a moment. That sound evokes a church choir and piano style that one might associate with a hymn.

Many other male singers capitalized on the same intensity of vocal emotion that made Jones so successful. Gary Stewart (1944–2003) sang with a quiver in his voice that sounded like he was on the verge of a breakdown—extremely effective in his heartbreak/honky-tonk tunes. Jack Greene (1930–2013) had a plaintive wail in his vocals, colored by a strong southern accent (he grew up in Tennessee and Georgia) that threatened to reduce the listener to tears in songs such as "There Goes My Everything." Moe Bandy (1944–) stuck to a much more stripped-down honky-tonk style, with more steel guitar, fiddle, and hard-core twang in his music than most of his contemporaries, but his vocals and song lyrics tugged on the same heartstrings. Whether adhering to a more Nashville-sound style like Greene or reviving a honky-tonk style like Bandy, the male stars relied heavily on the naturalized vocals that had characterized hard country music ever since the days of Hank Williams.

Like George Jones, Conway Twitty (1933–1993) had enjoyed two decades of a singing career before the classic country era. Born Harold Lloyd Jenkins in Mississippi, Twitty started out in rockabilly and signed with Sun Records in the 1950s. He had a few teen-crooner pop hits in the late 1950s along with a few appearances in films. In 1965, he headed to Nashville to reshape his career into that of a country singer, which is where he always claimed his musical heart was. Five years later, he released "Hello, Darlin'," a bitter ballad about a chance encounter with an ex that encapsulated everything the male voice of classic country music was about.

Twitty spent the next decade singing songs pitched predominantly toward a female audience. In those recordings, Twitty cultivated an identity as an imagined lover for women who were observing the sexual revolution and women's liberation movement from traditionally domestic vantage points in the 1970s. In other words, he fulfilled the fantasies of a middle-class, middle-aged housewife. His song lyrics delved frankly into female sexuality and desire ("You've Never Been This Far Before," see Listening Guide), portrayed a sensitive, vulnerable man deeply in love ("Touch the Hand," "I'm Not Through Loving You"), and offered wounded confessions of wrongdoing ("How Much More Can She Stand," "She Needs Someone to Hold Her [When She Cries]"). His songs frequently addressed the listener directly through second-person narration (singing to "you"), which let the listener imagine that she was the one to whom Twitty was speaking and gave the songs an added degree of intimacy. He even described his role explicitly in "See the Want To in Your Eyes," in which his lyrics address a married woman: "A woman wants a love, sweet and warm . . . how many men like me do they sleep with in their dreams? . . . I see the 'want to' in your eyes." Twitty's approach landed him twenty number one hits in the 1970s alone, and a dozen more in the next decade. Although the songs presented a male voice and perspective, they are, in fact, a revealing portrait of female country fans and their concerns, interests, and identity within the larger social context of the 1970s.

Kenny Rogers (1938–) followed a career trajectory similar to Twitty's. From the 1950s through the mid-'70s, Rogers tried a short-lived solo career as a rock singer, then performed with various doo-wop and rock groups, including the First Edition, who signed with Reprise Records and enjoyed several pop hits with a slight hippie vibe. In 1976, Rogers left the group to strike out on his own, slipping easily into the classic country vocal style. A year later, he scored his first number one hit with "Lucille" (see essay on Gender in Classic Country). In 1978, Rogers recorded songwriter Don Schlitz's "The Gambler," about a down-on-his-luck man who gets sage advice about the meaning of life from a gambler on a late-night train bound for "nowhere." For Rogers, it was a career-making hit that gave him a much rougher musical reputation than he had enjoyed prior to that time. It even tied him loosely to the outlaw movement (see Chapter 9) simply by the nature of its lyrics. Rogers capitalized on the song's success in a series of made-for-TV movies about the song's characters. He traded on his popularity to reshape his music career once again, and by 1980, Rogers had become one of the leading stars of the next pop-

Figure 8-5 Loretta Lynn and Conway Twitty, 1971.
Source: Courtesy of Country Music Hall of Fame and Museum.

crossover movement (see Chapter 10). But for a brief time in the late 1970s, Rogers's music was a quintessential part of the classic country sound.

Breaking Barriers

Two of the barriers that had long characterized country music were its association with a white racial identity and its perceived position of cultural inferiority to pop music. During the classic country era, both of those barriers were crossed in significant ways. Charley Pride (1938–) became the first black country star of the modern (post-television) era, and did so at a time with civil rights tensions were at an all-time high. Yet his career also highlights just how many hurdles were in place for a black star, and the complicated and conflicted ways in which the country music audience did and did not accept him. Pride grew up in a family of poor sharecroppers (as had Johnny Cash) in Mississippi. Like Roy Acuff before him (and Garth Brooks after him), Pride dreamed of a baseball career, but when

Listening Guide

"You've Never Been This Far Before" (1973)

PERFORMER: Conway Twitty

SONGWRITERS: Conway Twitty and L.E. White

ORIGINAL ALBUM: *You've Never Been This Far Before* (MCA 359)

FORM: AABA

STYLE: Classic country

Conway Twitty wrote this song with bluegrass fiddler L. E. White, who worked with Twitty for many years, wrote several of his biggest hits, and helped set up his publishing company. Both the lyrics and the music itself portray a sexual encounter in scandalous detail. Listen for the musical representation of the lovers' heartbeats, both in the steady pulse of the music and the "bum-bum-bum" utterances from Twitty. The musical texture increases and intensifies over the course of most of the song, building to a musical and metaphoric (sexual) climax, then dissipates as the last section of the song returns to a thinner musical texture and more relaxed, almost breathy vocal delivery. The song even changes chord progressions and keys, moving higher in pitch at the moments of greatest tension and lower in pitch after that peak.

This song was sufficiently graphic in its depiction that it was banned from some radio stations. It is also a prime example of how Conway Twitty's music fulfilled an escapist fantasy for many of his middle-aged female fans in the 1970s. Twitty both understood the drudgery of middle-class and working-class daily life, especially for a housewife who felt trapped by her domestic role during the rise of the women's liberation movement, and offered a three-minute indulgence in a sensuous and exciting world of illicit romance. The title of the song, which becomes a hook in the lyrics, has multiple meanings that are none too subtle; it refers to the passionate nature of the physical encounter and its conclusion, to the distance the woman has strayed from her previous relationship, and to the distance that the couple has traveled emotionally in what the singer claims to be love.

nothing came of that, he headed to Nashville to try for a music career instead. As it was for many young boys of his age from rural Mississippi, both black and white, country music was simply part of the soundscape in which he lived, and many of its topics about rural, working-class life matched his experiences. In 1966, Chet Atkins signed him, and Pride began recording songs in a classic country style that blended Atkins's refined Nashville sound production with the twang of the newer generation of singers.

From the outset of his career, Pride's identity as a black man was something that the country music industry grappled with. Pride's manager emphasized his moniker, "Country Charley Pride," in all marketing materials and deliberately refused to distribute any photographs of Pride for the first two years of his career, a move calculated to hide his African-American identity from the country fan base. The strategy worked; within a short time, Pride's songs, including the

The song's AABA form connects it to the popular songwriting traditions that were so prevalent in country music in the 1950s and '60s. It also allows for a continuous story line (rather than switching between verses and a chorus), which fits the content and meaning of the song.

TIME	FORM	LISTENING CUES	REFERENCES
0:00	Introduction	steel guitar	Common in traditionalist country.
0:07	A-section	"I can almost hear ..."	Listen for the steady pulse of the bass.
0:16		"bum-bum-bum"	The lyrics call to mind a heartbeat over and over in the song, sometimes echoed by the guitar
1:02	A-section	"I don't know what ..."	During this section, the background singers and instruments add more intensity to the texture. Notice that the song has sped up just a bit. The guitar picks up the "bum-bum-bum" idea, and then Twitty echoes it.
1:58	B-section	"And as I take the love ..."	The instruments and chords both intensify the emotional content. Listen for the tambourine and high, plucked strings. The background singers add louder "oohs" and "ahs" behind Twitty. Listen for the strained sound of Twitty's voice on "in your mind."
2:26	A-section (half)	"You have no way ..."	The texture simplifies. Background singers disappear, Twitty's voice cracks, and a sweet fiddle adds a few fills. This is only the last half of the typical A-section. At the very end [starting at 2:40], listen for the short, chirpy sounds from the strings that get quieter as the song ends.

warm and happy love songs such as "Amazing Love" and "Kiss an Angel Good Mornin'," had achieved widespread fame, and he was an accepted part of the country music family, but he achieved that in part by hiding the ways in which he was different.

Pride's country music career, which included induction into the Country Hall of Fame in 2000, highlights two important aspects of racial identity within country music. The first is that Pride's management and record label sensed the potential for rampant racial discrimination and went to great lengths to hide his identity until his career was well established. This speaks to the way that the audience's expectations are intertwined with ideas about an artist's identity, not just the sound of the music. The second aspect, however, is that to this black artist, country music represented something other than racial identity, a shared experience that despite all odds crossed racial lines in the South. Pride specifically wanted to be a country singer because, as he later explained, that was the genre that connected with his sense of who he was. Corresponding to that perspective, once the country fan base got beyond first impressions, many accepted Pride into the fold based on the sound, style, and performances he offered them. Yet Pride's acceptance as a country singer did not change the fundamental relationship between musical genre and racial identity.

Pride remained an anomaly: he was the sole instance of a black country singer gaining the highest levels of acclaim in country music in that era, and the general case of racial barriers in country music remained firmly in place. Many consider Price to be an exception that proves the still-present rule of country's whiteness. It is worth noting, however, that in the years just after the Civil Rights Act radically altered the social landscape of the South, country music offered a working-class, rurally grounded identity that occasionally reached across racial lines. In the years that followed, interactions and exchanges between black and white musicians, which had been present from the earliest days of country recordings, actually increased. But the corporate infrastructure of country music, and the majority of its audience, remain invested in the racial whiteness of the music into the present (see Chapter 14).

Figure 8-6 Charely Pride.

Source: Southern Folklife Collection, Wilson Library, The University of North Carolina at Chapel Hill.

The second barrier that was part of country music's identity was its perceived position of artistic inferiority to pop-rock music. The homegrown, homespun country industry that was originally tagged as "hillbilly" had been fighting this perception since the 1950s, but had not yet triumphed entirely over the widely held notion that country music was backward music for backward bumpkins, and unworthy of respect from outsiders. Yet in the 1970s, an influx of artists from other genres altered that perception. Some of those inroads were made by folk and country rock artists such as Bob Dylan and the Byrds (see Chapter 7). Yet others were made by entertainers who simply saw country music as a musical and aesthetic space in which they wanted to work, and Nashville as providing easy access to top-quality recording studios. A similar perspective would surface two decades later in the early 1990s, when noncountry artists and producers flocked to Nashville, accompanied by much harsh criticism over the lack of so-called authenticity they brought to the genre. In the late 1960s, the head of this trend was Glen Campbell (1936–2017).

Born in Arkansas, Campbell moved to Los Angeles in 1958 to work as a session guitarist in the booming music scene on the West Coast. He was hired to perform with the Beach Boys, both on their albums and on tour, and was highly regarded for his instrumental talent. He attempted to launch a solo career in 1962 and signed a record contract with Capitol Records, but with no commercial success. In 1967, he shifted his style toward more folk and country influences, which resulted in several hits. Campbell specialized in pop-infused country, borrowing heavily from the Nashville sound tradition and layering his recordings with strings and heavy backup vocals. He also recorded songs that were more musically complicated, especially those written by songwriter Jimmy Webb (best known for "MacArthur Park"). Campbell's recording of "Galveston" (1969), for instance, is highly acclaimed and appears on many critics' lists of the top ten country songs of all time, yet many country fans do not know the song at all, and upon hearing it, are either overwhelmed or merely unimpressed—its musical arrangement employs the excesses of the Nashville sound, its lyrics are more abstract than the typical country song, and Campbell's performance would be entirely at home in pop music. The song reached number two on the pop charts, something that was tolerated and even admired by the country fan base in the early 1960s but which had come to be a liability in the eyes of some country fans by 1969. Campbell's 1975 hit, "Rhinestone Cowboy," pushed even further into pop-crossover territory; it reached number one on both the country and pop charts. Its lyrics followed a man chasing dreams of success in the big city, hoping to wind up not like a traditional cowboy but like the glittery version seen in the "star-spangled" rodeos. With its pop beat and heavy strings, the recording illustrated the merging of pop and country in the mid-'70s, which drew the ire of many fans.

Other singers had similar relationships with country music, moving from pop into country because the 1970s country audience liked their music, even if it paid little allegiance to country traditions. This was the same environment in which the Eagles saw their biggest success in country music (see Chapter 7). John Denver was another such example; in the mid-1970s, he scored a number of top country hits with his soft-rock, singer-songwriter stylings about stereotypically rural topics such as "Country Roads, Take Me Home" and "Thank God I'm a Country Boy."

Such crossover success, where pop artists moved into country music, was not without controversy. Many country fans during these years, and to an even greater extent some established country artists, sought a type of lived experience in their country music, particularly in the way that the music connected to its own past. They were vocally resistant to crossover trends, framing their objections with the rhetoric of authenticity. Two particular flash points illustrate the heightened tensions about ideas of authenticity that emerged in the mid-1970s. In 1975, country star Charlie Rich came on stage at the CMA Awards to hand out the Entertainer of the Year accolade. When he opened the envelope and found the name of John Denver, Rich pulled a lighter out of his pocket and set the paper on fire in protest. Whatever Rich's motivations, many fans interpreted his actions as a protest against Denver's pop leanings and soft-rock reputation. Rich (1932–1995) himself had worked as a pop and jazz musician earlier in his own career. In the 1950s, he had made a string of little-known rockabilly and blues-infused records at Sun Records in Memphis. He then transitioned into classic country, where he became quite successful. His biggest country hit, "Behind Closed Doors" (1973) was a study in Billy Sherrill's Nashville-sound production, with syrupy strings and slip-note piano. But like George Jones's, Rich's vocal style was colored by honky-tonk, and he was highly respected and admired by traditional country fans. The responses to Rich's incident with the cigarette lighter highlighted the deep tensions regarding pop-crossover styles, commercial success, and issues of authenticity in country music of the '70s.

A similar controversy had occurred in 1974, when pop star Olivia Newton-John won the CMA Female Vocalist of the Year award for her own country recordings, which exhibited a similar soft-rock or pop style. Newton-John released a statement that she wanted to come to Nashville to meet Hank Williams, apparently so unfamiliar with country's past legends that she thought Williams was still alive. Established country stars offered scathing responses.

None of the tensions between pop-crossover and roots-oriented country music were new; they dated back essentially to the origins of the genre, when producers were looking for "old-time" songs that were also trendy, new, and commercially appealing. Yet these tensions reached a heightened fervor in the mid-1970s, when one strand of country music assimilated into pop, or, from a different perspective, pop music encroached on country's home territory. That crossover was a result of a shared audience between country and pop; many country listeners identified with the mainstream middle-class, a result of the shifting demographics from the past two decades. Although these pop-crossover recordings comprised a significant portion of country music in these years, they also prompted oppositional developments such as the outlaw movement (see Chapter 9), whose musical style was a direct response to these trends. In spite of the pervasive examples of pop-crossover country during the 1970s, the trend had not yet reached its peak, and it would even expand in the early 1980s (see Chapter 10).

The Duets and Ensembles

Amid all the developments of the classic country era, one of the most significant was the increased presence of vocal ensembles in the music. Many of the stars regularly recorded vocal duets (see essay on Gender in Classic Country). Working as a duet partner for an established singer was a practical means of gaining exposure in the music industry, and several future stars started out in those jobs. But beyond the commonplace male-female duets in this era, vocal ensembles carved out a niche in country during these years. The two best known were the Statler Brothers and the Oak Ridge Boys. These vocal ensembles relied on the traditions of four-part gospel harmony for their performances. Gospel harmonies had been a mainstay of blue-grass for several decades, but the four-part sound, especially with a low bass part, was seldom featured in mainstream country music (not counting the backup vocalists such as the Jordanaires, whose harmonies graced countless country recordings but who went largely unnoticed by the general audience). The Statlers and, a few years later, the Oak Ridge Boys, started singing for gospel audiences and chose to move into the country genre as a way of finding a bigger audience. Their gospel backgrounds gave them an entry point into country, given the historical connections between the two genres. But the success of these groups in the 1970s was also because of the rise in popularity of "bands" (as opposed to solo artists) and vocal ensembles in the rock scene. With hits such as the Statler Brothers' "The Class of '57" (1972) and the Oak Ridge Boys' "Y'All Come Back Saloon" (1977), these groups contributed significantly to the overall sound and legacy of the classic country era. They also paved the way for later country bands and ensembles, such as Alabama.

TV and Country Music

It would be hard to overstate the importance of television in the classic country era. In the late 1960s and early 1970s, just about every major male country star had his own television show: Johnny Cash, Glen Campbell, and Porter Wagoner, just to name a few. A spate of shows earlier in the 1960s, hosted by singers such as Jimmy Dean (*The Jimmy Dean Show*) and Redd Foley (*Ozark Jubilee*), had paved the way. As they proliferated, these shows became increasingly important in expanding the borders of country music while simultaneously bringing in new audiences. Johnny Cash, for instance, was famous for hosting noncountry guests, including Louis Armstrong and Bob Dylan, and pitched his show specifically to audiences beyond the country fan base. The most significant of these shows, however, amplified rather than challenged country stereotypes. *Hee Haw*, hosted by Buck Owens and Roy Clark, was broadcast on CBS from 1969 until 1971, when it went into syndication and remained popular for two more decades. The cast relied on hayseed stereotypes for humor, and the show featured plenty of bluegrass and hillbilly music. Later in his career, Owens reflected that his time hosting the show had overshadowed his more serious musical career that came before it, and he was probably right, as far as most country fans were concerned. For country fans, *Hee Haw* was a way to connect over a shared musical legacy. Its jokes, comedy skits, characters, and performances were a televised incarnation of the barn dance programs of the 1920s and '30s, complete with hillbilly rube characters. It reinforced "insider status" among country fans—those who got the jokes were part of the community. For noncountry fans, *Hee Haw* simply highlighted those aspects of the genre that appeared the most outrageous, backward, and embarrassing and appeared to reinforce negative stereotypes about country music.

Looking Back on Classic Country

This music remains an important part of the listening experience for today's country fan: is still heard on the radio, especially on "oldies" shows, Radio stations often dip back into that decade for "oldies" shows, and many of the artists still have active careers. It was a period when country music came to represent a large swath of Middle America, yet this decade enveloped that population in the concerns of the Vietnam War, a recession, and a radical reconfiguration of the social landscape in the wake of the 1960s Civil Rights and women's liberation movements.

All three main themes of our study are relevant for understanding classic country of the 1970s. Within the music itself, this was an era when the tensions reached a fevered pitch between pop-crossover trends that were commercially successful and roots-oriented styles that were strongly tied to tradition. Fans and artists alike expressed passionate opinions about what was or was not authentic country music, with several different concepts of what authenticity might mean all present in their rhetoric. Charley Pride offered a case study of race and country music. Meanwhile, the subject matter explored in the song lyrics focused largely on characters to whom their audience could relate: navigating new gender roles, differences in social class, and economic conditions that affected both the audience's lifestyles and who they saw as their chosen heroes. Finally, classic country music for the most part adopted a middle-aged perspective that was not particularly rebellious in its political nature or social outlook. That conservative outlook helped differentiate the genre at the time from pop and rock music. But it has also affected how later generations of country fans and musicians have treated the period. As we will see, many of today's artists trace their musical heritage not through the classic country era but instead through other strands of 1970s country music and even rock music for these reasons. Nonetheless, the stars of the classic country era remain some of the most influential and legendary individual figures in the genre.

✶ ESSAY: SONGWRITING

 # Truckin' Songs and the Open Road

Similar to the tradition of novelty songs that flourished in the 1950s and again in the 1960s, the classic country era was home to truckin' songs, country songs that celebrated the lure of the open road and the massive infrastructure of the American freeway system that not only connected communities but enabled the American way of life through the transportation of goods. Dave Dudley's recording of "Six Days on the Road" (1963) was an early instance, but the topic grew over the next two decades, with quite a few artists contributing along the way, including Merle Haggard's "White Line Fever" (1969).

In 1975, C. W. McCall (1928–) released a novelty song called "Convoy." Born William Dale Fries, McCall took a truck-driver character he had created when working in advertising and used it to create a stage persona for himself as a country singer. "Convoy" reached the top of the *Billboard* country charts and, more important, offered a new heroic figure to country music at a time when the genre's traditional masculine icons, such as the cowboy, the rounder, and the miner, had lost relevancy. The truck driver slid into that rhetorical space because he offered the same gateway to freedom as the rounders who hopped trains in the songs of the 1920s and '30s. In the song, the truckers defy governmental authority, much as the Wild West outlaws had done. And the convoy of truckers in the song embrace the concept of community; they even welcome a chartreuse microbus with "eleven long-haired friends of Jesus." The song captured the country fan base's attention, and three years later, a Hollywood film was released, starring Kris Kristofferson and Ali McGraw, based on the story line of the song.

The truckin' songs reached their peak in 1977 when Burt Reynolds headed up an all-star cast for the film *Smokey and the Bandit*. Country singer Jerry Reed (1937–2008) appeared in the film and also wrote and recorded its theme song, "East Bound and Down." That country hit put a truckin' song into the mainstream country music repertory and also solidified the association between the sound of banjos and the sight of car chases, which had been introduced earlier in songs such as "Foggy Mountain Breakdown" as used in *Bonnie and Clyde* (see Chapter 5).

✫ ESSAY: MUSICAL STYLE

 # Classic Country

Classic country music in the 1970s blends the Nashville sound from a decade earlier with the rhythms, ringing guitars, intricate rhythm guitar picking patterns, and use of electric instruments that were all common in Bakersfield, then adds a dose of traditional, twangy honky-tonk and bluegrass elements. The resulting musical style has many of the commercially popular features of the Nashville sound, a strong, audible commitment to country music's past, and a decidedly modern twist.

Revealing the Nashville sound's influence, the recordings feature lots of reverberation added to the singer's voice plus accompaniment by a large instrumental ensemble, often with piano and occasional hints of strings and backup singers. However, the excesses of strings and thick orchestrations common a decade earlier are largely gone. The catchy rhythmic grooves that emerged in the mid-1960s developments in Nashville (such as Roger Miller's music) as well as in Bakersfield are still present, and the prevalence of rhythmic hooks intensified in the early 1970s (listen, for instance, to Dolly Parton's recording of "Joshua"). Along with these elements came increased attention to the rhythm section of the band, especially drums and bass. Added to that mix, however, are banjos, steel guitars, and harmonicas—all instruments that have associations with twangy, roots-oriented styles such as honky-tonk and bluegrass and that were seldom present on Nashville sound recordings.

The role of the musical **arranger** became more important during this era. Classic country features the same arrangement techniques in so many songs that those techniques border on cliché. For instance, these classic country recordings commonly change keys (i.e., **modulate**) in the middle. This means that the entire collection of chords used in the song shifts. Within this musical style, the modulations are almost always to a higher key (in technical terms, up by either a step or a half-step), so the melody shifts to a higher set of notes. Arrangers also sometimes included novelty elements that were direct references to earlier country hits; listen, for instance, to Tom T. Hall's "Faster Horses (The Cowboy and the Poet)," which used trumpets (which are casually called "horns") that are reminiscent of the trumpets on Johnny Cash's "Ring of Fire" (1963).

The musical styles of classic country are most notable for their combination of both pop elements and traditional elements—the backup vocalists, electric bass, or keyboards, mixed up with the very traditional lyrics, steel guitars, banjos, etc. Yet one of the most distinctive elements in the musical style is the way that the singers' vocals stand out prominently from the accompaniment. These aspects combine to make 1970s classic country recordings very easy to recognize by ear.

✫ ESSAY: IDENTITY

 # Gender in Classic Country

One of the most prominent themes in classic country songs is the negotiation of gender roles that took place in the 1970s. Assumptions about how men and women behaved within working-class American society were suddenly called into question, and country music reflected those concerns. Among the most common topics were:

1. The prevalence of divorce and the idea that women were stepping outside of a marriage
2. An increasingly outspoken female perspective about both their sexual needs and respect for their role in the household
3. A male perspective of ambivalence and loneliness when abandoned by a woman

Collectively, classic country songs offer a window into a time when gendered roles had changed and people wrestled with how to make sense of the new social order.

Divorce songs appeared with increasing frequency throughout the 1970s, which is not surprising, given that divorce rates in the United States skyrocketed during that same period. The change in divorce rates reflected, among other things, laws that permitted no-fault divorce (on grounds such as "irreconcilable differences"); California's law went into effect in 1970, and several other states followed suit. Many classic country songs from these years explore the practical fallout of divorce, especially with regard to children ("D-I-V-O-R-C-E," "Six Weeks Every Summer (Christmas Every Other Year)," "Mommy, Can I Still Call Him Daddy?" "I Don't Wanna Play House," "The Games That Daddies Play"). Others explored a gloomy sense of inevitable failure that hung over a marriage ("Golden Ring") and the profound loss that accompanies separation ("I Will Always Love You").

The impact of the women's liberation movement on country music was profound, partly because it brought more attention to female singers and a female perspective. Certainly, classic country songs tended to express less radical ideas and philosophies affiliated with that movement than are found in other sections of popular culture; with varying amounts of humor, many female singers sang about sticking by one's man ("Run, Woman, Run," "Stand by Your Man"). Yet other songs demanded increased respect ("Don't Come Home A Drinkin' [With Lovin' On Your Mind]"), threatened rebellious behavior ("Your Good Girl's Gonna Go Bad"), and talked more openly about sexual needs ("The Pill") and the double standards of sexual promiscuity to which women were held ("Just Because I'm a Woman," "The Bridge"). Some of the most poignant songs from this era contemplate the challenges of balancing one's family responsibilities with the changing landscape of opportunity ("One's on the Way"). The most outspoken female voice during this era was Loretta Lynn, who, as wife, mother, and country star, sang about these issues with unparalleled conviction and passion.

The male perspective heard in country songs shifted during this era as well. With increasing frequency, men sang about the sense of loss and despair that followed a woman leaving. George Jones specialized in these songs, with tearjerkers such as "The Door" and "The Grand Tour." Songs sung by men frequently told tales of a woman stepping out to find love or satisfaction ("Tight Fittin' Jeans," "You've Never Been This Far Before"). Of those, Kenny Rogers's recording of "Lucille" (1976) stands out. In the song, a woman leaves her husband, children, and household responsibilities and winds up in a bar with a stranger. Her husband confronts them and—instead of hitting or attacking the stranger—breaks down, shaking and miserable. The song provokes conflicting emotional responses from the listener toward the three main characters: who's right, who's wrong, and what's the right thing for them to do remain ambiguous. The song is a good representation of the complicated responses to new gender roles, the instability of marriage, and the rising threats of infidelity that the country music audience faced during these years.

Male-female duets brought this larger conversation about gender roles together in individual songs. Most country stars in the classic country era also worked with a regular duet partner: Conway Twitty and Loretta Lynn; Dolly Parton and Porter Wagoner, then later Kenny Rogers; Dottie West and Kenny Rogers; George Jones and Melba Montgomery, then later Tammy Wynette, to name a few. While their duets covered a range of topics, one common theme was reflecting on a relationship gone bad ("The Last Thing On My Mind," "Two Story House," "After the Fire Is Gone," "As Soon As I Hang Up the Phone," "Just Someone I Used to Know").

Classic country music became a site for people to work out their emotions, frustrations, fears, and freedoms as they confronted a changing set of expectations about gender roles and relationships during the 1970s. From that perspective, the songs represent the general responses of a largely working- and middle-class white audience who were not on the front lines of these progressive social movements, but who felt their impact nonetheless.

Story Songs

During the late 1960s and 1970s, songwriting trends in country music turned to "story songs," which had longer plots with more action, more character development, and less reflection or repetition. These sorts of ballads—a term meaning lengthy narratives, as opposed to the way that people casually use the term today to mean "slow song"—have a long history in country music. In the earliest days of hillbilly recordings, they were frequently accounts of local events (the so-called event songs about train wrecks or murders, for instance). These sorts of story songs or narrative ballads became less common as country music grew into a commercial genre, partly because by their nature, story songs seldom emphasize a catchy chorus. They still appeared occasionally, however, especially in the cowboy and Old West traditions of "saga songs" (Marty Robbins's "El Paso," for instance).

Partly through the influence of folk music, which was extremely popular in the 1960s, and as a counterbalance to the increasingly recondite lyrics in rock music, country music rediscovered story songs in the late 1960s, and they became a hallmark of the genre. Songwriters in Nashville approached these songs as three-minute literary short stories. Their topics explored the general attitude of working-class and middle-class Americans during the 1960s and '70s: social change that followed the civil rights and women's liberation movements, along with how those revolutions affected one's personal philosophy.

Many of the story songs explored men's search for meaning in life ("[Old Dogs, Children, and] Watermelon Wine," "Faster Horses [The Cowboy and the Poet]," "The Gambler"). Other grappled with the social clashes between different cultural groups of that era: hippies versus cowboys or rednecks, or the social establishment versus rebellion ("Uneasy Rider"). Defense of masculine pride was a common theme as well ("Coward of the County," "A Boy Named Sue"). Female stars explored the emerging social roles for women and the controversies that came with them through story songs ("Harper Valley P.T.A.") These approaches to songwriting affected the form of the songs. Songs increasingly relied on long sets of verses to tell their stories, which was different than how most songs had been written in the Nashville sound era. Performers also more frequently used spoken recitation instead of singing the entire songs. Story songs often begin as if in the middle of a thought or tale and end just as abruptly, as if the story began prior to the audience entering and continues after the song stops. In this way, the story songs create a sense of endless continuity; the story is continually in progress (just like life), whereas the song briefly opens a window onto one short segment of it.

One of the masters of the story songs was songwriter Tom T. Hall (1936–). By the mid-1960s, Hall had moved to Nashville, and several of his songs had become modest hits for other country artists. His biggest success came when a then-unknown singer named Jeannie C. Riley recorded his "Harper Valley P.T.A." in 1968. As he became better known, record executives pushed him into a performing career, and he scored his first top ten hit as a singer with "The Ballad of Forty Dollars" that same year. Hall's specialty as a songwriter was rambling character sketches of working-class masculine ambivalence; an example is "A Week in a County Jail," in which the singer gets jailed for speeding in a small town, then sits in jail, where there is little to do but drink beer and wait a week for the judge to show up to process his release. Hall portrays the man's ambivalence about his self-worth (the sheriff was unimpressed by the man's identity and unconcerned that he was missing his "steady" job) and the meaningless passage of time.

Other songwriters who worked successfully in this style include Kris Kristofferson (1936–) and Shel Silverstein (1930–1999). Neither of them built their careers entirely in country music; Silverstein, for instance, is known for his children's books, cartoons, plays, and other projects. Neither of them claimed a stereotypical country biography either; Kristofferson was a Rhodes scholar who studied at Oxford University, while Silverstein was an active participant in the Greenwich Village folk revival scene. Yet the artistic climate in classic country, which was both receptive of outsiders and welcoming of popular culture beyond the borders of the country genre, allowed both to become quite successful as country songwriters. Kristofferson became part of the outlaw movement (see Chapter 9). Silverstein's classics include "One's on the Way" (Loretta Lynn), "25 Minutes to Go," and "A Boy Named Sue" (both Johnny Cash).

While story songs were by no means the only types of songs on the charts in the 1970s, they were a significant presence within the classic country era. They helped differentiate country music from the other popular genres of that era, and became a site wherein country fans could wrestle with the unsettling philosophical questions that troubled them during those years.

✱ ESSAY: CULTURE

 # The Opry Moves

On March 16, 1974, President Richard Nixon stood on the stage in a brand-new, state-of-the-art theater and, with one of the Opry's most senior performers, Roy Acuff, dedicated the new home of the Grand Ole Opry. The theater included an extensive backstage area with dressing rooms for performers; space and equipment for television productions; comfortable, climate-controlled seating for the audience; and ample parking. The theater was the centerpiece of Opryland, a Disney-style theme park that included family-oriented musical entertainment, rides, and a petting zoo. The new facilities offered much-needed amenities for the traditional barn-dance radio program that had been on the air since 1925, but the move also marked a change in the way country music was presented to the national audience.

The Opry was broadcast from the Ryman Auditorium in downtown Nashville from 1943 until the new facilities opened thirty-one years later. The Ryman, which had originally been built as a tabernacle for religious meetings by riverboat captain

Figure 8-7
President Richard Nixon at the piano, opening night of the new Opry House, with Roy Acuff on the right (in the dark jacket).
Source: Les Leverett photograph © Grand Ole Opry Archives.

Thomas Ryman, was a red-brick building with hard wooden pews, very sparse facilities backstage for the musicians, and no air-conditioning. Located on 5th Avenue in downtown Nashville, the Ryman was also plagued by a lack of parking and, by the 1960s, decaying urban surroundings. The neighborhood's run-down bars and XXX adult theaters were a far cry from what country music executives wanted to show audiences, many of whom traveled to Nashville specifically to attend the legendary broadcasts of country music's most famous program. Roy Acuff was particularly outspoken about wanting the music to be presented in a more high-class setting.

Although the Ryman's facilities were sorely lacking in amenities, the building itself had acquired symbolic meaning within country music. Widely known as the "Mother Church of Country Music," its stage represented ideas of tradition and of belonging to something wholesome and original, even sacred. The cast of the Opry and its most ardent fans valued the physical trappings of the Ryman because they associated them with country authenticity, down-home roots, and respect for musical lineage. For some performers and fans, the fact that Patsy Cline and Hank Williams and a young Roy Acuff had all stood on that physical stage outweighed the discomforts of the auditorium. Leaving the facility was difficult for the show's stars; Minnie Pearl cried onstage at the last Ryman performance, and stars who were not on the program that night showed up anyway just to experience what they felt was symbolically the end of an era.

Opry executives recognized the high value fans and performers had invested in the space itself, and worked very hard to preserve some of the show's traditions. They cut a ten-foot circle out of the oak stage from the Ryman and had it inlaid in the new Opry stage so that future generations of singers could still stand in the spotlight on the same wood where legends from the past had stood. The Opryland theme park's designers incorporated lots of antique and folksy images into the venue in an attempt to preserve an atmosphere of down-home rusticity and the traditional sense of community that was embedded in country music's lore, but all situated now in a suburban, middle-class, up-to-date environment. That tension—old vs. new—was at the heart of country music's struggle in the classic country era.

The results were both a modernization and a suburbanization of the Opry. Its shiny new suburban home fifteen miles from downtown became a compelling symbol for how the country audience's demographics had moved from working-class rural people in the early years of the Opry to mainstream, middle-class people living, eating, and shopping in suburbs and experiencing the homogenization of American culture. The theme park presented safe, sanitized, very white, family-friendly versions of rustic culture. The Opry itself continued its internal negotiations between tradition and innovation. Millions of visitors enjoyed the new location each year, but it severed a literal connection to country's past. In 1997, the theme park closed—replaced with an outlet mall (see Chapter 14)—and a few years later, the Opry management began periodically returning the show to the Ryman in an effort to recapture the cultural cachet that the building's history conveyed.

LISTEN SIDE-BY-SIDE

"Muleskinner Blues"
Songwriter (for all versions): Jimmie Rodgers
Dolly Parton, 1970 (on *The Best of Dolly Parton*, RCA Victor LSP-4449)

"Mule Skinner Blues"
Hank Williams, Jr., and Connie Francis, 1964 (on *Sing Great Country Favorites*, MGM SE 4251)

"Muleskinner Blues"
The Fendermen, 1960 (originally released on Cuca 1003, then Soma 1137)

"Mule Skinner Blues"
Bill Monroe, 1940 (originally released on Bluebird B-8568)

"Blue Yodel No. 8"
Jimmie Rodgers, 1930 (originally released on Victor 23503)

"MULESKINNER BLUES" shows up time and again in country music history, always in interesting contexts. By comparing different artists' versions of it, we can see how country music incorporates its past even while it is changing. The first version of the song was a 1930 recording by Jimmie Rodgers. Rodgers borrowed lyrics from several different black blues tunes and reworked them into a story about a muleskinner (a worker who drives a mule train). Rodgers recorded the song while accompanying himself on guitar. With Rodgers's trademark yodeling, the song was quite popular. In 1970, Dolly Parton recorded her version of it, which featured a full band, the sound effect of a whip cracking, and a shrill whistle. The recording rose to number three on the *Billboard* charts and became the breakthrough hit for Parton's solo career. For Dolly Parton, covering this song brought together all the basic elements of classic country music: a strong connection to the traditions of country music, a commercially savvy incorporation of both pop music and the crossover Nashville sound, and an exploration of social issues, most commonly gender roles.

"Muleskinner Blues" was known not only as a Jimmie Rodgers song but also as a huge hit for Bill Monroe. Monroe covered many of Rodgers's songs throughout his career, most famously

"Muleskinner Blues," which he used on his Grand Ole Opry debut in 1939. By 1970, the song was both an old hillbilly tune and, simultaneously, a standard within bluegrass. From that perspective, Parton was tapping into the rich roots of country traditionalism by covering the song.

Ironically, "Muleskinner Blues" also had a long history in pop music, the antithesis of its more traditional, bluegrass reputation. In 1960, two friends from Wisconsin known as the Fendermen recorded the song as a novelty rock 'n' roll number, accompanied by loud electric guitars. They clucked like chickens when singing about the "water bucket," and shouted "cha cha cha" at the end of the song. The Fendermen's recording became a number one pop hit. Four years later, pop singer Connie Francis recorded a duet version of the song with Hank Williams Jr., which had a whip-crack sound effect, some new lyrics for the verses, and a string section accompanying them, full Nashville-sound style. By the end of the 1960s, there were also versions by calypso star Harry Belafonte and even an easy-listening orchestra. From those perspectives, Parton was covering a well-worn pop song.

Finally, Parton's version of "Muleskinner Blues" crossed established lines of gender in country music. Although a few women had sung the song before her, the most famous versions were all by men, and the song's main character is a decidedly masculine muleskinner who hollers out and yodels boldly throughout the text. Parton emphasized her appropriation of that masculine role by changing the lyrics to say "I'm a *lady* muleskinner . . ." She also wrote a new verse for the end of the song, in which she sings about being a waitress (a traditionally female job) who is annoyed with her "no-good man" who takes all her money. The waitress declares she wanted to go be a muleskinner instead. Parton's vocal performance is bold and commanding. She used a two-finger wolf whistle to kick off the song, hollered out loud, and yodeled, all of which thwarted expectations of her as a feminine "girl singer," which was the term by which she was known back then. Those aspects of the performance undoubtedly helped catch the audience's attention and earned her respect as a solo performer.

Listen to as many different versions of "Muleskinner Blues" as you can find between Jimmie Rodgers's and Dolly Parton's versions. Notice how some aspects of the song stay the same, while many others change, like a musical chameleon, to match the cultural context of the performer and intended audience in each case. In this way, the song both connects new performers to the past and lets them do something original and different.

PLAYLIST

Oak Ridge Boys. "Y'All Come Back Saloon" (1977)

Parton, Dolly. "Muleskinner Blues" (1970)

Riley, Jeannie C. "Harper Valley P.T.A." (1968)

Rogers, Kenny. "The Gambler" (1978)

Twitty, Conway. "Hello, Darlin'" (1970)

Wynette, Tammy. "Stand by Your Man" (1968)

FOR MORE READING

Hall, Tom T. *The Storyteller's Nashville*. Garden City, NY: Doubleday, 1979.

Hill, Jeremy. *Country Comes to Town: The Music Industry and the Transformation of Nashville*. Amherst: University of Massachusetts Press, 2016.

Isenhour, Jack. *He Stopped Loving Her Today*. Jackson: University Press of Mississippi, 2011.

Kingsbury, Paul, ed. *Country: The Music and the Musicians (From the Beginnings to the '90s)*. New York: Abbeville Press, 1994.

Lynn, Loretta, with George Vecsey. *Loretta Lynn: Coal Miner's Daughter*. New York: Warner Books, 1976.

Nash, Alanna. *Dolly: The Biography*. Updated ed. New York: Cooper Square Press, 2002.

NAMES AND TERMS

arranger	Newton-John, Olivia	Silverstein, Shel
Campbell, Glen	Oak Ridge Boys	Statler Brothers
Denver, John	Opryland	story songs
girl singer	Parton, Dolly	truckin' songs
Hall, Tom T.	Pride, Charlie	Twitty, Conway
Hee Haw	Rich, Charlie	Wagoner, Porter
Jones, George	Rogers, Kenny	Wilburn Brothers
Lynn, Loretta	Ryman Auditorium	Wynette, Tammy
modulation	Sherrill, Billy	

REVIEW TOPICS

1. How did classic country employ signifiers of country tradition and authenticity, and why did those elements matter to country fans?

2. Discuss the relationship between classic country and the women's liberation movement.

3. How was the emerging suburban, middle-class identity of some country music in the 1970s reconciled with the genre's origins?

Outlaw Country and Southern Rock Rebellion

During the 1970s, two musical movements outside of Nashville had a profound impact on country music. The first was the outlaw movement, which found its geographic center in Austin, Texas. The second was the emergence of Southern rock, which developed across the South, particularly in Alabama and Georgia. The outlaw movement was an integrated part of the country genre; its artists, songwriters, and fans were deeply invested in country music. Southern rock, on the other hand, was not; for the most part, fans of Southern rock considered their music rock, not country. But a few of its artists and bands crossed over between the two genres, Southern rock claimed the same musical pedigree as country music, and its fans included a large portion of Southern, white, working-class people—the same general population who still listened to country music.

Outlaw country and Southern rock impacted the country music genre in five distinct ways:

1. The styles refocused attention on the performers as musical creators.
2. They drew the 1970s counterculture and youth into country, thereby expanding country music's audience dramatically.
3. They disrupted the corporate traditions that had become deeply entrenched in Nashville.
4. They spotlighted geographic centers for country music outside of Nashville.
5. They reintroduced an edgier, stripped-down, twang-driven, aggressive musical sound that counterbalanced the classic country style.

Outlaw country in particular resurrected many elements of honky-tonk that had drifted out of favor, and also provided a new image that country music fans found very appealing. Southern rock, on the other hand, became essential vital point of contact between rock and country. Later generations of country fans would retroactively claim Southern rock as an important part of their country music heritage.

As both outlaw country and Southern rock artists engaged with country music, they expanded the fan base in significant ways. This expansion primed country music for its largest period of crossover success to date, which would occur in the early 1980s (see Chapter 10). The image of the outlaw character stayed in country music and was co-opted by later generations of artists. And the role of bands (as opposed to solo artists), especially bands with a strong rock influence, grew in country music, largely as a result of Southern rock's impact.

The Emergence of Outlaw Country

In the late 1960s and early 1970s, a few well-established country singers began to chafe under the heavy-handed musical control that producers in Nashville asserted, while simultaneously expanding their interest in music with Texan and cowboy roots. At the front of this movement was Waylon Jennings (1937–2002), originally from Littlefield in West Texas. During the late 1950s, Jennings played with early rock 'n' roll star Buddy Holly; after Holly's death in 1959, Jennings moved to Arizona, where he worked as a DJ and eventually began performing again. In 1965, Jennings signed with producer Chet Atkins at RCA and moved to Nashville. His first recordings in Nashville were not very popular, but Jennings became friends with Tompall Glaser (1933–2013), part of the classic country group the Glaser Brothers, and Willie Nelson (1933–), who had been working primarily as a songwriter in Nashville since the early 1960s (see Artist Profile). The Glasers had already broken ranks with the corporate traditions of Nashville by launching their own publishing firm and by Tompall opening an independent studio, which his friends called "Hillbilly Central" and used as a place for socializing. In the early 1970s, a new generation of songwriters from Texas (including Willie Nelson, Kris Kristofferson, and Mickey Newbury) caught Jennings's interest, particularly with songs that focused on darker, more troubled personalities. Jennings put together an album from those songs, adopting their attitude by titling the project *Lonesome, On'ry, and Mean*. For these recordings, Jennings and his producers experimented with more sparse accompaniments that let his low baritone voice come through more dramatically.

Figure 9-1 Waylon Jennings.
Source: Courtesy of Country Music Hall of Fame and Museum.

In 1973, a reporter asked Nashville celebrity commentator and publicist Hazel Smith to describe the new sound that Jennings and others in his circle of friends were favoring. Smith recalled the album Jennings had released the previous year, titled *Ladies Love Outlaws* (also the title of its first track), and dubbed the music "outlaw." The term stuck, and branded the movement with an antiestablishment, rebellious image that appealed to listeners in the growing counterculture movement. Within the popular imagination, "outlaw" carried images of the Wild West, Texas, cowboys, independence, and breaking free from society's grasp. It also evoked notions of illicit behavior, underscored by Jennings's arrest for drug possession and well-publicized incidents of reckless behavior. At its heart, the outlaw movement in country music was less about any of those aspects than it was about changing the infrastructure of the music business (see essay on Behaving Like Outlaws), but that renegade, bad-boy image generated great publicity nonetheless.

The outlaw movement gained steam as musicians and record executives formed more professional ties between Nashville and a growing musical scene in Austin, Texas. Texas had always been home to a rich tradition of songwriting and had always supported a healthy live music scene. From the 1930s onward, the blended cultural traditions in Texas fostered social dancing, which thrived among the immigrant communities in the region, and brought together populations living in comparative geographic isolation. The popularity of dancing, in turn, supported local country music scenes. The Texan landscape—vast expanses that were barren, dry, and sometimes unforgiving and at the same time a rich resource for oil, ranchlands, and agriculture—inspired a rugged independence of character. Its political history played into its image. Texas was by nature a rebellious place, the only state to have ever been its own sovereign country, and was home to such legendary stories as the Alamo. Its country music traditions were uncompromising as well, both in their independence and their dominance. Jimmie Rodgers made it his adopted home; Bob Wills and Milton Brown conjured western swing, complete with drums and jazz tunes, in the dance halls of West Texas; Ernest Tubb and later Lefty Frizzell forged the rhythms of honky-tonk there; and Buddy Holly's blend of West Texan rockabilly and rock 'n' roll incited frenzy among the youth of his generation. Waylon Jennings and Willie Nelson claimed that musical lineage as their birthright.

Figure 9-2 Jerry Jeff Walker.

Source: Courtesy of Country Music Hall of Fame and Museum

Austin offered access to another music scene for country artists outside of Nashville in the 1970s. For more than a decade, Austin's musicians had fostered an easy kinship with the musicians and cultural scenes developing on the West Coast. Singer-songwriters involved in the folk-rock movement traveled easily between California and Austin, as did like-minded hippies looking for a space to claim as their own. Fed by this rock influence, many Texan musicians walked a fine line between rock and country, establishing their own brand of roots-rock that was steeped in traditional country music, combined with influences from Mexican and Tex-Mex music. Doug Sahm (1941–1999), for instance, grew up on traditional Texas country music, especially western swing, and was playing steel guitar in country bands as a young teen. In high school, his interests turned toward rockabilly and rock, and in his twenties, he was working as a rock musician. Jerry Jeff Walker (1942–) played mostly country music, but the songs he wrote wound up as major rock and folk-rock hits. In the Austin scene, distinctions between rock and country were essentially meaningless. Thus, Austin offered yet another point of connection between country music and the developments in rock and folk music, much as country rock artists such as the Byrds and the Nitty Gritty Dirt Band had done a few years earlier in California (see Chapter 7). In this Texan setting, where folk-rock, country rock, rockabilly, western swing, and traditional country music blended together, a movement broadly known as progressive country emerged. Progressive country welcomed the outlaw artists, and offered a more inclusive musical space and label for the songwriters, rock bands, country bands, and folk-rock singers who congregated there.

WRITING IN THE WINGS

Some of the most celebrated songwriters in country music, the so-called "musicians' musicians," are artists that casual country fans have never heard of. These songwriters work outside the core of the genre and seldom find widespread success with the country fan base. But they both influence and provide a sourcepool of songs for mainstream country stars, and are a vital part of the larger country music infrastructure.

John Prine (1946–) is a prime example of this phenomenon. His music has been covered by dozens of country artists. His most enthusiastic fans include Kris Kristofferson, who helped him get his first record contract, and Johnny Cash, who called him one of his "big four" songwriters. Literary scholars have analyzed his lyrics, and everyone from Miranda Lambert to George Strait has recorded songs of his. Prior to the installation of Americana as a genre in the American popular music landscape (see Chapter 13), though, fans had a hard time finding the vocabulary to describe these songwriters' genre. Prine won "folk" and "indie" awards but never, say, a CMA award, and profoundly influenced country music without any direct acknowledgement of his involvement in the genre.

That was exactly the musical environment that Willie Nelson and others were seeking. Nelson moved from Nashville back to Texas in 1971, and in 1973 began hosting summer concert events where he invited musicians from both the local rock-influenced scene and stars from the Grand Ole Opry to perform side by side. These and other concerts imported country stars from Nashville into a growing musical scene that was both thoroughly embedded in country music and overtly dismissive of the mainstream industry. At the same time, these events brought Texan musicians and songwriters to the attention of the big record labels and mainstream country stars. Although fans of outlaw country often describe the music as having been isolated from the corrupting forces of Nashville, in fact the outlaw movement maintained strong ties to Nashville and in some cases involved artists working entirely within Nashville's industry. Nashville's record labels had the money and distribution networks to promote and distribute their music. Furthermore, the major record labels were hungry for new and different music that would help them expand to a bigger audience, especially fans who were turned off by the trends in classic country. Austin appealed as a country music outpost, both to the artists and to the music industry.

In 1973, Jennings renegotiated his contract with RCA Records so that he had full artistic control to choose songs, to record in whatever studio he wanted, and to select the producer for his recordings. From that point forward, his recordings were steeped in the outlaw style that he had been cultivating: sparser textures, more of a rock influence, and edgier vocals. In 1975, Willie Nelson released *Red Headed Stranger* (see Listen Side by Side), and both country and rock audiences took note of the growing outlaw phenomenon. But the musical event that brought outlaw country into the mainstream—and, ironically, successfully exported country music to a large rock audience—was a calculated marketing gimmick from one of Nashville's top producers and record executives.

Jerry Bradley (1940–) had grown up in the country music business, the son of Owen Bradley, who had produced Patsy Cline for Decca Records and been instrumental in crafting the Nashville sound (see Chapter 6). In 1973, Jerry Bradley took over as head of RCA Records' Nashville office, a position formerly held by Chet Atkins. In his new role, Bradley was eager to make his mark, and among his goals was finding a way to attract rock audiences to country music. He recognized the outlaw movement had the potential to do this. In 1976, Bradley pulled out several recordings that RCA already had in its vaults—some that had already been released, and some unreleased—and assembled a concept album. He used recordings by Willie Nelson (who had long since moved to other record labels), Waylon Jennings, and Jessi Colter (1947–) (Jennings's wife, and the only female performer on the album), plus a pair of songs from Tompall Glaser, whom Bradley added at Jennings's request. Of the four artists, only Jennings was still under contract to RCA, so Bradley gave him top billing. Bradley also commissioned a set of liner notes from Chet Flippo, the same journalist who had written the notes for *Will the Circle Be Unbroken*, the Nitty Gritty Dirt Band's breakthrough country rock album (see Chapter 7). Flippo had become thoroughly entrenched in the country music scene, but he still retained credibility and a high reputation with rock audiences from his earlier writing for *Rolling Stone*. Bradley then capitalized

Willie Nelson (1933–)

illie Nelson has remained an iconic country star in spite of the fact that his musical projects—which span more than half a century—have frequently ventured outside of country music. He was born in Abbott, Texas, just south of Fort Worth. He and his sister Bobbie were raised mostly by his grandparents, who encouraged their musical interests from a young age. By high school, Nelson played the guitar, was working as a DJ, and had started writing songs. After graduation, he served briefly in the Air Force, but was discharged for health reasons. He moved briefly to Washington State, then back to Texas, working as a DJ and attempting to launch a solo career.

In 1960, Nelson moved to Nashville, where he became friends with many of the established artists and songwriters, including Ray Price and Hank Cochran. Nelson soon had a songwriting contract with Price's publishing firm, Pamper Music, where he wrote many of the biggest Nashville Sound era hits, including "Crazy," "Hello Walls," and "Funny How Time Slips Away." Nelson signed as a performer with Liberty Records in 1961 and released several records during the 1960s; none were very successful, and Nelson chafed under the restrictive and producer-centric studio model that was the norm in Nashville at the time. After his house burned to the ground, Nelson moved back to Texas permanently in 1971.

Nelson set up his home near Austin, changed record labels, and joined the active Austin music scene. After performing at music festivals in the area, in 1973 he launched his own annual outdoor music festival as a "4th of July Picnic," where he invited his friends from mainstream country music to perform alongside local musicians more in the folk-rock vein. These picnics moved Nelson into a role of facilitator and figurehead within the scene. In his recordings from the same time period, Nelson took full advantage of the artistic freedom his metaphoric distance from Nashville allowed.

In 1975, Nelson changed record labels once again, this time assuring himself full artistic control over his work—the hallmark of the outlaw movement's rebellion against the mainstream music industry. His first album, *Red Headed Stranger*, was an unexpected success. In its wake, Nashville's mainstream establishment jumped onto the outlaw movement's bandwagon. The late 1970s were a high point of Nelson's artistic and commercial success. He and Waylon Jennings collaborated on several projects. He cultivated his interest in collecting songs from all different genres and musical traditions. That was the attitude in which he conceived of his album *Stardust*, on which he reprised classics from the Golden Age of popular song, including

on the outlaw trend with the cover art, a sepia-toned "Wanted!" poster with burnt edges that offered a reward for the four performers, shown in unsmiling photographs, all the men with beards.

The strategy behind *Wanted! The Outlaws* worked; even though the compilation album contained older recordings, many of which were already available, it appeared just as interest in the rebellious, outsider "outlaw movement" was peaking

"Georgia on My Mind" and Broadway show tunes by composers such as George Gershwin and Irving Berlin. By this time in Nelson's career, he was paradoxically a huge star within country music and an artist who defiantly crossed genre boundaries in his own work.

In the 1980s, Nelson continued to experiment musically while venturing into film. Starting with 1978's *Electric Horseman* (starring Robert Redford), Nelson brought his eclectic country songwriter persona to the silver screen. In 1985, Nelson, Johnny Cash, Waylon Jennings, and Kris Kristofferson formed the supergroup the Highwaymen. This wildly popular project helped revive more traditional country music as the *Urban Cowboy* crossover era faded (see Chapter 10). Nelson also took up increasingly visible social causes, such as the Farm Aid concerts he founded.

At the height of country music's crossover popularity in the 1990s, the IRS charged Nelson with millions of dollars of unpaid back taxes. To pay off his debts, Nelson auctioned his possessions and recorded *The IRS Tapes: Who Will Buy My Memories*. The publicity surrounding his tax troubles and the album only added to his reputation as a free-spirited outlaw icon. The Country Music Hall of Fame inducted him in 1993. For the past three decades, he has focused primarily on joint musical projects with artists from all genres and styles, including Sheryl Crow, Winton Marsalis, Norah Jones, Bob Dylan, Paul Simon, and countless others.

Figure 9-3 Doug Sahm and Willie Nelson at Nelson's 4th of July Picnic, 1976.
Source: Ed Malcik / Austin American Statesman.

Nelson's musical stylings—both as a singer and as a songwriter—owe as much of a debt to jazz as they do to country music. He tends to sing musical phrases with a free, declamatory rhythm. The result is that his performances give the effect of him getting out of the way of the music and letting the song itself act as the central focus. That performance style relates closely to the work he has done in bringing old standards and songs from other genres to country audiences; he serves as a conduit delivering the song directly to the listener. As both the consummate country star and one whose career shows little concern for genre boundaries, Nelson remains a much-loved enigma.

and gave fans a single album to connect to. In November of 1976, it became the first indisputably country album to be certified platinum, which meant it achieved sales of one million units. It also marked the acceptance of outlaw country by the mainstream country establishment. A major record label had co-opted and profited from a trend that had started out as rebellion against the traditions that label represented. Nashville had effectively gone outlaw.

The same self-effacing use of irony that was common in the Bakersfield sound (see Chapter 7) made its way into the outlaw country movement in the mid-1970s. Its most poignant appearance is in "You Never Even Called Me by My Name" (1975). David Allan Coe (1939–) has long been regarded as a tangential part of the outlaw movement, an identity he has cultivated with autobiographical (and sometimes exaggerated) tales of serving prison time, and through his preference for a raw, honky-tonk–infused, sparse, "outlaw" musical style. Coe had been working in Nashville as a songwriter and country singer for more than half a decade when he recorded this song, written by singer/songwriter Steve Goodman. In it, Coe imitates the vocal styles of many of the best-known country stars from the early 1970s, including Conway Twitty, Waylon Jennings, Merle Haggard, and Charley Pride, while wryly commenting on his own comparable anonymity. Toward the end of the song, however, he recounts an exchange between the song's writer (Goodman) and himself, in which he claims that the song falls short of being the "perfect country and western song" because of its omission of stereotypical content, such as drinking, mama, trains, or prison. Goodman supplied him with another verse, Coe tells the listener, that rectifies those omissions. Coe then sings a verse that rolls all those topics into an insider's joke, a stinging mockery of what country music is supposed to be about. The verse's self-reflective and ironic commentary on country's stereotypes matched the underlying attitude of the outlaw movement. For decades, outsiders not steeped in country tradition have interpreted the song as a straight-up representation of country music and missed both the ironic tone and humor in the verse. Noncountry fans have used the verse as an illustration of country music's contents, while country fans have recognized and identified with the song as caricature. These opposing perspectives have made the song one of the most talked about in all of country music and an indicator of insider versus outsider status for country fans. The song also effectively illustrates the outlaw movement's attitude toward country as a genre, simultaneously claiming and parodying it.

Outlaw Country Runs Its Course

With its mainstream attention and acceptance, aspects of the outlaw movement worked their way into more areas of country music. Stars such as Kenny Rogers, whose work had been situated squarely in classic country, adopted outlaw themes more readily, as in his recording of "The Gambler" (see Chapter 8). Willie Nelson and Waylon Jennings in particular capitalized on their fame with a series of major hits and especially duets such as "Luckenbach, Texas (Back to the Basics of Love)" (see Listening Guide). Many of the outlaw artists also enjoyed crossover success with rock and pop audiences. And they expanded their careers into new media, most notably movies and television: Willie Nelson appeared in *The Electric Horseman*, starring Robert Redford, and Waylon Jennings sang the theme song for and narrated the TV show *The Dukes of Hazzard*.

IRONY OF IRONIES

The irony of outlaw country—an anti-establishment movement—going mainstream was not lost on the country singers, as they observed in their songwriting. In 1978, Jennings offered up a sardonic dismissal of the phenomenon with a song titled "Don't You Think This Outlaw Bit's Done Got Out of Hand?" To listeners, this song's criticism of the marketing blitz that turned outlaw country into a buzz word was, itself, a very "outlaw" attitude—and they loved it. Ironically, the "outlaw" song criticizing outlaw country's success reached number five on the *Billboard* country chart.

By the end of the 1970s, the movement's status as an outsider to mainstream country was essentially lost. Its leading figures, including both Nelson and Jennings, had moved beyond the themes and musical identity of outlaw country; Nelson, for instance, explored old pop standards, show tunes, and jazz. Even as they left outlaw themes behind, they retained their increased artistic freedom and creative control, the principles on which the movement had been founded.

The outlaw movement had three lasting effects on the musical geography of country music. The first was that it brought significant attention to the songwriting scene in Texas, which persists to the present day. The second was that it codified the idea that Texas, and Austin in particular, was a country music outpost that challenged the position of Nashville within the country music industry. Of course, the musical developments in Texas throughout the 1970s had strong and unrelenting ties to the mainstream Nashville industry and record labels, but the idea, if not the fact, that Austin was both different and distant became important. The third lasting effect was that new performance venues provided a national stage for Texas country music. In 1976, a PBS show called *Austin City Limits* debuted. Unlike the earlier generations of barn dances in radio formats, *Austin City Limits* was televised from its start. In the spirit of Texas's progressive country movement, the show did not limit its musical content to country. Instead, it sought to represent the music of a much more diverse and genre-crossing Texan scene, drawing from folk, rock, and country with a strong showing from the progressive country artists. The show adopted a theme song by progressive country songwriter Gary P. Nunn, and offered a mix of music that was more in tune with the younger audience's musical tastes in both rock and country than anything the more traditional Opry could present. *Austin City Limits*, which continues to air today, was an important both as a place for artists to perform and as a symbolic representative of Austin challenging Nashville's prominence.

By about 1980, the outlaw movement was no longer a separate and distinct strand of country music. Aspects of it had become fully embedded in the mainstream country sound, while its role as an oppositional front had simply faded. During its heyday, however, the whole outlaw and progressive country scene drastically altered the direction that country music as a genre was headed. It opened up new geographic spaces as important in country music, it bridged the gap between country and rock in a critical way, and it reconnected a younger, more liberal audience to country music.

Listening Guide

"Luckenbach, Texas (Back to the Basics of Love)" (1977)

PERFORMERS:
Waylon Jennings and
Willie Nelson

SONGWRITERS: Chips
Moman and Bobby
Emmons

ORIGINAL ALBUM: *Ol'
Waylon* (RCA Victor
APL1-2317)

FORM: Verse-chorus

STYLE: Outlaw
country

In 1977, the outlaw movement was at its peak. Just a year earlier, producer Jerry Bradley's *Wanted! The Outlaws* album had generated a buzz in both the country and rock scenes, and the careers of many of the outlaw stars were in full stride. This song was the first commercially released recorded duet for Waylon Jennings and Willie Nelson. And although their duets evoked the image for country audiences that they were listening to two legendary stars who were strumming guitars and singing songs together in the true spirit of outlaw country, most of the duets were overdubbed in separate sessions. Although Jennings and Nelson had both acquired more control of their own recording careers and were working on their own projects at this time, this duet was put together by RCA executive Jerry Bradley.

The song was written by two professional songwriters, neither of whom was linked with either the outlaw movement or traditional country music. Chips Moman was a highly respected producer who had worked in California in the early rock 'n' roll boom, then moved to Memphis, where he produced many of the most famous Southern soul records from the 1960s, and later worked with Elvis Presley. Moman moved to Nashville and integrated himself into the country music scene during the 1970s. Bobby Emmons, likewise, had spent many years in rock and soul recording studios, primarily as a session musician playing piano and organ. He moved to Nashville in the early 1970s and worked as both a songwriter and a session player. While neither Moman nor Emmons subscribed to the outlaw movement's artistic philosophy, their song captured the sentiments so well, and with such vivid images, that fans treated it as the commercial representative of the outlaw movement. The song reached the top of the *Billboard* country chart and number twenty-five on the pop chart.

The song relies heavily on references to places, people, and songs to convey its meaning. Luckenbach is a ghost town in central Texas, west of Austin, that represents not only getting away from urban growth but also the lore of Texas and its symbolic freedom of wide-open spaces, cowboys, independent spirits, and country music, with its emphasis on tradition, roots, the land itself, and simplicity. This image of Texas is contrasted with the story of the Hatfields and McCoys, which evokes the East Coast (specifically Appalachia), crowded spaces, restlessness, anger, and resentment over old issues. The Hatfields and McCoys were two families embroiled in a bitter and sometimes violent feud who lived on the border of West Virginia and Kentucky. Several generations had been fighting over a stolen pig, a romance that crossed family lines, and even which sides the families fought with during the Civil War.

The song's meaning emerges from a series of symbolic cultural references. Listeners who were already fans of the outlaw movement understood the references; others were drawn into the movement by the song, through which they learned about the scene. In that sense, the song was a powerful ambassador for outlaw country. Jennings and Nelson both name themselves in the song. The lyrics mention Mickey Newbury and Jerry Jeff Walker, neither of whom was well known as a country star but both of whom were highly regarded as songwriters and performers within the outlaw scene. Walker was also connected to Luckenbach—he and his Lost Gonzo Band had recorded the album *Viva Terlingua* there in 1973. Walker's album was a favorite among the outlaw musicians, which transformed the obscure town, completely devoid of modern, urban development or material wealth, into a representation of outlaw country. The lyrics also mention Hank Williams and "Blue Eyes Cryin' in the Rain." Hank Williams represented the idea of traditional, honky-tonk country music, and more importantly, living out one's personal experiences in song.

A year after this song's release, Jennings questioned the way the outlaw movement had become a mainstream fad—the antithesis of its origins. Jennings essentially disowned the identity with "Don't You Think This Outlaw Bit's Done Got Out of Hand." As for "Luckenbach," according to critic Peter Doggett, Jennings admitted, "The guys that wrote the thing have never been to Luckenbach. Neither have I." Jennings told audiences he hated the song. Given the ideology of the outlaw movement, any other response would have been out of character.

TIME	FORM	LISTENING CUES	DISCUSSION
0:00	Intro	"The only two things …"	Waylon Jennings's voice and an electric guitar are the only sounds at the beginning. Jennings sings with very free rhythms, almost like he is speaking as each thought comes to him. From the beginning, the song explores a philosophical outlook on life that values music and love over fame.
0:28	Chorus	"Let's go to Luckenbach …"	Vocal harmony enters here, along with drums, piano, and the steady sounds of rhythm guitars. The entire song relies on external references, starting with place (Luckenbach) and people (Waylon Jennings and Willie Nelson). The prominent electric bass is common to Jennings's outlaw sound.
1:01	Instrumental interlude	Piano and steel guitar	The steel guitar that rises in this short interlude evokes the traditional sound of honky-tonk, with its Texan associations.

Continued

Listening Guide

"Luckenbach, Texas (Back to the Basics of Love)" (1977) Continued

TIME	FORM	LISTENING CUES	DISCUSSION
1:09	Verse	"So, baby, let's sell . . ."	The verse sounds fresh and different here because it's the first time we have heard this melody in the song. The lyrics describe changing wardrobe as a symbolic way of changing value systems, and the new clothes are specifically boots and jeans. Here, conspicuous consumption is equated with both choking and crying, or in other words, physical misery. The simple life, represented by cowboy culture in Texas, equates to happiness.
1:46	Chorus	"Let's go to Luckenbach . . ."	Note the prominent steel guitar that we hear behind this chorus.
2:24	Chorus	"Let's go to Luckenbach . . ."	Willie Nelson sings lead on this chorus. Notice that he changes the order of the names to "Willie and Waylon and the boys . . ." Nelson's style of singing, with his free rhythmic phrasing, is strikingly different from Jennings's rich, sustained phrases. The juxtaposition of the two styles here highlights the different vocal styles within the outlaw movement.
3:00	Outro	steel guitar	The song's lilting rhythms and fade-out entice us to think the song flows on forever with its soothing promises of a better life.

Southern Rock and the Country Audience

While classic country music and the growing outlaw movement anchored the country genre in the 1970s, some country fans also developed an interest in rock bands. In particular, an emerging style known as Southern rock (see essay on Southern Rock) borrowed many of the same roots, ideals, and aspects of identity that had shaped country music for decades. These bands cultivated a working-class, Southern, and predominantly white identity with historical ties to honky-tonk and blues music. For younger country fans who did not relate well to the classic country artists and their songs about middle-aged themes, Southern rock was a satisfying alternative. For more socially liberal fans who were put off by country's mainstream conservatism, Southern rock was a space for freer expression. And for country musicians with a rebellious streak who did not fit comfortably into the outlaw movement, Southern rock was a welcoming place to explore their musical creativity.

From the vantage point of the rock genre, Southern rock was a movement that turned back to simpler musical chord progressions and forms, unpretentious artistry, and working-class aesthetics as a reaction to the progressive art-rock developments prevalent in the late 1960s and 1970s. From the vantage point of cultural history, Southern rock was the expression of a younger generation's frustrations at a changing social order—the teens' answer to what their parents found in classic country. From civil rights to women's liberation, to the fears brought on by the Vietnam draft, to the economic troubles that blanketed the South in the 1970s, Southern rock gathered that angst and unleashed it in a barrage of macho, blues-driven, distorted guitars. Some of the music professed an extreme right-wing political outlook, further differentiating it from other styles and movements. Many of the musicians in the movement had grown up on the 1950s and '60s country music that their parents liked. With that pedigree, Southern rock held obvious appeal for a segment of young fans who came from a country music lineage but were unmoved by the older conservatism, image, and themes of classic country.

Southern rock was never fully a part of the country genre; it remained squarely in the rock genre, as defined by its fans' sense of identity, by its cultural institutions such as record labels and trade magazines, and by its musical lineage. But some segments of the audience crossed over, and several individual musicians in the movement were embraced by both country and rock. Furthermore, a few country artists working in the 1970s, most notably Waylon Jennings, borrowed musical ideas from Southern rock and collaborated with Southern rock bands at various times. Southern rock also had a lasting effect on country music that only became apparent in subsequent years. For several decades, aspects of Southern rock slowly but persistently worked their way into mainstream country music, and individual songs were adopted as anthems within the country scene. Today, at local country bars, country bands routinely play Southern rock hits for country audiences. Finally, many emerging country stars in the 2000s have looked back in time for their musical inspirations. For many of them, the mainstream country sounds of the 1970s and early 1980s (when they were children) did not provide the musical references and ideology they were seeking, whereas the Southern rock bands did (see Chapter 14). Thus, Southern rock has been retroactively dragged into the accepted history of country music in interesting ways.

Southern rock originated with the Allman Brothers Band, formed by brothers Gregg and Duane Allman in 1969 in Jacksonville, Florida, along with guitarist Dickey Betts and three other bandmates. Their first commercial success came with a live album in 1971 recorded at the famous rock concert hall, New York's Fillmore East. In spite of the death of several band members, including lead guitarist Duane Allman in 1971, they achieved widespread fame with their 1973

Figure 9-4 Lynyrd Skynyrd, performing on stage in 1975 with a Confederate flag unfurled behind them, reinforcing cultural associations for southern rock; the band has explained that their record label made them do it against their will.

Source: Pictoral Press Ltd/Alamy Stock Photo.

album *Brothers and Sisters*, which included the hit song "Ramblin' Man." The song made reference to traditional country themes of the rootless "rambler" who lived on the fringes of society. Their sound combined traditional elements of blues and honky-tonk with close harmony in a roots-rock form that was unpretentious and centered on straightforward, memorable lyrics.

In the mid-1960s, another group of friends in Jacksonville, Florida, put together a rock band steeped in many of the same traditions. Over the next several years, Gary Rossington, Allen Collins, and Ronnie Van Zant changed the band's name several times, finally settling on Lynyrd Skynyrd, a lampoon of their high school gym teacher's name. In 1972, major label MCA Records signed Lynyrd Skynyrd. Their first MCA album appeared in 1973, with hits "Free Bird," "Gimme Three Steps," and "Simple Man." Their songs' lyrics celebrate the sharp wit and free spirits of the young, rambling generation, refusing to be tied down by responsibility. Their sound was aggressively rock in character. In concert, they sometimes used two drummers, and they filled out the band's lineup to include keyboards and three electric lead guitars. By 1974, the band had earned a substantial following. Their sophomore album included "Sweet Home, Alabama" (see Listening Guide), which, along with other songs and their stage personas, added a strong political twist to the identity of Southern rock. After that song, Southern rock was no longer simply a descriptor of a particular musical style in a place and time, but rather a label for music whose attitude ranged from mere antiestablishment rebellion to more extreme attitudes of Confederate pride and racial prejudice. Not all of Southern rock took on those associations. At their core, most of the Southern rock bands held primarily to a musical identity centered on overdriven guitars, raucous live shows, and twangy blues in their musical roots. But the pervasive understanding that Southern rock represented a white racial vantage point would inflect country music some four decades when Southern rock experienced a revival of sorts.

Two other Southern rock bands in the mid-1970s reached into country music in substantial ways: the Marhsall Tucker Band and Barefoot Jerry. In 1972, Toy Caldwell and George McCorkle assembled a band called the Marshall Tucker Band in Spartanburg, South Carolina. The Marshall Tucker Band included both folk and country rock elements in their sound, specifically flute, steel guitar, and piano. They also invited their friend, session musician/guitarist Charlie Daniels, to perform and record with them on several occasions. Southern rock fans liked them, but country fans also welcomed their easy-listening sound, which had a lot in common with California country rockers such as the Eagles (see Chapter 7) and which foreshadowed what country bands would do in the 1980s (see Chapter 10). In the mid-1970s, several of their songs appeared on both *Billboard*'s pop charts (which essentially tracked rock music) and country charts at the same time, most notably "Heard It in a Love Song" (1977).

The other Southern rock band that was closely tied to country music was Barefoot Jerry, fronted by Wayne Moss and launched in Nashville in 1971. Barefoot Jerry's band members included several of Nashville's top session musicians who were playing regularly on classic country albums. On the side, however, they were extremely interested in the sounds and styles of rock music. Barefoot Jerry won over a local following of audiences for whom classic country was not a match for their musical interests, and within a short time the group had made inroads into the Southern rock scene. The band also teamed up with Charlie Daniels to host live gatherings of rock bands in the hometown of country music, thereby giving Southern rock even more of a foothold in country.

Whereas the Marshall Tucker Band and Barefoot Jerry were primarily rock bands who delved a bit into country, two country musicians—Charlie Daniels and Hank Williams, Jr.--took an opposite approach, reaching from their home base in country music into the Southern rock scene. Their music created a permanent link between rock and country music and drastically changed the sound of country music in the early 1980s. Charlie Daniels (see Artist Profile) had already established himself as a highly respected guitarist in Nashville's session-musician community, but following his work with Bob Dylan in the late 1960s, Daniels's personal musical tastes shifted closer to the rock scene. Collaborations with the Marshall Tucker Band and with Barefoot Jerry, combined with the new sounds he cultivated with his own band, won him a strong following among Southern rock audiences. As a result, both in the 1970s and continuing to the present, country fans tend to think of him as a country musician, while rock fans tend to think of him as a Southern rocker. His acceptance in both genres illustrates how much Southern rock and country music overlapped in the 1970s.

Randall Hank Williams (1949–), the son of Hank and Audrey Williams (see Chapter 4), also found a shared musical identity in Southern rock, all while maintaining his birthright and role in country music. Hank Sr. gave his son the nickname Bocephus, which was the name of a ventriloquist's dummy on the Grand Ole Opry. The nickname presaged the way that Hank Jr.'s early career would go; he was a talking and singing mouthpiece for his father's music and legacy. After Hank Sr.'s death in 1953, Audrey styled her son in the image of his father. She took him on tour when he was only eight, where he sang his father's songs in the style that his father had made famous. Although his performances helped shore up the finances of Hank Sr.'s musical estate, Hank Jr. found the role stifling, and growing up in the spotlight was difficult. By the early 1970s, he had rebelled against his mother's wishes and recorded songs of his own that lashed out against his conscripted role as the son of Hank Williams Sr. This musical independence coincided with his growing interest

Listening Guide

"Sweet Home Alabama" (1974)

PERFORMERS: Lynyrd Skynyrd

SONGWRITER: Ronnie Van Zant, Gary Rossington, and Ed King

ORIGINAL ALBUM: *Second Helping* (MCA 1686)

FORM: Verse-chorus

STYLE: Southern rock

This Southern rock anthem is so well known that even a short fragment of its guitar introduction is enough to elicit cheers from fans. It has become a staple of cover bands in country bars coast-to-coast, and today's country singers refer to it in their lyrics regularly (see Chapter 14). Yet when it was recorded, it had almost no connections to country music other than the most broadly defined themes of Southern pride and working-class identity.

"Sweet Home Alabama" is laced with references to politics, other musicians, and other genres and styles. Band members penned the song in response to what they perceived as insults toward Southerners in Neil Young's "Southern Man" and "Alabama" recordings. The most controversial aspects of the song concern its position on Southern racism. The band frequently performed in the South with a Confederate flag on stage, and their reference to Governor George Wallace, a staunch segregationist, is open to interpretation as being either for or against Wallace's politics. Band members have gone to some length to defend themselves against those charges. They have explained that the song's lyrics point out that sometimes politicians make decisions that their constituents might not agree with, and they have also claimed that the Confederate flag was a gimmick added by their record label to increase their regional appeal.

Lead singer Ronnie Van Zant (1948–1977) grew up immersed in country music. His father was a fan of Merle Haggard, Conway Twitty, and Loretta Lynn, and Van Zant's style of songwriting, which favored telling stories about working-class daily life, was heavily indebted to country traditions. Van Zant and friends Gary Rossington (1951–) and Allen Collins (1952–1990) formed a band in Jacksonville, Florida, as teenagers, and signed a contract with MCA in 1972. As the Who's opening act a year later, the band earned national attention, and their first two albums sold exceptionally well. "Sweet Home Alabama" was their first single to break into the pop charts, peaking at number eight. Throughout the mid-1970s, the band was celebrated as the face of Southern rock, a reign that came to an end in 1977 when the band's plane crashed, killing Van Zant, guitarist Steve Gaines (who joined the band after "Sweet Home Alabama"), and backup singer Cassie Gaines (Steve's sister), along with the pilots and one of their managers.

Note how different "Sweet Home Alabama" sounds from the other mid-'70s recordings we have explored. If we compare it to Top 40 country music released after 2000, however, we find some recognizable similarities. This song's reception illustrates the way country musicians and fans actively reconstruct the genre's history in continually evolving ways.

TIME	FORM	LISTENING CUES	DISCUSSION
0:00	Intro	electric guitars, drums, bass	Guitarist Ed King counts the band in at the beginning, "1, 2, 3," and singer Ronnie Van Zant says "Turn it up" audibly as well. These bits, both of which were simply practical communication in the recording studio, make the recording more like a live performance and bring the audience closer to the band's experience.
0:23	Verse 1	"Big wheels …"	The opening line is a reference to the song "Proud Mary," from Creedence Clearwater Revival, later covered by Ike and Tina Turner. The verse also describes a Southerner who has left and is returning, both literally and figuratively. Ronnie Van Zant overdubbed his lead vocals, so we hear the same voice performing the song on top of itself.
0:42	Interlude	electric guitar	The piano adds an extra harmony part here.
0:52	Verse 2	"Well, I heard Mr. Young …"	Notice the backup vocalists' "oohs" here—the vocal harmonies suggest a sense of community. The most discussed line in the song is the reference to musician Neil Young, who has ties to the country rock scene, yet who also recorded two songs that were widely understood to be harsh condemnations of the South for its racist practices.
1:12	Chorus	"Sweet home, Alabama …"	Additional voices, including two women, join on the chorus.
1:32	Interlude	electric guitar solo	
1:41	Verse 3	"In Birmingham …"	Much of controversy surrounding the song comes from this verse, and questions of whether the band was endorsing Governor George Wallace's segregation policies or pointing out that politicians may be corrupt or have objectionable stances in many different settings, with the reference to President Nixon.
2:01	Chorus	"Sweet home, Alabama …"	Notice that the recording makes the electric guitars more prominent than the voices.
2:21	Interlude	electric guitar solo	The guitar solo here has distortion in its sound.
2:40	Instrumental chorus	electric guitar solo	Back-up singers enter with "Ah, ah, ah, Alabama."
3:00	Interlude	electric guitar solo	The music returns to the basic riff from the introduction.
3:10	Verse 4	"Now, Muscle Shoals …"	This verse contains another musical reference to the Southern soul that was recorded by the famous studio musicians, the Swampers, in Muscle Shoals.
3:29	Chorus	"Sweet home, Alabama …"	By this point in the song, the chorus is already highly familiar.
3:49	Chorus	"Sweet home, Alabama …"	Van Zant adds vocal interjections such as "Oh, sweet home!" and "Lordy" between lines of the chorus.
4:09	Instrumental verse	piano	The piano solo here evokes the sound of the boogie-woogie tradition. The recording fades out on the album, as it would when played on the radio.

Listening Guide

"The South's Gonna Do It" (1974)

PERFORMERS:
Charlie Daniels Band

SONGWRITER: Charlie Daniels

ORIGINAL ALBUM:
Fire on the Mountain
(Kama Sutra
KS-2604)

FORM: Verse-chorus
(twelve-bar blues)

STYLE: Outlaw
country

Fire on the Mountain, named for a famous old fiddle tune, was the fifth studio album that seasoned fiddler and session musician Charlie Daniels released with his own band. By 1974, Daniels was a highly respected part of the growing Southern rock scene, and to fans of that music, he was squarely in that tradition. However, Daniels was also a fiddler with traditional country roots who had been working in Nashville for a decade, and to country fans, Daniels was part of the burgeoning outlaw country movement. While for the most part country and Southern rock were distinct and separate musical worlds in the 1970s, this particular song illustrates one of the few points where the two intersected.

"The South's Gonna Do It" is based entirely on a twelve-bar blues progression (see Appendix A). Each section of the song—each verse, each chorus, and each instrumental solo that is marked separately in the Listening Guide—consists of twelve bars of music that follow the typical blues chord progression. The verses are a roll call of the biggest names in Southern rock during the mid-1970s. Much like the tradition in outlaw country of naming other artists in the songs, here the list helps to define and circumscribe the musical style and scene for its fans. The choruses, on the other hand, are more generic calls for Southern pride, especially endorsing the idea of being a rebel.

The recording has little in common with the musical style of Southern rock. Daniels's vocals are clear, with just a slight Southern twang. The electric guitar solos are boisterous, but never venture into either the distortion or the dominance heard on most Southern rock albums. The fiddling owes an obvious debt to western swing. Even the piano remains somewhere between rockabilly and boogie-woogie in its style. The lyrics—and Daniels's own popularity among Southern rock fans—turned the song into a Southern rock anthem. But other aspects of the recording all connected him loosely with country's outlaw movement: the song has a live aesthetic, Daniels released the song on his own independent record label, and Daniels was known for his rebellious attitude even while working inside the core of the Nashville music industry.

in rock music, and with this new style and approach, he found far greater commercial success. He moved to Alabama, physically leaving the country music nest that had been his home—both literally and metaphorically—his whole life. In Alabama, he became friends with and collaborated with Southern rock bands, including the Marshall Tucker Band. Like Waylon Jennings, Hank Williams Jr. never abandoned the essence of honky-tonk music in his own recordings, and the country heritage is audible in all his work. But he imported the vocal aggression, the drums and bass, the electric guitar styles, and the attitude from Southern rock.

TIME	FORM	LISTENING CUES	DISCUSSION
0:00	Intro	fiddle	Stop-time accompaniment with a fiddle solo, then the band joins in for the rest of the introduction.
0:23	Verse 1	"Well, the train to Grinder's Switch …"	References to Southern rock bands: Grinderswitch, Marshall Tucker Band, Lynyrd Skynyrd, and the Allman Brothers Band (with guitarist Dickey Betts).
0:40	Chorus	"So gather 'round …"	The piano is prominent during the chorus. Daniels mentions pride in being a Southern Rebel. His voice is very clear, with just a hint of Southern twang.
0:58	Instrumental verse	fiddle, then electric guitar	The fiddle solo here gives way to a electric guitar solo.
1:16	Instrumental verse	electric guitar	The guitar solo continues into another twelve-bar blues section here.
1:33	Instrumental verse	piano	The piano takes a boogie-style solo over this twelve-bar blues section.
1:51	Instrumental verse	piano	The piano switches to a higher register, and the fiddle re-enters for this twelve-bar blues section.
2:08	Verse 2	"Elvin Bishop's sittin'"	Southern rock bands include Elvin Bishop, ZZ Top, Wet Willie, Barefoot Jerry, and Charlie Daniels Band ("CDB").
2:25	Chorus	"Well, gather 'round …"	
2:43	Instrumental verse	fiddle	This fiddle solo is very similar in style to something one might hear in a mainstream country recording.
3:00	Instrumental verse	fiddle	The fiddle continues into a second twelve-bar blues section here.
3:18	Instrumental verse	fiddle and electric guitar	Here the fiddle introduces a high, repeated motive that acts like a "shout chorus" in a typical big-band jazz arrangement.
3:35	Instrumental verse	fiddle and electric guitar	The final twelve-bar blues section continues the "shout chorus" characteristics, plus a tag that the instruments all play together (at 3:50), serving as a bookend to the song's introduction.

Unlike Charlie Daniels, who was fully welcomed in to the Southern rock scene by rock fans and whose music in the mid-1970s appeared on the rock charts, Hank Williams Jr. remained essentially a country musician, and his fan base was essentially a country audience. He briefly ventured out of that role with his 1975 album, *Hank Williams Jr. and Friends*. That album included Charlie Daniels, Dickey Betts, and members of both the Allman Brothers Band and the Marshall Tucker Band, and has been described in reviews as country rock. For Hank Jr., it was the debut of a new and short-lived musical identity constructed out of Southern rock. Severe

Charlie Daniels (1936–)

harlie Daniels is one of the few musicians equally at home in rock and country music. The guitarist and fiddle player was raised in Wilmington, North Carolina, on a musical diet of country, gospel, and blues. He graduated from high school in 1955, just as the rock 'n' roll craze was sweeping the country. Daniels and some friends formed a rock 'n' roll band and headed west to California. Along the way, they met up-and-coming producer Bob Johnston, who would soon take over Columbia Records' country division from Don Law. Johnston helped launch Daniels's songwriting career by cowriting a tune for Elvis Presley, and he also encouraged Daniels to come to Nashville to work as a session musician.

In 1969, Daniels moved to Nashville, where he played on Bob Dylan's 1969 *Nashville Skyline* album (see Chapter 7), produced by Bob Johnston, and worked regularly as a session guitarist for mainstream country acts as well. He built more ties with the folk-rock scene and produced an album for the Youngbloods, one of the most successful of the folk-rock bands. At the same time, his own music drew increasingly from the Southern rock sound that was gaining popularity. He began to host annual jams in Nashville with Southern rockers Barefoot Jerry, and in 1971 launched his solo career on an independent label.

By the mid-1970s, Daniels had scored a few modest hits on both the country and rock charts. He was well known both in country circles, where he was treated as a core player in the music industry and still perceived as a slightly rebellious outsider, and in rock circles, where he was a celebrated part of the Southern rock scene. His breakthrough moment in country music came in 1979 when he wrote and recorded "The Devil Went Down to Georgia," a saga of a southern fiddler named Johnny besting the Devil in a fiddle contest, where the stakes were the boy's soul versus a golden fiddle. The recording pitched Daniels's hot fiddling solo against a screaming fiddle (the devil's solo) supported by a distorted bass (the "band of demons"). The results handed Daniels his first number one *Billboard* country hit, which also reached number three on the pop charts and turned a fiddle tune in which the performers even sing the names of fiddle tunes into a rock hit. His music was heard in the movie *Urban Cowboy* (see Chapter 10), which turned him into a household name.

In the mid-1980s, Daniels scored a few more radio-friendly country hits as country music turned back toward more traditional sounds, and in subsequent years he remained on the fringes of mainstream country. He has adopted a conservative political stance in his music, which

injuries from an accidental fall and the subsequent lengthy recovery period kept him out of the spotlight for two years, and when he returned, he reverted to a more country identity and released his seminal hard country anthems, "Family Tradition" (1979) and "Whiskey Bent and Hell Bound" (1979). In the 1980s, (see Chapter 10), this rock-infused country sound became a more significant part of mainstream country. Hank Williams Jr. infused his live performances with both the musical energy and Southern rock's crowd synergy. With that formula, he enjoyed even more mainstream country success, which culminated in a series of

Figure 9-5 Bob Dylan (left) and Charlie Daniels (right, with guitar) in the studio in 1969.
Source: Photo by Michael Ochs Archives / Getty Images.

resonated with some segments of the country audience in the years after September 11, 2001.

Daniels has always focused on live performance as the heart of his musical identity, even though he has logged many hours as a studio session musician and found several of his breaks through songwriting. For Southern rock, Daniels offers a connection to the region's roots of country music; for country music, Daniels invigorates the genre with the energy of a rock concert and the drive of a freight-train boogie. His dual images as conservative country fiddler and long-haired (to quote from his own song lyrics) Southern rocker represent the complex relationship that country music had with the cultural landscape of the 1970s.

"Entertainer of the Year" awards from both the Country Music Association and the Academy of Country Music.

While Southern rock remained part of the rock genre, functioning largely outside of country music, its impact on country was both significant and long-lasting. By the late 1970s, an increasing number of country artists were borrowing from the edgy, antagonistic attitudes found in rock music to create new sounds and identities within country music. Tanya Tucker (1958–), for instance, launched her career as a young teenager with classic country recordings in the early 1970s such as "Delta

Dawn" and "What's Your Mama's Name." But by 1978, she had restyled herself as a sexy rock star. Her album *TNT*—with a cover photo of Tucker in skin-tight black leather with a microphone cable pulled between her legs—was filled with covers of rock hits. Tucker's musical style and identity as a performer remained unquestionably country, but infused with blues and rock sounds, a similar approach to musical style as that of Hank Williams Jr.

Part of Southern rock's appeal was simply generational. Classic country in the 1970s was the domain of forty-year-old artists and audiences wrestling with midlife crises, divorces, and a changing economic landscape that threatened formerly steady employment. Southern rock, on the other hand, along with outlaw country to a lesser extent, was the domain of younger fans who had come of age during the rock era of the 1960s. Rock was their native musical language, and they used it to express their own generation's concerns, a situation that was similar to how rockabilly had reached a youth audience within the traditional country fan base in the 1950s. As had long been the tradition in country music, in the 1970s several different styles coexisted, sometimes in tension but often comfortably cohabitating, and became the musical legacy on which the next generations of country artists would build.

☆ ESSAY: MUSICAL STYLE

 # Outlaw Country

Like many other developments in country music, the outlaw movement of the 1970s was not tied to a single musical style or even a specific group of styles. Nonetheless, there are some stylistic features that stand out. Many of the outlaw country artists and recordings in the 1970s included:

- Themes and topics that resonated with the Old West, cowboy culture, or stubborn independence of character
- Increased use of electric guitars, loud drums, and bass, recreating a live-band sound
- An increased sense of sonic space, the use of silence, and a sparse texture
- Frequent use of steel guitar, harmonica, and tambourine
- A predominance of male artists and masculine styles of presentation

The two main stylistic prongs of outlaw country were the incorporation of rock styles of bass, drums, and electric guitar on the one hand, and the revival of various honky-tonk, stripped-down sounds on the other, including vocals that emphasized raw emotion over proficient technique. Because the outlaws connected with the singer-songwriter scene, especially in Texas, and celebrated the work of musicians who were not major commercial successes, they gravitated toward a live, minimalist sound, often emphasizing just guitar and vocals. The outlaw movement's emphasis on increased independence meant that many of the artists succeeded in reducing the role of Nashville's established producers in their recordings. That meant that the strings, backup vocalists, thick instrumentation, and polished studio sound that were commonplace on the classic country recordings (see Chapter 8) tended not to show up much on those of the outlaws. Although the sound of outlaw country recordings varied from one to the next, and there were no clear boundaries on what was and was not considered outlaw country (especially as songs moved from one artist to another), it is relatively easy to identify the sound of the core outlaw recordings, especially when compared to the classic country of the same time period.

✴ ESSAY: MUSICAL STYLE

Southern Rock

Most historians define Southern rock more by ideology and a band's biography or stated musical influences than by musical style. But there are certain musical characteristics that we can identify, particularly in the context of Southern rock's influence on country music:

- Southern rock bands in the 1970s built their music from the blues tradition, particularly in their choices of chord progressions and types of musical harmony, and from the musical forms of riff-based rock.
- The bands emphasized electric guitar—many bands having two or three featured players—and electric guitar solos that often displayed virtuosic talent.
- As in other close-knit musical scenes, including outlaw country, Southern rock bands frequently name-checked each other in their music ("The South's Gonna Do It" being the most extreme case, see Listening Guide).
- They featured loud drumming and sonic distortion in their recordings.
- Southern rock recordings attempted to capture the live sound of the band, representing on record most of what the audiences might experience at a concert. Live albums (such as Lynyrd Skynyrd's 1976 recording) were common within this style.
- To an even greater extent than the outlaw movement, Southern rock was a male scene of masculine posturing and identity.

Along with the live aesthetic, we can hear a blend of elements from gospel (such as organ), blues, jazz improvisation, and country (often in the lyrics, or by the inclusion of a fiddle) that give Southern rock its regionally specific character.

Southern rock songs were frequently built on short, memorable hooks—little bits of music, perhaps a few notes played on a guitar, that were extremely catchy. Extended jams—long sections of music featuring improvised instrumental solos—were common in their recordings and even more common in their live performances. The lyrics emphasized swaggering Southern pride, independence, rebellion against the establishment, and clever wit. Most of the bands featured vocal harmony and the tighter, shriller styles of singing common in rock, which were very different than the resonant, smooth baritone voices with vibrato heard in classic country. In some instances, as explored in this chapter, we find instruments such as the fiddle or steel guitar appearing in Southern rock recordings, but this illustrates occasional intersections between country and rock rather than the core of the Southern rock sound.

 # Behaving Like Outlaws

The word "outlaws" often conjures up images of Wild West bandits robbing banks and trains. Within country music, many famous outlaw artists are known for their bad-boy images, drug scandals, and reckless, sometimes self-destructive behavior. But neither of those images has anything to do with the heart of the outlaw movement in country music. What made them outlaws was their refusal to accept the conventional business approach to making country music.

In the years just prior to the rise of the outlaw movement of the 1970s, most country music was the artistic creation of record label executives and producers. The producers chose the songs, selected the studio musicians, decided on the style and feel of the musical arrangements, coached the stars' performances, and controlled every aspect of the music-making process. The payment structures for royalties funneled most of the songwriting profits into publishing firms (which were usually run by Nashville insiders) and, in some instances, into the hands of the record producers through various business contracts. Very little artistic control resided in the hands of the performers, or even the songwriters. The biggest record companies thought of their country divisions as small-stakes outposts and treated the artists accordingly; concert promoters figured that country acts could be booked cheaply into any old venue; and country stars had little idea how much commercial power they could actually wield if they tried.

The outlaws changed all of that, and their lasting impact on country music—which resonated far beyond the small circle of outlaw artists—was a change in the business model of country music. The change happened partly because many of the outlaw artists became friends with rock musicians and discovered just how artistically free and financially lucrative their contracts could be. They also realized how large the country market and country music business was. The big opportunity for change came when RCA executives forgot to automatically renew Waylon Jennings's contract in the early 1970s. Jennings found himself essentially a free agent, and had recently found out about the artistic freedom and perks that rock stars enjoyed regularly. Jennings negotiated heavily with RCA, and when he re-signed with the label, it was with unprecedented freedom to choose his own band, music, recording location, and marketing style. Willie Nelson executed a similar change when he switched labels in the mid-1970s. With these changes, the artists on the front lines of country music could take their road bands into whatever studio they wanted, choose their own songs, producers, and musical arrangements, and take chances with adventurous new artistic ideas, just as rock bands had been doing for years. They also discovered they could easily set up publishing companies and keep the publisher's share of royalties for songs they had written themselves. As the movement gained momentum, more independent publishers and recording studios made it easier for newcomers to avoid slipping into the old Nashville establishment's way of doing things.

The outlaws effectively broke down the music industry's barriers that had kept the country music recording business and concert scene both isolated and marginalized. With these changes, country acts were getting written up in *Rolling Stone* magazine and appearing on rock billings in rock venues (at rock-concert prices). Country music could no longer be figuratively tucked back into a corner, nor could the producers and record labels ever regain the level of control that had characterized Nashville for decades. Even artists with no affiliation with the outlaw movement jumped on the bandwagon; in the late 1970s, Dolly Parton, for instance, who was by no means part of outlaw country, switched to a New York–based management firm and set her sights on far more ambitious venues, record contracts, and artistic projects than would ever have been possible under the pre-outlaw regime of country music (see Chapter 8). The outlaw movement also made space in the country genre for rock music that the old-time country establishment did not particularly like—the shifting power structure meant that if the fans supported the music, Nashville's gatekeepers were no longer in a position to keep it out. Outlaw behavior, it turned out, had little to do with any sort of bad-boy image, and everything to do with a new ordering of artistic control and financial compensation, not really the stuff of Wild West legends, but instead the engine that keeps the music industry running.

☆ **ESSAY: CULTURE**

Long-Haired Rednecks, Hippies, and Cosmic Cowboys

Country music ran headlong into a clash between mainstream culture and counterculture in the 1970s. In the previous decade, the mainstream country music establishment had turned a cold shoulder to the youth culture movements that were adopting a hippie outlook. The Byrds' long hair helped get them booted from the Opry (see Chapter 7); Merle Haggard's "Okie From Muskogee" was interpreted by many country fans as an endorsement of the so-called silent majority, which endorsed conservative values, short hair, and rejection of the whole 1960s counterculture of drugs, free love, and rock 'n' roll. By the mid-1970s, however, the country music perspective had shifted. Rock and country music shared common ground. Most relevant, the country audience underwent an identity shift. As the Vietnam War had dragged on, more working-class Americans became more skeptical of the political establishment, and scandals such as Watergate tainted their opinions even more. Texas served as a gathering place for young musicians, hippies, and counterculture enthusiasts. Yet the music that those audiences embraced, which reflected their ideals of a rural, pastoral, folk-influenced society, sounded suspiciously like country music, which already had a dedicated fan base among the cowboys and working people who were not part of the counterculture. At Willie Nelson's 4th of July picnics and in the marijuana-induced haze of the big concert halls, cowboy culture and the counterculture joined forces.

Several songs from the 1970s illustrate country music's inclusion of a countercultural identity. Michael Martin Murphey's "Cosmic Cowboy" (1973) expressed the same sentiment heard in other outlaw recordings: taking up the cowboy life in Texas would be a great way to find ultimate freedom of personal expression ("riding the range and actin' strange"). The same year, Charlie Daniels wrote and recorded "Uneasy Rider," in which a long-haired adventurer with a peace sign on his car breaks down in the Deep South, and the protagonist heads into a "redneck-looking joint" to call for help. There he encounters some locals who, in the song's depiction, are the most extreme stereotypes of Southern rednecks. He raises their ire by poking fun at Governor George Wallace and the Ku Klux Klan and suggesting one of them might actually be a communist sympathizer—the ultimate insult. As he makes his escape, he hints that he might head west "via Omaha," just to avoid any more Southern encounters. What was particularly significant about "Uneasy Rider" was that country fans liked it—the song was Daniels's first hit on the *Billboard* country charts (although it did not get close to the top)—despite the fact that it was written so that the audience identified with the long-haired counterculture protagonist and flagrantly mocked the Southern working-class establishment. Two years later, Daniels followed it up with "Long-Haired Country Boy," a declaration of independence for anyone who chose to forge his own cultural path. In 1976, David Allan Coe released "Long Haired Redneck" on an album by the same title, a swaggering declaration that "my long hair just can't cover up my red neck." While singing about his rough-and-tumble persona and time served in prison, Coe asserts that his redneck identity trumps his counterculture "long hair" image. The song reinforces the point that country music's ideology had shifted to include a countercultural perspective.

The outlaw movement found common ground in, and created bridges between, the conventional, conservative country fan base and the growing countercultural movement. In so doing, these artists dramatically expanded the commercial reach of country music. They radically changed the cultural associations and accepted meaning of country music. They also paved the way for later generations of country fans and musicians to look back in history and claim both Southern rock and country rock, with all its Californian hippie associations, as part of the core country music lineage.

LISTEN SIDE-BY-SIDE

"Can I Sleep In Your Arms"
Songwriter: Hank Cochran
Jeannie Seely, 1973 (on *Can I Sleep In Your Arms/Lucky Ladies*, MCA Records)
Willie Nelson, 1975 (on *Red Headed Stranger*, Columbia)

"May I Sleep In Your Barn Tonight Mister"
Traditional
Hank Thompson, 1958 (originally released on Capitol EAP3-1246)

"Red River Valley"
Traditional
Gene Autry, 1946 (originally released on Columbia 37184)

When Willie Nelson recorded his concept album *Red Headed Stranger,* he started with songs already in existence. Thus, a comparison between Nelson's version and the original highlights the musical transformations that forged the outlaw style.

Jeannie Seely's original version, from just two years earlier, was written by her former husband Hank Cochran, one of the songwriters responsible for cranking out material for the Nashville Sound era. Seely's recording is classic country through and through, complete with the rich vocal harmony on the chorus, the intricate guitar parts, and the full texture of the band. In just about every way, this recording represents the themes, emotional tenor, and musical aesthetics of the classic country era.

"Can I Sleep in Your Arms" tells the first-person tale of assuaging heartbroken rejection in the arms of a stranger, a very 1970s outlaw and classic country theme. Cochran's song, however, has a much longer history. A folk song called "May I Sleep In Your Barn Tonight, Mister," sometimes phrased as "Can I sleep . . ." dates back to the earliest recordings of hillbilly music, with Charlie Pool, Vernon Dalhart, and Ernest Stoneman among those who recorded it. The melody and chords are identical, and the slip from "barn" to "arms" clearly links the refrain in the song's choruses. A completely different set of lyrics also used the same melody and chords: "Red River Valley," sometimes called the "Cowboy Love Song," was recorded by Gene Autry for use in one of his films, and by Carl T. Sprague and Jules Verne Allen in the 1920s, among many others. Folklorists have traced the song well into the nineteenth century in both published versions and oral traditions. Thus, "Can I Sleep in Your Arms" joins a tradition in country music of rewriting lyrics to an extant melody and collection of songs (see, for instance, "It Wasn't God Who Made Honky Tonk Angels" in Chapter 4). We can readily compare a singing cowboy and a honky tonk version of the song by listening to Gene Autry and Hank Thompson's recordings, or go back further to hear the hillbilly versions of these incredibly popular folk tunes.

Willie Nelson transforms the song for his outlaw project mainly through the use of silence. One of the key features of the outlaw movement was the musical use of space, sparse instrumentation, and silence that lets a listener penetrate all the way through the sound. Notice how few notes are played in the opening of this recording. The song becomes a musical gesture, more than a fleshed-out performance. Once the full band enters, we hear the harmonica as isolated, and individual guitar parts leap out of the texture with urgency and independence. Toward the end of the song, we hear a piano solo, tying it back into the story of the *Red Headed Stranger* album by evoking a saloon pianist from the Old West. The song ends with the same sparse minimalism with which it began.

LISTEN SIDE-BY-SIDE
Red Headed Stranger
(Columbia CK-33482, 1975)

Willie Nelson's album deserves to be heard as a complete musical work, one track right after another. Such an experience allows comparisons between the individual tracks as well as a far better sense of what made this album so unique in the world of country music.

In 1975, Willie Nelson went to Garland, Texas, just north of Dallas, and recorded a concept album with sparse instrumental accompaniments. Concept albums, which were common in rock music by then, feature a single theme or story line throughout the album so that, rather than a collection of ten or twelve random songs, the entire album's musical contents fit together to form a larger artistic work.

Nelson constructed a loose story line, set in the Old West, about a brokenhearted man setting out on a journey and searching for a way to ease his pain. He finds his former lover with another man in a tavern, kills them both, then continues on his way with his horses. The man takes comfort in the arms of a stranger, then leaves with a bittersweet parting. At the end of the album, he makes peace with himself. Nelson weaves most of the story together from existing country songs made famous by artists such as Eddy Arnold ("Red Headed Stranger"), Lulu Belle and Scotty ("Remember Me [When the Candle Lights Are Gleaming]"), and Jeannie Seely ("Can I Sleep In Your Arms Tonight"), along with old fiddle tunes (such as "Down Yonder," originally a barrelhouse ragtime number), folk tunes ("Bandera"), and gospel hymns ("Just As I Am"). He adds only a few bits of his own compositions. By constructing a single story line from a scattered selection of older songs, Nelson's album is itself artistic commentary on the genre of country music, namely a tale of lost love, a search through loneliness, and, ultimately, redemption. The entire album highlights Nelson's philosophical perspective on songs as individual works of art that are worthy of contemplation.

The music on *Red Headed Stranger* is sparse, haunting, and minimalist. The entire album uses only six instruments: guitar, bass, drums, piano, mandolin, and harmonica. Vocal harmony was kept to an absolute minimum. The biggest hit from the album was a tune penned by Fred Rose, "Blue Eyes Cryin' in the Rain," which became Nelson's first number one single on the *Billboard* country chart. The album features several instrumentals (tracks with no singing at all), and long instrumental sections at the ends of several other tracks. Its structure includes recurring refrains, where fragments of the same song return several times over the course of the album to create musical continuity across the whole work. The use of silence and minimalist accompaniment were both hallmarks of the outlaw country style.

Nelson recorded this album immediately after leaving Atlantic Records for Columbia, where his new contract granted him more artistic license and less oversight—the core values of outlaw country. When Nelson first delivered the album to Columbia, the country division's executives thought it was an unfinished demo album that clearly needed many layers of overdubbing in the recording studio to polish it up. Nelson, however, insisted that it was already in its final state, and under the aegis of Columbia's main New York offices (rather than their Nashville country offices), the album was released. It sold astonishingly well; in less than a year, the Recording Industry Association of America had certified its gold-record status.

PLAYLIST

Daniels, Charlie. "Uneasy Rider" (1973)

Jennings, Waylon. "Don't You Think This Outlaw Bit's Done Got Out of Hand?" (1978)

Nelson, Willie. "Georgia on My Mind" (1978)

Walker, Jerry Jeff. "Desperados Waiting For a Train" (1973)

Williams, Hank Jr. "Family Tradition" (1979)

FOR MORE READING

Doggett, Peter. *Are You Ready for the Country: Elvis, Dylan, Parsons and the Roots of Country Rock*. New York: Penguin Books, 2000.

Guralnick, Peter. *Lost Highway: Journeys and Arrivals of American Musicians*. Boston: Little, Brown, and Company, 1999. First ed., Boston: David R. Godine Publishers, 1979.

Kemp, Mark. *Dixie Lullaby: A Story of Music, Race, and New Beginnings in a New South*. New York: Free Press, 2004.

Reid, Jan. *The Improbable Rise of Redneck Rock: New Edition*. Austin: University of Texas Press, 2004.

Stimeling, Travis. *Cosmic Cowboys and New Hicks: The Countercultural Sounds of Austin's Progressive Country Music Scene*. New York: Oxford University Press, 2011.

NAMES AND TERMS

Allman Brothers	4th of July picnics	Nelson, Willie
Austin City Limits	Glaser, Tompall	outlaw country
Barefoot Jerry	Goodman, Steve	*Red Headed Stranger*
Bradley, Jerry	Jennings, Waylon	Southern rock
Coe, David Allan	Luckenbach, Texas	*Wanted! The Outlaws*
Colter, Jessi	Lynyrd Skynyrd	Williams, Hank Jr.
Daniels, Charlie	Marshall Tucker Band	

REVIEW TOPICS

1. What were the differences between the images and symbols associated with outlaw country and the images and symbols associated with classic country, and how did they relate to the meaning of the music?

2. In both Southern rock and outlaw country, how did the extensive use of references (of names, people, events, places, etc.) contribute to the "otherness" of the music?

3. How did the outlaw movement's campaign for artistic freedom correspond to the audience's conception of authenticity in these years?

PART IV

Expansion: Country Makes It Big-Time
(1980s and 1990s)

In the 1980s, political and economic trends in the United States created an environment in which mainstream America embraced country music. The result was country music's largest period of growth up to that time, and, shortly thereafter, a reactionary shift that took country music away from the mainstream.

The political climate changed significantly when, in 1980, Ronald Reagan entered the White House. Reagan had a bold charisma that had been cultivated and refined by his years as a movie star. His personality was that of the quintessential American cowboy hero of the old western movies (a role he had played on screen), even down to the boots he wore. In his rhetoric, and in the widely accepted perceptions of many of its citizens, America was an idyllic land of opportunity and a force for good throughout the world. It could triumph over the communist threat of the Cold War and remain a beacon for capitalism.

Economic policy reinforced this attitude. The general trends in popular culture were toward glamorous, bigger, and louder consumerism. MTV, which launched in 1981, added a continuous visual presence to popular music, and pop stars such as Michael Jackson and Madonna brought sizzling dance moves and tantalizing beats into musical fashion. Country music followed suit; by the early 1980s, the sound and images of country music had shifted toward a more glamorous version of pop-country, known as countrypolitan. The music combined the sonic aspects of 1970s and '80s pop with the idea of country as representing something grounded in the wholesome superiority of American traditions. These developments brought in listeners who were newcomers to the genre, and for a short while, country music merged with pop music. And for brief period of time, country songs were sitting at the very top of the pop charts.

By the mid-1980s, the interest in country music began to wane. As is common after a period of pop-crossover success, the country music industry experienced an internal revolution, sparked by a backlash against the pop-crossover success of the early 1980s. Styles of country music that were more strongly tied to tradition, especially honky-tonk and western swing, once again gained traction. Two major changes happened during the latter half of the 1980s. The first was that these neotraditionalist artists, as they were known, focused on connecting country music's present to its past in audible ways. The second—which was a direct corollary—was that country music was no longer as successful at crossing over to the pop charts; in other words, country music and popular music once again diverged.

In spite of the reduction in market share that country experienced in the late 1980s, the genre was rich with new talent. When the socioeconomic landscape brought a "New South" into the public limelight, New Country was poised to step up, rolling up market share in the process. Many historians see parallels between the rise of Bill Clinton to the presidency and beyond, and the rise of Garth Brooks to a dominant but fraught role in country music. For about a decade, country rode the wave of large market shares, general mainstream popularity, and a musical reputation that was inclusive of families, of suburban moms, and anyone who wanted their country music to unite rather than divide communities.

Part IV explores the various expansions of country music to the point that it encroached on pop music and drew the ire of traditional country fans along the way. The three major cycles in this time period are:

1. The urban cowboy era, sparked by the 1980 Hollywood film, during which country music became a national phenomenon. Although there were many different styles of country music thriving at the same time, the most prominent was the crossover style known as countrypolitan, which allowed some country singers to become mainstream pop stars.
2. The shift back toward harder-edged, twang-centered country music in the late 1980s, when country music regrouped and reaffirmed its distinction from pop music.
3. Building on that core, historically-informed country music, a new crop of artists found synergy with the political, social, and economic climate, and in the early 1990s pushed a style known as New Country into the national spotlight. New Country subsequently changed the look, sound, and class associations of country music permanently.

Urban Cowboys, Countrypolitan, and the Reagan Era

During the early 1980s, the cultural, political, and economic climates of the United States together fostered an environment in which country music became popular in mainstream culture. But the styles of country music that reached the wider audience were specifically those that had musical ties to other genres, notably rock and pop. The most popular of these styles continued in the vein of the smooth, pop-crossover Nashville sound from the 1960s, which had been incubating throughout the 1970s and emerged as the dominant sound of mainstream country in the late 1970s; we will call it countrypolitan (see essay on Countrypolitan). As this style of country music crossed over into mainstream American culture, it left behind many of the distinctive elements that had always been associated with its working-class and rural origins. Instead, it fused country with aspects of pop, dance music, and especially disco, which turned into a national craze in those years. Countrypolitan offered its listeners a palatable style of pop music whose allegiance to country was primarily displayed in its political and sociological content rather than in its musical style. The style's widespread acceptance among pop audiences threatened the "otherness" of country music, and that, in turn, prompted the development of a new country style in reaction to it.

The four most significant aspects of country music from 1980 to the middle of the decade were:

1. The country-pop crossover strands of the genre that had existed since the late '50s became the main sound of country music, though only as a short-lived fad.
2. Country music mirrored the mainstream cultural, political, and economic trends in middle-class America.
3. Several country stars expanded their careers beyond the borders of country music while still maintaining an ostensibly "country" identity.
4. As the countrypolitan fad passed, the extremes to which it had fused with pop culture alienated more traditional fans and helped fuel a countermovement that would become the main focus and style of country music for the rest of the 1980s.

History and Rise of Crossover Country

Country music's appeal to mainstream audiences was already well known in the late 1970s. The initial forays into pop-crossover styles occurred in the late 1950s with the invention of the Nashville sound, when country music from stars such as Patsy Cline

303

and Jim Reeves became the dominant sound within the genre while simultaneously reaching successfully into the pop mainstream (see Chapter 6). From that time forward, crossover styles of country music had persisted, if not to the same extent as during the heyday of the early 1960s. Those styles had always been characterized by such features as sophisticated piano parts, silky-smooth backup vocalists, strings, carefully handled studio arrangements, and vocal performances that were resonant, polished, and devoid of the extreme nasal aspects of honky-tonk. Crossover artists and recordings appeared sporadically throughout the late 1960s and '70s, often raising the hackles of traditionalists. Stars such as Glen Campbell ("Galveston"), Lynn Anderson ("I Never Promised You a Rose Garden"), Olivia Newton-John ("I Honestly Love You"), and John Denver ("I'm Sorry") found success on country radio in the those years. Those stars made no secret of their mainstream success or pop credentials, nor in most cases did they claim any traditional country lineage. Regardless of those factors, their sheer commercial appeal and ability to sell records was both noticed and appreciated by the country music infrastructure. By the end of the 1970s, more and more singers were shifting into a pop-infused style, and singers such as Barbara Mandrell (see Artist Profile) who had already cultivated that style earned even more publicity.

From the historical vantage point, countrypolitan was an accumulation of developments that had been in the works for two decades. Three characteristics in the late 1970s differentiated countrypolitan from the pop-crossover styles that had come before:

COUNTRY MEETS COSMOPOLITAN

The term "countrypolitan" showed up in 1966 in a *New York Times* article where journalist Thomas Buckley offered satirical commentary regarding radio station WJRZ (located in Newark, New Jersey) switching to country music. In so doing, WJRZ provided New York City's country fans—whose mere existence surprised some commentators—with local access to the genre. The station manager described WJRZ's format as "countrypolitan," meaning they aired country records whose style was most palatable to a mainstream audience. Buckley defined the "countrypolitan sound" as a synonym for the "Nashville sound," which aimed to attract the "largest possibly number of listeners" with a "sleek," "commercial," and, he pointed out, "lily-white" music. In the journalist's wry assessment, the music was "a good deal less bothersome than the shrieking disc jockeys, bells, sirens, and dismal wails of the rock 'n' roll stations here."

The term, a combination of "country" and "cosmopolitan," refers to the upscale makeover that mainstream country music underwent beginning in the late 1950s. However, the term did not appear frequently until the early 1980s. Some historians have used it retrospectively to describe the continuum of pop-crossover country music from the late 1950s to the present, others have used it as a synonym for the Nashville sound, and still others have used it more specifically for 1970s and '80s crossover music. For our purposes, it is an excellent descriptor of an audibly recognizable style, that of the crossover country music that was popular from about 1977 to 1985 (the same era in which the term came into common usage) and that incorporated elements of pop, soft rock, and disco.

- The pop-crossover strands that had been overshadowed for more than a decade by more classic, outlaw, and traditional styles of country music came into the spotlight as the dominant sound of country music;
- A significant number of stars who had established their reputations in classic country and other more traditional styles switched into countrypolitan;
- Disco and popular dance music infiltrated countrypolitan, giving the crossover style a noticeably different sound than the crossover country from the Nashville sound era and early 1970s.

Pop Culture, the Cowboy, and the Country Boy

In the late 1970s, cowboy and country images became increasingly popular in mainstream culture. They showed up in popular television shows, movies, and pop music hits, and also as celebrities, all of which brought more attention to country music. Yet the images represented in the popular media tended to be more glamorous versions of cowboys and country icons, symbolized by the "star-spangled" rodeo celebrity whom Glen Campbell sang about in his 1975 crossover hit "Rhinestone Cowboy." Collectively, these images played up the heroic appeal of cowboys and country culture while deemphasizing the rural and working-class origins of those characters.

On television, the prime-time soap opera *Dallas*, which aired from 1978 until 1991, captured the public's imagination with tales of a wealthy Texan family. With their boots and cowboy hats, gorgeous women and ruggedly handsome men, the family portrayed in the show made all things Texan seem larger than life, more dramatic, and more enticing. The state was portrayed as a mythic place of money, wealth, and power within the American landscape. *Dallas* was the top-rated program on all of television from 1980 to 1982 and again from 1983 to 1984, according to Nielsen Media Research. Meanwhile, *The Dukes of Hazzard*, which aired from 1979 until 1985, amplified a Southern country-boy image as rugged, heroic, independent, and loyal, relying on his wits to outsmart the establishment. The show, set in rural Georgia, had strong associations with country music; Waylon Jennings wrote and sang the theme song, "Good Ol' Boys," and provided the voice-overs for narration. The show's soundtrack relied on country styles, including bluegrass. In 1980, the show placed second (behind only *Dallas*) in the Nielsen ratings, which meant that an enormous segment of the American audience was watching and had become fans of these iconic country images.

The main catalyst for country's early-'80s crossover trend was the movie *Urban Cowboy* (see essay on Country Music on the Silver Screen). The film hitched John Travolta's substantial star power to a seductive story about working-class country nightclubs, tantalizing and tawdry trailer-park romances, and mechanical bulls. For an audience already intrigued by the country images of cowboys, good ol' boys, Texas, and the heroic American strength they represented, the movie was a how-to manual: it suggested that fans, too, could find their inner cowboy even in an urban environment by heading down to their local honky-tonk or nightclub.

Figure 10-1 Urban Cowboy became the symbolic representative of country music in the early 1980s.

Source: Photo by Hulton Archive / Getty Images.

Public interest in country nightclubs and especially country dancing had been building for some time, partly as a result of the growing popularity of social dancing in general. In particular, the rise of disco in the 1970s had a palpable effect on the country fan scene. Disco emerged as dance music in underground urban clubs that catered to black and Latino fans, as well as those that were popular with the gay population, in the late 1960s and early '70s. By the middle of the decade, disco spread beyond those communities, especially in New York, and *Rolling Stone* reported on the genre in 1973. The dance styles in these nightclubs included both partner dancing and line dancing. In 1975, R&B producer, songwriter, and recording artist Van McCoy released the song "The Hustle," inspired by disco partner dancing. The song catapulted disco into the pop music spotlight. Two years later, the disco craze had become a mainstream fad. Discos emphasized a constructed glamour: dress codes and social convention led patrons to deck themselves out, and disco clubs overwhelmed the senses with their pulsating lights and throbbing beats from DJs who overlapped recordings so that the music never stopped. Disco—and, by extension, the dancing—took on the symbolic meaning of upward class mobility, putting glamour and glitz within reach of the working class. The movie *Saturday Night Fever* (1977), starring John Travolta and filmed in a Brooklyn discotheque, was built on that story line. By 1977—the year that Studio 54, the most famous of New York's discotheques, opened—disco tunes routinely crested on the pop charts and artists such as Donna Summer reigned over popular music.

Country musicians and country fans alike took an interest in disco, whose themes of upward mobility registered with a population who had been on that path—and had been singing about it—since the 1960s. Furthermore, country was one of the few genres in popular music where partner dancing (such as waltzing, two-stepping, and swing dancing, where a couple is in physical contact) was still practiced. Partner dancing was a common social activity in American middle-class culture until the rise of rock 'n' roll. During rock's reign in the 1960s, it had largely disappeared in many communities, but it remained a vital part of country honky-tonk and Texas dance hall culture. Thus, when disco brought partner dancing back into vogue in mainstream culture, the country fan scene was poised to jump on the bandwagon.

In the 1970s, two new developments occurred in the country fan scene that affected the music. The first was that cavernous nightclubs transferred traditional honky-tonk into an urban setting. Country singer Mickey Gilley, for instance, opened Gilley's in 1971 in Pasadena (near Houston). The second was that other country nightclub owners merged conventional honky-tonks with the upscale appeal and nightclub environment of disco, creating "country discos" where fans of country music could indulge in the glamour and sophistication of disco while remaining loyal to their preferred music. In 1979, for instance, Cowboy opened in Houston as a self-proclaimed "country disco," as did Diamond Jim's in Dallas, and both were joined by a half-dozen other such establishments within a matter of months. In these clubs, country fans danced two-steps, polkas, and schottisches under glittering disco balls, all partner dances that had a long tradition in the Southwest and that reflected the influence of immigrant communities, especially German and Czech (see Chapter 3), that had long contributed to Texas culture. The *New York Times* reported on the trend and quoted a fan in 1979: "It used to be you went to a disco or a standard country dump. . . . There was no such thing as a classy country place." Now there was.

Country dancing spread beyond the boundaries of the conventional country fan base in the wake of *Urban Cowboy*. In the early 1980s, readily available books and videotapes offered instructions on how to do a two-step, how to dress when going to a country nightclub, and how to experience firsthand the country dance culture fans had seen in the movie. These books and videotapes, along with the proliferation of urban country nightclubs and country discos, indicated that newcomers who needed these sorts of instructions were joining the country fan scene. Indeed, sales of country music picked up, and country singers became increasingly visible as movie stars and as hosts of their own television shows.

Urban Cowboy became the widely accepted label and shorthand for the era from the film's release until the mid-1980s. Fans and writers used it to refer both to the time period and to the urbanization of country themes, most notably the countrypolitan crossover style that was so prominent. Although countrypolitan was the most publicized style of country music in those years, many other musical styles were also present during the *Urban Cowboy* era, just as they were on the film's soundtrack.

Politics, Economics, and the Appeal of the Urban Cowboy

The rise in country music's appeal and in the popularity of country and cowboy images in mainstream culture accompanied a shift in politics during the first few years of Ronald Reagan's presidency. Throughout the 1970s and into the first years of the 1980s, the economic turmoil continued, resulting from the rise in oil prices, sky-high inflation, high unemployment, and destabilization of the nation's job infrastructure (see Chapter 8). A particularly bad recession occurred in 1981–1982. In 1980, Ronald Reagan was elected president. Reagan had starred in western films in the 1940s and hosted popular television series, including one about the Wild West and the frontier, in the 1950s and '60s. From his polished cowboy boots to his square-shouldered good looks, Reagan embodied the movie-star cowboy, and he metaphorically rode into the White House on a landslide. Reagan promised to fix the economy by revving the engines of capitalism through supply-side economics. This was a version of the historical American dream that trumpeted the strength of individuals unfettered by governmental restrictions or limitations. The rugged independence of the cowboy or country boy matched that vision. Over the next few years, his foreign policies emphasized good-guy versus bad-guy themes through an arms race (the Strategic Defense Initiative, for instance, announced in 1983), while the general population imagined the Soviet Union as an ever-looming threat against the core American way of life.

In this political and economic climate, country music came to represent the very essence of the American dream. Specific songs trumpeted the strength and resilience of the American worker (Alabama's "40 Hour Week [For a Livin']," or the Oak Ridge Boys' "American Made") and raw patriotism (Lee Greenwood's "God Bless the U.S.A."), both of which appealed to audiences who were looking for a musical version of these philosophical positions. In these ways, country music and mainstream national identity fused in the early 1980s in an unprecedented way.

The countrypolitan style was absolutely critical in country music's widespread acceptance. During these years, the general audience sought a musical representation of patriotism and pride in the American dream, but that vision included an upward mobility and modern outlook that did not align with earlier, roots-oriented country identities. Countrypolitan offered them the right philosophical outlook, while its infusion of disco and pop elements eliminated any unpalatable twang and made the music sound current and forward-looking.

New Media and Breaking Down Genre Borders

Both fans and musicians challenged the borders of country music—sometimes literal and sometimes figurative—during this era, and four specific developments pushed country into mainstream acceptance: first, country stars sought careers outside of the genre; second, country stars upgraded their appearances; third; country, along with most of pop culture, adopted some features of R&B; and fourth, music videos and television connected country with pop.

In a very literal sense, country's international reach expanded tremendously during the 1980s (see essay on International Country). But more locally, much of countrypolitan's success was because of performers crossing fluidly between genres. This trend had existed in the 1970s, most notably between country and rock music, when country singers discovered the large potential audiences in rock as well as the artistic freedom and economic rewards typically granted to them (see Chapter 9). As the 1970s progressed, a few country artists moved into the Las Vegas scene to take their stage shows to wider audiences, including Dolly Parton and Barbara Mandrell; others launched careers as actors in film and television, including Kris Kristofferson, Willie Nelson, and Parton. For the individual performers, these were opportunities to expand both their audiences and their creative output. But for country music as a genre, these changes further reduced any lines of demarcation between pop and country genres.

Another trend that pushed country music into its crossover period was that country stars consciously upgraded their images. As they reached larger and more mainstream audiences, their performance wardrobes changed, with sequined evening gowns for the women and suits or even the occasional jumpsuit without any western styling for the men, similar to the outfits of country stars in the early 1960s. Any cowboy imagery that did show up was of the glitzy Hollywood variety, and even the stage sets for the ubiquitous televised variety shows that featured country singers seldom indulged in the sort of folksy backdrops that had been the norm a decade earlier.

All of these developments gained additional momentum from mainstream pop culture's embrace of rhythm and blues (R&B) styles. Specifically, the decades-old genre divisions between country, pop, and R&B broke down in terms of the sound of the music, although the racial distinctions persisted, most notably country's whiteness. As previously discussed, disco and funk had infiltrated the public's imagination so that syncopated dance rhythms were appealing in any form. Stars such as Michael Jackson transformed what had been traditionally black styles such as Motown (from his performances with the Jackson Five) into mainstream pop (his *Thriller* album from 1982, for instance, sold three million copies). Country entertainers were not immune to these developments. In the Nashville studios, the electric bass had been used for more than a decade, but producers made it more prominent in the sonic mix; syncopated rhythms and dance beats appeared that were borrowed from other genres. And individual country singers including Barbara Mandrell, Willie Nelson, and Dolly Parton looked more frequently to R&B and pop to find songs. The same trend would lead to the Bee Gees (of disco fame) writing and producing "Islands in the Stream" in 1983 for Parton and Kenny Rogers (see Listening Guide). In summary, country music joined in a larger trend where popular culture was embracing disco, dance beats, and R&B in general.

New media outlets contributed to these border-hoppings and blendings across genres. In the early 1980s, music videos became an increasingly essential component in how popular music was marketed. MTV ("Music Television") launched in 1981, turning the visual depiction of a song into a core part of its success (or failure). Just two years later, Country Music Television (CMT) debuted as a country version of MTV, airing historical footage, promotional short videos of country songs, and newer music videos created especially for the new medium. The popularity of music videos meant

Listening Guide

"Islands in the Stream" (1983)

PERFORMERS:
Kenny Rogers and
Dolly Parton

SONGWRITERS:
Barry, Robin, and
Maurice Gibb

ORIGINAL ALBUM:
*Eyes that See in the
Dark (RCA 4697)*

FORM: Verse-
prechorus-chorus

STYLE:
Countrypolitan

"Islands in the Stream" encapsulates countrypolitan as a musical style, as a cultural phenomenon, and as representative of a period in American history, all in one very popular recording. The hit was the joint product of two established country stars; Rogers had started his career in pop music singing with First Edition, and Parton had dabbled in pop as a young teen recording for the Goldband label. The recording was also the product of songwriters and producers best known for their work in disco. The resulting song epitomized crossover success in the most extreme case, where country literally became the new pop music, or, from a different perspective, pop music invaded and devoured the country genre.

In the late 1970s, former rock band the Bee Gees found superstardom as a disco act. Born on the Isle of Mann, three brothers, Barry, Robin, and Maurice Gibb, grew up in Australia, then moved back to England, where their rock band picked up a large following in the late 1960s. In 1975, they moved to Miami and began working in the American scene, shifting their sound toward disco. Their manager contracted them to create a soundtrack in 1977 for a film about the disco scene, *Saturday Night Fever*. At the time, the Bee Gees had passed the peak of their popularity as performers, but almost overnight, "Stayin' Alive" and other hits from the film turned the Bee Gees into the hottest disco phenomenon in popular music.

By the early 1980s, both Rogers and Parton had won over the country fan base and already stylistically departed from classic country. Rogers's success with "The Gambler" (1978) marked his shift into a soft-rock style that was a key element in countrypolitan, and he branched out into television by starring in a movie based on the song. Parton had pulled disco influences into her music as early as 1977, and when she starred in *9 to 5*, she broadened her fan base far beyond the borders of country music. Thus, their collaboration with the Bee Gees in 1983 made perfect sense in the path of their own musical careers and at a time when disco, country, and pop were merging.

"Islands in the Stream" topped both *Billboard*'s country chart and the "Hot 100" chart. The song lacks any of the stereotypical markers of traditional country music in its lyrics, instrumentation, vocal styles, or musical structure. It boasts instead the main stylistic features of countrypolitan: strings, horns, synthesized sounds, an active and pop-style drum part, vocals that slip into a breathy sound at places, and rhythmic syncopation. It is also one of the earliest instances of a song form that uses a prechorus—a short, clearly delineated segment of the song that comes after the verse and that ramps up the energy for the chorus—which is a structural indicator of its pop influences (see Appendix A). The song has remained an easy-listening classic in the decades since its release. The Bee Gees added it to their set list in live performances nearly twenty years later, and eventually released their own version of it.

Fifteen years after its initial release, the song resurfaced with different lyrics as the chorus to a hip-hop collaboration between Pras, Mya, and Ol' Dirty Bastard, called "Ghetto Supastar (That Is What You Are)" (1998), which became an extremely popular remixed club dance track. Unlike most cover versions of country songs, which in some way refer back to the original in a culturally meaningful way, "Ghetto Supastar" simply extracts the rhyme scheme and musical ingredients of a catchy pop hit and uses them as the foundation to build a new song. That in itself is perhaps rich cultural commentary on the original song, its role in country music, and the style of countrypolitan in general.

TIME	FORM	LISTENING CUES	DISCUSSION
0:00	Intro		The horns, synthesizers, and drums all match the pop styles of the early 1980s.
0:09	Verse 1	"Baby, when I met you …"	Listen to the sustained synthesizer chords behind Rogers's singing.
0:28	Verse 2	"You do something to me …"	Dolly Parton enters here, singing harmony above Rogers's melody. A Rhodes piano (electric, synthesized keyboard sound) becomes apparent in this section.
0:48	Prechorus	"Tender love is blind …"	The presence of a prechorus ties this song to the pop scene, as this structure was basically unheard of in country prior to this time period.
1:06	Chorus	"Islands in the stream …"	The most significant musical feature in the chorus is syncopation, where the accents of the singers are purposely off the beat of the music.
1:32	Verse 3	"I can't live without you …"	Dolly Parton takes over singing lead. The song changes key from C major to A-flat major (a modulation) so that Parton can now sing the melody in a range that is comfortable for her. These sorts of structural changes mark the song as pop.
1:51	Verse 4	"But that won't happen …"	Rogers joins in, singing harmony under Parton's melody.
2:09	Prechorus	"No more will you cry …"	Parton's voice changes from a brassy belt sound to a breathy warble in the span of just one phrase, the sort of vocal technique that matches pop-rock stars of the early 1980s.
2:28	Chorus	"Islands in the stream …"	During each chorus in the song, back-up vocalists thicken the musical texture.
2:52	Instrumental interlude	trumpets	Both Rogers and Parton add interjections here, "Sail away," and "Oh, come sail away …"
3:11	Chorus	"Islands in the stream …"	Strings become very apparent during this chorus.
3:37	Chorus	"Islands in the stream …"	Parton varies the melody slightly here for interest.
4:02	Chorus	"Islands …"	After just a few seconds, the song fades out.

Listening Guide

"I Was Country (When Country Wasn't Cool)" (1981)

PERFORMER:
Barbara Mandrell

SONGWRITERS:
Kye Fleming and
Dennis Morgan

ORIGINAL ALBUM:
*Barbara Mandrell
Live* (MCA 5243,
1981)

FORM: Verse-chorus

STYLE:
Countrypolitan

"I Was Country (When Country Wasn't Cool)" represents the paradox of countrypolitan in many different ways. The first single from Mandrell's live album, it appeared about a year after the *Urban Cowboy* craze had swept in, bringing new fans to country music and calling into question aspects of tradition in country music. The more pop-crossover sounds of countrypolitan became prevalent, the more fans and artists alike reaffirmed that this was, in their perception, still country music in the same traditions and with the same values as decades earlier.

For Mandrell, this song became her way of staking claim to being a "real" country singer, as determined by the codes of tradition that were part of the genre. The lyrics spoke of her childhood memories of culturally specific Southern and redneck traditions, from fashion (straight-leg Levis) to food (peanuts in her Coke) to favorites (the Opry and George Jones). The song called to mind a time when country music and, by extension, country fans, were treated as uncool outsiders by mainstream pop culture. It offered a way to reconcile country's newfound mainstream popularity and coolness with the way that country music had always relied on being marginalized, and actually valued that as a source of fierce pride. Now it was OK for country music to be popular and cool, the song suggests, because country music and country singers had not changed—they were holding fast to their traditional roots—even though the rest of popular culture had come over to join them.

George Jones's guest appearance on this recording had two effects. The obvious was an endorsement of Mandrell by one of the most respected country patriarchs, who represented the continuation of the honky-tonk tradition to his fans. But his participation also brought him into the new crossover spotlight, offering him exposure among the pop-country fans and newer listeners to countrypolitan, and simultaneously and subtly introducing those fans—who had fully embraced Mandrell—to Jones.

In spite of the song's apparent autobiographical nature and personal, confessional tone, it was the product of a professional songwriting team who were riding a wave of late-'70s countrypolitan hits when they crafted this one. Dennis Morgan and Kye Fleming, one of only a handful of successful female country songwriters from that era, scored their first success with "Sleepin' Single in a Double Bed" in 1978, shortly after both arrived in Nashville. By the early 1980s, the two were routinely winning the top awards in the songwriting industry and had made names for themselves with catchy lyrics about more traditional country topics set to music that melded effortlessly with the pop-crossover, hook-centered recordings that were in vogue. Both Morgan and Fleming also had a number of hits far outside the country genre, with artists ranging from Rod Stewart to Tina Turner. But with this particular song, they captured perfectly the essence of the countrypolitan era: lyrics that made overt claims on country traditions, packaged in a song that sounded entirely palatable to a noncountry listener. Note that the phrase which is both the title and hook ("I was country when country wasn't cool") saturates the song, appearing at the end of every verse and at both the beginning and end of the chorus.

The live elements of the recording—specifically, the crowd noise at the beginning, in the middle when George Jones enters, and at the end—have two major effects on the audience. The first is to invite the listeners to imagine that they, too, are hearing this testimonial about country tradition directly from Mandrell's own mouth, conveying the sense of a live concert setting where the singer is communicating directly to the listener and helping to mask the packaged and constructed nature of the recording. The second is to present not just Mandrell's and Jones's voices as the people who are laying claim to this country tradition, but rather a host of voices, all cheering loudly in affirmation of the same ideas. The crowd noise suggests that all the listeners are part of the "in" crowd of country fans who have been authentically country all along. As country crossed further into the mainstream culture during the early 1980s, and as the music became saturated with pop sounds, that sense of community became increasingly important as a means of preserving country as a genre.

TIME	FORM	LISTENING CUES	DISCUSSION
0:00	Intro	crowd noise, then the introduction begins at 0:04	The crowd noise creates a setting where Mandrell is literally communicating directly to her present, live listeners.
0:12	Verse 1	"I remember wearing . . ."	The first-person narration connects the song to Mandrell, even though she didn't write it. The Opry, mentioned in opposition to rock 'n' roll and R&B, is the most significant reference in this verse, although she also mentions singing cowboy star Roy Rogers.
0:49	Verse 2	"I remember circlin' . . ."	Note the foreshadowing in mentioning George Jones's name.
1:26	Chorus	"Ooh, I was country when . . ."	Right before this chorus, a soprano saxophone appears prominently in the band. Note that the backup singers' "Aah" and "Ooh" provide a smooth, pop sound behind Mandrell.
2:02	Instrumental verse (half)	electric guitar	Note the prominence of synthesized sounds and saxophone in this section, which forms the first half of the third verse.
2:21	Verse 3 (half)	"They called us country bumpkins . . ."	Mandrell enters in the middle of this verse, taking over from the instrumental solos. The lyrics pick up on major themes in country music: patriotism (specifically praising individual freedom of expression in America) and the way that country differentiates itself from mainstream pop by highlighting how a country identity has been "othered" or marginalized (through such labels as "country bumpkins").
2:39	Chorus	"Hey, I was country . . ."	George Jones enters, with the crowd cheering his arrival. At 2:58, Mandrell joins him in a duet, and they affirm the idea that "being country" requires consistency in both action and appearance.
3:16	Tag/Outro	"Yeah, I was country . . ."	The crowd's approval and applause are kept on the recording, so the listener hears, in effect, a crowd endorsing and agreeing with Mandrell's lyrics.

Figure 10-2
Producer George Martin, best known for his work with the Beatles, and singer Kenny Rogers in the studio; Martin produced an album for Rogers in 1985.

Source: Courtesy BenCar Archives.

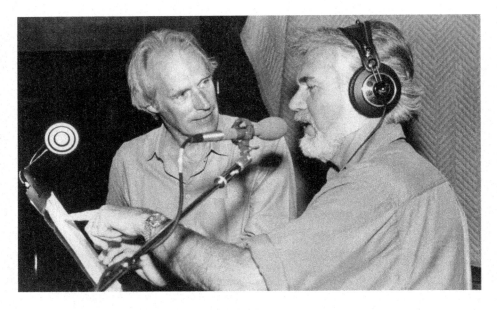

ARTIST PROFILE

Ronnie Milsap (1943–)

onnie Milsap's career offers a great illustration of how countrypolitan fits into the more general development of popular music in the 1970s and 80s. He started his professional musical career in R&B, then moved to Nashville in 1972 at the urging of producer Chips Moman, whose career had encompassed early rock 'n' roll and Elvis's later recordings. He situated himself in country music by simply shifting into the style, rather than weaving any sort of personal biography into his claim of being a country singer. His number-one country hits started in 1974, and by the end of the '80s, he had piled up 35 in all.

From Robbinsville, North Carolina, Milsap was blind from birth. Like most youth of his generation, he grew up on the rock 'n' roll of the 1950s, then shifted to the R&B and soul styles of the 1960s. In the meantime, he learned to play the piano, and worked at times as a session musician in recording studios. In 1972, as classic country was in full flourish and the

musical excesses of countrypolitan were starting to sneak into the music, Milsap moved to Nashville and inserted himself in country music.

His early country hits were all classic country in style, matching the core of what Conway Twitty, Kenny Rogers, and George Jones were doing during these years. His R&B roots were still present, as in "What A Difference You've Made in My Life," where he stops singing toward the end, calling out fragments of text while the backup singers sing the whole chorus, full gospel-style. Over time, those crossover aspects of his performances became more prominent. And as the 1980s loomed on the horizon, Milsap shifted his sound to more strings, more heavy-handed arrangements, and the pop grooves that he had absorbed from his days performing R&B.

The shift paid off: between 1980 and 1982, Milsap had ten of his songs in a row reach number one on the *Billboard* country charts, including "Smoky Mountain Rain" (1980) and "Any Day Now" (1982), by pop songwriters Burt Bacharach that country stars were under increased pressure to look good in performance, rather than just sound good. Audiences saw pop and country videos effectively juxtaposed, which motivated the country music industry to make sure their product appeared as polished, professional, sophisticated, and appealing to a general audience as possible.

The Stars and Songs of Urban Cowboy

The stars during the *Urban Cowboy* era brought a range of backgrounds and identities to country music, several of which we will consider briefly in turn.

1. Established pop-crossover singers enjoyed even greater success when countrypolitan gained popularity; these include Anne Murray, Ronnie Milsap, Eddie Rabbitt, and Barbara Mandrell.
2. A spate of newcomers arrived on the scene, along with a few singers who had not found much commercial success in the previous years, including Juice Newton, Janie Fricke, Sylvia, Crystal Gayle, and the most successful of all the 1980s performers, the band Alabama.

and Bob Hilliard. "Smoky Mountain Rain" was quintessential countrypolitan; its lyrics are full of references to country signifiers like hitchhiking, truck drivers, the Smoky Mountains, and heartache. The musical setting, however, consists of soft-rock drums and bass, syncopated piano parts, soaring washes of strings, surging textures, and chord progressions that used harmonies outside the country vocabulary. Like most countrypolitan singers, Milsap did not write his own songs. "Smoky Mountain Rain" was by Kye Fleming and Dennis Morgan, the same pair who wrote other Milsap hits such as "I Wouldn't Have Missed It for the World" as well as "I Was Country (When Country Wasn't Cool)" for Barbara Mandrell (see Listening Guide). As had been the case in the 1960s, a relatively small pool of professional songwriters, of whom Fleming and Morgan were a part, were the creative engine behind most of the music.

Many of his most prestigious industry awards came in the 1970s, when he was performing in between classic country and early countrypolitan. But his lasting impact on the genre was the string of early '80s recordings. Milsap never built the same level of fan commitment that some of his

Figure 10-3 Ronnie Milsap, in 2012, seated at a piano with a vocal mic in front of him, which is where he has spent nearly five decades as a musician.
Source: ZUMA Press, Inc./Alamy Stock Photo.

contemporaries did, leaving him further from the spotlight in recent years. But his ability to show up in Nashville, from an R&B musical past, and forge a place for himself in country helps explain how countrypolitan was an era focused on stylized performances laced with connections to the R&B and pop sounds

3. Some country singers who persisted with styles other than countrypolitan, including Conway Twitty, T. G. Sheppard, Emmylou Harris, and those with a country-rock hybrid sound, especially Charlie Daniels and Hank Williams, Jr.
4. Two stars in particular, Willie Nelson and Dolly Parton, navigated through countrypolitan with dual identities as definitively country singers but at the same time mainstream entertainers

Among those who had been successful for some time were Canadian singer Anne Murray (1945–). Murray's career epitomized the *Urban Cowboy* era. She was initially received as a pop singer whose songs routinely crossed into the country charts. In the

---

ARTIST PROFILE

Barbara Mandrell (1948–)

Barbara Mandrell is one of the most highly regarded entertainers and vocalists in all of country music. The peak of her career came at the height of countrypolitan, and her style was heavily inflected by R&B and soul music, both of which have heavily colored the way she is remembered within country music.

Born December 25, 1948, in Houston, Texas, Mandrell grew up in Southern California in a musical family. By age ten, she was already quite accomplished as a pedal steel guitar player, and within a few years she mastered several other instruments, including saxophone and banjo. Her father took her to Chicago to perform at a music trade show, where she impressed Chet Atkins and West Coast honky-tonk star Joe Maphis, among others. A string of television appearances followed, and in 1962 Johnny Cash hired her as part of his touring act, which also included Patsy Cline and George Jones. After the tour, Mandrell's father assembled a family band, in which she gained additional stage experience.

In 1969, she signed with Columbia Records, working with producer Billy Sherrill (who was largely responsible for Tammy Wynette's sound). With Sherrill, Mandrell had her first charting single, "I've Been Loving You Too Long (to Stop Now)," which had been a huge hit for African American soul star Otis Redding. Throughout the early 1970s, Mandrell scored several hits with the formula of Sherrill's Nashville sound accompaniment and R&B-inflected vocals.

Mandrell switched to Dot records in 1975, working with producer Tom Collins. Her basic sound stayed the same, but as the trends in country music moved toward the pop-crossover styles in which Mandrell specialized, her popularity surged. She continued to draw on soul music, covering songs such as "Woman to Woman" (a soul hit for Shirley Brown, which Mandrell took to number four on the country charts) and "(If Loving You Is Wrong) I Don't Want to Be Right" (a soul hit for Luther Ingram and several other singers, which earned Mandrell her second number one country recording). By the early 1980s, Mandrell was at the absolute top of country music stardom, touring extensively and routinely scoring top ten country hits, many of which also crossed over onto the pop charts. The Country Music Association awarded her the title of "Entertainer of the Year" twice in a row. In 1980, she and her sisters launched a television show on NBC that ran for two years, after which she starred in a Las

late 1970s, however, she scored number one country hits with songs such as "I Just Fall in Love Again" (1979), and became known more as a country singer whose songs happened to have crossover appeal in the pop market. Her vocal performances were entirely devoid of any Southern accent and featured a cultivated, carefully controlled and polished sound, backed by sophisticated studio arrangements.

Of the country artists who were already stars before the *Urban Cowboy* era, Barbara Mandrell was unquestionably the most significant (see Artist Profile and Listening Guide). Eddie Rabbitt (1941–1998) similarly had built a career with pop-crossover country for years, then capitalized on the whole countrypolitan trend even more with hits such as "Step by Step" (1981).

Vegas stage production. She also ventured into gospel, with an inspiration-themed album that won a Grammy. Throughout the countrypolitan era, Mandrell represented the most extreme version of bespangled, crossover country-pop performances with her long, sequined evening gowns and an image that denied any down-home country associations.

Mandrell's career was interrupted by a car accident in 1984 in which she was severely injured. By the time she returned to performing and recording a year later, the country music landscape had shifted toward the neotraditionalist style (see Chapter 11), and Mandrell's countrypolitan sound was no longer in demand. Her popularity began to wane, although she tried to fit into the new trends with a cover of an old Bakersfield shuffle classic by Harlan Howard, "I Wish That I Could Fall in Love Today." The effort succeeded in the short term, but by the early 1990s Mandrell was no longer part of the commercial scene. She shifted most of her attention to an acting career, with numerous guest appearances on television shows and the occasional made-for-TV movie, essentially retiring from recording and full-time touring.

Although she has enjoyed over four decades in the country music business, Mandrell's main contributions were the soul-infused countrypolitan that became so popular in the late 1970s and

Figure 10-4 Barbara Mandrell.
Source: Southern Folklife Collection, Wilson Library, The University of North Carolina at Chapel Hill.

defined commercial country for the first half of the 1980s. Her talent as a virtuosic instrumentalist and vocalist has earned her respect from critics and colleagues in spite of her crossover countrypolitan style, which has drawn the ire of staunch traditionalist country fans.

Other singers were relative newcomers to the country spotlight. Juice Newton (1952–), for instance, and Janie Fricke (or Frickie, as she was sometimes identified; 1947–) both launched their careers in the late 1970s when the tide was already turning toward countrypolitan. Stars such as Fricke who followed that career path presented very different biographies to the country audience than had the stars a decade earlier. For stars such as Loretta Lynn and Dolly Parton, their traditional country "roots"—where and how they were raised, who their family was, religion, poverty, and the country singers they idolized—had been essential in establishing their credibility and role within country music. In contrast, Newton and Fricke's generation of countrypolitan singers seldom marketed themselves by their biographies. During the *Urban Cowboy* era, fans paid far less attention to the characteristics by which previous generations of fans had weighed a country star's personal authenticity, partly because the fan base itself had changed in all the ways discussed above. Similarly, Sylvia (born Sylvia Jane Kirby, 1956–), Marie Osmond, and Crystal Gayle (1951–) were quite bold in claiming their status as simultaneous country and pop stars. Gayle, who is Loretta Lynn's younger sister by nearly two decades, cultivated a particularly pop-influenced stage presence, and on hits such as "Too Many Lovers" (1981), Gayle rocked syncopated vocals over heavy electric piano and pop-dance beats. Her biggest hit, "Don't It Make My Brown Eyes Blue" (1977) was simultaneously a country song, a soft-rock ("adult contemporary," in *Billboard's* categorization) song, and a pop song—appearing on three charts. Sylvia, on hits such as "Drifter" (1981) and "Nobody" (1982), pulled out the full arsenal of pop sound effects for her music.

A few singers' careers were the direct result of the movie *Urban Cowboy's* success. Johnny Lee (1946–), for instance, sang the soft-rock influenced theme song, "Lookin' for Love," in the film. Lee then parlayed that song's popularity into a string of country hits for himself in the early 1980s, but by the middle of the decade, his success was on the wane.

Both the band Alabama and Lee Greenwood (1942–) also arrived on the country music scene at the dawn of the *Urban Cowboy* era and rode the countrypolitan wave for nearly a decade. In the case of Alabama, the band's soft-rock approach to country music led to an astounding run of twenty-one singles in a row that reached the top of the country charts; they were, quite simply, the dominant sound of country radio during the *Urban Cowboy* era, and their style of country music was hand-in-hand the essence of countrypolitan: lyrics that reference country themes such as working-class identity ("Forty Hour Week [For a Livin']"), traditional country music ("If You're Gonna Play in Texas [You Gotta Have a Fiddle in the Band]," "Mountain Music"), heartbreak ("Lady Down on Love"); a rock band's rhythm section; chords and musical settings that bridge Southern rock and soft rock; and an updated, pop image. Lee Greenwood, originally from Sacramento, California, had been working as a pop singer in Las Vegas when, in 1981, he was offered a country record contract. That the audience not only accepted but actually embraced such recordings as "Somebody's Gonna Love You" (1983), saturated in electric piano and breathy vocals, is indicative of how the fans' concept of country music had changed in the *Urban Cowboy* era, and equally indicative of how the country fan base itself was no longer the same as it had been a decade prior.

Countrypolitan was not the only style on country radio or within the core of country music during the early 1980s. Some stars, including Conway Twitty and T. G. Sheppard (1944–), kept a more classic country sound in their recordings even as they continued to reach the top of the charts. Twitty's "Red Neckin' Love Makin' Night" (1981) and "Tight Fittin' Jeans" (1981) both stuck with stalwart, traditional country references in their lyrics and in their musical settings, while his vocals toyed with the twang of earlier decades. Sheppard, with hits such as "Do You Want to Go to Heaven" (1980), was a throwback to the classic country sounds with expressive vocals who still sounded like a genuine honky-tonk singer. Yet even Twitty and Sheppard incorporated a few of the pop trends in their musical arrangements. And Emmylou Harris even recorded a bluegrass album in 1980, a stark contrast to the country rock she had done and the country she would sing later that decade.

Country stars with Southern rock credibility, most notably Charlie Daniels and Hank Williams Jr. (see Chapter 9), had stellar successes during these years, with music that made no concessions to the countrypolitan trends. Instead, they stuck to the Southern rock hybrid of country music that was fully at home in live performances and honky-tonk venues. That sound had been richly represented in the movie *Urban Cowboy*, which featured the music of not only Charlie Daniels but also blues-rocker Bonnie Raitt (who also appeared on screen) and Jimmy Buffett in his more country-roots mode. In the early 1980s, the occasional anthem from Hank Williams Jr., such as "All My Rowdy Friends (Have Settled Down)" (1981), on the country charts and radio stations certainly helped balance out the waves of countrypolitan; that song also acknowledged in its lyrics that times had changed.

The two most interesting careers throughout this period were unquestionably those of Willie Nelson and Dolly Parton. Nelson, who had been one of the mainstays of the outlaw movement (see Chapter 9), had already captured a large audience in the rock genre and through his forays into Hollywood. He capitalized on that fame by stretching the boundaries of country music even further during the *Urban Cowboy* era. Unlike other singers whose style changed to a pop-crossover countrypolitan sound, Nelson kept his sparse, outlaw sound and explored jazz and pop standards from many decades earlier (albums such as *Somewhere Over the Rainbow* and *Always on My Mind*). Nelson's popularity translated into huge sales numbers: *Always on My Mind* (1982), for instance, sold over three million copies. Nelson also ventured into collaborations and duets that fell further afield from country, most famously "To All the Girls I've Loved Before" with Latin music sensation Julio Iglesias. The song was a major pop hit and matched what was happening with countrypolitan.

Dolly Parton (see Chapter 8), like Nelson, had already expanded her career beyond the borders of country music before the *Urban Cowboy* era arrived, and she simply continued in those same directions. She had changed producers in the late 1970s and covered songs from the R&B and pop traditions. By the time she starred in *9 to 5*, her music was already drenched in the countrypolitan style that was about to become the mainstay of country music. From the saxophone solo at the opening of "Single Women" (1981) to her recording of "Starting Over Again" (1980), a song by disco queen Donna Summers, or the disco jam "Baby, I'm Burning" (1978), Parton was entirely immersed in a pop-crossover sound.

Listening Guide

"Love in the First Degree" (1981)

PERFORMERS:
Alabama

SONGWRITERS: Tim
DuBois and Jim Hurt

ORIGINAL ALBUM:
Feels So Right (RCA
AHL1 - 3930)

FORM: Verse-chorus

STYLE:
Countrypolitan

In the early 1970s, Randy Owen, Teddy Gentry, and Jeff Cook—three cousins from Fort Payne, Alabama—decided to turn music making into a full-time job for themselves. They eventually settled on Alabama as a band name, and spent the rest of the decade playing clubs across the Southeast, honing a version of country music that was heavily indebted to the easy-listening sounds of the Eagles and country rock (see Chapter 8) as well as the more classic country vocal harmonies of groups such as the Oak Ridge Boys (see Chapter 9). With their propensity for live performances in rowdy clubs, the band also picked up some of the stage presence of the Southern rock acts from that era, most visible in their incorporation of the Confederate "Stars and Bars" flag in their logo and album covers in the 1980s. After a few short-lived contracts with small record labels and several years of managing their own promotion and marketing, Alabama signed with RCA records in 1980. By then, they were a seasoned road band who had already had a few modest successes.

With a major record contract, Alabama began churning out number one hits with a musical formula that combined token elements of country music with pop music, the basic approach that was sweeping country music in the early 1980s. Their close vocal harmony, smooth lead vocals, and liberal use of strings, keyboards, and rock beats fit perfectly into the country scene in the wake of *Urban Cowboy*. Even their musical choices matched that profile. The songwriters for their fifth number one single, "Love in the First Degree," were Jim Hurt and Tim DuBois. Hurt had spent many years in the music industry working as a demo singer and songwriter for both country and pop music, although his leanings were more toward the pop side of things. DuBois, an accountant and sometime university professor, had come to Nashville to pursue songwriting, and quickly slid into the role of staff writer for a major publishing firm. The musical characteristics of the song, most notably the rhythmic patterns, the instrumentation, and the chord progression, are a sharp departure from the classic country of Nashville in the early 1970s.

Like a high percentage of countrypolitan hits, "Love in the First Degree" is an upbeat song built on a clever lyric hook, in this case, wordplay on the "crime" of love, laced throughout with phrases such as "baby" and "oh yeah." None of the prominent signifiers of country music from past decades (such as names of places, clues about social class, employment, wardrobe, lifestyle, etc.) are audible in this song, one of the reasons why this and so many other hits from the countrypolitan era also scored well on the *Billboard* pop charts (number fifteen, in this particular case). Nonetheless, within the context of the early 1980s, this was indeed mainstream country music, and was widely accepted as such by both newer fans and many of the older fans of country, who saw the music simply developing in lockstep with modern life.

TIME	FORM	LISTENING CUES	DISCUSSION
0:00	Intro	electric guitars, electric bass, and drums	The extreme use of stereo separation (different sounds in the left and right speakers), the echo of the drums, and the click-track that emphasizes a steady, pop rhythm all mark this as 1980s countrypolitan.
0:05	Verse 1	"I once thought of love …"	The song's topic is a metaphoric interpretation of love as a crime, in which the perpetrator confesses his guilt.
0:23	Verse 2	"But you came, and I was …"	The band adds more guitar sounds here, thickening the musical texture.
0:42	Chorus	"Baby, you left me defenseless …"	Notice the strings that enter at the start of the chorus and continue to fill out the recording's sound. The band stops briefly ("stop-time") behind the song's title and hook. Alabama was known for their three-part vocal harmony, which is on clear display here.
1:05	Interlude	ringing chord on the guitar	
1:10	Verse 3	"I thought it would be so simple …"	An electric piano sound comes in at this point (audible at 1:14), which adds to the 1980s pop sound. Many of the sounds in this recording are synthesized rather than created by acoustic instruments, another feature of early 1980s pop.
1:28	Verse 4	"Now, babe, I'm not beggin' …"	Listen to the buildup, especially in the drums, at 1:45, that announces the arrival of the chorus.
1:47	Chorus	"Baby, you left me defenseless …"	In each chorus, the drums and bass pick up another 1980s pop rhythm: the Scotch snap, which sounds like a quick "ba-bump" rhythm at the start of each bar (a very short note right before the downbeat, then repeated on the downbeat).
2:10	Extension	"Love in the first degree …"	This is a little extension of the chorus that acts at first like a tag, but then launches another repetition of the chorus. Notice the vocal interjections, "Oh yeah," which again add a common pop-music element.
2:19	Chorus	"Baby, you left me defenseless …"	The chord progression in the chorus is atypical for traditional country music.
2:43	Tag	"Love in the first degree …"	Here, the band repeats the same music over and over behind the title of the song, setting it up for easy use on the radio, where DJs like fade-out endings.

Country songwriting in the *Urban Cowboy* era was drastically different than it had been in previous decades. Not only did the songs rely more heavily on short, catchy hooks or rhythmic patterns to appeal to the listeners, but they also used chord progressions (modal mixture, flat-side harmonies such as bVII and bIII, extended harmonies, modulations, etc.) and even song forms and patterns that had not been part of traditional country music. Country singers increasingly looked to songwriters who had specialized in both pop and R&B to find new material. Even after *Urban Cowboy* was long past, many of the changes in country songwriting stuck around.

The End of Urban Cowboy

For about a half decade, countrypolitan recordings and performances dominated country music. During this time, country sales expanded dramatically and country stars became both part of mainstream pop music and fixtures on television shows. Country music's share of the market for all music jumped substantially from 1980 to about 1983, when countrypolitan and the whole *Urban Cowboy* phenomenon sold lots of records. The expansion came at a price, however. One such cost was that the newfound country audience—from a different background and different socio-economic identity—was not as invested in ideas of tradition and the history of the genre, so they were not particularly troubled by the notion that country music had merged with pop. Thus, country music's commercial success further threatened its very existence as a distinct genre. Furthermore, the growth in the genre's popularity was largely the result of fad interests in a few cultural icons; as with all fads, this one was short-lived, and a drop in sales and popularity was inevitably on the horizon.

Meanwhile, more traditionally minded country singers and fans alike were dissatisfied with the countrypolitan style and the general direction in which country music had moved. Those fans wanted to hear music that was reminiscent of the older styles of country that they valued. Some country singers were in fact already making that sort of music, especially outside of Nashville. Texas and the West Coast both housed music scenes that nurtured younger performers playing older styles of country music.

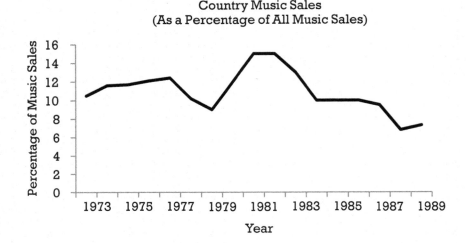

Figure 10-5 The market share of country music, according to data from the Recording Industry Association of America, showing a sharp increase from 1980 to 1983 during the countrypolitan fad.

The end of the *Urban Cowboy* era came on quite suddenly in the mid-1980s. Pop music moved away from country music, and the audience for country shrank rapidly. The national news media announced that country was in a decline, most famously in a *New York Times* article in 1985; sales plummeted; crossover hits became less common. Those stars who had built their careers with countrypolitan found their careers fading. Others, with a longer history in country music or more flexibility in their sound, changed styles once again to more traditional fare. In their wake, a new generation of stars emerged who had a radically different outlook on country music and eschewed the pop-crossover success that had come with countrypolitan. Yet this sudden and dramatic shift toward the more traditional styles of country music—whose stars were known as neotraditionalists (see Chapter 11)—was partly the result of countrypolitan and the whole *Urban Cowboy* era, which acted as its foil. Thus, in a strangely ironic way, the pop-crossover trends of the early 1980s, which tied together cultural, political, and economic forces into the countrypolitan fad, ended up propelling country music back toward its more traditional, twang-centered roots.

MAKING SENSE OF COUNTRYPOLITAN AS COUNTRY

It is easy and sometimes tempting for fans today to look back at the countrypolitan recordings and simply dismiss them as "not really country." That attitude misrepresents both the music and country as a genre. In order to understand countrypolitan as country music, one might recognize that a large part of the country audience—meaning people who described themselves as "country fans"—in the early 1980s heard in this music the same meaning and significance that other styles of country had had in previous decades. In the musical landscape of those years, the artists and recordings we now label as countrypolitan were indeed the country music of their day. When we look back in time, we weigh those recordings against what we know came later, or what we contrast it with what was happening in small Texas roadhouse honky-tonks and other places not on the commercial radar during the same years. But most of the country audience of the early 1980s had neither of those perspectives, and, many of them liked the commercial country music they were hearing and buying. Thus, it is not productive for purposes of our studies to try to label the music as country or not. Rather, we can try to understand how those recordings were part of the larger history of the genre, what their impact was, and how their audiences interpreted and valued them.

⋆ **ESSAY: MUSICAL STYLE**

 # Countrypolitan

Although the term "countrypolitan" has been used in some contexts to describe any country music with crossover appeal, we will use it to refer to the specific sound (musical style) of crossover country music that gained popularity during the mid- to late 1970s and became the mainstream country sound in the early 1980s. Its main musical characteristics include:

- Loud drums, electric bass, and additional percussion such as hand-claps, shakers, and tambourines
- Musical interjections from horns (trumpets, etc.), saxophones, electric guitars, and sometimes special-effects noises
- Strings that fill in the overall sonic landscape, along with smooth backup singers
- Electric piano, organ, and synthesizers
- Minimal use (and sometimes elimination) of traditional country fiddles and steel guitars
- Rhythmic grooves that rely on steady eighth notes and rock beats, along with lots of syncopation
- Lots of reverb and echo
- Chord progressions that extend far beyond the traditional patterns of classic country

The music revealed a strong influence from rhythm and blues, with a number of songs even borrowed straight from that genre. During the early 1980s, disco, pop, rock, and country all shared more musical characteristics than they had in the past or than they would a few years later. Even with this intersection of genres, one distinctive feature that allowed listeners to still differentiate among genres was the vocal performances: Southern accents and lyrics about traditionally country themes still appeared on the country recordings. Countrypolitan hits—like those in other early-'80s pop, R&B, and disco styles—involved significant sonic manipulation in the recording studio. Producers incorporated heavy reverberation and other special effects, careful layering of many instruments, and creative stereophonic mixing into the albums and singles. While one can find countrypolitan recordings with sad lyrics about heartbreak, drinking, and life's misery, there was also a strong trend toward more upbeat songs, both in their musical arrangements and in the topics of their lyrics, that matched the dance-friendly and pop-crossover character of the style.

✫ ESSAY: CULTURE

 # Country Music on the Silver Screen

Hollywood has long been fascinated by country music. Some movies have treated country music with great sympathy and affection; others have subjected it to mockery or satire; many have used it symbolically to represent various aspects of American culture. But regardless of the approach, movies about country music have had profound effects on the ways fans think about country music.

Most of the movies to use country music in the 1930s and '40s were westerns. The impact of the westerns was profound; they literally changed the sounds and images of country music (see Chapter 3). Along with the best-known singing cowboys such as Gene Autry and Roy Rogers, western swing musicians such as Bob Wills cultivated successful movie careers in those films—Wills and his band, for instance, were featured in over a dozen films in which Wills both acted and sang or fiddled with a band. Honky-tonk singer Faron Young also appeared in an outlaw-themed western in the mid-1950s. Other than the westerns, there were a few films during those years that centered on the institutions and traditions of country music. In 1940, for instance, Republic Pictures released *Grand Ole Opry*, a movie with a lighthearted plot that was mostly a chance to showcase Opry stars, including Roy Acuff and his Smoky Mountain Boys.

In the 1960s, movies began to make more frequent use of country music in their soundtracks, and many of the cultural associations that are still around today stem from those films. Bluegrass gained widespread exposure through the television shows and, subsequently, movies, especially *Bonnie and Clyde* (1967) and *Deliverance* (1972) (see Chapter 5). In the 1970s, classic country gained wide exposure through the soundtracks for truckin' films such as *Smokey and the Bandit* (1977) and its sequels, as well as *Convoy* (1978). Television shows including *The Dukes of Hazzard* (which began in 1979) certainly contributed on these fronts.

Hollywood had a greater impact on country music in the late 1970s and early 1980s, when several movies appeared that focused specifically on country music and country music venues. The earliest of these was also the most controversial: director Robert Altman's *Nashville* (1975) offered biting political satire and a cynic's view of the country music industry. Although it won rave reviews from critics, it alienated the country music establishment and reinforced the distance between country music and mainstream popular culture. A few years later, Loretta Lynn's biopic, *Coal Miner's Daughter* (1980), celebrated the themes that were most deeply embedded in country music's themes: a rags-to-riches story of self-made success, the triumph of talent, and loyalty to family and tradition. Later biopics such as *Sweet Dreams* (1985), about Patsy Cline, and the acclaimed *Walk the Line* (2005), about Johnny Cash, have similarly spread the legendary biographies of country singers to new generations of fans.

Also in 1980, John Travolta starred in *Urban Cowboy*, which had a substantial effect on country music. The plot was based on an article that journalist Aaron Latham published about cowboy culture transplanted into an urban nightclub. Travolta had recently become a pop-culture sensation through his performance in *Saturday Night Fever*, and *Urban Cowboy* artfully combined a country soundtrack, onscreen appearances by several musicians, and a seductive storyline of a good old boy triumphing over a hardened villain. The soundtrack featured a range of country styles, from honky-tonk twang to the rock-infused country of Charlie Daniels and Jimmy Buffet, bluegrass, and a hefty dose of smooth, crossover countrypolitan. The movie showed lots of two-stepping scenes, which affected the fan base's interest in country dancing. More recently, *O Brother, Where Art Thou* (2000) also had a catalytic effect on the country music fan base and industry, but with a slightly different outcome from *Urban Cowboy*; *O Brother* contributed to a roots revival within the genre (see Chapter 14) rather than a pop-crossover phenomenon, although in both cases, the movie brought a new audience into some form of country music.

Over the course of the 1980s and into the 1990s, quite a few movies centered on issues of authenticity in country music, with plots that revolved around so-called real country music presented as intrinsically better than some artificial imitation. In these instances, good country music is portrayed as coming from a performer's personal rural experiences and from eschewing the commercial aspects of the genre. Dolly Parton, for instance, turned Sylvester Stallone into a "real" country singer in *Rhinestone* (1984) by taking him home to a farm, where homemade biscuits and daily chores instilled the desired authenticity. A far better movie that played on the same themes was *Tender Mercies* (1983), in which Robert Duvall traded in his life as a major country star for small-town romance and music making with a local band. George Strait starred in *Pure Country* (1992), in which a country superstar realizes the artifice of his craft and heads to a Texas ranch, where horses, dancing, and true love restore his music to its supposedly authentic roots, although at the end of the film, the singer takes his newfound country soul back to the concert arena. River Phoenix and Samantha Mathis explored Nashville's songwriting scene in *The Thing Called Love* (1993), in which a country songwriter only reaches her artistic potential after personal heartbreak. The same tropes of authenticity resurface in *Crazy Heart* (2009), in which Jeff Bridges plays a hard country singer against the foil of an attractive young crowd-pleasing star who lacks country authenticity, and to a lesser extent in *Country Strong* (2011), as well as several other films.

Quite a few country singers have established careers as actors since the late 1970s, furthering the connection between Hollywood and Nashville. These instances where country stars have crafted careers as actors are another indicator of the way that country merged with mainstream pop culture during those years and that the genre boundaries were in flux. Dolly Parton and Willie Nelson were particularly successful, which helped expand their fame far beyond country audiences. Nelson carved out a niche playing essentially himself—a country singer/songwriter sidekick, first in *Electric Horseman* (1979, starring Robert Redford) and later in such movies as *Wag the Dog* (1997). Johnny Cash appeared in several movies in the 1980s, including the Civil War saga *North and South* (1985). Kenny Rogers appeared in a series of made-for-TV films during those years, while Kris Kristofferson and Dwight Yoakam both appeared in films that did not connect them to their country-music careers. Outside of that era, Waylon Jennings starred in *Nashville Rebel* (1966) and was featured in a few later films, as well. And in subsequent decades, Reba McEntire (*Tremors* [1990]), Faith Hill (*The Stepford Wives* [2004]), and Tim McGraw (*Flicka* [2006], *The Blind Side* [2009]), among others, have appeared in multiple movies. In each case, their acting careers expanded their fan base and name recognition within popular culture in general. The relationship between Nashville and Hollywood continues to thrive, as contemporary stars such as Taylor Swift (*Valentine's Day* [2010]) slide into acting roles, and as movies continue to exploit the culturally rich tropes of country music.

★ ESSAY: MUSIC BUSINESS

International Country

Although most of our attention in this book has been on American country music and its historical and cultural role within the United States, country music also has an extensive global presence. It exists in communities around the world in different versions and with many different relationships to American country music. The global presence of country music fits generally into four categories:

1. a preservation of traditional country music styles and songs, exported from American styles and artists in past decades;
2. music that represents the local, working-class identity of the people and places in which it is found, which is considered "country" because it adopts many of the same topics, meanings, and sounds as American country but is not directly derived from American country;
3. country music that is exported from America as a type of "foreign," exotic novelty entertainment;
4. American country stars with a substantial international fan base who view them as contemporary singers/entertainers.

Beginning in the 1920s, country music spread via American hillbilly recordings throughout the world, transmitted as sailors and other travelers took records home with them. Jimmie Rodgers's records were particularly well liked, and there is ample evidence that he had a growing fan base in Australia and the British Isles. Local musicians in those and other places remember their grandfathers bringing back hillbilly records from their travels. A second wave of exports took place during and after World War II, when American servicemen and women took their country music—both on records and in live performance—with them to foreign locations. After the war, the Armed Forces Radio Network routinely broadcast country music for the servicemen and women who were stationed abroad, which locals near American military bases readily picked up. These broadcasts converted droves of new foreign fans to country music. Those same military bases often supported a thriving nightlife as well as servicemen's bands. Countless country singers from the 1950s put together some of their first bands during their military service, especially in Europe, Johnny Cash among them. In this way, hillbilly, honky-tonk, and especially bluegrass made their way beyond the borders of the United States.

In many locations, local performers became fans of the American music and adopted that musical style for their own bands. With the passing decades, some performers stuck to the original styles they had learned. In Liverpool, England, for instance, and in smaller communities throughout the British Isles, local musicians who had been entranced by Jimmie Rodgers and Hank Williams kept their musical styles alive and active long after American country music had moved on.

In some places, initial contact with American country music in the 1920s was enough to launch a local version of country music that developed and thrived over the span of many decades. Canada has enjoyed a deeply intertwined relationship with

American country music in which artists move fluidly across that border (Hank Snow, Terri Clark, Shania Twain, etc.). But the same is true elsewhere. In Australia, for instance, Tex Morton and other musicians heard American hillbilly records in the 1920s, and within a few short years had developed their own version of country music that was built on the same source material but that took root as a native Australian musical genre. The musical evocation of wide open spaces, rural themes, working-class identity, and even the cowboy images all resonated with Australian culture, and over the span of the twentieth century, Australia developed its own robust country music scene, which parallels that in the United States. The U.S.-based Country Music Association has given a "Global Artist" award since 2003, and it is no surprise that, through 2010, all nine winners were either Canadian or Australian. Furthermore, a number of Australian country artists, including Keith Urban and Kasey Chambers, have found success in the United States, confirming a kinship between the two country music scenes. Like Canada, Australia has its own country music association and annual awards, and a genre of country is fully established within its national popular culture.

In Central and Eastern Europe and parts of Asia, bluegrass found a welcoming home from the mid-twentieth century on. In what is now the Czech Republic, for instance, bluegrass instruments were completely foreign when they first showed up as an imported form of American entertainment, but over the next decades, local musicians learned to play them and claimed them as their own. As the years passed, bluegrass—particularly five-string banjo—took on local meanings and significance, and today Prague and other cities are well known for hosting large bluegrass festivals. Similar developments in Scandinavian countries have led to a thriving country music festival scene. In Norway, for instance, large outdoor festivals feature country music—both American songs and styles and local styles—where a primarily (but not exclusively) working-class fan base gathers for music that celebrates the same core themes as its American counterpart, but in a locally specific version. In Japan, bluegrass has taken root even more emphatically, and Japanese bluegrass bands today are part of an active scene.

In some countries, music that shares many traits with American country music has developed independent of any American influence. This has long been the case in Brazil, for instance, where similar themes of an idealized rural past, connection to the land and traditions, and working-class identity are expressed through close vocal harmony and guitar-driven, folk-derived music. *Música sertaneja*, for instance, is a musical style in which male duets (often brothers) perform, accompanied mainly by ten-string guitars (called *violas*), and sing about those themes in music that is both traditional and still influenced by modern, cosmopolitan, and commercial musical developments. Although it is not specifically derived from American country music, it runs parallel to it, and is readily called "country music." Furthermore, there are several styles and genres of Latin American popular music that share musical elements with American country music of the Southwest, where immigrant populations have injected American country music with influences from Latin styles for decades—Bob Wills, for instance, hired and played with Mexican musicians in the 1920s, and brought the sound of mariachi trumpets into "New San Antonio Rose," which is only one of dozens of instances where that influence showed up in country music.

In some cases, American country music has been exported as a novelty, something so different and strange compared to local culture that it becomes a form of exotic entertainment. "Wild West" theme parks in Germany, for instance, allow fans to try dressing up as cowboys and other characters that are native to American country music but not to those locales. These sorts of novelty attractions featuring caricatures of American country music are popular around the world—in Kanchana-buri, Thailand, for instance, where many Thais choose to vacation, a country music bar features a Thai cover band performing American hits in a setting that is decorated as an extreme stereotype of a Texas roadhouse honky-tonk.

Part of the reason why these types of country music establishments exist is that American country music relies on characters, images, and themes that sometimes do not translate easily into foreign cultures, especially those of Europe. The cowboy is the most readily apparent example; several American country music executives have pointed out that a cowboy hat, straight-leg jeans, and boots would be so totally out of place as to imply "camp," a performance of such pretentious artifice and excessive bad taste that it makes a statement, often implying the performance of a gay or gender-bending identity. In that context, obviously it would be difficult for a middle-class European audience to find much sincerity in American country performers and traditions. Another reason why American country music has not always found a firm foothold in Western Europe is that the music and performers cultivate an unsophisticated identity—one that is in opposition to all things urban, global, and cosmopolitan—in their lyrics and self-presentation. Some stars have made public their discomfort in different cultural and culinary settings, which only adds to that reputation. More recently, many European audiences have identified American country music with conservative, Republican politics, personified by President George W. Bush, and where his popularity waned, so did the acceptance of American country music. One of the most famous international country music incidents occurred when the Dixie Chicks were performing in London and attempted to distance themselves from the strongly negative stereotypes of Texas politics that many European and British audiences held at the time (see Chapter 14). Yet in spite of these and other related hurdles, some American country stars have succeeded in building an enthusiastic and loyal fan base outside of the United States and Canada.

Many major country stars toured Europe in the years after World War II, often to perform on American military bases—as Hank Williams did in 1949, for instance. In subsequent years, stars who successfully cultivated general overseas audiences without the military links included Jim Reeves and George Hamilton IV, whose career began in the 1950s and who was a major figure during the Nashville sound era (see Chapter 6). Reeves toured both Europe and South Africa quite successfully prior to his death in 1964. In subsequent years, Hamilton worked tirelessly as an ambassador for country music. By the late 1960s, he had already moved into the folk scene, and established himself with a Canadian fan base. He toured England in 1967, and a few years later became the first American country artist to perform in the Soviet bloc. Other American stars also expanded their concert locations; Barbara Mandrell, for instance, played across Southeast Asia with her family's band in the 1960s. In subsequent decades, many more followed the precedents set by these artists.

The formula that many stars have followed in establishing their international careers is, ironically, to emphasize their identity as simply an entertainer, while downplaying their "country" status. Not surprisingly, many of the most successful have been crossover stars who are well known in either the pop or folk scene.

Taylor Swift and Shania Twain, for instance, both found a welcoming audience in Europe, but one that viewed them more as American pop artists than as country stars per se (or, in the case of Twain, simply as a pop artist, as Twain was actually Canadian). Even the most successful of these stars has faced surprising stereotypes among the foreign press; at the peak of his success, Garth Brooks undertook a world tour, during which he was taken aback and even offended by journalists and interviewers who confronted him with mock hillbilly stereotypes, accents, and costumes—worlds apart from his brand of modern country. But he persisted, and won a following not as a country star but rather as a music star. Similarly, both Dolly Parton and Emmylou Harris have toured Europe extensively, but drawing on their bluegrass, folk, and singer-songwriter personas more than their commercial country identities.

Outside the United States, the market share of country music is extremely low compared to other genres. Whereas an estimated 10% of the music sold in the United States today is country, in many European countries that number is only around 1%. Nonetheless, country enjoys a rich and diverse presence outside the United States in these four guises: the preservation of traditional hillbilly and honky-tonk styles; the adoption of country music as a new local genre; the importation of country music as an exotic and foreign form of entertainment; and the acceptance of American entertainers through downplaying their distinctive "country-ness."

For More Reading on International Country

The topic of country music outside the United States deserves its own full investigation. A few preliminary sources are listed here:

Bidgood, Lee. *Czech Bluegrass: Notes from the Heart of Europe.* Urbana-Champaign: University of Illinois Press, 2017.

Bidgood, Lee, and Shara Lange. *Banjo Romantika: American Bluegrass Music and the Czech* Imagination. Shara K. Lange, director. Johnson City, TN: A Light Projects Documentary, 2013.

Cohen, Sara. *Decline, Renewal, and the City in Popular Music Culture: Beyond the Beatles.* Hampshire, England: Ashgate, 2007.

Cusic, Don. "Country Music Internationally." In *Discovering Country Music*, chap. 11. Westport, CT: Praeger, 2008, pp. 149–158.

Dent, Alexander Sebastian. *River of Tears: Country Music, Memory, and Modernity in Brazil.* Durham: Duke University Press, 2009

Gibson, Nathan D. "What's International about International Country Music? Country Music and National Identity around the World." *The Oxford Handbook of Country Music*, ed. Travis D. Stimeling. New York: Oxford University Press, 2017, pp. 495–518.

Goertzen, Chris. "Popular Music Transfer and Transformation: The Case of American Country Music in Vienna." *Ethnomusicology* 32, no. 1 (1988): 1–21.

Gruber, Ruth Ellen. *sauerkrautcowboys* (blog), http://sauerkrautcowboys.blogspot.com/

Martin, Toby. *Yodelling Boundary Riders: Country Music in Australia since the 1920s.* Melbourne: Lyrebird Press, 2015.

Smith, Graeme. "Australian Country Music and the Hillbilly Yodel." *Popular Music* 13, no. 3 (1994): 297–311.

Solli, Kristin. "North of Nashville: Country Music, National Identity, and Class in Norway." PhD diss., University of Iowa, 2006.

LISTEN SIDE BY SIDE

"Baby I'm Burning"
Songwriter: Dolly Parton
Dolly Parton, 1978 (on *Heartbreaker*, RCA Records)

"Rosewood Casket"
Traditional
Dolly Parton, Emmylou Harris, and Linda Ronstadt, 1987 (on *Trio*, Warner Brothers)

"Nobody"
Songwriters: Kye Fleming and Dennis Morgan
Sylvia, 1982 (on *Just Sylvia*, RCA Records)

"Private Eyes"
Songwriters: Daryl Hall, Sara Allen, Janna Allen and Warren Pash
Hall & Oates, 1981 (on *Private Eyes*, RCA Records)

There are two types of side-by-side comparisons that highlight the range of styles in 1980s popular music. Both are well worth taking time to do carefully.

The first comparison juxtaposes country and pop/rock sounds from the same time period. Many fans talk about countrypolitan as if it were indistinguishable from other pop music in the early 1980s. But careful listening shows that there were differences in style between countrypolitan and the rest of pop. On the countrypolitan side, listen to the artist Sylvie's "Nobody" or "The Boy Gets Around," both by Kye Fleming and Dennis Morgan. On the pop side, duo Hall & Oates are a useful point of comparison because their music is infused with just enough folk that its melodies and chord structures are in the same general form as most country. Listen to their "Private Eyes." Both of these recordings have similar characteristics that identify them as part of the soundscape of early 1980s mainstream music, but especially the sound of the vocals (and sometimes the regional accents of the singers) and the way that the guitars are used differentiates between countrypolitan and other (non-country) styles of pop music.

The second way to explore the soundscape of countrypolitan is to listen to one artist whose music spans the whole countrypolitan fad. After more than a decade of recording, Dolly Parton moved into the crossover sounds of countrypolitan on the front end of that trend, releasing *Heartbreaker,* which amounted to a disco album with plenty of funk grooves, in 1978. Listen to the full brass section ("horns," specifically trumpets and trombones) that punctuates the song, the electric bass, and the dance groove that was heavily influenced by funk. The sound effects are particularly surprising and a stark departure from classic country music. Less than a decade later, Parton collaborated on *Trio*, a neotraditionalist, acoustic-styled album with Linda Ronstadt and Emmylou Harris, both artists who had acoustic bluegrass and alternative country rock lineages. On this album, Parton sang "Rosewood Casket," a traditional mountain ballad, accompanied by acoustic string instruments, including a hammered dulcimer, and with three-part bluegrass-style vocal harmony on the chorus. Note how one artist moved across the whole spectrum of country music, from countrypolitan to very traditional, old-time-influenced sounds.

These two comparative listenings, very different in their specifics, allow us to zero in on countrypolitan by illustrating first how countrypolitan compared to what else was happening in popular music in the early 1980s and, second, how countrypolitan relates to what came after it in country music.

PLAYLIST

Greenwood, Lee. "God Bless the U.S.A." (1984)

Harris, Emmylou. "Two More Bottles of Wine" (1978)

Lee, Johnny. "Looking for Love (In All the Wrong Places)" (1980)

Milsap, Ronnie. "Smoky Mountain Rain" (1980)

Newton, Juice. "Queen of Hearts" (1981)

FOR MORE READING

Brackett, David. "Banjos, Biopics, and Compilation Scores: The Movies Go Country." *American Music* 19, no. 3 (2001): 247–290.

Latham, Aaron. "The Ballad of the Urban Cowboy: America's Search for True Grit," *Esquire,* September 12, 1978, 21–30.

Mandrell, Barbara, with George Vecsey. *Get to the Heart: My Story.* New York: Bantam Books, 1990.

Tucker, Ken. "Contemporary Country Coast to Coast: How Dolly Parton and Willie Nelson Qualified for 'Lifestyles of the Rich and Famous.'" In *Country: The Music and the Musicians (From the Beginnings to the '90s)*, ed. Paul Kingsbury. New York: Abbeville Press, 1994.

NAMES AND TERMS

Alabama	*Dukes of Hazzard*	Morgan, Dennis
Armed Forces Radio Network	Fleming, Kye	MTV
	Fricke, Janie	Murray, Anne
Bee Gees	Greenwood, Lee	Newton, Juice
Campbell, Glen	Harris, Emmylou	Rabbitt, Eddie
CMT	Latham, Aaron	*Saturday Night Fever*
country discos	Mandrell, Barbara	*Urban Cowboy*
Dallas	Milsap, Ronnie	

REVIEW TOPICS

1. For country stars who were already established, what appeal did the countrypolitan style hold, and why did they switch to it?

2. How did the political climate of the early 1980s foster the development of countrypolitan?

3. What aspects of tradition were present and valued in the *Urban Cowboy* era?

Neotraditionalists and Remaking the Past

In the mid-1980s, musical styles and trends in country music moved sharply away from the countrypolitan that had thrived in the earlier parts of the decade. In its wake, a neotraditionalist movement that looked backward through time and anchored itself in older country music and traditions gained attention. The neotraditionalist trend was part of the natural cycle of country music's development; periods of crossover country are followed by more roots-oriented, traditional styles. This process is driven by the tension within country music between its commercial orientation and its need to remain distinct from pop music. And in keeping with that cycle, the neotraditionalist movement paved the way for the biggest commercial crossover period yet, which would arrive in the mid-1990s. The neotraditionalist era drew together a smaller but invested audience and reestablished a very distinctive look, sound, and attitude for country music that differentiated it from the rest of pop culture.

Countrypolitan Fades

The *Urban Cowboy* era had enticed new fans into country music who filled the cavernous dance clubs that opened coast-to-coast, mimicking Gilley's from the movie. Yet as with most pop-culture fads, this one was short-lived, and after a few years those fans moved on to other forms of entertainment. Although pop and country music had fused into a nearly indistinguishable sound for a brief time, pop music subsequently started to drift in different directions. Stars like Madonna and Michael Jackson appealed to younger audiences, while Whitney Houston (whose first number one pop hit appeared in 1985) increased pop music's alliance with R&B traditions. These developments were at odds with even the most countrypolitan of country music, and as a result, country and pop became more clearly differentiated once again.

Since its earliest days, country music has followed a natural cycle of extension into the pop market, followed by a retrenchment in more traditional styles, after which the cycle would begin again. Any time country music ventured too far toward pop assimilation, a core group of fans and artists voiced their concern, and those calls for roots-oriented country anchored in twang and tradition often motivated a change in style. By 1984, long-time fans of harder country styles were extremely dissatisfied with the state of country music. Bill C. Malone, the preeminent historian of country music, was so distressed by the extreme crossover sounds of countrypolitan recordings that he assessed the situation in 1984 with the Biblical admonition "What shall it profit a man if he gains the whole world and loses his own soul?" when he published a revision of his landmark book, *Country Music, U.S.A.*

His eloquent phrasing summed up the sentiments of many dedicated country fans, who were more than ready to throw their support behind any vanguard of twangy, honky-tonk influenced music that appeared to retain country's soul.

Record label executives also sensed the end of a fad and were ready to try something new and different, although they were motivated more by dwindling sales than any aesthetic loyalty to old country. Newspaper articles reported that during the height of the *Urban Cowboy* era (1981–1982), 24% of all record sales were country, whereas by 1985, that number had slipped to 18%. The Recording Industry Association of America (RIAA) released statistics with slightly lower percentages, but that still confirmed a major increase in sales in 1981–1983, followed by a sizeable drop-off. That downward trend would continue throughout the rest of the decade, winding up at around 7% by 1989. The audience had turned away from country and toward pop and rock music in huge numbers, and the few remaining country listeners were older—a most distressing fact in terms of sales, given that younger audiences buy the most records. In 1985, the average age of the country listener was forty, and heading upward. By 1988, 69% of the country audience was over thirty-five, which made their nostalgia for the sounds (and topics) of the past and distaste for glitzy countrypolitan all the more understandable. Market share had tumbled, the young fans had left the genre, and the stalwart traditionalists were fed up with the crossover trend. The subsequent neotraditionalist movement included a distinct musical sound, but equally important to the movement were the philosophies, outlooks, and rhetoric of the musicians and in the way that their fans thought about their music and found meaning in it

---

MULTIPLE STYLES, MULTIPLE CHOICES

Although we have described the early 1980s as dominated by countrypolitan and the late 1980s as featuring neotraditionalists, at any given time country music features multiple diverse styles. Anomalies and distinctive styles can be heard even within the relatively narrow confines of Top 40 country radio. That is also true of any individual singer's recordings. When we discuss trends and major developments, keep in mind that there are always counterexamples and opposing styles brewing. In some cases, those styles are cultivated in certain places or types of venues; for instance, Texas dance halls incubated honky-tonk music even while countrypolitan graced the airwaves. In some cases, those other styles are holdovers from earlier times; for instance, a few countrypolitan stars and recordings continued to appear at the top of the charts well into the late 1980s. Keep in mind that trends do not start or stop instantaneously.

Most recordings will have a few features or elements that make them just a little bit different than the "stylistic norm"; in some cases, recordings are even stylistic hybrids. Similarly, almost all artists explore different styles and combinations of styles over the span of their careers. As attentive listeners, we should adopt two approaches in our investigations. The first is to find the commonalities and the general stylistic features that are shared across a group of recordings. The second is to examine the aspects of a recording that are not the same as others in that style or, in other words, those features that make it stand out from the crowd. In combination, those two approaches let us see both the big picture of styles and trends and the details of individual works of art that may not conform to the larger trends at all.

Neotraditionalist Philosophy

The essence of the neotraditionalist movement was a concerted effort on the part of the musicians and fans alike to reclaim the past of country music for the present, to rekindle traditions that they felt had been lost. This perspective was motivated by a strong sense of nostalgia and the belief that countrypolitan had strayed from the core values and identity of country music or—worse yet—sold them out for monetary gain. In terms of the basic characteristics of country music, this movement prioritized tradition over innovation. It favored sharp distinctions between country and pop music and reintroduced older signifiers of country identity, particularly with regard to wardrobe, image, and biography. Rather than focusing on just one musical style, the movement embraced several different older country styles.

This idea of looking back to the past to define a musical style was relatively new in country music. In the 1940s and '50s, for instance, both bluegrass and honky tonk were new, contemporary innovations in musical style that responded to the changing interests, demographics, and modern lifestyles of country fans. Western swing had similarly been a progressive musical style, quick to embrace drums, electrified guitars, and then-contemporary jazz elements. But some thirty or forty years later, fans looked back to those musical styles and hailed them as worthy not only of celebration but of resurrection and preservation.

The neotraditionalist outlook also thought of country music not as something to be performed but rather as something that emerged as a natural, intrinsic extension of a musician's being. In other words, biography became very important. Where singers were from, what they had done while growing up, and how they were related to the symbolic markers of a country lifestyle (farming, ranching, rodeos, etc.) mattered, as did their knowledge of and reverence for early country stars. These aspects of the movement showed up in the form of cover songs (see essay on Cover Songs Revisited) and in frequent references to past stars and early hit songs in their lyrics, such as Vern Gosdin's recording, "Set 'Em Up Joe" (a number one hit in 1988), which quoted lines from Ernest Tubb's songs by way of tribute.

The main features of the neotraditionalist movement—its much smaller and older core audience, its reverence for the past, and its desire to reclaim the past for the present—reflected the political and cultural sentiments of the late 1980s. New technological developments had intruded on the "country" way of life as never before. There was widespread concern about the continued viability of family farms, leading both to political policy changes and to the much-publicized Farm Aid concerts, which began in 1985. Widespread

Figure 11-1 George Strait.

Source: Courtesy of Country Music Hall of Fame and Museum.

LISTENING GUIDE

"All My Ex's Live in Texas" (1987)

PERFORMER: George Strait

SONGWRITERS: Sanger D. Shafer and Linda J. Shafer

ORIGINAL ALBUM: *Ocean Front Property* (MCA 5913, 1987)

FORM: Verse-chorus

STYLE: Neotraditionalist

Like many other songs in the neotraditionalist era, "All My Ex's Live in Texas" was written by songwriters who also had their own small-scale performance careers but became a hit for a major star who did not write his own material. Sanger D. Shafer had been writing honky-tonk tunes in Nashville (for the Acuff-Rose publishing firm) since the early 1970s. For this tune, the native Texan collaborated with his fourth wife, Linda J. Shafer (his marital history and personal biography perhaps lending some credence to the song's lyrics). Shafer was also one of the songwriters to whom George Strait regularly turned for material; Strait had already recorded another half dozen of his songs when he cut this one.

The most relevant aspect of "All My Ex's . . ." to our study is its straightforward nature. As with most of the neotraditionalist recordings, the instrumentation relies heavily on guitar, steel guitar, fiddle, and piano played in a swing style. The fiddle player for this recording session was Johnny Gimble, who had played in Bob Wills's band in the late 1940s and had been a legend in Texas fiddling for more than four decades by then. Gimble's playing is one of the highlights of the entire album, not just this track. The song's verse-chorus form further reinforces the more traditional approach to country music.

The song's lyrics reinforce the tension between Tennessee and Texas as two symbolic locations in country music's history. Recall Jimmie Rodgers's "Blue Yodel" (1927): the opening line there was "T for Texas, T for Tennessee" (see Chapter 2). Strait's lyrics also play with the alliteration of the two states' names, as well as their literal and metaphoric distance. The singer longs to be in Texas but is stuck in Tennessee, which does not stop him from dreaming about Texas. Strait's musical style is clearly following in Texan traditions, most relevantly western swing, but also uses the expressive freedom of the outlaw movement, which also metaphorically pitted Texas against Tennessee in terms of their place in the country music industry.

The entire *Ocean Front Property* album captures the essence of a Texas dance hall. The majority of the tracks on the album, including "All My Ex's . . ." are the

economic growth, an attitude of materialism, low unemployment, and a generally optimistic outlook thrived in the popular mainstream, but for the core country audience, which was inherently skeptical of change, these trends merely fostered more nostalgia. People were now buying personal computers, and music was purchased on shiny new compact discs. While the pop audience dove enthusiastically into the future, hard-core country fans sought the familiar twang of days gone by.

right tempo and meter for two-stepping. One track has a country cha-cha rhythm, underscoring the influence of music from south of the border that had been part of Texan country music for decades; another, "Second Chances," is a slow waltz, something that was almost unheard of from countrypolitan artists but which was always part of a band's set list in a Texan dance hall; and the last track is a slow ballad.

TIME	FORM	LISTENING CUES	DISCUSSION
0:00	Intro	steel guitar	The steel guitar gives way to a Texas-style fiddle at 0:09. Note the swing beat and general feel of old western swing.
0:16	Chorus	"All my ex's . . ."	Like many of the old 1960s country songs, this one starts with the chorus so the first thing the listener hears is the hook and most memorable part of the song.
0:45	Verse 1	"Rosanna's down in . . ."	The steel guitar provides fills between the lines of text. The catalog of women's names and geographic references both have long traditions in country songwriting.
1:15	Chorus	"All my exes . . ."	A honky-tonk style acoustic piano provides fills between the lines of text here.
1:44	Interlude	steel guitar, then fiddle	The improvisational solos stay quite close to the song's main melody, again following a more classic western swing style.
1:59	Verse 2	"I remember that old . . ."	For this verse, the fiddle plays the fills between lines of text. The lyrics refer to Texas as a place to which one might go in one's imagination or dreams—a figurative destination as well as a literal one.
2:28	Chorus	"All my exes . . ."	Note how subtle the backup vocalists are, who on this song sing the lyrics along with Strait in rich harmonies reminiscent of the 1940s western swing vocal styles. There's a subtle change in the last line of this chorus (from the "hang my hat" line to "reside").
2:58	Tag	"Some folks think . . ."	The lyrics here add a bit more humor to the already light-hearted song.

Early Practitioners

The first wave of neotraditionalists appeared on country radio several years before the main movement coalesced. In 1980, classic country stars George Jones, Conway Twitty, and Bakersfield legend Merle Haggard were still very prominent in the country music scene. Twitty had embraced a slightly pop sound, and certainly Haggard's music varied in style during that period, but they and others still remained a strong, traditional presence. A younger generation of stars joined them. George Strait (see Artist Profile) released his debut single, "Unwound" (1981), which turned into a top ten hit with its refreshing brand of western swing. Strait's clean-cut image, Texas rancher roots, and musical honesty became hallmarks of the growing neotraditionalist trend. Joining him was Ricky Skaggs (1954–), who brought bluegrass to the table. The mandolin player grew up on the sounds of traditional bluegrass of the Flatt and Scruggs era and started performing on the radio and on television variety shows as a young teen. In 1971, Ralph Stanley hired him to play in the Clinch Mountain Boys, and later Skaggs joined Emmylou Harris's Hot Band. In 1981, he signed a major-label deal for himself, and that same year scored his first of five number one *Billboard* country hits in a row. Even during the reign of countrypolitan, country radio was serving up new versions of western swing and bluegrass-infused country.

Ricky Skaggs's story features all the elements of the neotraditionalist movement. From Cordell, Kentucky, he staked his claim on country music through his own biography and investment in traditional sounds of the 1950s. He paid his professional dues and learned his craft on stage with revered masters such as Ralph Stanley. He talked knowledgably and respectfully about the music's past. And his major-label debut album, *Waitin' for the Sun to Shine* (1981), was a collection of covers. Skaggs's songs drew from more than just first-generation bluegrass. His second and third number one singles were, respectively, an old Webb Pierce honky-tonk tune ("I Don't Care") and a song by Texas legend and outlaw country singer Guy Clark. For these recordings, Skaggs layered bluegrass instrumentals and a high lonesome style of singing over a thoroughly modern rhythm section of bass, drums, and guitars. The hybrid sound evoked and incorporated bluegrass without actually sticking to the traditional acoustic sound. It worked, and by the mid-1980s Skaggs was a huge commercial country star. His career did not maintain that commercial momentum, however, and a decade later, he returned to a more traditional bluegrass career outside the country mainstream.

John Anderson is often cited as the third pioneer (along with Skaggs and Strait) of the neotraditionalist sound in the 1980s. Anderson (1954–), from Orlando, Florida, moved to Nashville in 1971, but struggled without a hit until 1980. His first successes came with "She Just Started Liking Cheatin' Songs" (1980) and "1959" (1980). Anderson sang in a heavily naturalized, twang-inflected voice that reminded critics of a younger George Jones or Lefty Frizzell, which added to his credibility as a neotraditionalist. He cultivated an image as a country rebel, photographed with his cowboy hat, brooding expressions, and scraggly beard, all of which eschewed the glitz of countrypolitan. The songs he recorded were also steeped in themes of nostalgia and heartbreak. But the recordings themselves—especially "1959"—were saturated with pop-crossover musical elements: thick string sections, pop chord progressions, and heavy-handed production. He earned respect as a neotraditionalist for covering old songs (such as Lefty Frizzell's "I Love You a Thousand Ways"), and his hard-driving boogie-blues numbers could hold their own against the southern rockers (such as "Black Sheep," which reached number one in 1983). The comedy number "Chicken Truck" (number eight in 1981) was a similarly rock-influenced boogie number, with rockabilly-style piano, steel guitar, and electric guitar. Adding to its neotraditionalist appeal, for the introduction the electric guitar player quoted from the old, traditional Appalachian fiddle tune "Chicken Reel." Like Skaggs, Anderson saw his commercial appeal fade in the late 1980s when he was displaced by a younger wave of neotraditionalists, but he staged a successful comeback in the early 1990s.

Anderson's music is a great illustration of how his neotraditionalist identity still allowed him to perform music that was part of the crossover trend. Anderson's biggest hit of his entire career, "Swingin'" featured screaming horns, sultry backup vocals, organ, and all the pop elements of countrypolitan, and even briefly showed up on the pop charts. Nonetheless, Anderson's overall reception by the country audience was as a stalwart hard country singer.

By the mid-1980s, the Judds and Reba McEntire had joined the ranks of the neotraditionalists (see Listening Guides and Artist Profile). Like Anderson, the Judds and McEntire recorded in many different musical styles, and both indulged in plenty of crossover sounds. But also like Anderson, they cultivated overall musical reputations that were wedded to the past. McEntire, for instance, earned credibility as a neotraditionalist in 1984 not only for recording a traditional-sounding album but also because she was the one who had spear-headed the project. Meanwhile, Naomi Judd (1946–) and daughter Wynonna (1964–), from Ashland, Kentucky, played up old-time mountain music elements (including a dulcimer, for instance, on their albums *Rockin' with the Rhythm* and *Heartland*; see Listening Guide) and themes of family and nostalgia.

In 1985, four senior country stars—Johnny Cash, Waylon Jennings, Kris Kristofferson, and Willie Nelson—reemerged as the Highwaymen, a supergroup that added to the neotraditionalist momentum by offering up an album that featured

Figure 11-2 The Judds: Wynonna (left) and Naomi.

Source: Courtesy BenCar Archives

George Strait (1952–)

George Strait has singlehandedly become the representative for traditional country music in the contemporary era. He has amassed forty-four number one *Billboard* country hits as of 2011 (more than any other artist to date, including Conway Twitty) and had a song in the top ten for thirty straight years from 1981 to 2011. During the neotraditionalist heyday of the late 1980s, Straight scored eleven number one singles in a row. For his legions of loyal fans, Strait embodies their conception of "real" country music, and he has played an important role in the genre for the past three decades as both an anchor and foil for other major developments.

Born in Poteet, Texas, a small town south of San Antonio, Strait grew up working on his family's cattle ranch. He picked up the guitar in high school and performed 1960s rock music with various bands. After high school, he enlisted in the army, and while stationed in Hawaii began fronting a country band. During those years, Strait immersed himself in honky-tonk and western swing music and the long traditions of Texan country, along with Merle Haggard's Bakersfield sound. After his stint in the military, Strait earned a degree from Texas State University, and while there, performed regionally with the Ace in the Hole band. During these years of performing, Strait honed his ability to entertain a large crowd and keep a dance floor active, all while mastering the musical traditions of Texan country. He and the band also cut a few singles with a local record company.

In 1981, MCA record executives who had heard him play in Texas signed him to a major-label deal. His debut single reached number six on the *Billboard* country chart, and his first album fared well. His first number one single, "Fool Hearted Memory," featured a fiddle introduction, a steady honky-tonk beat that was perfect for two-stepping, plenty of steel guitar, and heartbreak lyrics that hearkened back to the 1960s. For country fans awash in the aftermath of the movie *Urban Cowboy*, Strait appeared to be the living, breathing version of the Texan honky-tonk singers who were on stage in the movie at Gilley's. Strait's success serves as a reminder that *Urban Cowboy* and the whole early 1980s country scene were not entirely centered on pop-crossover countrypolitan styles of music.

When the *Urban Cowboy* era faded, Strait had already established himself as the consummate honky-tonk and western swing revivalist. His biography, from his cattle-ranch roots to his team-roping rodeo abilities, matched the neotraditionalist emphasis on country singers having personal experience with the iconic lifestyles described in their songs. Like many of the other neotraditionalist singers, Strait rarely wrote his own material, but instead drew from a stable of the top country songwriters in the business, which gave him an endless supply of fresh songs that were always in keeping with subtle trends and developments. That approach got songs such as "The Chair" (1985) by Dean Dillon and Hank Cochran into his hands, and his performances were so compelling that most fans thought of those songs as "his," as if he were singing about his own personal experiences.

Strait also made frequent use of cover songs as a way of reaffirming his investment in country music's traditions. Just a few of his many covers include:

- "Our Paths May Never Cross" (1983), recorded by Merle Haggard in 1980
- "Right or Wrong" (1984), recorded by Bob Wills in 1936
- "Deep Water" (1986), recorded by Bob Wills in 1947, Ray Price in 1958, and Ferlin Husky in 1959
- "If You Ain't Lovin' (You Ain't Livin')" (1988), recorded by Faron Young in 1954
- "She Loves Me (She Don't Love You)" (1990), recorded by Waylon Jennings in 1967
- "Lovesick Blues" (1992), recorded by Hank Williams in 1949

While his reputation as a neotraditionalist, hat-wearing honky-tonk singer was unwavering, Strait's recordings occasionally dipped into the fringes of pop-crossover sounds, which meant that his songs fit comfortably into radio playlists.

In 1992, as Garth Brooks and the new country movement were ascending within country music (see Chapter 12), Strait starred in the Hollywood movie *Pure Country*, expanding his career into acting, as so many other country stars of his generation had done. *Pure Country* grossed just over $15 million, less than a third of *Urban Cowboy's* total earnings, but it was a critical step in Strait's career that helped him remain a viable commercial force even while country music's styles changed. In the film, Strait played a country star named Dusty who had let his career slide into a crossover phase. In the film, Dusty finds redemption by leaving the flashy concert scene and moving to a ranch, where he discovers real love (and dances with his girl in a Texas honky-tonk) and reconnects with country music as a rural expression of self.

Having rediscovered "real" country music, Dusty triumphantly returns to the concert stage, where he tells the crowd "I gotta do something a little different tonight," and brings his acoustic guitar to the front edge of the stage, as close as possible to his audience, and sings "I Cross My Heart." Ironically, about halfway through the song, the musical arrangement changes to a heavily produced, lush ballad laced with soaring strings, pop chord progressions, and a modulation. For early 1990s country fans, *Pure Country* depicted Strait denouncing the artifice of commercial country while singing a very polished, radio-friendly hit (the song reached the top of the *Billboard* country chart). The song is an example of how the country genre often embraces a rhetoric of tradition and authenticity within a commercial and pop-influenced setting.

Strait's tireless touring and dedication to live performance has sustained his career, now over four decades long. Garth Brooks mentioned his name in "Ain't Goin' Down ('Til the Sun Comes Up)" (number one in 1993), which helped transform him from a star into a legend. Younger generations of artists routinely drop references to him in their songs as metaphors for traditional country music and the elusive value of authenticity (as in the top ten singles Gretchen Wilson, "Redneck Woman" [2004]; Brooks & Dunn, "Play Something Country" [2005]; Eric Church, "Love Your Love the Most" [2009]; and Rodney Atkins, "Take a Back Road" [2011], to name just a few). He remains a highly revered figure in the genre, with fiercely loyal fans, and he was inducted into the Country Music Hall of Fame in 2006.

Listening Guide

"Grandpa (Tell Me 'Bout the Good Old Days)" (1986)

PERFORMERS: The Judds

SONGWRITER: Jamie O'Hara

ORIGINAL ALBUM: *Rockin' with the Rhythm* (RCA PCD1–7042, 1985)

FORM: Verse-chorus

STYLE: Neotraditionalist

The mother–daughter duo of Naomi and Wynonna Judd was a major part of the neotraditionalist movement. Even their mother–daughter relationship evoked ideas of early hillbilly family singing groups. Many of their early songs focused on topics of lasting love and nostalgia for rural life, which was depicted in their lyrics as more wholesome and fulfilling than city life (listen to "John Deere Tractor," for instance). The Judds also tapped into an older tradition of songwriting, as when they recorded several songs by Harlan Howard (who had written hits for Patsy Cline back in the 1960s). This song's writer, Jamie O'Hara, had been working in Nashville since the mid-1970s and was well established by the time he penned this hit, for which he won the Grammy for Best Country Song. This song was part of a long string of number ones for the Judds, who placed fourteen songs at the top of the *Billboard* country chart between 1984 and 1989.

The lyrics of this song obviously invoke nostalgia for an idyllic past, but that theme runs deeper than just the lyrics. In the song's music video, Wynonna appears in a gray and washed-out cityscape, caged in an elevator, confronting unsavory characters on the street, and staring out her small window at a wall of cubicle-sized apartments. The urban landscape and her bleak, lonely life contrasts even more strikingly with the warmth of a country home, family, and hearth depicted in the song's lyrics. The musical recording is deeply invested in the neotraditionalist approach. It features acoustic piano, steel guitar, and dulcimer, an instrument with a long history in the Appalachian Mountains whose very presence signifies a return to traditional musical roots.

The rest of the songs on this album, like most of their mid-1980s recordings, took a similar approach to musical depictions of old-time nostalgia. Several of the other tracks open with an acoustic accompaniment for nearly a minute of the song (listen to "Dream Chaser" and "River Roll On," for instance). The Judds' overall musical style during this period matched the general approach of most female country stars during this era: they blended an old-time musical approach with an undeniable investment in R&B. Along with all the old-time and mountain-music references on these early albums were plenty of tracks with hard-driving boogie or rock beats (listen to "Have Mercy" or "Cry Myself to Sleep"). Wynonna's vocals were heavily inflected by growling blues traditions at times, too. For "Grandpa (Tell Me 'Bout the Good Old Days)," even the song's form was part of the general trend toward simplicity and transparency that characterized the neotraditionalist artists: a verse-chorus form without any bridges, prechoruses, or other complicating elements. Furthermore, the extended playout here brings to mind an old-time front-porch pickin' session, where the music and its nostalgic message float on after the main body of the song is finished.

TIME	FORM	LISTENING CUES	DISCUSSION
0:00	Intro	acoustic	The guitar takes the melody here. The clearest indicator that this is a mid-80s recording is the loud "click" sound from the drums.
0:20	Verse 1	"Grandpa, tell me . . ."	The dulcimer is clearly audible at 0:42, evoking a mountain-music atmosphere.
0:58	Chorus	"Did lovers really . . ."	Note that the list of old-time events covers relationships, especially the lack of divorce; personal integrity; and religion.
1:36	Interlude	acoustic guitar plus piano and dulcimer	Although the playing here is excellent, there are no showy improvisational solos. All the instruments stay close to the melody.
1:56	Verse 2	"Grandpa, everything is changing . . ."	Note the sparse accompaniment here, with steel guitar interjections such as at 2:06 and 2:13. There is a clear rejection of modernism ("progress") in the lyrics.
2:34	Chorus	"Did lovers really . . ."	Wynonna's voice is smoky and breathy throughout this performance, suggesting reflection, introspection, and nostalgia. Lots of steel guitar here also evokes traditional country music.
3:11	Tag	"Woh-woh, Grandpa, tell me . . ."	This short tag moves into an extended instrumental playout.
3:41	Playout	humming	At the end of the recording, the humming evokes casual family music-making on a front porch, as well as the notion that the song's sentiment continues even after the song has ended.
4:00	Playout continued	"[Did] families really bow . . ."	Here again, we get the sense that the song (and the reminiscence and longing for the idyllic past) are still continuing, as the vocals reenter with a few lines of the chorus as the song fades out.

old covers and cowboy songs such as Ed Bruce's "The Last Cowboy Song" (Bruce also wrote "Mamas, Don't Let Your Babies Grow Up to Be Cowboys") and Eddy Arnold's "Jim, I Wore a Tie Today" (written by Cindy Walker). Cash, Jennings, Kristofferson, and Nelson's combined effort on this sparse, musically retro album brought the ghost of outlaw country back into the present, yet another evocation of the past that played into the current trends.

Neotraditionalism Takes Root

In 1986, the neotraditionalist movement blossomed into the dominant trend in country music. A number of younger artists made their national debuts that year, all under the banner of reviving country's honky-tonk past, while several established artists enjoyed increased attention. The two new artists who garnered the most attention were North Carolina native Randy Travis (1959–) and Kentucky native Dwight Yoakam (1956–). Travis (born Randy Traywick) left behind a criminal record as a teenager when he won a talent contest at a country bar in Charlotte, North Carolina, and became a professional entertainer. The club's manager helped him gain more experience singing in front of a dance crowd and, in 1982, Travis and his manager moved to Nashville. It took three years for him to get a major-label contract, but in 1986 he scored his first number one country hit, "On the Other Hand," and released his debut album to critical acclaim. That started a long streak of success for Travis, who was one of the biggest stars of the late 1980s. Unlike many of his neotraditionalist contemporaries, Travis was also a songwriter, and he did not specialize in cover songs. He wrote or co-wrote a couple of tracks on each of those 1980s albums. But his vocals had the naturalized diction of old honky-tonk and the low baritone range that recalled classic country singers such as George Jones. His musical style on was straight honky tonk, updated for the 1980s with a contemporary rhythm section.

Dwight Yoakam's biography included one additional aspect that played well with neotraditionalist audiences: he had come to Nashville in the 1970s with grand aspirations, but his brand of hard-edged honky-tonk failed to land him a record contract; in other words, he had been "too country" for Nashville. Yoakam moved to Los Angeles in 1978, where he played with rock bands while absorbing the traditions of Bakersfield country. In 1986, Reprise Records rereleased an album that Yoakam and a friend had recorded for a tiny independent label. On it, Yoakam blended the twang of Bakersfield with rockabilly's electric guitars. It was edgy, retro, and—in the neotraditionalist climate—wildly popular. Yoakam further played into the movement's philosophy with the cover songs he featured so prominently: Johnny Horton's "Honky Tonk Man" (1956), Ray Price's "Heartaches by the Number" (penned by Harlan Howard and a hit for Price in 1959), and Johnny Cash's "Ring of Fire." Yoakam talked openly about his disdain for pop-crossover country and his respect for older styles. In 1988, he recorded "Streets of Bakersfield" as a duet with Buck Owens, solidifying his reputation as a Bakersfield revivalist. The result was his first number one hit—Yoakam's revivalist attitude and retro music had found acceptance in the new era of commercial country.

Figure 11-3 Randy Travis.

Source: Courtesy of Country Music Hall of Fame and Museum

The most interesting contributions to the neotraditionalist scene came from musicians whose connection to commercial country was limited and who thrived in more alternative or independent scenes. Steve Earle (1955–) was born in Virginia but raised in San Antonio. He was part of the 1970s singer/songwriter scene in Texas in the era of progressive country (see Chapter 9). He came to Nashville in the mid-1970s, where he earned his living as a songwriter. In 1986, he released his debut solo album, *Guitar Town*. The stripped-down Texas honky-tonk sound, combined with his nasal vocal and rumbling electric guitars, was essentially Earle rebelliously confronting commercial country music. Earle saw little success on the country charts, and two albums later, he shifted to a rock identity. Yet later generations of country fans have reclaimed his legacy as part of country music, and "Copperhead Road" (1988), which was too rock for country music when it was released, has resurfaced as a mainstay on country radio and in country bars.

The Texan singer-songwriter scene was a major musical site in the neotraditionalist era. Also in 1986, Lyle Lovett (1957–), from Klein, Texas, released his first album. His singles showed up on country radio, but never turned into the sort of chart-topping hits that would have secured his future in mainstream country. Lovett's music was an intoxicating blend of western swing and honky-tonk, but toward the end of the 1980s, he veered off in other musical directions, exploring jazz and gospel projects. The independent/alternative audience embraced him. Lovett's friend Robert Earl Keen Jr. (1956–), from Houston, Texas, was also part of the 1970s

Reba McEntire (1955–)

Reba McEntire was the most successful female star of the neotraditionalist era, yet her music embraced more than one style. She has had one of the longest and most successful performance careers in the genre and heads an entertainment firm whose reach extends into almost all aspects of the music business. Her fans continue to celebrate her Oklahoma, rodeo-riding roots and regard her as a down-to-earth country star, even while her career and music have ventured far beyond the bounds of country music.

Raised on a cattle ranch in Oklahoma with a rodeo bull-riding father and a singer and schoolteacher mother, McEntire was part of her family's band that performed in the local area. Country entertainer and songwriter Red Steagall heard her perform the national anthem at a rodeo in 1974, encouraged her to come to Nashville, and helped her land a recording contract with Mercury Records. Her first several albums were produced in a light country-pop sound, moving toward the countrypolitan trends of the late 1970s. In the early 1980s, her vocal prowess won over country fans, and she enjoyed modest success with several countrypolitan recordings. During those years, McEntire included a few traditionally styled recordings on each album, such as the slow honky-tonk waltz "I'm Not That Lonely Yet" (1982) and the similarly styled

"You're the First Time I've Thought about Leaving" (1982), which was her second number one hit; those recordings established her credibility with the slowly emerging neotraditionalist movement.

In 1984, McEntire switched record companies, and shortly thereafter released *My Kind of Country*, which consisted mostly of neotraditionalist, twang-filled recordings, including covers of old country songs ("How Blue," for instance; see Listening Guide). The album foreshadowed the coming wave of neotraditionalists, established McEntire as a major star, and let her claim her place among the vanguard of country stars.

Toward the end of the 1980s and into the early 1990s, McEntire embraced music videos as a major part of her art, solidified her vocal style as a balance of pop-crossover and traditional sounds, and forged a bond with the female country audience that boosted her commercial success even further. From the mid-1980s on, McEntire treated her music videos as short movies with carefully molded storylines. These videos were a chance to showcase her formidable acting skills as well as giving her songs richer backstories and cultural contexts. Historians point to "Whoever's in New England" (1986) as a breakthrough in country videos for its depiction of a story line

singer-songwriter scene in Texas, and in 1986, he moved to Nashville with similar commercial country aspirations. Unlike Lovett, Keen did not get a chance to test out his music in the mainstream country market, and he returned to Texas two years later. There he built a substantial career as a songwriter and country musician, releasing an album for national distribution in 1989. While he never charted on country radio, he and others like him created an even broader fan base for roots-oriented that went beyond the song's lyrics: a housewife laments her husband's business travel, which covers for his affairs, but in the final scene he comes back to embrace her in a gesture that indicates his contrition. By the time McEntire filmed "Fancy" (1991) and "Is There Life Out There" (1992), her videos had a seasoned, artful maturity.

During these same years, from the late 1980s into the early 1990s, McEntire's music focused directly on the middle-aged female country audience, with songs that resonated with their concerns, experiences, and interests. Again, this was a prescient move on her part; that demographic became the focus of national attention in early 1990s politics and became a huge force in country music fandom (see Chapter 12). Her song lyrics covered divorce, social injustice, AIDS, infidelity, midlife crises, women's education, religious faith, and other topics with a depth of conviction that earned her very loyal fans. Yet her stage shows were displays of a consummate entertainer, involving the latest in technology, special effects, glitzy costumes, and McEntire's own masterful stage presence and vocal domination.

In the 2000s, McEntire ventured further into acting, starring on Broadway and in her own televised sitcom, *Reba*. She continued to balance dual identities as a more traditional country artist and pop-crossover singer throughout these years. Her duet ("Because of You" [2007]) and tour with American Idol

winner Kelly Clarkson, along with several of her later singles, were styled entirely as contemporary pop, while her 2009 album *Keep On Loving You* had a haunting murder ballad on it ("Maggie Creek Road") along with a western swing romp ("I'll Have What She's Having").

In spite of her adoption of pop-crossover stylings throughout her career, many other aspects of McEntire's professional life are heavily invested in the ideology of neotraditionalist country. Fans have always paid close attention to her biography, from her rodeo experiences in her youth to her owning a cattle ranch with first husband Charles Battle (whom she divorced in 1987) to her personal grief and its expression in her music after half her road band was killed in a plane crash in 1991. The extensive list of cover songs she has performed over the years tie her convincingly to her heroes from country's past, which is a critical part of the neotraditionalist perspective. McEntire has also focused on being a singer rather than a songwriter, and has relied on the top craftsmen in the songwriting business to supply her country material, as was common among the neotraditionalists. Finally, she has remained quite consistent in her musical style throughout her career. Her star power, both inside country music and beyond, is impressive; she was still placing songs on the *Billboard* country charts in 2017, more than four decades after her first chart single.

country music, especially a Texas sound grounded in the progressive country songwriting traditions of the 1960s and '70s. Some of Keen's fans, many of whom were invested in ideas of anticommercial authenticity, actually valued his music and artistic identity more for the fact that he had never been a commercial country star. In general, the fan base that supported the development of neotraditionalist country would play a critical in the emergence of alt-country in the mid-1990s (see Chapter 13).

LISTENING GUIDE

"How Blue" (1984)

PERFORMER: Reba McEntire

SONGWRITER: Hugh Moffatt

ORIGINAL ALBUM: *My Kind of Country* (MCA 5516, 1984)

FORM: Verse-chorus

STYLE: Neotraditionalist

Reba McEntire had been releasing country singles and albums since 1976, and had already had two number one hits, always striking a careful balance between pop-crossover countrypolitan recordings and a more retrospective approach to twangy country. In 1984, she switched record labels and was reportedly dissatisfied with the types of songs her new producers were bringing to her. Her producers wanted to mix traditional roots sounds into an overall pop-crossover approach, whereas McEntire was pushing for a more traditional country sound. This same conflict is a major part of Patsy Cline's legacy: Cline purportedly always wanted to sing more straight country, whereas her producer Owen Bradley was pushing her into a pop-crossover mold, and that tension is one of the most cited features of her career (see Chapter 6).

In the case of Reba McEntire, her 1984 album *My Kind of Country* became the touchstone for fans of more traditional country music: McEntire resisted the crossover approach and instead sought permission from Jimmy Bowen, then head of the record label (and also George Strait's producer), to find the songs for the

Figure 11-4 Reba McEntire had been on stage for years before her breakthrough in the mid-1980s.

Source: Courtesy of Country Music Hall of Fame and Museum

album. She insisted that the studio musicians stick to a more traditional, western swing style of accompaniment without the thick layers of strings or lush arrangements that were favored on countrypolitan sessions. The story that she was the one pushing the album back toward country traditions and refusing to indulge in pop-crossover trends was just as important as the recording itself; it gave her credibility with more traditionally minded fans, for whom the idea of authenticity in the mid-1980s was heavily tied to showing respect for country's past.

Songwriter Hugh Moffatt had been working in Nashville since the mid-1970s, and had already written classic hits for Tammy Wynette and Dolly Parton, among others. In the style of the old 1960s country songwriters, Moffatt stuck to straightforward heartache lyrics without any complicating structural features or elaborations in the song's form. "How Blue" is in verse-chorus form, and on this recording, the chorus appears first, with just two short verses tucked into the song. It has comparatively few lyrics and no complicated wordplay, but instead leaves plenty of time in the recording for instrumental solos, as was common in western swing.

The main style of this recording is neotraditionalist, drawing on western swing. Yet there are many other musical references in the performance, several of which are mentioned in the Listening Chart. The call-and-response vocals evoke gospel, and the way the single line of vocal harmony floats over the melody reminds the listener of the 1930s and '40s duet tradition as well as Bakersfield of the 1960s, where that approach became part of the style.

For these recording sessions, legendary western swing fiddler Johnny Gimble and newcomer Mark O'Connor teamed up with other topflight session musicians. The accompaniment, with its emphasis on acoustic instruments and swing rhythms, sounded fresh and novel in 1984. It won over the audience and sailed to the top of the *Billboard* country chart. For fans who were tired of countrypolitan, this sound was a welcome indicator that change might be on the horizon. The rest of the album contained cover songs by Ray Price, Connie Smith, and Loretta Lynn. She included Bakersfield shuffles (such as "Don't You Believe Him") and a honky-tonk waltz ("You've Got Me [Right Where You Want Me]"). She also featured new songs by long-established songwriters, including Harlan Howard, and marked them all with her distinctive Oklahoman accent. Historians and fans proclaimed that the whole album was on the front lines of the neotraditionalist movement.

"How Blue" was not, in fact, McEntire's first roots-oriented single; "You're the First Time I've Thought about Leaving" (1983) had been a steel-and-fiddle-driven retro waltz, for instance. But fans talked about "How Blue" as a turning point in her career. McEntire continued to indulge both her pop-crossover tendencies and her retro tastes. Her later albums feature twangy western swing cuts alongside honky-tonk weepers and plenty of retro country, but the majority of her subsequent hits featured R&B vocal stylings and pop-crossover studio production. Nonetheless, throughout her career, she retained her reputation as a neotraditionalist, which was earned largely on the merits of this one song.

Continued

Listening Guide

"Hallelujah Side" (1926) Continued

TIME	FORM	LISTENING CUES	DISCUSSION
0:00	Intro	acoustic guitar	Finger-picked acoustic guitar starts the song out, with just a hint of fiddle at the end of the introduction.
0:13	Chorus	"How blue can you make me ..."	Notice the single line of vocal harmony is above the melody, in a style reminiscent of the duet acts from the 1930s and '40s, or the classic 1960s Bakersfield technique of a single line of high vocal harmony. The harmony also comes in a call-and-response pattern, where the lead sings "how blue..." and then the harmony echoes after that, "how blue...," a technique common in the gospel singing of the 1930s and beyond. In other words, the vocal performance is very retro and traditional.
0:36	Verse 1	"Oh, honey, why did you ..."	The full band enters here, but the main sounds we hear are the vocals, fiddle, and guitar.
0:58	Chorus	"How blue ..."	The steel guitar fills in between the singer's lines in this chorus.
1:20	Instrumental interlude	fiddle	A western swing fiddle solo occupies the first half of this section, which is a variation on the chorus. An electric guitar plays the solo over the second half (starting at 1:31).
1:42	Verse 2	"If I sink any lower ..."	The electric guitar fills in between the singer's lines here, which pulls the performance into a more modern sound. At the end of this section (at 2:01), a rumbling electric guitar interjection reminds the listener that this is a thoroughly modern, radio-friendly recording in spite of its traditional dressing.
2:04	Chorus	"How blue ..."	The fiddle reappears, filling between the singer's lines.
2:25	Tag	"How can I go on ..."	The last two lines repeat here, with a twangy steel guitar interjection (at 2:30) and a classic western swing pattern from the fiddle at the end (2:34).

Co-opted, Conservative, and Commercial

By the end of the 1980s, neotraditionalism was no longer novel, rebellious, or refreshing, but instead had become the standard commercial face of country music. Kathy Mattea (1959–) turned out female versions of honky-tonk music with a strong dose of acoustic folk in them. Rosanne Cash scored a number one hit in 1987 with a cover of her father Johnny Cash's "Tennessee Flat Top Box." Rodney Crowell (Rosanne's husband at the time and an extremely successful longtime songwriter) recorded "I Couldn't Leave You If I Tried" (1988) as if it were lifted straight out of Bakersfield circa 1965. Keith Whitley, who had as stellar a bluegrass background as Ricky Skaggs, released honky-tonk twang with crying steel guitars, as in "I'm No Stranger to the Rain," to critical and popular acclaim. Other artists such as Dolly Parton jumped on the neotraditionalist bandwagon as well. Parton teamed up with Emmylou Harris and Linda Ronstadt for the *Trio* album (1987), which was a collection of old country covers sung in close harmony and laced with old-time sounds such as an autoharp (heard on "Wildflowers," for instance).

The revival attitude even made room, briefly, for k. d. lang, whose *Angel with a Lariat* album appeared in 1987. Lang was an enigma in the neotraditionalist country movement, because her biography and personal identity were at odds with the conservative, roots-oriented, tradition-laden movement. She started her musical career in Canada, then moved to Nashville in 1986. Critics heralded her vocal talent as simply astonishing, a smoky, bold voice with a huge range and all the nuances in performance of Patsy Cline at her best (lang's band was named the Reclines). Her first Nashville album, *Angel with a Lariat*, included covers of both Patsy Cline ("Three Cigarettes in an Ashtray") and Lynn Anderson ("Rose Garden," a 1970 number-one hit). Owen Bradley—who had shaped Patsy Cline's sound in the late 1950s—then produced her follow-up album, *Shadowland*, which included a collaboration with Loretta Lynn, Brenda Lee, and Kitty Wells along with a cover of "I'm Down to My Last Cigarette," a 1964 Bakersfield shuffle from Billy Walker (penned by Harlan Howard, produced by Don Law, and recorded by the top Nashville session musicians). Lang was situated in the middle of a network of classic country songwriters, producers, and stars.

Singles from the album *Shadowland* snuck onto the *Billboard* country chart, but lang did not find widespread acceptance among country fans. Lang's highest barrier to being accepted a mainstream country star was her androgynous image and her public identity as a lesbian. Especially in the neotraditionalist era, many fans equated musical authenticity with how closely a singer's biographical identity aligned with a prototype that was white, politically conservative, straight, Christian, and tied to rural, working-class roots. Gender roles in particular had been a major theme in the genre for decades, and the core fan base was highly resistant to anything that challenged those firmly established identities. Lang's album covers and personal style combined exaggerated camp (the cartoonish drawing on the cover of *A Truly Western Experience*, for instance) with androgyny (her Elvis Presley–style haircut on the cover of *Shadowland*). For many years, lang had deflected questions about her sexuality in interviews, resulting in an ambiguity that was not satisfactory to the country audience (lang came out in 1992). Although the musical community inside Nashville had accepted her, the fan base had not. By the end of the 1980s, lang had left country music and found a more enthusiastic audience in the alternative musical scene.

Lang's neotraditionalist recordings illustrate the relationship between musical style and genre. From the perspective of musical style, lang's mid- to late-'80s recordings are some of the finest neotraditionalist country ever recorded, and her musicianship and respect for country's past is profound and sincere. Yet from the perspective of genre, lang did not fit; the mainstream country audience was seeking a representation of identity and meaning beyond the actual sound of the music.

As the decade drew to a close, new country stars in the neotraditionalist mold appeared. The press dubbed them "hat acts," a reference to their propensity for wearing cowboy hats and western wardrobes. Critics sometimes used the term derisively to imply that the newcomers were copycats of stars such as George Strait, although fans were less judgmental. Ricky Van Shelton (1952–) was one of these newcomers. Among Van Shelton's hit singles were several covers of 1960s country tunes, including "Statue of a Fool" (1969 hit for Jack Greene) and "From a Jack to a King" (1962 hit for Ned Miller). The next generation of singers following this model, including Garth Brooks, would take the foundations of neotraditionalist country and transform it into the biggest pop-crossover trend that country music had ever witnessed (see Chapter 12).

The symbolic end of the neotraditionalist era came in 1989 when Keith Whitley died of acute alcohol poisoning. In the subsequent years, some of the movement's stars moved forward successfully into the next wave of developments; others found musical havens in the alternative and independent musical scenes outside of mainstream country; and yet others faded out of the performance scene entirely. The two major outcomes of the neotraditionalist movement were:

1. The completion of a natural cycle of country music's evolution, where a crossover period was followed by a return to the roots of country tradition;
2. The emergence of a few superstars who built their careers on a particular brand of authenticity.

The neotraditionalist era served as a retrenchment period for the genre. After countrypolitan threatened to blend country indecipherably into pop music, the neotraditionalists reaffirmed country's distinct "otherness" and reminded fans of the unique signifiers of the genre: the twang, the cowboy imagery, and the musical styles that had come to symbolize hard country, especially honky-tonk and Bakersfield. Stars such as George Strait and, to a lesser extent, Randy Travis and Reba McEntire, defined their careers on that particular definition of authenticity, including their biographies. That identity carried their careers through the next decade and beyond. They also served as symbolic anchors who kept country music tied to its past when other artists again moved into a pop-crossover style in the 1990s. Although the audience and record sales during this era were only a fraction of what they had been during the height of countrypolitan, the symbolic importance of this era to the overall evolution of country music was profound.

⋆ ESSAY: MUSICAL STYLE

 # Neotraditionalist Recordings

The recordings that became popular during the latter half of the 1980s tended to feature neotraditionalist musical styles. The main characteristics of these styles were an obvious and audible resurrection of earlier, distinctive styles of country music, updated with modern recording studio techniques. These imported styles are most often identified by their rhythmic characteristics and basic instrumentation.

The main styles that reappeared in the neotraditionalist era included honky-tonk, bluegrass, Bakersfield, and western swing. Some elements of outlaw country, especially its use of Old West and cowboy imagery, were also present, as was some rockabilly. The earlier styles that were assiduously avoided were the Nashville sound and any extension of it, along with the countrypolitan trends from earlier that decade.

The ensembles and texture of the neotraditionalist recordings were stripped down. Fiddle and steel guitar reappeared as prominent lead instruments. Vocal harmony shifted back to one, two, or three voices, usually singing the lyrics along with the soloist rather than filling in with nonsense syllables such as "ooh" or "ahh." Banjos and mandolins served as clear signifiers of a neotraditionalist attitude, as did the reappearance of instruments associated with hillbilly or folk traditions of the 1930s and earlier: the hammered dulcimer and mountain dulcimer heard on the Judds' *Rockin' with the Rhythm* album, for instance, or the autoharp (famously linked to the original Carter Family) heard on Dolly Parton, Linda Ronstadt, and Emmylou Harris's *Trio* album.

Rhythmic characteristics included songs based on the Bakersfield shuffle pattern, slow waltzes (which were rarities in countrypolitan), and the two-beat basic honky-tonk pattern that matched country dances such as the two-step. Bluegrass breakdowns reappeared, as did swing rhythms that evoked the jazz-influenced tradition of western swing. Both bluegrass and western swing featured instrumental solos throughout a song, another trait that reappeared in the neotraditionalist era.

Singers used a naturalized technique and allowed regional accents to be heard more prominently. However, this trend was balanced, especially on the part of the female country singers, by virtuosic displays of vocal gymnastics clearly influenced by R&B singers. There was a clear distinction between the male and female singers in this style, with the men remaining closer to traditional honky-tonk vocals and the women allocated more freedom to sing like a pop star.

As had occurred in the outlaw era of the mid-1970s, the neotraditionalist style was defined as much by what it lacked as by what it contained, in this instance the most obvious elements of countrypolitan. Electric keyboards were largely gone, as were the string sections (which had always been a signifier of crossover since they first appeared in the late 1950s), horns, layers of backup vocals, special effects, and extra percussion (hand-claps and tambourines, for instance). The forms of the songs were simpler, often just a verse-chorus pattern. Song topics and references in the lyrics also reverted to traditional signifiers like heartbreak, cheating, small-town and rural life, cowboy themes, and rodeos. Despite these differences from the previous era, electric guitars and electric basses remained in common use, and the drums continued to be placed prominently in the recording mix, often closely miked and with a lot of reverb. In fact, one can often identify a mid-1980s country recording simply by listening to the timbre of the drums. Overall, the neotraditionalist styles were a reconstruction of past hard country styles but redressed in a modern studio.

Branson, Missouri, and Country Music Tourism

Live performances and fans' first-hand access to country stars have been staples of the country genre since its conception. During the 1980s, the importance of live performance venues increased dramatically, however, due to several factors. The genre's commercial boom during the *Urban Cowboy* era increased the fan base interested in country music. More importantly, younger country fans who had grown up during the music's modern commercial phase of the 1950s and '60s were raising their own families, while the older ones were now nearing retirement, which meant there was a large country audience interested in travel and entertainment that would cater to families and seniors. Similarly, many of the country artists from the 1960s and '70s had slipped out of the ranks of contemporary radio stars yet still had large, active fan bases, and these artists were eager to continue their own careers, preferably under conditions that were less taxing than full-time touring. Branson, Missouri, located south of Springfield and near the Arkansas border, took on the role of providing family entertainment and access to yesteryear's country stars in a setting that brought to life the core values of country music. As religious studies scholar Aaron Ketchell has explained, people who visited the region found it "inherently imbued with the ability to enhance spiritual prowess and moral wherewithal

Country jamborees and regional Opry-style shows were common throughout the 1960s and '70s, especially in the region spanning Texas to the Midwest and beyond. Missouri was home to several of the better-known ones, including Buster Doss's Frontier Jamboree and Lee Mace's Ozark Opry. The Ozark Mountains had long been an incubator for country music, home to both national stars such as Porter Wagoner and countless family bands and local entertainers who graced the radio and television stations for decades there. The greater Springfield area had hosted the *Ozark Jubilee* television show in the late 1950s, an important early instance of country music on television. The region built a reputation on family-friendly Midwestern entertainment and became the hub for a booming country music tourism industry.

Branson had already cultivated a substantial tourist industry around natural caves, which had drawn paying visitors since the early 1900s and around which a theme park was built in 1960. For years, fans had flocked to the area seeking the setting of the 1907 novel *The Shepherd of the Hills*, which was turned into a movie starring John Wayne in 1941 and, subsequently, a huge outdoor drama, performed on the site that ran from 1960 to 2017. Locally based family entertainers thrived, including the Baldknobbers and the Presleys' Country Jubilee (no relation to Elvis), both of which expanded the entertainment infrastructure in the town when they moved into their own theaters in the 1960s. Similar growth continued through the 1970s, and in 1981, entertainment entrepreneur Chisai Childs opened the Starlite Theatre, a glitzy, upscale venue that captured the countrypolitan appeal of sequined country stars. All these theaters and shows provided ample booking opportunities for country singers, and just about every major 1980s country star has played the Branson region at some point in his or her career.

In the case of Branson, the growth of its entertainment scene prompted even more expansion. In 1983, Roy Clark opened a theater with his name on it in Branson. Clark had cohosted *Hee Haw* with Buck Owens and had an established fan base by that point, but his music was not getting radio airplay, and he was looking for a different way to continue his career as an entertainer. His theater brought a cavalcade of country stars in as guest performers, and within a few years many of them had also set up their own shows in Branson. Even Willie Nelson and Merle Haggard set up shows there in the early 1990s, although both were very short-lived ventures, primarily because the Branson audience was looking for more family-friendly, folksy entertainment than they could muster. In 1992, *Time* magazine heralded Branson as "country music's new Mecca."

The shows in Branson continue to feature local entertainers covering both classic and contemporary country music, guest stars, and resident country stars from previous generations and a host of other variety shows. Many of them include some "frontier" theme: chuck wagon suppers or trick-riding shows such as Dolly Parton's Dixie Stampede. The Sons of the Pioneers (of singing cowboy fame, having now passed through several generations of membership) are regularly in residence at the theme park in the summer. The idea of family-friendly country music tourism spread to other locales, as well; in 1986, Dolly Parton opened Dollywood in the Smoky Mountains, for instance, as a combination theme park that featured traditional crafts, foods, and representations of Appalachian life from bygone days, tons of family entertainment and rides, and, of course, live music venues.

The refrain that "today's music is not as good as the last decade's" is perennially part of the country fan base's beliefs. Until the rise of Branson, fans had few options, other than the Grand Ole Opry, where they could indulge their nostalgia for country from a bygone era. Country singers had been performing in Las Vegas for decades, but Vegas's wilder side was off-putting to the family-centric fan base. And Nashville of the 1980s and early 1990s offered little by way of family entertainment except the Opryland theme park, which was on the decline and would shutter its doors in 1997.

In the 1980s and early 1990s, Branson mattered to country music because its local entertainment industry picked up on the underlying themes of the genre. These included family, a religious outlook embedded in secular entertainment, and an idealized rural, Western frontier as a site of imagined escape. Branson gives fans a chance to see former generations of stars perform live, as well as a chance to visit a place that embraced a country-music philosophy wholeheartedly: sacred and secular entertainment merge in the town in a country music time capsule.

☆ **ESSAY: SONGWRITING**

Cover Songs Revisited

The neotraditionalist artists' attention to country music's past shows up in their frequent use of cover songs. Obviously, these songs provide literal ties to the styles, eras, and stars of earlier country music. But their frequent appearance in the 1980s also had broader implications for the country music industry and country music in general.

As explored in Chapter 2, when a singer "covers" a song, he or she performs a song that was already strongly associated with a different artist and a previous performance. This is different than merely performing a "standard," which is a term that music scholars use to refer to songs so popular and so widely performed that audiences do not associate them with any one particular artist or performance. Covers, on the other hand, are songs that fans think of as "belonging"—in a cultural sense, not in terms of legal copyright—to a particular artist. In country music, songs that have become big hits are readily associated with the star who performed them rather than the songwriter(s) who created them originally. For instance, country fans think of "Lovesick Blues" as a Hank Williams song, even though it was written by Cliff Friend and Irving Mills. Thus, when George Strait released a version of "Lovesick Blues," he was covering Hank Williams, and to fans, he was actually referring to Hank Williams and forging a connection with him through the very act of singing the song.

Prior to the neotraditionalist era, plenty of artists routinely covered earlier country songs. But In the mid-1980s, covering was part of a larger philosophical perspective that tried to bring the past of country music forward into the present. George Strait derived his musical style from Texas country of the past, but he also literally borrowed its songs. The majority of Dwight Yoakam's early hits were famous country songs by earlier artists, and he took the perspective a step further by bringing Buck Owens out of semiretirement to sing "Streets of Bakersfield" with him, connecting not only to the recording but also to the original artist in person. Reba McEntire constructed her neotraditionalist identity with covers on *My Kind of Country* (1984) and again later with her smash hits "Fancy" and "The Night the Lights Went Out in Georgia." When Ricky Skaggs made the transition from bluegrass to mainstream country, he tucked old songs from George Jones, Bill Monroe, and the Everly Brothers into his albums, along with plenty of other covers. Much of Ricky Van Shelton's career was built on his interpretations of old Bakersfield shuffles and classic country songs. Emmylou Harris and Dolly Parton did so as well during these years, and the list could go on.

The prevalent use of cover songs in the neotraditionalist era raises five major points:

1. Covers allowed those artists to assert a connection between themselves and the legends of the past, thereby paying tribute and laying claim to their figurative birthright of country music. This factor was extremely important to neotraditionalist stars and their fans.

2. Covers helped educate new generations of country fans about the references, songs, styles, and performers of the genre's past. This effect was significant, especially since fans in the late 1980s often had little or no personal connection to country music prior to that decade, and country's existence as a genre relies on a heavy investment in tradition.

3. The widespread use of covers occurred in the 1980s in a way that it would not today because key aspects of both the industry and the fan base have changed in the intervening years. In the '80s, artists were not under as much pressure from their record labels to record their own compositions. The artists stood to profit from writers' royalties if they did, but their record labels cared far less about who penned their songs because it did not affect their income. In today's industry, artists' contracts with record labels often include strong incentives for them to record songs they have written or cowritten. Furthermore, country fans in the 1980s had not yet equated authorship with authenticity. The indie rock and alternative music scenes of the 1990s changed this, however, and that philosophy spread to country music as well. From that time forward, country fans expected new country singers to write or co-write their own material at least most of the time, and only a few country stars (such as George Strait) were granted immunity. While professional songwriters are still the creative force behind much of country music, they now frequently co-write with the recording artists, and those collaborations are often initiated by the artists' record label or management. In the late 1980s, however, neither of these conditions was yet in place. In the late 1980s, about 20% of number one country hits were written or cowritten by the artist, whereas two decades later, that number was around 70%. Those conditions made cover songs more prevalent in the '80s.

4. Covers allowed artists to lay claim to one type of authenticity that 1980s country fans valued, specifically the notion that "authenticity" means "the established, traditional way." That perspective was the underlying force behind the entire neotraditionalist movement, namely that country music needed to return to something earlier, already established, and already vetted by history. This is, of course, only one of the definitions or values that that country fans have subsumed under the term "authenticity," but it was an important one in the late 1980s, given the cultural, political, and musical contexts in which that country music existed.

5. Ironically, however, cover songs also undercut the other type of authenticity that modern country fans value, which is the notion that something is authentic when it is the original creation of the presenter. That perspective on authenticity, which prioritizes originality over tradition, wants a musician to (a) do something different, unique, and innovative, and (b) do something that is invested with personal authorship, or in other words, write and sing songs that are generated from firsthand experience. Cover songs, and by extension, the whole neotraditionalist movement, denied that type of authenticity to the stars, who were instead focused on resurrecting earlier

styles and performing "someone else's song." Within a few years, those limitations would be responsible for driving new developments and artistic movements in country music, most notably the alt-country movement (see Chapter 13).

LISTEN-SIDE-BY-SIDE

"Deep Water"

Songwriter: Fred Rose
Bob Wills and His Texas Playboys, 1947
(originally released on Columbia 38137)
George Strait, 1986 (on *7*, MCA Records)

George Strait is known for bringing western swing back into country music in the 1980s. That is a style that was crafted in the 1930s and thrived in the years before and after WWII, linked geographically to Texas and the Southwest. But what does western swing sound like in the neotraditionalist version compared to the style that reverberated in dance halls a half-century earlier?

"Deep Water" links us to a time, place, and tradition in country music's past. Fred Rose wrote the song, bringing to bear all of his experience in the pop standards of the 1930s. Like many of the songs that Rose wrote with Hank Williams and other standards such as "Blue Eyes Crying in the Rain," this song's form is a "standard song form" AABA pattern, which would have a retro feel in the context of 1980s music. And even though casual fans would not necessarily know the songwriter's name, any listener steeped in country music history would recognize the song from earlier versions.

In 1947, Bob Wills's band was already in the process of condensing back to a string-band format, without the full horn sections he had hired before WWII. Here we find the signature twin-fiddles sound, plus steel guitar, supported by a typical rhythm section with piano, guitar, banjo, mandolin, bass, and drums. Tommy Duncan sings in his expected crooner style.

Almost four decades later, George Strait recorded the song at the moment that the neotraditionalist

movement was sliding into the dominant musical position. Strait's entire musical presence was built on the western swing sounds from his native Texas. But clearly, the sound of western swing in the mid-1980s is sonically distinct from its earlier incarnation. The basics of the style are present: a swing beat, twin fiddles, the same lyrics, melody, and chords. Even the instrumentation is largely the same. A piano is present, although layered so deep in the mix that only the most careful listening gives its presence away. What we hear most prominently is the difference in recording technologies and styles of blending and balancing the different instruments in the recording: Strait's recording has drums forward in the mix and miked to give a distinctive presence to each instrument in the drum kit. The stereo spread of the sound is also an instant reminder of when it was recorded. Finally, listen for musical precision: there are moments in the 1947 recording where an individual note is slightly out of tune or other imperfections exist. By 1986, the recording has the polish of studio work where every short fragment of the music can be corrected or overdubbed.

With a close comparison of these two versions of "Deep Water," we can hear the ways in which George Strait is tying himself to history through the essence of the song. We can also hear the commonalities that make Strait's recording a western swing revival and part of a tribute and link to Bob Wills. But most striking to our ears is the difference in recording procedure, the technology itself, and the way that the recorded tracks are blended or mixed together to create the final recording, each carefully positioned in volume and prominence in the final version. In other words, we can hear both the shared style of western swing and the forty years' difference in how records were made such that we would never mistake one for the other.

PLAYLIST

lang, k. d. "I'm Down to My Last Cigarette" (1988)

Mattea, Kathy. "Eighteen Wheels and a Dozen Roses" (1987)

Parton, Dolly, Linda Ronstadt, and Emmylou Harris, "Wildflowers" (*Trio* album) (1988)

Shelton, Ricky Van. "From a Jack to a King" (1988)

Travis, Randy. "Forever and Ever, Amen" (1987)

Yoakam, Dwight. "Little Ways" (1987)

FOR MORE READING

Bufwack, Mary A., and Robert K. Oermann. *Finding Her Voice: Women in Country Music, 1800–2000.* Nashville: Vanderbilt University Press, 2003.

Cusic, Don. *Randy Travis: King of the New Traditionalists.* New York: St. Martin's Press, 1993.

Gates, David. "Are You Sure Hank Done It This Way?" In *All That Glitters: Country Music in America,* ed. George H. Lewis. Bowling Green: Bowling Green State University Press, 1993, pp. 314–316.

Judd, Naomi, with Bud Schaetzle. *Love Can Build a Bridge.* New York: Fawcett Crest, 1993.

Ketchell, Aaron K. *Holy Hills of the Ozarks: Religion and Tourism in Branson, Missouri.* Baltimore: Johns Hopkins University Press, 2007.

Malone, Bill C., and Jocelyn R. Neal. "Tradition and Change: Country Music 1985–2002." In *Country Music U.S.A.*, 3rd rev. ed., chap. 12. Austin: University of Texas Press, 2010, pp. 417–465.

Wolff, Kurt, and Orla Duane. "Wild and Blue: Traditionalism Makes a Comeback." In *Country Music: The Rough Guide,* chap. 12. London: The Rough Guide Ltd, 2000, pp. 457–501.

NAMES AND TERMS

Anderson, John	Keen Jr., Robert Earl	Skaggs, Ricky
Branson	lang, k.d.	Strait, George
dulcimer	Lovett, Lyle	Travis, Randy
Earle, Steve	McEntire, Reba	Yoakam, Dwight
Highwaymen	RIAA	
Judds	Shelton, Ricky Van	

REVIEW TOPICS

1. Discuss the different definitions of authenticity that were relevant to the neo-traditionalist movement and how they had different effects on country music's development.

2. Identify and explore instances in country music where a song, artist, or album takes on simultaneously opposing meanings, such as occurred with "I Cross My Heart."

3. How did accepted gender roles affect the development of country music in the late 1980s?

The Commercial Country Explosion

Two major developments occurred in commercial country music during the 1990s. The first rode in on the heels of the 1980s neotraditionalist movement and launched country music once again into the American mainstream. The second occurred later in the decade, when country music embraced a new country-pop sound and again crossed over onto the pop charts, as it had done in the early 1980s. Along the way, new technologies changed how information about the music industry was collected and reported, how recording studios worked, and how fans accessed and interacted with the music, most notably due to the internet. By the turn of the twenty-first century, country music had enjoyed unprecedented commercial success and a boom period unrivaled by anything in its history. These developments had also pushed the boundaries of the genre to an unsustainable extreme, which would soon lead to substantial changes.

The Class of 1989 and "New Country"

The contemporary commercial country era began with a group of artists whom the press dubbed the "class of 1989." The neotraditionalist era of the late 1980s had brought back sounds, attitudes, images, and references from the early decades of country music, and the new artists of the next generation kept the honky-tonk sounds and cowboy hats that characterized those years. But four new factors changed the course of country music in the early 1990s:

1. An unprecedented group of exceptionally talented newcomers arrived on the scene.
2. These artists brought with them a new approach to the art of making and performing country music, largely informed by rock music.
3. New technologies inside the music industry helped rebrand country music.
4. The economic and cultural climate in the United States shifted dramatically, which made a large mainstream population more receptive to new styles of country music.

On May 9, 1989, neotraditionalist honky-tonk star Keith Whitley died from alcoholism, a moment that retrospectively marked the changing of an era. That same year, a new crop of talented singers arrived in Nashville or, in the case of some who were already there, finally got their big breaks within the music business. At the front of the male group were Garth Brooks (see Artist Profile), Alan Jackson (1958–), and Clint Black (1962–), all of whom cultivated a western image by donning cowboy hats and western wear. Their music continued the neotraditional honky-tonk sounds of Randy Travis and George Strait with fiddles, steel guitar, danceable two-step beats, and voices with an audible twang (see Chapter 11). Although Vince Gill (1957–) had been working in country music since the early 1980s, he moved to a whole new level of stardom when his album *When I Call Your Name* (1989) appeared. Over the next few years, the roster of male stars associated with this movement continued to grow. In 1990, Alan Jackson, Mark Chesnutt (1963), and Travis Tritt (1963–) each released their debut albums, with Tritt drawing on a Southern rock heritage in his music and image, while both Jackson and Chesnutt emulated honky-tonk styles. A year later, Brooks & Dunn (Kix Brooks [1955–] and Ronnie Dunn [1953–]), the group Diamond Rio, and Billy Ray Cyrus (1961–) arrived on the scene, as well. Within only three years, a whole new cast of extremely talented singers who would go on to enjoy long and influential careers had established themselves as the new voices of country music. Together with the few established stars such as John Anderson, Ricky Van Shelton, Randy Travis, and George Strait, whose careers continued to thrive, they shaped the contemporary commercial country of the early 1990s.

Several notable female stars emerged at the same time. Lorrie Morgan—who had been working in country music since the late 1970s and was the daughter of Opry member George Morgan—released her first major-label album in 1989, and Mary Chapin Carpenter, who likewise had been in the music business for years, saw her first major success with her 1989 album, *State of the Heart*. Two years later, Pam Tillis released her debut album. Like Morgan, Tillis was the daughter of a famous country singer, Mel Tillis, and like Morgan, she had been working in Nashville for nearly a decade. In 1991, newcomer Trisha Yearwood (1964–) launched her first album and single. A year later, after the Judds disbanded in the wake of Naomi's medical problems with hepatitis C, Wynonna (1964–) emerged as a solo act and joined the growing cadre of female voices in the new era, along with a couple of long-established stars such as Reba McEntire, who continued to enjoy commercial success.

This generation of singers, both male and female, brought a new approach and aesthetic perspective to country music from their own backgrounds as fans. As teens, they had been exposed to FM radio, rock bands, and music videos. Although many of them came from working-class backgrounds where country music was valued, many of them were also fans of rock and pop music. They had observed the appeal of both MTV and CMT and had seen how artists such as Michael Jackson and Madonna entertained thousands in stadium concerts and with music videos. The *Urban Cowboy* era had proved that the potential audience for country music was huge, but only if the music could reach out to the mainstream audience. This new generation of artists believed that they owed their fans an entertainment experience that rivaled the spectacle of other genres. This investment in the fans—something that country singers had cultivated since the 1920s—reached heightened levels in these years, and artists such as Alan Jackson and Garth Brooks displayed unprecedented allegiance to their fans and a sense of personal obligation to them.

Two new technologies altered the course of country music at the same time that these new performers arrived on the scene. On January 20, 1990, *Billboard* switched to Nielsen Broadcast Data Systems (BDS) as the method for collecting information about what songs were receiving radio airplay, from which they determined chart rankings. Prior to that date, the data for the "Hot Country Singles" chart was compiled by asking radio station personnel what they played, a system of human reporting that was prone to inconsistencies and errors. After that date, BDS electronically monitored the airwaves and relied on computers to compare what was broadcast to digital "fingerprints" from their database of songs, thereby producing information about what songs were actually played and how often. This new system drastically changed the public's awareness of what was on the radio, what was popular, and how new music was disseminated. For instance, prior to BDS's implementation, *Billboard's* "Hot Country Singles" chart typically showed approximately fifty different songs reaching the number one slot each year, which meant that a whole range of artists and songs were recognized with that top honor, and fans' attention was dispersed among many different singers. After BDS's implementation, however, between twenty and thirty songs made the top of the *Billboard* chart each year—about half the previous number. This new information revealed just how few songs were in heavy rotation on radio playlists. In other words, the attention of the fan base zeroed in on only a handful of singers whose songs were constantly on the radio. As fewer artists got more of the attention, country music culture moved further toward focusing on individual superstars.

The second technology that affected country music during this era was Sound-Scan, which began in 1991 to track actual sales of music. Like BDS, SoundScan allowed the music industry to collect data on the sales of country music recordings electronically, rather than by human reporting. And, like BDS, SoundScan revealed a very different picture of the state of country music than many had assumed. Prior to SoundScan, *Billboard* reported on music sales by phoning various "reporting" record stores and asking them each week what the most popular music was. Those record stores tended not to be the primary sites where country fans shopped, and many of those stores employed young staff who were, themselves, not fans of country music. Thus, country's reported sales always appeared low. SoundScan, however, kept track of actual sales electronically (through the barcodes on the products), and the stores they tracked included major discount retailers such as Wal-Mart, where a large percentage of country fans bought their music. The new data revealed what some people working inside the music industry had always known—country music was far more popular, and sold far more albums, than had previously been reported. Before SoundScan, country music was constrained by old stigmas or cultural prejudices; people—including many executives in the popular music industry—looked down their noses at the music and treated it like a marginal, backward, and insignificant music. Once its sales figures were electronically generated and openly reported, it became apparent that country was widely accepted within popular culture, and the genre wielded far more power than had been previously acknowledged. This realization prompted the rebranding of country music in the 1990s as something acceptable, popular, and modern.

These factors came together at an auspicious time in history for country music. The arrival of new talent, the singers' awareness of rock music aesthetics and styles of entertainment, and the technologies that reported just how popular country

Garth Brooks (1962–)

Garth Brooks had a monumental impact on country music in the 1990s. Over the span of his career, he has also become a highly polarizing figure. He has legions of fans who loyally declare his music the essence of country and the soundtrack to their lives, but equally vocal are those who believe he threw country music off its traditional course, corrupted the music's authenticity, and sold out to commercial interests. The Recording Industry Association of America certified him as the highest-selling (numbers of albums) solo act and second highest music act of all time, positions he held in 2017, with only the Beatles in front of him. These accolades fueled controversy, as some critics claimed he sought sales at the expense of his art. What remains undisputed, however, is that Brooks's music single-handedly changed country.

Born in Tulsa, Oklahoma, Troyal Garth Brooks was the youngest of six children. Brooks played football and baseball and participated in track and field. He graduated from Oklahoma State University with a degree in advertising. In 1985, he went to Nashville to explore possibilities in the music industry, but returned home less than a day after arriving. He married college girlfriend Sandy Mahl and, in 1987, the two moved to Nashville. Brooks was discovered singing at the Bluebird Cafe (see essay on Songwriting and Sophistication), and signed a contract with Capitol Records.

Brooks's self-titled debut album, which appeared in 1989, established him as a major star with a particular talent for connecting with his fans. With subsequent albums, *No Fences, Ropin' the Wind,* and *The Chase,* his domination of commercial country music continued. Among the factors that contributed to his success were a series of controversies and bold media maneuvers that earned him both fame and notoriety. His mother leaked the debut single from his second album to radio before its release date; he outed his sister as a lesbian on national television when discussing "We Shall Be Free"; and he provoked a boycott with his music video for "The Thunder Rolls," which depicts infidelity, spousal abuse, and the scorned wife shooting her husband (played by Brooks) in front of a child.

Brooks's reputation was built on fierce loyalty to his fans, which he viewed as a contract between himself as an entertainer and the people whom he entertained. That loyalty was his motivation when, in 1993, he had his manager book him and his band, Stillwater, into a tiny honky-tonk in Clovis, New Mexico, under a fake name so that he could recapture the experience of playing for regular fans in a local bar, or the oft-recounted time when he stood at Fan Fair and signed autographs for twenty-three hours straight in 1996 so as not to disappoint his fans who were waiting in line.

Another aspect of Brooks's reputation was that he was too deeply involved in marketing and the business side of music. As his musical success peaked in the middle of the decade, several of Brooks' public actions led fans to wonder if he was losing touch with his roots and focusing too much on his own success and commercial power. In 1993, he threatened to walk out of the Super Bowl halftime show, where he was scheduled to sing the national anthem, if the television station refused to broadcast his music video before the game. In 1996, he walked off stage at the American Music Awards after refusing the trophy for "Favorite Artist of the Year" on the grounds that he did not deserve it—a display of public humility that critics pilloried as a media stunt. In the wake of the release of

Fresh Horses (1995), Brooks publicly lambasted his record label, Capitol, for what he considered poor marketing and a lack of support. That was only one incident in a very long and public dispute with label head Jimmy Bowen, dating back to 1989. Bowen reportedly criticized Brooks's music and wanted to produce his records (whereas Brooks insisted on sticking with producer Allen Reynolds). After Bowen left the label in 1995, Brooks clashed with Bowen's replacement, Scott Hendricks. Conflicts between Brooks and label executives continued, and to the fans, these incidents suggested that Brooks emphasized "business" over "music."

In 1997, Brooks played a concert in New York's Central Park to an astonishingly large crowd, marking the high point of country music's acceptance as mainstream popular entertainment. However, two years later, he puzzled his fans by taking on the character of fictional rock star Chris Gaines and releasing what was supposedly a greatest hits album and retrospective of Gaines's career. He appeared on *Saturday Night Live* as host Garth Brooks, with musical guest Chris Gaines (Brooks, acting as the fictional star). To his loyal audience, the entire undertaking, which initially included plans for a movie, was seen as a self-indulgent artistic vanity project that sold out Brooks' country identity. In its wake, he announced his retirement.

Brooks rescinded his retirement in 2001 with the release of *Scarecrow*, an album on which he consciously resurrected images and sounds from his first few blockbuster albums. The album art showed Brooks in shirts, hats, and settings that matched the most famous photographs from his early career. Throughout his career, his marriage to Sandy had been a prominent feature in his public persona, so fans were also surprised when they announced their intention to divorce in 2000. In 2005, Brooks

Figure 12-1 Country comes to the city: the spectacle of Garth Brooks's free concert in Central Park, New York City, 1997.

Source: Photo by Bob Strong / Getty Images.

married his longtime friend and musical collaborator, Trisha Yearwood.

Throughout his career, Brooks has masterminded clever ways to connect with his fans while simultaneously bolstering sales numbers. He released a limited edition boxed set of his first six albums, making it an instant "collectible" for fans while driving sales by pricing it well below the market standard. He buried the masters for his greatest hits album in concrete to preserve its "limited edition" status. He brokered an exclusive distribution deal with Wal-Mart later in his career for another boxed set, along with an album of formerly unreleased tracks, thereby taking advantage of the strong connection between the discount retailer and the country music fan base. Although he remained in retirement, he occasionally released tribute songs

Continued

ARTIST PROFILE

Garth Brooks (1962–) **Continued**

and performed for charity. In 2010, he began performing in Las Vegas and, four years later, returned to the recording studio to release *Man Against Machine* (2014) and *Gunslinger* (2016), both on his label Pearl Records. Although both albums were ostensibly commercial country that sought radio airplay, their style remained quintessential New Country Garth, welcomed by Brooks's fans but too dated for any real radio success.

Brooks' biggest contribution to country music was his fusion of neotraditionalist honky-tonk with the entertainment appeal of stadium rock and a fiercely loyal bond with his fans. He modeled his sound on the neotraditionalist styles of George Strait and a lesser-known honky-tonk singer, Chris LeDoux, who was also a rodeo champion. Brooks included their names in song lyrics which, along with the style of Brooks's music, his wardrobe, and his ever-present hat, formed a cowboy identity. Although there were striking exceptions, the majority of his songs followed straightforward verse-chorus forms, with conventional honky-tonk lyrics, recorded with plenty of fiddle and steel guitar, even when there were additional layers of instruments in the accompaniment. Brooks's musical influences also included 1970s rock—Journey, Boston, Dan Fogelberg, and James Taylor—which showed up to some extent in his music but mainly in the way he conceived of concerts as full-scale stadium entertainment, complete with stage antics (he used a harness and suspension system to "fly" over the crowd in his Texas Stadium concerts in 1993) and special effects.

Brooks's ability to win over a live crowd was legendary. Yet his commercial success and career maneuvers led detractors, such as alternative country author David Goodman, to label him "the anti-Hank." In sum, Brooks' career offers an interesting case study of the main themes of this book. The first is how he managed to sell 128 million albums to Middle America and still maintain, in his fans' perceptions, his integrity as an authentic country singer. The second is the "otherness" of country—Brooks' career marks one point in twentieth-century history when country music became the mainstream sound and identity of popular culture, but without losing its distinctive "country" identity.

music really was all coincided with an economic downturn. That downturn was sparked by a savings and loan crisis in the late 1980s that resulted in the government spending millions of dollars to protect peoples' savings. It was compounded by the Persian Gulf War, which began in 1990 and led to an increase in oil prices, and by uncertainty about America's place in the global economy after the Berlin Wall fell in 1989 and the Soviet Union dissolved two years later. Under those political and economic conditions, more Americans turned toward conservative values and religious stances (see essay on Southernization and Soccer Moms), and for them, country music provided an appealing way to connect with ideas of roots, family, home, and patriotism.

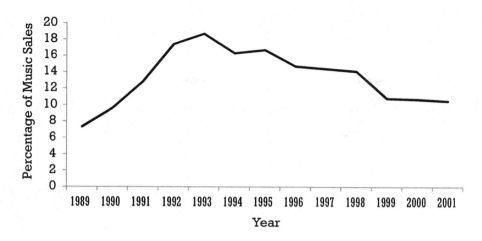

Figure 12-2
Country music as a percentage of all music sales, according to the Recording Industry Association of America (RIAA). The RIAA collected the information by surveying music consumers.

The results on country music's sales were dramatic. Data collected by the Recording Industry Association of America (RIAA) shows country as a percentage of all music sold. Even before SoundScan entered the picture, country's market share was rising. Between 1989 and 1998, country music more than doubled in popularity. By 1993, country accounted for almost one-fifth of all music sold—more than any other single genre.

The country stars who arrived on the scene with the class of 1989 and shortly thereafter were dubbed "new country," "new traditionalists" (a carryover from the previous decade), and "hat acts" by the media. Of these terms, "new country" generally carried positive associations and reassured fans that the music—which was extremely popular—no longer carried the stigmatizing markers of low-class hillbilly twang. It became the primary label for the new trend and style.

HIGHEST-SELLING COUNTRY ARTISTS

According to the RIAA's ranking and certification, as of September 2017, the following country artists have each sold more than 35 million albums (note that the rankings and list for digital single sales is very different):

Garth Brooks	148 million units
George Strait	69
Shania Twain	48
Kenny Rogers	47.5
Alabama	46.5
Alan Jackson	43.5
Reba McEntire	41
Tim McGraw	37.5

Listening Guide

"Friends in Low Places" (1990)

PERFORMER: Garth Brooks

SONGWRITERS: DeWayne Blackwell and Earl Bud Lee

ORIGINAL RELEASE: *No Fences* (Capitol Nashville 93866)

FORM: Verse-chorus

STYLE: New country (contemporary commercial country)

The debut single on Brooks's sophomore album, "Friends in Low Places" was his third number one hit and topped the *Billboard* country chart for four weeks. The song has become a barroom anthem celebrating working-class identity in country music and has remained one of Brooks's signature songs throughout his career. The song illustrates how and why Brooks became a country superstar in the early 1990s and what path new country followed during those years.

Brooks's performance combines both pathos and humor, the recipe that had been a staple of honky-tonk a half-century earlier. Listeners are invited to sympathize with the singer's bitter heartbreak, empathize with his working-class identity and the way it is demeaned by cultural outsiders, and revel in the low-class celebration that, according to the song's lyrics, is far more satisfying than any highbrow affair could ever be. This theme became one of the core ideas in early 1990s country music, in which song lyrics affirmed and celebrated working-class values and lifestyles. Musically, the song builds dramatic tension by beginning with a lonesome acoustic guitar, then allowing the verse to set up expectations for a miserable, tear-in-my-beer song. The chorus brings a musical transformation into a raucous celebration such that by the end of the song, a whole crowd of voices has joined in singing, effectively inviting the listener to participate, too. This sort of crowd enthusiasm—present both in his live performances and his recordings—helped propel Brooks to stardom. The recording also fuses distorted electric guitars, fiddling, and a crying steel guitar into a sonic blend of honky-tonk tradition and barroom rock. Brooks showcases his vocal range (singing an impressive low note on the word "low"), laughs in the middle of the second verse, and whoops along with the crowd in the playout, all of which put a very personal stamp on the performance.

Comparisons with two other versions of the song highlight the important features of this performance. In 1990, Mark Chesnutt released the song on his *Too Cold at Home* album. That recording amplifies the heartbroken honky-tonk features of the song. Without the crowd sing-along, the vocal humor (laughing and whooping), and the barroom revelry that takes the form of a driving bass and drums in the chorus, Chesnutt's version is a fine neotraditional honky-tonk specimen, but it illustrates what was different about Garth Brooks's approach to performance.

A second, contrasting version of the song is Brooks's live rendition. Beginning in 1991, in his concerts, Brooks added a newly penned third verse to the song, which he introduced with a short, spoken monologue about how the song seemed too tame and about how he would have reacted differently if he found himself confronting his ex at a high-society event. This monologue, followed by a new and humorous verse for the song, invokes David Allan Coe's iconic recording, "You Never Even Called Me by My Name" (see Chapter 9), also a barroom sing-along anthem. Brooks's third verse rewrites the storyline so that the singer tells off his ex, rather than leaving quietly; as Brooks sings, "You can kiss my . . ." the crowd roars its approval, drowning out the end of the phrase on the live version released to radio. Brooks also included a live recording on his 1998 *Double Live* album, with the crowd singing along on the third verse. The song's lyrics serve as a rallying cry for enthusiastic fans and illustrate the way that Brooks' career pulled together communities of listeners in a mass celebration of working-class identity, even when the fans themselves were firmly ensconced in the suburban middle class.

Figure 12-3 Garth Brooks performing, with his signature cowboy hat, headset-microphone, and Takamine dreadnought guitar.
Source: Rockstar Photography / Alamy Stock Photo

TIME	FORM	LISTENING CUES	DISCUSSION
0:00	Introduction	acoustic guitar	Evokes the idea of a heartbroken singer-songwriter, working acoustically.
0:10	Verse 1	"Blame it . . ."	Brooks' voice was at its strongest in these early years. The full band enters with a prominent steel guitar line at 0:28. Listen to the buildup to the chorus, starting at 0:37, where the bass, drums, and electric guitar build up the sonic tension.
0:46	Chorus	"'Cause I got friends . . ."	The chorus adopts a more energetic rhythmic groove and features prominent honky-tonk fiddling. Listen to Brooks' voice, which includes a growl (at 1:04) and a pronounced Southern twang.
1:22	Instrumental interlude	electric guitar	The electric guitar, then steel guitar play the last half of the chorus.
1:40	Verse 2	"I guess I was . . ."	Notice the piano that emerges from the mix. The buildup (at 2:08) to the chorus is even more pronounced this second time.
2:15	Chorus	"'Cause I got . . ."	The rhyme scheme in this chorus propels the song forward with run-on lines (poetic enjambment).
2:51	Chorus	"I got friends . . ."	Brooks' voice remains audible while a crowd (representing friends in the bar to which the story's protagonist retreats) sings the chorus. The recording even includes sound effects of cans being opened (at 3:19, for instance). This section evokes both a live-performance setting and a tight connection with fans, both of which were staples of Brooks' career.
3:26	Chorus	"I got friends . . ."	The sing-along version of the chorus repeats here, with more improvised hollering and whooping.
4:02	Chorus	"I got friends . . ."	A third iteration of the sing-along chorus begins, but then the song fades out, leaving the listener to assume that the song continues among the bar's patrons endlessly.

Themes in New Country

During the early 1990s, mainstream commercial country music and its audience evolved together. New listeners from different backgrounds than that of previous generations of fans grew interested in country music, and the songwriters and artists incorporated the concerns, interests, lifestyles, and memories of this new audience into their music. Three themes appeared prominently—a celebration of modern working-class lifestyles and values, often laced with humor; a growing attention to global and societal issues that affected the middle class; and a new wave of feminist themes and concerns.

During these years, songwriters churned out dozens of songs that celebrated different facets of working-class life. The theme resonated with the broader middle-class population because it represented the idea of having roots, resilience in the face of economic troubles, and strength—a working-class ethic within a middle-class existence. Many of the songs purposely inverted conventional markers of social achievement such as PhDs, law degrees, private-membership clubs, royalty, and celebrity status: "Working Man's Ph.D." (Aaron Tippin, 1993), "American Honky-Tonk Bar Association" (Garth Brooks, 1993), "Country Club" (Travis Tritt, 1989), "Queen of My Double Wide Trailer" (Sammy Kershaw, 1993), and "Life-styles of the Not So Rich and Famous" (Tracy Byrd, 1994) are examples. Plenty of other songs employed time-honored honky-tonk tales of broken hearts, love-gone-wrong, drinking, and down-and-out troubles to be shared with barroom buddies. Yet a large number of love songs picked up a story line that first appeared in the 1950s, that true romance is worth more than money and transcends all troubles; examples include "She Is His Only Need" (Wynonna, 1992), "Love, Me" (Collin Raye, 1991), "Where've You Been" (Kathy Mattea, 1989), "Two of a Kind, Workin' on a Full House" (Garth Brooks, 1990), and "Don't Take the Girl" (Tim McGraw, 1994). Taken together, these topics helped construct and defend an idealized working-class identity that appealed to legions of new fans in the economically lean years of the early 1990s.

The second theme that appeared in commercial country songs in the early 1990s was a growing recognition of global issues and societal problems that reached beyond small-town, honky-tonk concerns. These topics illustrated that country music was becoming increasingly connected to mainstream politics and culture, and that country singers and songwriters saw themselves as the voice of a broader community rather than just a solitary person reflecting inward on personal troubles. The music also embraced calls to action. These themes were most prevalent in Garth Brooks's music. "We Shall Be Free" (1992) evokes gospel music with an organ and gospel choir on the recording, a plea for a better world and the end of poverty; "The River" (1992) and "Standing Outside the Fire" (1993) both rally listeners toward activism. Reba McEntire confronted AIDS in "She Thinks His Name Was John" (1994) and social injustice in a cover of "The Night the Lights Went Out in Georgia" (1991), and Shania Twain closed her 1995 album with "God Bless the Child," a heart-wrenching plea for social justice for the poor.

"The Dance," by songwriter Tony Arata, was the fourth single from Garth Brooks's 1989 debut album, and the song that best epitomized this theme of global awareness in 1990s commercial country music. The lyrics reminisce about a dance with a loved one who is now gone. The song used the common metaphor of dancing to represent living life to the fullest extent possible and opening oneself up to love, even though that leaves one vulnerable to heartache. The music video, however, made an even bolder statement: it included footage of President John F. Kennedy; Dr. Martin Luther King Jr.; the crew of the space shuttle *Challenger*, which exploded on takeoff in 1986; actor John Wayne; and country singer Keith Whitley, among others. Brooks made the video, he explained, to honor the lives and contributions of those who had passed away before their time, pointing out that the "dance" had been worth it, even with the pain and mourning that came after their deaths. The video also marked an important change in country music's usual imagery; it drew on cultural icons far outside the conventional domain of country music. His inclusion of Dr. King was particularly noteworthy within a country music context. It was an ambitious move on the part of Garth Brooks, and revealed the dramatically expanding scope of country music's social and global outlook.

A third theme featured in contemporary commercial country songs was a strong female voice speaking out about gender-related issues. These songs represented the interests and concerns of middle-aged, middle-class women who were confronting the next wave of social changes. The songs of the 1970s (see Chapter 8) had begun to address the prevalence of divorce, the women's liberation movement, and—for many women—their initial forays into the workplace. The songs of the 1990s continued the dialogue with the next generation of audiences, addressing the balance of work and motherhood, partnership and respect within a marriage, and sacrifice of self for family. Songs such as "I Can't Do That Anymore" (Faith Hill, 1995), "He Thinks He'll Keep Her" (Mary Chapin Carpenter, 1993), and "Is There Life Out There" (Reba McEntire, 1992) all describe the dilemmas of the middle-aged housewife reexamining priorities, weighing sacrifices, pursuing education, seeking independence, and challenging gender roles in the cultural landscape of the 1990s.

These strong female voices and perspectives were even more remarkable given the male domination of country music during those years. In the late 1980s, women typically scored one-quarter of the number one hits in country music. But during the first few years of the 1990s, when country music's popularity was soaring, women very rarely had songs make it to the top of the *Billboard* charts. In 1991, for instance, only 10% of the number one songs were sung by a woman. The "hat act" generation not only featured mostly male singers but also shifted the music's identity so that its projected image was essentially working-class, male, and (still) white. In this context, the few female voices that did emerge sounded even more defiant and outspoken: "What Part of No Don't You Understand" (Lorrie Morgan, 1992), "Cleopatra, Queen of Denial" (Pam Tillis, 1993), and most notably, "Independence Day" (Martina McBride, 1994).

In "Independence Day," by songwriter Gretchen Peters, the singer recalls a Fourth of July celebration when she was eight years old. As an adult thinking back on the event, the singer realizes that her mother was the victim of a violently abusive, alcoholic husband. In desperation, her mother burned down the family's home around him. The song and video's graphic portrayal of domestic violence produced a firestorm of controversy, just as Garth Brooks's video for "The Thunder Rolls," in which an abused wife shoots her cheating husband, had a few years earlier. The song also

Listening Guide

"Gone Country" (1994)

PERFORMER: Alan Jackson

SONGWRITER: Bob McDill

ORIGINAL RELEASE: *Who I Am* (Arista 18759, 1994)

FORM: Verse-prechorus-chorus

STYLE: New country (contemporary commercial country)

"Gone Country" topped the *Billboard* country charts just after country music peaked in its popularity. Its lyrics offer an ironic commentary on the mid-'90s scene as they describe three individuals, all of whom decide to leave other genres and switch to country music. In its positive depiction of country music, the song refers to the way that the genre accepts older singers, the historical and ongoing links between country music and folk music, and the wholesome, family-oriented values that the music had come to represent. All of these characteristics run in parallel with the Southernization of America.

Also present in the lyrics is the observation that by 1994 Nashville had drawn in a huge population of musicians, songwriters, and producers who had not been longtime or traditional fans of the music and who had not paid their dues in the genre. This song was part of a groundswell opinion that country music had been diluted by this influx of outsiders, and the lyrics subtly criticize this development. In the song, the Las Vegas lounge singer writes her own version of a "simple, country" autobiography, based on growing up on Long Island. On the one hand, New York has often signified the antithesis of country authenticity, and this seems to highlight the singer's outsider status. But on the other hand, the lyrics also hint that country music and a country identity might be able to transcend conventional Southern geographic boundaries (that "country" lifestyles and values, especially simplicity, are found everywhere). Even during the 1920s, New Yorkers contributed to the fledgling genre's growth.

The most sophisticated irony in the song comes when it addresses financial success. Both the folk singer and the serious composer in the song's vignettes eschew material wealth ("wealth and privilege") and cling instead to music as a vehicle for social protest in one instance and unfettered artistic expression in the other. Yet both are drawn to country music for its promise of getting them "back in the money." Those lyrics address an intrinsic duality that has been part of country music since its earliest days; the music celebrates a working-class lifestyle without material wealth, presenting an artistic front showcased McBride's powerful voice and established her as a major star. Although "Independence Day" remains her signature, McBride has continued to choose songs that champion social justice, speak out against child abuse and domestic violence, and represent the perspective of the strong-minded, middle-aged female country fan. Collectively, these women's songs offer a perspective on the concerns of the 1990s female country fan base, seeking independence, respect, and self-fulfillment while still holding loyally to spouse and children within a working- or middle-class community.

that hides both the inner workings of the music business and the idea that music is product to be sold. This song reminds listeners, however, that the genre's booming commercial success is what is drawing outsiders into Nashville; in other words, from one perspective, country's popularity is proving its undoing.

When talking about this song, Jackson has carefully avoided any intimation that he was criticizing the country music industry of the '90s, its new stars, or its commercial boom; instead, he touted the positive appeal country music held for so many people during that time. But in spite of his claims of sincerity, fans interpreted the song as wry commentary in which Jackson was protesting the apparent artifice in the mid-'90s scene and reasserting his own role as both an insider and a traditionalist. The same wave of commercial success at which the lyrics poke fun was directly responsible for the success of Jackson's song, however. Millions of new fans, themselves recent converts to country music, sang along with no apparent awareness of self-referential irony. In that sense, the song is an insightful representation of the developments in country music during these years.

Figure 12-4 Alan Jackson performing on the Opry.
Source: Donny Beauchamp photograph © Grand Ole Opry Archives.

Continued

Listening Guide

"Gone Country" (1994) **Continued**

TIME	FORM	LISTENING CUES	DISCUSSION
0:00	Introduction	electric guitar, then steel guitar	The steel guitar (at 0:09) counterbalances the rock beat heard in the drums and the steady cowbell.
0:16	Verse 1	"She's been playing . . ."	The first of three vignettes relies on the contrast between the artifice of Las Vegas ("show business") and Nashville (country).
0:47	Prechorus	"So she packs . . ."	This section moves the song into the chorus, and—in its lyrics—moves the characters to Nashville.
0:54	Chorus	"She's gone country . . ."	The chorus relies on a repeated pattern of three chords, and repetition of the title line.
1:09	Instrumental interlude	steel guitar	This short interlude acts as a spacer before the next verse.
1:17	Verse 2	"Well, the folk scene's . . ."	This verse's vignette addresses the history of country music and folk music. The fiddle shows up between lines of text.
1:48	Prechorus	"I hear down there . . ."	Listen for the drums, which help build up the tension as the chorus approaches, then launch the chorus with a loud crash on the cymbals.
1:56	Chorus	"He's gone country . . ."	Notice that the description of "country" is anchored in clothing (boots and suits). Notice also the prominent fiddle during the chorus.
2:11	Instrumental chorus	steel guitar	The steel guitar plays an entire chorus.
2:26	Verse 3	"Well, he commutes . . ."	The piano (at 2:30) appears prominently in this verse.
2:56	Prechorus	"Lord, it sounds so easy . . ."	The piano contributes to the musical buildup here.
3:04	Chorus	"He's gone country . . ."	Fiddle and steel guitar interact during this verse.
3:20	Instrumental interlude	electric guitar	This section repeats the introduction.
3:27	Chorus/Playout	"He's gone country . . ."	This section repeats the chorus with new lyrics, then continues a playout, over which Jackson improvises on the song's title.

Stylistic Pendulums and Country-Pop

Shortly after country music sales peaked in 1993, a new style, known as country-pop, emerged that shaped mainstream commercial country music for the last half of the '90s. This style was, in part, a natural outgrowth of the popularity that country music enjoyed in the 1990s.

Since the 1950s, country music styles have cycled between more roots-oriented traditional music and more pop-infused crossover music. As country music adopted more pop-influenced sounds and musical approaches, it gained more fans, who in turn encouraged the music to move further toward a pop sound. At some point, these pop-infused trends would run their course, and country music experienced a counterbalancing shift toward more twang-centered roots styles, usually accompanied by a decline in the size of the fan base. The pop-infused styles and artists remained active, but fade into less prominent roles. These harder-edged country styles continued in the spotlight until some catalyst again moved the music toward crossover popularity, and the whole cycle began again. Of course, even during periods when country music's biggest stars were crossing over into pop, other artists were still playing harder honky-tonk styles. Periods of pop-crossover dominance occurred with the Nashville sound and with countrypolitan in the *Urban Cowboy* era. In the mid-1990s, there was another crossover era.

In 1995, while Garth Brooks was clashing with his record label, Capitol Records, and as country sales started to decline from their highest point, Shania Twain (see Artist Profile) released her groundbreaking album *The Woman in Me* with co-writer and producer (and then-husband) Robert John "Mutt" Lange. With that album, Twain spearheaded a major stylistic shift in country music toward country-pop, which found a waiting and welcoming audience among pop fans as well as country. The music was well suited for line dancing (see essay on Line Dancing), radio-friendly, mostly upbeat and optimistic in tone, and ready to ride the wave of country music's lingering popularity. Given the music's emphasis on hooks (brief, catchy musical patterns), sound effects, and unusual musical textures, the record producers played a prominent role in creating country-pop. Two producers in particular, Dann Huff and Mutt Lange, who worked respectively with Faith Hill and Shania Twain, were largely responsible for shaping the development of country-pop. But it was the singers rather than the producers who became household names during this era. Country-pop resulted in four major developments in country music:

1. Country music took on a brand new image that was far younger, sexier, and more glamorous than ever before.
2. Country music lyrics tended to avoid any overtly honky-tonk or redneck themes, and instead drifted toward an optimistic, philosophical outlook.
3. Female singers reappeared in large numbers on the radio, along with song topics about young women searching for personal fulfillment and independence.
4. Ironically, as country-pop drifted further away from harder-edged honky-tonk sounds and into the pop scene, it provoked contrary developments. Country-pop's success helped give rise to the alt-country scene (see Chapter 14), which defined itself as the antithesis of country-pop, and also set the stage for a subsequent shift in mainstream country toward more traditional, twangy, harder-edged styles.

ARTIST PROFILE

Shania Twain (1965–)

Shania Twain is an enigma in country music. She is a former pop singer from Canada who has outsold every other female country star; she is a sexy pin-up star whose self-penned lyrics contain overtly feminist themes; and she single-handedly transformed a genre that relies on down-home wisdom, age, and hillbilly roots into a youthful, glamorous version of itself, along the way incurring the ire of traditional country fans. Detractors have argued that her music simply was not country at all and have labeled her with derogatory terms such as "highest-paid lap dancer in Nashville." Yet to millions of fans, she was the face of country music and the voice responsible for bringing it into modern relevance.

Born Eilleen Regina Edwards in Ontario, Canada, Twain took her last name from her stepfather. She adopted the stage name of Shania, which fans believed meant "on my way" in Ojibwe, the language of her stepfather's Native American tribe, a connection that added exoticism to her appeal. In the mid-1980s, she cut a few demos in Nashville and made several pop and dance-track recordings, but none of them became successful. Her parents were killed in 1987, at which point Twain took over care of her younger siblings and landed a job singing pop music at a resort in a Las Vegas–style variety show where she honed her stage-craft. After her siblings left home, Twain moved to Nashville and signed a record contract with Mercury. Her self-titled debut appeared in 1993. It featured only one song that she had a hand in writing, and it was packaged with cover art that played up her Canadian identity—snow, a wolf, and Twain bundled in a parka, an image that was at odds with the hat act era of new country. Twain's vocals caught the attention of rock producer John Robert "Mutt" Lange, however, who was looking for an artist with whom he could break into the burgeoning country market.

Lange and Twain collaborated on her next album, *The Woman in Me* (1995), which effectively repackaged Twain as a classic western-style "country girl" (see Listening Guide for "Any Man of Mine") with honky-tonk–style hits that were subtly enhanced by Lange's experience in the stadium rock scene; he had produced such acts as Bryan Adams, the Cars, AC/DC, and Def Leppard before working with Twain, and he was known for his songwriting and ability to hook an audience's attention through studio production techniques. The album spawned eight successful radio singles. Their subsequent album, *Come On Over* (1997), was even more popular. For that project, Twain and Lange abandoned obvious country trappings, both in Twain's image and in the music, and ventured entirely into the world of country-pop crossover music. Twain became famous for her bare midriff (inspiring the term "navel acts"), sensuous image, and ability to entertain a crowd with a pop-styled stage presence. In 1999, both the Academy of Country Music and the Country Music Association awarded her Entertainer of the Year.

For *Come On Over*, Twain and Lange remixed the recordings in versions that were tailored to a pop style and released them to pop radio. These versions, which fans could buy as an imported "International Version" CD, were extremely popular on noncountry radio stations. The idea of tailoring a single song to different audiences reached an extreme with their next project, *Up!* Twain and Lange created three distinct mixes of each song, with different instrumental accompaniments and, in some cases, a different rhythmic groove and chord progression, as well. They released the three mixes on color-coded CDs: green for country, red for pop-rock, and blue for what Twain and Lange termed "world," each CD "dressing" the music in a different style and genre, just as Twain was dressed in a representative costume on each disc's album art. Each CD package contained two of the three CDs, which was an attempt to appease music fans who were complaining at the time about the high cost of CDs and the few songs on a typical album.

While *Up!* sold over 11 million copies and produced eight radio singles, it also marked the end of the country-pop heyday. Twain's approach to repackaging songs in different musical styles, her emphasis on short pop-dance hooks, and her sleek production values all were at odds with the rising trend toward more roots music and stronger connections to country's past in the early 2000s. Twain released a greatest hits album a few years later, but her reign over country radio had ended.

During her time on the charts, she blazed trails as a female country star in an era still dominated by male entertainers. She was both a performer and a songwriter. Her lyrics inverted gender roles in a feminist way, as in "Honey, I'm Home," in which a woman comes home from work and asks her man to bring her a beer, or "In My Car (I'll Be the Driver)." Yet all of those influences were subsumed in her overall stage presence, through which she made country music more youthful, sexy, and hip.

Figure 12-5 Shania Twain's Up! album packaging: cover art (top), and three different styles; country (center, note the cowboy hat), world (bottom left), and pop-rock (bottom right).

Source: Walter Everett

Listening Guide

"Any Man of Mine" (1995)

PERFORMER: Shania Twain

SONGWRITERS: Mutt Lange and Shania Twain

ORIGINAL RELEASE: *The Woman in Me* (Mercury 522886, 1995)

FORM: Verse-prechorus-chorus

STYLE: Country-pop

"Any Man of Mine" was Shania Twain's first number one country hit and a game-changing song in country music. This album's first single, "Whose Bed Have Your Boots Been Under?" established her as a major radio star, but "Any Man of Mine" tied together the appearance of glamour with the traditional country signifiers of jeans, ranches, and cowboy hats, the sounds of fiddles and steel guitars with pop accompaniments, and a sexy image with a new feminist twist on conventional gender roles in country music.

Twain's music video for the song cast her in jeans and a denim vest, with her signature bare midriff and big hair, on a cattle ranch, accompanied by signifiers of an idealized, bygone era (an old model truck, old-fashioned bathtub, wooden hay-wagon wheels). That visual setting merged with her own image as a glamorous and sexual pop-influenced singer to create the mid-'90s representation of country music—a nostalgic evocation of western ranches, small Texas towns, and country roots, but presented in a thoroughly modern, attractive, and popular package.

This album's music retains many of the traditional musical signifiers of country music (e.g., long-bow fiddling, crying steel guitar, acoustic guitar) but combines them with a musical accompaniment and arrangement designed to draw in listeners, evoke crowd participation, satisfy line dancers, and enhance the song with pop hooks. The most obvious of these is the "stomp-stomp-clap" rhythm, which is a reference to the rock band Queen's "We Will Rock You," and which had, by 1995, become a crowd favorite in sports stadiums and other such venues. Beyond the words, melody, and chords, the soundscape itself of the recording was part of its appeal, such as the stereo panning (in which the sounds were spread out in the right and left channels) and the special effects added to the instruments in the recording process. Backup singers popped in and out in different rhythmic patterns. Two other common Twain/Lange features appear in the song as well. One, the "pump-up" modulation, which raises the key of the song before the last chorus, is a cliché pop technique for making the end of a song sound more exciting. The second is the stop-time segment, where the band stops playing except for keeping the beat, which creates a striking change in texture that catches the listener's attention.

Unlike many of the countrypolitan hits in the early 1980s during the *Urban Cowboy* era, these mid-'90s commercial country recordings kept fiddles, two-step and shuffle beats, and other elements from country's past clearly audible. This recording features prominent fiddle, steel guitar, acoustic guitar, and a two-step beat in the chorus, fusing the pop and traditional country features into a single musical event. The song's rhythmic pattern and, most especially, Twain's spoken patter at the end of the song also connect it to the burgeoning line dance fad. This song was extremely popular among line dancers, with several different dances choreographed specifically for it (all of which emphasized the stomp-stomp-clap rhythm in their dance steps). Twain's music video for the song included two very brief shots of her doing steps from the best known of those line dances.

The biggest impact of this song in country music was its play on gender roles, through which it ushered in a new era of feminist themes in country music. Its defiant lyrics declare that any man the singer will keep must not measure her value against conventional feminine points of success—such as being a good cook or being physically beautiful, or against conventional insecurities such as being in-decisive. Although contrasting sharply with Twain's growing reputation as a gor-geous, midriff-bearing, sexy pin-up star, the song's lyrics ushered in a new wave of feminist country songs that challenged conventional gender roles and identities, culminating in Twain's own "Man! I Feel Like a Woman," wherein even the title played on those ideas.

TIME	FORM	LISTENING CUES	DISCUSSION
0:00	Introduction	acoustic guitar, fiddle, pop rhythm section, and vocal utterances	The acoustic guitar at the beginning connects with country tradition. Sound effects (at 0:05) herald the pop-crossover nature of the recording. The rhythm section (at 0:08) begins the stadium-rock "stomp-stomp-clap" pattern. Twain whoops, laughs, and talks over the intro, evoking the atmosphere of a live performance.
0:20	Verse 1	"Any man of mine better . . ."	Reverb-drenched vocals draw all the focus, with only a sparse percussion accompaniment.
0:32	Verse 2	"Any man of mine will say . . ."	Full band comes in at this point, layering classic coun-try fiddling over a pop-infused accompaniment.
0:44	Prechorus	"And if I change my mind . . ."	Electric guitar becomes more prominent, and this sec-tion builds the listener's expectation for the upcoming climax of the chorus. The repeated "Yeah" call and re-sponse (at 0:53) invites audience participation.
1:01	Chorus	"Any man of mine . . ."	The chorus is built on a steady, two-step dance rhythm, with lots of steel guitar fills, trading with fiddle (at 1:14). Stop-time (at 1:26) highlights the title of the song.
1:27	Interlude	fiddle plus full band	Twain whoops again during this section.
1:32	Verse 3	"Well, any man of mine better . . ."	The accompanying vocals drop in an out from the stereo mix to emphasize the "stomp-stomp-clap" rhythm.
1:46	Prechorus	"And if I change . . ."	
2:03	Chorus	"Any man of mine . . ."	

Listening Guide

"Any Man of Mine" (1995) **Continued**

TIME	FORM	LISTENING CUES	DISCUSSION
2:29	Instrumental prechorus	"Any man of mine ...," fiddle, "Let me hear you say ..."	This section overlaps the last line of the chorus with the beginning of an instrumental version of the prechorus, with Twain coming back in for the last few lines of the prechorus. This sort of manipulation of song-form is typical of Twain/Lange arrangements (see essay on Songwriting and Sophistication).
2:44	Stop-time interlude	"Any man, any man ..."	This stop-time vocal moment is accompanied by a shimmering cymbal roll, then a percussive crash and a sudden "pump-up" modulation that changes the key of the song from A-flat major to B-flat major. This section disrupts the steady flow of the song long enough to recapture the listener's attention.
2:49	Chorus	"Any man of mine ..."	In the new, higher key, the chorus sounds even more climactic. Twain holds out the word "kind," for dramatic effect.
3:16	Coda	fiddle plus full band	This extended coda features Twain chanting dance instructions in the tradition of a square-dance caller, but here the lyrics refer to line dancing. At the end of the coda, the steel guitar punctuates the recording, while Twain reiterates the statement from the introduction, "This is what a woman wants."

The first change to appear in the mid-1990s was that female country singers shed their middle-aged housewife image and adopted instead a sleek, glamorous appearance, symbolized by Shania Twain's often bare and very sculpted midriff. Youth, or at least the appearance of youth, became the new trend. Singers got younger and younger. Some, like Mindy McCready (1975–2013) and Bryan White (1974–), were in their early twenties, but many others, including LeAnn Rimes (1982–), Lila McCann (1981–), and Jessica Andrews (1984–), were young teens; in an extreme case, Billy Gilman (1988–) was barely twelve when his country album debuted. The change in the music reflected their ages; it switched from full-voiced, mature singers contemplating the concerns of middle age to teenage voices accompanied by electric fiddles and syncopated drum beats, singing lighthearted lyrics about exploring the world.

The scope of the trend was most apparent when, in 1998, Faith Hill (1967–) reappeared on the scene after a three-year hiatus. The singer, from Star, Mississippi, arrived in Nashville in the late '80s, and her debut album appeared in 1993 at the crest of country music's popularity. Like Martina McBride, Hill had a strong, belting vocal style that lent itself to the diva-heartbreak ballads popular in the early '90s. Her image, as seen on her first two album covers, played on the big-hair, redheaded, jeans-wearing look so common to stars of that era, and she made a name for herself singing from the perspective of a frustrated, heartbroken married woman experiencing what were conventionally midlife concerns. In 1996, she married fellow country music star and "hat act" Tim McGraw and soon had two babies. During those years, she was mostly absent from the country music scene. When she cut her third album in 1998, the country music landscape had changed, and Hill moved smoothly into the country-pop world. She reinvented herself as a blond bombshell, switched producers to Dann Huff (who had worked with Shania Twain), and chose songs that matched the trendy hooks and optimistic, youthful topics of country-pop ("This Kiss," "The Way You Love Me," "If My Heart Had Wings"). On her subsequent album, *Breathe*, she appeared in sensuous and revealing photographs, with cover art that was inspired by pop superstar Britney Spears's image. Like Shania Twain, Faith Hill found a welcoming audience in pop radio. At the height of her success, she recorded the soundtrack for the Hollywood blockbuster *Pearl Harbor* (a song that had no country affiliation) and moved into acting.

1993   1995   1998

1999   2002   2005

Figure 12-6 The cyclic evolution of mainstream country music through the 1990s, new country through country-pop and back to roots revival, can be seen in Faith Hill's album art. 1993: all smiles, jeans, white cotton shirts, big red hair, new country. 1998: blond, cute, crossover-pop. 2002: pink lipstick, pouty lips, sultry eyes, sexy wet photographs, all pop (and unpopular). 2005: back to all smiles, jeans, white cotton shirts, big red hair, and a roots-revival sound (see Chapter 14).

Song lyrics in country-pop veered away from traditional honky-tonk themes of drinking, lost love, working-class identity, and redneck roots. Instead, songs were optimistic and sweetly sentimental, like "I Love You" (Martina McBride, 1999); "You Had Me from Hello" (Kenny Chesney, 1999), whose title line comes from a Tom Cruise movie; and "I Don't Want to Miss a Thing" (Mark Chesnutt, 1999), a power-ballad cover of the rock band Aerosmith.

"I Don't Want to Miss a Thing" in particular underscores the fusion that occurred between country and pop-rock in the late 1990s. Its songwriter, Diane Warren, had won the ASCAP pop songwriter of the year award five times. Aerosmith had been at the front of the hard rock scene in the 1970s, but in the late '90s their music was featured in a Disney theme park ride, and they had graduated from rebellious rockers to senior entertainers by the time they recorded the song as part of a blockbuster movie's soundtrack. Mark Chesnutt's cover was simply one more incarnation of the song as a commercial product within popular culture at a time when country and pop were driven by the same music-industry engine of songwriters and producers.

The culmination of this trend was a Grammy-winning song by Mark D. Sanders and Tia Sillers, sung in 2000 by Lee Ann Womack, called "I Hope You Dance," whose lyrics take the form of a blessing of good wishes. As was common during this era, two different mixes of the song were released, one to country stations and one tweaked for easy-listening and pop stations. The song topped both the country and the "adult contemporary" charts. Country and pop had merged quite convincingly.

MIXING

Audio mixing is the process through which the separately recorded tracks of a song are combined to create the final product. This process is usually done after all the instruments and vocals for a song have been recorded. The way that those parts are combined is a big part of musical style. The balance between the parts, meaning which instruments are louder and which are quieter, and the effects added to the individual tracks are all part of a particular style at a particular time. Many fans used to think of an artist, a song, and a particular recording as fused together: there would be one version of a song by a particular artist, and the way it was mixed was just one more part of how we thought about the song. That is simply no longer the case: country music is part of the practice where more than one "mix" or version will be created from the same collection of recorded tracks, or, in many cases, with the addition and deletion of some instrumental tracks. Thus, the same artist, same vocals, and same song can exist in many styles, sometimes with only subtle distinctions, but sometimes radically different.

Even during the height of country-pop, a few country songs still amplified older, traditional honky-tonk themes and balanced out the country-pop trends. For example, George Strait and Alan Jackson both carved out roles for themselves during the late '90s as loyalists to traditional, twang-centered country music. Garth Brooks's "Two Piña Coladas" and "Longneck Bottle" also were in the honky-tonk tradition. Cover songs provided additional hard-country options while preserving the genre's ties to its past: "Who's Cheatin' Who" (Alan Jackson covering Charly McClain), "Six Days on the Road" (Sawyer Brown covering Dave Dudley), and "Today My World Slipped Away" (George Strait covering Vern Gosdin), for instance. Nonetheless, these were the exceptions in the country-pop era.

The number of women who reached the top of the country charts increased during the country-pop era. Whereas a few years earlier only 10% of the number one hits on the *Billboard* "Hot Country Singles and Tracks" chart were sung by women, by 1998 that number had increased to 52%. Although that was a substantial increase, those hits were sung by only a small handful of well-established artists; Trisha Yearwood, Reba McEntire, Faith Hill, Shania Twain, and Martina McBride accounted for most of them. Almost all the successful women in country fit in the glamorous country-pop style, although there were a few exceptions, including Canadian Terri Clark, whose cowboy hat lent her a slightly more traditional image. Although still few in number, female stars asserted a more prominent voice in the country-pop era than they had in the early '90s.

As had happened before, the popularity of country music and the country-pop style in the 1990s helped build a countermovement. As country music became more popular and assimilated into mainstream culture, some fans felt that the music had abandoned its core identity and was no longer really country music. The country-pop songs that Shania Twain and others were recording did not use the same references, signifiers, or sounds that had marked country in the past, and the audience to whom they were singing was no longer limited to a working-class population connected to small towns or rural America. This raised the question, how and why was this music country in the first place, an echo of the sorts of questions fans had asked in the early 1980s about countrypolitan. To some, who did not care for the styles, the answer was simple: they claimed it was not country and went looking elsewhere for music that satisfied their tastes. To millions of others, the answer was that country music reflected a shared but imagined sense of origin and a shared set of aesthetic and philosophical values. In other words, its fans found meaning in the idea, rather than the reality, of a working-class foundation, and in songs that focused on empathetic storytelling about daily family life in (white, socially conservative) middle America. But it was hard for some to accept the idea of country-pop styles *as* country music.

The End of the 1990s

By the end of the 1990s, country-pop had run its course, and by the first years of the next decade the trend was waning. Shania Twain's *Up!* (2002) sold 11 million copies, but that was down from the 20 million in U.S. sales of her previous release, *Come on Over*. Furthermore, by 2002, country radio and many country fans were turned off by the three different mixes of all songs (rock, country, and world) packaged and presented together on *Up!* The different mixes undercut the notion that country songs contain some aspects of genre identity at their core and suggested that rock and country were merely different dressings of the same thing. Faith Hill's *Cry* (2002) earned some of the worst reviews ever seen in print, and fans of country-pop were growing scarce. Country nightclubs shuttered their doors at an alarming rate, and television shows featuring country line dancing, such as TNN's *Club Dance* (see essay on Line Dancing), were canceled. Toward the end of the decade, country music began to make room for new artists who brought back more traditional, honky-tonk–influenced sounds. Such change was slow to come, of course, but another shift in the continuous cycle from crossover trends toward more roots-oriented, hard-edged country sounds was under way.

By the early years of the next century, country was in transition away from the country-pop style. Garth Brooks had retired (temporarily, it would turn out), and country music's market share had dropped to a much lower but steady level. More importantly, the broader landscape of popular music had also changed: hip-hop had shifted into the mainstream; the internet had radically altered how fans acquired, shared, and even created music; and a new crop of singer-songwriters were claiming fans' attention. Amid all these developments, country had passed through a full cycle of pop-crossover acceptance, and was poised to define a new place for itself in the new century.

☆ **ESSAY: MUSICAL STYLE**

 # New Country and Country-Pop

The two distinct musical styles dominating country radio during the 1990s, namely new country and country-pop, can each can be identified readily by ear. New country (or contemporary commercial country) arrived with the Class of '89 artists and amplified neotraditionalist features (see Chapter 11). Country-pop, from the mid-1990s onward, incorporated more elements from outside traditional country sounds. As had been the case during the 1980s, the musical styles favored by male and female country singers continued to differ during the 1990s.

During the early 1990s, contemporary commercial country kept the danceable, two-step rhythmic grooves and the occasional waltz rhythms from the neotraditionalists of the late 1980s, accompanied by prominent fiddles and steel guitars. The style favored simple verse-chorus song forms (see Appendix A). The biggest change was the increasing presence of distorted electric guitars playing long solos and crisper, drier, and sharper drums in the recordings, both of which betrayed the influence of stadium rock on the music. Many of the male vocalists (e.g., Clint Black, Garth Brooks, Tim McGraw, Alan Jackson, Mark Chesnutt, and Tracy Byrd) had resonant baritone voices that blended honky-tonk twang with smoother vocal artistry. Female vocalists (Reba McEntire in her '90s recordings, Martina McBride, Faith Hill on her first two albums, Wynonna Judd, Trisha Yearwood, etc.) favored a full, open-throated ballad style of singing that created a "big" sound. A surprising number of these hits incorporated aspects of Cajun music, most notably the bouncy Cajun two-beat rhythms, fiddling styles, and accordion sound (see Chapter 4). The Cajun rhythms are most apparent on songs such as Alan Jackson's "Tall, Tall Trees," Vince Gill's "One More Last Chance," and Garth Brooks's "Cowboy Cadillac." The topics of the songs, as discussed throughout this chapter, were also strong markers of the new country style in this era.

Country-pop, by contrast, borrowed syncopated pop riffs, more rhythmic electric guitar patterns, a stronger emphasis on the rhythm section, full harmony backing vocals, and extra sound effects. This music often featured highly contrasting bridge sections in the songs' forms (see Appendix A); short, memorable "hooks," especially in the guitar parts; and dense musical textures throughout the recording where the individual instruments blend into a constant sonic backdrop. This era was the first where vocals appeared with pitch-correction computer software (Auto-Tune), which not only adjusted the singer's pitch on each note but also altered the timbre (the "color" of the sound) in the recordings. Country-pop hits frequently featured lyrics with a feisty tone and a bounce-back attitude, even when singing about lost love or sadness. Line dancing terminology and instructions became part of the music's lyrics in many instances.

☆ ESSAY: CULTURE

 # Line Dancing

The way that country music fans interact with the music changed radically in the early 1990s because of the explosive popularity of line dancing. Although dancing in various forms had long been associated with some styles of country music, this new trend provided an extremely attractive business and marketing opportunity for the genre, made it easier for new fans to participate in the fan scene, and helped country music move closer to mainstream popular culture.

A line dance generally involves all participants standing in lines, performing a sequence of steps, turns, and other dance moves in unison. The choreographed pattern usually takes between twenty-four and ninety-six beats of music, at which point the dancers repeat the pattern, often turning so that they face a different direction each time the pattern starts over. The basic style of the dance allows novices to participate easily, while more advanced dancers can embellish or add personal flourishes to the choreography, thereby putting their skills on display. Unlike other styles of country dancing such as two-stepping, line dancing does not involve dance partners touching each other or leading and following different steps. Any number of men or women can participate at the same time, with no concerns over gender roles or the skill level of a prospective dance partner. This feature helps explain why line dancing caught on with different social groups. In the mid-'90s, it was common to find groups of women who might have attended a jazzercise class together a decade earlier now meeting at a local country bar to line dance. Men who were uneasy with other styles of dance or with having to lead in conventional partner dances were able to participate in line dancing with friends simply by following the prescribed steps.

Although various forms of choreographed patterns danced in lines are found in earlier traditions, including the swing and lindy hop dancing of the 1930s, country line dancing descended from disco line dances popular in the 1970s and early '80s. Soon thereafter, country dancers started doing dances such as the "Electric Slide" and the "Tush Push," which had originally been choreographed to noncountry music. Owners of the cavernous country nightclubs that had sprung up in many cities during the *Urban Cowboy* craze opened their doors to line dancers as a way to draw in much-needed patrons after attendance dropped off in the mid-'80s. The link between country music and line dancing was solidified in 1992 when Billy Ray Cyrus recorded "Achy Breaky Heart." As part of a marketing plan, his record label asked local Nashville choreographer Melanie Greenwood (wife of country singer Lee Greenwood) to choreograph a line dance specifically for Cyrus's song. That dance was incorporated into the music video, which was released along with the recording, dance steps, and an instructional video for the line dance. Fans saw the dance in the video and wanted to learn it, and sales of the instructional materials became a new source of revenue; once fans knew the dance, they requested that DJs play it more at their local clubs. "Achy Breaky Heart" became a huge hit in part because it connected music, video, and dance.

The business model behind line dancing proved highly successful during the 1990s. Because different line dances were associated with specific songs, each time a new song came out, fans had a new dance to learn. Large country nightclubs hired dance instructors to teach lessons, which drew people into those clubs each week, especially new fans of country music who had no prior dance experience. To help support this new fad, dance teachers released countless commercial instructional videos and line-dance books, which helped disseminate the dances even further while earning additional income for the dance teachers. For country singers, the obvious benefit of having a popular line dance connected to one's song was that fans would request that song repeatedly in the nightclubs. At its peak, country singers commonly referred to line dancing in their lyrics (see Listening Guide for "Any Man of Mine") or in their stage patter. Line dances had the potential to prolong a song's commercial life; Tracy Byrd's recording of "Watermelon Crawl" came out in 1994, but its corresponding line dance became a crowd favorite, and eight years later the song was still played every single night at country nightclubs across the Southeast.

In 1991, the cable station The Nashville Network (TNN) began broadcasting a reality-style television show called *Club Dance*. Filmed in Knoxville, Tennessee, *Club Dance* was set in a fake country nightclub called the White Horse Café, where "regulars" (mostly amateur country dancers who lived in or around Knoxville) danced just as they would at a country bar on a Saturday night, while hosts Phil Campbell and Shelley Mangrum chatted with the dancers and conducted friendly, conversation-style interviews with them. Dance clubs or teams from around the country frequently traveled to Knoxville to appear as guests on the show. *Club Dance* was instrumental in spreading dances from one part of the country to another and showing off trendy new line dances. In 1994, TNN added a second dance show, *The Wildhorse Saloon*. Filmed in Nashville, it helped disseminate line dances and new styles of dancing to even more viewers. Meanwhile, the United Country Western Dance Council, which had incorporated in 1989, helped transform country dance contests from homegrown two-step challenges on beer-soaked barroom floors into a highly competitive, formalized series of events that included line dancing. These and other similar organizations and television programs added an infrastructure to the country dance scene that helped spread the popularity of line dancing to even more fans, which encouraged the country music industry to release more country-pop music, which, in turn, fostered the dance scene.

Figure 12-7 Club Dance, filmed in Knoxville, Tennessee, put the new country dance scene (including line dancing) on television.
Source: Courtesy of Ross K. Bagwell.

Over the span of the 1990s, line dancing evolved in tandem with new country-pop styles, which incorporated more elements of pop music. Country line dance competitions began including categories of line dances known as "funky" and "Cuban," referring to the styles of motion and basic steps used in those dances, neither of which had any origins in traditional country music. In these ways, line dancing forged a bridge between country music and other genres, including hip hop, Latin, and pop, each of which also fostered line dancing. Ironically, this led to the common practice of country nightclubs playing noncountry music for their line dancers, who often requested noncountry songs from the DJs just so they could do a popular line dance. By the end of the 1990s, new line dances based on hip-hop styles of music and hip-hop dance steps surfaced among young fans, while country line dancing began to fade from popularity in the United States. Although some avid fans continued to dance after those years, country line dancing was more often found in middle-school physical education classes than in trendy country bars. But during the 1990s, it had been a major factor in the ongoing evolution of country music.

 # Songwriting and Sophistication

Few other genres celebrated the craft of songwriting as enthusiastically as country music, which has been a haven for professional songwriters since its earliest days. Many stars got their first professional breaks as songwriters, not singers. Hank Williams, for instance, caught Fred Rose's attention with his writing, and Willie Nelson spent the early years of his career as a Nashville songwriter, penning hits for others. During the 1960s, professional songwriters became increasingly important in the industry, and in 1967, three of Nashville's best-known writers, Buddy Mize, Eddie Miller, and Bill Brock, formed a professional trade organization, now known as Nashville Songwriters Association International. Three years later, the group established a songwriter's hall of fame, membership in which is considered one of the highest professional honors in country music.

While songwriters have been a vital part of country music from its beginning, their contributions began to change in the 1990s as commercial country music experienced its boom period. The developments in songwriting went hand in hand with other developments in country music, such as its acceptance by pop radio and its financial prosperity. As country songs crossed over onto the pop charts and became popular with noncountry audiences, songwriters began to adapt their songs to incorporate more pop features—similar to what had happened in the early 1980s countrypolitan era, but now to an even greater extent. New songwriters (some with experience in the pop genre) were attracted to country music because in its 1990s guise it was both lucrative and welcoming to people with pop credentials. These newcomers brought their craft, honed in pop music, into the genre. As a result, country songs in the 1990s featured more sophisticated song forms and arrangements, and songwriters took on more public roles within the music scene.

In terms of song form, in the 1990s country hits tended to feature either bridges or prechoruses (see Appendix A), whereas a decade earlier, songs in simple verse-chorus form had been the norm. More subtle plays on words, patter songs (which involved rapid-fire lyrics with intricate metric and rhyme structures), abstract metaphors, and songs that wove social commentary into their lyrics supplanted straightforward stories and confessionals with increasing frequency. These changes, especially in the area of song form, distinguished this period from earlier trends in country music.

Three additional developments during the 1990s made songwriters more visible within the industry. The first was the changes in technology that made it easier and cheaper for songwriters to produce and sell their own CDs, which gave the public direct access to the songwriters' own versions of the songs. The second development was the rise of country singers who co-wrote the majority of their own music. Just a decade earlier, the biggest stars, such as Reba McEntire, the Judds, and George Strait, made little or no effort to write their own material. But beginning with the class of 1989, major stars teamed up with professional songwriters in long-term collabora-tive associations, such as Garth Brooks with Kent Blazy and Pat Alger, Alan Jackson with Jim McBride, Brooks & Dunn with Don Cook, Shania Twain with Mutt Lange, and countless other pairings. These arrangements reflected a renewed emphasis in coun-try music on singers presenting first-person experiences, but it also indicated that artists were increasingly business-savvy—performance royalties, such as those paid when a song is played on the radio, go not to the singer but to the songwriter.

The third development that brought country songwriting into a brighter spotlight in the 1990s was the growing popularity of venues that featured songwriters "in the round," a style of performance in which several songwriters sit in a circle and take turns playing and singing acoustic versions of their own songs. The most famous venue for songwriters' performances is the Bluebird Cafe in Nashville, Tennessee, which began the "in the round" format in 1985. Songwriters began to get record deals based on their performances at the Bluebird, which drew even more aspiring musi-cians to their performances and garnered the club legendary status. In 1993, a Hol-lywood film called *The Thing Called Love* (starring River Phoenix and Samantha Mathis) chronicled two young songwriters in Nashville chasing their dreams, and used the Bluebird as its setting. For many aspiring country stars during these years, the dream of becoming a country songwriter supplanted the dream of becoming a country singer.

During the peak of country-pop's popularity and during the line dance craze of the 1990s, fans began to pay more attention to whether or not singers were writing or cowriting their own material and to the quality of the songs as compositions. The fans' attitude affected how country stars presented themselves and their music during these years, and inadvertently affected the song forms, musical structures, and creative process by which country songs were conceived.

In today's country music, many fans overlook the significance of the coun-try songwriting industry. The career path for many young country stars involves a songwriting contract long before a recording contract. Furthermore, fans continue to associate a song with its most famous singer rather than its writer, and the rhetoric with which they discuss songs implies that the singer owns the song. Yet Nashville itself remains a "writer's town," and one of the most revealing interview questions that journalists often ask songwriters is, "What songs do you wish *you* had written?"

⋇ **ESSAY: HISTORY**

Southernization and Soccer Moms

In 1996, President William Jefferson (Bill) Clinton faced reelection against longtime Republican senator Bob Dole. Clinton adopted a campaign strategy that champi-oned "family values" and targeted a segment of the voting population whom the press dubbed "soccer moms." The term referred to a stereotyped middle-class, middle-aged, usually white, married suburban woman driving her school-age children around in a minivan, whose primary concerns were how she would raise her family in the coming years and how the government could assist her in those efforts. The campaign emphasized topics such as school vouchers, student loan programs for college, and other family-oriented social policies. The strategy worked, and women voted more than two to one for Clinton, who swept both the popular vote and the electoral college.

That emphasis on family values, a renewed focus on religious life (especially in the form of Protestant worship), and overt displays of patriotism (which increased in the wake of the Persian Gulf War) were part of a larger trend that historians have dubbed the Southernization of America. Values that were conventionally associated with Southern lifestyles, culture, and politics became more prominent across the nation. Differences between regions lessened, with middle-class society widely adopting ideas that had formerly been associated with the South. This trend was amplified by an increasing number of nationally prominent politicians who were Southerners, including Vice President Al Gore (Tennessee), Speaker of the House Newt Gingrich (Georgia), and President Bill Clinton (Arkansas). Clinton in particular embodied a young, attractive Southerner with bold vision and excusably human character flaws who was in touch with middle-class Americans.

Country music, with its historically Southern association, capitalized on this trend. In its new incarnation in the 1990s, country music appeared to keep the ideas of homespun, traditional, rural-centered family values but packaged them in a way that eliminated the negative associations of a racist, low-class, uncouth, hillbilly-hayseed Southern identity. The soccer-mom population who had been the target of the 1996 election found this new version of country music appealing. Music industry executives consciously pitched their music to those listeners. Don Cook, who produced several new country stars and then became a senior executive at Sony, told writer Bruce Feiler, "It's our job to give radio songs that will get people's attention while they're driving their screaming kids down the freeway." The "people" to whom he was referring were country music's core audience, those soccer moms. During this time, parents of middle-class white suburban youth considered developments in other music genres, especially grunge and hip-hop, increasingly objectionable. To some, hip-hop, and especially some styles of rap, appeared particularly threatening because they represented an urban, predominantly black identity when the Los Angeles race riots of 1992 were fresh in their minds. For those parents, country music appeared to offer a more wholesome, family-centered, storytelling alternative that they could relate to and to which they gravitated. The music's appeal to that demographic grew by the late '90s, when country music updated its image as even fresher and more contemporary, and appealing to an ever-younger population. Over the span of the 1990s, country music lost its distinctive marginalization and embraced its role as the soundtrack for a Southernized middle-class suburban America.

LISTEN SIDE-BY-SIDE

"Amarillo by Morning"

Songwriters: Terry Stafford and Paul Frasier
George Strait, 1982 (on *Strait from the Heart*,
MCA Records)

"Much Too Young (to Feel This Damn Old)"

Songwriters: Randy Taylor and Garth Brooks
Garth Brooks, 1989 (on *Garth Brooks*, Capitol
Nashville)

"The Beaches of Cheyenne"

Songwriters: Dan Roberts, Bryan Kennedy, and
Garth Brooks

Garth Brooks, 1995 (on *Fresh Horses*, Capitol
Nashville)

"I Can Still Make Cheyenne"

Songwriters: Aaron Barker and Erv Woolsey
George Strait, 1996 (on *Blue Clear Sky*, MCA
Records)

"The Cowboy in Me"

Songwriters: Jeffrey Steele, Al Anderson, and
Craig Wiseman
Tim McGraw, 2001 (on *Set This Circus Down*,
Curb Records)

WHEN THE FIGURE of the cowboy entered country music in the 1920s and 30s, he (almost always in a male identity) stuck around as one of the stalwart personas that shaped the genre and differentiated it from other genres. In the neotraditionalist era, the cowboy persona rode front and center, with ranch imagery and cowboy outfits resurfacing. Although many historians have talked about the major changes that occurred as country rolled into the 1990s and the New Country style, the cowboy persona remained a prominent symbol of the genre even as those other changes occurred. George Strait, who seemed permanently ensconced in the Wranglers, western shirt, and cowboy hat, passed the metaphoric torch to Garth Brooks, who made the same outfit his uniform, turning the color-block western shirt into an icon. But the importance of the cowboy was not only the wardrobe and visual signifiers of the genre. Rather, it was deeply entrenched in the character of both singers and protagonists in the stories, and in the independent, aloof, mysterious and strong character that had resided in country songs, the target of Willie Nelson's "Mamas, Don't Let Your Babies Grow Up to Be Cowboys."

While most country fans today know about the close association between country music and cowboy imagery, thirty years after Garth Brooks arrived in Nashville, the cowboy persona has virtually faded from country music lyrics. But during the 1980s and 90s, cowboys rode through the songs with surprising frequency. Garth Brooks's first single, "Much Too Young (to Feel This Damn Old)" established him as a cowboy singer singing about cowboys. From the name-check of legendary bull rider Chris LeDoux to the story about the rodeo cowboy who heads to the next event, sure that his woman has left him. The same story is featured in George Strait's "I Can Still Make Cheyenne" (1996).

Brooks re-visited the rodeo theme with "Beaches of Cheyenne" (1995), in which a bull rider is killed in the arena, and his lover is haunted by the death, walking on the beaches of "Cheyenne," a land-locked town in Wyoming that hosts one of the biggest rodeos. Even Tim McGraw evoked the cowboy's persona in "The Cowboy in Me," his 2001 hit.

All of these rodeo cowboy songs echo George Strait's pathbreaking single, "Amarillo by

Morning," the lonely cowboy who lost his "wife and a girlfriend" to the itinerant lifestyle of the rodeo cowboy.

These songs let us hear the threads of continuity that weave throughout the neotraditionalist era and into the New Country styles, framing the 1980s and 90s country music scene with the cowboy identity. These songs help us hear Garth Brooks as continuing an established musical tradition, rather than disrupting the lineage of country music. The cowboy has not remained a central figure in country music since that time, however. Pay attention to how rodeo-themed songs about cowboys fade from the spotlight as country music moves into the 2000s, and how the basic list of references and images that we find in song lyrics changes, even among the singers who still sport the cowboy wardrobe some twenty years later.

PLAYLIST

Brooks, Garth. "The Dance" (1990)

Brooks, Garth. "We Shall Be Free" (1993)

Cyrus, Billy Ray. "Achy Breaky Heart" (1991)

Hill, Faith. "I Can't Do This Anymore" (1994)

McBride, Martina. "Independence Day" (1994)

McEntire, Reba. "Is There Life Out There" (1991)

Twain, Shania. "Man! I Feel Like a Woman" (1997)

FOR MORE READING

Cox, Patsi Bale. *The Garth Factor: The Career behind Country's Big Boom.* New York: Center Street, 2009.

Ellison, Curtis. *Country Music Culture: From Hard Times to Heaven.* Jackson: University Press of Mississippi, 1995.

Escott, Colin. "Stadium Country." In *Lost Highway: The True Story of Country Music,* chap. 20. Washington, DC: Smithsonian Books, 2003.

Feiler, Bruce. *Dreaming Out Loud: Garth Brooks, Wynonna Judd, Wade Hayes, and the Changing Face of Nashville.* New York: Avon Books, 1998.

Keel, Beverly. "Between Riot Grrrl and Quiet Girl: The New Women's Movement in Country Music." In *A Boy Named Sue: Gender and Country Music,* ed. Kristine McCusker and Diane Pecknold. Jackson: University Press of Mississippi, 2004, pp. 155–177.

NAMES AND TERMS

Black, Clint	Brooks & Dunn	Cyrus, Billy Ray
Bluebird Cafe	Brooks, Garth	Diamond Rio
Broadcast Data Systems	*Club Dance*	Gill, Vince

Hill, Faith
Huff, Dann
Jackson, Alan
Judd, Wynonna
Lange, Mutt
line dancing

McBride, Martina
McGraw, Tim
Morgan, Lorrie
Nashville Songwriters
    Association
    International

RIAA
soccer moms
SoundScan
Twain, Shania
Yearwood, Trisha

REVIEW TOPICS

1. Discuss the representation of gender in mainstream country music of the 1990s. What changes over the course of the decade, and how does it relate to the music's social role and identity?

2. What is the relationship of professional songwriters to the country genre during this era, and how does it affect fans' perception of the music?

3. Why was the mainstream middle-class audience so interested in country music during the 1990s?

PART V

Country Music Navigates Genre (1990s and 2000s)

Country music has always coexisted in a complicated relationship with other genres. At times it has borrowed heavily from rock; at other times, from R&B; at other times, from pop. Always at stake is its independence and musical autonomy, balanced with its role as a part of the fabric of popular culture. And always present is its role as an expression for middle-class and working-class people as they navigate a changing global economy, domestic and international crises, economic shifts, and restructuring of American society.

The story of the mid-1990s is one of technological change. Amazon.com, which launched online in 1995, let consumers order books and then music straight to their mailboxes, something that country music had long exploited with mail-order record distribution companies. But the new shift was the beginning of the end for many brick-and-mortar music stores. Music fans found ways to turn sound recordings into digital files on their personal computers, and file sharing became a new way to share music. In 2001, iPods and iTunes appeared, which moved the musical marketplace to one's computer and digital music players and away from physical media; when one buys a song on iTunes, one does not get a physical CD or LP to put on a shelf. The idea of owning music became even more tenuous when the music industry shifted toward streaming distribution models, and fewer fans purchased individual songs directly.

The biggest effect of these emergent technologies appeared in the alternative movements, because the internet allowed bands without a major-label record contract to communicate with fans and make and distribute their own music more widely. These technologies also empowered regular fans to shape the music scene. One of the most significant changes was the ability for amateur musicians and writers to share music and opinions. Over time, print publications lost readership and—more significant—lost cultural authority. Fans started looking to blogs and other sources for their music information. Blogs such as the9513.com (active from 2006 to 2011) and countryuniverse.net gained followers and became the nexus of country music writing, joined by online versions of formerly print publications that adapted to a blog style. Fans had a greater hand in choosing whose opinions they wanted to read, as opposed to the old model where music critics were employees of major newspapers or magazines.

For the past twenty years, the tone, content, reputation, and popularity of country music has continued to reflect the ups and downs of the American economy as well as the global political landscape. The terrorist attacks on September 11, 2001, plus other catalysts led to a roots revival in the early 2000s, which also connected to themes of home, family, and experiences associated with military service—highly relevant during the wars in Iraq and Afghanistan. That gave way to a return of redneck, rock, and honky-tonk themes for a few years. The subsequent resurgence of country-pop crossover music is another iteration in the ongoing cycle between crossover trends and roots revivals that has been part country music since the 1930s. More recently, the economic recession from the subprime mortgage crisis in 2008 and a subsequent change in national politics led to the rise of bro-country and a southern rock sound, finally giving way to hybrid styles that integrated hip-hop and R&B.

Any examination of country music during the past two decades should also consider its role in the larger context of popular music. One development that had a significant effect on country music was the rise of indie rock. In the 1980s, punk music gave way to indie rock bands who privileged a do-it-yourself attitude, outsider status, and antiestablishment rhetoric in their music. The scene nurtured alternative styles of country music when those rock musicians turned toward country roots and traditions as a source for the authenticity they sought. The relationship between alt-country, singer-songwriters, and indie rock is a close and complicated one, and some country music from the past twenty years can best be understood as straddling these worlds. But the biggest contextual shift has unquestionably been the role of hip-hop in American popular culture. In the 1980s, hip-hop, and especially the form of music within hip-hop culture known as rap, was still outside the musical mainstream for most white, suburban teenagers. Even into the 1990s, it remained marginalized; when *The Miseducation of Lauryn Hill*, a hip-hop album, won the 1998 Grammy album of the year award, many music fans were shocked. Hip-hop had not yet garnered mainstream acceptability, and had not yet infiltrated all of pop culture. A decade later, that had changed. These developments have affected the relationships between fans, music, and racial identity in all genres. Country music's position within this context deserves careful reflection, given historically ingrained associations with whiteness, the presence of black singer/songwriter Darius Rucker among the ranks of contemporary country stars, and the duets and collaborations between country and hip-hop or R&B singers that have become popular.

In the past two decades, country music has moved into a more active dialogue with the rest of pop music. Despite all the accompanying changes, the relevant issues within country music remain the same as they were at the genre's beginning, namely, how it yields to questions of identity, authenticity, and otherness:

- Who are today's country fans, why do they associate with the genre, and what meaning do they find in the music?
- What systems of values have fans constructed to ascribe authenticity to the music, and what do they reveal about the fans themselves?
- How does country defend its uniqueness and defy assimilation into pop music, while still reaching crossover fan bases and sharing common trends with other genres?

Alternative Country and Beyond

13

hile Garth Brooks, Shania Twain, and similar artists were ruling country radio in the 1990s, another thriving musical scene also laid claim to country music. Broadly identified as alternative country, or alt-country, the movement fed on themes of anticommercialism and musical independence, and earned a large and devoted following. Although its name implied a connection to the country genre, the fans of mainstream country and the fans of alt-country were different. Alt-country never settled on any one musical style, nor did it find the momentum to become a self-sustaining genre within popular culture, but it did have a lasting effect on country music. Toward the end of the 1990s, a new development in mainstream country drew heavily on the alt-country scene: commercial country music experienced a roots revival and a resurgence of interest in older, more traditional, twang-centered styles of country music, especially early hillbilly, honky-tonk, Bakersfield, and country rock. This roots revival began to take hold while country-pop was still on the top of the charts. It came to a head in 2000, when the soundtrack to the film *O Brother, Where Art Thou?* became an unexpected hit and turned unprecedented media attention toward country music, its contemporary styles, and its hillbilly roots.

Defining Alternative Country

The term "alt-country" arose from the internet discussion boards called "newsgroups" in the early 1990s. These newsgroups were indexed according to categories and subcategories. "Alt" newsgroups were those that fell outside the seven formally defined and monitored categories of Usenet newsgroups—a computer network that formed an early version of an internet community. The fans who posted to the "alt.country" newsgroup mostly preferred music that positioned itself ideologically against mainstream country, yet still claimed a lineage to hillbilly and honky-tonk roots. The alt-country movement centered around a handful of bands and record labels that shared common traits, but it also expanded to include a wide variety of music and musicians from different styles that were connected to country but not part of the commercial mainstream.

There had always been music that resided outside the commercial mainstream but still related to the genre, so that aspect of alt-country was not new. Singer-songwriters drawing on old honky-tonk or hillbilly tunes had always existed, bands playing retro styles in retro costumes had also been around for years, and the story of rock musicians discovering America's roots music through old, dusty records was similar to the story of folk musicians discovering the *Anthology of American Folk Music* (1952) and subsequently launching the folk revival (see Chapter 5).

Yet three major differences in the 1990s pulled these sorts of musicians into an identifiable movement:

1. With new technologies, fans and musicians could communicate across great distances with great ease and without any mediation from record labels or the mainstream media.
2. Mainstream country had reached unprecedented levels of commercial success, which alienated some country fans who thought "their" music had sold out and set them in search of different music.
3. Outsiders with little connection or investment in the country genre latched onto early styles of country music as representing an idealized anticommercial roots music.

These factors were enhanced by a general trend toward retro fashion, music, and dance that occurred in the 1990s. This trend included the swing dance craze that revived 1940s clothing and music among young people coast-to-coast and brought both rockabilly and western swing bands more exposure. Under these conditions, several different groups of musicians that existed outside of contemporary country radio found common ground in alt-country.

Alternative Country Origins

Alt-country emerged from the aftermath of the punk scene, when punk musicians gravitated toward early hillbilly recordings and the 1960s country rockers as icons of authenticity. The band generally cited as starting the alt-country movement is Uncle Tupelo. In 1987, Jeff Tweedy (1967–), Jay Farrar (1966–), and Mike Heidorn (1967–) transformed their punk band, the Primitives, into a band that paid homage to the sounds of hillbilly, folk, and country rock. Based in their hometown of Belleville, Illinois, Uncle Tupelo played songs written by Tweedy and Farrar that voiced the considerable angst and frustration of a young, working-class population trapped in middle America, searching for more tangible roots than the punk scene's disenfranchised attitude offered. They found their grounding in old styles of country music. To them, early hillbilly, blues, and folk recordings, along with Merle Haggard's Bakersfield sound and Gram Parson's country rock, sprang from some noncommercial fount of American identity. Critic David Goodman described Uncle Tupelo's style as an "alternation between or joining of grinding punk, country rock, and acoustic country" from a dark and brooding perspective. Uncle Tupelo released their debut album, *No Depression*, in 1990. Two more albums followed, juxtaposing punk-infused originals with acoustic hillbilly-styled covers. The band shifted to major label Sire Records for 1993's *Anodyne*. As had happened with so many of the country rock bands from the 1960s and early '70s, the personalities, tensions, and different musical interests that gave rise to the sound of Uncle Tupelo also threatened the stability of the band. Although they sounded tighter than ever in 1993, Tweedy and Farrar had clashed personally, and the band dissolved.

Uncle Tupelo became the symbolic origin for alt-country in part because they arrived at a critical moment in country's evolution, and then dissolved before the band wandered too far afield from their signature sound. After the breakup, Jay Farrar and drummer Mike Heidorn formed Son Volt, which kept the same formula of rock fused with twangy barroom country music. Jeff Tweedy formed Wilco, which, after its first album, quickly migrated toward an alternative rock sound. That split was representative of the fragmentation of the alt-country scene; fans continued to follow the music of both bands and apply the label alt-country to them, even when the music no longer bore any audible vestiges of country twang or hillbilly roots.

Uncle Tupelo was not the first band to combine rock (or, more specifically, punk) sounds with old country music. Within the rock scene there had always been musicians interested in country to varying degrees; Elvis Costello, for instance, had made an album of country covers in 1981 that exposed New Wave fans to country hits. In the early 1980s, punk bands from New York to California had taken to collecting country records and using them as a source for their music. The trend, often dubbed "cowpunk," was sufficiently widespread that the *New York Times* reported on it in 1984. Bands such as Rank and File (which included Alejandro Escovedo, who would be a major solo artist in the later alt-country scene), the Meat Puppets from Arizona, and Jason and the Scorchers, originally based in Nashville, released albums that were heavily laced with honky-tonk twang and sounded like a genuine homage to country's traditions, updated for a 1980s rock audience. Many Midwestern bands such as the Jayhawks, from Minneapolis, adopted an approach that combined heartland rock with country music.

Those formulas made sense for an audience where teenagers had grown up on their parents' Bakersfield country records but followed their own tastes toward Bruce Springsteen or Tom Petty, a similar situation to the way that Southern rock bands in the 1970s had grown up on their parents' honky-tonk but sought a rock identity for themselves. The Jayhawks, with Mark Olson and Gary Louris, released a self-titled record on an independent label in 1986 that brought those influences together. In some music scenes, various styles of music had gone even further with the blend of rock and country, such as the lurid extremes of punk and rockabilly ("psychobilly"). In other words, Uncle Tupelo was part of a bigger trend, but they happened to build a loyal fan base, break up before changing styles, and find fame at a moment when other factors came together to define a much larger movement. And whereas the 1980s rock/country hybrids had very little impact on country as a genre, the 1990s alt-country scene found far more points of intersection with mainstream country.

Alternative Country Coalesces

The heart of the alt-country movement was built on the sounds and ideology that Uncle Tupelo presented, as young musicians, disenchanted with both the social establishment and the commercial music industry, combined the aesthetics of punk with roots music. The characteristics included:

- Band members often had formerly played in punk or hard rock bands, and had little or no investment in contemporary country music as a genre.

Listening Guide

"No Depression" (1990)

PERFORMERS:
Uncle Tupelo

SONGWRITER:
A. P. Carter

ORIGINAL RELEASE:
No Depression
(Rockville Records
6050, 1990)

FORM: Verse-chorus

STYLE: Alt-country
(postpunk)

When Uncle Tupelo released their first album in 1990, the title track was a cover of folk revivalists the New Lost City Ramblers, who were in turn covering an old Carter Family song that had been published in a paperback hymnal in the 1930s. "No Depression" was the most acoustic and folk-influenced of the tracks on the album, much of which veered toward heavy guitar distortion, chord progressions borrowed straight from punk, and vocal expressions of raw angst. But the song solidified the connection between old-time country and the folk revival on the one hand, and Uncle Tupelo and the growing movement surrounding them on the other.

Uncle Tupelo regularly performed cover songs. *No Depression* included folk blues artist Lead Belly's version of "John Hardy"; later releases of bonus tracks and bootlegs featured songs from Woody Guthrie, the Byrds, the Flying Burrito Brothers, Bob Dylan, and Johnny Cash, along with punk and hard rock bands. These covers reinforced the complicated relationship that the band had with earlier musical styles, as they were simultaneously paying tribute and offering ironic commentary.

Both the Carters and the New Lost City Ramblers sang three verses on "No Depression." Uncle Tupelo omitted the one verse that touched on the description of real human compassion and the conditions of heaven, a "bright land" where orphans are not hungry and there are no weeping widows. Instead, the band kept only the verses that center on dark, oppressive moods: hurling storms, failing hearts, millions lost to their doom in the darkest of hours. In their hands, the song was less of an optimistic promise of glory days to come than a morbid description of a mundane present. Critics have noted that the album focused on an immediate sense of repetitive, meaningless, abject mundaneness, depicted in the songs through the modern forces of factory work and teen angst about the future. The balancing forces of age, religion, and family that were present in the early generations of folk and country music were mostly absent from this brand of alt-country.

- Instrumentation included distorted electric guitars, drums, electric bass, plus layers of country-style fiddling, steel guitar, and harmonica.
- Musicians adopted a DIY ("do it yourself") approach to music making, in which simple chord progressions and straightforward melodies are the norm. The DIY aesthetic also includes recording techniques that preserve a "live" and raw, unmediated sound.
- Singers favored emotional expressivity over technical control.
- Both musicians and fans adopted an attitude that disavowed the contemporary country music industry.

While "No Depression" became the symbolic identity of the emergent alt-country movement, Uncle Tupelo's other recordings are far more representative of the band's signature sound. Their first single, "I Got Drunk," for instance, epitomizes the punk drumming, guitar rhythms, and chord progressions that live audiences were used to.

TIME	FORM	LISTENING CUES	DISCUSSION
0:00	Introduction	guitars and bass	Uncle Tupelo copied the introduction, especially the guitar licks, from the New Lost City Ramblers' version of the song (1959). The melody of the song is played on the lower strings of the guitar, which is the "Carter scratch" or "thumb brush" style Maybelle Carter pioneered.
0:18	Verse 1	"Oh, fear the hearts..."	Jay Farrar's vocals are as rough and gritty, and he pronounces the words with an affectation of the Southern accent the Carters used and that the New Lost City Ramblers adopted.
0:34	Chorus	"I'm going where..."	Jeff Tweedy adds one line of vocal harmony over the melody, which is the standard approach used by many 1970s country rock bands. The tempo of this recording is faster than either the Carters or the New Lost City Ramblers.
0:51	Instrumental interlude	guitar	This instrumental interlude, which covers the chord progression of one chorus, evokes the sounds of the folk revival with the patterns played on the guitar.
1:08	Verse 2	"In this dark hour..."	The doomsday predictions of this verse match the weighty, gravelly sound of the band.
1:25	Chorus	"I'm going where..."	This chorus creates a sense of musical urgency.
1:42	Chorus		This chorus uses sustained bass notes and sparse guitar picking to change the mood of the song and create a moment of repose.
1:59	Chorus	"I'm going where..."	Stop-time at 2:08 creates a more dramatic ending.

- Songs were written by the band members themselves, and the idea that the songs represented personal experience was critical to the music's value. The exceptions to this were cover songs that connected the band directly to much older repertory.
- The musicians to whom the movement paid tribute were 1920s and '30s hillbilly singers like the Carter Family, pioneers of the folk movement like Woody Guthrie, honky-tonk stars like Hank Williams, country rockers like Gram Parsons, and country singers who were seen as defiant toward the mainstream industry, like Johnny Cash and Merle Haggard.

Ryan Adams (1974–)

hen the alt-country movement caught the attention of the national press in the mid-1990s, the band Whiskeytown and its front man, Ryan Adams, were tagged as the face, sound, and future of the movement. Whiskeytown did not last into the next decade, but after the band's demise, Adams struck out on his own to both critical and popular acclaim as a leading figure in alt-country. Within a few short years, he had left behind the country twang for an independent singer-songwriter rock identity. His music had little or no audible connection to country, and he was no longer engaging with an audience who thought of themselves as country fans.

Adams was born and raised in Jacksonville, North Carolina, a midsize town close to the U.S. Marine Corps' Camp Lejeune. He grew up listening to punk as well as heavy metal, and when he dropped out of high school, he joined the local punk band The Patty Duke Syndrome. A few years later, Adams and his bandmates moved to Raleigh, North Carolina, with its much larger music scene. Adams's songwriting turned toward country themes and sounds, and the punk band broke up. Shortly after, Adams formed Whiskeytown with drummer Eric

"Skillet" Gilmore, violinist Caitlin Cary, bassist Steve Grothman, and guitarist Phil Wandscher. Whiskeytown's sound grew out of Adams's interest in Gram Parsons, the stark individuality of each of the band's members, and the edgy, ironic punk attitude they layered over honky-tonk music, with distorted electric guitar mixed with fiddle and steel sounds.

In 1995, the fledgling alt-country magazine *No Depression* featured Whiskeytown in a profile that called the band "the most inspired" of a bunch of "ace country-rock bands." A wave of enthusiastic press followed their debut indie-label album, *Faithless Street*, and the band signed with a subsidiary of Geffen Records. With the backing of that major label, their next album, *Stranger's Almanac*, was far more refined and polished in its sonic mix, evoking comparisons to '70s rock band Fleetwood Mac. The band's personnel had already changed, and in spite of Whiskeytown's critical success, Adams and other band members were actively pursuing other projects. Within the active alt-country scene in North Carolina, Adams played in various lineups under different band names during this time, as is common in tight-knit musical scenes. Whiskeytown recorded a third album, *Pneumonia*, that drifted

By the early 1990s, the formula of former punk musicians exploring country roots had become quite common. The advent of the internet (see essay on the Internet Age) meant that bands without major record labels could generate grass-roots publicity, and fans could find out about hot bands more quickly and easily than before. Alt-country artists often declared that "Nashville" (a way to refer to the mainstream country music industry and country radio hits of the 1990s) was making shallow, cookie-cutter music that had lost its soul. For their fans, this explanation justified the alt-country bands' absence from the radio or major record labels, and also reassured their fans that they had discovered something untainted further toward '70s rock revival sounds and away from honky-tonk sounds, but before it was released, the band dissolved, and the album got trapped in corporate red tape involving a record-label merger. When it finally was released on a different label in 2001, the liner notes ended, "Thank you and goodnight"; Whiskeytown was really over.

By then, Adams had already gone solo and was riding the crest of the alt-country wave. In 1999, he toured extensively, sang with Emmylou Harris on a PBS television show tribute for Gram Parsons, and became friends with Gillian Welch and David Rawlings. They encouraged him to leave New York and head to Nashville, where he recorded *Heartbreaker* with guest vocals from both Harris and Welch. Released in 2000, the album recaptured Adams's earlier honky-tonk vulnerability, blended with 1970s country rock with a hint of folk. His musical associations with Harris and Welch added to his "country" affiliation, although the mainstream country fan base paid little attention. But after that, Adams's records turned away from any recognizable country styles. He left Nashville to live in New York and then Los Angeles, and within a few years had distanced himself entirely from country music. By 2010, his music was more connected to heavy metal, and his

Figure 13-1 Ryan Adams.
Source: Daniel Coston.

reign over the alt-country scene had ended. He has nonetheless maintained an active career with his core audience, and in 2015 enjoyed a brief return to the mainstream spotlight by recording a cover version of a Taylor Swift album, once again standing as an alternative foil to the mainstream music scene.

by commercial corruption and therefore better. Similarly, the DIY sound that was a hallmark of the alt-country bands was sometimes the result of very small production budgets and independent record labels rather than an aesthetic choice, but to alt-country's fans, that sound came to represent a new mode of authenticity.

As had happened in Austin in the 1960s and '70s, once the movement began to expand, the infrastructure of a music industry sprang up. Bloodshot Records, based in Chicago, launched in 1994 and specialized in "insurgent country" acts (their term for alt-country). A year later, Grant Alden and Peter Blackstock launched a bimonthly magazine called *No Depression*, which became the central trade publication for the alt-country scene. The magazine's initial tag line was "Alternative Country (Whatever That Is) . . . ," which expressed the scene's unwillingness to define its own musical borders. E-mail Listservs became a means for fans to discuss the burgeoning scene, which also gave them a sense of belonging to a (virtual) community. The best known was Postcard2, which started as a backup Listserv for Uncle Tupelo's fan list (called Postcard after one of the band's songs) but grew to be the central discussion forum for fans, critics, industry personnel, and journalists interested in alt-country. Sales charts and radio airplay charts also appeared, allowing the bands and fans to keep track of who was popular and measure commercial success. By the mid-1990s, an infrastructure was firmly in place to support the alt-country movement. Bands that garnered lots of attention included Whiskeytown (see Artist Profile: Ryan Adams), the Bottle Rockets, the Old 97's, Two Dollar Pistols, and Drive-By Truckers, along with solo artists including Alejandro Escovedo (1951–) and Robbie Fulks (1963–), who recorded "Fuck This Town" (1997) to share his opinion of Nashville and the mainstream country music industry.

For the most part, the fan base for alt-country was different than the core fan base for commercial country. The values that the postpunk alt-country bands instilled in their music were largely shared by their fans, who appreciated the intellectual stance of irony and the affectation of artistic ease in their performances. Like many of the musicians in the alt-country scene, many of the fans had little investment in country as a contemporary musical genre. Conversely, fans of commercial mainstream country found the alt scene at times pretentious and lacking in the direct sincerity that they valued in their music. These generalizations do not account for individual cases; any fan's connection to music is highly personal and may not match broader trends. But they do help explain the larger trends of alt-country and commercial country, along with their social meanings within popular culture.

A Broader Definition: Alternative Country as Musical Space

Although Uncle Tupelo, Whiskeytown, and other postpunk rockers who turned to country roots received a disproportionate amount of the alt-country scene's attention, their musical style was by no means dominant. Alt-country became a gathering place for musicians with country connections but working outside the mainstream, including but not limited to:

- Singer-songwriters working the independent coffee houses, college campus venues, and indie rock clubs
- Older country artists who had fallen off country radio playlists
- Bands that performed older or revivalist styles of country music
- Honky-tonk entertainers, especially in Texas, whose careers simply did not intersect with Nashville.

Singer-songwriter country artists who either had no interest in a major-label deal or whose music did not match the interests of mainstream country radio often had thriving careers with alt-country fans. Lucinda Williams (1953–), for instance, drew on her Texas country roots to create music that was strongly indebted to the outspoken female country stars of the 1960s and '70s, but with an indie rock twist. After more than two decades performing and recording, Williams earned critical acclaim and widespread attention for her 1998 alt-country album *Car Wheels on a Gravel Road*, which won a Grammy for Best Contemporary Folk Album, a category that illustrates just how difficult it is to formally define the boundaries of this alt-country movement.

Gillian Welch (1967–) followed a similar path to many of the musicians who moved from the folk revival scene into country music in the 1960s and '70s. Raised by professional musicians in California, Welch cultivated an interest in bluegrass, folk, and country rock. Her 1996 debut, *Revival*, drew heavily on acoustic folk music. She expressed little interest in commercial country, but an alt-country fan base, including intellectual hipsters to

Figure 13-2 Lucinda Williams on stage, 2001.
Source: Daniel Coston.

whom her music bespoke revivalist authenticity, adored her. Welch remained a leading figure throughout the alt-country era, falling under the banner of "contemporary folk," and was involved as both a performer and producer on the *O Brother, Where Art Thou?* soundtrack that catapulted the roots revival trend into the spotlight.

Like Welch, Tift Merritt (1975–) was another singer-songwriter who thrived in the alt-country scene even while she sometimes explained in interviews that she did not like that classification. Merritt's career began in Chapel Hill, North Carolina, where she fronted her own band, sang duets with John Howie Jr. of Two Dollar Pistols, and cultivated her songwriting. In 2000, she won the prestigious songwriting contest at Merlefest, the bluegrass festival that Doc Watson had started in 1988 (see Chapter 5). That accomplishment helped her land a contract with Lost Highway Records for her debut album, *Bramble Rose*. Although Merritt released a music video to Country Music Television, opened on stage for Willie Nelson, and pitched her music to country radio, she never dove into the mainstream country scene, nor did the fan base embrace her. Within a few albums, as was the case with so many artists who started out in the alt-country scene, her music had drifted away from any audible connection to its country roots.

Listening Guide

"Suppose Tonight Would Be Our Last" (1999)

PERFORMERS: Two
Dollar Pistols with
Tift Merritt

SONGWRITERS:
George Jones and
Melba Montgomery

ORIGINAL RELEASE:
*The Two Dollar Pistols
with Tift Merritt* (Yep
Roc Records, 1999)

FORM: AABA

STYLE: Retro
alt-country

In 1963, George Jones and Melba Montgomery (1938–) released a duet album that included a song the two had penned together. The song reflected the updated honky-tonk sound slipping over a Bakersfield shuffle with a crying steel guitar filling in between the voices. The Jones-Montgomery partnership was so successful that the two sang together regularly for the next several years until Jones met Tammy Wynette.

Three decades later, John Howie Jr. put together a retro honky-tonk band called Two Dollar Pistols in Carrboro, North Carolina. Howie had played drums in various punk and rock bands, but as the alt-country movement of the mid-1990s gained momentum, he made the leap into country music and switched from drums to singing. While changing personnel several times, Two Dollar Pistols released three albums and became local favorites in a thriving alt-country scene centered on Chapel Hill and Raleigh, North Carolina. Meanwhile, Tift Merritt (1975–), a songwriter and student at the University of North Carolina at Chapel Hill, began to perform locally. Merritt's sweet, Southern, soul-inflected voice won over a devoted local following, and in 1999, Howie and Merritt decided to make a set of duet recordings. The two pored over Howie's collection of classic country LPs, and picked this song. The resulting EP, *The Two Dollar Pistols with Tift Merritt*, appeared a year before Merritt won a major songwriting contest at Doc Watson's Merlefest festival and headed into a national career.

This recording captures the musical essence of a local alt-country scene: talented performers making a budget record that resurrects past country styles into the present. Compared to the Jones & Montgomery version (rereleased and readily available on *Vintage Collections* [Capitol Nashville 33832, 1996]), Howie and Merritt's version has less reverb on the vocals, which makes them sound closer and more directly connected to the listener, as opposed to the drenching reverb on the 1963 original, which conveys the sense of space and great distances between the singers and the listeners. Howie and Merritt's recording also has a purposeful imprecision—pitches slide a bit, the vocal rhythms are not quite synchronized at times, and the singers breathe at awkward places in some of the phrases. All of these factors fit into the DIY and live aesthetic of alt-country. To their devoted fans, this recording captured the feeling of the singers performing a bunch of classic country cover songs onstage at a local dive.

"Suppose Tonight Would Be Our Last" represents a fleeting, priceless moment in the history of alt-country when these musicians found new roots in old honky-tonk and thrilled local fans, who identified with the music as an idealized version of country music. Just a few years later, Merritt signed with Lost Highway Records and was exploring her sound, image, and audience through a series of critically acclaimed releases. A decade after the duet EP, she has mostly left country music behind. Two Dollar Pistols dissolved, and after a few years of trying out different collaborations and playing solo around the local area, Howie formed a new band, Rosewood Bluff, and started recording again, but heyday of the active local country scene had passed.

Song Form: This song is an excellent example of the hybrid AABA/verse-chorus form (see Appendix A). The song clearly follows the classic form of AABA, with an instrumental interlude, and then a repetition of the complete AABA structure. However, in the two halves of the song, the lyrics change for the first two sections, but they stay the same for the last two. Thus, the last two ("BA") serve as a type of chorus for the song:

Form	Hybrid Interpretation
A	"Verse"
A	
B	"Chorus"
A	
[INSTRUMENTAL INTERLUDE]	
A	"Verse"
A	
B	"Chorus"
A	

Figure 13-3 Tift Merritt and John Howie Jr. in the recording studio.

Source: Daniel Coston.

Continued

Listening Guide

"Suppose Tonight Would Be Our Last" (1999) Continued

TIME	FORM	LISTENING CUES	DISCUSSION
0:00	Introduction	fiddle	The opening fiddle notes are reminiscent of the honky-tonk and Bakersfield shuffle tunes of the late 1950s. Compare the introduction of Ray Price, "Heartaches by the Number" (1958).
0:09	A-section	"Suppose tonight..."	The way that the drums are miked reveals that this is a recording from the 1990s, not the 1960s. Notice that Merritt and Howie are rhythmically not quite together, which makes the recording sound both "live" and natural (unmediated).
0:23	A-section	"Would we laugh..."	Howie in particular slides through different pitches while singing, which makes his performance sound expressive and raw.
0:37	B-section	"I know I'd die..."	The steel guitar becomes more prominent here, while the band abandons their shuffle rhythm here. This makes the B section stand out from the rest of the song.
0:52	A-section	"If just..."	Merritt's voice includes a sultry singer-songwriter quality.
1:06	A-section instrumental	fiddle	As in the 1950s and early '60s, AABA song forms often feature two of the sections as instrumentals. Here, a very traditional honky-tonk fiddle takes a solo.
1:21	A-section instrumental	steel guitar	The steel guitar finishes the instrumental interludes with a solo that could have been lifted straight off a 1960s country record.
1:34	A-section	"I couldn't live..."	Notice how the steel guitar supports the vocals in this section.
1:49	A-section	"If just suppose..."	The same line of text appears here as at the end of the AABA unit, which plays with the listener's perception of the song's form.
2:03	B-section	"I know I'd die..."	This section showcases Merritt's vocals better than any other in the recording.
2:17	A-section	"If just suppose..."	The song ends quite simply at the conclusion of this section.

Some of the biggest stars within the alt-country scene were singers who had formerly been in the mainstream country spotlight, though with varying degrees of success. Artists such as Robert Earl Keen Jr. (1956–) and Lyle Lovett (1957–), both Texans who had tried their hand at mainstream country careers (see Chapter 11), built huge fan bases among alt-country listeners. Keen's concerts, in particular, drew a college crowd for whom commercial country held little appeal but who found Keen's music both intelligent and easy to relate to. By the early 1990s, Johnny Cash was no longer part of the mainstream commercial scene and did not have a

Figure 13-4 Johnny Cash at his last performance, July 2003.

Source: Daniel Coston.

record deal. His music and his persona, however, held great appeal to fans who saw the Man in Black's brooding, dark mix of rock, country, and an antiestablishment attitude as matching the aesthetic perspective of alt-country. Music producer Rick Rubin, who had started Def Jam Records with Russell Simmons in the 1980s and made some of the most successful early hip-hop records, was looking for a new project for his American Recordings record label. Rubin saw potential among the large and fractured alt-country audience for any artist whose music would fit into the broader philosophy of the movement, and Cash was the perfect match. Rubin and Cash's first collaboration, *American Recordings,* appeared in 1994.

Over the next few years, Rubin had Cash sing old, traditional songs or ones from his rockabilly days, covers of contemporary rock songs done in his sparse style, and duets with a variety of hip rock artists. The resulting albums were stark, raw, haunting, and edgy. In their marketing, Cash and Rubin played up the concepts of "real" and "authentic" against the foil of commercial country. For instance, when their second album, *Unchained,* won a Grammy, Cash's record label took out a full-page ad in *Billboard* that showed him in an angry pose flipping the bird to the camera (a photograph taken during a concert almost three decades earlier). The ad's text was a sarcastic condemnation of the contemporary country music industry for ignoring Cash's records. Ironically, the lack of mainstream success actually made his records far more popular among alt-country fans.

Other well-known senior country stars reappeared in the alt-country scene to great acclaim during these years. Emmylou Harris (1947–), who had been a mainstay of country radio in the 1980s and had won a CMA award, released *Wrecking Ball* in 1995 (see Listen Side by Side). Along similar lines, Roseanne Cash and

Figure 13-5 Emmylou Harris and Rodney Crowell perform in Berkeley, California, 1975; four decades later they released a duet album.

Loretta Lynn both won over new audiences long after they had slipped off mainstream radio. For Lynn's *Van Lear Rose* (2004) she worked with producer Jack White from the rock band the White Stripes, an instance of hip young rock artist collaborating with senior country artist, as was common in the alt-country scene.

Some bands that appealed to the alt-country fans resurrected past styles of country music in a retro style. The Derailers, a band that started in 1994 in Austin, Texas, not only play music that sounds like Buck Owens's Bakersfield shuffles and early George Jones recordings but also dress and act on stage like a 1960s country dance hall band. The Cigar Store Indians, from Crabapple, Georgia, launched in 1991 as a rockabilly band with a retro flair to their performances. Other bands, such as Big Sandy & His Fly-Rite Boys, opted for more of a western swing sound. These bands were not the first to take up a retro style; Asleep at the Wheel had been performing western swing since 1970, and rocker-guitarist Brian Setzer and the Stray Cats had been a rockabilly revival band since 1980. But in the early 1990s, the alt-country audience was looking for more musicians who could channel the past of country music, which helped the careers of these bands quite a bit, as did the swing dance revival that was generating performance opportunities.

On occasion, singers who were popular in the alt-country scene caught the attention of a major record label. These moments in their careers often created a dilemma for the artists. Many of them had built their reputations among alternative fans by eschewing Nashville, the mainstream record industry, and country radio, yet now they faced a golden opportunity to get their music distributed more widely and with more financial support. If they made that career transition, however, their original fans might accuse them of selling out, or abandoning their musical ideology in exchange for money. Only a few artists, such as Texan honky-tonk songwriter Pat Green (1972–), made the transition reasonably successfully.

The most difficult challenge that alt-country faced was sustainability. Because the fans in particular defined the movement as an anticommercial opposition to something else (in this case, commercial country), it was threatened any time its musicians became too commercially successful, or when the mainstream music establishment welcomed it into the fold. Nonetheless, alt-country as an inclusive musical space that functioned outside the mainstream country industry persisted through the decade and beyond.

Americana

In the mid-1990s, a few radio stations adopted the term "Americana" to describe a new format. The term became a new descriptor for much of the music that was popular among alt-country fans. The word had been used before; it showed up in record label catalogs in the 1950s and '60s to describe folk, country, and pop music that sounded like old storytelling ballads, and forty years later it was back. The term downplayed the oppositional nature that was implied by alt-country (an "alternative" positioned itself against some other option), and described music that claimed American folk styles (including both hillbilly and blues, white and black) as its roots without venturing into pop music. Essentially, Americana described the gentler side of alt-country, plus modern folk singers, blues-and gospel-influenced singer-songwriters, old country singers from past generations, and rock musicians who held to a sparse, 1950s-influenced approach. By removing the notion that this music was an "alternative" to commercial country, the term also freed the music from its tethers to the country genre. Music and institutions such as Garrison Keillor's *A Prairie Home Companion* radio show and his house band fit this definition. Unlike alt-country, which evoked a sense of oppositional, disenfranchised angst, Americana came to represent simplicity, native identity, originality, and a homegrown, noncommercial authenticity. Radio stations and organizations still identify with the term, as do younger musicians and bands who assiduously avoid calling themselves "country" because of its commercial and sometimes anti-intellectual associations.

Another Alternative: Bluegrass

While the alt-country scene was flourishing, bluegrass was experiencing a resurgence of interest outside of mainstream country music. Many of the same factors contributed to this trend as to alt-country, including the dominance of pop cross-over styles in mainstream country. Since the early '50s, bluegrass bands, both more traditional and more progressive, had existed in all regions of the country, nurtured by a small but dedicated audience and a large network of festivals. The division between country and bluegrass had started in the 1950s, solidified in the 1960s folk revival era, and been further entrenched in the 1980s. fairly recently, bluegrass musicians and fans had taken steps to expand the infrastructure supporting the genre. The International Bluegrass Music Association (IBMA) was formed in 1985, with many of the same motivations that the Country Music Association had held in the late 1950s. These included goals to promote the music, to educate potential consumers in an effort to transcend negative stereotypes about the music's culture, to connect the different components of the bluegrass music industry to each other, and to cultivate high standards of professionalism within the musical community. The IBMA organized annual awards beginning in 1990, with categories such as Female and Male Vocalists of the Year just like the CMA Awards.

Throughout the 1990s, bluegrass music held a similar relationship to country as did alt-country: it offered an alternative musical space that claimed the same roots (in this case, string band and hillbilly stars along with Bill Monroe and

Flatt & Scruggs) but presented music that purported to be less commercial, more celebratory of instrumental virtuosity, and closely tied to an idea of folk music. Middle-class and upper-middle-class audiences who did not like commercial country music found satisfaction in getting back to the musical earth through bluegrass. It also provided a useful parallel musical scene as an alternative to commercial country music.

Country artists who were no longer receiving airplay on mainstream radio found that a lateral move into bluegrass offered the same sort of career renewal that Johnny Cash had found by sliding into rock-infused alt-country. The bluegrass audience was, in large part, very different from the commercial country audience. The bluegrass fan base generally sought music that, to them, represented an idea of imagined escape from modern life, whereas the country audience sought music that instantiated their present existence, although of course any such generalizations did not account for all music and all fans. Thus, bluegrass welcomed artists whose music failed to connect with the literalist country audience. Bluegrass's anticommercial rhetoric also meant that bluegrass artists had to adopt fewer traits of pop music to be successful than did their country music peers. In practical terms, this meant bluegrass welcomed older stars and stars whose stage presence lacked glamour. Ricky Skaggs, Dolly Parton, and Patty Loveless were just a few of the older commercial country stars who reinvented themselves musically in bluegrass. Dolly Parton in particular redefined herself as a bluegrass singer in the late 1990s, explaining to interviewers that she had started out singing bluegrass some three decades earlier and had now returned to her musical home. In 1999, Parton signed with Sugar Hill Records, known for their acoustic and bluegrass offerings, and released *The Grass Is Blue*. Her silvery soprano voice melded easily with the acoustic backings of a traditional bluegrass band, and the album stood in stark contrast to the countrypolitan music that Parton had been singing just a decade earlier. Parton's transformation from pop-crossover star to bluegrass singer won over fans, who perceived her new music as down-home and real. In no small irony, Parton was defining herself against the foil of pop-crossover artists of the very sort that she herself had been just a few years earlier. Parton won several IBMA awards and recorded two more albums that were essentially bluegrass in style.

The Impact on Mainstream Country

The developments in alt-country and bluegrass music in the 1990s had a substantial impact on mainstream commercial country music, even while the contemporary commercial country and country-pop styles remained the prominent sounds in the genre. Although both bluegrass and alt-country defined themselves in opposition to commercial country music, they actually coexisted in a complex, symbiotic relationship. Alt-country and bluegrass needed commercial country, and mainstream commercial country needed both alt-country and bluegrass.

Alt-country offered a musical space for singer-songwriters to develop their music and sustain themselves with live performances and independent albums.

Yet it also provided a source pool of songs for commercial country artists. Many songwriters, like Darrell Scott (1959–), toured and released independent albums of their material, which major country stars like Travis Tritt then mined for potential hit songs. In other words, alt-country served an important purpose within the business infrastructure of commercial country. Along the same lines, alt-country venues and audiences allowed emerging or future commercial artists such as Pat Green to hone their skills in front of live audiences and figuratively pay their dues in honky-tonks.

Particularly in the mid-1990s, record labels that had strong reputations in commercial country went looking for new acts that would help project the importance of tradition on which country music relies. For these labels, musicians with alt-country or bluegrass credentials provided an essential counterbalance to the country-pop identity that was thriving within country music at that time. BR5-49 was one such example. Nashville musicians Chuck Mead and Gary Bennett organized the band in 1993, and they landed a gig as the house band for Robert's Western Wear, a clothing store turned honky-tonk located on Broadway in downtown Nashville that catered to both tourists and locals. Their retro-styled band combined honky-tonk sounds with western swing rhythms, and soon they were playing to packed crowds. In 1995, Arista Records signed the band, and a year later, their first full-length album appeared. They had a few songs on the *Billboard* charts and caught the attention of the mainstream country audience.

BR5-49 resurrected a much more stereotyped image of Southern, rural country music even in the band's choice of name, which they lifted from a comedy routine on the television show *Hee Haw*. One of their most popular songs poked fun at the very country scene in which they resided: "Little Ramona," which sounds like a rockabilly swing tune, describes a fan abandoning her mosh-pit punk interests and taking up an obsession with old honky-tonk, basically a summation of the alt-country storyline. The punk cultural references include the name Ramona (the Ramones were a famous American punk band), safety-pin T-shirts, Doc Martin shoes, and thrashing, all of which Ramona trades in for Hank Williams records, "kicker" boots, and swing dancing. In an unusual about-face, a song on mainstream country radio offered tongue-in-cheek mockery of the postpunk alt-country scene.

For a record label like Arista, signing a band with an alt-country identity offered a way to renew the connections between contemporary commercial country music and traditional country music. This would allow them to reconnect with fans who were turned off by country-pop (and sell them records). Not all record labels were successful in these attempts, but some of their efforts paid off. For example, bluegrass singer Alison Krauss (see Artist Profile) covered "When You Say Nothing at All," for a tribute album to Keith Whitley in 1994, and country fans loved it. Other artists also moved from alternative styles into the mainstream, which was the exact opposite of what Johnny Cash, Dolly Parton, and Loretta Lynn were doing at the time. All together, these instances illustrate the interdependence and interconnected nature of mainstream, commercial country music and the scenes of alt-country, bluegrass, and Americana.

Alison Krauss (1971–)

Alison Krauss's career flows continuously between bluegrass, mainstream country, and Americana, illustrating just how interrelated those musical worlds are. Different audiences know different facets of her career: champion bluegrass fiddler, Americana vocalist, country star, and producer. In combination, she is one of the most formidable stars of the current Americana scene, holding 27 Grammys, 14 IBMA awards, and 8 CMA awards.

Raised in Illinois, Krauss garnered significant attention at fiddle contests by the time she was twelve, and at age fifteen, she signed with Rounder Records, who hoped to market her as an instrumental virtuoso. Her first album, *Too Late to Cry* (1987), was recorded with Nashville session players and featured her singing as well as playing, a nod to the commercial preference for vocals over pure instrumentals. Shortly after that, she put together a backing band, Union Station, and shifted her focus to recording albums with the band. Fans unfamiliar with her earliest recordings would be surprised to hear her early singing style. Her first albums feature a belting, brash vocal typical of female bluegrass vocalists. Both her fiddle playing and her singing found enthusiastic audiences, and in the early 1990s, she earned accolades in bluegrass, firmly establishing herself as a star within that scene.

Over the span of her first four albums, Krauss changed her singing style into a sweet, airy soprano. The shift in tone moved her further away from traditional bluegrass and gave her a very distinctive and instantly recognizable sound, both features that would help launch the next phase of her career.

The always fluid boundaries between bluegrass and country were particularly important in the 1980s neotraditionalist era, when a large number of bluegrass singers slid into major country careers, including Ricky Skaggs, Vince Gill, and Keith Whitley, among many others. Thus, in 1994, when Whitley's widow and fellow country singer Lorrie Morgan organized a tribute album, she included a long roster of top country stars, but also bluegrass musicians, including Alison Krauss. Krauss's recording of Whitley's hit, "When You Say Nothing at All," put her in front of a mainstream country audience, who loved her performance. This success let Krauss migrate into a mainstream country career while still maintaining her bluegrass credentials. Female singers shifting from bluegrass to country was, in itself, a tried and true practice, from Delia Bell to Rhonda Vincent, who had tried to make that move just a few years earlier. Seldom did the shift last (both Bell and Vincent returned to their bluegrass fan bases, describing their forays into country as if they were musical excursions to a foreign land), but Krauss was the exception. Over the next decade, she continued to perform

Changes in Commercial Country

In the late 1990s, mainstream country music was dominated by country-pop, but that trend was fading, and country music was beginning to show signs of shifting back to a more roots-oriented, hard-edged country sound. That change would mainstream country duets and participate in the scene, albeit without ever diving fully into the center of the genre.

Krauss was a well-known performer with an excellent reputation when she was tapped to participate in the *O Brother* soundtrack. The astonishing success of that album (see essay on the *O Brother* phenomenon) solidified her identity as one of the biggest stars in the amorphous Americana/alt-country/bluegrass musical world that was getting an unprecedented amount of attention.

Krauss also shifted into a new role within the music industry—that of producer. From her position as an established senior performer, she began cultivating younger musicians whose interests were similarly rooted in bluegrass but directed well beyond the bounds of that scene. In 2000, she produced the debut album for a young California trio known as Nickel Creek. Their mandolin player, Chris Thile, would continue on a career trajectory that defied any categorization by genre and represented the most ambitious realization of Americana. As an aside, Thile's work fronting the Punch Brothers, his collaborations with fellow virtuosic string players Edgar Meyer, Yo-Yo Ma, and Stuart Duncan called *The Goat Rodeo Sessions*, and his eventual selection to replace Garrison Keillor as host for the radio show *A Prairie Home Companion* radio speak to the profoundly wide range for a musical career from that starting point.

Krauss has continued a practice she established early in her recording career, namely alternating between making solo records and making bluegrass records with Union Station. Of significance, Krauss's more recent solo recordings have reached well beyond the bounds of bluegrass, embracing pop, jazz, and a host of other styles. *Windy City* (2017), for instance, features covers of classic country and pop songs, performed with an army of session players, and the overall effect is a blend of acoustic Americana and classic country. "Goodbye and So Long to You" on that album is a prime illustration, with an unexpected combination of western swing and New Orleans bounce that pulls in trumpets, piano, and, as one reviewer put it, "everything including the kitchen sink." The album as a whole is musically beyond reproach—and simply stunning. But the fact that she is still regarded primarily as a bluegrass star is a testament to the loyalty of the bluegrass world toward stars who "paid their dues," professionally speaking. It also speaks to the shortcomings of genre labels and the limitations such categorizations would place on musicians who, like Krauss, as well as others like Chris Thile and Rhiannon Giddens, have visions and musical ideas that simply cannot be circumscribed with commonplace genre labels. Understanding how their careers emerged from alternative, acoustic, and Americana scenes helps explain how to conceptualize their music within the framework of today's popular music.

continue the cyclic pattern of country music styles over the previous decades, when eras of pop-crossover success were followed by a return to more traditional, honky-tonk, and twangy sounds, which then evolved into another period of crossover success. The tensions between these various styles prompted new developments in the music, and by the late 1990s, a major shift was on the horizon.

A new act appeared in mainstream commercial country in 1998 that foreshadowed this change, which took the form of a roots revival. They were decidedly not part of the alt-country scene, yet they shared values and approaches in common with it. Sisters Emily Strayer (1972–, née Erwin) and Martie Maguire (1969–, née Erwin) founded the Dixie Chicks in the late 1980s near Dallas, Texas, as a four-member, all-girl bluegrass band with Robin Lynn Macy and Laura Lynch. Savvy business skills combined with musical talent led to the group's success in the local market. The Dixie Chicks cut three independent-label albums, which included yodeling songs, instrumental tracks, and a rousing tribute to Hollywood cowgirl Dale Evans. Some of their song choices drew from outside country music, including a Sam Cooke soul number and a cover of Ray Charles's R&B "Hallelujah I Love Her So," but their approach to the recordings was mainly a combination of bluegrass and close-harmony, singing-cowboy styles.

In 1995, after several personnel changes, vocalist Natalie Maines joined the two sisters in the new lineup. Executives from Monument Records heard the group play in Austin and signed them—yet another instance in the mid-1990s of a major label seeking new talent from within the alternative and bluegrass scenes. Their debut major-label album, *Wide Open Spaces* (1998), was an immediate success. The record label marketed the group as a refreshing alternative to country-pop, emphasizing the women's instrumental talent (McGuire was a champion fiddler, and Strayer brought the Dobro back into the country music spotlight) and the gutsy style of Maines's singing, which was reminiscent of Tanya Tucker. Their songs included traditional country themes and sounds, including a Bakersfield shuffle, "Tonight the Heartache's on Me," with honky-tonk–styled lyrics. But for all the talk about their bluegrass roots and traditionalist leanings, the Dixie Chicks balanced their traditional musical roots with plenty of country-pop. From 1997 through 2002, every single they released appeared on both the country and the "Hot 100" (pop) charts; the band signed endorsements for trendy Candie's shoes; and they appeared on the Lilith Fair tour alongside pop, rock, and folk-influenced singer-songwriters. A substantial number of their fans did not associate them strongly with country music during these first years of national attention, even as both their record label and many country fans heralded them as a return to roots tradition in country music.

Their second album, *Fly* (1999), brought more attention to both the band and the country genre with the song "Goodbye Earl," written by Dennis Linde. The recording, with an accompanying campy music video, presented a murder ballad as a macabre comedy that played on Southern redneck stereotypes while highlighting the serious problem of spousal abuse. In spite of the comedic presentation, the song disturbed some fans, and a few country radio stations even resisted playing it. The song charted nonetheless, and "Goodbye Earl," along with the Dixie Chicks' bad-girl romp "Sin Wagon," placed twangy, roots-oriented sounds with banjos, fiddling, and themes that resonated with wild honky-tonk stereotypes, back on country radio. From 1998 until about 2001, the Dixie Chicks melded country-pop with sounds and topics that were hard-core country. Their music enjoyed crossover success like the rest of the country-pop scene, but they—along with a few other bands and singers—were also on the front lines of a looming roots revival.

"Murder on Music Row": The Turning Tide

The long-standing tension between fans' perceptions of authenticity (music that appears to stick to its origins) and commercialization (music that sells) came to a head in the late 1990s. Country-pop artists drew criticisms from fans who felt that the music had gone too far in the direction of commercialization at the expense of its roots. One of the longstanding traditions in country music, however, has been to sing songs bemoaning how country music has gotten too commercial—and then to have those songs played on the radio. In these instances, fans generally disregard the irony of listening to a radio hit with lyrics that complain about how bad (meaning fake, shallow, or insincere) the country music on radio is. They suspend disbelief regarding the obvious commercial appeal of these songs and embrace them as affirmation of country music's commitment to traditionalism.

SONGWRITING ABOUT COUNTRY MUSIC

Country songwriters often write songs about a subject they know well: songwriting. In some instances, the lyrics criticize commercial country music, especially radio, but do so in the form of a radio-friendly, commercial country song. In others, they comment reflexively on the role of professional songwriters in a genre where songs are celebrated for their simplicity or as poetry of the everyday person. Collectively, these songs are an important way in which the genre navigates the tension that comes from its representation of itself as an unmediated expression of art, presented through a commercial medium. A few such examples follow:

Willie Nelson, "Sad Songs and Waltzes" (1973)

Darrell Scott, "Title of the Song" (1997)

Alan Jackson, "Three Minute Positive Not Too Country Up-tempo Love Song" (2000)

George Strait and Alan Jackson, "Murder on Music Row" (2000) (written by Larry Cordle and Larry Shell)

Dixie Chicks, "Long Time Gone" (2003) (written by Darrell Scott)

Alan Jackson, "The Talkin' Song Repair Blues" (2005)

Joey + Rory, "Play the Song" (2008) (written by Rory Lee Feek)

One such occurrence was the duet that George Strait and Alan Jackson sang at the CMA awards in 1999 and released a year later. The song, titled "Murder on Music Row," bemoaned the current state of country music. "Music Row" is the nickname for Nashville's 16th Avenue, the location of many music publishers and record companies' offices, which had become a symbol of the modern country music industry. In the song, Strait and Jackson lament that country radio has turned its back on the likes of Hank Williams, Merle Haggard, and George Jones (referred to in the song by his nickname, Possum), and that someone has "committed murder" and killed the very heart and soul of country music. Drums and "rock 'n' roll guitars" have replaced steel guitars and fiddles in the search for commercial success and fame, the song's lyrics complain. Strait and Jackson's recording features lots of steel guitar and fiddle and a steady, two-beat, two-step rhythm straight out of the honky-tonk tradition.

Strait and Jackson got the song from a Nashville-based bluegrass band, Larry Cordle and Lonesome Standard Time, who released it on their 1999 album titled *Murder on Music Row*. Cowritten by Cordle and Larry Shell, the song makes perfect sense when sung by either a bluegrass band or an alt-country band, or any band, for that matter, that has been left out of the commercial mainstream. However, at the time George Strait and Alan Jackson were two of the most prominent figures in commercial country music. Although they both cultivated a more traditional sound in their recordings than the leading country-pop stars, their songs routinely topped the *Billboard* charts. Jackson had thirty-four top ten hits between 1990 and 2000, while Strait had thirty-six.

Strait and Jackson's record label did not send the song to country radio stations. But country DJs found it on the *Latest, Greatest, Straitest* album and added it to their playlists anyway. Country radio stations were promoting a recording by two of country's biggest commercial stars, laced with steel guitar and fiddle solos, singing about how country radio no longer played any good country music because that music had been violently killed by the music industry. The obvious irony was compounded when the Country Music Association gave a CMA Award to the recording in 2000, a moment in which all of the superstars of contemporary country music (whose songs are routinely on the radio) stood and applauded. In other words, the song illustrated how espousing anticommercial ideas and overt nostalgia is actually part of the practice and tradition of commercial country music itself.

"Murder on Music Row" was one more sign that the stylistic trends in country music were slowly shifting away from country-pop. The biggest catalyst in that shift, however, was a movie soundtrack full of bluegrass recordings. Released in December 2000 on Lost Highway Records, the soundtrack to *O Brother, Where Art Thou?* caught the attention of the national media as well as millions of listeners who enthusiastically declared themselves to be new fans of both bluegrass and old-time country music (see essay on the *O Brother* Phenomenon). This turn of events was linked to the economic environment and cultural context of that time. In 2000, the "dot-com" financial bubble, which was based on unsupportable growth in stocks and speculations about new technologies, burst. The value of tech stocks tumbled, countless start-up internet companies went under, and the entire economy experienced a shake-up. In that climate, bluegrass music symbolized an imagined simpler, better, rural way of life isolated from material concerns and modernist technologies. The soundtrack sold eight million copies, earned countless industry awards, including a Grammy, and brought stardom to its performers. While *O Brother* had

Figure 13-6 Patty Loveless, Ralph Stanley, and Emmylou Harris performing in the Down from the Mountain tour in the wake of O Brother, Where Art Thou's success, 2002.

Source: Daniel Coston.

little immediate impact on country radio or commercial country music and was not marketed as commercial country on its release, the publicity that it garnered pushed bluegrass and Americana into the national spotlight and fostered significant growth in those areas.

Much of the rhetoric surrounding the *O Brother* phenomenon was the same as what had fueled the alt-country movement: pronouncements that commercial country music has lost touch with its roots, celebrations of homegrown music, acoustic performances, revival of lost styles and legendary performers, and claims that this was "real" country music. *O Brother* symbolized the moment when country-pop gave way to twangy, roots-oriented country music as the trending style, even though it would take a few years to hear its full effects. It also represented a metaphoric high point in the history of the alt-country movement. Bluegrass was front-page news, Whiskeytown's Ryan Adams had just gone solo, aging Ralph Stanley released a brand-new CD and went on tour, *No Depression* magazine had hit its stride, and more traditional styles of country music were popping up on country radio.

Listening Guide

"Man of Constant Sorrow" (band version) (2000)

PERFORMERS:
The Soggy Bottom
Boys (Dan Tyminski,
Harley Allen, and Pat
Enright)

SONGWRITERS:
Traditional

ORIGINAL RELEASE:
*O Brother, Where
Art Thou?* (Mercury
Nashville 170069,
2000)

FORM: Strophic

STYLE: Traditional
bluegrass

Although the album's producer claimed he did not intend for "Man of Constant Sorrow" to become a theme song for the movie, soon after its release it took on that role. The song appears in four different versions on the soundtrack. Track 16 features the full band accompanying the vocal trio; this track received some radio airplay, partly because its steady beat, up-tempo rhythmic pattern, and accompaniment made it closer to contemporary popular music than anything else on the album.

The song was originally derived from an old Baptist hymn called "Wandering Boy." Hillbilly songwriter Dick Burnett, a blind musician from Kentucky, printed it in a songbook sometime before 1920. Several musicians recorded it shortly thereafter, including Sarah Ogan Gunning and Emry Arthur. Three decades later, it became a standard in the folk scene, performed by many musicians, including Bob Dylan and the Stanley Brothers, whose version was the model for the arrangement on the soundtrack.

The strophic form of the song means that there is no high point in the form of a chorus or climax in the recording. Instead, the recording creates a sense of stasis, as one verse follows another and another, spaced only by very unobtrusive instrumental solos. Its minor mode (which uses a different scale than the more common major mode) gives it a haunting quality and makes it sound even more foreign and musically distant to a contemporary audience.

TIME	FORM	LISTENING CUES	DISCUSSION
0:00	Introduction	acoustic guitar	Notice the layers of string instruments: mandolin, fiddle, banjo, Dobro, and guitar.
0:15	Refrain	"In constant..."	This refrain wraps up each verse in the song and breaks up the form's monotony.
0:21	Verse 1	"I am a man..."	Tyminski sings in a high, lonesome style. The song is performed in the minor mode, which gives it a forlorn musical quality.
0:48	Refrain	"The place where..."	
0:55	Instrumental interlude	slide guitar	Throughout the song, the instruments take turns playing instrumental solos, but the solos remain embedded in the band's musical texture and do not stand out much at all.
1:09	Verse 2	"For six long years..."	Each verse consists of two long lines that rhyme.
1:36	Refrain	"He has no friends..."	
1:43	Instrumental interlude	banjo	
1:57	Verse 3	"Hence, fare thee well..."	Repetition becomes an important factor in how the listener hears this piece by this point in the song. The lack of a chorus becomes even more apparent at this point.
2:25	Refrain	"Perhaps he'll die..."	
2:31	Instrumental interlude	mandolin	
2:45	Verse 4	"You can bury me..."	Tyminski changes very little in the melody from one verse to the next.
3:13	Refrain	"While he is sleeping..."	This is the darkest text in the song's lyrics.
3:19	Instrumental interlude	fiddle	The fiddle stands out more from the band's texture than the other solo instruments.
3:33	Verse 5	"Maybe your friends..."	The gospel theme of the lyrics comes out clearly at the end of the song.
4:01	Refrain	"He'll meet you on..."	Notice how the last notes of the recording are allowed to ring for about five seconds, with the sound fading and trailing off slowly and hauntingly.

The O Brother Phenomenon

O Brother, Where Art Thou?—a film that was written, produced, and directed by Joel and Ethan Coen in 2000—earned rave reviews for its retelling of Homer's *The Odyssey*, set in 1930s rural Mississippi. The film, which stars George Clooney and Holly Hunter, follows the exploits of three ex-cons as they make their way across the South. Their journey is peppered with musical encounters, from sirens singing at the river to a revivalist baptism to a chanting lynch mob. The group ends up making a recording as the "Soggy Bottom Boys," and the climax of the film involves the trio masquerading as old-time entertainers singing on stage at a political rally, where they ham up a cover of a Jimmie Rodgers' song.

While the movie was fairly successful, its soundtrack stunned observers of popular culture by turning into a cult phenomenon. Produced by singer/songwriter T-Bone Burnett, the album gathered old and new recordings together into a mainly bluegrass collection of old-time music, combined with several blues tracks. The sources of songs and the performers on the album varied. Among them was an actual 1928 recording by Harry McClintock, who recorded mainly cowboy and hobo songs for Victor records in the 1920s and '30s; a black gospel number from the Fairfield Four, who were honored by the National Endowment for the Arts in 1989 for their decades-long career; a Primitive Baptist a cappella rendition of "O Death" from bluegrass patriarch Ralph Stanley; and haunting vocal harmonies from Emmylou Harris, Gillian Welch, and Alison Krauss, all three highly respected country, folk, and bluegrass performers. Throughout the recording and film, bluegrass musician Dan Tyminski (1967–), who is a member of Alison Krauss's band Union Station, provided all the singing for George Clooney's character.

The Coen Brothers helped fund the soundtrack, which appeared on Lost Highway Records, and were actively involved in its creation. Media outlets that are not known for their attention to country music, such as NPR and the *New York Times*, took notice of the album, and four months after its release, it had sold more than a million copies. People who had never listened to bluegrass, country, or old-time music caught wind of it and bought a copy of the CD, which came with a sticker that declared it "the ultimate American roots music collection." Critics were shocked when the soundtrack won the 2002 Grammy for Album of the Year, and by 2007 it had been certified eight times platinum (sales of 8 million copies).

The artists involved in the recording capitalized on its unexpected success. They performed a "Down from the Mountain" concert at the Ryman Auditorium (historic home of the Grand Ole Opry), which turned into both a CD and a DVD. They then launched an extended concert tour that sold out Carnegie Hall in New York City and grossed over $10 million by the end of the summer. Other record labels and artists saw the potential for new sales here, and related albums were rushed to the market: *O Sister*, which was an album of bluegrass women, and countless compilations of bluegrass such as Sugar Hill's *Cool, Blue, and Lonesome* and *Cool, Blue Outlaws*,

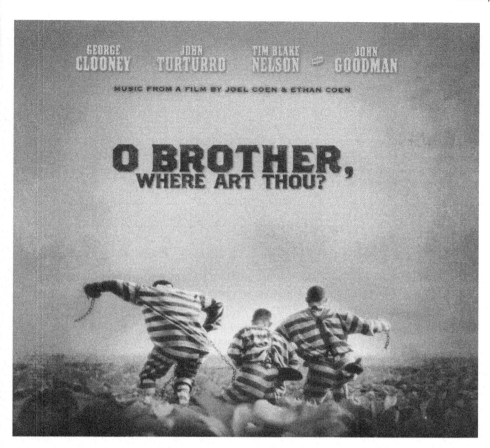

Figure 13-8 Cover art for the O Brother, Where Art Thou? soundtrack.

all of which were aimed at the new fans who wanted more of the music to which they had just been introduced. Ralph Stanley, who was in his mid-seventies, came back into the spotlight and recorded several new albums. Bluegrass festivals saw a jump in attendance, and new artists such as the California trio Nickel Creek found waiting audiences hungry for any acoustic-based, bluegrass-influenced music that reminded them of the soundtrack. The soundtrack's cover art, with a sepia-toned sky, open fields of rural America, and a light hidden over the horizon, spawned many imitations in both album covers and music videos.

In the wake of this success, critics and journalists picked up on a recurring theme—why was country radio not playing this album, and for that matter, why didn't country music today sound like what was on the recording? For millions of fans, this soundtrack represented the ideal version of country music, and commercial country music failed to measure up to its standards, in their opinion. The only track from the album that got much radio airplay was the full band version of "Man of Constant Sorrow." But the rest, one music industry executive explained, simply was not the sort of music that the country radio audience wanted.

The *O Brother* soundtrack brought a huge new audience to bluegrass and acoustic styles of music, at least in the short term. It dramatically expanded the public's awareness of old-time and bluegrass music at a time in history when Americans were looking for popular music that would represent wholesome, folk-oriented values. And it sparked further criticism, albeit from outside the core country fan community, of the extremes to which country-pop had traveled, a refrain that had been sounding for nearly a decade by then. Country radio did not change its course immediately, but over the next few years, the impact of *O Brother* was felt as country music continued to shift away from country-pop crossover sounds toward a retrenchment of tradition.

☆ ESSAY: MUSICAL STYLE

What Alt-Country Doesn't Sound Like

The alt-country movement encompasses many different and sometimes opposing musical styles. Simply put, alt-country does not sound like what is on mainstream country radio—at least not most of the time. Nonetheless, one can learn to recognize certain common styles that appear within the alt-country movement.

The postpunk alt-country bands tend to feature distorted electric guitars, heavy drums, and a give-and-take attitude between acoustic moments and full-on, assaulting band sounds. Instrumentation often includes steel guitar, fiddle, or harmonica. Vocals are often naturalized and gravelly, with lots of sonic texture. The retro-style alt-country bands tend to feature less vocal resonance than recordings of actual 1950s honky-tonk or western swing. They also often use more rock-styled drums than the traditional styles featured. On the singer-songwriter side of alt-country, one often finds thinner textures, fewer instruments, and acoustic accompaniment as dominant features. Throughout the alt-country movement, one often hears combinations of two distinct traditions merging, whether punk and old-time hillbilly, rockabilly and heartland rock, or bluegrass and psychedelic jam bands. One also hears different time periods contrasting in the sound, which creates a sense of temporal fusion and sometimes confusion—modern elements positioned in a retro context, old groups of instruments accompanying songs with abstract lyrics, and hillbilly covers of industrial metal-band songs.

The one audible characteristic that spans these different approaches is the do-it-yourself (DIY) aesthetic, which means some element in the recording that portrays a sense of homegrown, self-made music. This feature is sometimes the result of alt-country bands working with small budgets and fewer layers in the process of making, recording, mixing, and mastering the CD. But even bands who had more resources at their disposal sometimes cultivated that sense in their recordings. This quality often is conveyed through such things as sudden changes in musical texture, unexpected balances between the different instruments, wide ranges of dynamics, and close-miked vocals without either pitch or resonance enhancements. Yet the overarching definition of the sound of alt-country is that, in whatever way the musicians can convey this, it does not sound like what is selling on mainstream country radio.

The Internet Age

Throughout country music's history, there have been singers and songwriters working outside the commercial mainstream. But what brought them together in a 1990s movement was access to new recording, communication, and music-access technologies, primarily through the internet. It is no coincidence that the alt-country movement emerged at the same time that technology radically changed the ways that musicians created, recorded, and distributed their music and that fans received, discussed, and shared it. The advent of the internet, and fans' access to it, completely changed the available business models. Prior to the internet, record companies served as gatekeepers between musicians and potential fans. Hundreds of singers and songwriters vied for the attention of the record labels, who selected a few of them to make records. Those labels then promoted the records to fans, whose options were generally limited to whatever their local record store stocked or what they could get through mail-order catalogs. Outside of the record labels, musicians were limited in how effectively they could market their own music. Live performances, flyers taped to telephone poles, newspaper ads and articles, etc., were means available to them. Fans had few ways of connecting with the musicians or each other, and most commonly overcame this through a centrally run "fan club" with newsletters and the promise of backstage "meet and greets."

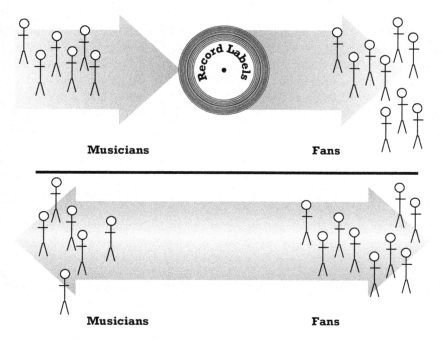

Figure 13-7
The relationship between musicians and fans before and after the internet.

The internet changed the music business model to allow for more effective direct marketing (see Figure 13-7). Musicians could advertise their music not just to fans who lived in their local area, but anywhere, without regard for geographic distance. All musicians with access to the internet had the same opportunities to get their music heard. By the end of the 1990s, countless websites offered aspiring musicians the chance to post recordings of their music for free. Fans could browse any of the music, not just the few recordings that a record label pitched to them. Such a system of distribution and marketing had its drawbacks; without record labels filtering the music, fans were deluged by recordings of wildly varying qualities, and few artists managed to garner any significant attention through those methods. But what did work was that fans could now communicate directly with each other, even across large geographic distances. The fact that alt-country's name came from a newsgroup discussion board is evidence that the movement coalesced through the internet. The communications in all directions increased: musicians could send music to the fans, along with various types of journal entries, newsletter updates, and so on, and the fans could then post comments in response.

Technological advances also changed the ability of homegrown musicians to make records. Two decades ago, making a recording required extremely expensive equipment generally not available outside the professional recording studio. The first recordable CDs appeared in 1990. Three years later, the MP3 codec was released, shrinking the size of digital music files and thereby making it practical for people to store and play music on their computers. Software advanced to the point that by the end of the 1990s, musicians could create a decent-quality recording using reasonably affordable equipment and a home computer, and small companies were happy to make the actual CDs from that recording for a modest price. Just about any singer or band could now self-produce and publish a CD to sell at concerts or distribute by the internet. The entire infrastructure of the music business created new ways for musicians to navigate the legal aspects of making a recording without the support of a record label. For instance, the Harry Fox Agency, which handles licenses and fees whenever a musician records someone else's song, set up a new system in 1999 that was designed as an easy way for anyone making fewer than 2,500 copies of a CD to get the required license.

Peer-to-peer (P2P) file-sharing networks also radically affected the alt-country scene. Of all the P2Ps, the most famous was Napster, which launched in 1999. Using Napster, fans could search for and download any digitized music that another user had uploaded. This system led to rampant copyright infringement, but for users who were unconcerned about the illegality of digitally copying, uploading, and downloading music files, the P2P networks provided a way to get and share rare, out-of-print, or indie music that simply was not available in stores or through catalogs. This offered a way for fans to hear music by alternative bands where the physical CDs or LPs were difficult to find, all of which helped build fans' enthusiasm for certain alt-country bands.

☆ **ESSAY: CULTURE**

Gay Line Dancing

While alt-country music emerged from the musical fringe in the 1990s, gay country fans also became more visible participants in the larger country music fan scene. One such form of participation was gay country line dancing, which became extremely popular among many gay country fans. By the end of the decade, they had created a network of bars and dance clubs that formed a different kind of "alternative" country scene. Some, such as the 3 Legged Cowboy (formerly known as Hoedowns, in Atlanta) are actual venues, whereas others, such as Big Apple Ranch (New York) and Southern Country (Charlotte) are organizations that hold special dances and events at various locations. The culture even made its way into Hollywood film, with a gay country bar in Texas figuring into the plot of *Happy, Texas*.

Cowboys have long been iconic figures within some segments of gay culture, where the lonesome independence, rugged masculinity, and physicality represented by the cowboy are celebrated. Gay rodeos first appeared in the mid-1970s, and by the end of the 1980s the International Gay Rodeo Association oversaw several major events each year, some of which started to include dance contests. Various styles of country dancing appealed to fans in gay bars for many of the same reasons they appealed to fans in straight bars: they offered an activity in the nightclubs that let fans collaborate as a group while still showing individuality, and line dancing was even more appealing on these fronts. In 1993, the International Association of Gay/Lesbian Country Western Dance Clubs was established to promote awareness and communication among groups, to oversee a growing network of cities and communities where gay dancing was popular, and to set up rules for dance contests, which attract huge crowds and exceptionally talented contestants.

The country music fan community includes some populations that are openly anti-gay, and regions of the country that are the least progressive on gay rights are also some of the areas where country music thrives. Although there is a distinct group of gay country singers who make records specifically for the gay community, few mainstream country singers are openly gay, and the lyrics in most commercial country songs offer a decidedly heterosexual perspective on relationships, families, and community life. Nonetheless, gay country dancers generally play mainstream commercial country music in their clubs and use many of the same dance steps and patterns that are common in the straight clubs. For many of them, their participation in the country dance scene provides a way to claim a metaphoric space in a musical genre and—in many cases—a region and community that has not traditionally been very welcoming to gays and lesbians. Although in recent years line dancing has fallen out of fashion at many straight country bars, gay country bars continue to host large populations of enthusiastic line dancers.

LISTEN SIDE-BY-SIDE

"Waltz Across Texas Tonight"
Songwriters: Emmylou Harris and Rodney Crowell
Emmylou Harris, 1995 (on *Wrecking Ball*,
Nonesuch Records)

"Waltz Across Texas"
Songwriter: Billy Talmadge
Ernest Tubb, 1965 (original release: single,
Decca 31824)

EMMYLOU HARRIS (1947–) has had a musical career that is the epitome of the alt-country biography. The album that marked her entrance into the alt-country scene, *Wrecking Ball*, was acclaimed by critics and fans alike for its musical content, but its impact was all the greater because of her musical background and all that the album represented beyond just the sound of its recordings.

Since her first recordings in the 1970s, Harris's music has been remarkable for the wide range of styles in which she has worked. Born in Birmingham, Alabama, Harris grew up in North Carolina and Virginia, then headed to college to pursue drama and music professionally. Her musical interests were very much in the folk genre, following Bob Dylan and Joan Baez. Harris dropped out of school to start performing in New York's Greenwich Village folk scene, eventually moving to Washington, D.C., where she met Gram Parsons (see Chapter 7). Parsons and Harris began touring and recording together for his *Grievous Angel* album. Most significant for her future career, Parsons taught Harris lots of traditional country music.

Following Parsons's death in 1973, Harris began performing and recording solo and forged a unique identity within country music with her haunting, shimmering voice. Her records drew equally from traditional country music, with covers of old Louvin Brothers and Merle Haggard songs and both rock and folk, such as her covers of the Beatles and Bob Dylan. She cultivated a crossover audience that was composed more of rock fans than of pop fans.

By the late 1970s, Harris had assembled the Hot Band, an exceptionally skilled group of musicians for both touring and recording. Her music pulled heavily from blues (such as her hard-rocking Southern blues version of Delbert McClinton's

"Two More Bottles of Wine") and country rock in the shadow of Gram Parsons ("Easy from Now On"), along with bluegrass-folk sounds ("Roses in the Snow").

During the heyday of countrypolitan in the early 1980s, Harris branched out into her own brand of countrypolitan music with hits such as the 1960s girl-group pop tune "Mr. Sandman," a remake of Floyd Cramer's schmaltzy Nashville-sound hit "Last Date," and a duet with Roy Orbison. That eclecticism kept her from being absorbed into any one trend in country music. But, at times, such as in "In My Dreams" (1983), Harris indulged in the same musical excesses of pop-driven countrypolitan as did other stars.

Her singing earned her a Grammy and a CMA female vocalist of the year award, marking her as a significant mainstream country star. Yet her demonstrated interest in older country hits and credibility as a bluegrass artist allowed her to transition into the neotraditional movement of the mid-1980s (see Chapter 11). In 1987, she collaborated with Dolly Parton and Linda Ronstadt on one of the best-known neotraditionalist albums, *Trio*.

By the early 1990s, commercial country music had evolved into a younger scene, and Harris was no longer placing songs on the charts. She turned toward the emerging alt-country scene, and signed a deal with Nonesuch Records, a label that was known for both classical music and off-beat eclecticism. *Wrecking Ball* turned entirely away from the dominant New Country sounds of the mid-90s, instead diving into an indie-rock creativity. And for the first, time, Harris took on the role of songwriter, penning most of the tracks for her new album and thus embracing the singer-songwriter aesthetic that was part of alt-country.

Harris co-wrote "Waltz Across Texas Tonight," with Rodney Crowell, who had sung harmony vocals for her as a member of her Hot Band two decades earlier. Crowell, like Harris, had enjoyed a mainstream country career in the 1980s and early 1990s, and would similarly move into the alt-country and then Americana space. "Waltz Across Texas Tonight" is a waltz-time record (where the music is counted 1-2-3), with longing, haunted vocals. The musical accompaniment is layered with independent rhythmic patterns that throw the listener a tad off balance, while the lyrics delve into both the clichés of moons and bright stars and the personal touch of a lover's hand. The reference to Texas situates the song in a place of independence, away from Nashville. But most notable is the song's refrain, which echoes an old country song.

In 1965, honky-tonk founder Ernest Tubb recorded "Waltz Across Texas," a slow waltz written by his nephew that mentions both stars in "her eyes" and "your hand in mine." Produced by Owen Bradley, the recording aligns with the second generation of the Nashville Sound: saturated with steel guitar, but also featuring the reverb, elaborate acoustic guitar parts, and schmaltzy production of the Nashville Sound era. Yet the song's simplicity and Tubb's own identity link it even further back in history, to the essence of honky-tonk. Harris's recording is not in any direct sense a cover of "Waltz Across Texas," but the shared themes and images, and the nearly identical title, make it feel like it is almost a cover.

Emmylou Harris's recording is thus a rich, multilayered invocation of the idea and sound of alt-country. She is a direct link to Gram Parsons and the country rock music from which the alt-country scene drew its ideology. Her past career success drew attention to the new alt-country scene, while her eclecticism and her frequent incorporation of both rock and acoustic styles gave creditability with the alt-country audience. She was now writing her own music. And finally, this song drew a direct line to the roots of country music by evoking honky-tonk legend Ernest Tubb's own famous recording.

PLAYLIST

Adams, Ryan. "Oh My Sweet Carolina" (1999)

Cash, Johnny. "Delia's Gone" (1994)

Dixie Chicks. "Goodbye Earl" (1999)

Krauss, Alison. "Baby, now that I've Found You" (1995)

Strait, George, and Alan Jackson, "Murder on Music Row" (2000)

Various artists, *O Brother, Where Art Thou?* (album) (2000)

Whiskeytown. "Hard Luck Story" (1996)

FOR MORE READING

Alden, Grant, and Peter Blackstock. *The Best of No Depression: Writing about American Music.* Austin: University of Texas Press, 2005.

Fox, Aaron A. "'Alternative' to What? 'O Brother,' September 11th, and the Politics of Country Music." In C. Wolfe and J. Akenson, eds., *Country Music Goes to War.* Lexington: University Press of Kentucky, 2005.

Fox, Pamela, and Barbara Ching, eds. *Old Roots, New Routes: The Cultural Politics of Alt. Country Music.* Ann Arbor: University of Michigan Press, 2008.

Goodman, David. *Modern Twang: An Alternative Country Music Guide & Directory*. Nashville: Dowling Press, 1999.

Gray, Christopher. "Down from the Mountain and into Wal-Mart," *Austin Chronicle*, July 19, 2002.

Strauss, Neil. "The Country Music Country Radio Ignores," *New York Times*, March 24, 2002.

NAMES AND TERMS

Adams, Ryan	Harris, Emmylou	Rubin, Rick
Americana	IBMA	Thile, Chris
Bloodshot Records	Jayhawks	Uncle Tupelo
BR5-49	Krauss, Alison	Usenet newsgroups
cowpunk	Merritt, Tift	Welch, Gillian
Derailers	Music Row	Whiskeytown
Dixie Chicks	*No Depression*	Williams, Lucinda
DIY	*Prairie Home Companion, A*	
Green, Pat	P2P file-sharing	

REVIEW TOPICS

1. How did social and economic conditions in the early 1990s foster the development of the alt-country scene?

2. How did alt-country benefit directly and indirectly from mainstream commercial country, and, conversely, how did mainstream commercial country benefit from alt-country?

3. Why did the alt-country scene favor performers who wrote their own songs, and how does that relate to the trends in commercial country during those years?

Redefining Country in a New Millennium

14

As country music entered the twenty-first century, the country-pop trend was past its prime, and *O Brother, Where Art Thou?* had increased fans' interest in more traditional styles of country music. In the subsequent decade, four major developments occurred:

1. Global political and economic events pushed country music into the spotlight, and Nashville responded with songs that addressed those events both directly and indirectly.
2. A new generation of stars reintroduced more traditional, twangy styles, stereotypically redneck themes, and references to Southern rock.
3. The alt-country movement dissipated into a broader "roots" music scene, with a few artists moving closer to mainstream country but most shifting closer to indie rock.
4. Country music became more integrated into contemporary popular culture, especially through an increased presence in reality television contests and a new generation of crossover stars.

Some of these developments occurred simultaneously, so as is usually the case, more than one style was alive and well within country music at the same time. Throughout all of these changes, the same internal tensions and issues have remained that first shaped country music in the 1920s.

Country Music in the Spotlight

On September 11, 2001, terrorists attacked New York City and Washington, D.C. In the months that followed, the general mood of many Americans turned toward reflections on family, home, and faith, along with bold expressions of patriotism and national pride. Country music was pulled into the spotlight as a musical expression of many of those emotions. "God Bless the U.S.A." (1984), from countrypolitan star Lee Greenwood, reappeared almost immediately on radio playlists, on television programs, and in concerts. Two months after the attacks, Alan Jackson appeared on the CMA Awards and sang a song he had recently written, "Where Were You (When the World Stopped Turning)," that took on a role as an anthem for the nation, even among noncountry fans. Country music's ideology had always incorporated elements of religious faith and of pride in working-class Americans. At a time when the nation was both mourning and celebrating firefighters, police officers, and emergency workers, and emphasizing patriotism and the strength of families, country music provided a ready-made soundtrack.

433

Brad Paisley (1972–)

Brad Paisley showed up toward the end of the reign of country-pop and squarely established himself as a voice of tradition within the roots revival movement. Over the years, as he has become one of the biggest stars in country music, he has balanced the role of staunch traditionalist with songwriting that abandons conventional country topics for commentary on popular culture.

Born in Glen Dale, West Virginia, Paisley grew up on traditional country music, especially Bakersfield artists, and learned to play the guitar as a child. By the time he reached high school, he had already put together a band and had joined the regular lineup on Wheeling's *Jamboree U.S.A.*, a radio barn dance that had been on the air since 1933. After high school, Paisley spent two years in college in West Virginia, then headed to Belmont University's music business program in Nashville. While there, he met several of his future songwriting partners and made connections in the music industry. After college, Paisley signed a contract as a songwriter with a publishing house, and a few years later got a record deal. His first album, *Who Needs Pictures* (1999), introduced Paisley's blistering guitar talent, honest baritone voice, and a strong neotraditionalist streak in the form of Bakersfield shuffles, honky-tonk laments, and comedy numbers, all of which he wrote or co-wrote.

Paisley was inducted into the Opry in 2001, by which time he had earned a reputation as a musical traditionalist, bolstered by recordings such as "Too Country," on which Buck Owens, Bill Anderson, and George Jones sang with him. Even his image, with a 1960s Fender electric guitar (the Pink Paisley model), western-cut jackets that follow Nudie suit designs, and an ever-present hat, declares his musical stance as firmly grounded in twangy, older styles of country music. As the full effect of *O Brother* hit the music industry, and as

Other factors also contributed to the widespread attention to country music. In 2000, Americans elected George W. Bush president, a conservative Republican and self-professed Christian, and the 2002 election season returned control of the Senate to the Republicans. These events were indicative of the general outlook of people who were increasingly able to relate to country music's reputation as a holdout of conservative values and a nostalgic embrace of a family, home, and an idealized past. A turn toward more traditional roots sounds had already begun in the late 1990s (see Chapter 13), when artists such as the Dixie Chicks and Brad Paisley (1972–) forecast a larger trend (see Artist Profile). The combination of the economic downturn of 2000–2001, the surge of interest in old-time music prompted by the *O Brother* phenomenon, and the global impact of the terrorist attacks simultaneously changed the sound of mainstream country and turned the attention of Middle America toward the genre.

During those years, common topics of country songs shifted toward warm, wholesome reflections and away from honky-tonk beer-drenched laments and hellraising songs. "Blessed" (Martina McBride), "My List" (Toby Keith), "The Good

Gretchen Wilson and others brought a stark twang back to the radio in 2004, Paisley was the man of the hour who could legitimately say he had been playing that sort of roots-oriented, twangy country music all along. He recorded haunting old-time duets with bluegrass legend Alison Krauss ("Whiskey Lullaby," see Listening Guide) and with country royalty Dolly Parton, which further secured his position. A streak of nine number ones in a row followed, along with the honor of hosting the ACM awards and other high-profile activities within the industry.

While Paisley has become one of the strongest voices for country traditionalism in the genre, his songwriting features another thread as well. Many of his songs in the 2005–2011 era played with ideas from pop culture that are not tied to traditional country ideology; for instance, "American Saturday Night" mentions the cosmopolitan experience and musical taste of country fans, name-checking the Beatles rather than, say, Merle Haggard, and "Online" riffs on people who lead a fantasy life on the internet.

This follows the tradition of country songwriting that addresses present-day culture, but it does so from a decidedly middle- or upper-middle-class perspective, and with references to events such as starlets' scandals, mentioned in the song "Celebrity," that sound dated or are just plain forgotten within a few years. With this strategy, Paisley has simultaneously carried the torch of country tradition and offered up country music that is closely tied to pop culture "in the moment." He reveres the genre ("This is Country Music," 2010), even while his songs about prom dresses sewn from camouflage (2011) and checking his date for ticks (2007) poke fun at country music and become inside jokes for his audience. One reason for his success is his astute balance of tradition and modernism; Paisley understands that his fan base takes country tradition as a symbolic part of their identity, while many of his songs relate directly to the daily lives of the middle- and upper-middle-class suburban demographic that makes up a large part of his audience.

Stuff" (Kenny Chesney), "Front Porch Looking In" (Lonestar), "Life Happened" (Tammy Cochran), and countless other songs from 2001 to 2003 focused on the importance of home and family. Although only a few songs addressed September 11, 2001, directly, many others focused on military service and the Iraq War's effects on American families (see Listening Guide for "Whiskey Lullaby"). Commercial country song lyrics tended to offer a slightly older person's perspective than had been the norm just a few years earlier in country pop; they addressed jobs and children rather than nights out partying or searching for young romance.

Expressions of Christian faith showed up more frequently and in more direct statements than they had in the recent past. Although country music's philosophical base has always included an evangelical belief structure, the prevalence of such lyrics on country radio was something new; "Three Wooden Crosses" brought Randy Travis back into the spotlight, and "Help Pour Out the Rain (Lacey's Song)," performed by Buddy Jewell, was one of many songs that touched on faith and prayer. Contemporary Christian band Mercy Me even landed their song "I Can Only Imagine" on country radio in 2001. Songs calling for social activism—usually

Listening Guide

"Whiskey Lullaby" (2004)

PERFORMERS: Brad Paisley with Alison Krauss

SONGWRITERS: Bill Anderson and Jon Randall

ORIGINAL RELEASE: *Mud on the Tires* (Arista 50605, 2003)

FORM: Verse-prechorus-chorus

STYLE: Commercial country / roots revival

"Whiskey Lullaby" is a haunting acoustic ballad about a couple who end up drinking themselves to death over their broken hearts. The themes of abject loneliness, misunderstandings left uncorrected and unresolved, and carrying a broken heart to the grave all resonate with the tradition of honky-tonk. The acoustic accompaniment, especially the distinctive wail of the Dobro (played by bluegrass legend Jerry Douglas on this recording), plus the close vocal harmony used throughout the chorus also evoke images of old-time music. Throughout the recording, the use of reverberation, echo, sparse accompaniment, and melodies in the minor mode all evoke text painting, or the technique where the sounds themselves help to convey the emotional and literal story line and the setting. Note that the recording, which reached number three on the *Billboard* country chart, is a stark and striking contrast to the country-pop that was dominant only a few years earlier. This recording was part of the roots revival that took place in country music in the years after *O Brother*, when an acoustic, minor-mode ballad about drinking oneself to death, sung by a bluegrass star, was a huge radio hit.

Songwriters Bill Anderson and Jon Randall are both veterans of the country music business. Anderson, known as "Whispering Bill," is a long-time fixture on the Grand Ole Opry and is known for a traditionalist perspective in country music. Jon Randall recounted the autobiographical source of this song: they wrote it shortly after Randall divorced country singer Lorrie Morgan, and during a time when he had neither a recording contract nor a songwriting contract and was drinking heavily. The song's lyrics cast the couple in the third person ("he" and "she"), but invite the singers and the listeners into the intimate center of the story through the narrator's use of "we:" "we watched him," "we found her," "we buried him," "we laid her . . ."

The music video sets the scene as a World War II story in which a soldier comes home to find his lover with another man. Although the lyrics alone do not specify a wartime setting, the video connected the song to a larger trend in country music of songs addressing war, servicemen and women, and the effect of war on families. Starting in 2002, when increasing numbers of U.S. troops were deployed to war zones, country music took up the theme regularly; "Travelin' Soldier" (Dixie Chicks), "Come Home Soon" (SHeDaisy), "Just a Dream" (Carrie Underwood), "If You're Reading This" (Tim McGraw), and "Letters from Home" (John Michael Montgomery) are only a handful of the country songs recorded during the wars in Iraq and Afghanistan. Some songs that had been released before the military conflicts began, most notably Lonestar's "I'm Already There," were also adopted after the fact as anthems for military families. With a large working-class, politically conservative and patriotic audience, country music has been a natural home for songs that both celebrate military service and sympathize with its impact on soldiers and those left behind. The songs and videos in several cases approach the present war obliquely by using stories about past wars and military conflicts ("Travelin' Soldier" and Montgomery Gentry's "Something to Be Proud Of," David Ball's "Riding with Private Malone," and the video to "Just a Dream" all refer to the Vietnam era, while "Whiskey Lullaby" is set in the 1940s). This strategy distanced the songs from the politically charged and polarizing debates about the present conflicts while still employing themes of war, service, sacrifice, and patriotism.

TIME	FORM	LISTENING CUES	DISCUSSION
0:00	Introduction	acoustic guitar plus Dobro	The introduction suggests haunting, old-time mountain music in a minor mode.
0:12	Verse 1	"She put him out…"	Paisley's vocals and the acoustic guitar accompaniment suggest an intimate, singer-songwriter-style performance.
0:33	Prechorus	"We watched him…"	The text here brings the listener into the story in a very personal way: "we" invites the audience into the scene, and suggests "we" are witnessing the tragic fate of the couple in the story firsthand.
0:48	Chorus	"He put that bottle…"	When songwriter Jon Randall recorded the song, he sang "blew away…"; here, Paisley and Krauss sing "drank away…" Paisley's wording suggests that the man in the story drank himself to death, an image that resonates with country music's history. Randall's version loses that coherence.
1:37	Refrain	"La la la…"	Listen to the echo and resonance in the recording here. It suggests wide-open space.
1:56	Verse 2	"The rumors flew…"	Krauss's voice is both thin and distinctive. It keeps the attention on the story line rather than on any vocal gymnastics. The song's lyrics, which describe first the man and then the woman in separate verses, invite the duet performance.
2:15	Prechorus	"She finally drank…"	The lyrics suggest abject loneliness here, as does the way the melody extends high in Krauss's range.
2:31	Chorus	"She put that bottle…"	Krauss sings the melody here, while Paisley switches to the vocal harmony. It's uncommon for a singer to switch from melody to harmony in a duet recording as is done here.

Continued

Listening Guide

"Whiskey Lullaby" (2004) **Continued**

TIME	FORM	LISTENING CUES	DISCUSSION
3:21	Refrain	"La la la…"	The vocalists sing the "la la la" refrain, then the Dobro answers it. This back-and-forth echo suggests absence, as if the singers are fading into and out of view in the song.
3:59	Refrain	"La la la…"	The refrain appears over long, sustained chords and then one time unaccompanied. It ends on an unresolved chord, as if the song slipped out of view but never concluded.

Figure 14-1 Brad Paisley and Alison Krauss, 2005.
Source: Billy Kingsley photograph © Grand Ole Opry Archives.

regarding poverty or charity toward strangers—also appeared in increasing numbers, such as "Grown Men Don't Cry" (Tim McGraw), "Thicker than Blood" (Garth Brooks), and "Almost Home" (Craig Morgan). Patriotic themes surfaced in songs such as "American Child" (Phil Vassar) and "Where the Stars and the Stripes and the Eagle Fly" (Aaron Tippin).

The musical sound of the recordings also started to change during those years, a result of the roots revival that had emerged in the late 1990s (see Chapter 13). Traditional string instruments were more audible in commercial country recordings than they had been in previous years. While the change was subtle and slow in coming, mandolins and banjos in particular began to show up in radio hits (banjo heard in Dierks Bentley, "What Was I Thinkin'" [2003], for instance, and mandolin in Brad Paisley, "I Wish You'd Stay" [2002]). This shift was partly the effect of *O Brother*, which made those instruments hip again. Musicians such as mandolinist Chris Thile, who first earned fame though his work with Nickel Creek, became sought-after guests on recording sessions.

In January of 1999, the Grand Ole Opry returned to the Ryman Auditorium in downtown Nashville for two broadcasts, a move instigated by Steve Buchanan, the Opry business organization's newly appointed president. Although the Opry's primary home remained its theater in the suburbs, the Opryland theme park, which had entertained tourists with rides, attractions, and country music shows since 1972, had gone out of business in 1997, symbolic of the shift in the tourist industry that supported country music in Nashville and the end of an era of suburban focus. Over the next several years the Opry returned more with increasing frequency to the Ryman, reconnecting both with the legacy of that building and with the downtown heart of the city.

Following suit, in 2001 the Country Music Hall of Fame and Museum moved from its 1960s building on Music Row, several miles west of downtown, to a new, state-of-the-art building just a few blocks south of downtown and walking distance from the Ryman. That same year, Fan Fair, the annual ritual gathering of country fans and stars, was also relocated to downtown Nashville. Within just a few years, even the International Bluegrass Music Association (IBMA) had moved its annual meeting and convention to Nashville, where it would stay from 2005 to 2012. Country music appeared to once again be taking root in the heart of Nashville.

All of these changes reflected corporate intentions, within the music industry, toward bringing fans together and rebranding Nashville as once again a center for music making. From the mid-1980s, when Branson, Missouri, and other locations had started to woo tourists with promises of live country music entertainment, Nashville had lost some of its appeal to country music fans. With the push to return country music to downtown, some detractors had predicted the demise of all local establishments, but instead, country music's institutions, such as Tootsies Orchid Lounge and Robert's Western World (formerly Robert's Western Wear) that were the face of Lower Broadway not only stayed in business but gained stature as prime hosts of live music.

Country tradition was briefly threatened when Gaylord Entertainment, which owned historic radio station and home of the Opry WSM, considered a proposal to change the station from classic country to an all-sports format. Reporters caught wind of the move, which subsequently drew vigorous protests from country music fans as well as more traditionally styled country stars, including Brad Paisley, and whatever plans might have existed were scrapped in the face of the outcry.

With the Opry nestled into the Ryman (at least occasionally), WSM secure in its country music format, and both Fan Fair (which became the CMA Music Festival in 2004) and the Hall of Fame and Museum drawing in audiences, downtown Nashville was once again a symbolic center for country music. Country had come home, and just as the song lyrics and performances were grounding themselves in the same ideas of home and roots, Middle America was nesting comfortably with country music as the soundtrack of modern life.

Return of Roots and Rednecks

From 2001 to 2003, the main country trend had been toward warm, wholesome lyrics sung by a well-established, even urbane, group of stars, and the music had increasingly focused on middle-class, middle-aged Middle America. During those years, however, country's percentage of all music sales had sunk to its lowest level in a decade (see Figure 14-1). At the same time, the total amount of music being sold dropped, too, so country music was getting an ever-smaller piece of a shrinking pie. The biggest problem facing the country music industry during these years was the lack of new breakout stars. Most of the major stars during this period had been on the radio since the mid-1990s or earlier and appeared stable, mature, and predictable (Alan Jackson, George Strait, and Brooks & Dunn, for instance). The stars whose careers saw the biggest gains during those years included Tim McGraw, whose breakout single "Indian Outlaw" came in 1994 and who had become a fixture on country radio in the early 2000s. Similarly, Toby Keith had been active on the scene since 1993, but his music became exceptionally popular in 2000–2003. Keith Urban, who had also been working in Nashville since the early 1990s, scored his first number one song in 2000 and continued with a great run of hits. In other words,

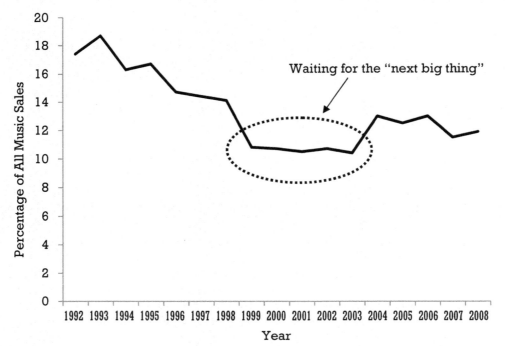

Figure 14-2 From 2000-2004, the country music industry was searching for the "next big thing" as its market-share flat-lined (data from the RIAA).

Waiting for the "next big thing"

none of those artists was really all that new. Among the women, both Sara Evans and Martina McBride continued to earn quite a bit of attention. But no group of artists offered much that was viewed as fresh, unpredictable, or exciting, or, in other words, the "next big thing." Unquestionably, country music was ready for a change. The artistic movement that would bring about that change was already brewing.

In 2004, song themes and images began to shift in four specific directions:

1. Anticommercial rhetoric
2. Redneck imagery
3. Southern rock references
4. South-of-the-border and beach references

Taken together, these themes and images reflected a move away from country's middle-class mainstream identity and into the territory of twang: a revival of honky-tonk themes and aesthetics. This was unquestionably an evolution and extension of the smaller roots revival that had started in the late 1990s and continued through the *O Brother* period. The heightened return of these themes once again delineated country more clearly as an "other" genre and pulled in a younger audience with a distinctly "country" identity.

Nashville's MuzikMafia was partly responsible for the first wave of change. Founded in October 2001, MuzikMafia was a collective of musicians—several of whom had been working successfully in commercial country in previous years—who happened to wind up disenfranchised by the mainstream country music industry. They began to host Tuesday night "happenings" at the Pub of Love on 12th Avenue in Nashville to explore new artistic directions, inviting like-minded musicians along with poets, painters, and an array of other artists to participate. Four original members, Cory Gierman, Jon Nicholson, John Rich (1974–), and William Kenny "Big Kenny" Alphin (1963–), adopted the moniker of "Godfathers" and coined the acronym "mafia" to stand for "musically artistic friends in alliance." The group's motto was "music without prejudice," and as word grew about their weekly gatherings, they began to emphasize their interest in music that crossed over or defied the boundaries between genres. The group also advertised their identity as "outsiders" to the mainstream music industry, which they accused of having sold out to commercial interests and created an artifice of genre boundaries. The idea of the disenfranchised musician building an audience for music that crossed genre boundaries was not new, and the MuzikMafia appropriated the cultural roles of musical mavericks, or outlaws, as other generations of musicians had done before them.

Before long, the grassroots audiences who came to their weekly shows had outstripped the size of the venue where the MuzikMafia gathered, and they moved to successively larger locations. The group also expanded; John Rich, former lead singer for the band Lonestar, met a bartender named Gretchen Wilson (1973–) at a club in Nashville and invited her to join the collective. Wilson had grown up in Pocahontas, Illinois, the daughter of an unmarried teenage mother. She dropped out of high school and sang with the house band at a local bar before heading to Nashville. There, she teamed up with Rich as a songwriting partner and began performing with the MuzikMafia. Local record executives caught wind of the

Listening Guide

"Redneck Woman" (2004)

PERFORMER:
Gretchen Wilson

SONGWRITER: John
Rich and Gretchen
Wilson

ORIGINAL RELEASE:
Here for the Party
(Epic 90903, 2004)

FORM: Verse-chorus

STYLE: Commercial
country/honky-tonk
revival

Figure 14-3 Gretchen Wilson,
performing in her signature black tee
and jeans.
Source: The Photo Access/Alamy Stock Photo.

"Redneck Woman," cowritten by John Rich and Gretchen Wilson, was heralded as the song that put working-class women back in country music and women back on top of the charts. Wilson was the first woman to reach that position in over two years, and her lyrics—as well as the crowd joining her to holler "Hell, yeah!"—seemed not only down-to-earth but a brazen dismissal of genteel middle-class values, lifestyle, and behavior. The song's lyrics define the musical lineage in which Gretchen Wilson placed herself: Tanya Tucker (the sexy, bad-girl singer with a honky-tonk "cry" in her vocal sound), George Strait (country music royalty), Kid Rock (roots rocker and sometime rapper, who represented a working-class, hard rock image), Lynyrd Skynyrd (the most famous of the Southern rock bands), Charlie Daniels (part outlaw, part Southern rock), and Bocephus (Hank Williams Jr.'s nickname). Wilson's music stuck very much to the tradition of honky-tonk, with its simple song form (verse-chorus) and its steady two-step beat. But Wilson was consciously channeling the attitude and appeal of Southern rock in her music.

The contemporary links between Southern rock and country came partly from the rock side of the tracks. In the early 2000s, Kid Rock (1971–) declared that he was a fan of the country outlaws, most specifically Hank Williams Jr. The two performed together on the CMA Awards in 2002, and a year later Kid Rock released a duet of himself with Sheryl Crow to country radio, where audiences accepted it as country. Since then, Southern rock has provided a way for country music fans to claim a wilder and more rebellious past than was found in the conventional lineage through the traditionalist era. Wilson tapped into that idea just as it was coming into vogue, and "Redneck Woman" became a hugely important catalyst in country music's next development.

TIME	FORM	LISTENING CUES	DISCUSSION
0:00	Pre-introduction	crowd noise	The audible crowd noise creates the effect of a live recording and suggests Wilson is just "one of the girls."
0:07	Introduction	bass, drums, guitar	Although the song is basically a jacked-up honky-tonk number, the heavy, pounding drums at the beginning, with the microphone capturing every echo, sounds like it comes out of hard rock, more specifically, Southern rock. Compare the sound to the opening of Tim McGraw's "Indian Outlaw," which borrowed from a rock song made famous by Paul Revere and the Raiders.
0:18	Verse 1	"Well, I ain't never…"	Wilson's voice is accompanied by a low, growling, distorted electric guitar, which adds to the song's attitude.
0:49	Chorus	"'Cause I'm a redneck…"	The song uses a slight variation on a twelve-bar blues pattern (see Appendix A), which ties it to both the Southern rock musical tradition (which was heavily indebted to blues), and to earlier hillbilly blues.
1:26	Verse 2	"Victoria's Secret…"	Even more than the first verse, this one established a social-class identity.
1:56	Chorus	"Hey, I'm a redneck…"	Notice the interesting timbre on "Let me get a big 'Hell, yeah!'" This comes from vocal harmony, placed exactly an octave under Wilson's melody. This is a nonstandard approach to harmony in country music, and is found instead in rock traditions.
2:28	Instrumental interlude	electric guitar, then fiddle	The juxtaposition of electric guitar and fiddle capture the essence of this song: hard rock meets honky-tonk.
2:46	Chorus	"I'm a redneck…"	This is a stop-time version of the chorus, a very standard arrangement technique that adds interest to a song. Notice the prominent banjo and honky-tonk piano behind this section of vocals, and the complete stop-time moment at 2:54.
3:18	Tag	"Hell, yeah!"	The song ends by evoking a live performance again.

group's grass-roots success and, in 2003, Wilson signed with Epic Records. By that time, Wilson had successfully made connections within the music community in Nashville, honed her performance skills on stages for years, and shaped her identity as the trash-talking, trailer-park–living, working-class antithesis of the polished, classy country-pop singers who had graced the airwaves for the past few years. Wilson's debut single, "Redneck Woman" (see Listening Guide), changed the course of country music.

Big & Rich, the duo of John Rich and "Big Kenny" Alphin, also landed a major-label record deal, which they leveraged into access to every corner of the music business. Fans flocked to their concerts, where the novelty aspects of their performances (such as including a dwarf on stage) were matched only by the raucous quality of their music. Rich became the hottest songwriter in Nashville, writing or co-writing new material for both new and established singers (such as Faith Hill). The group signed their own television show with CMT, and Rich also slipped into the role of one of the judges on *Nashville Star*, a country version of the televised singing contest *American Idol*. Within the span of only a few years, the antiestablishment and genre-defying ideals of the MuzikMafia had become a very successful commercial brand within country music. The impact on the genre as a whole was noticeable; sales increased, and country music experienced a boost in general popularity.

Gretchen Wilson's "Redneck Woman," along with her biography, reinserted "redneck" into the common country music lexicon. In the early 1990s, the contemporary commercial country stars had emphasized country's relevance to middle-class Americans from all walks of life, and over the next decade country songs had drifted toward more universal images and lyrics. Those elements matched the demographics of the country audience, which had largely shed its own affiliations with the rural Southern identity that previous generations of fans had cultivated. But now, the emphasis on social class distinction and "othered" identity was once again front and center. Song lyrics reflected this trend; in 2005 and 2006, "Honky Tonk Badonkadonk" (Trace Adkins) was joined by a host of other songs reveling in inebriated barroom behavior and small-town craziness (for example, Neal McCoy's "Billy's Got His Beer Goggles On," Joe Nichols's "Tequila Makes Her Clothes Fall Off," Little Big Town's "Boondocks," etc.). Another honky-tonk theme that returned to the airwaves was cheatin' songs, specifically from the perspective of a scorned woman whose feisty response would give Loretta Lynn a run for her money (Sara Evans's "Cheatin'," Gretchen Wilson's "Homewrecker," Carrie Underwood's "Before He Cheats"). Country had rediscovered its inner redneck; a younger country fan base who similarly embraced this working-class identity rallied around the music.

During these years, country music redefined its own history, most specifically pulling 1970s Southern rock into the direct lineage of contemporary country music and de-emphasizing its heritage of classic country. This shift happened both in the musical style (chord progressions, guitar timbres, and rhythmic patterns) and in the references found in lyrics: singing about Southern rock songs, bands, and iconic places became the norm. Gretchen Wilson name-checked Charlie Daniels and Lynyrd Skynyrd in "Redneck Woman." Rodney Atkins quoted famous Skynyrd songs in "These Are My People" (2007). Kid Rock scored a top-ten hit on the "Hot Country Songs" chart with "All Summer Long" (2008), which is about Skynyrd's song "Sweet Home Alabama." Trace Adkins sings about a radio "blarin' Lynyrd Skynyrd" in "Ladies Love Country Boys" (2006). Even Lady Antebellum mentioned Skynyrd's "The Ballad of Curtis Loew" in their song "Perfect Day."

This shift reflected a change in how the fan base of contemporary country music thought about their musical history. Especially for the younger fans, the image of Conway Twitty in a tuxedo or of Kenny Rogers singing "Islands in the Stream" was hopelessly beyond redemption. Rock, on the other hand, was still rebelliously cool, and both Southern rock and heartland rock particularly appealing (Bruce Springsteen's name pops up in both Eric Church, "Springsteen," and Montgomery Gentry, "Hell Yeah," for instance). Demographic research sponsored by the Country Radio Broadcasters (CRB) and CMA in 2011 confirmed this: the country radio audience's second-favorite station choice by a very wide margin was classic rock, while hip-hop, R&B, Christian, jazz, and gospel formats ranked well below. It is interesting to note that in order for country singers in the mid-2000s to reestablish country music's distinct identity, they had to invoke musicians from the 1970s who were working outside country music's traditions.

Along with the redneck imagery and rock references, country music exhibited another trend in these years: south-of-the-border and waterfront images that gave rise to beach country. The new locale that symbolized escapism from daily life was no longer the farm, the ranch, the small town, or the open road, but rather the beach. Isolated instances of these themes are found in earlier country, all the way back to Gene Autry's recording of "South of the Border (Down Mexico Way)" (1939) or, more recently in fans' memories, Garth Brooks's "Two Piña Coladas" (1997). But these themes showed up with stunning frequency as country music let its wilder redneck side show in the mid-2000s. From "Redneck Yacht Club" to "Some Beach," "Stays in Mexico," or the steel drums in "When the Sun Goes Down" (a duet from Kenny Chesney and Uncle Kracker), Latin and specifically Caribbean sounds and images became a part of country music's core identity that would persist for years (e.g., the Zac Brown Band's "Toes" [2009]). This shift in imagery persisted in country music—a decade later, beachfront imagery had become more common in country music videos than cowboys, ranches, or even small-town middle America. Streaming radio outlets had stations called "Island Beach Country" that focused on these songs.

One of the most interesting case studies in artistic identity during this era is Faith Hill, a star who first appeared in the early 1990s in the commercial boom period, then reinvented herself as a country-pop star in the late '90s, extended her career beyond country music and into Hollywood, then pushed the country-pop limits to such extremes that she lost her fan base and position of authority within country music (see Chapter 12). Hill staged a comeback that illustrated the major changes that had taken place in country music between 2001 and 2005. In the album art for *Fireflies* (2005), Hill appeared in denim jeans and a white cotton shirt, with the big-haired, redheaded look that represented a return to her first style. Hill released "Mississippi Girl," penned by John Rich and Adam Shoenfeld, as the album's

Listening Guide

"Long Time Gone" (2002)

PERFORMERS: Dixie
Chicks

SONGWRITER: Darrell
Scott

ORIGINAL RELEASE:
Home (Open Wide/
Monument/Columbia
86840, 2002)

FORM:
Verse-chorus-bridge

STYLE: Commercial
country/roots revival

"Long Time Gone" was the Dixie Chicks' lead single from their third album, *Home*. Appearing after their self-imposed hiatus from recording, the whole album showed the effects of the roots revival in mainstream country music, as well as the impact of *O Brother*. One of those effects is seen in the lyrics, which deride contemporary country radio for having "no soul" and not playing good country music. The lyrics make clever puns on the names of Johnny Cash, Merle Haggard, and Hank Williams, casting them as country legends the likes of which are nowhere to be found on contemporary radio. The song features acoustic instrumentation, opening with banjo, mandolin, and acoustic guitar, followed by fiddle. The string band and percussion settle into a very catchy Cajun groove as the accompaniment behind Natalie Maines's vocals and the close harmony provided by Emily Robison and Martie Maguire. The song also features a lot of **syncopation** and rhythmic ingenuity.

Darrell Scott, a Kentucky native who had established himself as one of the preeminent songwriters in Nashville in the late 1990s, wrote the song. Its story traces the singer from his childhood home on a tobacco farm to Nashville, where he attempts to break into the music business only to find it offers nothing but empty promises. He then returns home to his small town, where he and Delia, the girl who sings in the church choir, settle into watching their children grow up and lament that Cash, Haggard, and Williams are a "long time gone" from country music. Scott and fellow songwriter and bluegrass musician Tim O'Brien put the song on their live album, *Real Time*, which they released in 2000 on a small indie label. The Dixie Chicks learned it from that album and kept the musical arrangement the same for their version.

In spite of the song's complaints about the "soulless" state of country radio, the song became a smash hit on country radio, scaling the *Billboard* chart extremely quickly. Its acoustic, banjo-infused sound thus continued the country tradition of self-referential irony, as seen in "Murder on Music Row" (see Chapter 13). What was most unusual about the song, however, was that Natalie Maines kept the lyrics the same as Scott's originals, which meant that the singer sang in the first person about a female love interest. Fans were faced with four ways of interpreting this: they could simply ignore the conundrum entirely, as many did; they could assume that the relationship was merely platonic; they could interpret it as a lesbian relationship; or they could recognize that Maines was singing "someone else's song." Within the majority of the country music fan base, the idea of a lesbian relationship being described in mainstream, radio-friendly country music did not even register as a possibility. Plenty of fans ignored the situation, and others assumed that the relationship was platonic. But others heard Maines's performance as separating the singer from the protagonist—in other words, undoing the critical connection between singer and song that had been forged by country music pioneers, most especially Hank Williams. In other words, Maines was clearly singing *Scott's* song, which made sense, since most of the album paid homage to famous songwriters that the Dixie Chicks admired. Yet this was a radical moment in country music: it reintroduced to the mainstream audience the idea of the songwriters behind the scenes, and turned the singers back into performers rather than surrogate authors of the songs.

TIME	FORM	LISTENING CUES	DISCUSSION
0:00	Introduction	banjo, acoustic guitar, mandolin, and fiddle stand out	The song sets up a Cajun groove.
0:23	Verse 1	"Daddy sits…"	The imagery here is the same nostalgia for a rural past, described as a tobacco farm, that defines country music.
0:45	Chorus	"Been a long…"	This song uses a changing chorus (see Appendix A), which means that each time the chorus appears, the words change slightly to refer to the previous verse.
0:56	Instrumental interlude	fiddle and banjo	Especially in 2002, this much fiddle and banjo prominently played in an acoustic recording was a novelty on country radio.
1:06	Verse 2	"Delia plays…"	This verse sets up the love interest for the singer and raises the conundrum about gender and the connection between the singer and the first-person character presented in the song.
1:29	Chorus	"Been a long…"	Notice the text changes to fit the second verse.
1:40	Instrumental interlude	fiddle	The fiddle (Martie Maguire) plays through a full verse of the song.
2:03	Bridge	"Now me…"	The bridge depicts the singer heading to Nashville to attempt to make it big. Nashville represents both the music industry in the song and the general case of an urban environment (inferior, according to the lyrics).
2:20	Verse 3	"Now me and…"	The first half of this verse involves stop-time, where the instruments drop out and let the vocals stand over just a few rhythmic patterns.
2:43	Chorus	"The rest is a long…"	This chorus is first extended and then merged into a long playout.
3:02	Playout	fiddle, then vocal improvisation	This section lasts for almost a full minute, which is a significant portion of the song. The musicians improvise here in an extended jam that also features lots of sophisticated syncopation.

first single. The song was blatantly autobiographical and a direct rebuttal to critics' accusations that Hill had left behind her country identity in the wake of her stardom. In the lyrics, Hill sang about being a regular mom next door with small-town roots, declaring that success had not altered her down-home, Southern identity. Rich's contributions to the album as a songwriter gave it street cred with current country fans who were under the spell of Big & Rich and Gretchen Wilson's redneck revival. Hill's album included a humorous romp through a Cajun country hoedown, "Dearly Beloved," that invoked more Southern redneck stereotypes than a Jeff Foxworthy comedy routine. Hill's transformation was successful, and her music was once again viewed as relevant by the country fan base.

In the years that followed, a spate of mostly male country singers released songs that define real country music against a foil of some unspecified "fake" country. Easton Corbin ("A Little More Country Than That," 2009), Billy Currington ("That's How Country Boys Roll," 2009), Eric Church ("Lotta Boot Left to Fill," 2009), and Jason Aldean ("She's Country," 2009) are just a few of the singers whose lyrics focused on establishing their own authenticity or country credentials, often by implying that the unspecified "rest of country music" does not measure up to those standards. It is a rhetorical strategy similar to that used in the early 2000s by songs that were part of the roots revival, including "Murder on Music Row" (see Chapter 13) and "Long Time Gone" (see Listening Guide). At the same time, many of these songs are musically closer to Southern rock and 1980s heartland rock in their instrumentation, harmonies, and guitar licks than to anything that could be labeled traditional or classic country. This is further evidence that these songs are drawing their definition of "country" from a different lineage than the Nashville-centric music of the 1970s.

Within the larger scope of country music, songs that claim to define "country" are part of a continual process by which genre borders are continuously reaffirmed. These songs and artists act as anchors for the genre and counterbalance the country singers whose music crosses over fluidly into the pop scene. In other words, these "chicken-fried," self-proclaimed-redneck, boots-wearing country-boy songs act as cultural markers of identity for the genre and for the audience as a whole. Brantley Gilbert's "Country Must Be Country Wide" (2011), for instance, presents a checklist of ways in which country fans assert their affiliation with the genre: praying, listening to "Cash, Hank, Willie, and Waylon," and self-identifying as "cowboys" and "hillbillies." Particularly at a time when pop-crossover artists such as Taylor Swift were a prominent part of commercial country music, these songs played a crucial role in defending the "otherness" and distinctiveness of the genre.

Americana and Alternative?

Alt-country failed to cohere as a genre in the years following *O Brother, Where Art Thou?* The artists whom critics had dubbed the most promising, the future of the movement, including Tift Merritt, Wilco, and Ryan Adams, headed off in the direction of indie rock and the singer-songwriter scene (see Chapter 13). Bluegrass-influenced bands like Nickel Creek dissolved as the individual members struck out on solo projects. Artists such as Gillian Welch, who had enjoyed a boost in fame from the *O Brother* phenomenon, continued to have a very loyal core group of fans, but as the years passed, these artists lost the widespread celebrity attention that had come from the soundtrack and the short-lived craze for roots music. Only a few artists, most notably Alison Krauss, succeeded in integrating into the country mainstream. Her 2000 duet with Kenny Rogers, "Buy Me a Rose," reached number one on the *Billboard* charts, and she continued to record occasional duets and singles that were successful on country radio.

The magazine *No Depression* even dropped "alternative country" from its tag line, adopting instead an ever-changing set of phrases that poked fun at its own inability to define the movement. The magazine finally settled on a broad identity, "Surveying the past, present, and future of American music." The vanguard publication of the movement no longer focused its coverage on either alt-country or country music in any explicit way, although the phrase "American music" in this context carried implications of country, folk, indie rock, and singer-songwriters working in mostly white, mostly vernacular styles. Certainly, the broader reaches of "American music," including classical, were not within the purview of the magazine or the music scene.

A SAMPLE OF THE CHANGING TAG LINES ON *NO DEPRESSION'S* COVERS

"The Alt.Country (Whatever That Is) Bimonthly Named Sue" (Nov–Dec 2002) *with cover photo of Johnny Cash*

"Don't Call What You're Wearing Alt.Country" (Bimonthly) (Jul–Aug 2003)

"Failing to Define Alt.Country Music for Eight Years" (Sep–Oct 2003)

"Climbing the Alt.Country Mountain (Wherever That Is) Since 1995" (Jan–Feb 2004)

"Happy Acting as an Alt.Country Bimonthly (Whatever That May Be)" (Mar–Apr 2005)

"Surveying the Past, Present, and Future of American Music (Whatever That Is)" (May–Jun 2007)

In spite of the general dissolution of the movement, many of the bands and styles that had been its core were still flourishing individually. With even more technological resources at their disposal, the bands were able to reach fans, build a following, and market themselves without the trappings of an organized movement. First Myspace and later Facebook, along with other social media websites, became the ultimate press kit for these bands, and fans could access that information without the intervention of the conventional press. Furthermore, although a few bands such as the Jayhawks (*Rainy Day Music* [2003]) returned to their earlier country-roots sound for new albums during those years, more artists, including Ryan Adams, found that they did not fit inside the constraints of even the broadest definition of country music. They broke away and headed in new directions, partly because country music required such strong allegiance to ideas of tradition. The movement that started out embracing connections with hillbilly traditional music now had many of its biggest names shying away from the alt-country label because those traditional roots proved too restrictive.

One of the ways that bands outside the country mainstream continue to build audiences and win over fans is through music festivals, which have grown in number and prominence since the early 2000s. Most of the festivals are anchored in rock, folk, or bluegrass identities, which merely reinforces the broader association of most alt-country and Americana bands with those genres. But a growing trend is for these festivals to actively promote listening across conventional genre borders. For instance, Bonnaroo, held in Manchester, Tennessee, since 2002, has a primarily rock profile but included Tift Merritt, Lucinda Williams, Robert Earl Keen, Merle Haggard, and the Del McCoury Band (bluegrass) on its varied 2009 lineup. One of the best known and oldest of the music festivals is Austin's South by Southwest (SXSW), which began in 1987. The event—which is now an astronomically large festival with little of its original home-grown flavor—has, in the past, showcased a number of bands who straddle the rock/country border. These festivals fill an important role for musicians working in alternative styles, because the people who attend live festivals often do so for the express purpose of hearing music that is not on the radio, and for whom distinctions between rock and country matter little.

Another trend outside the mainstream country scene that gained prominence after *O Brother* is a modern incarnation of old-time string band and bluegrass music, recast for younger, indie and alternative rock audiences. Old Crow Medicine Show, based in Nashville, Tennessee, often records with string-band instruments, but their live shows are irreverent explorations of jam band music, and their vocal styles are more indebted to Bob Dylan than Bill Monroe, as heard on recordings such as "Methamphetamine." Yonder Mountain String Band, from Colorado, has also succeeded in making progressive bluegrass music appealing to college-age audiences who have little or no affection for mainstream country music. And bands such as the Avett Brothers, including brothers Seth (1980–) and Scott Avett (1976–), from Concord, North Carolina, borrow bluegrass instrumentation to play music equally indebted to their grunge and metal musical influences and admiration for banjo legends. In spite of their obvious musical connections with bluegrass and old-time music, in most cases these bands have rejected terms such as bluegrass and country as identifiers for their music, which indicates that the terms still carry social stigmas that limit their acceptability to the younger, rock-oriented audiences.

The term "alt-country," which had emerged as an intertwined genre with country music in the 1990s, lost most of its relevance in 2006 and 2007, when two major media outlets challenged its usefulness. The *New York Times* directly posed the question when it published "Recalling the Twang that Was Alt-Country," with the subheading: "Bands like the Jayhawks and Uncle Tupelo flourished in the 90's; Has the genre ridden into the Sunset?" In the article, journalist Jesse Fox Mayshark pointed out that many of the artists labeled as alt-country had always found the term "suspect" and suggested that it was merely a now-obsolete musical gathering space for bands and singers who did not fit in the core commercial genres.

In their May–June 2007 issue, *No Depression's* editors put a photo of Miranda Lambert (1983–) on the cover and featured laudatory article about her (see Chapter 15). To diehard alternative fans, this was tantamount to heresy, because Lambert was a major country star whose first album had gone platinum, who had songs on the *Billboard* charts, and whose second album debuted in the number one chart spot. In other words, Lambert was a face and voice of the commercial mainstream country music establishment, fronting the magazine that had once defined itself in fierce opposition to that. Lambert herself saw no conflict of interest. In that 2007 interview with journalist Barry Mazor, Miranda Lambert talked about the attitudes of working musicians in the Texas scene, the singer-songwriters, the local and regional bands: "I'd be playing at one of the Texas music shows in a tent . . . where people would be chanting, literally, 'Nashville sucks! Nashville sucks!' And I was thinking that any one of us would take a record deal in a heartbeat. . . . Why *wouldn't* you want to get our kind of music out there?" Indeed, Lambert had succeeded in doing just that. The magazine's editor, Grant Alden, declared it a victory: "that battle [between alt-country and the mainstream] is largely over and, fundamentally, we won."

What had actually happened was neither that simple nor that closely linked to *No Depression.* Country music's natural cycle between pop-crossover styles and harder-edged twangy, roots-oriented styles and honky-tonk or redneck references had simply run its course, moving into a redneck phase where artists like Gretchen Wilson and Lambert were embraced by the mainstream. Between 2005 and 2008, the alt-country term drifted out of use; musicians who formerly would have been associated with it either moved beyond any bounds of country music and into indie rock, or else they got major-label recording contracts and started putting out mainstream hit records, as was the case with musicians such as Gretchen Wilson, Big & Rich, and Miranda Lambert. And of course, the singer-songwriters, bluegrass musicians, western swing revival bands, and other assorted musicians who had gathered under the alt-country banner for a few years simply continued to make their music and connect with their fans through the internet, summer festivals, and small-venue concerts as they always had.

The one major exception was found in Texas and Oklahoma, which continued to support a healthy alternative music scene that seamlessly blended retro honky-tonk and rock. Texas fans remained fiercely loyal to their local brand of country music, and the rivalry between Texas and Nashville routinely surfaced in their rhetoric. Texas also housed a thriving live-performance scene of large dance halls and nightclubs, and fans pay attention to independent charts published for song rankings such as the "Texas Regional Radio Report" and "Texas Music Chart." Bands such as Cross Canadian Ragweed have continued to play country-infused rock while distancing themselves from Nashville and mainstream country. And the scene still holds great appeal for many artists. Pat Greene (see Chapter 13), who began his career there and then moved into mainstream success in the mid-2000s, announced in 2011 that he planned to return to an independent-label career and go back to Texas, both metaphorically and literally.

Carrie Underwood (1983–)

arrie Underwood's career shows the ways that fans' perceptions are continually changing with regard to an artist's role in country music. When she broke into country music, fresh off her win on *American Idol in* 2005, Underwood was widely regarded as a pop star moving into country just to capture an available audience. Yet over the next few years, that perception shifted to the point that some fans considered her the standard by which to judge other singers' authenticity.

Born in Muskogee, Oklahoma, a town made famous by Merle Haggard's song Underwood grew up in Checotah, the youngest of three children and daughter of a teacher and a paper mill worker. She sang at local events and church all through high school, and continued performing while a student at Northeastern State University, where she earned a degree in communication. In 2004, she auditioned for a slot on the fourth season of *American Idol.* While on the show, she sang several country songs, including a memorable rendition of "Independence Day." She won the contest in May 2005, with over 60 million votes cast in the finale, and released her first single, "Inside Your Heaven," which did well on the pop charts.

Underwood and her label, Arista Records, steered her first album toward the country market, a genre that Underwood claimed in interviews as her musical home. She was still a child when Garth Brooks ushered in the new country boom period, and she grew up on the sounds of Reba McEntire, Martina McBride, and Trisha Yearwood, all women with great big diva voices whom Underwood admired, and after whom she patterned her style. Her first single after *American Idol*, "Jesus, Take the Wheel," soared to the top of the *Billboard* country chart, bolstered both by the name recognition that came from winning *Idol* and by her subsequent access to the top songwriters and producers in the industry. Unsurprisingly, many skeptical country fans still saw her as an outsider, especially when they compared her biography and image with those of other then-current stars like Gretchen Wilson.

Just a year after her debut, Underwood started winning the top industry awards, to the surprise of many longtime country fans. At the CMAs in 2006, cameras captured Faith Hill looking stunned and dismayed when the newcomer took home the Female Vocalist of the Year award, which Underwood swept at both the CMAs and ACMs for the next three years straight. Yet Underwood executed a careful shift in her career that transformed many country fans' perceptions of her from a pop-star outsider to an accepted part of country tradition. Her sophomore album, *Carnival Ride* (2007),

Pop Culture Lays Claim to Country Music

A short time after the MuzikMafia crashed onto the national scene in 2004 and sparked a redneck roots revival, a major crossover movement within country music emerged. Three indicators of this were:

1. The prominence of country music on the televised reality contest *American Idol.*
2. A surprising number of pop artists attempting to cross over *into* country music.
3. A new generation of country singers whom fans have accepted as crossover pop stars.

included a cover of "I Told You So," by neo-traditionalist Randy Travis. In March of 2008, Travis walked out on stage while she was performing at the Grand Ole Opry and invited her to become a member of the Opry. A few months later, Garth Brooks inducted her into that venerated institution. More than any of the industry awards she had received, it was the highest mark of acceptance by the country music establishment. It correspondingly gave the Opry—which had a reputation among some fans as an aging museum piece—a bright, young, attractive superstar with wide audience appeal (a win-win situation). The following spring, Underwood returned to *American Idol* as a guest performer. Travis was the "mentor" for country week that season, which coincided with the release of his greatest-hits album. The pair sang a duet version of "I Told You So." For Underwood, the duet staked her claim to a traditionalist country identity on the very stage that had launched her career. Her record label released a digital, downloadable version of the duet within twenty-four hours to meet the huge demand for the performance.

By 2009, Underwood had three albums' worth of country hits under her belt, and the ways in which many country fans talked about her started to change. On blogs and in website comments, where country fans had once complained endlessly about her artifice, they began referring to her as a "real" country star

Figure 14-4 Garth Brooks inducted fellow Oklahoman Carrie Underwood into the Grand Ole Opry March 15, 2008.

Source: Chris Hollo photograph © Grand Ole Opry Archives.

in comparison to greener pop-crossover artists. Yet once that base was firmly established, Underwood moved yet again into a more pop-crossover phase that saw unprecedented commercial success. By the time she performed "The Fighter" with Keith Urban at the 2017 Grammy awards, she had built an anomalous career as a country singer with high standing in the pop music community, or in other words, exactly the same identity she had forged at the start of her career.

By 2010, country music was home to hugely successful crossover artists working in a range of styles from catchy indie-rock to the slickest pop.

Country music's inclusion on *American Idol* connected the genre further to mainstream pop culture and introduced a new crop of country stars who had already secured a large noncountry following. *American Idol* debuted on the Fox network in 2002. Based on a British televised reality contest, the show featured singers in a quest to become the next "American idol," or pop star. A panel of judges critiqued the singers, and audiences voted for their favorites. In its second season, the show began to include a "country week" in its format, during which the contestants sang covers of country songs. A few seasons later, the show began bringing in a country star to mentor the contestants and perform on the awards broadcast. Guests included Kenny Rogers, Martina McBride, Dolly Parton, Randy Travis, and Shania Twain. While some viewers made fun of country week and judge Simon Cowell repeatedly stated that he did not like it, the show set country music on an equal footing with other genres of popular music. When the contestants—often a mix of races and ethnicities, from musical backgrounds ranging from soul to hard rock—were all singing country songs on the show, the "otherness" of those songs, along with any hillbilly twang, basically disappeared. In other words, "country" became just another generic category of songs. The show brought aging country stars who were no longer on the top of the charts back into the public consciousness, but more important to the development of country music, it launched the careers of several singers who became dominant figures within country music.

Carrie Underwood (see Artist Profile) went from being Season 5's winner of *American Idol* to a country star in a very short span of time, and along the way took care to remind audiences that she had always seen herself as a country singer. Yet she was far from the only *American Idol* contestant to claim that identity; Scotty McCreery, Kellie Pickler, Bucky Covington, Lauren Alaina, and Josh Gracin have also fared remarkably well as country artists, along with a few others who have had some success in country. The *American Idol* contestants obviously had an advantage when they launched their careers, enjoying widespread name recognition from the television show, which had supplied them with millions of viewers each week. Predictably, many traditional and hard-core country fans saw the entrance of these contestants into country music as diluting the music's core identity, but the influx of attention that the contestants brought to country music helped sustain the genre's popularity over the coming years.

Televised reality contests about country music pushed the genre even further into mainstream pop culture. A country version of *American Idol* called *Nashville Star* appeared on cable television's USA Network in 2003 and lasted five seasons there, finally making the leap to major broadcast network NBC in 2009, where it aired for one season. Along with a host of lesser-known shows (such as CMT's *Can You Duet?*), these shows allowed the general public to gain exposure to country music. They have also been the way that some of the most hard-edged, twangy, roots-oriented artists have been discovered in recent years. Miranda Lambert, for instance, placed third on *Nashville Star*, and Joey + Rory, whose bib-overall-wearing banjo breakdown "Cheater, Cheater" was the novelty hit of 2008, took third on *Can You Duet?*

With country music appearing through the lens of *American Idol* as just another collection of songs and musical style, a significant number of pop stars attempted to move into the country genre in the late 2000s, with varying levels of success. These transitions were also prompted by the fact that country fans were still buying CDs and listening to the radio, generally speaking, even while much of the rest of the popular music landscape appeared to be shifting away from those models. Jewel attempted the genre-shift, based on her singer-songwriter background and her yodeling abilities, with the country album *Perfectly Clear* (2008). Jessica Simpson parlayed her role as Daisy Duke in a Hollywood film version of the old TV show *The Dukes of Hazzard* into a country album in 2008. Academy Award winner Gwyneth

Paltrow played a country singer in the 2011 film *Country Strong*, and released the title song from the film to country radio as a single; she performed (with Vince Gill on stage with her) on the 2010 CMA Awards show. None of these efforts resulted in acceptance from the country fan base.

Others were more successful. Darius Rucker (see essay on Race in Country Music), who had been the lead singer for pop-rock band Hootie and the Blowfish, made the leap into country, largely by releasing radio-friendly country singles with little fanfare about his personal life. Rock artist and sometime rapper Kid Rock placed several songs on the country charts. Collaboration projects also brought rock musicians into country radio and into the ears of country fans: the rock band Bon Jovi released a duet with Jennifer Nettles (from the country band Sugarland). Country star and hat act Kenny Chesney scored hits with duets, in one instance with Uncle Kracker and in another with Dave Matthews. Alison Krauss recorded a duet album with Robert Plant (of Led Zeppelin) that critics raved about. These collaborations were in line with the CMT television show *Crossroads*, which began in 2002. The show pairs country stars with noncountry stars, aiming for jarring juxtapositions out of which the artists find common ground, and that idea took on a life of its own in country music. It even led to country stars performing more rock music, such as Martina McBride adding 1980s pop star Pat Benatar's "Hit Me with Your Best Shot" to her live concerts, further blurring boundaries.

Carrie Underwood's entrance into country music in 2005 set in motion a steady trajectory toward more crossover styles that became the dominant story in country music for that time period. Certainly, some artists and songs have continued in that vein ever since the late 1990s. Rascal Flatts, for instance, has maintained a reputation as both country and pop, with songs routinely on both charts and with fans squarely situated in both camps. Sugarland, consisting of Jennifer Nettles and Christian Bush, has been similarly successful with crossover country-pop since their start in 2003. But the magnitude of the trend increased from about 2005 to around 2010. Most notably, Taylor Swift, Lady Antebellum, and the Zac Brown Band have built country careers while enjoying parallel successes in the pop and rock worlds.

Taylor Swift (1989–) illustrates how country music's identity evolved between 2005 and 2010. As a teen songwriter in Nashville, she was "discovered" at the famed Bluebird Café. Shortly thereafter, she began releasing teen-romance songs such as "Love Story" (2008) with a slick, heavily produced sound. Blond and cute, with up-tempo songs reflecting American middle-class teenagers' concerns, Swift brought thousands of teenage girls into the ranks of country fans. Long-time country fans considered her an easy target for their predictable complaints about the current state of country music, which they decried as too pop, too trite, too produced, and too lacking in honky-tonk authenticity. Swift exported her brand of country music to a pop audience who received it on much the same terms as "country week" on *American Idol*—simply another musical style to be enjoyed from an enthusiastic young singer. On the question of country authenticity, the respected country journalist Chet Flippo weighed in with the opinion that Swift's skill as a songwriter (she writes or co-writes almost everything she sings) earned her a large measure of credibility within country music.

Figure 14-5 Taylor Swift, with her boots and acoustic guitar, 2009.
Source: Photo by Rahav Segev/Getty Images.

This trend toward crossover country expanded well beyond Taylor Swift. Nashville's Lady Antebellum, consisting of Hillary Scott, Charles Kelley, and Dave Haywood, similarly created a reputation as a country band singing pop music. Their debut album appeared in 2008, and within two years they had scored four number one country songs, all of which were also pop hits. In 2011, they won Grammys for both song of the year and record of the year, not in any "country" category but rather across all music. It was an astonishing feat for a band that claimed country as its home genre, and marked an apex of crossover success.

The Zac Brown Band, from Georgia, took a different path, though with a similar crossover reputation. Zac Brown formed the band in 2002, and for several years they played music festivals and small-venue clubs, gathering loyal fans from their live performances. They released several albums on their own independent record label, a method of building a musical career that is common within rock and the alt-country movement, but less so in commercial country music. From there, major record labels took notice of the band, and in 2008 Atlantic Records released their first major-label, nationally marketed album. Like Lady Antebellum, they scored four number one country hits in two years, and those singles crossed over onto the pop chart as well. Their musical identity, however, is more closely linked to indie rock. The Zac Brown Band has played festivals, including Bonnaroo (generally described as more of a rock festival) and Telluride (ostensibly bluegrass). Yet in spite of their crossover appeal—especially with rock fans and on their later albums—they periodically re-established their connections to country music. For instance, on their 2010 album *You Get What You Give*, traditionalist Alan Jackson sang a duet, "As She's Walking Away."

The whole *American Idol* generation of country music has two very different, yet equally significant, facets. One of those is that country music has become just another part of mainstream pop culture. Pop audiences are embracing country singers and country songs in all sorts of situations, from television shows to music festivals, that mix singers and bands from all genres. But the other facet is a portion of mainstream commercial country music that has actually returned to the sounds and styles of its roots. Artists are writing more of their own songs, and bands with Southern rock influences are showing up on the charts. Miranda Lambert and Zac Brown are shifting what would have been an alt-country biography a decade ago into the center of mainstream country music. That duality—some artists being accepted by the mainstream with a pop-crossover sound while others are resurrecting its twangy traditions—is one of the ways that country balances its otherness with commercial viability.

Reflecting and Projecting Meaning

In the decade following *O Brother*, country fans continued to embrace music that reflected their concerns, which on a large scale remained tied to matters of politics, global events, economic conditions, and social change. The demographics of the country audience have been constantly shifting since the 1950s, and six decades later, survey data suggests that the fan base is different than that to which the music is directly marketed: better educated, more affluent, and more suburban, but still unarguably white. As country music moved ever closer to mainstream pop with crossover stars, the discrepancy between the stereotyped image of country music fans and the reality of who listened to the music was best described as cognitive dissonance.

The gendered identity of country music even varied during the 2000s. In the years immediately after September 11, 2001, the commercial scene was dominated by male voices to a more extreme extent than in the early 1990s. Of the twenty-two and twenty songs that made it to number one on the *Billboard* country chart in 2002 and 2003, only two and one, respectively, featured female singers. Women regained footing, however, helped in large part by the stylistic shift toward crossover country. In a typical week in 2009, more than 20% of the songs on the *Billboard* country chart were sung by women, with Lady Antebellum (featuring Hillary Scott), Taylor Swift, Carrie Underwood, Miranda Lambert, and Reba McEntire accounting for many of those. But that gain was short-lived. Just two years later, for a brief period, there were no solo female artists at all in the top thirty *Billboard* songs, a fact that provoked accusations from several journalists that the genre was biased against women, especially in light of the fact that the audience included more female than male fans. The "redneck" female persona that Gretchen Wilson made popular in 2004 stuck around in various guises within country music as a balance for the classy and glamorous images of many of the genre's crossover stars, but ultimately even that image faded into the background of the scene.

Country fans continued to project their own concerns onto the music, which served the important social role of reflecting back and endorsing the listener's own identity. In the years following the subprime mortgage crisis and economic meltdown of 2008, middle-class Americans found themselves squeezed in an economic recession with high unemployment, while working-class people were hit even harder because of the number of jobs lost. Many in the country fan base found themselves out of work, broke, and devalued by society at large, and the unemployment rate affected men worse than women because of the kinds of jobs that disappeared. Two of the characteristics by which middle-class Americans define their identity—namely vocation and consumerism—were threatened. And the gender disparity in unemployment would be reflected in the song lyrics of this era.

Country music reflected these concerns directly in a number of songs, including Ronnie Dunn's "Cost of Living" (2011), Craig Campbell's "Family Man" (2011), Pistol Annie's "Housewife's Prayer" (2011), and John Rich's "Shuttin' Detroit Down" (2009), all of which discussed the lack of work, rising costs, "bills to pay," and loss of domestic manufacturing. A wave of songs also appeared about macho posturing and rough-and-tumble country boys driving big trucks out in the country, as far back as a dirt road will take them. Songs by Jake Owen, "Barefoot Blue Jean Night" (2011); Rodney Atkins, "Take a Back Road" (2011); and Jason Aldean, "Dirt Road Anthem" (2011); to name just a few, reflected a growing movement that would soon become the dominant sound of country music (see Chapter 15). Journalist Chet Flippo derided the trend as a "series of mini-scripts for manly TV commercials . . . for suburban wannabe country boys . . . [in] a race to out-macho the next guy." These songs reflected societal insecurities at a time when many men found themselves out of work and unable to provide for their families in the conventional modes, and they served as a way of reaffirming or shoring up a sense of secure masculinity for their audience.

The whole trend is summed up eloquently by Alan Jackson's "Hard Hat and a Hammer" (2010), an endorsement of working-class male identity that calls to mind the songs in the early 1990s on similar topics (such as Travis Tritt, "Lord Have Mercy on the Working Man" [1992]; see Chapter 12). Even though the country audience is no longer composed exclusively of the working-class audience to whom the industry first pitched the music in the 1920s and '30s, listeners still find deep symbolic value in constructing their identity on those characterizations.

☆ ESSAY: CULTURE

Dixie Chicks and Politics

Country music has always been tangled up with politics, from the 1920s and '30s, when hillbilly musicians worked the campaign trail, to the way that country singers have addressed wars, called for social justice, and spoken their minds on public policies for nearly a century. Yet the biggest political scandal to rock country music started at a Dixie Chicks concert in 2003.

The Dixie Chicks (see Chapter 13) emerged on the national scene after years of playing bluegrass and commercial country music in the Dallas area. Their first two albums each achieved "diamond" certification (sales of over 10 million albums) by the RIAA. They caught the attention of a pop audience as well as country, and by all outward appearances, their career was going exceptionally well. After *Fly* (1999), however, the band took a brief hiatus that kept them out of the country spotlight for a few years. When they returned, both they and the country music landscape had changed.

After their second album appeared, the Dixie Chicks sued their record label, arguing that their recording contract was too restrictive and unfair and that they should have more artistic control over their music as well as better compensation for their success. While their lawyers and the attorneys for Sony Music sorted out the suit, the three women held their ground back in their native Texas. No new record would be forthcoming until the suit was settled. In 2002, a resolution was reached, and the Dixie Chicks released their third album, *Home*, on their new imprint, Open Wide Records.

The group's new control over their career paralleled a change in their musical direction. By 2000, the Dixie Chicks had pushed their music so far into the pop arena and toured so extensively that they individually and collectively expressed the desire to regroup and revive the heart and spirit of their music. They went home to Texas, where they attended to family matters, had babies, enjoyed "picking sessions," and sang all sorts of songs, both new ones they had written and older bluegrass and folk songs, on which they had originally founded their musical identity. Meanwhile, the *O Brother* phenomenon had served as a catalyst to bring the county-pop era to a close, and bluegrass, acoustic music, and anything that sounded like "roots music" was all the rage. The Dixie Chicks asked lead singer Natalie Maines's dad, steel guitar legend Lloyd Maines, to record a bunch of their favorite songs in stripped-down, acoustic versions that emphasized close harmony, twang-tinged vocals, and raw instrumental virtuosity. The result was *Home*.

With its sepia-toned cover that depicted the three women standing on a Texas highway, the album invoked associations with the roots music and legends of old-time hillbilly blues. The hand-stitched "fabric label" shown on the cover furthered the association with homespun handi-work. On the back of the liner notes, a photograph of a roadside diner's sign declared, "We are changing the way we do business." The double meaning— a new business contract as well as a renewed dedication to heartfelt, roots-oriented music making—was apparent.

Figure 14-6 Cover art and back of liner notes for the Dixie Chicks' Home album.

Home's lead single, "Long Time Gone" (see Listening Guide), was an instant success. They followed it by releasing a cover of '70s rockers

Figure 14-7 Protestor at the opening night of the Dixie Chicks' US tour, 2003, in Greenville, South Carolina.

Source: Daniel Coston.

Fleetwood Mac's "Landslide." Their third single from the album, "Travelin' Soldier," reached the top of the *Billboard* chart. The song told of a young girl who mourns the death of a soldier in Vietnam. With the United States already at war in Afghanistan and the Iraq war just weeks away, the song appeared timely.

In the midst of their success, the group suddenly sparked a major controversy. On March 10, 2003, on stage in London, Natalie Maines quipped, "Just so you know . . . we're ashamed the president of the United States is from Texas." The press reported the comment, and within days, a firestorm ripped through the country music community. Country radio stations pulled their songs from their playlists, slipping in a conveniently conservative and apparently pro-war track from Darryl Worley, "Have You Forgotten," which had the side effect of giving his career a huge boost. Radio talk show hosts and DJs fanned the flames with staged events at which they destroyed Dixie Chicks CDs (which, unlike vinyl records, inconveniently do not burn, thereby forcing the organizers to come up with other methods). Meanwhile, Toby Keith had released "Courtesy of the Red, White, and Blue (The Angry American)," a song he penned in response to September 11 that describes a swift and violent response to the attacks, including the now-infamous phrase "put a boot in your ass." Maines criticized the song, and a very public feud between Keith and the Dixie Chicks ensued. As the Dixie Chicks were about to embark on a major U.S. tour, conservative commentators stirred up even more press by calling for a boycott of the concert tour and staging protests; in the most extreme case, the band received an anonymous death threat.

The issue was the political inclinations of the audience, as well as their tolerance for their music mixing with politics. Although the genre had strong populist leanings in its first few decades, by the 1980s, the bulk of the audience had changed to a socially conservative, mostly Republican demographic, in parallel with political changes in the South. In the national media, by the time the Dixie Chicks hit the scene, country music was described as right-wing Republican, religiously conservative, and pro-military. References in articles about politics frequently cited Merle Haggard's "Okie from Muskogee" and Tammy Wynette's "Stand by Your Man" as evidence of the music's political leanings on matters of social change, military support, and family values. At the Republican National Conventions in 2004 and 2008, country stars headlined as entertainers, and Gretchen Wilson performed for Sarah Palin's campaign in 2008. Furthermore, journalist Chet Flippo explained, the country music audience expects loyalty from its country stars on political topics, and the appearance of dissent is generally not tolerated.

Yet the politics of country music are not as simplistic as these portrayals suggest. Not all country singers are Republicans, nor are all country listeners, although demographic surveys confirm that the country radio audience resides disproportionately in so-called "red" states (those that vote Republican). As author Chris Willman has documented, the songwriting community from which most country hits emerge leans the opposite way. What remains constant in today's music is that, with the exception of concert appearances at campaign events in election years, most country musicians and country songs avoid partisan politics in their music and public personas. The Dixie Chicks violated that taboo, which caused such an outcry that they have not been embraced by the country music fan base in its entirety since. The lead single off their next album, *Taking the Long Way* (2006), titled "Not Ready to Make Nice," confirmed that they had not retracted their opinions, and since that time, the band has resided on the fringes of country music (without releasing any more records), acclaimed by critics and devoted fans but treated as a cautionary tale within the community.

Figure 14-8 Supporter at the opening night of the Dixie Chicks' US tour, 2003, in Greenville, South Carolina.
Source: Daniel Coston.

Race in Contemporary Country

In 2008, Darius Rucker (1966–), best known as lead singer for the pop-rock band Hootie and the Blowfish, released a country single titled "Don't Think I Don't Think About It." Rucker's record rose to the top spot on the *Billboard* country chart, something that no black singer had done since Charley Pride's last number one, "Night Games," in 1983. Rucker's success focused attention once again on race and country music. Country music has a reputation as white music and, especially to noncountry fans, the music embodies a white, working-class, rebellious Southern identity, with all the baggage that entails. Yet a study of race in country music is well worth undertaking for all that it can reveal about the culture in which the music was created and the people who invest in it.

The history of white country musicians learning and borrowing from African American traditions continued throughout the genre's history; Elvis Presley covering Roy Brown is one of the better known instances. There is also a history of black musicians borrowing from and performing country: Chuck Berry made known his affinity for hillbilly music, Isaac Hayes covered Glen Campbell, and Ray Charles released a country album in 1962. Country has had a few black stars, most notably DeFord Bailey on

Figure 14-9 Darius Rucker with his acoustic guitar and fiddle player on stage. August 2010.
Source: Daniel Coston.

the Opry, rockabilly's Big Al Downing, and of course Charley Pride, who had thirty-six number one country hits. Dona Mason had a minor country hit in the 1980s, as well. Collaborations abound: Ray Charles and Willie Nelson had a hit in the 1980s, and Louis Armstrong reprised his Jimmie Rodgers duet with Johnny Cash on television in 1969. Garth Brooks, Shania Twain, and Reba McEntire have all recorded with gospel choirs. In 2004, R&B star Nelly invited Tim McGraw to record a duet, "Over and Over," that reached number three on the *Billboard* "Hot 100." Yet at its core, country musicians and audiences remain mostly white, and racial identity and country music have become fodder for comedy. Popular movies, including *Remember the Titans* (2000) and *Soul Men* (2008), have even exploited that affiliation in their plots.

The first African American country artist signed to a major-label record contract since Charley Pride was Troy Coleman (1970–), known as Cowboy Troy. Part of the MuzikMafia, Cowboy Troy coined the terms "blackneck" and "hick-hop" to describe who he was and the music that he made. In interviews, he suggested that he was not the only person who enjoyed listening to both country and rap, and that his fusion of the two was a reflection of the contemporary audience's tastes. In his stage act, his recordings, and his interviews, Cowboy Troy continually emphasized racial difference and sings lyrics such as "I'm big and black, clickety-clack."

Darius Rucker adopted a very different strategy. After achieving fame with Hootie and the Blowfish, Rucker attempted to launch a solo R&B career with *Back to Then*, which appeared in 2002 but garnered little attention. In 2008, with very little fanfare, he released a country album that featured songs cowritten by some of Nashville's hottest writers. The album included several radio-friendly tracks that had clear crossover appeal, as well as a few harder-edged country shuffles and honky-tonk novelty numbers. In the rounds of interviews that Rucker did after the album came out, he described his synergy with country music as stemming from his youth in South Carolina, where he described growing up "country." He also suggested that he had always been a country fan and a country singer because of that background and declared that this album was finally an expression of his true identity. Race was rarely mentioned at all in his interviews. Rather than highlight his differences with the majority of the country audience, he laid claim to country music through the shared Southern, rural, working-class experience that spans both black and white racial identities and underpins the music.

The idea of defining a country identity through social class, geography, and work experience is not new. It allows space for both black artists and black fans, and there is a small African-American contingent among the country audience. Black fans who listen to country music have explained that their shared experience with small-town Southern or rural life trumps the racial affiliations of the music. For instance, LZ Granderson, a black journalist who writes for CNN, defended his affinity for the genre in a 2011 op-ed piece: "My family is from rural Mississippi and I spent a lot of my childhood playing on the dirt roads south of Greenwood. I have an uncle who has yet to recover from his time in Vietnam. So I know full well the world many country artists sing about: the watering holes, eating fried chicken, going to church, God, war. When Rodney Atkins sings, 'these are my people' I think: 'yes they are.'"

That perspective on race, however, denies the fact that country's whiteness has been consistently preserved by the fan base at large. During the eras of rampant genre crossing, white artists appeared on the pop and, occasionally, R&B charts, but black artists with a similar sound did not appear on the country charts and—with very few exceptions—country radio has not played black artists.

Country's relationship to racial identity deserves exploration beyond the duality of black and white, as well. In some parts of Texas, New Mexico, and Southern California, for instance, local clubs feature bands whose sounds blend country with Tejano and *norteño* music effortlessly, and those influences have made their way into (white) country performers' styles. Hispanic fans have appropriated the music as meaningful within their lives and communities, but Hispanic country stars are largely absent from country radio. Similar situations arise on the musical borders of country and Cajun.

Rucker's success may be attributed to the way he has de-emphasized racial difference in his music at the same time that the audience has expanded beyond its core constituency, courtesy of crossover acts. Anomalous cases such as his, however, do not change the fact that musical genre and racial identity are deeply intertwined, and for decades country music has used whiteness as one of its border-defining features. The relationship between race, ethnicity, and musical genre deserves thorough and reflective investigation.

✶ ESSAY: TECHNOLOGY

MP3s Please

The way that listeners got their music changed significantly between 2001 and 2010. In 2001, Apple released its first iPod, a device that had become ubiquitous among college students a decade later. The number of country music fans who owned iPods increased dramatically during the same time that stars such as Carrie Underwood and Taylor Swift appeared on the scene; in 2005, only 17% of country listeners had one, but that grew to 42% by 2007 and 61% by 2009. The music industry in general (not just country) shifted its focus to digital music. For all genres together, there were approximately 1.2 billion singles, albums, and videos downloaded in 2009, whereas fewer than 300 million CDs were shipped to stores. Yet the dollar value of all digital downloads was barely over $2 billion, whereas the dollar value of the CDs and other physical sales was over $4.5 billion. In other words, the media format shifted from physical CDs to digital files far faster than the business models could keep up.

In the very early days of MP3 players and cell phones with music capabilities, many users thought of MP3s as just a way of carrying songs from their physical CD collections around more conveniently. These technologies gave way to rampant file-sharing, particularly through Napster from 1999–2001. A decade after the introduction of the iPod, however, the technology had actually changed the way that music fans thought of "owning" a recording or getting access to music. As CD sales declined, music companies first tried to figure out ways to stop fans from ripping MP3s from their CDs, then ways to sell them digital recordings, and only after some extended time, ways to stream music via subscription services. These changes in the industry had corresponding seismic changes in the way that record labels and artists generated revenue streams. Many of the streaming services, for instance, paid far, far lower amounts than the royalties that were distributed for physical CD sales, leading eventually to artists' complaints about "micropenny" payments from companies such as Spotify, which started in 2008. It took some time for the economic models in the music industry to adjust to the new technologies, too.

One effect of digital music distribution is that record labels could now make recordings instantly available exclusively via download, so in a growing number of instances, there was no physical media to buy. If a live performance or duet suddenly caught the attention of lots of listeners, record labels could move quickly to release it as a digital single. But digital downloads also separated the music from other components that were associated with it in CD form. CDs included cover art, liner notes, discographical information, and a collection of songs that went together to form a larger creative work, namely an album. Digital music was divorced from all those other components. This allowed music to cross genre boundaries more easily, because songs were not packaged with other songs, the appearance of the artist, or cover art, or stocked in one particular category in a record store. It also changed the focus for the artists from creating a great album to just creating a great single.

The rapid shift to new technology across the music industry proved tricky for country music, and thus sparked a large number of surveys and studies, all aimed at figuring out who was listening to country music and how they were acquiring their music. These surveys inadvertently helped identify ways in which country fans were different from other genres. For instance, a survey conducted by the Country Radio Broadcasters (CRB) in 2007 found that 65% of country fans were at least thirty-five years old, and neither the country singers nor the country audience were, for the most part, on the cutting edge of developments in social networking, making country slower in many ways to gain footing in the new scene.

The rise of digital downloads had another effect on country music: fans could connect with individual artists via their social media, thereby having what felt like a direct-access lines of communication. These methods circumvent traditional channels for both distribution and criticism, such as record stores and print magazines. This artist-centered idea means that fans can claim loyalty to an individual musician rather than to a genre, and artists are actually freer to move beyond, around, and across genre boundaries. The CRB survey pointed out, for instance, that in 2011 Taylor Swift's fans did not necessarily think of themselves as country fans, nor did they necessarily like other country artists besides Swift. Fans' access to music and artists via social media also means that more artists are free to self-promote and market their music without having to categorize it by genre at all.

LISTEN-SIDE-BY-SIDE

"Independence Day"
Songwriter: Gretchen Peters
Martina McBride, 1994 (on *The Way That I Am*, RCA Records)

"Broken Wing"
Songwriters: Phil Barnhart, Sam Hogin, James House
Martina McBride, 1997 (on *Evolution*, RCA Records)

"Goodbye Earl"
Songwriter: Dennis Linde
The Dixie Chicks, 1999 (on Fly, Monument Records)

"Gunpowder & Lead"
Songwriters: Miranda Lambert and Heather Little

Miranda Lambert, 2007 (on *Crazy Ex-Girlfriend*, Columbia Nashville)

"Maggie Creek Road"
Songwriters: Karyn Rochelle and James T. Slater
Reba McEntire, 2009 (on *Keep On Loving You*, Starstruck/Valory)

"Blown Away"
Songwriters: Chris Tompkins and Josh Kear
Carrie Underwood, 2011 (on *Blown Away*, Arista Nashville)

"Church Bells"
Songwriters: Zach Crowell, Brett James, and Hillary Lindsey
Carrie Underwood, 2016 (on *Storyteller*, Arista Nashville)

Within country music, the same broad narratives or stories show up time and again in song lyrics. Songwriters even talk about the importance of knowing traditional stories in the genre and of the craft of re-telling those stories from a new angle or perspective. These generalized stories, from which many individuals derive, can be called **metanarratives**. One of these metanarratives that surfaced repeatedly in the New Country era through the present is a tale of a woman avenging abuse she suffered at the hands of a violent man. These six recordings, all by different songwriters and performed by different artists, reveal this common thread throughout two decades of country music.

Metanarratives tie together a genre: they let fans generalize about the topics or themes of country music, for instance, and they forge implicit connections between songs that were recorded at different times.

They reiterate similar ideas, which give those ideas more weight within the musical discourse. For fans, they are an appealing combination of new and familiar: new in that each song is its own artistic entity; familiar in that the stories are well-trod territory for the listener. Most important,

these metanarratives usually echo songs or themes that have been part of country music's fabric since its earliest recordings.

These seven tales of avenging domestic violence resonate with the tradition of murder ballads that has been a part of country music from its earliest recordings. The first generation of country recordings included several of these ballads from earlier centuries, passed around by oral tradition, and often telling the tale of a man who killed his lover or betrothed, often with graphic depictions of the violent act and death of the woman in the lyrics. "The Knoxville Girl" (The Blue Sky Boys), "Pretty Polly" (The Coon Creek Girls), and "Delia's Gone" (part of several ballad collections and later recorded by Johnny Cash) are three such examples. Only a few ballads told instead of a woman killing her lover or husband, such as "Frankie and Johnny" (Jimmie Rodgers). Given the ubiquity of the first type, those few songs act as a general answer song to the historical narrative.

Martina McBride's "Independence Day" was groundbreaking in its poignant treatment of the subject of domestic violence and a woman avenging her abuse. In 1994, it rode the wave of the feminist new awakening in country music. The song's craft and nuance was heralded: the story told from the perspective of the child, the double meaning of the song's title, and the subtle ambiguity that kept the full plot of the song inferred rather than stated outright. In the song, a daughter recalls the day her mother burned down her house around her drunk and abusive father. While it may seem incongruous to have such a serious story told in a very popular song, it also reveals the serious side of country music that has always confronted social justice issues. McBride continued recording songs that addressed these sorts of issues, and repeated the theme of a woman escaping an abusive relationship with "A Broken Wing" just a few years later.

Several common elements appear across these seven songs, most notably distrust of the law or authorities to protect the women; and solidarity, sisterhood, and assistance from friends and female family members. By the time Carrie Underwood recorded "Church Bells" in 2016, fans could hear the song as part of a long tradition of this metanarrative, interwoven with another prominent metanarrative in which a poor girl catches the eye of a rich man, and he lifts her out of poverty ("Fancy," recorded both by Bobby Gentry and Reba McEntire, for instance).

The presence of these songs on country radio and on the country charts is evidence of a very serious side of country music. The metanarrative links together that aspect of the genre across time, across different artists, and across the various trends and fads that threaten to saturate the market with superficial songs. To whatever extent country music is the poetic voice of its people, these songs tell a tale of women's empowerment and of distrust for authority that, together, help depict the identity of country music in the contemporary era.

PLAYLIST

Chesney, Kenny, with Uncle Kracker, "When the Sun Goes Down" (2004)

Keith, Toby. "Courtesy of the Red, White, and Blue (The Angry American)" (2002)

Lambert, Miranda. "The House that Built Me" (2010)

Rucker, Darius. "All I Want" (2008)

Swift, Taylor. "Love Story" (2008)

Underwood, Carrie, with Randy Travis, "I Told You So" (2009)

FOR MORE READING

Cusic, Don. *Discovering Country Music*. Westport, CT: Praeger, 2008.

Flippo, Chet. "News Flash: Women Still Recording Country Music," *Nashville Skyline*, May 20, 2004, cmt.com, available at http://www.cmt.com/news/nashville-skyline/1487148/nashville-skyline-news-flash-women-still-recording-country-music.jhtml

Mayshark, Jesse Fox. "Recalling the Twang that Was Alt-Country: Bands like the Jayhawks and Uncle Tupelo Flourished in the 90's. Has the Genre Ridden into the Sunset?" *New York Times* (July 16, 2006): A26.

Mazor, Barry. "Miranda Lambert: Nashville Lonestar," *No Depression* #69 (May–June 2007): 56–63.

Pruett, David B. *MuzikMafia: From the Local Nashville Scene to the National Mainstream.* Jackson: University Press of Mississippi, 2010.

Willman, Chris. *Rednecks & Bluenecks: The Politics of Country Music.* New York: The New Press, 2005.

NAMES AND TERMS

American Idol	Krauss, Alison	Paisley, Brad
Avett Brothers	Lady Antebellum	Rich, John
Bonnaroo	Lambert, Miranda	Swift, Taylor
Dixie Chicks	Metanarrative	Wilson, Gretchen
IBMA	MuzikMafia	Zac Brown Band
Jackson, Alan	*Nashville Star*	

REVIEW TOPICS

1. What cultural associations do people within your community or circle of friends have, and how do they correspond to the current music's lyrics, the information we have about audience demographics, and the history of the genre?

2. In the 2000s, why did so many artists from outside the country genre make recordings—either duet projects or solo albums—that were presented as country music?

3. Are there newly released songs that address the main topics presented in this chapter, and are there other topics that you can find based on our five themes of investigation?

Breaking Borders

On May 2, 2013, Alan Jackson stepped onto the stage of the Grand Ole Opry and solemnly sang "He Stopped Loving Her Today," a final farewell to George Jones, who had passed away six days earlier. Jones's funeral, held at the Opry, bound together the genre's present and past, a stately reminder that, in country music, the lines between sacred and secular are thin, indeed. For young fans who watched the service on television or via the internet, it was an extraordinary history lesson; for old fans who longed for the days when Jones's voice poured out of their radios, it was a reassurance that whatever country music sounded like at the present, it still honored its legacy.

A number of the performers at Jones's funeral were essentially retired, musicians whose heyday was many decades in the past. But several were also part of the current scene, with songs on the radio and albums on the charts. Their presence was a stalwart reminder that country music has always had a traditional core. Ever since the 1950s, that core has had elements of honky tonk, plaintive singing, story-telling, and a lack of pretense over genre labels. Alan Jackson filled that role in the New Country era of the early 1990s; a decade later Brad Paisley joined him, fortuitously arriving on the scene just as the roots revival was cresting. A full decade later, both of those performers were still on stage in their white cowboy hats, singing music that eschewed any short-term style trends in honor of one of their musical heroes.

The Past Is Alive and Well

One of the basic principles of country music is that no matter the innovations or changes that color public perceptions of country music, there is always some space on the charts and in the venues for a sound that traces its history through the same set of styles that formed the base of the neotraditionalist sound: classic country, Bakersfield, honky tonk, and western swing. George Strait has single-handedly embodied this role of a keeper of tradition throughout his career; he was still placing songs on the charts in 2015 in his neotraditionalist style. Yet it is equally true that these artists seldom get enough attention from the media and the fans to rise to the top of the industry. Only when the timing of their careers happens to align with a more general shift toward roots-oriented and older classic and honky-tonk styles are they likely to earn real staying power.

In most cases, these core artists' albums contain a range of musical styles, from the more traditional to some that contain pop-styled elements. Sitting squarely in this position are Blake Shelton (see Artist Profile) and Justin Moore. With a string of successes and obvious staying power since his debut in 2009, Moore has kept songs such as "If You Don't Like My Twang" and "Kinda Don't Care" in the mix. Eric Church has also cast his music in this general mold, with songs like "Give Me Back My Hometown" and "Talladega." And as one might expect, many other artists have showed up on the scene with an album or two, rotating in and out of the spotlight fairly quickly but contributing a steady diet of hard-core country songs tied to the neotraditionalist past.

Figure 15-1 Travis Tritt sang "Why Me, Lord," at George Jones's funeral.
Source: Rick Diamond/Staff.

Another throwback to the past in the early 2010s was the reappearance of Garth Brooks. Following his (second) retirement in 2004, Brooks had slid into a legacy role. He spent several years performing in Las Vegas, letting the contemporary world of country music pass him by. But in 2014, he reemerged with a new album and the stated intention of making himself and his music relevant to the commercial scene again. He launched a world tour and released *Man Against Machine*. Two years later, he followed that up with *Gunslinger*. In both cases, the albums were stacked with songs that sounded like Garth Brooks circa 1995, still steeped in the New Country style that he helped to invent. Yet what had sounded new and adventurous more than two decades earlier now appeared comfortingly traditional and familiar, a touchstone for core country music in a time when most attention was focused on crossover styles and hip-hop making its way into the genre.

Brooks's relationship with streaming technology also underwent a radical change: Brooks had held out for many years and refused to make his music available through third-party streaming companies. He even went so far as to launch his own music distribution service called GhostTunes. In 2017, however, Brooks's service closed its doors, and Brooks reached an agreement by which his music could stream via Amazon. Even those aspects of country music that are resistant to change sometimes succumb to new ways of doing business.

New Directions

Five major trends have characterized country music since 2010, each of which is an extension of a development that started in the early 2000s:

1. Country music became fodder for other popular media and cultural institutions, notably the televised drama *Nashville*.
2. A new style, dubbed "bro-country," overtook the genre for a short period.
3. Female singer-songwriters gained attention as harbingers of change with regard to country music's engagement with gender.
4. The trend toward crossover styles picked up hip-hop.
5. Two singers with reputations as musical outsiders upended country music, captured the media's attention, and challenged the music's crossover direction.

In country music, the biggest story of this decade has unquestionably been a major shift in the direction of pop-crossover and hybrid styles. From the perspective of the stylistic pendulum, always oscillating between roots-oriented movements and pop-crossover movements (see chapter 12), the current phase is decidedly in the crossover portion of the cycle.

Nashville on Screen

The drama of country music got big-screen exposure in 2010's *Country Strong*, a movie starring Gwyneth Paltrow and Tim McGraw. Similar to Robert Altman's 1976 film *Nashville*, this movie used characters who were scripted on stock types in country music. Although *Country Strong* failed either to garner the critical acclaim of *Nashville* or to launch Paltrow as a country singer, it reacquainted the public with country music as a backdrop for scripted dramas.

Just two years later, the songwriters' scene in Nashville got unexpected public attention from a television show. In October 2012, a new television drama debuted on ABC called *Nashville*. The show starred Connie Britton as a middle-aged country star with allegiances to the music's traditions and Hayden Panettiere playing a much younger, much blonder country singer who leans toward crossover country-pop. Set in the present, the show also featured several characters who were songwriters, and much of the drama in each episode centered around how individual songs were created. The show also lifted real-world controversies from country music and used them for plot devices, including a country star coming out as gay and singers launching record labels. Although its popularity dipped after a few seasons and ABC dropped the show in 2016, for several years it was a very public representation of the genre. Through it, viewers tapped into the idea of getting to know songwriters, their original versions of hits, and their personalities.

Country got another public boost of attention in the form of *The Voice*, a televised singing contest that was the heir-apparent to *American Idol* in its popularity. Unlike *Idol*, which had a complicated and occasionally ambivalent relationship with country music, *The Voice* brought on Blake Shelton as one of its four judges from the first season. Together, *The Voice* and *Nashville* kept country music situated squarely in the center of popular culture. In these shows, the genre was populated with hip, attractive young people who used one particular style of music as a form of artistic expression. This portrayal diminished the sense that country music was something foreign to mainstream culture, performed by people separated by social class and outlook from the rest of the population.

The Rise of Bro-Country

The biggest stylistic development of the decade was dubbed "bro-country" by Jody Rosen in 2013 (see essay on The Splintering of Country). By the time the term was coined, this trend had been firmly entrenched in the genre for several years. Bro-country was a hyper-masculine sound that built on the already-present elements of southern rock, layered them with lyrics about dirt roads and tailgates in the South, added just enough banjo to signify that this was "country music," and delivered it all with sass and defiance.

The attitude was an important characteristic of the music that helped explain what made it so successful. Country music has mirrored the economic conditions of the working- and middle-class population since its inception. In 2008, the subprime mortgage crisis undercut both the public's faith in the largest financial institutions in this country and their own financial stability. The first response in country music was a wave of songs about the plight of the working man (see Chapter 14). As time moved

ARTIST PROFILE

Blake Shelton (b. 1976)

In many ways, Blake Shelton is an anomaly as a country star, especially in the twenty-first century. He does not write his own music, and he is best-known for his long-term role as a judge on the reality television singing contest *The Voice*. Nonetheless, since his debut in 2001, Shelton has had 24 number one hits, including a streak of 17 consecutive ones. He was the five-time winner of Male Vocalist of the Year at the Country Music Association awards (2110–2014) and crowned Entertainer of the Year for 2012.

Shelton was born and raised in Oklahoma, and after high school, came to Nashville to pursue music full-time. As is common among artists who end up "making it" in country music, he had some support and mentoring early on, in his case from songwriter Bobby Braddock. Within a few years, Shelton had signed a production contract with a major-label; a recording contract followed shortly afterward with Giant Records, and from there he moved on to Warner Brothers.

Shelton's music tends toward honky tonk, at least in its story lines about drinking, love affairs, and heartbreak ("The More I Drink," "Came Here to Forget"). He has, for the most part, avoided delving into bro-country (with the exception of "Boys 'Round Here"), a move that has protected him from some of the harsher criticism launched at that movement. Detractors, however, are quick to deride his success by crediting it to his rugged good looks and good ol' boy charm rather than in his music. And, in a time when almost all country singers co-write the majority of their music, fans are often surprised to find out he does not write his hits. The only exception to that was "Over You," a song about the death of Shelton's little brother that he co-wrote with then-wife Miranda Lambert, and which Lambert (rather than Shelton) recorded.

Shelton's career highlights the splintering of country music into more distinctive subgenres. Since 2013—when *Billboard* started reporting country radio airplay on a separate chart than the broader category "Hot Country Songs"—Shelton's songs have been staples of country radio, which relies on a base of male, feel-good drinking songs. By contrast, none of his singles since 2013 have reached the top of the "Hot Country Songs" chart, which accounts for segments of the country audience who are interested in country music that is notably different than Shelton's.

In 2011, Shelton became a judge on NBC's *The Voice*, a reality-style singing competition that emphasizes pop music and spans multiple genres. His role on this popular show made him a household name amongst people who would otherwise never pay attention to country music. As the music industry has discovered repeatedly over the years, numbers matter; for any artists, the more people who know their names and have heard their music in any setting, the higher the likelihood of career success. Shelton's exposure on *The Voice* has definitely supported his country music stardom.

And therein lies the dichotomy that is most interesting—Blake Shelton, who in many ways is not the most likely figurehead for country music, has ended up in that role—the one country singer that non-country fans may know and even watch weekly. And Shelton knows how to dispense his hard-country and redneck persona just a little at a time to shore up his credentials as a country singer for the audience who cares about that while charming but not alienating his non-country fans. It's a negotiation that requires some finesse, which Shelton definitely has.

on and as people got a better sense of what had happened and why, the message that emerged was that regular working people had been suckered into taking out large mortgages that they could not afford. When the crisis reached a breaking point, the financial institutions were bailed out by the government while the working people suffered. The white Southern male persona—the demographic that mirrored those who had been hit the hardest by the economic conditions and unemployment—showed up in these songs with a new attitude (see Chapter 14). "He" (the protagonist in the songs) metaphorically grabbed a ball cap, some beer, and set out on a dirt road to go fishing. Country song lyrics offered a solution for their disenfranchisement. These men were enacting a modern version of Johnny Paycheck's 1977 hit, "Take This Job and Shove It," abdicating their modern suburban responsibilities and escaping to a tailgate party.

Rosen revealed in an interview that he had almost called this music "frat country," a jab at the way that this attitude and music seemed sidelined in a permanent party, and that it found resonance with a lot of listeners who were not actually working-class at all.

Dirt-road, country-drive, tailgate, devil-may-care, and female-as-accessory songs emerged as a trend in the late 2000s and crested in 2012 and 2013. A sample of them includes:

ARTIST	SONG	DATE
Lost Trailers	"Holler Back"	2008
Currington, Billy	"That's How Country Boys Roll"	2009
Moore, Justin	"Backwoods"	2010
Shelton, Blake	"Kiss My Country Ass"	2010
Aldean, Jason	"Dirt Road Anthem"	2011
Atkins, Rodney	"Take a Back Road"	2011
Bryan, Luke	"Country Girl (Shake It for Me)"	2011
Campbell, Craig	"Fish"	2011
Owen, Jake	"Barefoot Blue Jean Night"	2011
Abbott, Josh	"I'll Sing About Mine"	2012
Aldean, Jason, with Luke Bryan, and Eric Church	"The Only Way I Know"	2012
Bentley, Dierks	"Tip It on Back"	2012
Florida Georgia Line	"Cruise"	2012
Gilbert, Brantley	"Bottoms Up"	2013
Florida Georgia Line, ft. Luke Bryan	"This Is How We Roll"	2014
Moore, Kip	"Dirt Road"	2014

Listening Guide

"Cruise" remix ft. Nelly (2013)

PERFORMERS:
Florida Georgia Line,
Nelly

SONGWRITERS: Brian
Kelley, Tyler Hubbard,
Joey Moi, Chase
Rice, and Jesse Rice
(produced by Joey
Moi, remix produced
by Jason Nevins)

ORIGINAL RELEASE:
Digital single, April
2013, from Big Loud
Mountain/Republic
Nashville

FORM:
Verse-chorus-bridge

STYLE: Bro-country

Party anthems and summer hits are a longstanding tradition in country music; almost every year has one light-hearted, party-themed track dominating the radio playlists. The upstart duo Florida Georgia Line's song "Cruise" owned that slot in 2013, setting records both for its total 7 million downloads and its 24 weeks at the top of the *Billboard* "Hot Country Songs" chart, as well as peaking at number four on the *Billboard* "Hot 100" chart. It saturated the soundscape for the better part of the year.

Brian Kelley and Tyler Hubbard, who together are Florida Georgia Line, represented a large swath of the country audience in the early 2010s. Raised on equal parts hip hop and country music, they settled into a public reputation as rebellious country singers who wanted to stake their claim to the genre while making music with the processes and outcomes of hip hop and dance music—detailed studio production, layering, and controlling the overall mix to generate different effects throughout the song. They teamed up with producer Joey Moi, who had made his mark in rock rather than country, and crafted their first single, "Cruise," with that process in mind. They released it in August 2012, and on the strength of its appeal, signed a record deal.

The original single relied on the same "stomp-stomp-clap" rhythmic reference to Queen's "We Will Rock You" that Shania Twain and Mutt Lange had deployed to rally a huge audience in the late 1990s. The most common description of the musical style of "Cruise" was dance-friendly pop with banjos, a nod to the audible combination of mainstream pop styles with a few instruments that tagged it as "country." The musical lineage of the song matched the interviews that Moi gave, in which he said his goal was to craft a hook and a chorus the way that metal band Def Leppard had done in the 1980s, an outlook in line with country pop and crossover country since the boom of the early 1990s.

Florida Georgia Line wanted to extend the reach of their song beyond the boundaries of country music. Nelly was signed to the same label at the time, and as has happened throughout the history of country music, labelmates were encouraged to collaborate on a project that would appeal to both sets of fans. With a new producer, Jason Nevins, working on the track, they created a remix that featured a rap bridge in the middle and a very different overall sound for the chorus. Note, for instance, that the stomp-stomp-clap drum pattern from the original was replaced with a much more complicated and syncopated hip-hop beat. The result continued in the long tradition of country records reappearing in pop remixes (see Shania Twain, Chapter 12, for instance, or dance remixes of Wynonna Judd's hits)—although this one had been nearly pop to begin with, and moved further along the spectrum of genres toward rap in its new version.

The remix appeared in April 2013, coinciding with a general boost in the presence of the white, Southern, working-class male protagonist singing about dirt roads and partying. "Cruise" was that brand of country in image and the performers' identity, but hip-hop in its sound and musical style. The formula worked, and Florida Georgia Line garnered a loyal fan base for their style of country.

TIME	FORM	LISTENING CUES	DISCUSSION
0:00	Introduction	Hook, "Baby you a song …"	The song starts with the hook line from the chorus, and then an introduction is constructed from a repeating segment that will become the post-chorus, which features the line "get your radio up," a version of calling for fans to put their hands in the air. The performers call out to each other over the introduction, and their vocal asides are audible. Notice that Nelly's name is heard, foregrounding the role of the rapper in the song.
0:19	Verse	"Yeah, when I first saw that bikini top …"	Tyler Hubbard sings the first verse, which establishes place ("South Georgia") and describes the woman by her clothing and "long, tan legs," as was common in bro-country lyrics. The bass drum is far more active than in the original version of this song, part of the shift to a hip-hop influenced style.
0:32	Chorus	"Baby you a song …"	The chorus drops in with a full texture on the first beat of this section. The catalog of images in the chorus (back roads, Chevy "with a lift kit," woman accessorizing the truck) become stock references.
0:58	Post-chorus	"I got my windows down …"	The short section after the chorus, known as a post-chorus, is a feature in electronic dance music that migrated into mainstream pop. It shows up in crossover country from around 2010 and later. Note the word-play of "down" / "up" and the shift in timbre to heavily processed Auto-tune vocal sounds.
1:04	Verse 2	"Yeah, she was sippin' on Southern and singing Marshall Tucker …"	More details of musical lineage and identity appear with the reference to Southern Rockers Marshall tucker band. The band texture thins out after to differentiate the verse from the previous thicker chorus. Brian Kelly sings harmony with Hubbard on this verse, evoking the long-standing tradition of male duets in country music.
1:18	Chorus	"Baby you a song …"	The texture intensifies again with the drop into the chorus. Note the shout-outs of "come on!" over the chorus, that were part of the remix.
1:43	Bridge / Rap	"My window down, my seat back, my music up and we ride …"	The electric guitar solo from the original is replaced with a rapped bridge from Nelly. The end of each line is double-tracked with extra voices audible on the last few words. At the end of this section, Nelly inserts the band's name, "Whippin' cross the border, *Florida* into *Georgia.*"

Continued

Listening Guide

"Cruise" remix ft. Nelly (2013) Continued

TIME	FORM	LISTENING CUES	DISCUSSION
2:12	Chorus	"'Cause baby you a song …"	This chorus is a "pull-back" chorus where the texture thins out to a bare minimum. Nelly alters the lyrics to add "every hood or town" to the images that are all "back roads" in the other choruses. The end of the chorus features scratching and a stutter (repeating "roll my, roll my …") to build up to the next chorus.
2:38	Chorus	"Baby you a song …"	This chorus drops in with the full band texture, which stands out in contrast to the previous section which did not have the full band.
2:38	Chorus	"Baby you a song …"	This chorus drops in with the full band texture, which stands out in contrast to the previous section which did not have the full band. The band drops out again at 2:54, for a moment of "break time" where the vocals stand out all alone.
3:04	Post-chorus	"I got my windows down…"	The post-chorus repeats, first with the full band, and then once with the drums and bass missing, ending with just an echo effect. The recording ends in the middle of the post-chorus, and the lingering echo suggests that the song might be continuing on forever, just heading on down the road out of earshot.

Jason Aldean, with his "Dirt Road Anthem," and Luke Bryan, with "Country Girl (Shake It For Me)," were two of the most successful purveyors of bro-country until Florida Georgia Line's "Cruise" (see Listening Guide) was released. Country artists expressed almost universal dislike for the term "bro-country," which was seldom used as anything but a pejorative description, arguing that it was an implicit criticism from people who were resistant to country music's natural evolution. Critics also pointed out a sameness in the lyrics across many of these songs, decrying what they heard as a copycat approach to songwriting. Indeed, a relatively small team of songwriters was producing a relatively large proportion of these songs, including the Peach Pickers, consisting of Dallas Davidson, Rhett Atkins, and Ben Hayslip. A small cadre of songwriters working behind the scenes to create a dominant theme in country music is also an age-old tradition in the genre. Yet here there was some irony that all the critical attention paid to bro-country ended up drawing attention to the songwriting community that had been existing largely outside the public eye.

The conversation around bro-country took an interesting turn in the summer of 2014 when Maddie & Tae, a new duo consisting of Madison Marlow and Taylor Dye, released "Girl in a Country Song," which they co-wrote with Aaron Scherz. Its lyrics take excerpts from other songs, mostly in the bro-country vein, that describe women, and rebut them. Florida Georgia Line's "Get Your Shine On," includes the lyric "Slide that little sugar shaker over here"; Maddie & Tae answer it with "There ain't no sugar for you in this shaker of mine." Their music video presents a comic gender-reversal: men dressed up in stereotypical female costumes, including cut-offs and bikinis, copying iconic sexy scenes from videos and films, such as washing a car.

Fans loved the entry of women's voices into the bro-country conversation, and critics saw parallels with country's tradition of answer songs (see Chapter 4), the feminist voice of the 1970s (see Chapter 8) and even the gender-role reversal songs from the 1990s (see Chapter 12). Maddie & Tae, on the other hand, tread lightly on the subject in interviews, keeping their responses extremely positive, avoiding any historical comparisons, and talking about how much they loved the songs and music at which "Girl in a Country Song" poked fun. Their attitude disappointed some fans who were looking for outspoken feminism, but it protected the interests of their fledgling career; the landscape of country music meant that the duo needed support from the same artists they were calling out in their song. The next summer, for instance, they opened on tour for Dierks Bentley and Kip Moore.

Promises Unfulfilled

The year 2012 held a lot of promise for women in country music. The big three, Taylor Swift, Miranda Lambert, and Carrie Underwood, were at the top of their game, and Swift was still releasing country-genre singles from her album *Speak Now*. Underwood's *Blown Away* had taken the scene by storm (including her tornado-themed song), and Lambert (see Artist Profile) was well on her way to selling a million copies of *Four the Record*, which would be the last album she released to go platinum for several years. Women fronting bands was also big news. The Band Perry, Lady Antebellum, and Gloriana were all examples. Little Big Town was getting increasing amounts of attention, which would culminate in the media storm around their sensual lyrics in "Girl Crush" a few years later (see Listening Guide). And there was a stable of newer female artists who were getting positive media attention (see essay on Tomato-gate).

Kacey Musgraves added her voice to the scene in 2012 with "Merry Go 'Round," a stunning about-face in a genre that was known for waxing nostalgic for small-town America. Musgraves gave candid interviews about her rebellious lyrics, punctuated by the occasional swear word; she wrote her own songs; and she and thwarted conventions of both lyric-writing and performance styles. She was heralded as the harbinger of change, as one more sign that mainstream country music was opening up to artists and music that had formerly been relegated to the margins and alternative scenes. Musgraves's song recounted the socio-economic limitations and personal frustrations of small-town America, where life goes 'round and 'round. She followed that up with songs that endorsed loving whomever one wants to love, smoking marijuana, and poking fun at Southern beauty pageants. She was writing in a circle of songwriters that included Shane McAnally and Brandy Clark, voices whose output stood in stark contrast to the bro-country being produced by other songwriters. Musgraves represented a possible sea change in country music toward more liberal viewpoints, more female-centric lyrics, and more singer-songwriter styled material.

Listening Guide

"Girl Crush" (2014)

PERFORMER: Little Big Town

SONGWRITERS: Lori McKenna, Hillary Lindsay, and Liz Rose

ORIGINAL RELEASE: digital single, December 2014, from Capitol Nashville

FORM: Verse-chorus

STYLE: Contemporary country

Country music loves a good media controversy. When "Girl Crush" was first released on radio, the media reported that country fans were objecting to what they thought was a song about a lesbian affair. News outlets including the *Washington Post* reported that program directors would be pulling it from airplay. Later reports revealed that the controversy was almost entirely fabricated and that fans were not responding negatively to the song. This flare-up had revealed yet again how socially conservative the country fan base was reported to be (purportedly riled up over a lyric that referred to a woman tasting another woman's lips) and subsequently affirming how much acceptance there was within the fan base for an artistic project of the caliber of this song.

Like much of what was happening in country music at this time, "Girl Crush" linked into a longstanding tradition in classic country music while at the same time presenting itself as in a pop form that appeared to be lacking any country signifiers at all. In terms of tradition, country is full of songs written from the perspective of a woman jealous of another woman who is with the man she desires. The best known of these is Dolly Parton's "Jolene," in which the lyrics paint a sensual portrait of the "other woman's" appearance, much like the lyrics in "Girl Crush." Classic country is full of these types of songs: Tammy Wynette's "Run, Woman, Run" and "Woman to Woman," Reba McEntire and Linda Davis's "Does He Love You," Patsy Cline's "She's Got You" and "You Took Him off My Hands," and the close match of Terri Clark's "If I Were You," just to name a few.

Yet even while tapping into that tradition, "Girl Crush" appeared with almost no visual or audible links to country as a genre. The video was shot in black and white, the band presenting a retro glamour; the lyrics avoid any genre-specific references to people, places, music, things, or attitudes. And when the songwriters played the song and talked about it at various writer's showcases, they said nothing to pigeon-hole it in country music. This trend toward country songs that passed in all respects as pop coexisted with the bro-country exaggeration of stereotyped class and culture markers that were distinctly and unapologetically "country."

The song's form contributes to its effect: The haunting ballad, sung in a triple meter, sounds retro in comparison to what else was happening in country music at the time. The performance clearly sets off a "chorus" within a verse-chorus form, but there are hybrid aspects to the form; the two-part verses followed by the chorus sounds a bit like a modified, hybrid AABA form (see Appendix A), where the final BA is the chorus. More significant is the wrap-around form at the end of the song: The last thing we hear is the first verse starting over, and the song ending in the middle of that verse. As the song seems to begin again, the form contributes to the sense that the singer is trapped in an endless, repeating loop of her obsession, jealousy, and heartbreak.

The song won a series of major awards, including a Grammy for "Best Country Song" and the CMA award for "Song of the Year." Critics pointed out that the song stood out from the typical mix of radio fare, in particular in contrast to descriptions of the other trends of the time. It helped solidify Little Big Town's reputation for stellar vocal harmony, and it reminds its audiences that today's country music has a complicated relationship with its own past.

TIME	FORM	LISTENING CUES	DISCUSSION
0:00	Introduction	(guitar)	This intro is very sparse, a combination of just a few arpeggiated chords on an electric bass guitar with echo added to the sound that mixes the effect of singer-songwriter simplicity and modern studio production.
0:08	Verse 1	"I've got a girl crush …"	Karen Fairchild starts singing expressively, almost in a singer-songwriter style.
0:25	Verse 1 continues	"I got it real bad …"	The melody for this section is the same as the beginning of the first verse, suggesting a retro form to the song.
0:41	Chorus	"I wanna taste her lips …"	Four voices enter in harmony here, along with more instrumental sounds, filling out the texture.
1:14	Chorus continues	"I got a girl crush, I got a girl crush …"	After the title line of the song, the singer takes along pause, leaving the idea hanging in the air.
1:31	Verse 2	"I don't get no sleep …"	The full band, including drums comes in at this point.
1:48	Verse 2 continues	"The way that she's whisperin' …"	Synthesized sounds are layered behind the vocals.
2:04	Chorus	"I wanna taste her lips …"	This section returns to familiar lyrics from earlier in the song, with the support of the vocal harmony. The lyrics draw the focus of the audience into intimate details: lips, long hair, and fingers representing the "other woman."
2:37	Chorus continues	"I got a girl crush."	This time, the end of the chorus only presents the title line one time instead of two; the extra musical space is occupied by an electric guitar solo.
2:46	Instrumental interlude	Electric guitar	This song has comparatively few sections; its long verses and the introspective tempo and mood result in little space for instrumental solos. Here the guitar fills the space that earlier in the song was the end of the chorus.
2:54	Verse 1 (incomplete)	"I've got a girl crush …"	The first verse repeats, while most of the band drops out, leaving only a few sustained notes from a synthesizer behind the vocals. The song ends after just the first half of the verse, creating a wrap-around form that suggests the song (and the singer's obsession) repeats in an infinite loop.

In spite of the critical embrace of individual songwriters in this scene—also including Angaleena Presley and Ashley Monroe—and in spite of the momentum that seemed to gather at various moments, country proved highly resistant to long-term change, and the potential these artists offered was never fully realized.

Along similar lines, the Dixie Chicks—one of the most celebrated female groups in all of country music—appeared to be active once again. The three women had been almost entirely underground in the American popular music world since 2006, working on separate individual projects and keeping a low public profile. But in 2013 they scheduled a tour in Canada. European performances followed, and in 2016, the trio undertook an American leg of their World Tour. There was no new album,

ARTIST PROFILE

Miranda Lambert (b. 1983)

Miranda Lambert has forged a career in country music that has many facets. She has dominated mainstream commercial country music for the past decade. Yet she has also been heralded as an outsider to Nashville, with roots in the Texas country scene and a rebellious streak in her music that thwarts country's conventions. She is both songwriter and entertainer. Her personal life has been subjected to intense public scrutiny, allowing fans to draw connections between her music and her biography that lend her music even more substantive weight.

Raised in Lindale, Texas, Lambert grew up in a family that enjoyed a mostly middle-class existence with some periods of economic hardship. After high school, she started building a music career by performing at local venues and opening shows for more established artists. In 2003, she auditioned for *Nashville Star*, a televised singing competition in the style of *American Idol* but focused exclusively on country music. Lambert placed third on the show, which earned her both national name recognition and the attention of Sony Records, who offered her a deal.

Lambert infused her music with notable elements from rock, including an edgy public attitude and songs accompanied by distorted electric guitars and aggressive drums, such as "Gunpowder and Lead" and "Kerosene," which appeared on her first album in 2007. Texas country music has a long tradition of fostering a rock-country hybrid, and Lambert amplified it, admitting to an interviewer, "I guess I've kind of put myself in this niche of 'rocker chick.'" The combination of her image and songwriting helped her stand out and earn a reputation as a "new alternative" in mainstream country music against a foil of pop-influenced country. Her first number one song, "The House That Built Me," was a first-person reflection on childhood, regrets, and reminiscence that seemed to give an intimate peek inside her own life and experiences (although in this rare instance, she was singing a song she had not written). She also co-founded a female trio, the Pistol Annies, with songwriters Ashley Monroe and Angaleena Presley, bringing even more attention to her profile as a songwriter and musician's musician.

In 2011, Lambert married fellow country star Blake Shelton (see Artist Profile), joining the ranks of country music couples such as George Jones and Tammy Wynette, and Tim McGraw and Faith Hill, whose biographies are and the tour centered on mid-sized venues, all casting the concerts in the light of singer-songwriter indie artists. But it was still a welcome signal to fans that they had rejoined the scene. The culmination of their re-entry was a performance at the 2016 CMA Awards show but, again, that marked an end of their run and another retreat from the spotlight.

During the early years of the 2010s, much hope had also been placed in the independent journalism that arose after the decimation of traditional print publications. Talented writers were freelancing, ambitious entrepreneurs built websites, and a new brand of criticism emerged, much of it dedicated to championing the musical underdogs with indie and alterative leanings. Two of the most highly

woven into the fabric of the genre. The pair split just four years later, though, in a very public divorce. Lambert's subsequent album, *The Weight of These Wings*, a two-album set on which she co-wrote twenty songs, was received by fans as her private story of heartbreak told through song. The widely acclaimed album increased her already significant status as a singer-songwriter and artist who was somehow different from the country-pop stars and possessed more of that nebulous quality of authenticity. She punctuated that reputation by performing a solo acoustic version of "Tin Man" at the Academy of Country Music Awards in 2017 (see Listening Guide). On that show, where performers typically pull out all the stops with special effects and lavish productions, her plaintive version accompanied only by her own guitar was heralded by fans and critics alike as bold, raw, deeply personal, and a display of unparalleled talent.

Figure 15-2 Miranda Lambert performing in 2007, the same year she appeared on the cover of *No Depression*.

Lambert was crowned Female Vocalist of the Year for six years in a row, from 2010 to 2015, by the Country Music Association, and an even more impressive record-setting eight years, from 2010 to 2017, from the Academy of Country Music. This level of dominance over the scene certainly underscores her important presence and musical output. But it also subtly highlights a stagnation in commercial country music, which is amplified for female singers given how few get any attention at all. Even with Lambert's obvious star status, critics have noted that her songs get relatively little airplay. Nonetheless, her career has balanced the alternative, singer-songwriter street cred among fans with an impressive reign over the commercial country scene, illustrating the complex musical identity of country music in the past decade.

Listening Guide

"Tin Man" (2017)

PERFORMER:
Miranda Lambert

SONGWRITERS:
Miranda Lambert,
Jack Ingram, and Jon
Randall

ORIGINAL RELEASE:
digital single, April
2017, from RCA
Nashville

FORM: Strophic (all
verses)

STYLE: Country with
singer-songwriter
characteristics

The second disc of Miranda Lambert's two-disc album *The Weight of These Wings* is titled "The Heart," a collection of twelve songs co-written by Lambert, all working through her emotional recovery process after she split from husband Blake Shelton. Both in Lambert's interviews and in critics' discussions, the album earned a reputation as a work of art imbued with personal meaning, much more so than her previous releases had been.

"Tin Man" opens the "Heart" half of the project. It is framed as a conversation between the heartbroken Lambert and the heartless Tin Man from the classic film *The Wizard of Oz* and weaves wordplay throughout the song. Folktales, films, and legends are common source material in country songwriting (Garth Brooks's "It's Midnight Cinderella" is just one such example).

Lambert sang an entirely acoustic version of the song at the Academy of Country Music awards in April 2017, then released it as the third single from her album the subsequent day. The song's pathos and mid-tempo acoustic-ballad style was unquestionably at odds with country radio playlists that were ramping up for summer; the song made a respectable showing on the *Billboard* airplay chart (#31), but became fodder for conversations about how few women were getting commercial attention and how limited the musical scope of commercially successful country was. Lambert followed up the single with an acoustic-version music video. Shot in black and white, it simply shows Lambert and her guitar sitting in a shower, and the stark minimalism of both the visual and audio performance stand out.

The song, co-written by two long-time songwriters who, like Lambert, are from Texas, matches the minimalism in its form and structure. The song is strophic in form, consisting of three verses that each begin with the refrain, "Hey there, Mr. Tin Man," and end with an expressive, mournful melody that Lambert sings without text, just vocalizing on "ooo." Country songs without a chorus are exceptionally rare in 2017, lending a retro and anti-commercial accent to the song simply through its form. The song also lacks the usual changes in dynamics and texture that are featured throughout most contemporary country songs—instead, "Tin Man" remains very steady and unchanging in its musical substance throughout, with minimal accompaniment from the band. And Lambert's acoustic performance, both at the ACMs and in the music video, pull the listener's attention both to the song's narrative and to her voice, fully exposed without the trappings of a band wrapped around it. That acoustic approach zeroes in on the song's story; other musicians used the same strategy to similarly establish themselves as singer-songwriters, including the Dixie Chicks on their acoustic-framed album *Home* (2002), and much of what was recorded during the Outlaw movement.. Most significantly, "Tin Man" serves as an essential counterbalance to the crossover-oriented country-pop and hip-hop-infused, highly produced country tracks on country radio. That check-and-balance system, where alternatives to country-pop find occasional acceptance, is one of the most important ways that country music maintains its distinctiveness as a genre.

TIME	FORM	LISTENING CUES	DISCUSSION
0:00	Introduction	Atmospheric sounds, plus acoustic guitar	The guitar suggests the minimalist, acoustic nature of this recording, while the atmospheric sounds of the synthesizer mix that with a modern, crossover-country style.
0:18	Verse 1	"Hey there, Mr. Tin Man …"	The song opens as a conversation between the singer and the character from *The Wizard of Oz* who wanted to have a heart. Each vocal phrase is followed by a long pause, which gives the song the character of an emotionally fraught and introspective conversation.
0:42	Verse 1 (continued)	"Every time you're feeling empty …"	The word-play on "empty"—the tin man's chest, and the emotional state of the singer—is subtle but characteristic of the writing throughout this song.
1:07	Refrain	"Ooo …"	The refrain that concludes each verse is short here – only one iteration of the melody.
1:19	Verse 1	"Hey there, Mr. Tin Man …"	The "road" in the song is both the famed yellow brick road and the metaphoric journey of the singer. The guitar accompaniment features occasional short solos or licks that act as "responses" to the singer's phrases.
1:43	Verse 2 (continued)	"You ain't missing nothing …"	The singer calls the Tin Man darling, revealing her empathy. At the end of this section, the atmospheric accompaniment swells, creating a very subtle climax for the song and punctuating the line "You don't want a heart."
2:08	Refrain	"Ooo …"	Here the refrain is twice as long as the first time—the melody heard twice. This expansion stretches out in a long-range pattern the song as it unfolds.
2:32	Verse 3	"Hey there, Mr. Tin Man …"	The implied conversation ("glad we talked this out") fits in the long pauses between each vocal phrase.
2:56	Verse 3 (continued)	"By the way there, Mr. Tin Man …"	The denouement of the song is saved for the last line, where the singer offers to trade her (broken and scarred) heart for what she really wants: his armor. This final line is a fitting and emotionally powerful cadence for the song.
3:20	Refrain	"Ooo …"	The refrain cycles through four phrases, once again doubling the length of the previous refrain, and ending with a faint note from Lambert and a single guitar chord.

regarded were The 9513.com and Engine 145, both of which housed a huge quantity of reviews and op-eds. But these independent journalism sites lacked long-term sustainable business models and shuttered their websites, The9513 in 2011 and Engine 145 in 2013, with no archives left behind as a record of their contents. That same year, journalist Chet Flippo, whose *Nashville Skyline* column had been a stalwart presence in country journalism, passed away, leaving another hole in the coverage of country music. In their wake, others have emerged, notably SavingCountryMusic.com, with a similar indie critic vibe. *No Depression* remained a thriving website and announced a return to print format in 2015. And closely related genres and musical scenes were ensconced in their own publications—*Bluegrass Today* emerged in 2011, for instance. But the enthusiasm around indie journalism had unquestionably cooled off.

Crossover and Hip-Hop-ification

In the 2010s, country music featured an even greater number of songs, styles, and artists moving fluidly between the genres of country and pop, and country and hip-hop, than ever before. In the simplest cases, singers left behind country and moved into careers in other genres. In the more complicated instances, musicians changed the formula by which they claimed country music as their home base, singing songs that were devoid of traditional country references but still claiming the overall identity. But the most unexpected instances of genre-crossing occurred when non-country singers showed up as duet partners with country singers. Those combined performances highlight the cultural hierarchy in which country remains "othered," the outsider to mainstream culture.

Taylor Swift bid farewell to country music between her albums *Red* (2012), which still showed some ties to the genre, and *1989* (2014), which unapologetically moved on. For fans who came to know her music after 2012, when her celebrity persona dwarfed her music, it might be hard to imagine she was ever really part of country music, so complete was the exodus.

But Swift was the exception; most other country singers who drifted toward pop careers kept one foot in each camp. Carrie Underwood, for instance, had kept a loyal audience that extended well beyond country music ever since her days on *American Idol*. Her albums *Blown Away* (2012) and *Storyteller* (2015) fed those fans a hefty dose of pop-influenced material, and the music videos and accompanying images had no visible country signifiers. The music video for "Something in the Water," for instance, used classically trained dancers performing a modern dance number.

Yet Underwood maintained a core set of themes and narratives in her music that tethered her to country music. "Church Bells" (2015) is a prime examples, a tale of a poor girl who marries a rich man, is the victim of domestic violence, and then kills him. "Church Bells" does not have to reach that far back for its forerunners; it sounds like an echo of "Fancy," first a hit for Bobbie Gentry in 1969 and then remade into a signature song by Reba McEntire in 1991. Tales of women killing abusive partners include Miranda Lambert's "Gunpowder and Lead" (2007) and, most famously, the Dixie Chicks' "Goodbye Earl" (1999). Underwood's recording also connects to past themes in her own music, particularly through the use of church imagery, choirs, bells, and religious faith ("Jesus Take the Wheel"). There are many similarities between "Just a Dream" and "Church Bells"— a white wedding dress turning into a black mourning dress; the church choir singing in the background. In other words, in spite of all her pop sensibilities and glamorous presentation, Underwood maintains strong ties in her music both to her own past and to country music history.

The most unexpected crossover artist of this time period was Sam Hunt (b. 1984) from Georgia. Like many country singers before him, his entry into the genre was as a songwriter, writing hits for Keith Urban and other established stars. When his first single, "Leave the Night On," came out in 2014, it caught the ear of fans with an infusion of smooth R&B. The track's producer Zach Crowell had a successful history of producing everything from rap to country-pop, and on Sam Hunt's records, he shaped each recording like a hip-hop track: catchy beats; the expected changes in the density of the sound through the pre-chorus; and dropping the beat with the chorus—a typical feature of contemporary pop music where the rhythm section is mostly absent from the sound for a short stretch and then comes back in strongly at a significant moment in the song. Their approach worked: "Body like a Back Road" (2017) stayed at the top of the *Billboard* "Hot Country Songs" chart for a record-breaking 34 weeks—well over half a year.

Hunt's music found an enthusiastic reception from fans, especially those for whom the more traditional core of country music was too, well, "country." Hunt offered no cowboy hats or boots, no cows in his music videos (which Blake Shelton had done), and no overt references to past country songs, singers, or history. Critics described his songs as "wordy" and his delivery technique as "rapping." On stage, his wardrobe and demeanor are essentially indistinguishable from hip hop stars. His music is basically country music for people who like the idea of country music without all the aspects that made it so very different from mainstream pop. While Hunt has been either ignored or criticized by country traditionalists, his success is evidence of the large fan base who like their country music to be the experience of R&B-styled pop but wrapped in a package that claims a country identity.

A parade of pop and rap stars appeared on country stages at the same time that Sam Hunt dominated the airwaves. Duets between artists from seemingly disparate genres had long been a novelty feature in country music.

Figure 15-3 Alison Krauss and Robert Plant.
Source: Kristoffer Tripplaar/Alamy Stock Photo.

Led Zeppelin's Robert Plant and bluegrass star Alison Krauss's duet album *Raising Sand* (2007), for instance, was critically acclaimed as a major artistic undertaking. But the newer occurrences were slightly different, both in frequency and in the way fans treated them. For the most part, these appearances highlighted that country fans were listening to music that sounded like pop, rock, and hip-hop, but still identified as country music fans. In most cases, the pop, hip-hop, and rap artists involved said that they are simply fans of the country artists with whom they are collaborating and have some shared connection—the place where they grew up or small town identity, for instance.

BANJO IN HEAVY METAL

The acoustic instruments and sounds associated with folk traditions, string bands, and even bluegrass show up with surprising frequency in styles of music that fans usually think of as the polar opposite. For instance, many listeners think of Led Zeppelin as a blues-based hard rock band that features Robert Plant's swagger and near-screaming vocals. As rock scholar John Covach points out, it has frustrated both guitarist Jimmy Page and lead singer Robert Plant "over the years that listeners and critics seem to focus on the heavier elements . . . forgetting how much of their total output is acoustically based." From "Gallows Pole" to "The Ballad of Evermore," their music is full of folk references to traditional Irish musics (roots that bluegrass clearly shares) and features banjo, mandolin, and even dulcimer. Led Zeppelin is far from the only hard rock band to incorporate such elements. And these sorts of musical intersections mean that seemingly anomalous combinations, such as Dolly Parton doing a bluegrass version of "Stairway to Heaven," or Robert Plant and Alison Krauss making an album together, often have rich backstories.

Some of these appearances lean toward pure novelty: Taylor Swift rapped "Thug Story" with T-Pain as an opening video for the 2009 CMT Music Awards show. The rap was a parody of Swift's hit "Love Story" and featured plenty of self-deprecating comedy from Swift. The resulting collaboration was never released as a single and was seen as a quirky bit of humor by most fans of each genre.

The CMT Music Awards were again the site of a country-rap collaboration in 2011, although this one was entirely different in its reception by fans. Jason Aldean was scheduled to perform, and the organizers of the show approached him about adding a rap collaborator. Aldean reportedly told CMT it would depend on who the rap artist was, as he was only willing to do it if the artist was someone "more mainstream." CMT proposed rapper Ludacris, and Aldean agreed. The two artists share a common home town, Atlanta, Georgia, and both represent a particularly southern identity within their genres. Aldean's song "Dirt Road Anthem," written by Brantley Gilbert and Colt Ford, features a spoken-word rap verse that Aldean delivers in a very rhythmically straight style, so the song already had a reputation within country music for borrowing rap style. For the CMT show, Ludacris wrote his own rap verse for "Dirt Road Anthem" that name-checked country singer Kenny Rogers and fit the overall narrative of the song. Ludacris and Aldean did not know each other prior to the performance, but their duet remix appeared for sale on iTunes immediately after the CMT appearance. On May 18, 2012, Ludacris showed up as a surprise guest at Aldean's Atlanta concert. The crowd went wild, and the two singers reprised that act at several of Aldean's later concerts.

A remix of a song is a new version that retains the vocal performance and basic musical arrangement but adds a new rhythmic layer under the vocals, often with different instrumentation and a different rhythmic groove. The producer who creates the remix is viewed today as part of the artistic team, and songs are often marketed with the producer's name alongside the singer's name. Remixes in country often include a duet artist, and the song's arrangement is sometimes altered to allow for an additional verse, bridge, or interpolation by the duet artist. Remixes also sometimes alter the form of the song with breaks, repetitions of short segments, and other changes that imitate the way that DJs manipulate records in hip-hop and dance scenes.

Rapper Nelly's collaboration with Florida Georgia Line on the remix of "Cruise" followed a similar track (see Listening Guide). Florida Georgia Line had already incorporated a fair amount of hip hop and hip-hop culture into their music, even in such small ways as the spelling of their first EP, *It'z Just What We Do.* "Cruise" was already highly popular when their record label engineered the collaboration for a remix with Nelly, who had dabbled in country collaborations with Tim McGraw in 2004. In the video for the "Cruise" remix, the St. Louis–born rapper is seen phoning Florida Georgia Line's Kelley and Hubbard. Nelly mentions their existing video for the song "Cruise"—"That thing' the deal . . ." he says, "I think we can turn it up, though. What'cha think?" What is perhaps most interesting in this introductory scene is that the rap-infused remix is "turned up," or in other words, higher on some cultural scale than the country-only version.

In 2013, Brad Paisley released "Accidental Racist" with LL Cool J (b, 1968), a rapper best known for his 1990s work. Unlike the guest appearances in the form of re-mixes, this track was a duet from the outset, with Paisley and LL credited as co-writers. And unlike the other two collaborations discussed here, this one met with harsh criticism and negative reviews. Some critics simply said it was a poorly executed song; others blasted its shallow treatment of racism, with lyrics from excuses for wearing a confederate flag to forgetting about iron chains (of slavery). Two other factors are important in understanding the song's chilly reception. One is that LL Cool J did not have the same commercial presence or young fan base. His most successful releases had been twenty years in the past, and he had not had a song on the charts in half a decade. The other is that Paisley had held the role of country traditionalist in the current scene, part of the roots revival of the early 2000s and steering clear of the sorts of crossover and genre-mixing that Aldean and Florida Georgia Line were doing. Thus, Paisley's fan base was not likely to include fans of LL Cool J to begin with, and there was no ready enthusiasm for their collaboration.

> ### DODGING POLITICS
>
> In 2016, Donald J. Trump was elected president of the United States. His campaign was highly divisive, and he lost the popular vote. In the wake of these seismic events, the identity of the "Trump voter" became entangled with the idea of the "country fan" in the popular imagination. Journalists called up country music writers, critics, and scholars, seeking insight into the mind of the Trump voter.
>
> The politics of country fans, unsurprisingly, are not so monolithic or simple. Although country music has always expressed unfettered opinions on various subjects of social justice, labor rights, and community support, it also has a long tradition of dodging partisan politics of this sort, a tradition that the genre mostly upheld. The most telling insight from the aftermath of the 2016 presidential election was merely a reminder that the country music audience is a complicated, multifaceted, heterogeneous group in many respects, obviously less so in terms of race, but in terms of politics and gender theories.

Pop singers have also followed suit, appearing as guests on country awards shows. Two recent occurrences garnered a lot of attention. The first was Chris Stapleton's eight-minute segment on the 2015 CMA Awards, which featured Justin Timberlake (see Listen Side by Side). The second was Florida Georgia Line's appearance on the Academy of Country Music's 2017 award show with the Backstreet Boys, one of the most acclaimed boy-band pop acts of the 1990s and early 2000s. When Backstreet's Nick Carter and the rest of the group appeared in the middle of "God, Your Mama, and Me," the audience cheered, and when the combined groups broke into the Backstreet Boys' hit "Everybody (Backstreet's Back)" from 1998, country stars were seen in the awards show audience singing and dancing along.

Clearly, the awards shows benefit from guest appearances by pop and hip-hop stars. They draw attention to the shows through the publicity leading up to the appearances and draw in curious audiences who otherwise would not watch. The pop stars get a platform to present their own music or stir up interest in their current projects. And the country stars get a similar boost of publicity. The usual criticism from country fans is that the guest appearances dilute the authenticity and tradition of country music,

Figure 15-4 Chris Stapleton.

Source: Daniel Coston.

threatening its otherness. But this criticism is answered with the recurring refrains that country music is constantly changing, that country music has always been an interactive part of popular music in general, and that musical collaborations between any two talented singers should be honored for their artistic merit.

The cultural hierarchy that positions contemporary commercial country music as a subset subsumed within the larger scene of popular music is also on display in these collaborations. It is hard to imagine that a country singer who made a pop-up surprise appearance at a rap concert would receive the same ovation that Ludacris did at Jason Aldean's concert; some country fans like pop, rock, and/ or hip-hop, but the reverse is not necessarily true. And country singers regularly tap into that relationship in their own performances. At a recent country concert in Charlotte, North Carolina, nearly 20,000 country fans came out to sing along with Dustin Lynch and Brad Paisley. Yet when Lynch wanted to get the crowd pumped up during his performance, he launched into a series of 1980s hard rock covers, including AC/DC's "Back in Black" and Def Leppard's "Pour Some Sugar On Me." The fans erupted, screaming and cheering and singing along. The same phenomenon, where country music sits in a subsidiary position to popular music in general, is invoked every time a country singer name-checks a rock band in their lyrics. In 2016, Thomas Rhett described his ideal girl as one who looked as though she was in a "Guns 'n' Roses video," for instance. As with most things in country music, this type of reference has been present for a long time; Hank Williams Jr. sang about liking Van Halen in 1988, for instance. But it is more prevalent than it was in the past, a marker of the shifting relationship between country and mainstream pop/rock music.

Dark Horse Surprises

The country audience was caught off guard by the unanticipated rise of two artists in recent years. The first was Chris Stapleton (b. 1978), with his debut solo album *Traveller* (2015). Stapleton had worked for some time in the country music industry as a songwriter and as a singer with the bluegrass band SteelDrivers, where his vocals were decidedly not in the high lonesome tradition. SteelDrivers found an audience in the Americana scene that liked its bluegrass mixed with blues. His solo album became a critics' favorite, and he was seen as a musician's musician, the sort of artist who deserved acclaim but was hidden behind the mass of bro-country pop-influenced stars. Stapleton's personal style—which channeled southern rock and served as a foil to the clean-shaven, pretty-boy appearances of so many country stars of the day—only enhanced his reputation as someone working outside the trends and fads. *Traveller* and Stapleton swept the awards shows, claiming both album of the year and male vocalist of the year at the ACMs and CMAs, and the Grammy for best country album. The general country audience had not caught up with the critics, and searches for "Who is Chris Stapleton" trended among Google searches. Stapleton continued a run of number-one hits on country radio, and *Traveller* was tagged as a symbolic change of direction for the genre.

Figure 15-5 Sturgill Simpson.

Source: Daniel Coston.

The second surprise was Sturgill Simpson (b. 1978), a singer from Kentucky who moved to Nashville in 2012 and released a couple of independent albums while building a reputation among fans of Americana and the remnants of the alt-country scene that thrived in small-venues. Simpson was one of several artists such as Corey Smith, Jason Isbell, and the critics' favorite Margo Price, who held loose ties to mainstream country but functioned mostly independently. What made Simpson different was that he got a foot in the door with the mainstream country audience.

Simpson's second album, *Metamodern Sounds in Country Music* (2014), caught the ear of several music critics while also evoking Ray Charles's famous *Modern Sounds in Country and Western Music* (1962; see Chapter 6). From that success, Simpson got a deal with major label Atlantic Records, the historical home of R&B and soul music who also kept a small roster of country singers. With Atlantic's budget and prestige backing him, Simpson recorded *A Sailor's Guide to Earth* (2016). The album was a self-consciously artistic project, with lyrics that are more abstract than found in mainstream country music. Simpson brought in the Dap-Kings, a New York–based funk and soul band, to play on the album, evoking references to Lyle Lovett's creative projects in the 1990s that combined big band sounds with country music.

Sturgill Simpson seemed poised to step into the mainstream country limelight. However, in April 2016, Simpson posted a rant online against the Academy of Country Music's "Merle Haggard Spirit Award," echoing the age-old complaint that contemporary country music was not true to its past and was ignoring "real country music." Haggard had passed away earlier that month, and his death was heralded as a great loss by the entire country fan base. Simpson's rant was, in part, an outcry against country radio and the core establishment for ignoring Simpson's own music. Sturgill wrote that the ACM should drop all the "formulaic cannon fodder bullshit they've been pumping down rural America's throat for the last 30 years along with all the high school pageantry, meat parade award show bullshit and start dedicating their programs to more actual Country Music."

This colorful tirade rallied musicians and fans alike whose tastes sat outside the mainstream. It also invoked the ire of the mainstream industry, which not only had been expanding its musical palette with the likes of Chris Stapleton but also had heard this cycle of complaints before and recognized them as their own tradition—Johnny Cash's extended middle finger in a *Billboard* ad in 1998 or Robbie Fulks's recording "Fuck This Town" (1997), for example. Simpson took home the Grammy for Best Country Album, got a lot of publicity, and sold a lot of records in the wake of his tirade, but he did not collect any nominations from either the ACM or CMA. Instead, he helped rebuild the boundary line between Americana's country scene and the mainstream country scene.

The trends in country music—both in the mainstream, radio-friendly arenas and in the alternative and Americana arenas—pointed in the same general direction: an incorporation of R&B and hip-hop styles into country. This concept is as old as country itself, from Jimmie Rodgers's duets with an African-American jug band to Elvis Presley's musical stylings that helped launch rockabilly, as well as much of Barbara Mandrell's output (see Chapter 10). This new iteration showed up in Sam Hunt's smooth styles, in Chris Stapleton's soul-tinged covers, in Sturgill Simpson's Dap Kings' accompaniments, and in every hip-hop/country collaboration. But such acceptance of hybrid and borrowed styles reached a breaking point in 2016 when Beyoncé performance at the CMA Awards.

Beyoncé (b. 1981) is an R&B and urban contemporary star who has been lauded as the highest paid female entertainer; her star power and celebrity status outstrips any figure in country music. She appeared at the 2016 CMA Awards on stage in a special duet performance. Her collaborators were the Dixie Chicks, who had only recently reacquired a tenuous connection to country music. The performance was built around Beyoncé's song "Daddy Lessons," a track from her 2016 album *Lemonade*, that was one of the most successful and talked-about releases of 2016. From the moment of its release, fans and critics alike touted the apparent resonance that "Daddy Lessons" had with country music: the song's story is about a daddy teaching his little girl how to shoot and defend herself, he said, when "men like me come around." With the setting of the story explicitly Texas, with an acoustic guitar laying down a shuffle groove, the country references were audible even amongst the New Orleans–style horns and roots vibe of the whole song. But was it "country"?

Beyoncé's public activism and platform that aligned with the Black Lives Matter movement added both a racial and political angle to this discussion, further amplified by the positive reviews for *Lemonade*. The Dixie Chicks added an acoustic cover of the song to their tour that summer. Some country fans loved it; most ignored it or were completely unaware of it, as the song got no formal acknowledgment through media outlets that funnel country music to its fans. Some of Beyoncé's fans applauded the connection; others were equally oblivious to the discussion.

For their 50th anniversary awards show, the CMAs brought Beyoncé and the formerly exiled Dixie Chicks on stage together, backed by a huge horn section, dressed in stunning black and white outfits (Beyoncé wearing a white gown that evoking the sorts of ornately beaded, mutton-sleeve dresses that Loretta Lynn made famous; the Dixie Chicks all in black). They rocked through a duet version of "Daddy Lessons" and slid seamlessly into a cover of the Dixie Chicks' "Long Time Gone" (see Chapter 14). The audience was on its feet, heralding what appeared to be a triumphant performance. After the performance, however, Twitter

Figure 15-6 Beyoncé and the Dixie Chicks performing at the 50th Anniversary CMAs.

Source: Image Group LA/Contributor.

and on-line commentary took an ugly but not unexpected turn. Country fans who are deeply invested in their music's distinctiveness from pop complained about the corruption of country music's identity through the incorporation of an R&B/pop star of that caliber, along with hateful, racist comments. Adding fuel to the fire, media reported that the CMAs had stripped references to Beyoncé and the performance from their social media and web presence, reports that the CMA later denied and said were misunderstandings when a single promotional video had been taken down for licensing reasons.

The performance served as a litmus test for country music's genre boundaries in 2016: would the mainstream country fan base accept Beyoncé's performance as "country?" The response indicated that the answer was a resounding "no": even fans who liked the performance did not talk about it as "country," per se. The politics of genre and investment in the genre's otherness, specifically defined as distinct from mainstream pop, combined with the comments that revealed yet again the level of racially motivated hate found in some segments of the fan base, showed just how far country could—or could not—stretch in its musical inclusivity.

Through the Lenses

Nearly a century after the first country recordings were made, the lenses through which we view the music's history and present day forms help explain how the genre retains a cohesive identity even with all the changes it has undergone. Issues of identity in country music remain tightly linked to both socioeconomic class and race. Just as the music labels marketed records according to the race of the performers in the 1920s, performances that cross racial boundaries in the 2010s still evoke politics of difference. For country music, both the audience and the roster of performers remain overwhelmingly white. Many young fans who listen to country music also listen to hip hop, rap, R&B, and pop styles and like artists of many different racial and ethnic identities. In conversations with these fans, they often express surprise that audiences self-identify along lines of racial difference. Yet the statistics confirm that audiences who identify themselves as country fans are overwhelmingly white. And while the country audience has a socioeconomic profile on par with national averages, the music remains heavily marked by working-class narratives and themes. Both of these factors contribute to the music's status as "othered," or distinct and separate from mainstream culture.

The irony of this situation is, of course, that when a song or artist is particularly successful, they move into that more central role within pop culture, which threatens their distinctive country identity. Such has been the case with Taylor Swift, who abandoned country music altogether, and Carrie Underwood; others, such as Blake Shelton, take active steps to renew their "country-ness," in song lyrics, in videos, and through the way they talk and dress. Note that there is a distinctly gendered nature to how stars do and do not move from country into mainstream pop, with women making this transition far more often than men. That point reveals how the core of contemporary country music is cast in a very masculine role, in spite of the strong presence of a few female artists.

No concept looms larger in the formation and definition of country music than that of "authenticity," an elusive description of a value system projected onto the music by its fans. What is authentic to one fan is a sell-out or poser to another. Yet that debate actually helps country music remain a vibrant and defined genre because it acknowledges the vital role that fans have in constructing and redefining genre.

In conclusion, this book offers ways of thinking about music and its relationship to people, culture, and history that can be extracted and applied to different artists, songs, time periods, and events. It is an attempt to account for the establishment, evolution, and present-day instance of a genre of music that has shaped and been shaped by a century of lived experience for its fans. Technology has changed radically in that century. Musical styles have come and gone, sometimes resurrected later and in other forms. Where this book ends, its ideas of how to make sense of music and culture can continue: Take these approaches and pathways of interpretation and apply them to whatever forms of country music exist. Reflect on what country music can teach us about history, its fans and creators and—more importantly—ourselves. For that is the real value of any study of the arts.

☆ ESSAY: IDENTITY

Tomato-Gate and the Women of Country

"If you want to make ratings in country radio, take females out. . . . Trust me, I play great female records, and we've got some right now; they're just not the lettuce in our salad. The lettuce is Luke Bryan and Blake Shelton, Keith Urban and artists like that. The tomatoes of our salad are the females," explained radio consultant Keith Hill to *Country Aircheck,* a trade publication, in May 2015. Hill's comment started a "food fight" on Music Row, as journalist Beverly Keel dubbed it. "Tomato-gate," as it came to be known, brought the discussion about gender in country music to the forefront once again. Why were more male artists getting radio airplay and commercial recognition? Did women have to compete with each other for a limited number of "slots" in any given format or playlist? Why were consultants and program directors adamant that fans did not want to hear too many female artists on the radio, especially since the majority of the country radio audience was female?

The dearth of women in country music in 2015 was even more surprising because critics had been predicting a turning of the tide. Two years earlier, Ann Powers, critic for National Public Radio, had dubbed 2013 "Country Music's Year of the Woman," writing about the depth of talent that was bubbling up from songwriters such as Kacey Musgraves, Brandy Clark, Ashley Monroe, and more. Powers noted artists such as Ashton Shepherd, who she thought deserved far more recognition, along with the prominence of powerhouse female voices in bands such as Sugarland, Little Big Town, and Lady Antebellum. All this attention was echoed by critics' accolades for work such as Kellie Pickler's album *100 Proof*. But in spite of such bold declarations and predictions, and regardless of the talent pool poised for bigger things, the sea change obviously did not happen.

The imbalance in gender in country music goes back to the earliest days of records and radio shows, and has been a recurring theme throughout the century. Certainly during the early days, life on the road with a band, and the social mores that applied to entertainers, made it more difficult for women to have prominent careers. But the dominant presence of men on the *Billboard* charts, on radio playlists, and within industry awards has persisted. Only during the late 1990s did the gap close, and only for a very brief period. By the early 2000s, once again numbers were skewed sharply toward male entertainers; it was big news when Gretchen Wilson broke a long stretch during which no women at all were at the top of the country charts. Although the successes of a few women in the early 2000s, notably Carrie Underwood and Taylor Swift, and—slightly later—Miranda Lambert, was widely reported, their presence overshadowed the news that there were very few other women among the ranks of country stars. Even those at the top were still getting only a fraction of the airtime and attention of their male counterparts. The Country Music Association's Entertainer of the Year, for instance, was awarded to women only three times between 2000 and 2016.

The immediate responses to "tomato-gate" ranged from humorous to serious, with Martina McBride selling "tomato lover" tee-shirts, and threats directed toward Keith Hill. As the dust settled, however, other radio programmers quietly confirmed that yes, reducing the ratio of female to male artists in playlists increased station ratings, and both artists and industry personnel noted echoes of the past throughout the conversations: in 2016, Maren Morris was the first female artist to have a debut hit reach the top of the charts since Carrie Underwood had done it in 2005, for instance. And yet, to people in the business, none of this was all that surprising.

A few senior figures in country music had already spearheaded efforts to address the situation. Leslie Fram, a senior vice president at CMT, launched a franchise and campaign in 2013 called "The Next Women of Country," which inducted a "class" each year, produced concerts, and worked on promotion for female artists. And Fram, along with Beverly Keel, a professor and highly acclaimed journalist, and Tracy Gershon, a record company executive, founded "Change the Conversation," a collective whose goals were to shift the industry's treatment of female artists by being able to answer rumors with irrefutable market research, support artists with mentoring, and engineer real-world solutions to address the gender imbalance.

None of their efforts, however, addressed the underlying causes that had created the situation in the first place. Many people agreed that some level of basic sexism was to blame. But there was more to it than just that. One contributing factor was that country music and its audience had inscribed more limits on what sort of image female singers could present, and what they could sing about. Within these narrow confines, it was harder for women to gain a commercial foothold. Maren Morris explained in a *Rolling Stone* interview that country music did not allow female artists to express their sexuality the way that men could; the boundaries on what female country artists could sing about were often set at flirting, or other light-hearted and light-weight topics, thereby handicapping female artists who wanted more freedom of expression in their songs.

A second contributing factor is that the entire concept of country music is expressed through a lens of masculinity: countless songs cast a male protagonist as the "real" country persona, who interacts with or often seduces either a nameless female character who is referred to only through the form of her body parts and clothing (little tank top, tan legs, red lips, cut-off shorts), or a female character who is not described as country (the visiting city girl, the "high class" woman who needs to experience "real country.") This theme runs deep in the genre, at the level of abstraction that is not even part of the average fan's conscious understanding of the music. But even though it is embedded deep underneath the everyday awareness of most fans, it makes it very challenging for female artists to navigate the genre successfully. None of these characteristics are unique to the country genre. And over the years, many women have successfully overcome the challenges to establish themselves as major stars. But the fact that a majority-female audience continues to listen to and buy this music, and that the core group of female artists and executives have had to mobilize to address this situation, should prompt ongoing discussion.

☆ ESSAY: MUSICAL STYLE

 # The Splintering of Country

On October 20, 2012, *Billboard* reconfigured its "Hot Country Songs" chart to incorporate digital download sales, streaming data, and airplay in determining songs' positions. A new chart, "Country Airplay," debuted to track only radio airplay. This change revealed that the industry was aware of and interested in tracking the way that country music had splintered in different directions: that country radio was no longer viewed as representative of the genre, and that other access points for country music might draw different country fans who wanted to hear different kinds of country music.

Country music has always served as an umbrella for many different styles of music, which coexist and influence each other. This development, however, was slightly different. The change arose from the freedom and flexibility fans finally had to circumvent restricted channels for accessing music. Particularly in the form of streaming services such as Pandora and Spotify, fans had the ability to create custom stations that used the listener's input to figure out what else the person might want to hear, regardless of the genre of the music. And since the creation of modern social media, fans have had the means to connect with their favorite artists directly without necessarily identifying with any particular genre. All of these changes have resulted in a more splintered genre, with substantial overlaps between country and Americana, and with a lot of baggage tied to the label "country."

The dominant musical style for country radio from about 2010 to 2015 was bro-country. These songs used some variation on a stock narrative: good ol' boy seeks dirt road, tail-gate party, and beer to reaffirm his Southern masculinity, usually in the company of a nameless but very attractive female. The songs layer stadium rock rhythm sections with highly produced hooks, just enough banjo to mark their genre as country, and entirely extroverted narratives, usually with a hint of defiance. Chet Flippo's 2011 assessment of the music as "manly TV commercials . . . for suburban wannabe country boys" proved prescient well before *New York Magazine* writer Jody Rosen christened it bro-country.

Beyond Nashville's indulgence in bro-country, three other musical styles have gained prominence. The Americana music scene has grown into its own genre with an awards show, a trade association, and a loyal fan base. Most significantly, as the support base around Americana developed and matured, it absorbed much of the attitude and musical aesthetics that had been part of alt-country in the early 2000s. By 2017, the Americana music awards were packed with artists whose indie rock influences, Texas honky-tonk attitudes, and self-consciously artistic versions of country music were transplanted straight from the alt-country heyday. Nominees for awards even included alt-country alumni Ryan Adams and the Drive-By Truckers, along with Texas staple Jason Isbell, post-punk rocker Billy Bragg, former mainstream country star Marty Stuart – a veritable roll-call of the former alt-country scene. The acoustic/folk side of Americana is still present with stars such as roots musician Rhiannon Giddens, but occupies a smaller portion of the scene. And country and Americana continue to overlap in complicated ways: for instance, songwriter Lori McKenna is a favorite in Americana, but also the source of a number of mainstream country hits, and the inimitable Sturgill Simpson is an enigmatic star in both scenes.

The bluegrass and old-time music scenes have continued to expand, and the gulf between those musical worlds and mainstream country has widened to the point that few musicians and fans venture across the borders. Although banjos still grace the mainstream country recordings coming out of Nashville, the days of country fans taking on a bluegrass album—or of bluegrass stars getting pulled into a mainstream country record—have faded. Alan Jackson's *The Bluegrass Album* (2013) was the very tail end of the trend that had run through the early 2000s. And the old-time world is even more insulated from mainstream country.

After bro-country began to recede from the limelight, the dominant style to take its place was a crossover style fully invested in contemporary hip hop and pop. Sam Hunt's "Break Up in a Small Town," with his spoken narrative, hip-hop styled beat, and heavy-handed studio production was the most obvious example; Carrie Underwood and Keith Urban's duet "The Fighter" is another example. These recordings match the sounds of contemporary pop and hip hop very well. While country music crossing into mainstream pop is nothing new, the degree to which these artists are finding acceptance with a pop audience is unprecedented. In many cases, the recordings contain no audible ties to country's past at all. In these instances, the country identity comes not from the recordings or even the artists themselves, but rather from the fans' own sense of where they see themselves fitting in a musical landscape. In other words, "The Fighter" is part of country music for little reason other than its fans think of themselves as "country fans."

☆ ESSAY: IDENTITY

 # Who Listens to Country?

"Country must be country wide," "we all got a hillbilly bone down deep inside," and "we're one big country nation," declare the lyrics in a roster of country hits from the past decade. In spite of these assertions of inclusivity, not everyone is a country fan, and the music industry spends a lot of time, energy, and money trying to figure out who their audience really is. No two surveys come up with identical results, but we can get a good sense of the audience's profile nonetheless.

Most information about country music audiences is collected through research surveys conducted by Nielsen Media Research, the company that has produced Nielsen Ratings for television shows since 1951, or GfK MRI, a market research institute. Trade organizations such as the Country Music Association commission research studies for the purpose of understanding how better to market country music and to persuade radio stations or music distributors that country music should be their primary format. A number of major consumer surveys were done between about 2005 and 2011, as the music industry sought to stabilize itself in a new, digital-media landscape. Since then, surveys have largely focused on the media through which consumers get their music (comparing various streaming services, for instance).

While country music is by no means a "universal" music for the American public, it does have widespread popularity. Approximately 42% of all Americans age 12 and older consume country music (i.e., choose to listen to it or buy it). Nielsen's radio format surveys confirm that country music is the number one radio format, based on percentage of overall listening, a position it has held since 2009. Approximately 14% of all radio-listening is to country music. The country music audience is also still willing to purchase physical albums (basically CDs); 37% of all country music is bought in this format, as opposed to digital downloads. In terms of total overall music consumption, which includes physical albums people buy, digital tracks they buy, and digital streaming, country music held an 11.2% market share in 2014, fell to only 8.5% in 2015, but was back up to 10% in 2016. These numbers have held comparatively steady for the past fifteen years or so, with country's market share bouncing around one-tenth of all music consumed.

So who are these country listeners? They are spread across all age groups, more so than with other genres, with 51% of the audience under age 45, and 49% of them over age 45, equally spread out across all ages. They are largely white; the percentage of country listeners who identify as white varies from year to year, but it has been in the general range of 88–93% for some time. About 5% of the country audience identifies as Hispanic, and just over 2% identifies as black. And the majority of the country audience is female—about 54%—a number that has held steady for a long time.

The Country Music Association has been touting the economic status of the country music listener since the 1960s, always in an effort to persuade radio stations and music outlets that the country fan base would appeal to their advertisers. In 2017, the CMA report cited that country music listeners had an average household income of $81.5K, that 71% own a home, 56% are married, and 57% are college-educated. These numbers are designed to project a sense of stable consumers with disposable income. Note, for instance, that the education statistic is for people with any sort of college education, rather than for people who hold at least a four-year degree; that number is actually closer to 24%, just a tad under the national average. And the CMA report downplays the racial homogeneity of country music: It points out that African American listenership is up 33% from the previous year but does not mention what a very small portion of the country audience it is in the first place.

Maps of where the country audience are located support the history of the music; the populations with the highest percentage of country fans are the Midwest and the region comprised of Kentucky, Tennessee, Alabama, and Mississippi.

The characteristics of country music fans that are perhaps most interest in relation to the common narratives and themes in the music are seldom displayed in these surveys, namely religion, sexual orientation, and political viewpoints. One survey from 2004 found that 60% of country fans were Republicans, a lower percentage than many journalists assume when writing about the music. But other than the information about the number of married fans, none of the major surveys report on these descriptors.

In sum, today's country audience, statistically speaking, is a portrait of middle-class, fly-over states, populated by mostly white Americans. The audience for commercial country music is not predominantly working-class, nor are they living in remote, rural areas. They connect to country music through a sense of personal values they believe the music reflects back to them and through a sense of metaphor. The lifestyles, situations, and experiences in the songs represent to them a life with which they identify. There are significant variations in demographics in different regions; in the Southwest, the percentage of Hispanic listeners is far higher, for instance. And in some regions, country music is simply unmarked by genre; in other words, people think of it as the "generic" form of popular music, rather than specifically as "country." It is the most common music used in public spaces without anyone thinking of it as specifically country. It is important to keep in mind that while surveys and reports can present the big picture, they do nothing to explain how any one community, or how any one individual, connects with a genre, an artist, or a song.

LISTEN-SIDE-BY-SIDE

"Tennessee Whiskey"

Songwriters: Dean Dillon and Linda Hargrove
David Allan Coe, 1981 (on *Tennessee Whiskey*, CBS Records 37454)
George Jones, 1983 (on *Shine On*, Epic FE-38406)
Chris Stapleton, 2015 (on *Traveller*, Mercury Nashville 3757743)
Chris Stapleton and Justin Timberlake, 2015 (live, November 4, 2015, Bridgestone Arena, Nashville, TN)

At the 49th annual Country Music Association awards show, Chris Stapleton and Justin Timberlake performed an eight-minute, two-song duet that showcased country music's outlook at the time: a contradictory combination of sliding toward the popular mainstream while claiming allegiance to its distinctive traditions.

"Tennessee Whiskey" was written by Linda Hargrove, whose career peaked with a string of classic country hits in the 1970s, and Dean Dillon, who would become a staple of the 1980s neotraditionalist

scene, including co-writing George Strait's hit "The Chair" (see chapter 11). The song was first recorded by David Allan Coe in 1981, and garnered little commercial attention. With its steel guitar, electric bass, and two-beat rhythms, the recording sits squarely in the sound of classic country. The subtle inclusion of electric piano suggests that this recording falls toward the end of the classic country period. The lyrics are a series of similes, comparing a woman's love to alcohol, concluding with the hook "I stay stoned on your love all the time."

Two years later, George Jones recorded it for an album and released it as a single, which reached number two on the *Billboard* country chart. A bona fide hit, this version featured both harmonica and strings, two hallmarks of Jones's sound that had been prominent on "He Stopped Loving Her Today" (see Chapter 8). With Jones's personal reputation for alcohol consumption and widely publicized love life, fans made easy connections between the lyrics and the singer. The recording was in the classic country style, in its arrangement (including the use of harmonica), Jones's plaintive vocals, even the change in keys (at 1:22), and sounded retro, part of Jones's career revival in the early 1980s.

Chris Stapleton's debut solo album, *Traveller*, was a classic instance of a "debut" coming after nearly fifteen years of a professional career in Nashville. As was the trend in 2015, the musical underpinnings of his album were pure Southern Rock in vocal timbre, instrumentation, and musical style. Also in keeping with what else was happening in country music, Stapleton wrote or co-wrote 12 of the album's tracks. The other two were covers that defined his musical lineage and linked him to country traditions. One cover was a Charlie Daniels record, "Was It 26." The other was "Tennessee Whiskey."

Stapleton's choice of songs connected him to the classic country lineage of legends such as George Jones. However, he transformed the style of the song entirely, shifting to a shuffle groove and changing the vocal harmonies and chord progression with an infusion of soul and the R&B styles that had mixed with southern rock in the1960s and 70s, largely in Texas. The song combined an invocation of classic country traditions with a very modern country sound that was indebted entirely to southern rock and soul.

When Stapleton was nominated for several CMA awards, he arranged for his performance on the awards show to include a duet performance with his friend Justin Timberlake, former star of the boy band NSYNC. Timberlake had launched an extremely successful solo career with R&B and

soul albums backed by his pop star celebrity status. Stapleton and Timberlake together completed the song's transformation into a soul cover by bringing Timberlake's horn section on stage and freeing up the rhythms of the vocals.

The results were a performance that brought down the house; as the camera panned the audience, the biggest stars of country music were seen taking video and pictures, and when Timberlake stepped up the mic for his solo verse, the crowd erupted in cheers. Stapleton took home two CMA awards that evening, and their performance spiked "Tennessee Whiskey" onto the *Billboard 200* list.

This performance highlights two important aspects of country music in 2015. The first is that even as the rhetoric among many country musicians turned toward wanting to reestablish the presence of traditional, hard-core honky-tonk influences in country music, the sound drifted increasingly toward R&B influences and pop styles. Even this cover of a George Jones hit, arguably the most traditional "classic country" sound one could find in the post-millennial scene, had its style radically changed so that it was classic country dressed entirely in soul.

The second aspect is that in spite of its large market share by many different standards of measurement, its continued presence on radio and its loyal fans, country remains a sidelined genre that wields only limited star power in the larger marketplace of popular music. The audience's response made it clear that in the grand scheme of popular entertainment, country can't compete with big league stars such as Timberlake. That is an ever-present theme in this era of country music, repeated time and again with different pop stars guesting on country shows. In a revealing follow-up interview in *Billboard*, Stapleton was asked why he doesn't tour with a horn section; he replied that he "certainly couldn't afford . . . one" and acknowledged the boost he got from all the attention Timberlake garnered. The fact that they were allocated an eight-minute segment for their performance—an eternity, in the timeline of an awards show—was because of the presence of Timberlake and his overall audience appeal inside *and* outside country, and the irony of that much time being allocated to a non-country star at the country awards show was not lost on fans. Yet at the same time, Timberlake unquestionably enjoyed the publicity boost from the event and got to present his own single, "Drink You Away," to a country audience, further evidence of the complex intersections and interactions of genres.

PLAYLIST

Hunt, Sam. "Take Your Time" (2014)

Lambert, Miranda. "The House that Built Me" (2010)

Morris, Maren. "My Church" (2016)

Musgraves, Kacey. "Merry Go 'Round" (2012)

Shelton, Blake. "Boys 'Round Here" (2013)

Simpson, Sturgill. "Keep It Between the Lines" (2016)

FOR MORE READING

Fry, Robert W. *Performing Nashville: Music Tourism and Country Music's Main Street.* London: Palgrave Macmillan, 2017.

Hight, Jewly. "Beyoncé and the Dixie Chicks Offer Up Lessons on Country Music's Past (And Future)." *The Record: Music News from NPR*, November 4, 2016, http://www .npr.org/sections/therecord/2016/11/04/500562813/beyonc-and-the-dixie-chicks-offer-up-lessons-on-country-musics-past-and-future

Keel, Beverly. "Sexist 'Tomato' Barb Launches Food Fight on Music Row." *The Tennessean*, May 29, 2015, http://www.tennessean.com/story/entertainment/music/.../ sexist-tomato-barb.../28036657/

Pecknold, Diane, and Kristine M. McCusker. *Country Boys and Redneck Women: New Essays on Gender and Country Music.* Jackson, Miss.: University Press of Mississippi, 2016.

Rosen, Jody. "Does Country Music Have a Problem with Women?" *Vulture*, September 12, 2013, http://www.vulture.com/2013/09/rosen-on-country-musics-women-problem.html

Rosen, Jody. "On the Rise of Bro-Country." *New York Magazine* via *Vulture*, August 11, 2013, http://www.vulture.com/2013/08/rise-of-bro-country-florida-georgia-line .html

NAMES AND TERMS

Aldean, Jason	Lambert, Miranda	Shelton, Blake
Bro-country	Little Big Town	Simpson, Sturgill
Brooks, Garth	Moore, Jason	Stapleton, Chris
Florida Georgia Line	Musgraves, Kacey	Swift, Taylor
Hip-hop collaborations	Remix	

REVIEW TOPICS

1. What did pop and hip hop artists have to gain from doing country duets? What did country artists have to gain?

2. What themes are still present in country music today that have persisted throughout the twentieth century?

3. Why do country audiences keep bringing the genre back to a relatively narrow persona in terms of race, class, and gender?

Song Form

In order to make sense of a song that they hear, listeners need to be able to hear the discrete sections of a song, the way the sections relate to each other, and the way that the sections combine to form the complete song. Listeners also need to recognize the common patterns formed by these sections, and how those patterns are used in many different songs. The study of these sections, their relationships to each other, and the common patterns in which they occur is the study of song form.

Most people who listen to music have at least a casual understanding of song form; we use terms like "verse" and "chorus" in informal conversations, for instance. These terms and others can be used in more specific and technical ways, however, to identify song form, to explain the way individual songs convey their message to their listener and the way that songwriters employ common patterns or models.

Why Study Form?

Studying song form allows us to:

1. spot patterns and trends within country music that are part of the genre's identity
2. describe features of a song in a technically specific and accurate way, which helps us communicate our ideas to others
3. identify and account for changes in songwriting practices that have occurred over time
4. explain how and why some songs stand out from others or have a particular effect on their listeners.

The Elements of a Song

In most instances, songs consist of three basic elements: the melody (the tune, with its specific pitches and rhythms), the harmony (the chords that go with that melody), and the lyrics (the words, although in some instances a recording may be of a piece of music without words). Combined, these three elements form the basic components of a song.

Most songs are constructed from distinct sections, each of which has an identifiable character of melody, harmony, and text (if present). The first step to analyze a song's form is to identify those sections. The divisions between sections are the natural breaks in the flow of the song. Evidence that determines the boundaries of each section might include a change in instrumentation, a change in the overall texture of the performance, or a change in the text to a new idea or perspective, similar to the division between stanzas in a poem. One of the most perceptible ways that listeners

identify the sections of a song is by listening for repetition: a return to a melody, a chord progression, or text that was heard before. Most main sections of a country song will be between 10 and 35 seconds long. Based on our general exposure to popular music, we generally expect to hear several different sections in a song, and we are used to identifying the sections even if only subconsciously.

The sections of a song relate to each other in terms of similarity and contrast: how similar or different are the melody, chords, and lyrics from one section compared to another. But even more significant to the study of form is the way that a particular section contributes to the overall meaning or effect of a song.

This introduction to song form relies on what music analysts call "theoretical models." Models illustrate a norm, or, in other words, what happens most of the time and in most cases. They do not necessarily describe what happens in every individual case, nor do they account for all songs. In many cases, a song will adhere quite closely to a model but still have some unique feature that is not represented by the model. These cases are interesting, and can lead to further analysis and discovery.

The Building Blocks

Three basic types of song sections, which one can think of as building blocks for a song, are:

Verse: A verse is the most fundamental building block of a song. The verse is typically where the plot of the song develops, or where we get basic information about the song's subject. When there is more than one verse in a song, each verse usually has the same melody and harmony but different lyrics. The end of the verse can sound finished (sometimes described as "harmonically closed"), or it can sound like there's more to come (sometimes described as "harmonically open"). The first verse in Garth Brooks, "Friends in Low Places" (Chapter 12 Listening Guide) begins, "Blame it all on my roots . . ."

Chorus: The chorus is the central point of reflection in a song; it contains the main idea, and acts as a timeless "big idea" in the song. Not all songs have choruses; at certain times in country music's history, songs tended to be written without choruses. When the chorus is heard more than once in a song, it usually (but not always) repeats the same lyrics, melody, and harmony. Choruses do not typically advance the plot of the song directly. The end of a chorus typically sounds finished (harmonically closed). If a song's form contains a chorus, then the chorus will typically be the last section of the song. The chorus in Garth Brooks, "Friends in Low Places" (Chapter 12 Listening Guide) begins, "I've got friends in low places . . ."

Bridge: A bridge is the section of a song that provides contrast to the other sections. A bridge typically occurs only once in a song, and has noticeably different melody, harmony, and lyrics than the other sections. A bridge sounds unfinished at the end (harmonically open), and it leads into another section of the song. Not all songs have bridges. The bridge in the Dixie Chicks, "Long Time Gone" (Chapter 14 Listening Guide) begins, "Now me, I went to Nashville . . ."

Along with these three basic sections are many other supplemental sections that enhance the song forms. These include:

Introduction: The introduction, often just called the intro, is the opening of the song before the main melody or lyrics appear. It usually is performed by instruments with no vocals. When a song is played on the radio, this may be the part that the DJ talks over.

Outro: The outro is the other bookend of the song that matches the role of the intro. An outro is a brief instrumental section that simply wraps up the song after the melody and lyrics have concluded.

Playout: A playout is an outro that extends into its own lengthy section, often showcasing instrumental improvisation by one or more soloists.

Prechorus: A prechorus is a very short section of a song, usually consisting of just two rhyming lines of text, that forms a link between a verse and a chorus. It builds up the energy of the song to launch the chorus. It is also called a ramp, a climb, or a transitional bridge by some songwriters, and all of these terms are metaphors for this section's role in the overall song: to prepare the launch of the chorus.

Postchorus: A postchorus is a short, catchy section that follows a chorus and typically features short repeating phrases or no lyrics at all. Postchoruses are common in electronic dance music, and often begin at the moment that the drums and bass "drop" into the song, creating a sense of climax. Postchoruses are not common in country songs and appear mostly in crossover country that borrows heavily from pop styles and mixing techniques from pop and hip hop, largely after 2010. Some music theorists call this section a "second chorus."

Instrumental: This is a generally vague, catchall label for any section of a song where the lyrics are not present but where one or more instruments is taking a solo role. An instrumental section can be any of the sections of a song, where an instrumental solo substitutes for the expected vocalist. When analyzing song form, we typically label these instrumental sections by whatever the underlying elements of the section are, such as an "instrumental chorus" or "instrumental verse." To determine the type of section, listeners focus on the chord progression and the basic melody, which they can then match to another section of the song.

Instrumental Interlude: An instrumental interlude is a brief section of music, usually only a few measures, that simply serves as a spacer between more substantial sections. This allows a song to breathe, or sometimes literally allows the singer to catch his or her breath.

Additional terms are used to describe parts of a song that *are not independent sections* but that are instead simply components *within a section.* These include:

Tag: A tag typically occurs in the very last section of a song, when the singer repeats the last line or two of the song as a form of punctuation to wrap up the performance.

Hook: A hook for a song is the single most memorable, repeatable fragment of the song; it often contains the essence of the song. This term is used very inconsistently by analysts and songwriters. In many instances, it is the title line of the song or the refrain.

Refrain: The refrain is a single line of the song that is repeated many times, possibly even showing up in different sections of the song (such as both the verses and the choruses). Note that the term "refrain" is used by music analysts to mean something very different when talking about other genres of music besides country and pop.

Basic Song Form Models

There are five commonly used song form models in country music. Each of these is defined by its use of the basic sections or building blocks of song forms. Supplemental sections such as an intro or an outro, or the presence or absence of a refrain or tag, do *not* change these basic models.

1. Strophic Song Form

A strophic song consists of all verses: a single type of song section that uses the same basic melody and harmony, while the lyrics change from one section to the next. A strophic song has neither a chorus nor a bridge (contrasting section). Typically, strophic song forms appear in long ballads that tell an elaborate story and in blues songs. Strophic songs are exceptionally rare in contemporary commercial country music—listeners are unlikely to hear them on country radio stations or on major stars' albums, for instance.

EXAMPLES

"Blue Yodel" (Jimmie Rodgers), Chapter 2 Listening Guide.
"Coal Miner's Daughter" (Loretta Lynn), Chapter 8 Listening Guide.
This is an example of a long strophic song with six distinct verses.
"Foggy Mountain Breakdown" (Flatt and Scruggs), Chapter 5 Listening Guide.
This is an example of a strophic song without lyrics.

2. Two-Part Sectional, or Binary, Form

Two-part sectional form, also called binary form, is one of the oldest song forms we find in country music. It was used in traditional dance music of the 18th century in Europe, and is most commonly found today in bluegrass and old-time country music performances of traditional songs called "fiddle tunes" (even when not played by a fiddle). The form consists of two distinct sections each with its own melody and harmony. The two sections do not have the characteristic relationship of a verse and a chorus, but rather are simply two independent yet related halves of a song. The two sections are typically labeled "A" and "B," and in these instances, the labels carry no connotations of verses or bridges. Specifically, these B-sections are not points of contrast that drive the song to return to the familiar A-section, but rather an equal and balanced half of the song. Each section contains a musically satisfying ending (they are harmonically closed), and they are the same length, typically 8 measures.

Performers usually repeat each section before moving onto the next, then continue alternating AABBAABB . . . until they conclude the performance, ending with a B section. Each instrumentalist in the band takes a turn playing an improvised solo for an AABB segment, then a different soloist will take over, continuing until everyone in the band has had that opportunity. Although many of these traditional fiddle tunes have lyrics, very few contemporary performances include any vocals at all, and many musicians who can play the songs do not know the words.

EXAMPLES

"Billy in the Low Ground" (traditional)
"Whiskey Before Breakfast" (traditional)
"St. Anne's Reel" (traditional)
"Arkansas Traveler" (traditional)
"Blackberry Blossom" (Doc Watson and Merle Watson).

This traditional fiddle tune, played here on two guitars, offers a very clear illustration of the form because the harmony and melody in the two sections are noticeably different. The form is shown below:

TIME	FORM	DISCUSSION
0:00	A-section	
0:09	A-section	The performers repeat the A-section, but with embellishments and variations on the melody each time.
0:16	B-section	Notice the easily perceptible change in the chords here: this fiddle tune has a very distinctive beginning to its B-section, making it easy to hear the form.
0:24	B-section	
0:31	A-section	Performers switch roles between soloist and accompanist. Note the return of the opening melody, but with different aspects of improvisation that make it different each time we hear it.
. . .	etc.	Performers continue to alternate who is playing the solo and who is playing the accompanying chords, repeating the pattern AABB.
. . .	etc.	
2:47	B-section	
2:54	B-section	Note that the last complete section we hear is a B-section.
3:02	Tag	Each performer plays a short melodic pattern that signals the end of the song and wraps it up with a flourish.

3. Standard AABA Song Form

A standard AABA song form, often referred to as just "AABA form," consists of verses and bridges. These songs do not contain a chorus. AABA song form was commonly used in popular-style songs written for Broadway shows and stage shows in the early twentieth century. The term "AABA" describes the pattern of song sections: four equal-length sections (traditionally eight measures of music per section), where the first, second, and fourth (the "A-sections," which can also be called verses) use the same melody and harmony but have different lyrics, whereas the third section (the "B-section") is radically different (the bridge). Note that unlike two-part sectional form, in these AABA forms, the B-section sounds unfinished (harmonically open), and cannot serve as the ending point for the song.

Standard AABA song forms show up occasionally in early country music, but they became extremely common in the 1950s and '60s, when pop songwriters (such as Fred Rose) were active in country songwriting and when country songwriters started writing tunes that they hoped would cross over to the pop market. Standard AABA song forms often use a refrain, which is a single line of text that appears at the end of each A-section. Standard AABA song forms are not common among today's country music, but when they do show up, they often sound very retro.

In many cases, an AABA song form is not long enough for a country recording. Thus, it is very common for a performer either to repeat the whole AABA pattern (i.e., AABA AABA) in a performance, or to repeat just the last half (i.e., AABA BA). In the first instance, instrumental solos often substitute for the singer when the pattern repeats, so the results are:

A   A   B   A   A (instrumental)   A (instrumental)   B (singer)   A (singer)

Instrumental sections can also appear at other places in the form. Clues that indicate AABA form include a recording that ends with the same section it starts with (the A-section), a strong contrast in the third section (the B-section) that fails to come to a conclusive ending, and a clear sense of "return to the familiar tune" at the fourth section.

EXAMPLES

"He'll Have to Go" (Jim Reeves), Chapter 6 Listening Guide.

This is an example of a straightforward AABA form, with no major sections repeated.

"Blue Moon of Kentucky" (Bill Monroe), Chapter 5 Listening Guide.

"Your Cheatin' Heart" (Hank Williams), Chapter 4 Listening Guide.

This is a more elaborate use of the AABA form, where the entire AABA unit repeats.

"Easy Living" (Miranda Lambert).

This is an example of an AABA song in contemporary country music. Note that the song uses a refrain to conclude each A-section: "'Cause it's easy living, easy loving you." The song ends with an instrumental A-section as a playout, with Lambert singing the last bit of the refrain at the end of the instrumental A-section as a tag.

The recording begins with sound-effects of dialing through radio stations, which evokes the atmosphere of a past sonic landscape. The acoustic bass also hints at an older style. These elements add to the retro sensibilities of this song, which are further reinforced by the song's form itself, a throw-back to an earlier era in country music.

TIME	FORM	LYRICS
0:00	Intro	
0:38	Verse (A-section)	"The weather man..."
1:03	Verse (A-section)	"People keep searching..."
1:28	Bridge (B-section)	"Talk show's talkin'..."
1:45	Verse (A-section)	"Tomorrow that ol' sun..."
2:10	Playout (instrumental A-section)	(Guitar and whistling)

4. Verse-Chorus Form

Verse-chorus forms consist of any combination of verses and choruses, in any pattern. The chorus is almost always the last section in these forms. In more traditional country music, a verse usually occurs first, but there are some eras when it became quite fashionable to open with a chorus (several of Buck Owens's Bakersfield hits, for instance). In some instances, this form also includes a prechorus before each statement of the chorus, and in this book we have identified these special cases of verse-chorus form as verse-prechorus-chorus.

EXAMPLES

"Keep on the Sunny Side" (Carter Family), Chapter 2 Listening Guide.

This song is a very typical verse-chorus form, with instrumental verses spaced throughout the song.

"Can the Circle Be Unbroken (Bye and Bye)" (Carter Family), Chapter 2 Listening Guide.

This song uses the same melody for both the verses and the chorus. The simplest way to tell the sections apart is by listening to the lyrics. The verses tell the story; the chorus repeats the same lyrics to comment on the verses.

"How Blue" (Reba McEntire), Chapter 11 Listening Guide.

Like most of the songs in the neotraditionalist era, this one is in verse-chorus form. Here, as with "All My Ex's Live in Texas," (George Strait; Chapter 11 Listening Guide), the chorus appears first, which kicks off the song with its most memorable part (both the title and the hook).

"Islands in the Stream" (Kenny Rogers and Dolly Parton), Chapter 8 Listening Guide.

This song uses a very distinctive prechorus. The underlying form is verse-chorus, but the prechorus stands out. Prechoruses were quite common in countrypolitan songs as well as in the new country era.

5. Verse-Chorus-Bridge Form

This form uses verses and a chorus, along with a bridge, which typically occurs in after the midpoint of the song. A typical pattern might be V-V-C-B-C, or perhaps V-C-V-C-B-C. These verse-chorus-bridge forms are a comparatively modern feature in country music, appearing mostly after 1980. They are especially prevalent in the past twenty years in pop-influenced country music.

EXAMPLES

"Long Time Gone" (Dixie Chicks), Chapter 14 Listening Guide.

This song uses a bridge in its form that contrasts in melody, harmony, lyrics, and plot. In this case the bridge is followed by an instrumental solo and then another verse. This song also uses a changing chorus (discussed below).

"The House that Built Me" (Miranda Lambert).

This is a straightforward illustration of a verse-chorus-bridge form, as shown below. One might identify the section from 0:21 to 1:08 as one verse, but it makes more sense to label it as two verses when comparing it to the length of the verse that appears later in the song.

TIME	FORM	LYRICS
0:00	Intro	
0:21	Verse 1	"I know they say..."
0:45	Verse 2	"Up those stairs..."
1:08	Chorus	"I thought if I could..."
1:47	Verse 3	"Mama cut out..."
2:11	Chorus	"I thought if I could..."
2:49	Bridge	"You leave home..."
3:04	Chorus	"I thought if I could..."
3:43	Outro	

Special Case: Blues Form

One of the most commonly described forms in popular music is twelve-bar blues. The term "blues" can have many varied meanings, ranging from a particular expression of emotion, to the cultural background of the performer or songwriter, to a specific use of musical scales and pitches, to forms and patterns of lyrics, melodies, and harmonies. The phrase "twelve-bar blues," however, describes a specific pattern that occurs as a single section of a song. The pattern carries cultural, historical, and musical significance in popular music, and is worth studying at some length.

"Twelve-bar blues" describes a song that has a fixed and unchanging pattern of chords that is twelve bars long. This pattern then repeats for the duration of the song. Each twelve-bar blues section features a set of lyrics or a melody that also follows a prescribed pattern. Listeners can recognize the chord progression. In its basic form, it uses only three chords, those built on the first, fourth, and fifth notes of the key of the music. Using Roman numerals to represent those three chords, the following chart illustrates the fixed chord progression for twelve-bar blues:

I	I	I	I
IV	IV	I	I
V	IV	I	I

There are many common variations on this pattern, but the essence of the pattern remains as shown here.

Over this pattern, there are a few different ways that melodies and lyrics appear. The most common of those is three lines of text: an initial statement, a repetition of that statement, and then a contrasting response to that statement. See, for instance, "T for Texas" as recorded by Lynyrd Skynyrd. A different pattern of lyrics uses four lines of text arranged as two rhyming couplets. See, for instance, "Folsom Prison Blues," as recorded by Johnny Cash.

Keep in mind that the twelve-bar blues pattern describes what happens within a single section of the song. The majority of blues songs in country music are strophic in their overall form: they consist only of verses, and each verse uses the twelve-bar blues pattern. In other cases, the twelve-bar blues pattern might show up as the chorus in a verse-chorus song. An example of this is the Dixie Chicks, "Some Days You Gotta Dance" (on *Fly*, 1999); the chorus ("Some days you gotta dance . . ." heard at 0:39, 1:21, 1:38 [an instrumental chorus], and 1:56 [a stop-time chorus]) is in the twelve-bar form, while the verses are not.

Formal Relationships: AABA Standard Song Form and Verse-Chorus Form

Several of the song-form models discussed here share various underlying features in common, and relate to each other in ways that complicate the analysis of form. One such relationship occurs between the AABA Standard Song Form model, and the Verse-Chorus song form model. In many cases, an AABA Standard Song Form model song treats the first "AA" segment as two verses, and the subsequent "BA" segment as if it were a chorus. If that "BA" segment appears again in the song with the same words, listeners might notice that the lyrics repeat and interpret that section as a chorus. But the underlying structure, including the proportions of the sections and the chords, are constructed on the AABA model.

Listeners can spot the AABA standard song form in these instances by listening very carefully for the return of the "A-section" melody after a contrasting bridge, rather than focusing on which sections of the lyrics do or do not repeat.

EXAMPLES
"Your Cheatin' Heart" (Hank Williams), Chapter 4 Listening Guide.
"Suppose Tonight Would Be Our Last" (Two Dollar Pistols with Tift Merritt), Chapter 13 Listening Guide.
"We Must Have Been Out of Our Minds" (George Jones and Melba Montgomery).

These songs' AABA form and its relationship to verse-chorus form is as follows:

A	A	B	A	A	A	B	A
"Verse"	"Verse"	"Chorus"		"Verse"	"Verse"	"Chorus"	

In many instances, the AABA standard song form is performed with just the last "BA" segment repeating. In these cases, we may still hear some implication of "chorus" simply because the "BA" segment repeats. "She's Got You (Patsy Cline), along with many of Cline's other recordings, and "Nothing Fancy" (Alan Jackson). The form for "Nothing Fancy" is shown here:

TIME	FORM	CORRESPONDING IMPLIED VERSE-CHORUS PATTERN	LYRICS
0:00	Intro		
0:21	A-section	"verse"	"No candlelight..."
0:42	A-section	"verse"	"Don't need no..."
1:03	B-section	"chorus"	"Girl, this is everything..."
1:22	A-section		"So I hope it's still..."
1:43	Instrumental		
1:58	B-section	"chorus repeated"	"Girl, this is everything..."
2:21	A-section		"So I hope it's still..."

Formal Relationships: Verse-Chorus-Bridge Form and AABA Standard Song Form

The Verse-Chorus-Bridge form shares a structural similarity with the AABA standard song form, a relationship that some music theorists have identified as a "hybrid" form. The basic relationship can be summarized as a pattern of "same-same-different-same."

Within a verse-chorus-bridge song, a listener can think of the segment "verse-chorus" as behaving like an A-section of an AABA song, and the bridge as behaving like a B-section. The relationship is even more pronounced when we consider that in AABA standard song forms, the A-section often has a refrain at the end, which, if it were lengthened, would resemble a chorus. The resulting patterns are:

Verse	Chorus	Verse	Chorus	Bridge	Verse	Chorus
"A-section"		"A-section"		"B-section"	"A-section"	

EXAMPLES

"Long Time Gone" (The Dixie Chicks), Chapter 14 Listening Guide.

"Welcome to the Future" (Brad Paisley).

"Love and War" (Brad Paisley and John Fogerty).

The verse-chorus-bridge form of this song and its correspondence to AABA form is shown here:

TIME	FORM	CORRESPONDING AABA PATTERN	LYRICS
0:00	Intro		
0:21	Verse 1	"A-section"	"He was nineteen. . ."
0:36	Chorus		"They say all. . ."
1:00	Verse 2	"A-section"	"He was nineteen. . ."
1:16	Chorus		"They say all. . ."
1:34	Bridge	"B-section"	"And the nightmares. . ."
1:57	Instrumental		
2:34	Verse 3	"A-section"	"They call 'em. . ."
2:50	Chorus		"They say all. . ."
3:06	Chorus (repeats)		"They say all. . ."
3:22	Chorus (repeats)		"They say all. . ."

In many other songs, no verses appear after the bridge, but the underlying relationship still remains, merely with the final A-section shorter than the others. This relationship is important in understanding how song forms have evolved from one pattern into another over time.

Special Case: Song Form Variants

Within country songwriting traditions, there are several common variations that appear in song forms. One of the most common in contemporary country songwriting is a "changing chorus." In these songs, each iteration of the chorus uses slightly different lyrics. This approach allows songwriters to give listeners the familiarity of a returning chorus, with the central theme of the song, the musical climax, and the reflective content, while at the same time letting the plot and the song's meaning continue to develop through the chorus sections of the song. Changing choruses are found regularly in contemporary songwriting. Compare the choruses in "Long Time Gone" (Dixie Chicks, Chapter 14 Listening Guide), for instance, to see how they vary from one to the next. Other famous examples include "Love Story" (Taylor Swift) and "Don't Take the Girl" (Tim McGraw).

Another variation on typical song form models is the "wraparound" song form, in which the song ends by returning to some or all of the first verse. The resulting effect is that the song goes on forever: as it ends, it appears to begin again. Examples of wraparound forms include "The Grand Tour" (George Jones) and "Don't' Take the Girl" (Tim McGraw).

A third variation in country's song form is the use of a "narrative shift" chorus. These songs exploit multiple meanings of the same text, usually in the chorus. The first time the listener hears the chorus, it means one thing, but then when it reappears later in the song, the same lyrics take on a very different meaning. One famous example is "The One I Loved Back Then (The Corvette Song) (George Jones), where the same text first describes a sports car. The song then shifts contexts such that the same words describe an attractive woman. Other examples include "How Can I Help You Say Goodbye" (Patty Loveless), "Don't Take the Girl" (Tim McGraw), and "All Over Me" (Blake Shelton).

Songwriters employ many other variations and relationships within and between these models. The main point to remember is that song form is a way of approaching analysis; you can describe the form of a song in order to show:

- patterns in country songwriting and how a particular song matches those patterns.
- how a song's parts fit together to tell a story through a particular musical journey.
- where a song fits in a country music timeline and what its historical influences are.
- Unique features of a song that stand out.

A Song-Form Time Line

In-depth analysis of song forms in country music reveals that they have changed over time. Strophic forms were common in the early days of country music, and they reappeared frequently in the classic country era (1970s) with the rise of story songs (see Chapter 8). Standard AABA song forms were common in the 1950s and '60s, especially in Nashville sound recordings (Chapter 6), but are rare in 1990s and 2000s country. Verse-chorus forms have been the staple of more traditional country music, resurfacing in the neotraditionalist era as well as in the roots revival after 2000. Note that many of the more roots-revival, twang-focused hits today use verse-chorus form, compared to the more pop-crossover songs that tend to rely more on verse-chorus-bridge forms. Verse-chorus-bridge forms are a fairly contemporary form, present mostly in the 1990s and beyond, and especially in pop-crossover songs. Prechoruses surface in the 1980s with the countrypolitan trend, and again in 1990s country-pop. While these generalizations are extremely broad and one can certainly find exceptions, they help illustrate how song form is an integral part of country music's identity and ongoing evolution through time.

HOW TO IDENTIFY FORM

You can identify the form of a song with careful listening and comparison to the models presented here. Keep in mind that some songs will not adhere strictly to any model, but will include variations. Most country songs, however, follow the models outlined here.

1.   **Transcribe the lyrics**. This transcription is a working draft of the song. Mark the timings from the recording throughout the lyrics.

2.   **Divide the song into sections**. Use the natural divisions in the lyrics, pauses from the singer, or changes in instrumentation, texture, rhythmic groove. Moments that sound like something has "started over" are also likely candidates for a division between sections. Listen for the start and end of different instrumental solos. Keep in mind that most song sections are in the range of 15-45 seconds long.

3.   **Study the lyrics**. Mark sections that use the same lyrics. Look for a refrain. Find the title of the song, main idea, or hook and see where it appears. Determine which sections of the lyrics advance the main plot. Look for sections of the lyrics that provide a contrasting perspective or a change of narrative voice.

4.   **Study the melody**. Try singing along with the song: this will help you find sections that have the same melody and sections that have different melodies. Mark those that use the same melody.

5.   **Listen for conclusions**. How "finished" does each section sound? Look closely at the end of the song: what other sections in the song match its lyrics and/or its melody?

6.   **Compare your information to the five basic song forms**. Review the definitions of the different types of song sections as you work. Determine what song form model describes the features of your song and label it accordingly, keeping in mind that some songs employ unique or unusual forms.

7.   **Look for variations and special features**. Now that you have identified the basic form, carefully compare the song to the model that best describes it, and notice any ways in which it is different than the model. What are the particular structural features of the song that make it unique? How do these unique characteristics relate to the rest of the song?

Song List for Appendix A

Brooks, Garth. "Friends in Low Places" (1990), by Dewayne Blackwell and Earl Bud Lee.

Carter Family. "Can the Circle Be Unbroken (Bye and Bye)" (1935), by the Carter Family.

Carter Family. "Keep on the Sunny Side" (1928), by the Carter Family.

Cash, Johnny. "Folsom Prison Blues" (1955), by Johnny Cash.

Cline, Patsy. "She's Got You" (1962), by Hank Cochran.

Dixie Chicks. "Some Days You Gotta Dance" (1999), by Troy Johnson and Marshall Morgan.

Dixie Chicks. "Long Time Gone" (2003), by Darrell Scott.

Flatt and Scruggs. "Foggy Mountain Breakdown" (1949), by Earl Scruggs.

Jackson, Alan. "Nothing Fancy" (2012), by Jay Knowles and Adam Wright.

Jones, George, and Melba Montgomery. "We Must Have Been Out of Our Minds" (1963), by Melba Montgomery.

Jones, George. "The Grand Tour" (1974), by Norro Wilson, Carmol Taylor, and George Richey.

Jones, George. "The One I Loved Back Then (The Corvette Song)" (1985), by Gary Gentry.

Lambert, Miranda. "Easy Living" (2011), by Miranda Lambert and Scotty Wray.

Lambert, Miranda. "The House that Built Me" (2009), by Tom Douglas and Allen Shamblin.

Loveless, Patty. "How Can I Help You Say Goodbye" (1993), by Karen Taylor-Good and Burton Banks Collins.

Lynn, Loretta. "Coal Miner's Daughter" (1969), by Loretta Lynn.

Lynyrd Skynyrd. "T for Texas" (1976), by Jimmie Rodgers.

McEntire, Reba. "How Blue" (1984), by John Moffat.

McGraw, Tim. "Don't Take the Girl" (1994), by Craig Martin and Larry W. Johnson.

Monroe, Bill. "Blue Moon of Kentucky" (1946), by Bill Monroe.

Paisley, Brad. "Love and War" (2017), by John Fogerty and Brad Paisley.

Paisley, Brad. "Welcome to the Future" (2009), by Chris DuBois and Brad Paisley.

Reeves, Jim. "He'll Have to Go" (1959), by Joe Allison and Audrey Allison.

Rodgers, Jimmie. "Blue Yodel" (1927), by Jimmie Rodgers.

Rogers, Kenny, and Dolly Parton. "Islands in the Stream" (1983), by Barry, Robin, and Maurice Gibb.

Shelton, Blake. "All Over Me" (2001), by Earl Thomas Conley, Mike Pyle, and Blake Shelton.

Strait George. "All My Ex's Live in Texas" (1987), by Sanger D. Shafer and Linda J. Shafer.

Swift, Taylor. "Love Story" (2008), by Taylor Swift.

Two Dollar Pistols with Tift Merritt, "Suppose Tonight Would Be Our Last" (1999), by George Jones and Melba Montgomery.

Traditional, "Arkansas Traveler."

Traditional, "Billy in the Low Ground."

Traditional, "St. Anne's Reel."

Traditional, "Whiskey Before Breakfast."

Watson, Doc, and Merle Watson. "Blackberry Blossom" (2006), traditional.

Williams, Hank. "Your Cheatin' Heart" (1952), by Hank Williams.

Country Instruments

This brief list of instruments commonly used in country music is intended only as the barest introduction for newcomers to the genre. In each description, you will find suggestions about where or when the instrument commonly appears within the history of country music and, where relevant, the names of major performers and suggestions on where to start listening for it. This list does not attempt to be comprehensive; plenty of instruments appear in country recordings that are not covered here. Furthermore, readers are warmly encouraged to undertake more in-depth explorations of these instruments, their history, and the ways they are used in country music from other sources.

Keep in mind that "families" of instruments may contain different instruments that are related by their technical features, which makes it harder to learn to identify them by sound. Instruments within the same family, or sometimes the same instrument, can sound radically different depending on how they are played and how they are recorded. Thus, it is essential to listen to a wide range of contexts and performance styles for each instrument, as well as to discuss what you have heard with both your instructor and classmates.

ACCORDION

Accordions, sometimes casually called squeezeboxes, show up only sporadically in country music. They appear in the traditional dance music of immigrants who moved to Texas and the Southwest from the areas that now are part of Germany and the Czech Republic During the 1930s and '40s, the large piano accordion—with a piano-style keyboard—became popular across many styles of music, including the singing cowboys and the

Figure B-1 Pappy Howard playing a piano accordion.

western swing bands working on the West Coast. Listen, for instance, to Tex Williams's "I Got Texas in My Soul" (1946). Sally Ann Forrester, the first woman in Bill Monroe's bluegrass band, played the accordion with him until about 1946.

A smaller type of accordion—often called a button accordion, because it features buttons rather than piano keys to play individual notes—is one of the main melodic instruments used in Cajun music; thus, by extension, it appears in country recordings that draw on Cajun traditions. This type of accordion is quite common in commercial country in the 1990s (the most obvious example is Mary Chapin Carpenter's "Down at the Twist and Shout") because of the general trend toward Cajun-influenced sounds and rhythms during that time. It can also be clearly heard on Alan Jackson's "Tall, Tall Trees" (1995).

Autoharp

The autoharp is a type of zither, an instrument that originated in Eastern Europe and is designed to be strummed or plucked. The autoharp, which was invented in America in 1882, includes a mechanism that allows the musician to play different chords by pressing buttons. Each button determines which strings on the instrument are allowed to ring (thereby creating the chord) and which strings are dampened, or stopped from ringing. Many Appalachian performers hold the instrument against their chest and use their left hand to press the different chord buttons while strumming or picking the strings with their right hand. The autoharp is relatively easy to learn to play well enough to accompany one's singing, and became quite popular among Appalachian musicians in the early twentieth century. Autoharp in country recordings often is played in a treble (higher) register, and many listeners describe it as having a distinctive "buzz" or "zing" in its sound. The instrument is most strongly associated with Sara Carter of the Carter Family; many other hillbilly performers used in on their recordings including Ernest Stoneman (notably on his 1925 sessions).

The autoharp was seldom heard on commercial country recordings after the 1930s, but more traditional and folk-influenced performers continued to use it. June Carter played it frequently onstage when touring in the 1950s and '60s (the film *Walk the Line* [2005] depicts Carter, played by actress Reese Witherspoon, playing it onstage in several scenes). Autoharp can also be heard on "Wildflowers" (Dolly Parton, Linda Ronstadt, and Emmylou Harris on the *Trio* album [1987]) and on June Carter Cash's last solo album, *Wildwood Flower* (2003). In its modern appearances, the instrument invokes a strong sense of Appalachian tradition and old-time performance.

Banjo

There are many different types of banjos, but the one that appears most commonly in country music is a five-string instrument with a round body. One of the strings is shorter than the rest and acts as a drone, remaining on the same pitch even when the player changes the pitches of the other strings to make different chords. During the first two decades of country recording, some banjo players used a frailing or clawhammer style, in which the performer struck the strings with the right hand to play chords. Other banjo players used a modified technique in which they also plucked individual strings with one or two fingers, combining melody and chords. In the 1940s, Earl Scruggs refined a technique that was used in western North Carolina for playing energized, syncopated patterns of individual notes on the banjo (heard on "Foggy Mountain Breakdown"). This technique, which is associated with bluegrass, is called "three-finger roll" or "Scruggs-style." Banjo players typically wear finger picks on their right hands (small plastic or metal picks on two fingers and the thumb) to perform in this style. The banjo has been a staple of bluegrass since its conception and in all its subsequent developments.

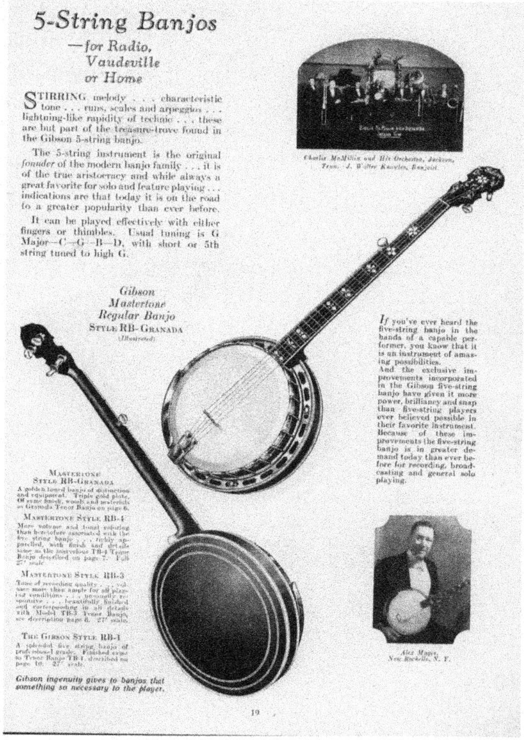

Banjos also show up frequently on neotraditionalist recordings (listen to Dolly Parton's "Time for Me to Fly" [1989] or Ricky Skaggs's "Country Boy" [1985]) and in the various roots revival recordings since 2000 (listen to the Dixie Chicks' "White Trash Wedding" [2002]). In its contemporary uses, the banjo usually is heard in up-tempo songs and strongly references old-time country, although it has also become common in more commercial and even crossover country in recent years (such as Taylor Swift's "Our Song" on *Taylor Swift* [2006, throughout, but particularly easy to hear in the introduction and at 2:25]).

Figure B-2 An advertisement for a Gibson banjo.

BASS, ACOUSTIC

Sometimes called the upright bass or even the doghouse bass, the acoustic bass is a large, four-stringed instrument with a hollow wooden body. In country music, performers usually pluck the strings with their right hands (as opposed to playing the strings with a bow). The bass was seldom heard in early hillbilly recordings or string bands, partly because its size made it difficult to transport. From the mid-1930s onward, it became increasingly common, and by the 1940s it was ubiquitous in almost all styles of country music. During those years, the bass provided the lowest notes in the band, usually playing just two notes per measure in a way that both supported the chord and kept a steady rhythm for the band. Western swing introduced a "walking bass" technique into country music, borrowed from jazz, in which the bass player played four notes instead of two in each measure (heard, for instance, on Bob Wills's "Deep Water" [1947]). Walking bass became part of the shuffle sound (such as Ray Price's "Crazy Arms" [1956]). Rockabilly bass players sometimes used a more aggressive technique, known as slap bass, that involved snapping the strings off the fingerboard and adding percussive thumps and pops to the music. The acoustic bass was a staple of country music through the 1960s. Since then, it has remained in acoustic-based styles (most notably bluegrass) but has been largely replaced by electric basses in other styles.

BASS, ELECTRIC

The electric bass, or electric bass guitar, shows up in country music gradually, but by the 1970s had supplanted the acoustic bass in all but a few select styles. The electric bass typically has four strings and looks much like a solid-body electric guitar; its notes ring longer than an acoustic bass's notes, and each pitch has a more consistent volume and tone. Since the 1970s, it has appeared in almost all styles of country music, the only exceptions being acoustic styles such as bluegrass (although some progressive and newgrass bands use electric bass) and folk-infused performances.

BASS, TIC-TAC

Tic-tac bass is not actually an instrument, but instead a technique used in the studio to make the lowest notes of a recording stand out more. Devised in the Nashville sound era and commonly associated with session player Harold Bradley, tic-tac bass involves an acoustic bass plus an electric guitar. The electric guitar—often a baritone guitar or a six-string short-scale electric bass guitar—plays the same notes at the same time as the acoustic bass, but with the strings muted so they only vibrate a little. The result is a "pop" or "tic" at the beginning of each bass note. This technique is easily heard on Nashville sound recordings from around 1960, such as Patsy Cline's "Back in Baby's Arms" (1962).

DOBRO

See Guitar, resonator.

DRUMS

Drums first appeared in western swing, when Bob Wills hired Smokey Dacus in 1935. Drums were considered controversial and unacceptable in mainstream traditional country music (for instance, they were banned from the Opry stage, with only rare exceptions, until the 1970s). Their next appearance outside of western swing was as a novelty sound in later honky-tonk (Hank Williams's "Kaw-liga" [1952], for instance), gradually becoming more common (Carl Smith's "Loose Talk" [1954]). Drums became fully accepted in Nashville sound recordings, when drummer Buddy Harman was part of the A-list of session players who accompanied all major country stars. Drums also showed up in rockabilly in the late 1950s, and Johnny Cash hired drummer W. S. Holland as part of his stage and recording band in 1960. From that time forward, drums have been present in most country recordings, the only exception being styles such as bluegrass that emphasize an acoustic identity. Unlike other genres, however, country recordings almost never feature drum solos.

FIDDLE

The fiddle, more formally called a violin, is a four-stringed instrument played most commonly with a bow. The term "fiddle" typically implies that the instrument is being used in a vernacular context and played in a particular way, with folk techniques and improvisation, as opposed to formal training and classical technique. The fiddle was the first instrument to appear on country recordings (Eck Robertson's 1922 "Sallie Gooden") and was a staple of string bands and local entertainers of all sorts in rural regions. Western swing bands usually featured fiddles in a lead role (Bob Wills, for instance). Fiddles were a core part of both bluegrass (Chubby Wise, for instance, played for Bill Monroe's band from 1942 until 1948) and honky-tonk (Jerry Rivers played in Hank Williams' Drifting Cowboys). The tradition of solo or duo fiddling was replaced by carefully orchestrated string sections during the Nashville sound era, but fiddling reappeared in Bakersfield recordings and has remained a core part of all styles of country music ever since, the only exception being those styles most heavily derived from southern rock and the most extreme examples of pop-crossover such as countrypolitan. The fiddle was a major feature of neotraditionalist recordings (such as George Strait's "Amarillo by Morning" [1983]). Famous fiddle players include western swing star Johnny Gimble, Charlie Daniels ("The Devil Went Down to Georgia" [1979]), contemporary solo artist and session musician Mark O'Connor, and bluegrass star Alison Krauss.

GUITAR, ACOUSTIC

The acoustic guitar is the most iconic instrument in country music. When hillbilly musicians began using it in the 1920s, it was a relatively new addition to their music-making: fiddles and banjos had been far more prevalent in the nineteenth century, but guitars began to enter the tradition, often when rural musicians ordered them via mail-order catalogs. Both Jimmie Rodgers and Maybelle Carter played in distinctive styles, which helped establish the guitar as more than just an accompaniment for singers. Hollywood's singing cowboys turned the guitar into a visual icon for country singers (prior to those movies, actual working cowboys had been more likely to favor a fiddle over a guitar, if only because of its more convenient size). Guitar virtuosos appeared in the 1940s and '50s in country music, most notably Merle Travis and Chet Atkins. The guitar was also a core instrument in bluegrass (Lester Flatt pioneered its more prominent role within the style).

The acoustic guitar, with six strings and a resonant body, is not a particularly loud instrument, and thus requires amplification in most country-band settings. When the electric guitar was invented, the acoustic guitar moved into a more supporting role in many styles, often referred to as "rhythm guitar," where it was mainly used to strum chords and help establish the song's rhythm. In contemporary country music, stars often perform while playing acoustic guitar, because the image of a singer strumming a guitar has been so firmly embedded in the genre's identity. The sound of an acoustic guitar can change radically depending on how it is played (such as with a single flat-pick, with fingers plucking the strings, or a combination of the two, sometimes called chickin' pickin') and what kind of strings are used on it.

GUITAR, ELECTRIC

Unlike an acoustic guitar, an electric guitar uses an electrical pickup (a device consisting of wire coils and magnets) to transfer the vibrations of the strings into electrical signals, which are then sent through an electric amplifier and speakers. Early models of electric guitars appeared in honky-tonk (most famously on Ernest Tubb's "Walking the Floor Over You" [1941]). In the late 1940s and early 1950s, guitar manufacturers introduced various solid-body electric guitars, whose main body was a solid piece of wood (or other material) cut into an interesting shape. In 1949, the Fender guitar company began selling a mass-produced solid-body electric guitar with two pickups, called the Telecaster. It was relatively affordable and offered a range of sounds to the performer, including a biting, gravelly tone that worked well in rowdy honky-tonks and dance halls. The Telecaster—and later the Stratocaster, which had a different pickup design—became essential features of Bakersfield country. Since then, electric guitars have been ever present in country music, played in a variety of ways and with a huge range of expressive qualities. Contemporary country singers known for their virtuosic playing include Brad Paisley, Vince Gill, and Keith Urban, among many others.

GUITAR, RESONATOR

Resonator guitars were invented in the late 1920s as a way to make a guitar louder and its sound ring longer; they are part of the family of slide guitars. They look like regular acoustic guitars but with a metal circle in the center of the guitar's top. The guitar's bridge is placed on this metal plate, which covers one or more metal cones that amplify the sound acoustically (rather than electrically). For many decades, resonator guitars have casually been identified as Dobros, which is a specific brand of resonator guitars (the Gibson guitar company currently owns the rights to the name). The instrument is held on the player's lap or supported by a strap around the player's neck, with the guitar's body parallel to the floor. The performer's left hand slides a metal bar up and down the strings to change the notes.

Resonator guitars are heard in the 1930s traditional hillbilly string bands, such as Roy Acuff's. "The Great Speckled Bird" features James Clell Summey's Dobro accompanying Acuff, for instance. In 1955, Flatt and Scruggs hired a Dobro player for their bluegrass band, and from that time forward, bluegrass ensembles have routinely included Dobros. Note that many discographies and reference sources do not differentiate between types of slide guitars, sometimes referring to them all as steel guitars (see separate entry).

GUITAR, STEEL

Steel guitars are the most complicated family of instruments in country music. The term generally refers to any guitar that is played with a metal bar in the left hand, which is slid up and down the strings to change the pitch. Early steel guitars (also broadly known as slide guitars) were often imported from Hawaiian traditions, and the term is sometimes also used to describe Dobros or resonator guitars (both acoustic instruments), especially in 1930s country.

In 1934, western swing musician Bob Dunn modified his steel guitar to include electric pickups, thereby becoming the first musician to play an electric guitar of any sort in country music. By the 1940s, the term "steel guitar" usually referred to an electrified instrument, either held on the lap or sitting on its own frame (a console). With the electric pickups, the instrument no longer needed any sort of resonant box to generate the sound acoustically, and so the instrument's design switched to just the neck of a guitar, lying parallel to the floor, without any traditional guitar body. Steel guitar designs also evolved to include more than one grouping of strings, or necks, to allow for a wider range of chords and pitches to be played. Don Helms, for instance, who played on Hank Williams's recordings, used a double-neck steel guitar. The steel guitar's ability to scoop or slide into notes and between different notes gave it a reputation

Figure B-3 Speedy West and his double-neck steel guitar; West played on western swing and honky-tonk recordings made in Los Angeles in the 1950s.

for "crying" in country music. The quintessential steel guitar sound of honky-tonk is heard in the introduction to "Your Cheatin' Heart" (1952). Steel guitar players often play more than one note at a time, which also adds to the instrument's distinctive sound.

In the early 1950s, Bud Isaacs modified his instrument by adding foot pedals, which could be used to change the tuning of the strings while notes were being played. The newly invented pedal steel guitar could play more complicated melodies and add more extensive scoops and bends to the notes. Isaacs used the new instrument on Webb Pierce's "Slowly," (1953), which motivated countless other players to do the same. From that time forward, the pedal steel has symbolized honky-tonk influences, heartbreak, and emotional strain in country music; it is heard, for instance, on "I Told You So," both Randy Travis's 1988 solo version (throughout, but especially audible at 1:08) and Carrie Underwood and Travis's 2009 duet version (in the introduction and throughout).

In contemporary descriptions, the term "steel guitar" generally refers to a pedal steel. The instrument is considered devilishly difficult to master. Song lyrics frequently make reference to steel guitars as a way of invoking a sense of honky-tonk tradition (as in Alan Jackson and George Strait's recording of "Murder on Music Row" [2000]).

HARMONICA

Casually called a harp or mouth organ, the harmonica shows up in early hillbilly recordings. Doc Humphrey Bates was a harmonica player, as was DeFord Bailey, whose "Pan American Blues" was an elaborate imitation of train sounds and one of the most popular numbers performed on the Grand Ole Opry. The harmonica reappeared at 1960s Nashville recording sessions and also prominently in the outlaw movement of the 1970s, as part of the Texas progressive country sound. The instrument is featured on Willie Nelson's *Red Headed Stranger* album. Harmonicas also show up on classic country recordings that evoke aspects of honky-tonk, most notably George Jones's "He Stopped Loving Her Today." Within today's country music, harmonicas are generally linked to either the blues or Texas outlaw styles.

Figure B-4 Mandolin.

MANDOLIN

The mandolin is a small, teardrop-shaped instrument with eight strings. It is pitched in the treble (high) register, and its sound decays quickly, which means that when a note is played, its sound fades rapidly to silence. That aspect of the instrument means that it is often played with a tremolo technique, where the player rapidly plucks the same note over and over so that it continues to be heard. Mandolin shows up prominently among brothers acts in the 1930s. Bill Monroe is the most famous mandolin player in country music history, and the instrument has been a staple in bluegrass as a direct result of Monroe. The opening of "Bluegrass Breakdown" (1947) features one of Monroe's most famous mandolin solos. Mandolins resurfaced in the neotraditionalist era, and again in the roots-influenced country after 2000. Chris Thile of Nickel Creek cultivated a large fan base in the early 2000s, and was featured on the Dixie Chicks' *Home* (2002) (for instance, on "Travelin' Soldier"). Mandolin also appears in contemporary radio-friendly commercial country music, including such hits as Darius Rucker's "This" (2010), on which bluegrass legend Sam Bush plays mandolin (note the solo starting at 2:16).

PIANO

Piano appeared in western swing recordings of the 1930s. Its next common use in country music was in the later honky-tonk recordings, heard in recordings such as Lefty Frizzell's "If You've Got the Money I've Got the Time" (1950, note the piano solo at 1:01) and Carl Smith's "Loose Talk" (1954, listen starting at 0:27), as well as some later rockabilly recordings. During the Nashville sound era, famous pianists such as Floyd Cramer adopted a new style of playing, known as slip-note piano (heard on Cramer's "Last Date" [1960]). This style imitated the way guitar players slid from one note to the next in country blues and the slides or "cries" of the pedal steel guitar. Since then, piano has reappeared in many different styles of country music, both those that are tied to honky-tonk traditions (including outlaw) and those that draw on pop-crossover trends. Electric pianos (especially the Fender Rhodes piano) show up in countrypolitan. And pianos are often used to accompany slow country ballads (as in the opening of Taylor Swift's "You're Not Sorry").

STRINGS

"Strings," as used to describe instrumentation in country music, is not an instrument but rather a collection of instruments played in a specific way. The term shows up in reference to late 1950s Nashville sound recordings, and refers to a combination of violins and sometimes violas and even cellos, the traditional "string section" of a classical orchestra. These instruments are played in a classical way, with vibrato (a shimmering sound created by wavering the pitch of each note very slightly), and with prearranged and written-out musical parts (as opposed to improvised parts). Strings are featured in Patsy Cline's "Sweet Dreams" (1963), especially the opening few seconds. Strings are used to add a thicker texture (a "wash" of sound) and a lush character to the overall recordings, and are often associated with pop-crossover trends in country music. Other distinctive appearances of strings include George Jones's "He Stopped Loving Her Today" (1980) (listen at the beginning of the chorus, around 1:50).

TRUMPET

Trumpets have had very limited use in country music's history. They first appeared in western swing bands such as those fronted by Bob Wills and Milton Brown. In that role, they brought the traditions of jazz (and, particularly, the sound of big band dance music) into country music. They are easily heard on "New San Antonio Rose" (Bob Wills and his Texas Playboys), where they evoke mariachi music. Trumpets also appear in Nashville sound recordings made in the early 1960s. Producer Don Law used them on Johnny Cash's "Ring of Fire" (1963), again in a mariachi-influenced arrangement. Trumpets are heard on countrypolitan recordings as well, such as Dolly Parton's "9 to 5." The presence of trumpets (or, more generally, "horns," which could include saxophones and trombones) often indicates a crossover style of country music.

Glossary

A&R: The corporate department at a record label responsible for "artists and repertoire." An A&R person is generally responsible for signing new talent, which means locating promising musicians and issuing them a recording contract. A&R people remain the point of contact between performers and their labels, and historically have also maintained contacts with publishing firms.

Answer song: A song that uses the melody, topic, and story line of an existing song, but with the lyrics rewritten from the opposite gender's perspective.

Arranger: The person responsible for the specific roles and musical parts of the different instruments for a song's performance. The songwriter generally comes up with the melody, lyrics, and chords for a song, and sometimes specifies other musical parts as well. The arranger determines which instruments will play on which sections of the song, which notes of the chord different instruments will play, and who will play the fills behind the singer. The arranger also determines what sections of the song will be repeated and can add modulations or other musical enhancements. In some styles, the arranger writes out elaborate and specific parts for the instruments to play. In a recording session, the producer might take on some of the arranger's roles, as might some of the session musicians.

Authenticity: A quality or value that fans ascribe to music based on two general considerations: first, the perception that the music is traditional, and second, the perception that the music is original (as opposed to a copy or facsimile), genuine (as opposed to artificial), and honest.

Border stations: Radio stations in Mexico, close to the U.S. border, that the U.S. government, especially the Federal Communications Commission, could not regulate. These stations therefore operated at much higher wattages than their U.S. counterparts, which let them blanket the United States with their signals.

Bristol Sessions: Recordings sessions held from July 25 to August 5, 1927, in Bristol, Tennessee, by Ralph Peer for Victor records. The Carter Family and Jimmie Rodgers were among the nineteen acts recorded at these sessions, which have become mythologized as the origin of country music.

Clear-channel status: A condition in which an AM radio station is granted the sole right to broadcast at a particular frequency. Clear-channel stations enjoy minimal interference from other radio stations and can thus be heard across much greater geographic regions. Atmospheric conditions at night allow these stations to be heard at even greater distances. Many of the significant stations in early country music, including WLS and WSM, were granted clear-channel status, and anecdotal accounts confirm that they could at times be heard thousands of miles away.

Concept album: An album with a central story or narrative that runs throughout all the songs.

Country: A commercial genre that claims a lineage from early-twentieth-century, rural, white, mostly Southern, working-class popular music. It incorporates accepted symbols such as the

cowboy, stock references, a collection of specific musical styles, and specific performance traditions. The fans of this music also play an important role in determining what is and is not considered country.

Cover song: A performance of a song that refers to or is derived from an earlier performance of the same song by a different artist. The earlier performance is often called the original or the model for the cover song.

Crossover: A recording that appeared on a trade chart in a category to which it was not initially marketed; examples include a country recording appearing as a pop hit or an R&B hit.

Genre: A category of popular music defined by the interactions of fans, the commercial music industry, and musicians. Genres include country, jazz, pop, rock, folk, world, etc.

Hillbilly: A reference to a white, Southern, backwoods, and culturally unsophisticated person. In the context of country music, however, the term more frequently refers to the style and musical practices of the 1920s and early '30s, specifically folk-influenced music performed by working-class white people with a connection to the rural South (see chapter 1). Although initially a pejorative label, the term has been reclaimed by the people to whom it was initially applied as a defensive rhetorical strategy. In this book, we use it to identify a particular musical style, without any derogatory inferences.

Hit: A recording that has achieved commercial success, usually signaling its appearance on a major trade publication's chart that indicates extensive airplay or high sales numbers.

Improvisation: The creation of a new melody or new lyrics in the moment of performance to fit in an existing song. The performer makes up a new melody to fit the existing chords in the song, or new lyrics to fit the existing melody. In popular music (including country), sometimes a musician will improvise an initial solo, but in subsequent performances of the song will reuse the same solo. Instrumental solos in the middle of performances are often improvised.

Medicine show: A salesman and his accompanying entertainers who traveled from town to town, using the musicians to draw in an audience so the salesman could pitch supposedly miraculous elixirs. Medicine shows were common from the late nineteenth century into the early twentieth century.

Minstrel show: A traveling theater troupe that performed a set of songs, dances, skits, and speeches in blackface, portraying harshly stereotyped African-American characters. Minstrel shows emerged in the early nineteenth century and flourished after the Civil War, continuing into the early twentieth century.

Modulation: a change in the home key, or tonic, of a recording. When a song modulates, the pitch level of the entire song moves up or down (most frequently up). The chord that serves as the reference or home chord (tonic, in music-theory terms) and the specific chords that provide the song's harmony in relation to that tonic also change.

Multitrack recording: the practice where several individual tracks or storage-spaces on the recording device each holds a recording of a musical performance. These tracks are combined in the mixing process to be played back as if they were one performance. This practice allows individual instruments to be recorded one at a time for a song, for instance.

Naturalized: A description of a vocal style that conveys the sense of an untrained, unmediated direct communication from singer to listener. A major feature of honky-tonk music, this style of singing allow cracks, pops, cries, quivers and breaks in vocal performances, along with dramatic changes the timbre, or tone color, from one note to the next. Naturalized vocals often feature a bright, nasal tone, which adds to the perception that the singers are "everyday folk" telling a story that just happens to be conveyed through music, rather than a structured, formal, artistic performance that would take the music out of the "ordinary" or "everyday" context.

Pop music: One genre of popular music. Pop music was originally the category of music that was pitched for mass acceptance by a large, predominantly white, mainstream audience. In contemporary definitions, pop is associated with mass marketing toward mainstream youth without the markings of race or musical style that characterize hip-hop and R&B.

Popular music: Commercially produced and disseminated music that is linked to its audiences' sense of identity (see Introduction).

Producer: A record producer is responsible for the creation of a recording and is the direct point of contact between an artist and a record label. In the earliest decades of country music, this role involved the physical setup and operation of recording equipment, along with coaching performers in their choices of songs. As the music industry evolved, the producer's tasks expanded to include selecting songs, hiring session musicians, booking a studio, overseeing the recording sessions, determining the overall sound of the performances, and guiding the recording through the processes of mixing and mastering.

Publisher: Historically, a person or company that reproduced a song on sheet music or in music books for distribution and sales. The publisher typically negotiated with the songwriter for the right to publish the song, licensing the copyright so that a large portion of the royalties earned by the song became income for the publisher. In the mid-twentieth century, the sale of sheet music declined dramatically as records became commonplace and cultural habits of music making changed. From that time forward, publishers no longer sold large quantities of sheet music, but they continued to manage much of the business of getting artists to record a song, and they continued to receive royalties based on the song's copyright.

Remix: A recording's main vocals and instrumental parts are kept, but a new combination of the tracks, or individual parts, is made, often with additional instrumental recordings added in. The term remix is most often associated with a hip hop or rap producer, who typical changes the rhythmic feel of the song when creating a new version. "Mixing" a recording is the process of combining all the individually recorded parts, deciding on their balance in relation to each other, and shaping the recording. Remixing is generally done to create a second, noticeably different version of the song. It has strong connotations of rap and hip hop practices.

Saga song: A song with a long narrative, usually involving a heroic account set in a previous era. Within country music, these often involved nostalgic depictions of the Old West, cowboys, and legendary folk heroes.

Single: a recording released either for sale to the public or for promotion to radio stations, consisting of one song. Not all songs on an artist's album are released as singles. Top 40 radio stations generally construct their playlist from songs released as singles, although they sometimes also select tracks from an album that were not released as singles. Singles that were records (as opposed to cassettes or CDs) had two songs on them: an A-side (the song that was most heavily promoted by the record label) and a B-side.

Slant rhyme: The relationship between two words that share the same vowel sound but different consonant sounds. Slant rhymes are common in country music, because they balance the formal structure of rhymed poetry with a more conversational, informal quality of speech. Examples include the opening rhyme in "Folsom Prison Blues," between "bend" and "when."

Style: the combination of instruments, how they are played, musical arrangement, and musical characteristics of rhythm, melody, and harmony that together describe a category within a genre based on what one can actually hear. Styles in country music include honky-tonk, Nashville sound, etc.

Syncopation: A rhythmic and metric phenomenon. Syncopation occurs when the music's rhythms set up a pulse that contradicts or clashes with the underlying beat of the music. In its simplest form, syncopation consists of musical accents between the beats. Syncopation was a key characteristic of ragtime and jazz; it became important in many different styles of country music, including western swing, country boogie, and bluegrass.

Twang: A description of a quality of a sound. With voices, it refers to a nasal, pinched sound, often combined with a Southern accent or drawl. In instrumental contexts, it refers to stringed instruments that are plucked hard enough so that the pitch of the note changes as it is sounding and so that the instrument's ambient noises are heard in the performance. In other contexts, it refers to the presence of certain instruments, most commonly the steel guitar, fiddle, or banjo, played so that they stand out from the texture of the band. Finally, twang is used to identify musical performances that fans perceive as unrefined, raw, or uncorrupted by the commercial recording process; antonyms might include "polished" or "schmaltzy." In combination, these aspects of twang describe the overall characteristic or quality of the sound in a country music performance. Noncountry fans often criticize the music as "too twangy"; fans, on the other hand, often treasure that quality of "twang" in the music's sound and actively seek it.

Selected Bibliography

Alden, Grant, and Peter Blackstock. *The Best of No Depression: Writing about American Music*. Austin: University of Texas Press, 2005.

Ackerman, Chris, and Sam Milkman. "Country P1 Consumer & New Media Study," sponsored by the Country Radio Broadcasters, Inc., and the Country Music Association. Raleigh, NC: Coleman Insights Media Research, 2011.

Berry, Chad. *Southern Migrants, Northern Exiles*. Urbana: University of Illinois Press, 2000.

Berry, Chad, ed. *The Hayloft Gang: The Story of the National Barn Dance*. Urbana: University of Illinois Press, 2008.

Bertrand, Michael. *Race, Rock, and Elvis*. Urbana: University of Illinois Press, 2000.

Bidgood, Lee. "'America Is All Around Here': An Ethnography of Bluegrass Music in the Contemporary Czech Republic." PhD diss., University of Virginia, 2011.

Bidgood, Lee. *Czech Bluegrass: Notes from the Heart of Europe*. Urbana-Champaign: University of Illinois Press, 2017.

Boyd, Jean A. *The Jazz of the Southwest: An Oral History of Western Swing*. Austin: University of Texas Press, 1998.

Brackett, David. "Banjos, Biopics, and Compilation Scores: The Movies Go Country." *American Music* 19, no. 3 (2001): 247–90.

Brasseaux, Ryan André. *Cajun Breakdown: The Emergence of an American-Made Music*. New York: Oxford University Press, 2009.

Brown, Maxine. *Looking Back to See: A Country Music Memoir*. Fayetteville: University of Arkansas Press, 2005.

Buckley, Thomas "Who Likes Country Music? City Folk, It Says Here." *New York Times*, June 5, 1966.

Bufwack, Mary A., and Robert K. Oermann. *Finding Her Voice: Women in Country Music, 1800–2000*. Nashville: Vanderbilt University Press, 2003.

Cantwell, Robert. *Bluegrass Breakdown: The Making of the Old Southern Sound*. Urbana: University of Illinois Press, 1984.

Carlin, Richard. *Country Music: The People, Places, and Moments that Shaped the Country Sound*. New York: Black Dog & Leventhal, 2006.

Carr, Joe, and Alan Munde. *Prairie Nights to Neon Lights: The Story of Country Music in West Texas*. Lubbock: Texas Tech University Press, 1995.

Cohen, Ronald D. *Rainbow Quest: The Folk Music Revival and American Society, 1940–1970*. Amherst: University of Massachusetts Press, 2002.

Cohen, Sara. *Decline, Renewal, and the City in Popular Music Culture: Beyond the Beatles*. Hampshire, England: Ashgate, 2007.

Coleman Insights Media Research. *Country P1 Consumer & New Media Study*. Commissioned by the Country Radio Broadcasters, Inc., and Country Music Association. March 2011.

Cox, Patsi Bale. *The Garth Factor: The Career behind Country's Big Boom*. New York: Center Street, 2009.

Cusic, Don. *Discovering Country Music*. Westport, CT: Praeger, 2008.

Cusic, Don. *Randy Travis: King of the New Traditionalists*. New York: St. Martin's Press, 1993.

Dawidoff, Nicholas. *In the Country of Country: People and Places in American Music*. New York: Pantheon Books, 1997.

Dent, Alexander Sebastian. *River of Tears: Country Music, Memory, and Modernity in Brazil*. Durham: Duke University Press, 2009.

Dicaire, David. *The First Generation of Country Music Stars: Biographies of 50 Artists Born Before 1940*. Jefferson, NC: McFarland and Company, 2007.

Doggett, Peter. *Are You Ready for the Country: Elvis, Dylan, Parsons and the Roots of Country Rock*. New York: Penguin Books, 2000.

Einarson, John. *Desperados: The Roots of Country Rock*. New York: Cooper Square Press, 2000.

Ellison, Curtis. *Country Music Culture: From Hard Times to Heaven*. Jackson: University Press of Mississippi, 1995.

Escott, Colin. *Lost Highway: The True Story of Country Music*. Washington, DC: Smithsonian Books, 2003.

Escott, Colin. *Good Rockin' Tonight: Sun Records and the Birth of Rock 'n' Roll*. New York: St. Martin's Press, 1992.

Escott, Colin. *Hank Williams: The Biography*. Boston: Little, Brown, and Company, 1995.

Feiler, Bruce. *Dreaming Out Loud: Garth Brooks, Wynonna Judd, Wade Hayes, and the Changing Face of Nashville*. New York: Avon Books, 1998.

Flippo, Chet. "If Miranda Lambert Can Make It, Why Can't You?: Country Music's Dirty Little Secret About Women, " *Nashville Skyline*, August 4, 2011, available at cmt.com http://www.cmt.com/news/nashville-skyline/1668497/nashville-skyline-if-miranda-lambert-can-make-it-why-cant-you.jhtml.

Flippo, Chet. "News Flash: Women Still Recording Country Music," *Nashville Skyline* 20 May 2004, CMT.com, available at http://www.cmt.com/news/nashville-skyline/1487148/nashville-skyline-news-flash-women-still-recording-country-music.jhtml.

Fox, Aaron. *Real Country: Music and Language in Working-Class Culture*. Durham: Duke University Press, 2004.

Fox, Pamela. *Natural Acts: Gender, Race, and Rusticity in Country Music*. Ann Arbor: University of Michigan, 2009.

Fox, Pamela, and Barbara Ching, eds. *Old Roots, New Routes: The Cultural Politics of Alt.Country Music*. Ann Arbor: University of Michigan Press, 2008.

Goertzen, Chris. "Popular Music Transfer and Transformation: The Case of American Country Music in Vienna." *Ethnomusicology* 32, no. 1 (1988): 1–21.

Goodman, David. *Modern Twang: An Alternative Country Music Guide & Directory*. Nashville: Dowling Press, 1999.

Gray, Christopher. "Down from the Mountain and into Wal-Mart," *Austin Chronicle*, July 19, 2002.

Green, Douglas B. *Singing in the Saddle: The History of the Singing Cowboy*. Nashville: Country Music Foundation Press and Vanderbilt University Press, 2002.

Greenway, John. "Jimmie Rodgers—A Folksong Catalyst," *Journal of American Folklore* 70, no.277 (Jul–Sept 1957): 231–234.

Gruber, Ruth Ellen. *sauerkrautcowboys* (blog), http://sauerkrautcowboys.blogspot.com/.

Guralnick, Peter. *Lost Highway: Journeys and Arrivals of American Musicians*. Boston: Little, Brown, and Company, 1999. First ed., Boston: David R. Godine Publishers, 1979.

Hall, Tom T. *The Storyteller's Nashville*. Garden City, NY: Doubleday, 1979.

Haslam, Gerald W. *Workin' Man Blues: Country Music in California*. Berkeley: University of California Press, 1999.

Henry, Murphy Hicks. *Pretty Good for a Girl: Women in Bluegrass*. Urbana: University of Illinois Press, 2013.

Hubbs, Nadine. *Rednecks, Queers, and Country Music*. Berkeley: University of California Press, 2014.

Huber, Patrick. *Linthead Stomp: The Creation of Country Music in the Piedmont South*. Chapel Hill: University of North Carolina Press, 2008.

Hughes, Charles. *Country Soul: Making Music and Making Race in the American South*. Chapel Hill: University of North Carolina Press, 2015.

Hume, Martha. *You're so Cold I'm Turnin' Blue: Martha Hume's Guide to the Greatest in Country Music*. New York: Penguin, 1982.

Isenhour, Jack. *He Stopped Loving Her Today*. Jackson: University of Mississippi Press, 2011.

Jensen, Joli. *The Nashville Sound: Authenticity, Commercialization, and Country Music*. Nashville: Vanderbilt University Press, 1998.

Jones, George. *I Lived to Tell It All*. New York: Villard, 1996.

Jones, Margaret. *Patsy: The Life and Times of Patsy Cline*. New York: Da Capo Press, 1999 (originally published New York: HarperCollins, 1994).

Kemp, Mark. *Dixie Lullaby: A Story of Music, Race, and New Beginnings in a New South*. New York: Free Press, 2004.

Ketchell, Aaron K. *Holy Hills of the Ozarks: Religion and Tourism in Branson, Missouri*. Baltimore: Johns Hopkins University Press, 2007.

Kienzle, Rich. *Southwest Shuffle: Pioneers of Honky-Tonk, Western Swing, and Country Jazz*. New York: Routledge, 2003.

Kingsbury, Paul, ed. *Country: The Music and the Musicians (From the Beginnings to the '90s)*. New York: Abbeville Press, 1994.

Kosser, Michael. *How Nashville Became Music City U.S.A.: 50 Years of Music Row*. New York: Hal Leonard, 2006.

La Chapelle, Peter. *Proud to Be an Okie: Cultural Politics, Country Music, and Migration to Southern California*. Berkeley: University of California Press, 2007.

Laird, Tracey E. W. *Louisiana Hayride: Radio & Roots Music along the Red River*. New York: Oxford University Press, 2005.

Lang, Jeffrey J. *Smile When You Call Me a Hillbilly: Country Music's Struggle for Respectability, 1939–1954*. Athens: University of Georgia Press, 2004.

Latham, Aaron. "The Ballad of the Urban Cowboy: America's Search for True Grit," *Esquire*, September 12, 1978, 21–30.

Lewis, George H., ed. *All That Glitters: Country Music in America*. Bowling Green: Bowling Green State University Press, 1993.

Lynn, Loretta, with George Vecsey. *Loretta Lynn: Coal Miner's Daughter*. New York: Warner Books, 1976.

Malone, Bill C. *Don't Get above Your Raisin': Country Music and the Southern Working Class*. Urbana: University of Illinois Press, 2002.

Malone, Bill C., and David Stricklin. *Southern Music/American Music, revised ed.* Lexington: University Press of Kentucky, 2003.

Malone, Bill C., and Jocelyn R. Neal. *Country Music U.S.A., 3rd rev. ed.* Austin: University of Texas Press, 2010.

Mazor, Barry. *Meeting Jimmie Rodgers: How America's Original Roots Music Hero Changed the Pop Sounds of a Century*. New York: Oxford University Press, 2009.

Mazor, Barry. "Miranda Lambert: Nashville Lone Star," *No Depression* #69 (May–June 2007): 56–63.

McCusker, Kristine M. *Lonesome Cowgirls and Honky-Tonk Angels: The Women of Barn Dance Radio*. Urbana: University of Illinois Press, 2008.

McCusker, Kristine, and Diane Pecknold, eds. *A Boy Named Sue: Gender and Country Music*. Jackson: University Press of Mississippi, 2004.

McCusker, Kristine, and Diane Pecknold, eds. *Country Boys and Redneck Women: New Essays in Gender and Country Music*. Jackson: University Press of Mississippi, 2016.

Meyer, David. *Twenty Thousand Roads: The Ballad of Gram Parsons and His Cosmic American Music*. New York: Villard Books, 2007.

Miller, Karl Hagstrom. *Segregating Sound: Inventing Folk and Pop Music in the Age of Jim Crow*. Durham: Duke University Press, 2010.

Morrison, Craig. *Go Cat Go! Rockabilly Music and Its Makers*. Urbana: University of Illinois Press, 1996.

Nash, Alanna. *Dolly: The Biography*. Updated ed. New York: Cooper Square Press, 2002.

Neal, Jocelyn. *The Songs of Jimmie Rodgers: A Legacy in Country Music*. Bloomington: Indiana University Press, 2009.

Pecknold, Diane, ed. *Hidden in the Mix: The African American Presence in Country Music*. Durham: Duke University Press, 2013.

Pecknold, Diane. *The Selling Sound: The Rise of the Country Music Industry*. Durham: Duke University Press, 2007.

Peterson, Richard A. *Creating Country Music: Fabricating Authenticity*. Chicago: University of Chicago Press, 1997.

Porterfield, Nolan. *Jimmie Rodgers: The Life and Times of America's Blue Yodeler*. Rev. ed. Urbana: University of Illinois Press, 1992; reprinted, Jackson: University Press of Mississippi, 2007.

Price, Robert. *The Bakersfield Sound: How a Generation of Displaced Okies Revolutionized American Music*. Berkeley: Heyday, 2018.

Pruett, David B. *MuzikMafia: From the Local Nashville Scene to the National Mainstream*. Jackson: University Press of Mississippi, 2010.

Reid, Jan. *The Improbable Rise of Redneck Rock: New Edition*. Austin: University of Texas Press, 2004.

Rodgers, Jimmie. *The Singing Brakeman* (short film). Columbia, 1929. In *Times Ain't Like They Used to Be: Early Rural and Popular Music, 1928–1935*. Newark: Yazoo Video, 2000.

Rogers, Jimmie N. *The Country Music Message: Revisited*. Fayetteville: The University of Arkansas Press, 1989.

Rosenberg, Neil V. *Bluegrass: A History*, rev. ed. Urbana: University of Illinois Press, 2005.

Russell, Tony. *Country Music Originals: The Legends and the Lost*. New York: Oxford University Press, 2007.

Sisk, Eileen. *Buck Owens: The Biography*. Chicago: Chicago Review Press, 2010.

Smith, Graeme. "Australian Country Music and the Hillbilly Yodel." *Popular Music* 13, no. 3 (1994): 297–311.

Smith, Richard D. *Can't You Hear Me Callin': The Life of Bill Monroe, Father of Bluegrass*. Boston: Little, Brown, 2000.

Solli, Kristin. "North of Nashville: Country Music, National Identity, and Class in Norway." PhD diss., University of Iowa, 2006.

Stanley, Ralph. *Man of Constant Sorrow: My Life and Times*. New York: Gotham Books, 2009.

Stimeling, Travis. *Cosmic Cowboys and New Hicks: The Countercultural Sounds of Austin's Progressive Country Music Scene*. New York: Oxford University Press, 2011.

Stimeling, Travis D. ed. *The Oxford Handbook of Country Music*. New York: Oxford University Press, 2017.

Strauss, Neil. "The Country Music Country Radio Ignores," *New York Times*, March 24, 2002.

Streissguth, Michael. *Eddy Arnold: Pioneer of the Nashville Sound*. Jackson: University Press of Mississippi, 2009.

Streissguth, Michael. *Johnny Cash: The Biography*. Cambridge, MA: Da Capo Press, 2006.

Taylor, Sarah Love. "The Nitty Gritty Dirt Band's *Will the Circle Be Unbroken* Album: An Accidental Success?" undergraduate honors thesis, University of North Carolina at Chapel Hill, 2003.

Tribe, Ivan M. *The Stonemans: An Appalachian Family and the Music That Shaped Their Lives*. Urbana: University of Illinois Press, 1993.

Whiteside, Jonny. *Ramblin' Rose: The Life and Career of Rose Maddox*. Nashville: Vanderbilt University Press, 1997.

Willman, Chris. *Rednecks & Bluenecks: The Politics of Country Music*. New York: The New Press, 2005.

Wolfe, Charles K. *Classic Country: Legends of Country Music*. New York: Routledge, 2001.

Wolfe, Charles K. *A Good-Natured Riot: The Birth of the Grand Ole Opry*. Nashville: Country Music Foundation Press, 1999.

Wolfe, Charles K., and James E. Akenson, eds. *Country Music Annual 2002*. Lexington: University Press of Kentucky, 2002.

Wolfe, Charles K., and James E. Akenson, eds., *Country Music Goes to War*. Lexington: University Press of Kentucky, 2005.

Wolff, Kurt, and Orla Duane. *Country Music: The Rough Guide*. London: The Rough Guide Ltd, 2000.

Zwonitzer, Mark with Charles Hirshberg. *Will You Miss Me When I'm Gone? The Carter Family and Their Legacy in American Music*. New York: Simon & Schuster, 2002.

Index